Seventh Edition

E-MARKETING

Judy Strauss
*Associate Professor of Marketing,
University of Nevada, Reno*

Raymond Frost
*Professor of Management Information Systems,
Ohio University*

Boston Columbus Indianapolis New York San Francisco Upper Saddle River
Amsterdam Cape Town Dubai London Madrid Milan Munich Paris Montréal
Toronto Delhi Mexico City São Paulo Sydney Hong Kong Seoul Singapore Taipei Tokyo

Editor in Chief: Stephanie Wall
Director of Editorial Services: Ashley Santora
Editorial Project Manager: Lynn M. Savino
Editorial Assistant: Jacob Garber
Director of Marketing: Maggie Moylan
Executive Marketing Manager: Anne Falhgren
Senior Managing Editor: Judy Leale
Production Project Manager: Tom Benfatti
Operations Specialist: Tom Benfatti
Creative Director: Jayne Conte
Cover Designer: Suzanne Behnke
Cover Art: Sergey Nevins
Full-Service Project Management: Sudip Singh at PreMediaGlobal, Inc.
Composition: PreMediaGlobal, Inc.
Printer/Binder: Courier/Westford
Cover Printer: Courier/Westford
Text Font: 10/12 Times

Credits and acknowledgments borrowed from other sources and reproduced, with permission, in this textbook appear on the appropriate page within text.

Photo Credits: All part and chapter opener photos are from Fotolia.

Library of Congress Cataloging-in-Publication Data
Strauss, Judy.
E-marketing / Judy Strauss, Associate Professor of Marketing, University of Nevada, Reno, Raymond Frost, Professor of Management Information Systems, Ohio University. — Seventh edition.
pages cm
Includes bibliographical references and index.
ISBN-13: 978-0-13-295344-3
ISBN-10: 0-13-295344-7
1. Internet marketing. I. Frost, Raymond, II. Title.
HF5415.1265.S774 2014
658.8'72—dc23
2013010934

10 9 8 7 6 5 4 3 2 1

ISBN 10: 0-13-295344-7
ISBN 13: 978-0-13-295344-3

Judy: To my girls, Cyndi and Malia

Raymond: To my boys, David, Raymond, and Luke

BRIEF CONTENTS

CONTENTS

Part 2 E-Marketing Environment 73

PREFACE

WHAT'S NEW IN THIS EDITION

This book presents e-marketing planning and marketing mix tactics from a strategic and tactical perspective. Part 1 begins with setting the context for marketing planning. Part 2 discusses legal and global environments. Part 3 begins the e-marketing strategy discussion in depth, and Part 4 continues with marketing mix and customer relationship management strategy and implementation issues.

This edition reflects the disruption to the marketing field based on social media. The seventh edition is a major revision from the sixth. There are many new topics, as dictated by changes in e-marketing practice in the past 2 years. The following are important changes for this edition:

- The previous edition social media chapter was deleted so this topic could be more appropriately integrated throughout the text.
- Many new business models were added and described in detail, such as social commerce (and Facebook commerce), mobile commerce and mobile marketing, social CRM, crowdsourcing, and many important but less pervasive models (e.g., crowdfunding, freemium, flash sales).
- Chapters 12, 13, and 14 were completely rewritten to reflect the move from traditional marketing communication tools to the way practitioners currently describe IMC online: owned, paid, and earned media.
- Chapter 1 includes many new and interesting technologies providing marketing opportunities, both in the Web 2.0 and in 3.0 sections.
- Statistics about internet use and strategy effectiveness were extensively updated throughout every chapter.
- There are two new chapter-opening vignettes, many new images in every chapter, and updated "Let's Get Technical" boxes.
- There are new discussion questions about each chapter opening vignette.
- A few of the additional chapter specific additions include more social media performance metrics (Chapter 2), "big data" and social media content analysis (Chapter 6), new consumer behavior theory and "online giving" as a new exchange activity (Chapter 7), social media for brand building (Chapter 9), and app pricing and Web page pricing tactics (Chapter 10).

FOCUS OF THIS BOOK

The internet, combined with other information technologies, created many interesting and innovative ways to provide customer value since its inception in 1969. Social media for marketing communication, commerce and customer support; one-to-one communication to many different receiving devices; mobile computing; search engine optimization; consumer behavior insights based on offline and online data combination; inventory optimization through CRM–SCM integration; a single-minded focus on ROI and associated performance metrics and the explosion of social media are all on the cutting edge of e-marketing as we write the seventh edition of this textbook and they continue to develop as important strategies.

As internet adoption matured at about 85 percent in the United States in the past few years, we thought things would be pretty quiet on the internet frontier. Then the social media appeared, holding marketers to their Holy Grail that customer needs and wants are paramount. High-readership blogs, social networks (such as Facebook, Twitter and LinkedIn), microblogs (such as Tumblr), and online communities (such as YouTube and ePinions.com) give consumers the opportunity to be heard in large numbers and to begin controlling brand conversations. A.C. Nielsen and others have discovered that consumers trust each other more than they trust companies, fueling the growth of social media and sending more traffic to some Web sites than does Google. Further, search engines are reputation engines, ranking Web sites partially according to popularity and relevancy. A simple brand misstep can appear as an online video showing a product malfunction or in the words posted by thousands of disgruntled customers. Conversely, marketers can use the Web, e-mail, and social media to build stellar brand images online and increase sales both online and offline. To do this, marketers must now learn how to engage and listen to buyers, and use what they learn to improve their offerings. This book tells you how to do this.

The book you have in your hands is the seventh edition of *E-Marketing* (the first edition was named *Marketing on the Internet*). This textbook is different from others in the following important ways:

- We wrote the first edition of this book in 1996, providing a long-term perspective on e-marketing not available in any other book.

- We explain electronic marketing not simply as a list of ideas, strategies, and techniques, but as part of a larger set of concepts and theories in the marketing discipline. In writing this book, we discovered that most new terminology could be put into traditional marketing frameworks for your greater understanding.
- The text focuses on cutting-edge business strategies that generate revenue while delivering customer value. As well, we reflect current practice by devoting many pages to performance metrics that monitor the success of those strategies.
- We highly recommend that marketers learn a bit about the technology behind the internet, something most of us are not drawn to naturally. For example, knowledge of the possibilities for mobile commerce will give savvy marketers an advantage in the marketplace. This book attempts to educate you, the future marketers, gently in important technology issues, showing the relevance of each concept.
- This book describes e-marketing practices in the United States, but it also takes a global perspective in describing market developments in both emerging and developed nations. Much can be learned from other industrialized nations that lead in certain technologies, such as wireless internet access and faster broadband connectivity.
- Most e-marketing books do not devote much space to law and ethics; we devote an entire chapter to this, contributed by a practicing attorney.

HOW TO USE THIS BOOK

Read, think, explore, and learn. This is not a typical book because the internet is a quickly and ever-changing landscape. Each time we write a new edition we know that by the time it is published some things will already be outdated. To be successful in this course, read and study the material and then go online to learn more about topics that interest you. Think about your use of the internet, the iPhone, iPad, and other technologies and how e-marketers use them to gain your attention, interest, and dollars. Next time you visit Facebook.com, see what kind of ads are there and think about why they were shown to you and not to some of your friends. If you use Hulu.com, Netflix, or a DVR and skip television commercials, think about how producers can afford to provide free programming if consumers don't view the ads that support the production costs.

This kind of critical thinking and attention to your own online behavior will help you understand the e-marketer's perspective, strategies, and tactics better. You likely know a lot about the internet that is not in this book, so work to compare and contrast it to the ideas we present and you'll have a really broad and deep perspective on e-marketing. Most importantly, think like a marketer when you read this book.

HOW THE BOOK HELPS YOU LEARN

Here are some things in this book that may help your learning of e-marketing concepts:

- ***Marketing concept grounding.*** In each chapter we structure material around a principle of marketing framework and then tell how the internet changed the structure or practices. This technique provides a bridge from previously learned material and presents it in a framework for easier learning. In addition, as things change on the internet, you will understand the new ideas based on underlying concepts. Although social media has really disrupted the marketing field, our basic processes remain the same (e.g., understanding markets through research and developing products that add value).
- ***Learning objectives.*** Each chapter begins with a list of objectives that, after studying the chapter, you should be able to accomplish.
- ***Best practices from real companies.*** A company success story starts each chapter. You will find these to be exciting introductions to the material, so don't skip them. New case histories for this edition offer current examples of firms that do it right.
- ***Graphical frameworks in each chapter.*** We created unique e-marketing visual models to show how each chapter fits among other chapters in the entire part. In addition, several chapters feature models for within-chapter understanding. We hope these help you tie the concepts together.
- ***Chapter summaries.*** Each chapter ends with a summary of its contents. Although these summaries capsulate the chapter guts, they were not created so that you will read them in lieu of the chapter content. Use them as refreshers of the material.
- ***Key terms.*** These terms are set in bold text within the chapter to signal their importance and Appendix B is a complete glossary.

- ***Review and discussion questions.*** Questions at the chapter end will help you refresh and think more deeply about the material. Check them out, even if your instructor doesn't assign them because they will likely help you study for an exam.
- ***Web activities.*** When you become actively engaged in the material, learning is enhanced. To this end we included several activities and internet exercises at the end of each chapter.
- ***Appendices.*** Most people don't brag about appendices, but we included three important ones: internet adoption statistics, a thorough glossary, and book references.

We hope you enjoy reading this book as much as we enjoy writing it!

ACKNOWLEDGMENTS

The most pleasant task in this project is expressing our appreciation to the many individuals who helped us create this work. We are always amazed that the scope of the job requires us to request, plead, cajole, and charm a number of folks into helping us. Our gratitude is enormous.

First, we would like to thank our students over the years. We teach primarily because we love working with our students. They inspire us, teach us, and keep us on our toes. Next we want to thank Pearson Education, Inc., for giving us a place to showcase our ideas. Project Manager, Lynn Savino, was extremely helpful. Brooks Hill-Whilton was amazingly responsive with copyright permissions and other questions. We also appreciate the many reviewers who gave us excellent suggestions for improving the sixth edition—we've used nearly all of them in writing the seventh edition. We could not have written this book without the support of our institutions, the University of Nevada, Reno, and Ohio University.

Other individuals contributed significantly to this book's content. The late Brian O'Connell contributed the interesting and timely "Ethical and Legal Issues" chapter for the fourth edition, and Lara Pearson and Inna Wood revised it for this edition. Al Rosenbloom wrote the fascinating chapter on "Global eMarkets 3.0." Special thanks to Adel I. El-Ansary at the University of North Florida and Brett J. Trout, Esq., for their expert assistance on earlier editions of this book. Cyndi Jakus single-handedly obtained permission to reprint many of the images in this book. Marian Wood also assisted with some of the material in the book. We also acknowledge the contribution of Jacqueline Pike to the "Let's Get Technical" boxes. Finally special thanks to Henry Mason, Global Head of Research and Managing Partner of Trendwatching.com, for his generosity in providing cutting edge text and examples to begin each chapter.

Finally, support and encouragement to accomplish a major piece of work come from friends and family. To them we are indebted beyond words.

ABOUT THE AUTHORS

Judy Strauss and Raymond Frost have collaborated on Web development, academic papers, practitioner seminars, and three books in 12 editions since 1995. They also developed a new course in 1996, "Marketing in Cyberspace." This book grew out of that course and has significantly evolved along with changes in e-marketing.

Judy Strauss is associate professor of marketing at the University of Nevada, Reno. She is an award-winning author of four books and numerous academic papers on internet marketing, advertising, and marketing education. Strauss is coauthor of the trade book *Radically Transparent: Monitoring and Managing Reputations Online*, and textbooks *Building Effective Web Sites* and the *E-Marketing Guide*. She has had many years of professional experience in marketing, serving as entrepreneur as well as marketing director of two firms. She currently teaches undergraduate courses in marketing communications, internet marketing, and principles of marketing and has won two college-wide teaching awards, a Lifetime Achievement in Marketing Award from the Reno-Tahoe American Marketing Association, and the 2008 Helen Williams Award for Excellence in Collegiate Independent Study. Strauss earned a doctorate in marketing at Southern Illinois University and a finance MBA and marketing BBA at the University of North Texas. Contact: jstrauss@unr.edu.

Raymond Frost is professor of management information systems at Ohio University. He has published scholarly papers in the fields of information systems and marketing. Frost is coauthor of *Business Information Systems: Design an App for That*. Dr. Frost teaches business information systems, information management, and information design courses. He has received Ohio University's Presidential, University Professor, College of Business, and Senior Class teaching awards. He was also named Computer Educator of the Year in 2010 by the International Association of Computer Information Systems (IACIS). Dr. Frost chairs the College of Business Teaching and Learning Continuous Improvement Team. He is currently working on improving learning outcomes by flipping the classroom in combination with team based learning. Dr. Frost earned a doctorate in business administration, an MS in computer science at the University of Miami (Florida), and received his BA in philosophy at Swarthmore College.

PART 1

E-Marketing in Context

CHAPTER

1

Past, Present, and Future

The key objective of this chapter is to develop an understanding of the background, current state, and future potential of e-marketing. You will learn about e-marketing's important role in a company's overall integrated marketing strategy.

After reading this chapter, you will be able to:

- Explain how the advances in internet and information technology offer benefits and challenges to consumers, businesses, marketers, and society.
- Distinguish between e-business and e-marketing.
- Explain how increasing buyer control is changing the marketing landscape.
- Understand the distinction between information or entertainment as data and the information-receiving appliance used to view or hear it.
- Identify several trends that may shape the future of e-marketing, including the semantic Web.

- If 'transparency 1.0' was all about the excitement at being able to see exactly what other (real!) people thought about products or services; 'transparency 2.0' saw this become just a default element of decision-making; now **'transparency 3.0'** will be about making almost all aspects of the transaction *and* experience transparent: manufacturing, pricing, reviews, popularity, and even personal relevance.

- February 2012 saw KLM roll out its ***Meet & Seat*** initiative. The optional service allows passengers to link their booking to their Facebook or LinkedIn profile and select a seat next to the individuals they find most interesting

The Barack Obama Campaign Story

U.S. President Obama made history by his use of e-marketing to win the election in 2008, and his 2012 efforts added higher levels of sophistication. His 2008 campaign used a mix of media: broadcast ($244.6 million), print ($20.5 million), internet ($26.6 million), and miscellaneous ($133.2 million), according to OpenSecrets.org. In 2012, both presidential candidates spent an average of 28.7 percent of their media dollars on internet strategies (an increase from 6.3 percent in 2008). They also used door-to-door personal selling, public relations when interviewed by the media and speaking at events, radio ads, e-mail, a poster, t-shirts, a campaign song, a slogan, and the now famous Obama chant—"Yes We Can."

Many of Obama's 2008 and 2012 internet strategies targeted 18- to 29-year-old voters, because 93 percent of this market is online and uses the internet to get information, upload content, and connect with friends. They are heavy smartphone and social media users. Obama's campaigns brilliantly mobilized this market through forums and social networks, such as Facebook and Twitter. A special 2008 community site where users could create a profile and connect with others was designed. The headline of this page read "It is About You" and continues as a space for supporters to create change in America.

In 2012, Obama dug more deeply into social media. He shared playlists on Spotify, posted recipes on Pinterest, and showed heartwarming, small family video clips on Tumblr. Both candidates maintained Twitter accounts to interact with voters. Obama's campaign staff built a digital database with information about millions of supporters. This allowed for personal communication targeting. The campaign managers were also very careful to guard the privacy of these data.

Knowing the heavy use of mobile phones in this market, Team Obama used mobile devices for text messaging, interactive voice response, and mobile banner ads. Obama reached voters via opt-in text messages in 2008, such as mobile banner ads inviting users to sign up to receive a text message as soon as the team selected its vice presidential candidate. "Be the first to know," the banner ad said. This line showed Obama's astuteness because he tapped into a key value in the target market. Obama was honest, direct, personable, and up front in his campaign, and this generated trust in this young-voter market. It worked in both elections, as evidenced by the following performance metrics:

- 2008: The vice president opt-in text banner resulted in the database capture of 2.9 million cell phone numbers from supporters, according to mobilemarketer.com.
- 2008: During the campaign, My.BarackObama.com hosted nearly 10,000 local groups, 20,000 volunteer blog pages, and 4,000 special-interest groups, according to WiderFunnel.com.
- 2008: Two-thirds of all the campaign funds raised came from the online channel ($500 million of $750 million total), according to Desktop-Wealth.com.
- 2012: Obama's Facebook account displayed over 33 million "likes" and 1.5 million talking about it.
- 2012: The Obama YouTube video channel had over 286,000 subscribers and 288 million upload views.
- 2012: Some of Obama's Tumblr posts received over 70,000 "notes," "likes," or reposts.

Why do we begin this book with a campaign story? Because politicians are products, promoting their benefits to consumers in hopes that they'll "purchase" with a vote. Obama's use of e-marketing is a stellar example for businesses and demonstrates the internet's changing landscape. Obama's campaign selected an important target market, made it all about them (the customers), reached them via the media they prefer (social media and mobile), and created a dialog with them, often initiated by them—versus the corporate one-way monologue on many Web sites. The 2008 campaign successfully mobilized voters to start the conversations themselves and build their own groups, both online and offline, in a perfect example of creating brand advocates. Finally, both campaigns used performance metrics to measure the success of their strategies and tactics. And it worked, because Obama made the sale twice: Nominee Obama became President Obama.

Sources: NYTimes.com, politico.com, candidates' social media pages, and others listed within this text.

E-MARKETING LANDSCAPE

The Obama example demonstrates that some marketing principles never change. Companies must meet the needs of their customers. Further, markets always welcome good products and demand good company–customer communication. Customers trust well-respected brands and talk to other people about them. What is new is that these classic concepts are enhanced and often more challenging when applied to social media, huge databases, mobile devices, and other internet technologies.

What Works?

The rapid growth of the World Wide Web (basis for "www.") in the 1990s, the subsequent bursting of the dot-com bubble, and mainstreaming of the internet and related technologies created today's climate: the comprehensive integration of e-marketing and traditional marketing to create seamless strategies and tactics. This provides plenty of profitable opportunities, as discussed in the following sections. This chapter is just a sampling of what you'll find in later chapters.

- ***The customer is CEO.*** After all those years of marketers talking about the customer being their focus, finally this has become a reality. The consumer is now in charge. This power shift means that companies must be transparent, be authentic, monitor online discussion about brands, and engage customers to help improve products (a strategy called crowdsourcing).
- ***E-commerce.*** U.S. consumers spent an estimated $194.3 billion online during 2011, representing 4.6 percent of all retail sales and a 16 percent increase over 2010. Over 70 percent of connected consumers

use the internet to buy products, bank, make travel reservations, or research products before buying. Mobile commerce sales in 2012 were predicted to reach $11.6 billion, growing to $31 billion by 2015.

- ***Advertising online.*** Online advertising is a bigger part of advertisers' media budgets than every other medium except television. Marketers spent $31 billion on online advertising in the United States in 2011. Mobile advertising is the fastest growing category, nearly doubling from the first half of 2011 to 2012 (from $636 million to $1.2 billion).
- ***Search engine marketing.*** This marketing tactic is hugely important. Paid search accounts for 47 percent of online advertising budgets (i.e., purchasing keywords that present ads on search engine results pages). Google gets the lion's share of the user search market at 67 percent, and most e-marketers use search engine optimization to be sure their sites appear near the top of the first page of the search engine results pages for natural searches.
- ***Owned, paid, and earned media.*** Marketing communication planning now involves owned (e.g., Web sites), paid (e.g., banner ads), and earned (e.g., blogs and Facebook posts) media. The traditional marketing communication tools of advertising, sales promotion, personal selling, direct marketing, and public relations are used within this new context to generate earned media.
- ***Mobile marketing.*** Seventy-seven percent of American adults now have mobile phones, providing plenty of profitable opportunities for smartphone applications and advertising. When added to mobile computing (iPads and netbooks), the wireless internet offers users anytime, anywhere access for consumers—and where consumers go, marketers follow.
- ***User-generated content.*** Now a huge part of online content, this includes everything from consumer-created commercials and product improvement suggestions to YouTube videos, Flickr photos, iTunes podcasts, as well as all the text on blogs, social networks, and user review sites (such as the Amazon.com book reviews).
- ***Social media communities.*** These communities gather users with like-minded interests for conversation and networking. This includes social networking sites such as LinkedIn, Twitter, and Facebook and social media sites such as Wikipedia, YouTube, Yahoo! Answers, and more. Marketers use these sites to build brands and engage customers.
- ***Content marketing.*** Marketers are becoming publishers, creating content on Web sites and in social media to attract and engage prospects and customers. Some companies publish small items, such as videos, press releases, and blog posts. Others create lengthy white papers, infographics, and eBooks. Content is king and customer engagement online is queen.
- ***Local and location-based marketing.*** These efforts work well online, thanks to Google local search, Foursquare, eBay classifieds, and the hugely popular Craigslist. Smartphone users can easily find a local business with a global positioning system (GPS) and the Google application or check into local businesses with Foursquare.
- ***Brand transparency.*** This means that marketers are rewarded for being honest, open, and transparent in their communication with internet users. Those who are not get called out under the bright lights of the blogosphere, product review sites, and elsewhere in the social media.
- ***Inbound marketing.*** The days of "interrupt" marketing are waning, such as spam and television commercials. Consumers are not waiting for marketing messages. Inbound marketing strategies are about enticing consumers to find companies online (more in this chapter).
- ***Metrics rule.*** Web analytics and many other techniques allow marketers to keep track of every mouse click and use it to improve strategy efficiency and effectiveness. There

are millions of metrics and marketers select the most appropriate for their objectives and tactics and follow them daily.

Internet 101

Technically speaking, the **internet** is a global network of interconnected networks. This includes millions of corporate, government, organizational, and private networks. Many of the servers (hard drives and software) in these networks hold files, such as Web pages and videos, that can be accessed by all networked computers. Every computer, cell phone, or other networked device can send and receive data in the form of e-mail or other digital files over the internet. These data move over phone lines, cables, and satellites from sender to receiver. One way to understand this process is to consider the internet as having three technical roles: (1) content providers who create information, entertainment, and so forth that reside on Web servers or computers with network access; (2) users (also known as *client* computers) who access content and send e-mail and other content over the network (such as a Facebook comment); and (3) technology infrastructure to move, create, and view or listen to the content (the software and hardware). Note that individuals can be both users and content providers at various times so the line between roles 1 and 2 is slowly disappearing. In *E-Marketing* we stopped capitalizing the word *internet*. Following *Wired Magazine*'s suggestion, we agree that the internet is not a place (requiring a proper noun's capitalization) but a medium, similar to radio and television.

There are three types of access to the internet:

1. ***Public internet***—The global network that is accessible by anyone, anywhere, anytime.
2. ***Intranet***—A network that runs internally in a corporation but uses internet standards such as HTML and browsers. Thus, an intranet is like a mini-internet but with password protection for internal corporate consumption.
3. ***Extranet***—Two or more proprietary networks that are joined for the purpose of sharing information. If two companies, or a company and its suppliers or customers, link their intranets, they would have an extranet. Access is limited to extranet members.

E-business, e-marketing, and e-commerce are internet applications. **E-business** is the optimization of a company's business activities using digital technology. Digital technologies include products and services, such as computers and the internet, which allow the storage and transmission of data in digital formats (1s and 0s). In this book, we use the terms *digital technology* and *information technology* interchangeably. E-business involves attracting and retaining the right customers and business partners. It permeates business processes, such as product buying and selling. It includes digital communication, e-commerce, and online research, and it is used in every business discipline. **E-commerce** is the subset of e-business focused on transactions that include buying/selling online, digital value creation, virtual marketplaces and storefronts, and new distribution channel intermediaries. Mobile commerce (M-commerce) and social commerce are subsets of e-commerce (discussed in Chapter 11).

E-marketing is only one part of an organization's e-business activities. **E-marketing** is the *use of information technology* for the marketing activity, and the processes for creating, communicating, delivering, and exchanging offerings that have value for customers, clients, partners, and society at large. More simply defined, *e-marketing* is the result of information technology applied to traditional marketing. E-marketing affects traditional marketing in two ways. First, it increases efficiency and effectiveness in traditional marketing functions. Second, the technology of e-marketing transforms many marketing strategies, as shown in the Obama example. This transformation also results in new business models that add customer value and/or increase company profitability, such as the highly successful Craigslist, Facebook, Twitter, and Google AdSense advertising models.

However, e-marketing involves much more than these basic technologies and applications.

E-Marketing Is Bigger than the Web

The Web is the portion of the internet that supports a graphical user interface for hypertext navigation, with browsers such as Internet Explorer and Mozilla Firefox. The Web is what most people think about when they think of the internet. Electronic marketing reaches far beyond the Web. First, many e-marketing technologies exist without the Web, which include mobile apps, software and hardware used in customer relationship management, supply chain management, and electronic data interchange arrangements predating the Web. Second, non-Web internet communications such as e-mail, internet telephony (e.g., Skype), and text messaging are effective avenues for marketing. Some of these services can also use the Web, such as Web-based e-mail; however, most professionals do not use the Web for e-mail (preferring software such as Microsoft Outlook). Third, the internet delivers text, video, audio, and graphics to many more information-receiving appliances than simply personal computers (PCs). As shown in Exhibit 1.1, these forms of digital content also go over the internet infrastructure to the television, personal digital assistants, cell phones, and even the refrigerator or automobile. Finally, offline electronic data-collection devices, such as bar-code scanners and databases, receive and send data about customers and products over an intranet.

It is helpful to think of it this way: Content providers create digital text, video, audio, and graphics to send over the internet infrastructure to users who receive it as information, entertainment, or communication on many types of appliances. As marketers think outside of the Web and realize that most users are also now content providers, they find many new possibilities for creating products that provide value and communicate in ways that build relationships with customers.

E-Marketing Is Bigger than Technology

The internet is like a watering hole for humans. We come for easy, inexpensive, and quick access to digital information, connections, and entertainment, and in turn it transforms individuals, businesses, economies, and societies. This book focuses on the union of technology and marketing; however, a brief overview of the big picture is useful for understanding e-marketing's impact.

INDIVIDUALS The internet provides individual users with convenient and continuous access to information, entertainment, networking, and communication. If "information is power," individuals have more power than ever before, as many companies experience. Consumers compare product features and prices using search engines and read product reviews from other consumers at epinions.com, Facebook, and other sites. Further, consumers use the internet to bring music, movies, and other types of entertainment

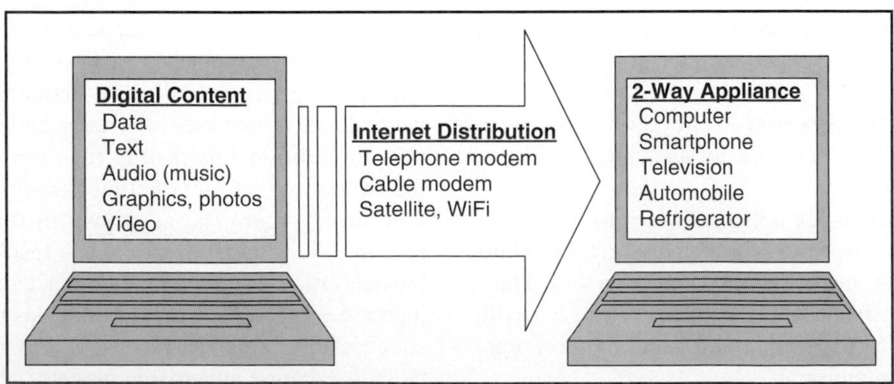

EXHIBIT 1.1 The Web Is Only One Aspect of E-Marketing

directly to their PCs, iPads, and televisions—on their schedule and preferred receiving device, not those of the medium distributor. Finally, the internet enables multimedia one-to-one communication through e-mail, internet-based telephone services, collaborative software such as NetMeeting, and more. The internet continues to affect the way many individuals work, communicate, and consume, and marketers scramble to provide value and earn a piece of the profits.

COMMUNITIES Strangers in countries worldwide form online communities to discuss a variety of things, facilitated by the internet. Consumers pay fees to compete in highly engaging multimedia games as mobile apps or on the Web and virtual worlds online, such as Second Life. Communities form around shared photos (Flickr), videos (YouTube), and individual or company profiles (Facebook). See Exhibit 1.2 for an idea of the huge number of internet users belonging to online communities. Companies and consultants gain exposure to customers on Web logs (blogs). **Blogs** are online diaries, or journals, frequently updated on Web pages. Micro sites and micro blogs, such as tumblr.com and twitter.com, allow individuals to follow each other's short posts and link uploads. Business communities also abound online, especially around shared industries or professions (such as ELMAR for marketing professors). Another example of online communities is auctions in both business and consumer markets. Finally, independent, private communities have formed around peer-to-peer file sharing. Individuals upload, share, and collaborate on documents and files at Google Docs and Dropbox from far away geographic locations.

BUSINESSES The digital environment enhances business processes and activities across the entire organization. Employees across disciplines work together in cross-functional teams worldwide using computer networks to share and apply knowledge for increased efficiency and profitability. Financial experts communicate shareholder information and file required government statements online. Human resources personnel use the internet for electronic recruiting and training—in

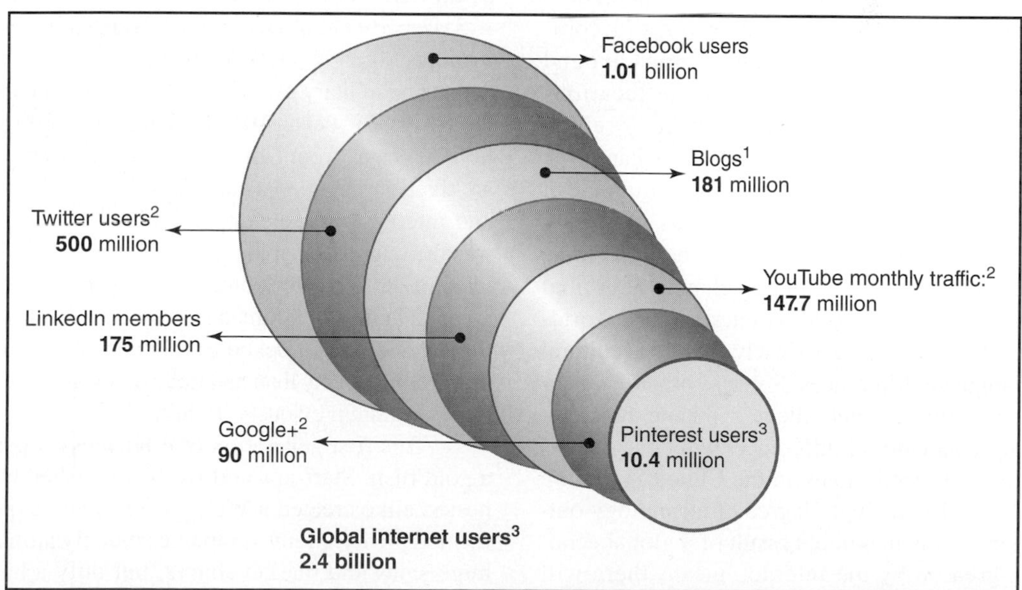

EXHIBIT 1.2 Internet Communities in 2012 *Sources*: [1] "Buzz in the Blogosphere," 2012. Available at blog.nielsen.com [2] Miel Opstal, "10 Social Networks and a Bunch of Stats," 2012. Available at slideshare.net [3] internetworldstats.com. All those without footnotes were obtained from the sites themselves.

fact, 89 percent of recruiters use search engines to learn more about candidates and 70 percent have eliminated prospects based on what they found (according to CareerThoughtLeaders.com). Production and operations managers adjust manufacturing based on the internet's ability to give immediate sales feedback—resulting in just-in-time inventory and building products to order.

Strategists at top corporate levels leverage computer networks to apply a firm's knowledge in building and maintaining a competitive edge. Digital tools allow executives easy access to data from their desktops and show results of the firm's strategies at the click of a mouse.

SOCIETIES Digital information enhances economies through more efficient markets, more jobs, information access, communication globalization, lower barriers to foreign trade and investment, and more. The internet's impact is not evenly distributed across the globe. The top 10 nations account for 56 percent of all usage (see Appendix A). In these countries, adoption rates range from 10 percent (India) to 84 percent (United Kingdom). Asia has the highest proportion of all internet users, at 45 percent—the next closest is Europe at 22 percent (according to internetworldstats.com). Stories abound about indigenous peoples in remote locations gaining health, legal, and other advice or selling native products using the internet (see Chapter 4). Clearly, the internet is having a huge, but unequal, worldwide impact on various societies.

A networked world creates effects that some see as undesirable. Societies change as global communities form based on interests, and worldwide information access slowly decreases cultural and language differences. Some say that the existence of a truly global village will have the effect of removing cultural differences, which is seen as negative. As well, many in the United States are concerned by the high degree of technology outsourcing. This inevitable result of a global economy, greased by the internet, means there will continue to be big changes in many countries.

Easy computer networking on mobile devices from any location means that work and home boundaries are blurring. Although this option makes working more convenient, it may encourage more workaholism and less time with friends and family. Yet another issue is the digital divide—the idea that internet adoption occurs when folks have enough money to buy a computer, the literacy to read what is on Web pages, and the education to be motivated to do it. Internet critics are justifiably concerned that class divisions will grow, preventing the upward mobility of people on lower socioeconomic levels and even in entire developing countries. Meantime, governments are working to solve some of these problems, but they have other important worries, such as how to collect taxes and tariffs when transactions occur in cyberspace in a borderless world. Finally, the problems of **spam** (unsolicited e-mail), online fraud, and computer viruses slow down the positive impact of the internet and e-marketing practices. These kinds of problems are the unavoidable results of all new technologies.

E-MARKETING'S PAST: WEB 1.0

The internet is over 40 years old. Started in 1969 as the ARPANET, it was commissioned by the U.S. Department of Defense's Advanced Research Projects Agency (ARPA) as a network for academic and military use. The first online community, the **USENET**, began 10 years later. Over 800 million messages from that early community are now archived in Google Groups. The first Web pages and internet browsers appeared in 1993 and that was the internet's tipping point. This was Web 1.0: Organizations created content on Web pages and in e-mail and users consumed the content. Companies, media, and users flocked to this new Web, and it grew more quickly than had radio, television, or any other medium previously (Exhibit 1.3).

This first generation of e-business was like a gold rush. Start-ups and well-established businesses alike created a Web presence and experimented plenty. Many companies quickly attracted huge sales and market shares, but only a handful brought anything to the bottom line. In early 2000, many firms experienced 12-month sales growth between 100 percent and 500 percent

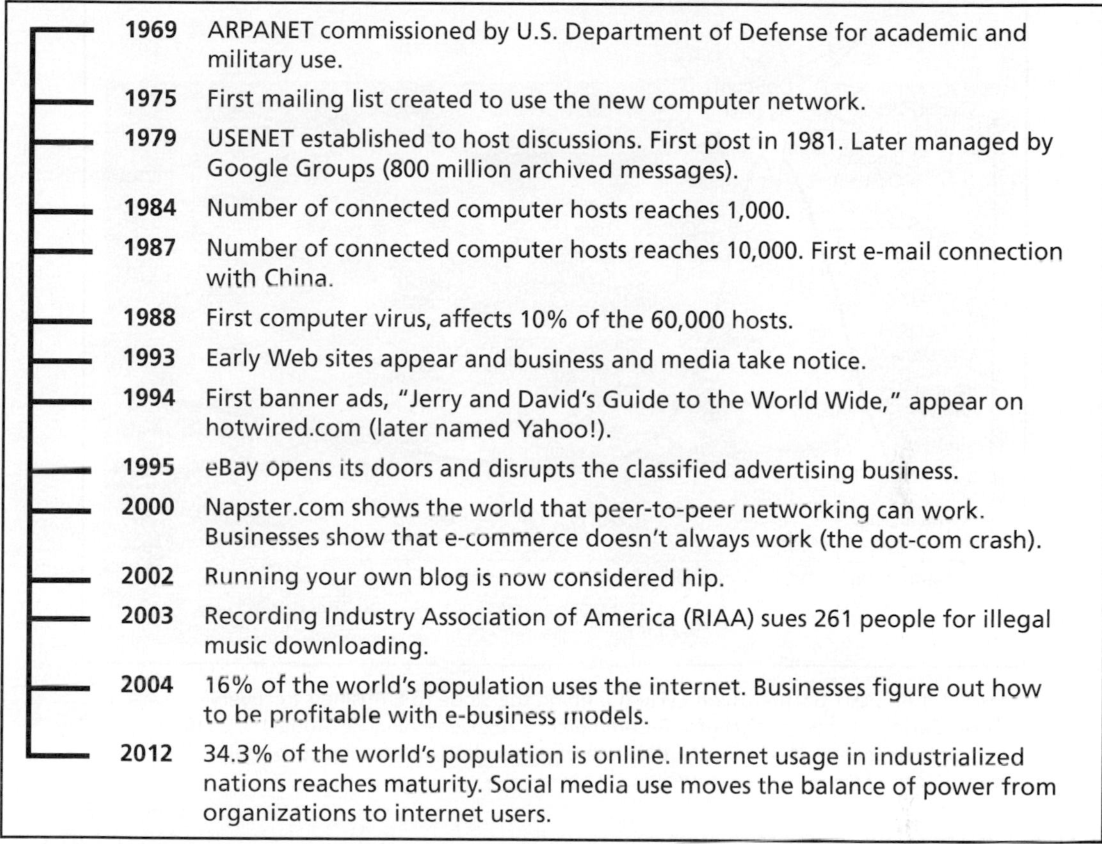

1969 ARPANET commissioned by U.S. Department of Defense for academic and military use.
1975 First mailing list created to use the new computer network.
1979 USENET established to host discussions. First post in 1981. Later managed by Google Groups (800 million archived messages).
1984 Number of connected computer hosts reaches 1,000.
1987 Number of connected computer hosts reaches 10,000. First e-mail connection with China.
1988 First computer virus, affects 10% of the 60,000 hosts.
1993 Early Web sites appear and business and media take notice.
1994 First banner ads, "Jerry and David's Guide to the World Wide," appear on hotwired.com (later named Yahoo!).
1995 eBay opens its doors and disrupts the classified advertising business.
2000 Napster.com shows the world that peer-to-peer networking can work. Businesses show that e-commerce doesn't always work (the dot-com crash).
2002 Running your own blog is now considered hip.
2003 Recording Industry Association of America (RIAA) sues 261 people for illegal music downloading.
2004 16% of the world's population uses the internet. Businesses figure out how to be profitable with e-business models.
2012 34.3% of the world's population is online. Internet usage in industrialized nations reaches maturity. Social media use moves the balance of power from organizations to internet users.

EXHIBIT 1.3 Internet Timeline for Interesting and Amusing Facts *Source*: Some of this information is from Hobbes's Internet Timeline (available at zakon.org). Internet adoption rates are from internetworldstats.com.

with negative profits. Between early 2000 and 2002, however, more than 500 internet firms shut down in the United States alone, owing to the so-called dot-com bust. After the bust dust had settled, almost 60 percent of the public dot-com companies making it through hard times were profitable by the fourth quarter of 2003.

Brick-and-mortar retailers, such as the bookseller Barnes & Noble and Wall Street investment firms, may have felt relief as their online competitors were failing, but quickly noted that internet technologies had fundamentally changed the structure of their and several other industries. In what *BusinessWeek* called the "first wave of internet disruption," firms such as Amazon, Expedia, E*TRADE, and the former CDNow (purchased by Amazon) transformed the way books, travel, investments, and music were sold ("E-Biz Strikes . . ." 2004). Disrupted industries in the first wave generally offered tangible products that were easily compared online and purchased for the lowest price.

Having gone through the boom and the bust in developed nations (the internet is still booming in many emerging economies), businesses then entered what Gartner, Inc., called the *slope of enlightenment* (Exhibit 1.4). It was a time when marketers returned to their traditional roots, relying on well-grounded strategy and sound marketing practices, but using information technology in ways that increased the company's profit—no more throwing money at ideas that don't return a desired amount on investment. During the dot-com shakeout from 2000 to 2002, industries

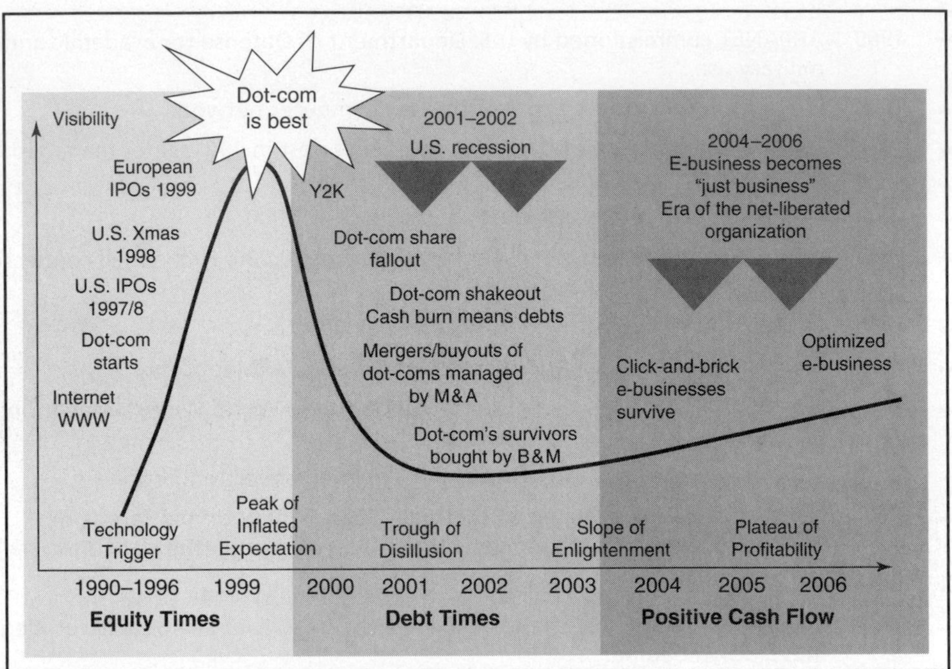

EXHIBIT 1.4 2001 Gartner Hype Cycle (Climbing the Slope to E-Business Recovery)
Source: Gartner, Inc. Hype Cycle for E-Commerce, 2010, Gene Alvarez, August 3, 2010.
Note: Gartner material speaks as of the date of publication and is subject to change without notice.

experienced much consolidation (the Gartner "Peak of Inflated Expectation" and subsequent "Trough of Disillusionment" in Exhibit 1.4). Some firms, such as Levi Strauss, stopped selling online both because it was not efficient and because it created *channel conflict* between manufacturer Sears Roebuck and Company and other long-time retail customers. Other firms merged, with the stronger firms typically acquiring smaller ones.

The *E* Drops from E-Marketing

Gartner predicted that the *e* would drop, making electronic business just part of the way things are done (refer to Exhibit 1.4). This means that e-business is just business, and e-marketing is just marketing. This is now mostly true, as evidenced by the majority of marketing managers and executives who say that online marketing is an integral part of the company's marketing effort. However, e-business and e-marketing will always have their unique models, concepts, and practices (and that is why we've not dropped the *E* from the name of this book).

Markets and traditional marketing practices continue to change, sometimes in fundamental ways, due to information technology. For instance, the concept of online search is intrinsic to e-marketing, continues to evolve, and has important implications that marketers must understand. However, most marketing processes stand the test of time—technology has just given them a new twist. Marketing research is greatly enhanced with online data collection, but the process of identifying research problems, collecting data, and using the results to make marketing decisions will never change. In short, marketers must stay well grounded in the discipline and simultaneously be current on new information technologies and changing e-marketing concepts to remain competitive. This is necessary because the moment marketers feel comfortable about the *e* dropping, new technologies will challenge traditional practices. For example, the e-marketing landscape is now changing rapidly due to consumer-generated content, mobile internet access, social media, and many disruptive technologies.

An example of a company that has already gone through the entire Gartner cycle is Charles Schwab, which allowed e.Schwab.com to cannibalize the larger brick-and-mortar securities firm in 1998. Dubbed "eat your own DNA" by former CEO, Jack Welch of General Electric, Schwab astutely pitted the online and offline business models against each other and allowed the most profitable methods to win. The e.Schwab model resulted in lower prices, incorporation of successful e-marketing strategies, and faster-growing accounts and assets. For this brokerage firm, e-business is just business.

Marketing Implications of Internet Technologies

Early marketers who grasped what internet technologies could do were better poised to integrate information technology into marketing practice. Compare the properties in Exhibit 1.5 to those of the telephone. The telephone is a mediating technology, has global reach, and has network

Property	Marketing Implications
Bits, not Atoms	Information, products, and communication in digital form can be stored, sent, and received nearly instantaneously. Text, audio, video, graphics, and photos can all be digitized, but digital products cannot be touched, tasted, or smelled.
Mediating Technology	Peer-to-peer relationships, such as auctions, social networks, and business partnerships, can be formed regardless of geographic location. Technology allows timely communication and data sharing, as with businesses in a supply chain.
Global Reach	Opens new markets and allows for worldwide partnerships, employee collaboration, and salesperson telecommuting.
Network Externality	Businesses can reach more of their markets with automated communication, and consumers can disseminate brand opinions worldwide in an instant.
Time Moderator	Consumers hold higher expectations about communication with companies and faster work processes within companies.
Information Equalizer	Companies employ mass customization of communication, and consumers have more access to product information and pricing.
Scalable Capacity	Companies pay for only as much data storage or server space as needed for profitable operations and can store huge amounts of data.
Open Standard	Companies can access each other's databases for establishing a smooth supply chain and customer relationship management, which connects both large and small firms.
Market Deconstruction	Many distribution channel functions are performed by nontraditional firms (e.g., Edmunds.com and online travel agents) and new industries emerged (e.g., internet service providers).
Task Automation	Self-service online lowers costs and makes automated transactions, payment, and fulfillment possible.

EXHIBIT 1.5 Internet Properties and Marketing Implications *Source*: Properties adapted from Allan Afuah and Christopher Tucci, *Internet Business Models and Strategies* (New York: McGraw-Hill/Irwin, 2001).

externality. In contrast, the internet has properties that create opportunities beyond those possible with the telephone, television, postal mail, or other communication media. It is these differences that excited early marketers and had them wondering how to best capitalize on them.

These internet properties not only allow for more effective and efficient marketing strategy and tactical implementation but also actually changed the way marketing is conducted. For example, the fundamental idea of digitizing data (bits, not atoms) has transformed media, software, and music delivery methods, as well as created a new transaction channel. This is why the traditional newspaper circulation is declining in comparison with the digital online versions. Also, the internet as an information equalizer has shifted the balance of power from marketer to consumer.

Marketers must understand internet technology to harness its power. They do not have to personally develop the technologies, but they need to know enough to select appropriate suppliers and direct technology professionals.

Gov.uk, a government site in the United Kingdom, assists marketers by summarizing e-business and e-marketing opportunities flowing from the internet's unique properties:

- ***Lower costs.*** Reach the right customers at a much lower cost than with traditional marketing methods.
- ***Trackable, measurable results.*** Obtain detailed data about customer responses to marketing campaigns.
- ***Global reach.*** Access new markets across the globe.
- ***Personalization.*** Connecting a database to a Web site allows for individually targeted offers. The more consumers and businesses buy, the better the data and more effective the marketing.
- ***One-to-one marketing.*** Gain instant access to individual customers on computers and mobile phones.
- ***More interesting campaigns.*** Use creative multimedia content to engage customers.
- ***Better conversion rates (increased purchases).*** Online customers are only a few clicks from a purchase, whereas when offline they must make a phone call or visit a store.
- ***Twenty-four-hour marketing.*** Allows 24/7 access to the firm's products and services, even when the office is closed.

E-MARKETING TODAY: WEB 2.0

The unique properties and strengths of internet technologies provided a springboard from the first to the second generation (Web 2.0), as described by NetLingo:

> The components of Web 2.0 sites (and the popularity of blogs and social networking) exist because of the ability to offer mini-homepages, a gig of storage, your own e-mail, a music player and photo, video and bookmark sharing . . . all of which were initially "first-generation" technologies. (netlingo.com)

Technology only opens the window of opportunity. Marketers and their markets create hot new products that capitalize on Web 2.0 technologies. Whereas Web 1.0 connected users to computer networks for receiving content, Web 2.0 technologies also connect people with each other for producing and sharing content. Collectively called social media, these are Web pages allowing social networking and are primarily authored by internet users (also called user-generated media [UGM] or consumer-generated media [CGM]). Social media sites are increasing in number and attracting users more quickly than are traditional media sites (such as CNN.com). And with any new technology, this creates opportunities and challenges for marketers, some of which are outlined next.

Power Shift from Sellers to Buyers

As noted previously, the connected customer is now the CEO online. "Marketers of all sorts are now being urged to give up the steering wheel to a new breed of consumers who want more control over the ways products are peddled to them," according to Stuart Elliott, a *New York Times* columnist (Elliott, 2009). Both individual and business buyers are more demanding than ever because they are just one click away from a plethora of global competitors, all vying for their business. As well, the internet's social media provide a communication platform where individual comments about products can spread like wildfire in a short time and quickly either enhance or damage a brand's image. Consumers and business customers' word of mouth has long been a powerful market force, but now individuals are not limited to their friends, colleagues, and families. The internet allows a disgruntled customer to tell a few thousand friends with one mouse click: word of mouth on steroids.

This phenomenon is only one part of a trend that has been growing for years because of the internet—the power balance has finally shifted from companies to individuals, as shown in Exhibit 1.6. How did this happen? It started with consumer control of both the television remote control and the computer mouse. This meant that marketers could no longer hold an individual captive for 30 seconds in front of a television screen or even for 10 seconds in front of a computer screen. With **digital video recorders (DVRs)**, consumers can easily pause, rewind, or record hundreds of hours of live television programming for later viewing—fast-forwarding through commercials. DVRs enjoy only about 40 percent penetration but their use is growing rapidly, according to the Nielsen Company. As well, consumers can now get entertainment and information on demand, anytime, anywhere through iTunes, Hulu.com, and television networks' Web sites. See the "Let's Get Technical" box for details on the TiVo DVR.

Other trends affecting consumer attention are as follows (and many more throughout this book):

- ***Consumers trust each other more than companies.*** In its 2012 Trust Barometer, public relations company Edelman asked survey respondents in developed nations who they thought provided the most credible information. Sixty-five percent said they find "a person like yourself" to be most trustworthy—higher than for any company CEO or government official. A "person like yourself" is someone who

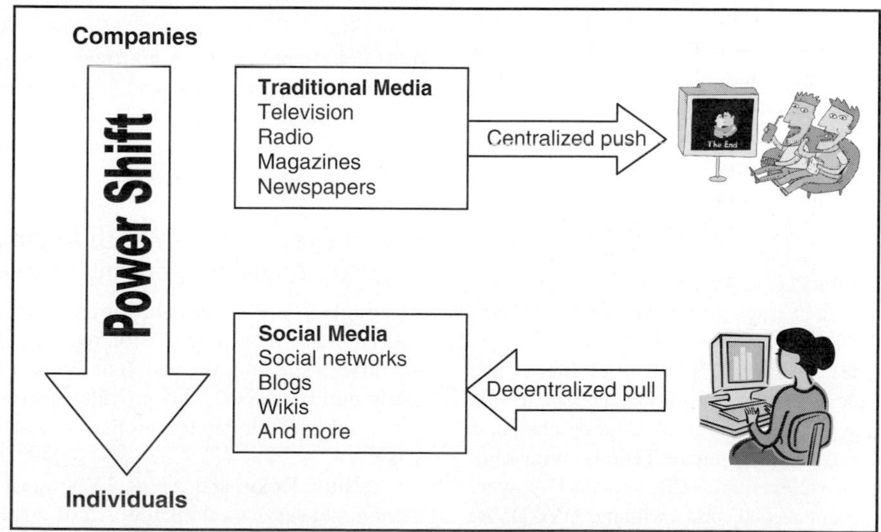

EXHIBIT 1.6 Power Shift from Companies to Individuals *Source*: Based on Dion Hinchcliffe's ideas (web2.socialcomputingmagazine.com).

LET'S GET TECHNICAL

DVR vs. Internet Television

It is Saturday night at 7:50 P.M. Your friends want you to go with them to the 8:30 showing of the latest movie, and you know that your favorite actor is the lead. However, you also do not want to miss the season finale of your favorite reality show, which airs at 8:00 P.M. With little time to get ready, programming your VCR is not an option. The thought of missing the show truly annoys you because you have seen all 13 episodes leading up to it. If only you had asked for a digital video recorder for your birthday last month ...

DVR

Founded in 1997, TiVo provides today's television viewer what he or she has long wished for: ultimate control. TiVo is a provider of television services for the digital video recorder (DVR)—which is a growing category of consumer electronics. In its most basic form, a DVR allows television viewers to record programs and play them back later. According to the company's Web site, the TiVo philosophy is "Watch what you want, when you want."

Now a public company, TiVo was a pioneer in television services for DVRs. The company quickly beat out its competition in the United States and recorded one of the fastest adoption rates in the history of consumer electronics. According to surveys conducted by TiVo in 2003, 98 percent of TiVo subscribers said they could not live without the TiVo service and more than 40 percent said they would choose to disconnect their cell phone over "unplugging" TiVo.

TiVo's target market consists of technologically comfortable 25- to 45-year-olds who are married and have an average yearly income of $70,000 to $100,000.

In order to have TiVo, five elements are required: a television, the TiVo DVR, a phone line or an internet connection, a TiVo subscription plan, and a television programming source. TiVo is compatible with nearly any television, VCR, and DVD player, and all equipment needed comes with the TiVo DVR. The programming source may be an antenna, a satellite dish, or a cable television.

Similar technology and services are offered by cable companies, such as Time Warner, and satellite companies, such as DirecTV. Most offer the following benefits:

- *Season Pass*: Automatically records all episodes of a show for the entire season.
- *Wish List*: Records any program containing a specified keyword, such as an actor's name.
- *Smart Recording*: Detects changes in programming schedules and changes recording time accordingly.
- *Internet Programming*: Allows you to program the television from your desktop at work.
- *Parental Controls*: Allows parents to establish limits on programs available to children.

With the control over programming in the hands of the television viewer, television marketers are faced with additional challenges. For example, when playing back an episode of a sitcom that aired an hour before, the viewer has the option to skip the commercials. However, the commercials provide the revenue needed to pay for the sitcom. The producers and purchasers of the commercials are paying for the contact with the potential consumers, who are bypassing the contact. This has led to an enormous increase in product placement.

Since TiVo's invention, it has received a frenzy of attention. The word *tivo* has even become a verb in popular media—"Did you tivo that football game on Sunday?" On the popular talk show *Live with Regis and Kelly*, host Kelly Ripa frequently discusses how she uses and loves her TiVo.

Internet Television—Watch Anything, Anytime, Anywhere, on Any Device

Although TiVo has revolutionized the way that television is watched, television over the internet is the future. The internet, which in the past was used solely through the PC, may provide viewers with the opportunity to sidestep traditional cable and satellite services.

Hulu, Roku, and Apple TV are just a few of the internet services available. All of these services require some sort of box that receives and decodes the internet signal. The box also verifies access rights for premium services. The data pathway is internet to your cable modem, cable modem to your router, and then either a wired or WiFi connection to the box.

However, television vendors are now creating internet-ready televisions that have one or more of the boxes built into the television itself. Just plug in the television, give it the password to your wireless router, and the service is ready to go.

One huge advantage for advertisers is that commercials cannot be skipped online. The content is not recorded locally on your box—it is recorded on massive hard drives maintained on the internet by the service. The content is then delivered to you upon request with the commercials interspersed. The vendors usually don't allow you to record the content locally. In this sense, it is like watching a YouTube video. In fact, ads can even run around the window where the content appears. It is small wonder then that the networks promote online viewing even during their broadcast episodes.

The great advantage of internet television for consumers is the ability to watch anything, anytime, anywhere, on any device. Unlike using a DVR, the consumer does not have to remember to program the show in advance. Just find it online and watch it on the platform of choice to match your device—whether that is an iPod, an iPhone, an iPad, a laptop, or even a regular, old television.

What Will Apple Do?

Apple offers a low-cost ($99) box as previously mentioned. The box communicates with the internet with no computer required. It allows connection to iTunes movies, YouTube, and Netflix. However, Apple's AirPlay mirroring allows any Apple computer, iPhone, or iPad in the home to stream whatever is on its screen to the television. So, for example, if you are watching a video on your Apple Computer, you can send it wirelessly to the television through the Apple TV box. Many think that this may be a precursor to Apple simply selling a television with the box included. Such a television might be like a giant iPad hanging on the wall. To control it, you might just talk to it using the Siri interface. If you need a keyboard, just use your iPhone, iPad, or Macbook nearby.

shares values and interests. For example, the TripAdvisor.com site allows travelers to review hotels worldwide, and other travelers rely upon it to pick hotels for upcoming trips—they trust it more than the corporate sales monologue they see at the hotels' Web sites.

- ***Market and media fragmentation.*** The mass market has been slowly disintegrating since about 1992, as evidenced by the decline in prime-time television ratings, growth of cable television, and increasing number of special-interest magazines. The internet put finality to this trend by extending it to its ultimate—a market size of one customer—and prompted marketers to create products, mobile apps, Web pages, and communication for small target groups.
- ***Connections are critical.*** Social networking is the name of the game today. Job recruiters scour social networks for job candidates, and business deals are made among LinkedIn members who have never met in person. Lady Gaga has over 31 million followers on Twitter and this has helped her to build her music empire. It is about whom you know online and what they say about you.
- ***Everyone is a content producer.*** Consumer-generated content also includes multimedia material. With smartphones, consumers always have the ability to take photos and videos and instantly upload to Facebook, Instagram, and other sites. Wearable recording devices open the door to action footage while skiing or during other activities. This helps to spread images of products that customers enjoy or ones that do not meet expectations and can be shown malfunctioning in YouTube videos.
- ***Information transparency.*** Because consumers write online product reviews and share other information, marketers must be authentic with brand and company information or they will be exposed in social media. The same holds true for consumers,

who present much personal information in social network profiles and wall posts.

- ***Social commerce.*** This is an evolution of e-commerce, using social media and consumer interactions to facilitate online sales. Customers chat about products online while they are shopping and post products they like on sites like Pinterest.

Voice of the customer is "a systematic approach for incorporating the needs of customers into the design of customer experiences," according to Brude Temkin at Forrester Research. Forrester outlines five components: relationship tracking, interaction monitoring, continuous listening, project infusion (including customer insights into strategies and tactics), and periodic immersion (by employees with customer interactions). Companies are buzzing about this new technique for capturing a 360-degree view of customer preferences and behavior in every online and offline channel. Forrester's Voice of the Customer Award recognizes companies who listen, analyze, and respond to customer feedback. The three winners in 2012 were Barclaycard US (partially for introducing a crowdsourced customer credit card), Cisco Systems (for integrating customer input from social media and other channels and resolving 81 percent of customer problems online), and the Vanguard Group (for passive and active listening techniques to create a holistic customer perspective) (see forrester.com).

Many years of exposure to marketing strategies have made consumers more demanding and more sophisticated, and marketers will continue to become better at delivering customer value.

Customer Engagement

What do marketers do when this new breed of consumer finds their Web properties? Marketers are in a "new age of engagement, participation, and co-creation," according to Nielsen Media ("Super Buzz or Super. . ." 2008). **Engagement** occurs when internet users connect or collaborate with brands, companies, or each other. This involves connecting with a user emotionally and intellectually. Online engagement is analogous to offline experience marketing, such as the famous Build-A-Bear retailers or Disney theme parks. Online marketers engage users by enticing them to participate in their content or media (as seen in Exhibit 1.7).

One way to engage online users is through **Crowdsourcing**. This is the practice of outsourcing ads, product development, and other tasks to a people outside the organization. For example, Doritos holds an annual contest where users create 30-second television commercials. Site visitors vote on the finalists and the winner's ad is shown during the Super Bowl game. Marketers capitalize on consumer desires for control by soliciting input on product development (such as mystarbucksidea.force.com).

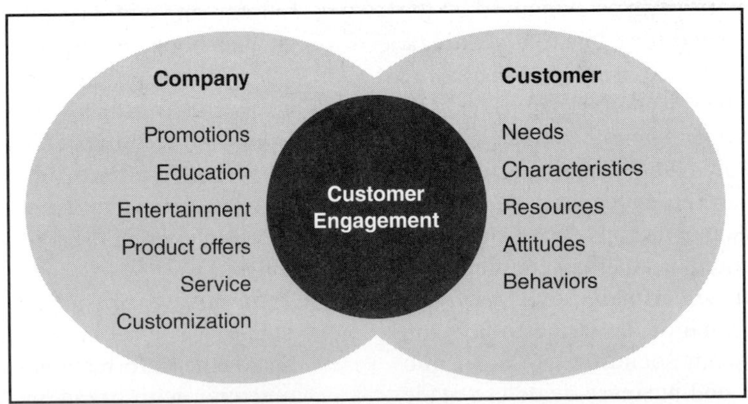

EXHIBIT 1.7 Customer Engagement Connects Company Content with Consumer Characteristics

Software developers ask users to test beta versions of Web sites or next-version software and suggest improvements. Customer engagement via crowdsourcing also involves consumers uploading videos or photos, posting comments on a blog, becoming a fan of the brand's Facebook page, and so forth. Inventors also ask consumers to help fund new products through sites such as kickstarter.com (sometimes called crowdfunding). When buyers are engaged with a company's content, they become more attentive and often feel more favorable toward the brand.

Content Marketing

In addition to crowdsourcing, marketers use their own content to engage users online. **Content marketing** is a strategy involving creating and publishing content on Web sites and in social media. All online content can be considered content marketing and it ranges from Web sites, social network pages, and blog posts to videos, white papers, and eBooks. When businesses receive an e-mail offering a free white paper about a hot topic, this engages them to click on the link and download the paper. In the process, the marketer receives the user's e-mail address and can follow up with a sales e-mail or call. Although the consumer is the CEO, content is the king online. What is new about this is that marketers are beginning to see themselves as publishers, creating engaging content and enticing users to visit and consume the information or entertainment.

Inbound Marketing

Customers are seldom reachable in large quantities in traditional media, such as television, and they are all over the internet in social media. As well, customers no longer appreciate marketing messages that interrupt them from what they are doing. This is why the U.S. government's "do not call" list has effectively killed the telemarketing industry and DVR adoption and television-commercial skipping continue to grow. Today, marketers need to ask for permission to deliver communication if they want it to be attended and generally give customers what they want when they want it.

This change in customer behavior gave rise to the concept of **inbound marketing**—getting found online, as opposed to interrupting customers with outbound marketing to get them to pay attention to the ads, Web site, products, and so forth. Outbound tactics include traditional and online media advertising, telephone calling prospects, trade shows, and e-mail blasts. The components of inbound marketing are content (e.g., blogs, videos, eBooks, white paper pdf files), social networks (e.g., Twitter, Facebook, blogs), and search engine optimization techniques to help get the social media or Web site come up on the first page of results for a keyword search.

Inbound marketing works. In 2010, 46 percent of companies claimed to gain a customer from their blog, 44 percent from a Facebook page, and 41 percent from LinkedIn and Twitter accounts ("The State of Inbound . . .," 2010). Those proportions have surely increased by now, as evidenced by the large number of companies participating in daily inbound marketing activities: 57 percent in search engine optimization, 54 percent in site analytics, 48 percent in social marketing, and 24 percent in content marketing, according to a study by SEOmoz in 2012 (seomoz.org).

One challenge for marketers involves developing new metrics to monitor the success of inbound marketing's social media tactics. The internet allows for tracking every mouse click, and marketers now have well-established measures for online tactics (as outlined in Chapter 2 and throughout the book). However, the standard measurement of number of site visitors or click-throughs from an ad does not measure site engagement well. Nielsen Media and others are now measuring the length of time spent on a site, number of comments posted, time spent watching a video, and other metrics to determine site engagement. Other performance metrics used by marketers include the amount of conversation about a topic for a specific time period; the number and growth of fans, friends, or followers and "likes" on a social network page; rate of pass-along for videos and other content; number of downloads or uploads of content; number of ratings, reviews, subscriptions, or social bookmarks; amount of interaction with a Web page; and many more.

New Technologies

Marketers constantly watch technology advances that spawn new marketing tactics. In this section, we discuss only a few important recent changes that affect internet technologies.

WIRELESS NETWORKING AND MOBILE COMPUTING 4G is a fourth-generation high-speed, wireless technology that replaces 3G (third generation). Although there are over a billion 3G subscribers worldwide, faster technology always gains adoption eventually. Mobile phones, tablets, and laptop computer technologies support a wide range of bandwidths for receiving and sending e-mail and large amounts of data, and for Web browsing in many different countries.

Using wireless mobile devices, customers check e-mail at Starbucks in Shanghai, receive flight information in the smallest of airports, and catch the latest sports scores while at the Gare du Nord train station in France (Exhibit 1.8). Wireless nodes are multiplying like rabbits. Consider the following:

- Several major airlines offer internet connections on airplanes.
- Autonet Mobile offers an in-car router and service that turns an automobile into a WiFi hot spot.
- Sprint and other mobile carriers offer USB modems, allowing users to create an internet bubble around them anytime, anywhere.
- Coffee drinkers listening to music in Starbucks can instantly identify the artist, track, and album via the Shazam app and download a copy to their iPods or iPhones via the iTunes WiFi Music Store.
- There are over 1 million WiFi access points worldwide and that is expected to grow to 5.8 million by 2015 (reuters.com).

EXHIBIT 1.8 WiFi at the Gare du Nord Train Station in France *Source*: Courtesy of Reinier Evers (trendwatching.com).

The rapid growth of wireless access points, when coupled with the large number of individuals worldwide owning mobile phones and the huge numbers owning smartphones, tablets, or notebook computers, indicates a continuing growth in wireless networking. As this trend plays out, customers will demand information, entertainment, and communication whenever and however they desire and in small file sizes for fast downloading. We discuss many mobile strategies in this book, such as the Square device that allows businesses to swipe credit cards from their iPhones.

CUTTING THE CORD In 2002, the number of mobile subscriptions began to surpass landline telephones (Meeker, 2012). Consumers are increasingly cutting the cord on their landline phones and moving to purely mobile phone use. They are also cutting the cable to their televisions. Nearly one-third of households with broadband internet access now watch videos on their televisions and 14 percent have eliminated the cable services altogether ("21% of US Pay . . . ," 2012).

Cutting the cords is an indication of the huge disruption in entertainment industries. Pandora, Spotify, and iTunes have kicked most physical CDs into a grave. Devices like the iPod and other MP3 players and digital music downloads have changed the music industry. The same is beginning to happen with the movie and television programming models: Streaming on-demand video from Netflix and others via WiFi to televisions and other receiving appliances has changed the business models in these industries.

APPLIANCE CONVERGENCE Digital media are simply data that can be sent to viewers by a number of ways, as seen in Exhibit 1.1. Television programs, radio shows, news, movies, books, and photos are sent by their creators in electronic form via satellite, telephone wires, or cable, which are then viewed by the audience on receiving appliances such as televisions, computers, radios, smartphones, and others. Contrary to popular terminology usage, the receiving appliance is separate from the media type. In other words, watching a television set doesn't mean one must be viewing television programming—many watch YouTube videos on their televisions via WiFi connections in their homes. Computers can receive digital radio and television transmissions, and television sets can receive the Web and satellite radio content. Some appliances, such as radio and fax machines, have limited receiving capabilities, while others are more flexible.

The idea of separating the medium from the appliance is both mind-boggling and exciting because of the business opportunities. It opens the door to new types of receiving appliances that are also "smart," allowing for saving, editing, and sending transmissions. For instance, LG Electronics currently sells an internet refrigerator (lg.com). Consumers can view television programs, movies, family photos, and Web pages on the refrigerator's 15.1-inch touch screen; read e-mail and handwritten or typed messages entered by the family; listen to downloaded music and recorded messages from the family; and track the food inventory in the refrigerator; by the way, it also keeps food cold.

The LG internet refrigerator is a good example of receiving-appliance convergence—many digital appliances in one. Another example is the convergence of cell phone and digital still and video cameras. Finally, consider the automobile. The Lincoln LS owner can watch a movie, use the telephone, listen to music on disk or from radio station transmission, view the time, and communicate using a GPS. If the car is involved in an accident or needs repair, it will automatically send a message to the nearest Lincoln dealer via the internet. So, the next time you think of television programming, remember that by U.S. law it is all simply digitized video that can be sent through several ways to a number of receiving devices such as a television, a computer, and even a refrigerator. This convergence trend is far from over—many opportunities still exist for new technology and appliance development.

What does this mean for marketers? They currently allocate advertising budgets by media type such as newspaper, television, or internet. Conversely, audiences don't discriminate between the same video advertising they see on the NBC broadcast news, the MSNBC cable news, the MSNBC.com Web site news, and YouTube. Similarly, the newspaper classifieds are equivalent to those on Craigslist.org, and magazine ads can be found as display ads on the magazine's or other Web sites. Individuals record television commercials, manipulate them using video software, and upload to video-posting sites or their own Web sites. Media editorial already appears both online and offline, paralleling the blurring of media advertising. Appliance convergence means that both editorial and advertising content are already viewed on a myriad of mobile and stationary devices. Marketers now realize that the medium and the appliance are no longer the defining way to reach customers (i.e., the term *television commercial* will soon lose its meaning). Instead, marketers will create multimedia communication for distribution to audience members anytime, anywhere, to any device—on demand by the user. In this light, social media and traditional media become simply media.

Exciting New Technology-Based Strategies

Demanding consumers jump on anything that saves them time. One new idea that works is one-click delivery:

- Uber Technologies, Inc., offers an iPhone and Android app that allows consumers to simply tap once and a taxi or luxury car with driver will arrive to pick them up (uber.com). This is currently available in San Francisco and other major cities.
- Red Tomato Pizza in Dubai offers a special "VIP fridge magnet" to its loyal customers (Exhibit 1.9). The hungry consumer simply taps the magnet, Red Tomato receives a signal and makes a pizza, and then the customer's favorite pizza is delivered (and a text message order confirmation). No phone call is required. This feature works using the customer's Bluetooth on a smartphone, WiFi technology, and the internet. However, no app is needed—just an initial Bluetooth connection with the magnet (see the video explanation on YouTube).
- Evian Chez Vous plans a similar magnet-based service to deliver bottled water to Paris residents and businesses (see trendwatching.com).

EXHIBIT 1.9 Red Tomato Pizza's VIP Fridge Magnet
Source: Tbwa\Raad – Dubai. Creative Team: Preethi Mariappan / Rafael Guida / Melanie Clancy

Voice navigation is another development, initiated by the iPhone's Siri software. Acting on a user's voice commend, Siri can send an e-mail or text message, make a phone call, add a calendar item, check the weather, or answer many questions using the Web. Siri decides which app or Web site will best answer the user's question and presents this to the user. The implications for marketers are huge. For example, if the user asks Siri for the best Thai restaurant, Siri might check Yelp for the answer, as opposed to a Google search (thus ignoring a marketer's search engine optimization efforts). Also, Google's Android plans a similar voice-recognition device and may use its database instead of Yelp. Stay tuned to see how this plays out.

There are a few physical objects that connect with a user's smartphone in interesting ways:

- Audi's e-bike, Wörthersee, comes with a computer that sends challenges and performance tips to the rider's smartphone as she is on the bike. It is also a social device because riders can compare their results on the challenges with other cyclists (progress.audiusa.com).
- Babolat Play & Connect has sensors on tennis racquets that give feedback to improve the player's technique and compare with other players online (babolat.com).
- Richard Nicoll and Vodafone UK created a handbag with a battery that can charge one's mobile phone; the handbag, fully charged, can provides two days' worth of on-the-go power to the phone (richardnicoll.com).
- Softbank has a smartphone in Japan with a Geiger counter built into it. Based on the Android system, it can measure radiation with 20 percent accuracy. It is not an app, but the user simply presses a button on the phone to read the radiation levels (mb.softbank.jp/en/).

By the time you read this book, there are bound to be many more exciting products and strategies capitalizing on internet technologies. A good place to view them is trendwatching.com.

Other Opportunities and Challenges in Web 2.0

Let's examine some of the other key elements of today's Web 2.0 landscape.

- ***Internet adoption matures.*** Today, the internet has matured in industrialized nations. High adoption rates have leveled and heavy Web and e-mail use are commonplace.
- ***Online retail sales mature.*** Although retail sales online continue to grow, they continue to hover at a little over 4 percent of all U.S. retail sales. With user adoption stabilized in industrialized nations, online retailers must compete with each other for sales because they can't count on many new internet users to find them.
- ***Search engines are now reputation engines.*** Relevance is one of Google's search algorithm variables. The more high-traffic, similar-topic Web pages that point to a site, the higher it appears on search engine results pages (SERPs) for specific keywords—meaning it is more relevant to the user. Popularity, as measured by incoming links, improves brand exposure, awareness, image, site traffic, and ultimately sales. Search marketing is now a key part of online marketer budget.
- ***Image recognition takes root.*** **Image recognition** is a technology that sees the content within an image. TinEye is an image-recognition search engine that will find images online based on their content, not on text-based keywords or metatags describing the image. This service has indexed over 2 billion images and can help users locate copies of pictures of themselves or any other object (tineye.com).
- ***Improved online and offline strategy integration.*** This integration is especially evident in **multichannel marketing**—offering customers more than one way to buy something, such as a Web site, retail store, and catalog. Retailers manage customers via databases accessible by all employees. To cite a media example, NBC allows its 13.5 million online users to subscribe to the site content; download widgets; add content to wikis, message boards, and the corporate blog; and view video clips through the site, as well as through iTunes and YouTube.
- ***Intellectual capital rules.*** Imagination, creativity, and entrepreneurship are more important resources than financial capital. This was true of the first-generation internet and continues to this day. The difference today is that marketers now know how to use solid marketing and business principles to monetize creative ideas.
- ***Decline of print media.*** In early 2012, the *Encyclopedia Britannica* announced that it will no longer produce a printed version (the first edition was published in 1768). Printed newspapers are also declining in number due to subscriber and advertiser declines. Wikipedia's start in 2001 paved the way for growth in digital encyclopedia content with online access. This applies to other areas as well, such as Twitter, YouTube, and e-mail for breaking news and digital book readers for longer texts (such as Amazon's Kindle).
- ***Online fund-raising increases.*** As you read in the opening Obama story, marketers use the internet to raise funds for political campaigns (nonprofits also do this well). Kickstarter.com allows inventors to raise funds from users for innovative new products (crowdfunding).
- ***Location-based services.*** Many companies use the smartphone's GPS (global positioning system) feature to provide local search, such as Google local search. Others also allow user check-in so friends can see where they are: for example, Facebook and Foursquare. There are also GPS pet-tracking collars now.
- ***The long tail.*** Made famous by Chris Anderson's book, this term refers to the economy of abundance and explains how cheap computing and storage make it possible to increase revenue by selling small

quantities of a large number of products online. For example, in 2004, Amazon.com had 2.3 million books in inventory as compared to 130,000 at a typical Barnes & Noble brick-and-mortar store. Amazon is able to sell a large variety of hard-to-find books in smaller quantities, and the sale of products not available in offline bookstores comprises 57 percent of Amazon's total sales. This idea has turned economic models upside down.

- ***Everything is "FSTR."*** Everything is faster in the Web 2.0 environment. Users are overloaded with entertainment and information opportunities and marketers need to be fast to gain their attention.

Many of these changes made traditional marketing more efficient and effective in reaching and selling to markets. However, some truly changed traditional marketing in fundamental and critical ways. The opportunities are stimulating and marketers must be ever vigilant to capitalize on the internet's new frontiers.

THE FUTURE: WEB 3.0

Plenty of other thrilling new opportunities lie ahead, but companies move with caution, watching the results of every goal, strategy, and tactic for signs of effectiveness. In the following sections, we describe several important trends that will further solidify in the near future and some that may take 10 to 15 years to do so.

Semantic Web

Conceptualizing information and entertainment as data that are separate from the receiving appliance is one way that marketers can give customers exactly what they want, when they want it, and where they want it. If the Web consisted of pure data that could be found, presented as required words and images on pages, texts, or e-mail, and shared based on its type and context, this would be Web 3.0. For example, you could ask your semantic Web electronic agent to book a flight to see a client on Monday in San Francisco, California. The agent would book a flight via the airline databases early in the morning with an aisle seat because the databases have stored your preferences. The agent would further charge your credit card and bill the flight to the client's account in your software program. Then the agent would remind you that you will miss a dentist appointment at home on Monday and ask if you'd like it cancelled in the dentist's database. Exhibit 1.10 displays the evolution from Web 1.0 (content creator makes a Web page and the content consumer views it) to Web 2.0 (every user is both content creator and consumer and they share with one another) and Web 3.0 (individual data presented and shared as desired). One thing keeping this from being a reality is that computer software cannot interpret data meaning based on the context, as in this example. Enter the semantic Web.

Sir Tim Berners-Lee, the World Wide Web's coinventor, has been working with many others since 2001 on the technology to organize the Web's data for greater user convenience. His idea, the **semantic Web**, is an extension of the current Web, in which information is given a well-defined meaning through HTML-like tags. The current Web carries text documents, photos, graphics, and audio and video files embedded in Web pages that search engines struggle to catalog for users to find. The semantic Web will make the search easier by providing a standard definition protocol so that users can easily find information based on its type, such as a person's name (e.g., in the HTML code), the next available appointment for a particular doctor (found by searching the doctor's database), details on an upcoming concert, the hours of the library, the menu at the local restaurant, and so forth (for more information, see Berners-Lee, Hendler, and Lassila, 2001 and w3.org).

The value of the semantic Web is truly information on demand. Using an analogy, think for a minute about the development of time-telling devices. All clocks before 1929 required user effort to find the time. The sundial took a lot of user effort, to go look at the time and reposition the instrument as the sun's position changed.

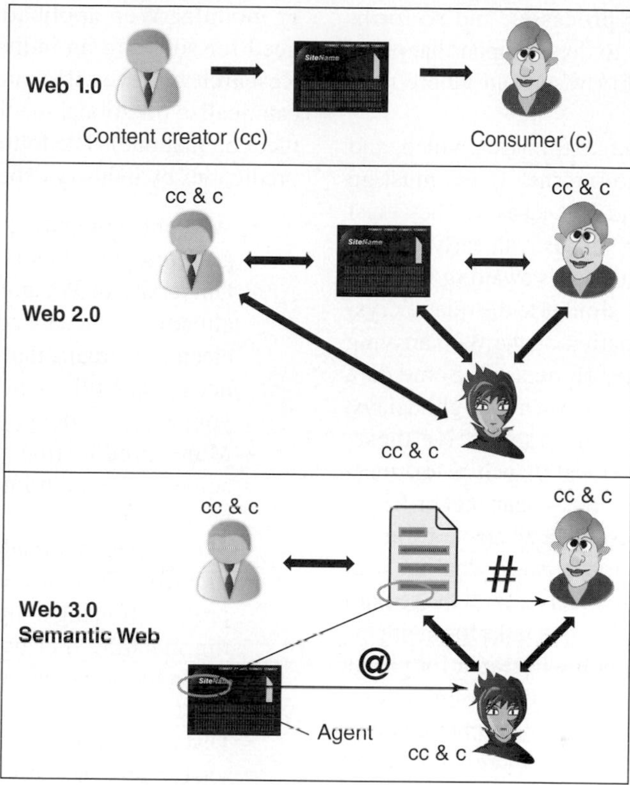

EXHIBIT 1.10 Evolution From Web 1.0 To Web 3.0

Later, mechanical, wind-up clocks displayed time only if the user wound the watch or clock pendulum to keep it running (Exhibit 1.11). In 1929, the quartz crystal changed things dramatically. From that point, the piece of data called *time* was pushed to users on demand with no effort on their part, a fundamental change from a user finding or pulling the time to automated delivery of the time data. Afterward, time appeared in lots of devices, controlling lawn sprinklers, microwave

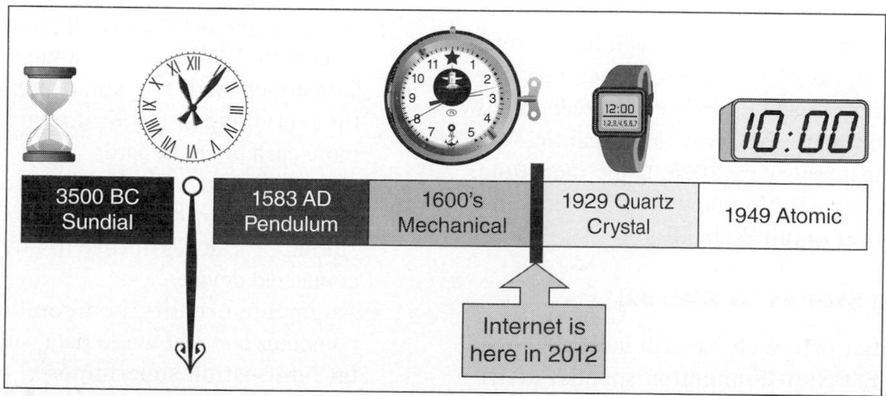

EXHIBIT 1.11 Internet–Time Analogy: Awaiting the Next Technological Breakthrough

ovens, manufacturing processes, and so forth. Individuals have come to depend upon that piece of data arriving reliably when and where they want it.

Now, think of the text, images, video, and audio available via the internet. Users must go find what they want, and it is not easy: They must spend effort searching, just as with early clocks. We believe that the internet is awaiting the next big technological leap, similar to the quartz crystal. Imagine the information on the Web arriving just as reliably as time, on demand. Some data are available this way now, such as flight delays, but consumers must sign up to receive these. Other data arrive automatically, such as text messages, e-mail, and Facebook comments or friend requests. However, these data all arrive from the source with no distinction between what the user wants or doesn't want to receive. With the semantic Web, consumers will define tasks for their personal digital agents, which will search for pieces of data and return them as movies to the television set, appointments to the smartphone calendar, contact information to the address book, and more. The semantic Web holds the promise of being this next huge advance: worldwide access to data on demand without effort. Get ready for the internet's "quartz crystal" and the next wave of disruption.

The semantic Web is only one view of the future, and 41 percent of experts believe it will be achieved and make a significant difference to internet users by 2020, according to a Pew Internet & American Life Project study in 2010 (note that 47 percent doubted it will be as effective as hoped) (available at pewinternet.org). The Gartner Group, a leading information technology research company, believes the semantic Web will become a reality by 2026. In the meantime, there are many exciting new developments that move us closer to full Web 3.0

Stepping Stones to Web 3.0

Many predict that Web 3.0 will include higher bandwidth, faster connection speeds, artificial intelligence, seamless social networking, or modular Web applications eliminating the need for software on individual PCs. Forrester Research believes that interactive media will cannibalize traditional media (and we are almost there on that one). The following are some of the predictions by industry experts:

- Wearable computing will deliver data into goggles, wristbands, and other devices. University of Washington researches have already produced a contact lens containing electrical circuits that can receive the internet via a WiFi connection (the internet in your eye) (see dailyuw.com).
- Many predict that mobile devices will someday be the primary devices for internet access.
- 3D printing is already available and close to hitting the consumer markets. This is a process of using a digital design in a printing machine that builds up a 3D object, layer by layer (using liquid, powder, or sheets of plastic and other material).
- Distance online education will become pervasive and perhaps eventually make the traditional university obsolete.
- "Big data" refers to the sea of information available about consumers, organizations, and all internet users. Some predict that these data will provide more transparency online and create better productivity and marketing strategies. Marketers currently struggle to shape this sea into usable customer insights.
- Some people believe that applications such as Google Wallet will become ubiquitous. Consumers will use smartphones to pay for everything in physical retail stores: no more cash or credit cards.
- Cloud computing will continue to grow, such that most data will be stored in the "cloud" for accessibility to any internet-connected device.
- Augmented reality is a combination of computer and real world data, such as digital information superimposed on reality. The digital information can be graphics,

text, sound, or video. For example, a person might be in the stands watching a football game and see a red line across the field to indicate where the ball needs to go for a first down. Augmented reality can also be viewed on a mobile device or computer. Marketers use augmented reality to display what is inside a package or to integrate traditional print and digital advertising. Expect to see more of this.

The Gartner Group creates a new "hype cycle" each year (beginning in 2001: Exhibit 1.4). See Exhibit 1.12 for Gartner's 2012 hype cycle. It presents Gartner's view of new technologies and when they will become mainstream (from less than 2 years to over 10 years). The important themes in this hype cycle include extensions of social media, cloud computing, and mobile internet access. Key technologies that affect marketing strategies follow:

- **Any channel, any device, anywhere—Bring your own everything.** This refers to the idea that employees can bring personal smartphones, tablet computing, and other devices into the workplace. This is feasible because cloud computing and other technologies are available on any device.
- **Smarter things.** Big data, machine-to-machine communication (e.g., internet television), better databases, and better analytics will help everyone in their daily lives.
- **Big data and global scale computing at small prices.** This predicts the growth of data and computing to improve consumer understanding and help to reduce online fraud, all with a small price tag.

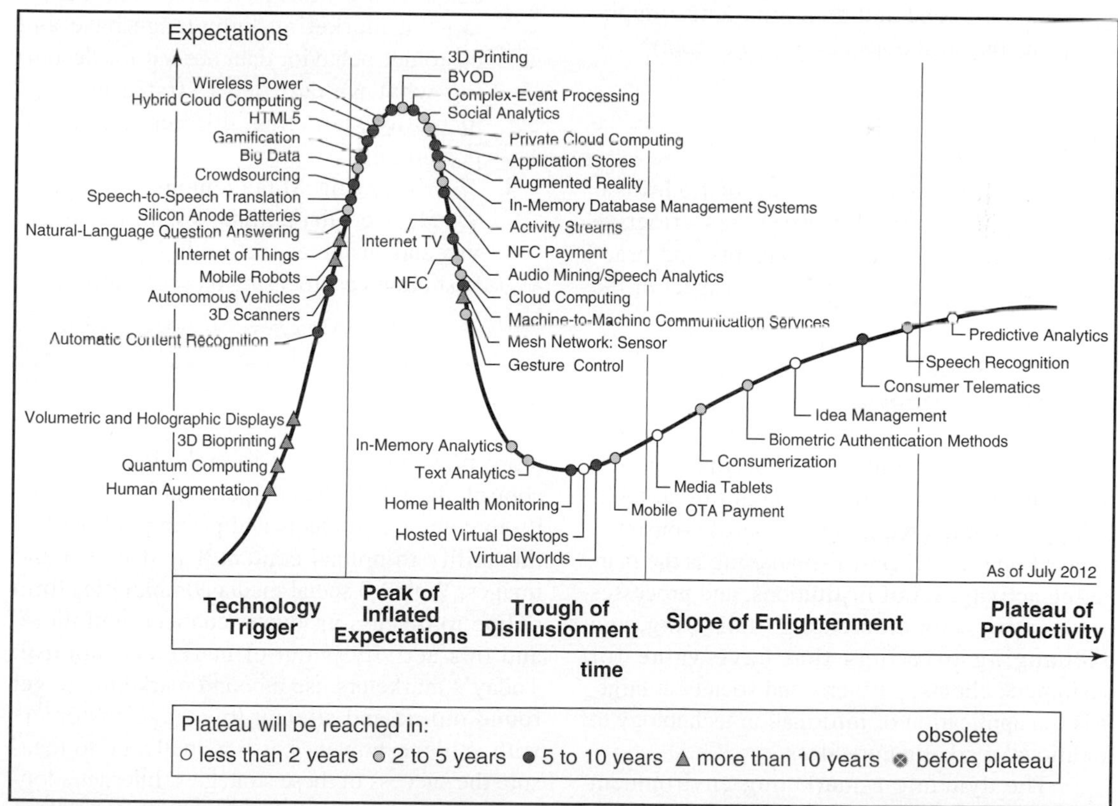

EXHIBIT 1.12 2012 Hype Cycle for Emerging Technologies *Source*: Gartner, Inc. Available at gartner.com
Note: Gartner material speaks as of the date of publication and is subject to change without notice.

- **The human way to interact with technology.** Holographs, speech recognition (e.g., Siri), augmented reality, and biometric authentication methods (like a fingerprint) mean that people will interact more naturally with machines.
- **What payment could really become. Near field communication** will facilitate consumer payments (e.g., holding a smartphone near a payment terminal as with the Google digital wallet). Gartner predicts a cashless world.
- **The voice of the customer is on file.** This relates to the semantic Web, cloud computing, better social analytics, and the ability to mine and analyze audio files in a database.
- **3D print at home.** As previously discussed, consumers will soon have 3D printers at home, and they can scan objects with a smartphone and then print a near duplicate physical object (see gartner.com).

READ ON

This book follows the structure of traditional marketing processes but discusses effective and efficient e-marketing concepts and practices. Technology is an important aspect of the e-marketing environment, and because it is critical for marketers to understand it, we integrate "Let's Get Technical" boxes throughout the text to help marketers understand some of the basics. *E-Marketing* is organized into four parts.

1. "E-Marketing in Context" (Chapters 1–3) introduces strategic e-marketing and the e-marketing plan. The discussions include e-business models, performance metrics for measuring e-marketing success, and the steps involved in an e-marketing plan.
2. "E-Marketing Environment" (Chapters 4 and 5) explains the legal and global environments that are critical to the success of any e-marketing effort. We place special emphasis on the next frontier: emerging and important markets, such as China.
3. "E-Marketing Strategy" (Chapters 6–8) deals with e-strategy formulation, including the marketing knowledge base and customer behavior data needed for designing what we call tier 1 strategies: segmentation, targeting, differentiation, and positioning.
4. "E-Marketing Management" (Chapters 9–15) covers tier 2 strategies: the marketing mix and customer relationship management best practices, focusing on social media.

Chapter Summary

E-business is the continuous optimization of a firm's business activities through digital technology. E-commerce is the subset of e-business focused on transactions. E-marketing is the marketing activity, set of institutions, and processes for creating, communicating, delivering, and exchanging offerings that have value for customers, clients, partners, and society at large. It is the application of information technology to traditional marketing practices.

The dynamic e-marketing environment offers opportunities to develop new products, new strategies and tactics, new markets, new media, and new channels. Individual buyers have more power because of the television remote control, the DVR, the computer mouse, the ability to compare products and pricing online, and the ability to upload content that affects brand images. Web 2.0 social media communities form online to discuss products, connect, and more, and this activity is out of marketers' control. Today's marketers use inbound marketing to get found online and attempt to engage customers with content; however, it is a challenge to measure the success of these strategies. Internet adoption and retail sales in most industrialized nations have reached maturity levels. The internet deeply affects the citizens of many countries.

The internet consists of computers with data, users who send and receive the data files on a myriad of receiving appliances, and technology infrastructure to move, create, and view or listen to the content. An intranet is a network that runs internally in a corporation using internet standards. An extranet is an intranet to which proprietary networks are joined for the purpose of sharing information. The Web is the part of the internet that supports a graphical user interface for hypertext navigation with a browser. The internet's properties allow for a more effective and efficient marketing strategy and tactical implementation and are changing marketing in Web 2.0 by realizing that customers trust each other more than companies; increasing market and media fragmentations, inbound marketing, and customer engagement; shifting power from sellers to buyers; empowering search engines as reputation engines; improving social commerce; and improving online and offline strategy integration (especially multichannel marketing). Content is still king online, but connections are critical in this climate of high broadband connectivity and intellectual capital rules. In the Web 2.0 environment, companies try to engage customers through content marketing, crowdsourcing, and inbound marketing. Finally, new technologies, such as wireless networking, cutting the cord, appliance convergence, and many other exciting inventions, open the door to new marketing strategies and tactics.

The internet has evolved from Web 1.0 (content creator makes a Web page and the content consumer views it) to Web 2.0 (every user is both content creator and consumer and they share with one another), and to the future Web 3.0 (individual data presented and shared as desired).

Web 3.0 will be a time of continued receiving-appliance convergence, merging of traditional and social media, increased wireless networking, wearable internet devices, big data, and cloud computing. As well, the semantic Web will change the marketing landscape. It is essential for marketers to realize that television programs, radio shows, news, movies, many books, and photos are simply digital data sent by their creators in electronic form via satellite, telephone wires, or cable and then viewed by the audience on receiving appliances such as televisions, computers, radios, cell phones, smartphones, and other devices. This understanding opens the door for many new product opportunities that provide value to the demanding customers of the future. Web 3.0 will be defined by better technology and Web applications, and automatic receipt of individual data to any connected device.

Exercises

REVIEW QUESTIONS

1. Define *e-business* and *e-marketing*.
2. What are metrics and why are they important?
3. How does technology change traditional marketing?
4. As a technology, how does the internet compare with the telephone?
5. What are some of the marketing implications of internet technologies?
6. In the context of e-marketing, what does "the medium is not the appliance" mean?
7. Describe the important internet properties that affect marketing.
8. What fundamental changes has the internet brought to marketing?
9. What is the difference between inbound and outbound marketing?
10. What are the key elements of Web 2.0?
11. What are the key elements of Web 3.0?

DISCUSSION QUESTIONS

12. **The Barack Obama Campaign Story.** Explain how Obama's 2008 and 2012 campaign capitalized on Web 2.0 properties and trends.
13. **The Barack Obama Campaign Story.** In 20 years, when Web 3.0 is a reality, what additional tactics will political campaigns use (also refer to Exhibit 1.12 ideas)?
14. What are the implications of the differences in various countries' internet adoptions?

15. As a consumer, what difference does it make if e-business is "just business"? Explain your answer.

16. Some economists suggest that the increase in e-commerce within the business-to-business (B2B) market will lead to greater competition and more goods and services becoming commodities, meaning they will compete solely on price. How do you think this competition is likely to affect buyers within the B2B market? How would it affect sellers?

17. What concerns about consumer privacy are raised by the increased use of wireless computing and handheld devices outside the home or workplace?

18. As a consumer, how will your life change when the semantic Web becomes a reality?

19. How do social media and consumer-generated content change the way marketers operate? Explain.

20. As a consumer who is in control, what would you like to see for the future Web 3.0?

WEB ACTIVITIES

21. See if you can find the portion of your university's Web site that is for students and employees only (intranet). What information is contained on those pages? Should outsiders be excluded from accessing these pages? Why or why not?

22. Visit the McDonald's Web site. List each stakeholder it reaches and tell what basic content is targeted to each stakeholder.

23. Visit Facebook.com and find a company's profile. How many friends does it have? Why would Facebook customers want to befriend a company, especially in light of the Edelman Trust Barometer findings?

24. Search gartnergroup.com for the latest Hype Cycle (sometimes available in a Google image search). What is in store for the future?

CHAPTER

2

Strategic E-Marketing and Performance Metrics

The main goal of this chapter is to help you understand strategic planning and the way companies seek to achieve their objectives through strategies and tactics involving e-business and e-marketing. You will become familiar with common e-business models implemented at different organizational levels and with the application of performance metrics to monitor progress toward objective accomplishment.

After reading this chapter, you will be able to:

- Explain the importance of strategic planning, strategy, e-business strategy, and e-marketing strategy.
- Identify the main e-business models at the activity, business process, and enterprise levels.
- Discuss the use of performance metrics and the Balanced Scorecard to measure e-business and e-marketing performance.
- Enumerate key performance metrics for social media communication.

- Now, with more consumers than ever pretty much constantly online and plugged into social networks, it's never been easier for shoppers to harness the power of the crowd in new and innovative ways (crowdsourcing).

- Australian site ***FlightFox*** allows travelers to set up a contest where online travel experts can compete to find the best available prices for future trips. Users pay an AUD 29 'finders fee' (refundable if a cheaper flight is found within 48 hours), and the site claims to save people AUD 369 per trip on average.

The Amazon Story

After opening its virtual doors in 1995, Amazon.com was one of the first to prove that the online retailing business model can be profitable, reporting its first-ever net profit in the fourth quarter of 2001 ($3.1 billion in net sales). Now a Fortune 500 company, in 2011 Amazon.com announced $48.1 billion net sales (41% growth from 2010) and $631 million in net income—an impressive growth rate. Amazon's strong customer service strategy (focusing on consumers, companies, e-commerce sellers, and content creators) has paid off big time.

Amazon, a dot-com survivor, is quite adept at leveraging its competencies into many different e-business models. It started as the world's biggest bookstore, but soon branched out into the "everything store." First is its core business—online retailing. Amazon sells merchandise and content purchased from manufacturers and resellers to consumer markets. Sales of paper books, electronic books through its Kindle platform, music, and DVDs account for the large proportion of Amazon's sales, but nonmedia sales now comprise 60 percent of all sales (toys, tools, health and beauty aids, prescription drugs, home furnishing, electronics, apparel, and more). Amazon also began renting textbooks in 2012. A truly global organization, 44.5 percent of all its sales occur outside of North America.

Second are Amazon's e-commerce partnerships with many retailers. These partnerships bring revenue through differing commitments, but they typically involve Amazon earning fixed fees, sales commissions, or per-unit activity fees by offering third-party merchandise on the Amazon.com Web site. Customers can purchase items in dozens of product categories and complete the transaction in one checkout process. Amazon also offers to undertake marketing, customer service, and product fulfillment services (inventory storage and delivery) on behalf of its partners. This partnership business model can be more profitable than the pure retailing model because Amazon earns a fee by leveraging its automated services, e-commerce experience, and huge customer base.

Amazon has evolved from online retailer, to e-commerce partner, and now to developer service provider. It sells many different Web services and space for computing, storing, and retrieving data from anywhere on the Web through its Amazon Web Services (AWS) business. Amazon offers 28 different Web services in 190 countries.

Amazon is also a content provider, offering authors and publishing companies an online platform for selling digital content for the Kindle. Authors receive 70 percent royalties and some have realized handsome revenues from this. Musicians and film makers also sell content through Amazon's CreateSpace.

Amazon also uses another important e-business model. It created the first affiliate program (called Amazon Associates), giving hundreds of thousands of Web site owners up to 15 percent commission for referring customers who purchase at Amazon. These partners integrate merchandise seamlessly into their Web sites via Amazon's Associate program. It is like having lots of sales people all over the world, and in fact, Amazon classifies this commission as a marketing expense in its annual reports.

According to founder and CEO Jeff Bezos, Amazon is not interested in expanding to the physical world because the company cannot differentiate Amazon-branded brick-and-mortar stores from well-established physical bookstores in a meaningful way. Amazon's success is based on selection, lower prices, better availability, solid and innovative technology, and better product information. Amazon's use of customer product reviews and product suggestions based on collective purchasing behavior also places it a cut above other retailers. It wins with low capital and high return business models. Amazon's future success seems certain because it knows how to capitalize on its unique capabilities through strategic planning and with careful management of its existing business models—and it remains customer-obsessed.

Sources: Amazon.com media kit (housed at phx.corporate-ir.net/) and annual report (annualreports.com).

STRATEGIC PLANNING

Amazon, like every other marketer, uses strategic planning for a profitable and sustainable business future. **Strategic planning** is the "process of developing and maintaining a strategic fit between the organization's goals and capabilities and its changing market opportunities" (Kotler and Armstrong, 2010). Part of this process is to identify the company's goals, such as the following:

- ***Growth.*** How much can the company reasonably expect to grow in terms of revenues, and how fast? The answer to these questions involves a thorough understanding of the competition, product life cycles, and market factors.
- ***Competitive position.*** How should the company position itself against other firms in the industry? Viable positions are industry leader (Google), price leader (Priceline), quality leader (Mercedes), niche company (eMarketer), best customer service (Amazon), and so forth.
- ***Geographic scope.*** Where should the company serve its customers on the continuum of local to multinational? Is the company prepared to ship tangible products purchased online to foreign countries?
- ***Other objectives.*** Companies often set objectives for the number of industries they will enter, the range of products they will offer, the types of channels they will use, ways to reduce costs, and so on.

For example, Facebook switched strategic direction in 2007, choosing to open its network to third-party developers—expanding customer benefits in the process. In 2008, Starbucks initiated "My Starbucks Idea" Web site to engage customers, increase sales, get new product ideas, and build its reputation online. As of August 2012, users had submitted 84,776 product ideas, 21,563 experience ideas and 19,309 ideas for community involvement (see mystarbucksidea .force.com).

Environment, Strategy, and Performance

The e-marketing plan is normally a part of an organization's overall marketing plan, flowing from its overall goals and strategies. For better understanding, we discuss the e-marketing plan in isolation in this book (Chapter 3). As depicted in Exhibit 2.1, it starts with the business environment, where legal, ethical, technological, competitive, market-related, and other environmental factors external to the company create both opportunities and threats. Organizations perform SWOT (strengths, weaknesses, opportunities, threats) analyses to discover what strengths and weaknesses they have to deploy against threats and opportunities, leading to e-business and e-marketing strategies. Organizations select e-business models, and then marketers formulate strategy and create marketing plans that will help the firm accomplish its overall goals. The final step is to determine the success of the strategies and plans by measuring results. **Performance metrics** are specific measures designed to evaluate the effectiveness and efficiency of the e-business and e-marketing operations.

The environment-strategy-performance (ESP) model might just as easily depict a brick-and-mortar business process—by removing a few Es (e.g., "e-marketing plan" for online strategy and tactics is simply a "marketing plan" offline). It underscores the idea that businesses are built not only on sound practices and proven processes but also with important technology transformations and e-marketing practices, as discussed in this book.

This chapter and Chapter 3 describe e-business and e-marketing strategies, the e-marketing plan, and performance metrics. Chapters 4 and 5 explore environmental factors particularly important for e-marketing and leading to the SWOT analysis.

Strategy

The term *strategy* has been used to describe everything from "the course we chart, the journey we imagine and, at the same time, the course we steer, and the trip we actually make" (Nickols, 2000, p. 6). Although the term is used in many different contexts to mean many different things, most strategists agree that **strategy** is the means to achieve a goal. It is concerned with how the company will achieve its *objectives*, not what its goals are. Interestingly, strategy has its roots in military action. For example, if a country's objective is to win a war, its strategy will be to deploy troops to a particular country, and its tactics will be to land a particular battalion in a specific location

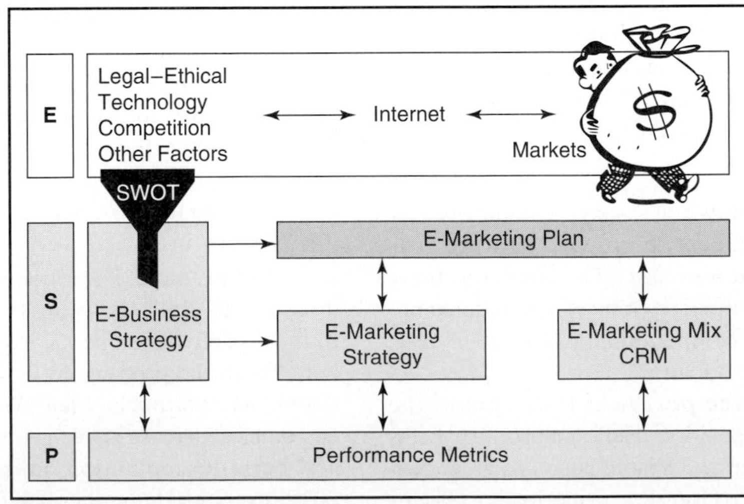

EXHIBIT 2.1 Focusing on Strategy and Performance

at a specified day and time. This process translates well to business strategy because the company sets its growth and other objectives and then decides which strategies it will use to accomplish them. The tactics are detailed plans to implement the strategies. For example, Starbucks's objective might have been to improve its product mix using a strategy of seeking product ideas from consumers and then creating the My Starbucks Idea Web site as a tactic to achieve this objective.

It is important to note that objectives, strategies, and tactics can exist at many different levels in a company. Thus far, we've been discussing high-level corporate strategic planning. Functional areas within a company also develop goals, strategies, and tactics to support corporate-level objectives. If a company wants to grow by 10 percent in the coming year, the marketing function may set supporting goals to engage customers in social media and increase market share. Similarly, finance, human resources, and other functional areas set goals to help achieve the company's overall objectives.

FROM STRATEGY TO ELECTRONIC STRATEGY

How does traditional strategy differ from e-business strategy? **E-business strategy** is the deployment of enterprise resources to capitalize on technologies for reaching specified objectives that ultimately improve performance and create sustainable competitive advantage. Thus, when corporate-level (also called *enterprise-level*) business strategies include information technology components (social media, digital data, databases, etc.), they become e-business strategies. As an example, Tchibo, the German retailer, has two key strategies for reaching its growth goals: First is the corporate-level business strategy of building new retail stores in selected European cities, and second is the e-business strategy of selling products on its Web site. Using strategic planning, Tchibo elected to use an e-business strategy only after careful analysis of its internal capabilities and the needs of its customers, retail competitors, and other environmental issues.

In a parallel fashion, marketing strategy becomes e-marketing strategy when marketers use digital technology to implement the strategy. **E-marketing strategy** is the design of marketing strategy that capitalizes on the organization's electronic or information technology capabilities to reach specified objectives. In essence, e-marketing strategy is where technology strategy and marketing strategy wed.

For example, Grupo Posados, with over 100 hotel properties in South America, maintains a sophisticated, large customer database. It is able to send customized e-mails by customer segments, such as customers who are high value, who are recent visitors, or who booked through a travel agent. By targeting special offers to relevant customers, it has increased its hotel bookings and profits. This relevant targeting keeps customers happy and supports Grupo Posados's customer relationship management (CRM) e-marketing strategy—ultimately supporting the corporate growth strategy.

Most strategic plans explain the rationale for the chosen objectives and strategies. They are especially important for a single e-business project trying to win its share of corporate resources and top-management support. Consider the following types of rationale managers must consider:

- *Financial justification*, such as break-even analyses, cost–benefit analysis, and return on investment (ROI), often leads the argument to gain funds for tactical implementation.
- *Operational justification* is also important: Does the company have the staff capability to engage customers in social media?
- *Organizational justification* involves the corporate culture and its fit with the new strategy.
- *Strategic justification* involves the strategy fit with the organization's overall mission, goals, and strategies.
- Finally, *technical justification* is hugely important for internet projects. For example, does the company have the technical expertise needed to implement big databases for a CRM program?

FROM BUSINESS MODELS TO E-BUSINESS MODELS

One more piece of this puzzle needs to be explained before we get into the really interesting content of e-business and e-marketing strategies. The term *business model* is often mentioned in print and by executives. Based on current use of the term, we suggest that a **business model** is a method by which the organization sustains itself in the long term and includes its value proposition for partners and customers as well as its revenue streams.

A business model does not exist in a vacuum. It relates to strategy in that a company will select one or more business models as strategies to accomplish enterprise goals. For instance, if the firm's goal is to position itself as a high-tech, innovative company, it might decide to use the internet to connect and communicate with its suppliers and customers, as does technology company Dell.

Presented with many opportunities, how does a company select the best business models? The authors of *Internet Business Models and Strategies* suggest the following time-tested components as critical to appraising the fit of a business model for the company and its environment (Afuah and Tucci, 2001):

- ***Customer value.*** Does the model create value through its product offerings that is differentiated in some way from that of its competitors?
- ***Scope.*** Which markets does the company serve, and are they growing? Are these markets currently served by the company, or will they be higher-risk new markets?
- ***Price.*** Are the company's products priced to appeal to markets and also achieve company share and profit objectives?
- ***Revenue sources.*** Where is the money coming from? Is it plentiful enough to sustain growth and profit objectives over time? Many dot-com failures, for example, overlook this element.
- ***Connected activities.*** What activities will the company need to perform to create the value described in the model? Does the company have these capabilities? For example, if 24/7 customer service is part of the value, the company must be prepared to deliver it.
- ***Implementation.*** The company must have the ability to actually make it happen, which involves the firm's systems, people, culture, and so on.
- ***Capabilities.*** Does the company have the resources (finance, core competencies, etc.) to make the selected models work?
- ***Sustainability.*** The e-business model is particularly appropriate if it can create a competitive advantage over time. Will it be difficult to imitate, and will the environment be attractive for maintaining the model over time?

E-BUSINESS MODELS

Traditional business models such as retailing, selling advertising, and auctions have been around ever since the first business set up shop. What makes a business model an e-business model is the use of information technology. Thus, an **e-business model** is a method by which the organization sustains itself in the long term using information technology, which includes its value proposition for partners and customers as well as its **revenue streams**. For example, the internet allows education, music, video, and software firms to deliver their products online, thus creating a new distribution model that cuts costs and increases value. E-business models successfully take advantage of the internet properties described in Chapter 1 (global reach, time moderator, etc.).

E-business models can capitalize on digital data collection and distribution techniques without using the internet. For example, when retailers scan products and customer data or reward cards at the checkout, these data can become a rich source of knowledge for inventory management and promotional offers—e-marketing without the internet. Similarly, when these data are available through the company's proprietary computer network (intranet), the firm is applying e-marketing without the public internet. For simplicity, we use the term *e-business models* to include both internet and offline digital models throughout the rest of our discussion.

Value and Revenue

As part of its e-business model, an organization describes the ways in which it creates value for customers and partners. This description is in line with the **marketing concept**, which suggests that the social and economic justification for an organization's existence is the satisfaction of customer wants and needs while meeting organizational objectives. And at no time is this truer than right now. Customers discuss brands on social media, and if companies do not satisfy customer needs the world will hear about it in a second and this often hinders the companies' goal achievement.

Business customers and partners might include supply chain members such as suppliers, wholesalers, and retailers, or firms with which the company joins forces to create new brands (such as the Microsoft and NBC alliance to create MSNBC). Organizations deliver stakeholder value through e-business models by using digital products and processes. Whether online or offline, the value proposition involves knowing what is important to the customer or partner and delivering it better than other organizations. **Value** encompasses the customer's perceptions of the product's benefits, specifically its attributes, brand name, and support services. Subtracted from benefits are the costs involved in acquiring the product, such as money, time, energy, and psychic costs. Like customers, partners evaluate value by determining whether the partnership provides more benefits than costs. This concept is shown as follows:

Value = Benefits – Costs

Information technology usually, but not always, increases benefits and lowers costs to stakeholders. Conversely, it can decrease value when Web sites are complex, information is hard to locate, and technical difficulties interrupt data access or shopping transactions.

As shown in Exhibit 2.2, e-business strategies help organizations to decrease internal costs,

E-Marketing Increases Benefits

- Online mass customization (different products and messages to different stakeholders)
- Personalization (giving stakeholders relevant information)
- 24/7 convenience
- Self-service ordering and tracking
- One-stop shopping
- Learning, engaging, and communicating with customers on social networking sites

E-Marketing Decreases Costs

- Low-cost distribution of communication messages (e.g., e-mail)
- Low-cost distribution channel for digital products
- Lowers costs for transaction processing
- Lowers costs for knowledge acquisition (e.g., research and customer feedback)
- Creates efficiencies in supply chain (through communication and inventory optimization)
- Decreases the cost of customer service

E-Marketing Increases Revenues

- Online transaction revenues such as product, information, advertising, and subscription fees; or commission/fee on a transaction or referral
- Adds value to products/services and increase prices (e.g., online FAQ and customer support)
- Increases customer base by reaching out to new markets
- Builds customer relationships and, thus, increases current customer spending (share of wallet)

EXHIBIT 2.2 E-Marketing Contributes to the E-Business Model

often improving the value proposition for customers and partners. They can also increase the enterprise revenue stream, an important part of the e-business model.

Menu of Strategic E-Business Models

A key element in setting strategic objectives is to take stock of the company's current situation and decide the level of commitment to e-business in general and e-marketing in particular. The possible levels of commitment fall along a continuum that is appropriately represented as a pyramid because fewer businesses occupy the top position (Exhibit 2.3). As a general rule, the higher the company travels up the pyramid, the greater its level of commitment to e-business, the more its strategies are integrated with information technology, and the greater the impact on the organization. Also, the more strategic moves are at the top, while the more tactical activities are at lower levels; as a result, higher levels carry more risk and have higher positive impact than lower levels for most companies.

Bear in mind that one company's activity may be another's enterprise-level strategy. For example, e-commerce or m-commerce (e.g., selling products on a Web site or mobile device) may be a small activity for a ski shop with 1 percent of its business from the online channel, but it is an enterprise-level activity for FedEx, the package delivery service.

It is also important to note that the lowest level of commitment—not shown on the pyramid—is no e-business involvement at all. Many small local retailers and other small businesses are at this level and should remain there because of their capabilities. For example, it is unlikely that the local independently owned dry cleaner could benefit much from e-business strategies.

Each level of the pyramid in Exhibit 2.3 indicates a number of opportunities for the company to provide stakeholder value and generate revenue streams using information technology. Because no single, comprehensive, ideal taxonomy of e-business models is available, we categorize the most commonly used models based on the company's level of commitment (Exhibit 2.4). This scheme is not perfect either, because the level of commitment for each model varies by company, as previously mentioned. Also, the activity-level items generally add value by saving costs but may not generate a direct revenue stream—although evidence shows that blogs and Twitter activity can result in sales and build customer loyalty. Nonetheless, we present it as a good menu of strategic opportunities, arranged by level of commitment to e-business, focusing primarily on models that involve e-marketing. We'll briefly

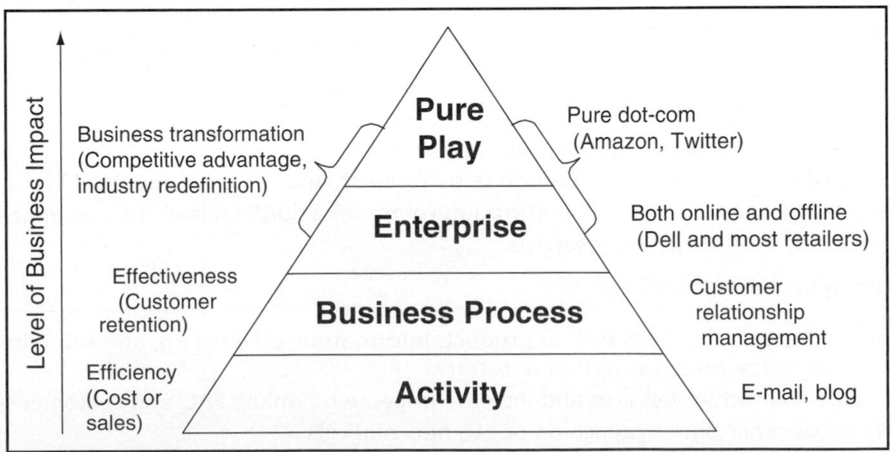

EXHIBIT 2.3 Level of Commitment to E-Business *Source*: Adapted from www.mohansawhney.com.

Activity Level	Business Process Level	Enterprise Level
1. Order processing 2. Online purchasing 3. E-mail 4. Content publishing 5. Business intelligence (BI) 6. Online advertising and public relations (PR) 7. Online sales promotions 8. Dynamic pricing strategies online 9. Social media communication 10. Search marketing.	1. Customer relationship management (CRM) and Social CRM 2. Knowledge management (KM) 3. Supply chain management (SCM) 4. Community building online 5. Database marketing 6. Enterprise resource planning (ERP) 7. Mass customization 8. Crowdsourcing 9. Freemium	1. E-commerce, social commerce, direct selling, content sponsorship 2. Portal 3. Social networking 4. Broker models • Online exchange, hub • Online auction 5. Agent models • Manufacturer's/selling agents • Shopping agent • Reverse auction

EXHIBIT 2.4 E-Business Model Classification

describe many models here and expand upon them in later chapters.

Although we are discussing individual e-business models, many companies combine two or more e-business models. For example, Yahoo! is both an online retailer and a content publisher. It also uses many processes and activities listed in Exhibit 2.4, such as e-mail and CRM.

ACTIVITY-LEVEL E-BUSINESS MODELS The lowest level of the pyramid affects individual business activities that can save the firm money if these activities are automated using information technology or the internet. In this low-risk area, the firm realizes cost reductions through e-business efficiencies (e.g., order processing, **competitive intelligence**, or surveys online). The following is a brief description of activity-level models:

1. ***Online purchasing.*** Companies can use the Web to place orders with suppliers, thus automating the activity. Normally this activity is not a marketing function, but when retailers such as Wal-Mart created automated order processing throughout the supply chain, it had a huge impact on marketing. While this is called e-commerce from the seller's perspective, here we only consider the business customer's online purchasing activity.
2. ***Order processing.*** This model occurs when online retailers automate internet transactions created by customers.
3. ***E-mail.*** When organizations send e-mail communications to stakeholders, they save printing and mailing costs.
4. ***Content publishing.*** In this model, companies create valuable content or services on their Web sites, draw lots of traffic, and sell advertising or generate sales leads. In another type of content publishing, the firm posts information about its offerings on a Web site, thus saving printing costs. See the "Let's Get Technical" box for streaming audio as subscription-based content (and online retailing).
5. ***Business intelligence (BI).*** This activity refers to the low-cost online gathering of secondary and primary information about competitors, markets, customers, and other entities.
6. ***Online advertising and public relations (PR).*** As an activity, the company buys

LET'S GET TECHNICAL

Streaming Music—Pandora

> You are at the office and, well, a little bored. A little music would really spice up your day. A colleague told you about a new group that really rocks. You're wishing now that you had the CD to run on your computer's speakers. Suddenly you remember that a colleague telling you about Pandora, a free online streaming music service.

Streaming music is a service that allows listening to music while it is still being downloaded. In other words, you don't have to wait for the entire track to download before it begins playing. Streaming music services are ideal for users who are nearly always near a computer or an iPhone, like to experiment with different kinds of music, and prefer the try-before-you-buy model.

The beauty of Pandora is that it learns your music preferences and delivers the music you love most. Pandora uses musicians to classify songs on 400 dimensions. The listener rates songs as they are served up by Pandora. "Thumbs up" means play more of the same. "Thumbs down" means don't play again and avoid songs that sound like it.

The Pandora service requires three technologies—a music server, a high-speed internet connection (wired or wireless), and security software to prevent unauthorized access and duplication of the music.

The music server is where the music is actually stored. When Pandora is activated, the music begins to stream onto the user's computer. When enough of the track has arrived (the music gets buffered in memory), it begins to play while the rest of it continues to stream. If the internet connection slows down, the song may actually catch up to the stream and briefly stop until more has been buffered.

Pandora's conceptual model is that the user creates customized radio stations. Each station streams a different genre of music depending on the listener's mood. Like a radio station, there are repeats. However, if you tire of a song, you can banish it for a month until you are ready to listen with fresh ears. If you just don't like a song you can skip it with a "thumbs down." However, to preserve copyright laws, Pandora allows only a limited number of skipped songs per hour.

Pandora makes money whenever the user decides to purchase a track. It is the consummate try-before-you-buy, promotional sampling model. It also makes money by offering a premium service that allows more skipped songs per hour and a cool desktop client.

Pandora provides mini-reviews and artist suggestions based on listening preferences. The usability and slickness of the Pandora interface are key differentiators.

Because of the buffering issue, streaming music is only advisable over a high-speed internet connection. However, mobile users can even stream to an iPhone on faster 3G and 4G cell phone networks.

Other streaming music services such as Rhapsody use a music library as a conceptual model. For a monthly fee, users can listen to complete albums or make their own playlists.

Security with streaming music is important to the record companies, who do not want unauthorized duplication of their music. Most streaming music services do not allow a user to log in from two computers simultaneously. Additionally, security software will not allow the music to be permanently captured on the user's computer without the user purchasing the track.

From a user's perspective, the major limiting factor used to be the restriction of proximity to a computer. However, some add-on technologies allow a computer to wirelessly send its music data to remote speakers located in another room. Furthermore, expect more streaming music to iPhone-type devices.

The possibilities of using the smartphone as a music source have not been lost on auto manufacturers. Earlier you had to plug your smartphone into the car's radio to hear it through the car's speakers. However, now with optional Bluetooth services, you can play Pandora wirelessly through your car's speakers. What's more, Pandora can report the current song and artist playing on your car's dashboard display. The integration of the two systems is so complete that Pandora will pause automatically when you turn off your car and then start again in the same place when you resume your journey!

advertising on someone else's e-mail or Web site. When the company sells advertising, it is engaging in content sponsorship, a higher-level process. Online PR includes a company's own Web site, as well as online press releases, and more.

7. ***Online sales promotions.*** Companies use the internet to send samples of digital products (e.g., music or software) or to run sweepstakes, among other tactics. Group promotions include coupons that provide deep discounts on products if a required number of people purchased it (such as Groupon.com).
8. ***Pricing strategies.*** With dynamic pricing, a company presents different prices to various groups of customers, even at the individual level. Online negotiation through auctions is one type of dynamic pricing initiated by the buyer instead of the seller. Technology allows this activity to be automated.
9. ***Social media communication.*** Companies use Facebook pages, Twitter streams, blogs, and more to engage and build relationships with customers and prospects.
10. ***Search marketing.*** It is all about getting found online and the search engines are one key tool for inbound marketing. Organizations optimize Web sites and incoming links and place content all over the social media so they can appear high in a search engine's results page for relevant key words.

BUSINESS PROCESS–LEVEL E-BUSINESS MODELS The next level of the pyramid changes business processes to increase the company's effectiveness.

Customer relationship management (CRM) involves retaining and growing business and individual customers through strategies that ensure their satisfaction with the company and its products. CRM seeks to keep customers for the long term and to increase the number and frequency of their transactions with the company. In the context of e-business, CRM uses digital processes and integrates customer information collected at every customer "touch point." Customers interact with organizations in person at retail stores or company offices, by mail, via telephone, or over the internet. The results of interactions at all these touch points are integrated to build a complete picture of customer characteristics, behavior, and preferences—all stored in electronic databases. Social CRM (SCRM) adds a new dimension when companies interact with customers as they chat about products in social media.

Knowledge management (KM) is a combination of a company's database contents, the technology used to create the system, and the transformation of data into useful information and knowledge. KM systems create a storehouse of reports, customer account information, product sales, and other valuable information managers can use to make decisions.

Supply chain management (SCM) involves coordination of the suppliers and distribution channel to deliver products more effectively and efficiently to customers. For example, when a customer orders from particular retail Web sites, FedEx's computers receive the instruction to pick up product from a warehouse and deliver it quickly to the customer. Similarly, when consumers buy a product at the grocery store, the bar-code scanner at the checkout signals the store's computer to reduce the inventory count by one and then automatically orders more cases of the product from warehouses or suppliers if inventory in the back room is low.

With **community building**, companies build social media Web pages to draw groups of special-interest users. In this model, firms invite users to chat and post comments on their Web sites, social media pages, or blogs with the purpose of building a buzz online and attracting potential customers to the site (**Blogs** are Web pages where entries are listed in reverse chronological order, with the most recent post at the top). Firms often contribute content on community and social networking sites that their customers frequent. Through community building, marketers can create social bonds that enhance customer relationships while building their images as experts in specific knowledge areas.

Affiliate programs occur when companies put a link to someone else's retail Web site and earn a commission on all purchases by referred customers. Amazon.com pioneered this e-business model. When viewed from an Amazon affiliate's perspective, the affiliate is operating as a selling agent for Amazon's products.

Database marketing involves collecting, analyzing, and disseminating electronic information about customers, prospects, and products to increase profits. It is one of the oldest and most important strategies for e-marketers. Database marketing systems can be a part of the company's overall knowledge management system.

Enterprise resource planning (ERP) refers to a back-office system for order entry, purchasing, invoicing, and inventory control. ERP systems allow organizations to optimize business processes while lowering costs. Many ERP systems predate the Web. ERP is not a marketing function, but it is so important that it must be included in this list.

Mass customization refers to the internet's unique ability to customize marketing mixes electronically and automatically to the individual level. Companies use this practice when they collect information from customers and prospects, and use it to customize products and communication on an individual basis for a large number of people.

Crowdsourcing is the practice of outsourcing ads, product development, and other tasks to a people outside the organization. Starbucks did this when setting up Idea Storm so the public could make product suggestions on its Web site.

Freemium is a combination of "free" and "premium," where companies offer a basic product for free and then provide upgraded versions for a fee. For example, customers can use some basic software for free but need to upgrade and pay for more functionality. This can be contrasted to a sales promotion sampling technique or a pricing strategy.

Location-based marketing delivers local and relevant content to a user's mobile device using GPS (global positioning system) technology. The content can include promotional offers designed to motivate the user to visit a retail store, restaurant, bar, or other business.

ENTERPRISE-LEVEL E-BUSINESS MODELS At the enterprise level of the pyramid, the company automates many business processes in a unified system—demonstrating a significant commitment to e-business. Firms relying heavily on these models (such as Dell, Google, and Facebook) believe that their future will depend on e-business activities.

E-commerce refers to online transactions: selling goods and services on the internet, either in one transaction or over time with an ongoing subscription price (e.g., *Wall Street Journal Online*). Following traditional marketing terminology, online retailers are firms that buy products and resell them online. However, any company that sells online, whether it produces its own products or purchases products for resale, is commonly known as an online retailer. One type of online retailer sells physical products and uses traditional transportation methods to deliver them. The other type sells digital products such as information, software, and music and delivers them via the internet (and usually ground transportation too). Many online retailers maintain brick-and-mortar stores as well. **Virtual worlds** often create revenue through subscriptions—these are sites where users can take the form of avatars and socialize in an online space of their own making. Second Life is the most well known of these; Webkinz and the Club Penguin are very popular with children.

Social commerce is one type of e-commerce that uses social media and consumer interactions to facilitate online sales. Tactics include "buy now" widgets on social media pages and software agents that put buyers and sellers together on social sites, such as online travel site Tripadvisor.com.

Direct distribution refers to a type of e-commerce in which manufacturers sell directly to consumers, eliminating intermediaries such as retailers (the Dell model—although Dell also sells through brick-and-mortar retailers).

Content sponsorship online is a form of e-commerce in which companies sell advertising on their Web pages, YouTube videos, or other online media. It is called content sponsorship because this model sprang from the media, which depends on advertising sales to pay for editorial content. Today, many sites use consumer-generated content to build their sites—for example, Yahoo!'s Flickr, the digital photo hosting site.

A **portal** is a point of entry to the internet that combines diverse content from many sources, such as the Yahoo!, Netvibes, and AOL Web sites. They are portals because they provide many services in addition to search capabilities. They are destinations for news, games, maps, shopping, mail, and so forth, in addition to being jump-off points for content provided by others. AOL uses its portal to communicate with members, help them find other Web sites, offer entertaining content, and conduct e-commerce—driving tens of billions of dollars in sales per year to its partner merchants. Some portals focus on vertical industries, such as government portals, Edmunds.com for automobiles, and TheKnot.com for couples planning a wedding. Portals are a viable business model, with the top four (Google, Yahoo!, Microsoft, and AOL) receiving an estimated 57 percent of all U.S. online advertising revenue ("Portals Vital for Users," 2010).

Social network sites are those that bring users together to share interests and personal or professional profiles. They use the community-building model previously described, but social network site owners are creating and hosting communities with the purpose of connecting like-minded individuals for friendship or business—such as LinkedIn for professionals and Facebook for businesses, nonprofits, or simply friends and family. Social network site owners monetize this model by selling advertising, charging recruiters for searching profiles, or by partnering with third-party developers for adding valuable applications to benefit users.

Online brokers are intermediaries who assist in the purchase negotiations without actually representing either buyers or sellers. The revenue stream in these models is commission or fee based. Examples of companies using the brokerage model are E*TRADE (**online exchange**), Guru.com (exchange for freelancers looking to connect with project managers), and eBay (**online auction**). Brokers usually create a market space for exchanges to occur, taking a piece of the action. A **business-to-business (B2B) exchange** is a special place because it allows buyers and sellers in a specific industry to quickly get connected. Online auctions occur in both B2B and B2C (business-to-consumer) markets, with the online broker providing the Web site and technology in exchange for a commission on all sales.

Unlike brokers, **online agents** tend to represent either the buyer or the seller and earn a commission for their work. **Selling agents** help a seller move product (such as real estate agents). Many selling agents work in the B2B market. In the B2C market, affiliate programs, discussed earlier, are also examples of the selling agent model.

Manufacturer's agents represent more than one seller. In traditional marketing, they often represent manufacturing companies that sell complementary products to avoid conflicts of interest. However, in the virtual world, they generally create Web sites to help an entire industry sell products. For example, Expedia.com, the online travel agent, is a manufacturer's agent in the travel industry (as well as a social network and recommendation site).

Purchasing agents represent buyers. In traditional marketing, they often forge long-term relationships with one or more firms; on the internet, however, they represent any number of buyers, often anonymously. For example, **shopping agents** help individual consumers find specific products and the best prices online (e.g., bizrate.com with its tagline, "Search, Compare, Conquer"). Another model, the **reverse auction**, allows individual buyers to enter the price they will pay for particular items at the purchasing agent's Web site, and sellers can choose to agree or not (e.g., Priceline.com). Purchasing agents often help buyers form cooperatives online for the purpose of buying in larger quantities to reduce prices (such as Groupon.com).

PURE PLAY The final level of the pyramid is comprised of internet pure plays. **Pure plays** are businesses that began on the internet, even if they subsequently added a brick-and-mortar presence. We did not include pure plays in Exhibit 2.4 because they start right at the top of the pyramid with a very distinct business model, rather than progressing upward, as do traditional brick-and-mortar companies. For example, E*TRADE is a pure play, beginning with only online trading.

Pure plays face significant challenges: They must compete as new brands and take customers away from established brick-and-mortar or online businesses. The successful ones have been able to do so by industry redefinition (i.e., changing the rules of the game) (Modahl, 2000). One way to change the rules is to invent a new e-business model, as Yahoo!, Google, Twitter, Flickr, and eBay did. The key to pure play success is offering greater customer value. For example, Rakuten.com increases customer value by using a content sponsorship model combined with direct sales. The ad inventory sold on the site helps to subsidize prices for the consumer.

PERFORMANCE METRICS INFORM STRATEGY

The only way to know whether a company has reached its objectives is to measure its results. **Performance metrics**, also called key performance indicators (KPIs), are specific measures designed to evaluate the effectiveness and efficiency of an organization's operations, both online and offline. For example, if the company strategy calls for 30 percent of its sales to come from the online channel, the company needs to continually measure revenue from various channels to determine whether it is achieving this goal. Note that this means monitoring sales from brick-and-mortar stores too and integrating online/offline metrics for the entire business success. The managers also monitor all the tactics used to drive sales to the online channel to see which ones are working well. Armed with this information, the company can make tactical corrections to make sure it accomplishes the goal.

For instance, grocery retailer Schwans.com had 40.6 percent of its site visitors convert to purchasers on the site in March 2010, according to the Nielsen Company. Schwans is excellent at converting Web site visitors to buyers and constantly watches this metric, making tactical refinements to improve performance. Schwans would also likely integrate its online data with offline data from brick-and-mortar operations to get the full picture of its strategy and tactic effectiveness.

Because strategy is the means to the end (the way of accomplishing objectives), performance metrics should be defined along with the strategy formulation so that the entire organization will know what results constitute successful performance. (Refer to Exhibit 2.1 for the role of performance.) Albert Einstein famously noted: "Not everything that can be counted counts, and not everything that counts can be counted." Marketers are drowning in metrics and many go for the easy metrics, such as number of clicks. It is critical for them to be effective and efficient in metric selection and measurement so that the results of their efforts will help improve marketing communications toward meeting the company goals.

When a company designates the performance metrics it will use to measure its strategy effectiveness, it does four important things:

1. It translates its vision, strategy, or e-business model into components with measurable outcomes. Some e-marketing goals needing metrics include attracting visitors to the Web site for selling more advertising or converting them to sales and building visitor loyalty to the site.
2. The performance metrics must be easy to understand and use. They should be accessible to employees using them for decision making. It is difficult to choose from among all the available data, so organizations often settle on KPIs to monitor progress toward important goals.
3. Metrics must be actionable. Companies use benchmarking and last year's metrics to decide where they are, after which they can set metric goals for the future (such as increase

the amount of time visitors spend on the site from 5 minutes to 10 minutes per session).

4. Finally, when employee evaluations are tied to the metrics, people will be motivated to make decisions that lead to the desired outcomes. Even though the metrics are usually set by top management, successful companies collect employee input throughout the process so that the measurements are relevant and the organization gains consensus on their importance. Thus, the adage, "What you measure is what you get."

Web analytics is the e-marketing term for the study of user behavior on Web pages. Companies collect data as users click through pages and take actions, such as registration or purchase. Companies use these data to optimize their online investments. These metrics help firms manage Web content, improve user targeting and personalization, and increase user engagement (and much more). Commonly collected metrics include which tactics generated the site traffic (e.g., click-throughs from online advertising or search engine optimization), which pages are viewed most often, how many comments were posted on a blog, and how many fans there are on a company Facebook page. Of course, a key metric involves conversions to sales or other desired behaviors, such as signing up for an e-mail newsletter. Finally, organizations want to know which of their new tactics are working well—things such as a new one-day shipping price or special promotion on the site to increase sales. These data for Web analytics are collected in several ways:

- Web site server logs record the user's IP (internet protocol) address, which browser the visitor is using, his or her location before arriving at the company site, the time of the day, and every click-through of the user while on the site. The IP address helps companies understand where users live (e.g., .jp for Japan).
- **Cookie files** are small data files written to a user's hard drive when visiting a site. They are necessary for using shopping carts and other operations at a site. When customers return, the cookie file data are retrieved and used to understand how many visitors are returning. Amazon.com uses cookie file data to display the user name on its home page instantaneously.
- **Page tags** are one pixel on a page that is invisible to users (a pixel is one dot of light on a computer screen). Page tags activate a special script when users are on the page, providing information such as when items are removed from a shopping cart. Tags can also be activated based on cookie files on the visitor's hard drive from a previous visit—creating data about the return visit and what the user did.
- **Geolocation**, uses many different technologies to locate an internet-enabled device (and its owner) at its physical world address: For example WiFi, GPS (global positioning satellite coordinates), or simply IP addresses. Marketers can use this for market segmentation when they observe consumer behavior from various countries or other more precise locations.

Web analytics software helps companies analyze all these data on server logs to uncover usage patterns. They can do this through free services or through purchased software. E-marketers use thousands of different performance metrics, often causing them to be lost in a sea of data. In fact, a 2012 study revealed fewer than half of all Web analytics collected by marketers is useful for decision making and only 10 percent of the respondents thought that most of their analytics were useful ("Marketers Find Less . . .," 2012). See Exhibit 2.5 for the heavily used online metrics, according to a survey of 550 market research professionals. ("2011 Annual Survey . . .," 2011).

In this chapter you'll learn the basics and see examples, and throughout this book you'll find many more very specific metrics for each type of tactic. Next time you purchase something online, think about how you found the site and navigated through it to the product you bought. Know that the company is tracking your every move and click in order to both optimize its tactics and be more relevant to your needs.

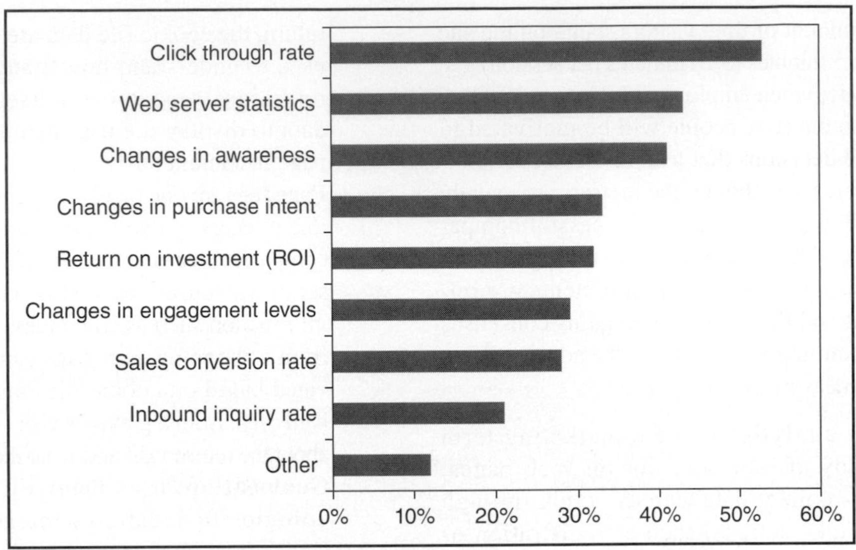

EXHIBIT 2.5 Metrics Used to Measure Internet Marketing (percentage of customers using the metric) *Source:* "2011 Annual Survey. . ." 2011

THE BALANCED SCORECARD

Several well-known performance metrics systems include these data in dashboards individualized to an organization's needs. The Balanced Scorecard is a good framework for understanding e-marketing metrics; thus, we present it as an organizational scheme for many important performance metrics.

For years, organizations valued financial performance or market share as the most important success measure. Large companies fostered competition among their brand groups or retail outlets and measured success by the bottom line (profits). Many still do so. During the mid- to late 1990s, the dot-com firms ignored financial measures and focused on growth, much to their dismay. These approaches are narrowly focused and place more weight on short-term results rather than on addressing the company's long-term sustainability through customer retention strategies and more.

These weaknesses paved the way for enterprise performance management systems that measure many aspects of a company's achievements. The **Balanced Scorecard**, developed by two Harvard Business School professors in 1990, is one such system with a huge adoption rate (over 50% of large enterprises according to estimates as reported at balancedscorecard.org). The scorecard approach links strategy to measurement by asking companies to consider their vision, critical success factors for accomplishing it, and subsequent performance metrics in four areas: customer, internal, learning and growth, and financial (Exhibit 2.6). In the following sections, we describe the typical goals and e-business

Customer Perspective		Internal Business Perspective		Learning and Growth Perspective		Financial Perspective	
Goals	Measures	Goals	Measures	Goals	Measures	Goals	Measures

EXHIBIT 2.6 The Four Perspectives of the Balanced Scorecard

metrics in each perspective. We start with the basic definitions and then adapt the system for e-marketers. However, it is important to remember that each company defines the specific measures for each box—the system is very flexible.

Four Perspectives

The customer perspective uses measures of the value delivered to customers. These metrics tend to fall into four general areas: time, quality, performance and service, and cost. They also include measures such as time from order to delivery, customer satisfaction levels with product performance, amount of sales from new products, and industry-specific metrics such as equipment uptime percentage or number of service calls.

The internal perspective evaluates a company's success at meeting customer expectations through its internal processes. The items with greatest impact in this area include cycle time (how long it takes to make the product), manufacturing quality, and employee skills and productivity. Information systems are a critical component of the internal perspective for e-business companies.

The learning and growth perspective, sometimes called the growth perspective, is one of the Balanced Scorecard's unique contributions. Here, companies place value on continuous improvement to existing products and services as well as on innovation in new products. These activities take employees away from their daily work of selling products, asking them to pay attention to factors critical to the company's long-term sustainability, which is especially important for e-business organizations. Measures in this area include a number of new products and the percentage of sales attributable to each, penetration of new markets, and the improvement of processes such as CRM or SCM initiatives.

If the projected outcomes result from the previous perspectives and performance metrics, the financial perspective will be on target too. Financial measures include income and expense metrics as well as ROI, sales, and market share growth. Companies must be careful to relate measurements from the first three perspectives to the financial area whenever possible.

Each company will select metrics for the four perspectives based on its objectives, business model, strategies, industry, and so forth. The point is to understand what the company wants to accomplish and devise performance metrics to monitor the progress and see that the goals are reached.

A U.S. regional airline developed a Balanced Scorecard to build and sustain its unique position as a high-frequency, short-haul carrier (see balancedscorecard.org for more examples). Consider the performance metrics goals it associated with each goal:

- ***Customer perspective.*** On-time flights, more customers, and lower prices. Metrics included being the first in the industry according to the Federal Aviation Administration on-time arrival ratings, customer satisfaction rankings of 98 percent, and a healthy percentage change in number of customers.
- ***Internal perspective.*** Improve turnaround time as measured by on-ground time of less than 25 minutes and 93 percent accurate departure time.
- ***Learning and growth perspective.*** Align ground crews better with company goals, measured by the percentage of ground crew who are trained and the percentage of ground crew who are stockholders. The airline wanted 70 percent of one-year employees, 90 percent of four-year employees, and all of six-year employees to own the company's stock.
- ***Financial perspective.*** Profitability increase of 25 percent per year, lower costs, and increased revenue (based on market value, seat revenue, and plane lease cost).

Applying the Balanced Scorecard to E-Business and E-Marketing

We'll say it again: E-marketers are swimming in data. They have huge databases full of customer information, Web site logs that automatically record every click of every visitor and how long the user stays, customer service records, sales data from many different channels, number of comments from a blog post, and so forth. One service company's manager reported: "Since I've got all these things to measure, I'm paralyzed by all the opportunities." In spite of these difficulties, measurement is vital to success.

METRICS FOR THE CUSTOMER PERSPECTIVE The most important of these metrics measure customer loyalty/retention and lifetime value. However, many other metrics can help a company optimize customer value, for example, customer perceptions of product value, appropriateness of selected targets, and customer browsing and buying patterns. The company must also measure value created for partners and other supply chain members because many can easily partner elsewhere if they are not satisfied. Customer engagement online is an important metric involving the number of comments, photos, videos, or other user-generated content posted to a site, among other things. As an example, Exhibit 2.7 displays several possible measures for some customer goals of a company employing e-business models.

Customer Perspective	
Example Goals	**Possible Measures**
Build awareness of a new Web site service	Survey target awareness of service Number of visitors to the site
Engage customers on a site	Number of comments, photos, or videos posted
Increase number of software downloads from the Web site	Number from Web site log
High customer satisfaction with Web site	Survey of target at Web site Number of visits and activity at site
High customer satisfaction with value of online purchasing	Number of complaints received (via e-mail, phone) Number of abandoned shopping carts Sales of online versus offline for same products
Increase the amount or frequency of online sales from current customers	Mine the database for change in frequency of purchases over time
Build customer relationships	Number of purchases per customer over time (using cookie data) Customer retention percentage
Appropriate target markets	Data mining to find purchase patterns by targeting criteria
Buy-to-delivery time faster than competition	Number of days from order to delivery Competition delivery times
Increased visits from sweepstake offers	Number who enter
Build communities on the site	Number of registrations/friends in community Amount of content uploaded to user profiles
Value for Business Partners	
Increase number of affiliates in program	Number of affiliates over time
Cross-sell to partner sites	Number of visitors to partner site from our site

EXHIBIT 2.7 Customer Perspective Scorecard for E-Business Company

METRICS FOR THE INTERNAL PERSPECTIVE The internal perspective is critical to a successful e-business. Many goals in this perspective affect human resources, information technology, and other areas that directly and indirectly affect marketing. Of particular note is that the entire supply chain is considered *internal* in this analysis. Obviously the manufacturing company cannot control the employees of its online retailers. At the same time, neither business customers nor consumers differentiate among organizations in a supply chain—they just want quality products on demand. Thus, recent work on the Balanced Scorecard includes measures for the entire supply chain. See Exhibit 2.8 for examples of goals and measures in the internal perspective.

METRICS FOR THE LEARNING AND GROWTH PERSPECTIVE The learning and growth perspective typically falls under the human resources umbrella. Two exceptions include product innovation and continuous improvement

Internal Perspective	
Example Goals	**Possible Measures**
Improve the quality of online service	Target market survey
	Number of customers who use the service
	Number of complaints in social media
Quality online technical help	Amount of time to answer customer e-mail
	Number of contacts to solve a problem
	Number of problems covered by Web site FAQ
	Customer follow-up survey
High product quality for online service	Product test statistics on specific performance measures
Web server size adequate and operational 24/7	Number of actual simultaneous Web page requests divided by maximum possible
	Percentage of uptime for server
	Number of mirrored or backup sites
Optimized number of customer service reps responding to online help	Number of inquiries to customer service rep ratio
	Number of chat sessions with site visitors
Superior Web site content management	Number of updates per day
	Web site log traffic pattern statistics
Optimized inventory levels	Average number of items in warehouse
	Inventory turnover
	Supplier speed to deliver product
Supply Chain Value to Company	
High supplier satisfaction	Supplier profits from our firm's orders
Partner value	Number of visitors from partner site to ours and number who purchase
	Partner contribution to product design

EXHIBIT 2.8 Internal Perspective Scorecard for E-Business Company

Learning and Growth Perspective	
Example Goals	**Possible Measures**
Online service innovation	Number of new service products to market in a year Number of new service features not offered by competitive offerings Percent of sales from new services
Continuous improvement in CRM system	Number of customer complaints and fixes Number/type of improvements over time
High internet lead-to-sales conversion	Revenue per sales employee from internet leads Number of conversions from online leads
Increased value in knowledge management system	Number of accesses by employees Number of knowledge contributions by employees
Successful penetration of new markets	Percentage of the firm's sales in each new market

EXHIBIT 2.9 Learning and Growth Scorecard for E-Business Company

of marketing processes, both of which are important for e-business firms due to rapid changes in technology. Exhibit 2.9 includes a few sample goals and measures affecting e-marketers.

METRICS FOR THE FINANCIAL PERSPECTIVE Marketing strategies clearly drive revenues, online and offline. They can affect profits as well, but other operational factors enter the equation when figuring company expenses. Nevertheless, marketers who manage brands have responsibility for their profits. When marketers propose new products or online services, they must forecast the potential sales over time, estimate the expenses to deliver that level of sales, and project the amount of time needed to break even (create enough revenues to cover expenses and start-up investments). In most cases, the product or internal project with the fastest break-even period or best potential for meeting the company's ROI hurdle will get funded.

Two of the most frequently used metrics are profits and ROI (or return on marketing investment [ROMI]). This section will outline basic ideas without considering taxes and other details. Net profits are revenues minus expenses. Revenues are the actual amount of dollars customers give the company in exchange for its products. Expenses include many things, most commonly the variable costs for producing the product, the selling costs (advertising, free product giveaways, and other customer acquisition costs (CAC), delivery, customer support, and other administrative costs.

Return on investment (ROI) is calculated by dividing net profit by total assets (fixed plus current). Marketers often evaluate ROI for specific e-business projects by dividing the project's profits by its investment dollars, such as the research, development, and the testing funds needed to introduce the new service. As an example, a company might invest $100,000 in software to analyze Web traffic patterns, use the results, change the Web site for better usability, and realize an additional $75,000 in e-commerce revenues: a 75 percent ROI. Marketing ROI was the most important measure used by marketing executives in 2010, followed closely by customer retention, brand loyalty, and positioning/differentiation ("Marketers Buzz about ROI," 2010).

The financial perspective scorecard relies heavily on sales, profit, and return figures. Exhibit 2.10 presents some common financial perspective performance metrics used by e-marketers.

Financial Perspective	
Example Goals	**Possible Measures**
Increase market share for online products	Market share percentage (firm's sales as percentage of industry sales)
Double-digit sales growth	Dollar volume of sales from one time period to the next
Target 10% ROI within one year for each new Product	ROI
Lower customer acquisition costs (CAC) in online channel	CAC (costs for advertising, and so forth, divided by number of customers)
Increase conversion rates at Web site	Number of orders divided by number of visitors to site
Increase individual customer profit	Average order value
	Profit contribution over time less CAC
Achieve at least a 10% net profit in first year of new product	Net profit as percentage of sales

EXHIBIT 2.10 Financial Perspective Scorecard for E-Business Company

SOCIAL MEDIA PERFORMANCE METRICS

Social media metrics are different from most standard Web site metrics because users interact with branded social media in many different ways. For example, when an internet user views an online video, he or she might spend 4 minutes viewing it, but another might stop it immediately. And if the user uploads, comments on, or shares a branded video, how can this brand interaction be counted? For example, Starbucks wanted to engage customers and learn ways to better meet their needs at physical stores through its My Starbucks Idea microsite. Starbucks can count the number of suggestions, measure the sentiment (as positive/negative), and identify the number of product changes to see if its engagement and learning goals were achieved. This is quite different from the metrics Starbucks might use on its main Web site (such as impressions and conversions to purchase). We will discuss strategy, tactics, and specific social media measurement items more thoroughly in Chapters 12, 13, and 14; however, this section presents a general framework and some popular metrics for measuring the success of communication efforts through social media.

As with all performance measurement, it is important to select metrics that can easily be measured on a continuous basis and apply them directly to the organization's social media objectives. Exhibit 2.11 displays five general measurement areas, from awareness through innovation, along with sample metrics used in each area. The pyramid shape represents the fact that the number of people decreases at higher levels: for example (1) most people will become aware of a viral video (awareness/exposure), (2) fewer will like or dislike and post positive or negative comments about it (brand health), (3) fewer still engage more deeply with the brand by sharing or using social bookmarking to tag the video (engagement), (4) even fewer visit the video sponsor's site to read about the products and purchase one (action), and (5) the smallest number are loyal customers who post collaborative type comments that the company can use to improve the product (innovation).

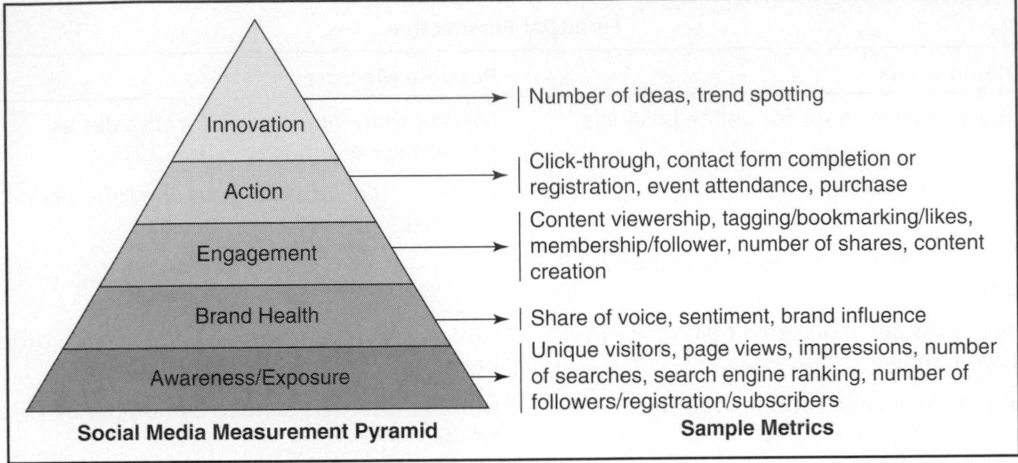

EXHIBIT 2.11 Social Media Measurement Areas

We next describe some exemplary metrics at each pyramid level. Note that companies also use many of these metrics to monitor their competition.

Awareness/Exposure Metrics

The most accurate way to measure an increase in brand awareness is to conduct survey research using a representative sample from the company's target market. However, this is very expensive and difficult to accomplish due to declining response rates on surveys, so organizations use many other proxy metrics to gain some measure of progress toward this goal. These metrics assume that if users land on an organization's Facebook page or other social media content, they will become aware of the product features discussed in an ad or on the pages:

- *Unique visitors* measures the number of visitors—without repetition— who access a site, application, video, or other social media content within a specific period of time. Unique visitors is measured by user registration, cookie files, or by a third-party measurement service such as Nielsen or comScore. Unique visitors additionally are categorized as either new or repeat visitors. Search engines also visit these sites, so companies must filter out visits from automated "bots." Video views on YouTube are visible for all to see under the video itself.
- *Page views* refers to single pages that are viewed on a social media site. For example, one unique visitor can view many different blog entries on one blog site. Obviously, the more pages users view, the longer they are on the site learning about the brand.
- *Impressions* refers to the number of times an ad loads on a user's screen. Marketers use this popular metric for all Web properties.
- *Number of searches* measures the number of times users search for the brand, company, or associated key words selected by the organization while typing the key words in a search engine.
- *Search engine ranking* evaluates where the organization's social media content appears in the search engine results pages for desired key words. For instance, if a user types in the name of the company, brands, or executives, ideally the links will appear in the first 10 links/page one of the results page.
- *Number of followers, registrations, or subscribers* to the blog, social network page, video channel, or other content. These are also used to measure earned media engagement.

Brand Health Metrics

In this category, companies want to measure the influence their brand and communications have on consumers. *Brand health* refers to the amount of conversation and what proportion of the sentiment is positive or negative—and more. Measures in this area include the following:

- ***Share of voice (SOV)*** is the proportion of online conversations about one brand versus its competitors. In the offline world, SOV measures the weight of advertising space in traditional media, but in the social media, it usually is only measured by conversation. For example, iStrategyLabs found the SOV for shoe brands over a one-month period in 2009: Nike (57%), Adidas (22%), Converse (15%), New Balance (4%) and Under Armour (2%) ("Social Media Share . . .," 2009).
- ***Sentiment*** refers to the proportion of online conversation about a brand that is positive, negative, or neutral. On August 11, 2012, we typed "Nike" into the social media search box at socialmention.com and got the following results (number of mentions): positive (116), neutral (409), and negative (27). The site calculated brand strength at 27 percent due to a 4:1 positive to negative conversation. This site reviews conversation "across the universe" of over 100 social media properties and also measures SOV.
- *Brand influence* can include a number of other metrics, including number of inbound links to a social media property, number of Twitter links that are retweeted, number of comments on posts, and number of times content is shared or linked (Jones, 2011).

Engagement Metrics

There are many ways to engage social media users, as discussed in later chapters. Engagement metrics are endless, and the ones companies select depend on the specific content, promotion, or other communication tactics. Following are some of the most common measures, relating to the depth of engagement:

- *Content viewership* refers to the number of visitors who consume content, such as by reading a blog (page views), watching videos or listening to podcasts, and downloading white papers.
- *Tagging, bookmarking*, or "likes" for content can be counted.
- *Membership/Follower* metrics count the number of RSS (Really Simple Syndication) subscribers, members in a community, such as a LinkedIn or Meetup.com group, or number of followers on Twitter.
- *Number of shares* measures how many times viral content is shared with others.
- *Content creation* counts the number of visitors who upload ads for a contest, such as the Frito Lay Super Bowl promotion. Companies can also measure the number of visitors who rate or review products, write comments on blogs or videos, or also retweet and other content-related items measured in previous categories.

Action Metrics

Although engagement metrics demonstrate actions taken by users, this category steps it up to a higher level of action (closer to purchase):

- *Click-through* to an advertiser's site. This is measured by the proportion of all people who are exposed to a communication message and those who click to visit the site.
- *Contact form completion* or *registration*, allowing the company to add the person to their database of names, e-mail addresses, and more.
- *Event attendance* online or offline, based on a social media promotion for a Webinar or other event.
- *Purchase* is the ultimate goal for company marketers. Companies measure conversion rates (proportion of all site visitors who purchase), number of purchases, average order value, and many other metrics that evaluate

communication effectiveness toward this goal. Note that many other factors lead to purchase, such as product quality, price, and availability; however, social media communication (especially discount promotions) can play an important role in motivating purchase.

Innovation Metrics

In this category, companies want to know if their social media communications are driving customers to comment and review in ways that help the company improve its products and services. Many of these metrics are also included in other categories, but we single innovation out because it is a very high level of brand engagement and builds customer loyalty. A few measures include the following:

- *Number of ideas* shared in a company's social media site (such as My Starbucks Idea).
- *Trend spotting* helps companies know what is hot in their target markets. Google Trends displays "hot" search key words and allows users to search trends. Trendsmap displays real-time Twitter trends worldwide, and many blogs and other sites provide word cloud displays of the most popular words in posts. Many other companies report social media trends.

MEASUREMENT TOOLS

Many companies offer excellent tools for measuring the previously mentioned and many other metrics. Companies select from free Google or other tools or use more sophisticated analytic dashboards that are continuously populated with metrics of choice. These tools help companies monitor progress toward objectives and tactical effectiveness, and help them catch negative conversations about their products as they occur, which is just as important.

Perhaps the simplest free tool is Google Alerts. Anyone can use this tool by entering the topic for monitoring and desired sources (video, blogs, news, or discussions), and Google will send e-mails based on the selected criteria at the requested frequency (as it happens, daily, weekly). Companies monitor their names, brand names, executive names, and tag lines or slogans in advertising campaigns. Google also provides free Web site or blog analytics to measure the awareness metrics, such as page views and action level click-throughs (Google Analytics). When companies advertise on Facebook, they get metrics from Facebook about number of impressions and clicks and more. Many social media sites provide various measures for their users.

Beyond that are complex dashboards, such as those provided for a fee by Alterian, Sysomos, Radian6, TrackUR, and many more. To view many dashboard samples, simply type "social media dashboard" into a Google image search.

Although performance metrics affect the entire organization, this book focuses on e-marketing metrics. Many of the measures mentioned earlier will be described in more detail in later chapters.

In Chapter 3, we move to the e-marketing plan and discuss how this plan flows from corporate e-business strategies, and how the marketing mix and CRM enter the picture. The e-marketing plan is a management guide and road map that paves the way to achieving performance goals.

Chapter Summary

A business or e-business needs strategic planning to develop and maintain the proper fit between the organization's objectives, skills, and resources and its ever-changing market opportunities. Key goals for growth, competitive position, geographic scope, and other areas must be determined.

Strategy is defined as the means to achieve a goal. E-business strategy is the deployment of enterprise resources to capitalize on technologies for reaching specified objectives that ultimately improve performance and create sustainable competitive advantage. E-marketing strategy is the design of marketing strategy that capitalizes on the organization's electronic or information technology capabilities to reach specified objectives.

An e-business model is a method by which the organization sustains itself in the long term using information technology, including its value proposition for partners and customers as well as its revenue streams. Companies deliver value by providing more benefits in relation to costs, as perceived by customers and partners. E-marketing improves the value proposition by increasing benefits, decreasing costs, and increasing revenues.

Companies can become involved in e-business at the activity level, business process level, enterprise level, or through a pure play. Commitment and risk are lower at the activity level and rise with each level. The main e-business models at the activity level include online purchasing, order processing, e-mail, content publishing, business intelligence, online advertising, online sales promotion, dynamic pricing strategies, and social media communication. The main e-business models at the business process level are customer relationship management, knowledge management, supply chain management, community building online, database marketing, enterprise resource planning, and mass customization. The main e-business models at the enterprise level are e-commerce, portal, social networking, online broker (online exchange and online auction), and online agent (manufacturer's agent, shopping agent, and reverse auction).

Performance metrics are specific measures designed to evaluate the effectiveness and efficiency of an organization's operations. Web analytics helps to analyze user behavior on a Web site by using server logs, cookie files, and page tags.

The Balanced Scorecard links strategy to measurement by asking companies to consider their vision, critical success factors for accomplishing it, and subsequent performance metrics in four areas: customer, internal, learning and growth, and financial. The customer perspective uses measures of the value delivered to customers. The internal perspective evaluates a company's success at meeting customer expectations through its internal processes. The learning and growth perspective looks at continuous improvement to existing products and services as well as innovation in new products. The financial perspective looks at income and expense metrics as well as return on investment, sales, and market share growth. Each company selects metrics for the four perspectives based on its objectives, business model, strategies, industry, and so forth. In this way, the company can measure progress toward achieving its objectives.

Organizations using social media require many different types of performance metrics because they want to measure levels of user engagement and how that influences brand awareness and product purchase. This chapter discusses exemplary metrics in five areas: awareness/exposure, brand health, engagement, action, and innovation. The chapter concludes with mention of various free and paid services that help marketers track performance metrics.

Exercises

REVIEW QUESTIONS

1. What is strategic planning, and why do companies prepare a SWOT analysis during the strategic planning process?
2. How does e-business strategy relate to strategy on the corporate level?
3. Define *e-marketing strategy* and explain how it is used.
4. Give examples of e-business models.
5. What is the formula for determining value?
6. What are the four levels of commitment to e-business? Give some examples of each.
7. What is customer relationship management (CRM), and why do companies create strategies in this area?
8. How is *e-commerce* defined?

9. What is an internet pure play and what are some examples?
10. What are the four ways of collecting Web analytics?
11. What is the Balanced Scorecard, and how do companies use it in e-business?
12. List six important social media awareness/exposure metrics.
13. List three important social media brand health metrics.
14. List four important social media engagement metrics.
15. List four important social media action metrics.
16. List two important social media innovation metrics.

DISCUSSION QUESTIONS

17. **Amazon story.** identify the business models Amazon used and at which level of e-business commitment each falls (Exhibit 2.3).
18. **Amazon story.** What performance metrics might Amazon use to measure progress toward its growth and customer service objectives?
19. Why is it important for an e-business model to create value in a way that is differentiated from the way competitors' models create value?
20. Based on the opening vignette and your examination of the Amazon.com site (or your experience as a customer), what strategic objectives do you think are appropriate for this e-business? What performance metrics would you use to measure progress toward achieving these objectives—and why?
21. The Balanced Scorecard helps e-businesses examine results from four perspectives. Would you recommend that e-businesses also look at results from a societal perspective? Explain your response.
22. Should e-businesses strive to build community with noncustomers as well as customers? Why or why not?
23. Do you agree or disagree that the page view metric is nearly useless in the Web 2.0 environment?
24. If you were to write a blog about your experiences at the university you attend to help high school students understand what college was like, which metrics would you use to measure the blog's success, and why?

WEB ACTIVITIES

25. Visit Dell.com. Write down what you think the company's goals are for its Web site. Then make a list recommending relevant performance metrics from each of the four perspectives.
26. Visit bizrate.com. Do a search for this book (*E-Marketing*). What is the lowest price available for the book? The highest? Compare these prices with those found at the brick-and-mortar stores Border's and Barnes & Noble. Check out the used bookstore site half.ebay.com (partnered with eBay). Explain in terms of value why customers might buy the book at a higher price.
27. Search Google images for "social media dashboards." Look at the dashboards and follow their links to the companies that created them. Which one do you think is best for a large consumer goods company, such as Coca-Cola? Why do you recommend the one you do?

The E-Marketing Plan

The primary goal of this chapter is to explain the importance of creating an e-marketing plan and present the seven steps in the e-marketing planning process. You will see how marketers incorporate information technology in plans for effectively and efficiently achieving e-business objectives such as increasing revenues and slashing costs.

After reading this chapter, you will be able to:

- Discuss the nature and importance of an e-marketing plan and outline its seven steps.
- Show the form of an e-marketing objective and explain the use of an objective-strategy matrix.
- Describe the tasks that marketers complete in tiers 1 and 2 as they create e-marketing strategies.
- List some key revenues and costs identified during the budgeting step of the e-marketing planning process.

- In today's 'expectation economy', consumers demand the best, they want it now and first, and they want real, human connection, too. Thanks to crowdsourcing platforms consumers are able to satisfy those demands through engagement with products and services pre-launch.

- By April 2012, there were 452 crowdfunding platforms operating globally, up from 100 in 2007. In 2011 crowdfunded platforms raised USD 1.4 billion. This year, that's on track to double to USD 2.8 billion (Source: Massolution/The Economist, May 2012). Examples: Kickstarter, the Porthole, Sedition Wars, Roominate, Matter, CashewChemists, DemoHour, CrowdCube, Indiegogo, and FreeBread Inc..

The Twitter Story

How did a brand-new internet concept go from an idea in a brainstorming meeting in 2006 to the second most popular social network six years later? Twitter is a social networking and microblogging service using instant messaging, a Web interface, or short message service (SMS), commonly called "texting." Jack Dorsey recalls the naming of his brainchild:

> We wanted to capture that feeling: the physical sensation that you're buzzing your friend's pocket. It's like buzzing all over the world. So we did a bunch of name-storming, and we came up with the word "twitch," because the phone kind of vibrates when it moves. But "twitch" is not a good product name because it doesn't bring up the right imagery. So we looked in the dictionary for words around it, and we came across the word "twitter," and it was just perfect. The definition was "a short burst of inconsequential information," and "chirps from birds." And that's exactly what the product was. (Sarno, 2009)

Twitter traffic took off after a South by Southwest (SXSW) festival in 2007, where attendees were sending text messages that displayed on 60-inch plasma screen televisions at the conference. The number of tweets grew from 2 million in all of 2007 to 340 billion per day from 140 million registered users in March 2012 (Palis, 2012). Twitter continues to grow, enabling users to stream tweets into their WordPress blogs and even into presentations using Prezi's online presentation software. Astounding growth, and reminiscent of the internet's early dot-com land rush.

Twitter began its business with venture capital. This begged the questions: What is its business model, and where is its revenue stream? However, with an increasing number of tweets and users, Twitter found a way to monetize this traffic: selling advertising. In 2012, Twitter was successfully selling these ad products: promoted Tweets, promoted trends, and promoted accounts. Following the Google AdWords model, these products target users based on their Twitter site searches. That should be interesting, considering the nature of the 140-character tweets: worth reading (36%), not worth reading (25%), and "okay" (39%) (according to a study done by university researchers and cited in Palis [2012]). Yet, Dorsey maintains that these ads get between 1 percent and 5 percent engagement from users (Sloan, 2011).

Twitter has a serious side, as well. It has been used for education (in China, the United Kingdom, Austria, and the United States) for reporting in emergency situations, for gathering opinions in surveys, for business fund-raising and public relations, and for news announcements. Many companies also use Twitter for customer service (such as Best Buy).

With this much activity, customer value, and media recognition, Twitter is sure to build its revenue from the business model to pay off those venture capitalists (VCs). How can it go wrong when it has celebrity followers, such as Lady Gaga who brings her 28.3 million Twitter followers to the site (see twitaholic.com for a list of top Twitter accounts)? It is a great example of an internet start-up trying to develop its marketing plan as the game is played. What an exciting ride for Dorsey and the rest of his staff.

OVERVIEW OF THE E-MARKETING PLANNING PROCESS

How can information technologies assist marketers in building revenues and market share or lowering costs? How can firms identify a sustainable competitive advantage with the internet when the landscape is constantly changing and filled with international competitors? The answer lies in determining how to apply digital data and information technologies both effectively and efficiently. The best firms have clear visions that they translate, through the marketing process, from e-business objectives and strategies into e-marketing goals and well-executed strategies and tactics for achieving those goals. This marketing process entails three steps: marketing plan creation, plan implementation, and plan evaluation/corrective action (using performance metrics, as discussed in Chapter 2). This chapter examines the first of these steps: the e-marketing plan.

CREATING AN E-MARKETING PLAN

The e-marketing plan is a blueprint for e-marketing strategy formulation and implementation. It is a guiding, dynamic document that links the firm's e-business strategy (e-business models) with technology-driven marketing strategies and lays out details for plan implementation through marketing management. It is usually integrated with the firm's overall marketing plan. The marketing plan guides delivery of the desired results, measured by performance metrics, according to the specifications of the e-business model embedded in the firm's e-business strategy. Exhibit 3.1 shows where the e-marketing plan fits in the process.

The e-marketing plan serves as a road map to guide the firm in the direction it wishes to take and helps it allocate resources and makes adjustments as needed. Many companies short-circuit this process and develop strategies ad hoc. For example, Twitter's Jack Dorsey says that his company's business model is based on "serendipity." Some of the companies are successful like Twitter, but many more fail. The Gartner Group correctly predicted that up to 75 percent of all e-business projects prior to 2002 would fail due to fundamental flaws in planning (Gartner, Inc. 2010). Nonetheless, some of the best firms discover successful e-commerce tactics accidentally and then use those experiences to build a bottom–up plan. Such was the case with Schwab, the online stock trading firm, which allowed its online channel successes to change the entire brick-and-mortar firm. Whether top–down or bottom–up planning, firms must plan for long-term sustainability.

This chapter is structured around a seven-step traditional marketing plan. It presents a generic plan that includes a menu of tasks from

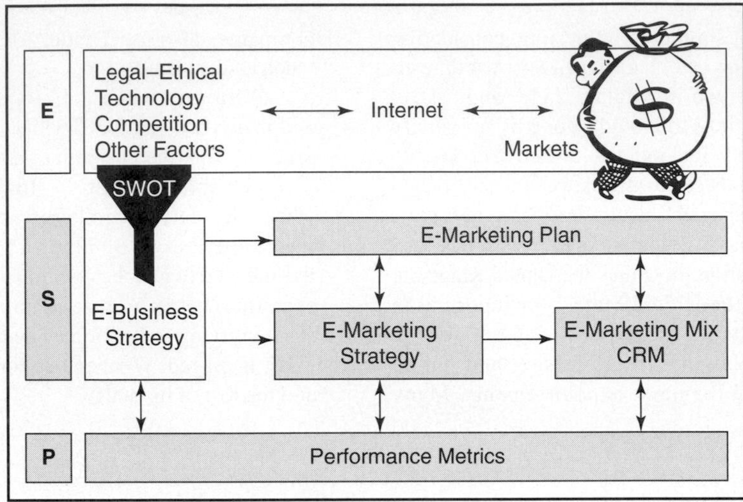

EXHIBIT 3.1 Focusing on the E-Marketing Plan

which marketers can select activities relevant to their firm, industry, brands, and internal processes. It assumes that a higher-level corporate plan is already in place, outlining the firm's goals, e-business strategies, and selected enterprise-level e-business models. If such a plan has not already been formulated, marketers must go through the **environmental scan** and SWOT (strengths, weaknesses, opportunities, threats) analyses prior to creating the plan. Two common types of e-marketing plans are the napkin plan and the venture capital e-marketing plan, discussed next.

The Napkin Plan

In what one marketer calls the *napkin plan*, many entrepreneurs simply jot their ideas on a napkin over lunch or cocktails and then run off to find financing. See the 2006 social network blueprint sketch created by Twitter's founder Jack Dorsey on Wikipedia (search for "Twitter"). It is simply a white legal-pad sketch that inspired this great company. Dorsey went on to create Square—the card reader that allows smartphone users to swipe credit cards for product purchases—in a similar fashion. The big-company version of this process is the just-do-it, activity-based, bottom–up plan. As an example, Kevin Rose of Digg.com had an idea about how to set up a Web site to host the most-liked stories of the day, and he just built this now hugely successful site. In another example, an e-marketing university student who works for a local ski shop approached the owner, asking for $500 for software and $50 a month for Web hosting to start an experimental e-commerce site. He placed a few pictures of skis on the site and included information about how to call the store to order. The site brought in several orders a week, quickly paying off the investment. These ad hoc plans sometimes work and are sometimes even necessary, given a stodgy corporate culture; but they are not recommended when substantial resources are involved. Sound planning and thoughtful implementation are needed for both raising capital and long-term success in business and e-business—a principle that became increasingly evident during the dot-com shakeout.

The Venture Capital E-Marketing Plan

Small to mid-sized firms and entrepreneurs with start-up ideas often begin with a *napkin plan* and do not initially go through the entire traditional marketing planning process. One reason is that one or two leaders generally plan the whole venture, intuitively understanding the marketing environment and how their hot new idea is positioned for success. Such was the case for Jerry Yang and Dave Filo when in 1994 they started "Jerry's Guide to the World Wide Web"—later named Yahoo! However, as the company grew and needed capital, Jerry and Dave had to put together a comprehensive e-marketing plan. Without an emphasis on strategic planning, Yahoo! would not have been an internet survivor.

Where does an entrepreneur go for capital? Some of it is debt financed through bank loans, though most of it is equity financed. Start-up companies tap private funds (friends and family), angel investors, and VCs. Angel investors provide funds with fewer requirements than those of VCs. In general, friends and family are the smallest sources of capital; angel investors invest hundreds of thousands of dollars; and VCs invest millions of dollars. Some banks, corporations, and consulting firms have established venture capital branches to finance internet start-ups. Some VCs even finance companies operated out of college dorm rooms.

Plenty of money is available to e-business entrepreneurs, and 2007 through 2010 saw an increasing number of e-businesses that were venture funded—largely due to the social media boom. That wave continued with 997 Web start-ups funding to the tune of $6.9 billion in 2011, an increase of 68 percent from 2010 (Taylor, 2012). The conventional wisdom is that money is scarce, but the most scarce resource is the talent. Obviously, investors aren't stupid. They are looking for a well-composed business plan, and more importantly, a good team to implement it. After all, it was Steve Jobs who drove Apple Computer to be the success it was.

This kind of thinking relieves some of the planning pressure on entrepreneurs but does not eliminate the need for planning to maximize organizational resources. The plan prepared by entrepreneurs for VCs should be about 8 to 10 pages long and contain enough data and logic to prove that (1) the e-business idea is solid and (2) the entrepreneur has some idea of how to run the business. In addition to product benefits and costs, it should include information about the competition, the target market and its potential, and the cost to acquire and retain customers.

VCs typically look for an exit plan—a way to get their money and profits out of the venture within a few years. The golden exit plan is to go public and issue stock in an initial public offering (IPO). As soon as the stock price rises sufficiently, the VC cashes out and moves on to another investment. VCs don't even pretend that all their investments will be successful. But even if 1 out of 20 is an Amazon.com or Facebook.com, the risk is well worth the reward. The employees of these start-ups typically work for very low wages—deferring their compensation in stock options. Of particular interest to investors are projects that tap new markets with high margins. First came a boom in B2C (business-to-consumer) investments, and then B2B (business-to-business) investments, and now social media investments. As soon as observers feel that the markets are becoming saturated, another opportunity arises. Now it is mobile marketing that is taking off.

A SEVEN-STEP E-MARKETING PLAN

The seven key planning elements are a **situation analysis**, an e-marketing strategic planning, the plan objectives, an e-marketing strategy, an implementation plan, the budget, and a plan for evaluating success (Exhibit 3.2). We cannot overemphasize the need to include feedback mechanisms to assess the plan's success and to use in making course corrections along the way, especially in the fast-paced e-business environment. In fact, some marketers recommend contingency plans and "trigger points" that if reached will invoke strategy refinement.

A good way to think about the marketing plan is through the analogy of preparing for a football game. While reviewing game films, a situation analysis reveals each team's strengths and weaknesses (e.g., the home team has a good passing game, the visitors have an excellent run defense). A likely objective would then be to win the game by throwing the ball. Strategies are developed to meet this objective (e.g., use play action to draw in the coverage, throw deep). Next, tactics implement the strategies (e.g., use a play action pass on first down, run on second down to keep them honest, pass on third down).

Step	Tasks
1. Situation analysis	Review the firm's environmental and SWOT analyses. Review the existing marketing plan and any other information that can be obtained about the company and its brands. Review the firm's e-business objectives, strategies, and performance metrics.
2. E-marketing strategic planning	Determine the fit between the organization and its strategic planning changing market opportunities. Perform marketing opportunity analysis, demand and supply analyses, and segment analysis. **Tier 1 Strategies** • Segmentation • Targeting • Differentiation • Positioning
3. Objectives	Identify general goals flowing from e-business strategy.
4. E-marketing strategy	Identify revenue streams suggested by e-business models. **Tier 2 Strategies** Design the basic offer, value, distribution, communication, and market/partner relationship management strategies to create a competitive edge. Modify objectives as warranted.
5. Implementation plan	Design e-marketing mix tactics: • Product/service offering • Pricing/valuation • Distribution/supply chain • Integrated communication mix Design relationship management tactics. Design information gathering tactics. Design organizational structures for implementing the plan.
6. Budget	Forecast revenues. Evaluate costs to reach goals.
7. Evaluation plan	Identify appropriate performance metrics.

EXHIBIT 3.2 E-Marketing Plan Process

Finally, Monday morning quarterbacking provides the postgame evaluation.

STEP 1—SITUATION ANALYSIS

Some people feel that planning for e-marketing means starting from the napkin plan. Nothing could be further from the truth for most companies. Working with existing business, e-business, and marketing plans is an excellent place to find opportunities.

The marketing environment is ever changing, providing plenty of opportunities to develop new products, new markets, and new media to communicate with customers, plus new channels to reach business partners. At the same time, the environment poses competitive, economic, and other threats. Three key **environmental factors** that affect e-marketing and are part of any situation analysis are legal, technological, and market-related factors. They are covered in depth in Chapters 4, 5, and 7, as well as in the "Let's Get Technical" boxes throughout the text.

The **SWOT** analysis flows from a situation analysis that examines the company's internal strengths and weaknesses with respect to the environment and the competition and looks at external opportunities and threats. Opportunities may help to define a target market or identify new product opportunities, while threats are areas of exposure. For example, when Amazon.com seized the opportunity to sell online, it had no significant competition. Its biggest threat was a full-scale push by one of the large bookstore chains to claim the online market. The company's greatest weakness was that it had no experience selling books or even processing credit card transactions. What's more, it had no experience boxing books for shipment and originally packed them on the floor until a visiting carpenter suggested building packing tables (Spector, 2000). The company's greatest strength was a smart and talented team that stayed focused and learned what it didn't know. Fortunately for Amazon, the big stores were caught napping. The delay by the bookstore chains gave Amazon the opportunity to establish its brand online. Barnes & Noble (barnesandnoble.com) did not fight back until Amazon was on the eve of a stock offering. By then it was too late. Further proving Amazon's strategy skills, CEO Jeff Bezos states that the company will not open brick-and-mortar stores because it has no way to differentiate itself from the current players. However, the threats are not over for Amazon or any company. Amazon's 2011 annual report lists no fewer than 24 potential risk factors, from competition to data security and foreign currency exchange rate fluctuations (search for Amazon at annualreports.com).

Bear in mind that a company's strengths and weaknesses in the online world may be somewhat different from its strengths and weaknesses in the brick-and-mortar world. For example, Amazon is worried about data security and intellectual property. Barnes & Noble has enormous strengths in the brick-and-mortar world, but it did not necessarily translate into strengths in the online world. Barnes & Noble can easily find itself in the unfortunate position of channel conflict—having to explain to channel partners why customers can purchase for less online than in the store. However, Amazon has less potential channel conflict because it sells only online.

STEP 2—E-MARKETING STRATEGIC PLANNING

After reviewing the situation analysis and currently used marketing plans, marketers engage in strategic planning. As you recall from Chapter 2, the strategic planning process involves determining the fit between the organization's objectives, skills, and resources and its changing market opportunities. For clarification throughout the book, we present these tasks as *tier 1 strategies*, including segmentation, targeting, differentiation, and positioning. During this phase, marketers uncover opportunities that help formulate the e-marketing objectives.

Marketers conduct a **market opportunity analysis (MOA)**, including both demand and supply analyses, for *segmenting* and *targeting*. The demand analysis portion includes market segmentation analyses to describe and evaluate the potential profitability, sustainability, accessibility, and size of various potential segments. Segment analysis in the B2C market uses descriptors such as demographic characteristics, geographic location, selected psychographic characteristics (such as attitude toward technology and mobile communication device ownership), and past behavior toward the product (such as purchasing patterns online and offline). B2B descriptors include the firm's location, size, industry, type of need, whether it is technologically savvy, and more. These descriptors help firms identify potentially attractive markets. Firms must also understand segment trends—are they growing or declining in absolute size and product use?

Companies use traditional segmentation analyses when they enter new markets through the online channel; however, if the firm plans to serve current markets online, it will delve more deeply into these customers' needs. Which of the firm's customers will want to use the internet? How do the needs of customers using the organization's Web site differ from those of other customers? For example, most internet users expect e-mails to be answered within 48 hours but will be satisfied if a postal letter is answered within weeks. In addition, firms often discover new markets as these customers find their way to the Facebook or other social media site, such as Pinterest. Marketers can use Web analytics to discover how best to serve these new markets.

The purpose of a supply analysis is to assist in forecasting segment profitability as well as to find competitive advantages to exploit in the online market. Only by carefully analyzing competitive strengths and weaknesses can a firm find its own performance advantages. Therefore, companies should review the competition, their e-marketing initiatives, and their strengths and weaknesses prior to developing e-marketing initiatives. They must also try to identify future industry changes—which new firms might appear online, and which will drop away? For example, who could have envisioned Facebook's success in 2005–2008 when MySpace was the hugely popular social network?

With a thorough MOA, a company can select its target market and understand its characteristics, behavior, and desires in the firm's product category. Furthermore, firms will want to understand the value proposition for each market. For example, marketers might decide to target several Hispanic markets (Exhibit 3.3).

Another tier 1 step in e-marketing strategic planning is identifying brand *differentiation* variables and *positioning* strategies. Based on an understanding of both the competition and the target(s), marketers must decide how to differentiate their products from competitors' products in a way that provides benefits perceived as important by the target. In the case of Facebook, management opted to add third-party applications to differentiate the site from its competitor, MySpace (which is now known as the best network for musicians). Flowing from this differentiation is the positioning statement: the desired image for the brand relative to the competition. If this positioning strategy was already decided upon in the traditional marketing plan, e-marketers must decide whether it will be effective online as well. If planning for a new brand or market, e-marketers must decide on branding strategies of differentiation and positioning at this point in the process.

Opportunities	**Threats**
1. Hispanic markets growing and untapped in our industry	1. Pending security law means costly software upgrades
2. Save postage costs through Facebook marketing	2. Competitor X is aggressively using Facebook e-commerce
Strengths	**Weaknesses**
1. Strong customer service department	1. Low-tech corporate culture
2. Excellent Web/social media sites and database system	2. Seasonal business: Peaks during summer months
E-Marketing Objective: $500,000 in revenues from e-commerce in one year	

EXHIBIT 3.3 SWOT Analysis Leading to E-Marketing Objective

STEP 3—OBJECTIVES

In general, the objective in an e-marketing plan takes a form that includes the following aspects:

- Task (what is to be accomplished)
- Measurable quantity (how much)
- Time frame (by when)

Assume that Pontiac wants to increase the number of avatar visitors to its Motari Island property in virtual world Second Life from 5,000 to 6,000 in one year. This type of objective is easy to evaluate and is a critical part of the e-marketing plan. The plan will often include the rationale for setting each objective—why each is desirable and achievable given the situation analysis findings, e-marketing, and e-business strategy.

Even though e-commerce transactions are a revenue-producing and an exciting dimension of an e-business presence, other objectives are also worthwhile, especially when the firm is using technology only to create internal efficiencies such as target market communication to build long-term customer relationships. In fact, most e-marketing plans aim to accomplish multiple objectives, such as the following:

- Increase market share.
- Increase the number of comments left on a blog.
- Increase the sentiment of comments to 5:1 (positive:negative).
- Increase sales revenue (measured in dollars or units).
- Reduce costs (such as distribution or promotion costs).
- Achieve branding goals (such as increasing brand awareness).
- Increase database size.
- Achieve customer relationship management (CRM) goals (such as increasing customer satisfaction, frequency of purchases, or customer retention rates).
- Improve supply chain management (SCM; such as by enhancing member coordination, adding partners, or optimizing inventory levels).

An important part of the planning process is to define potential revenue streams, using a viable business model from Chapter 2. The organizational e-business plan might contain a SWOT analysis similar to the example depicted in Exhibit 3.3, leading to the firm adopting an e-business model of e-commerce. E-marketers take over from here, setting a measurable objective of generating $500,000 from e-commerce sales within the first year.

STEP 4—E-MARKETING STRATEGIES

Next, marketers craft strategies regarding the four Ps and relationship management to achieve plan objectives regarding the offer (product), value (pricing), distribution/supply chain (place), and communication (promotion). Further, marketers design CRM and partner relationship management (PRM) strategies. For clarification, we call these *tier 2 strategies* throughout the book. In practice, tier 1 and tier 2 strategies are interrelated (Exhibit 3.4). For example, marketers select the best target market and identify a competitive product position, which dictates the ideal type of advertising, pricing, and so forth. Steps 2, 3, and 4 are an iterative process because it is difficult to know what the brand position should be without understanding the offer that comprises the brand promise (i.e., the benefits the firm promises to customers). Following are some of the tier 2 strategies covered in detail in subsequent chapters.

The Offer: Product Strategies

The organization can sell merchandise, content, services, or advertising on its Web site. It can adopt one of the e-business models discussed in Chapter 2, such as *online auctions*, to generate a revenue stream. The firm can create new brands for the online market or simply sell selected current or enhanced products in that channel. Obviously, the previous analyses will reveal many opportunities. If the firm offers current brands online, it will need to solve many different problems, such as the way colors appear differently on a computer screen than in print. The most astute

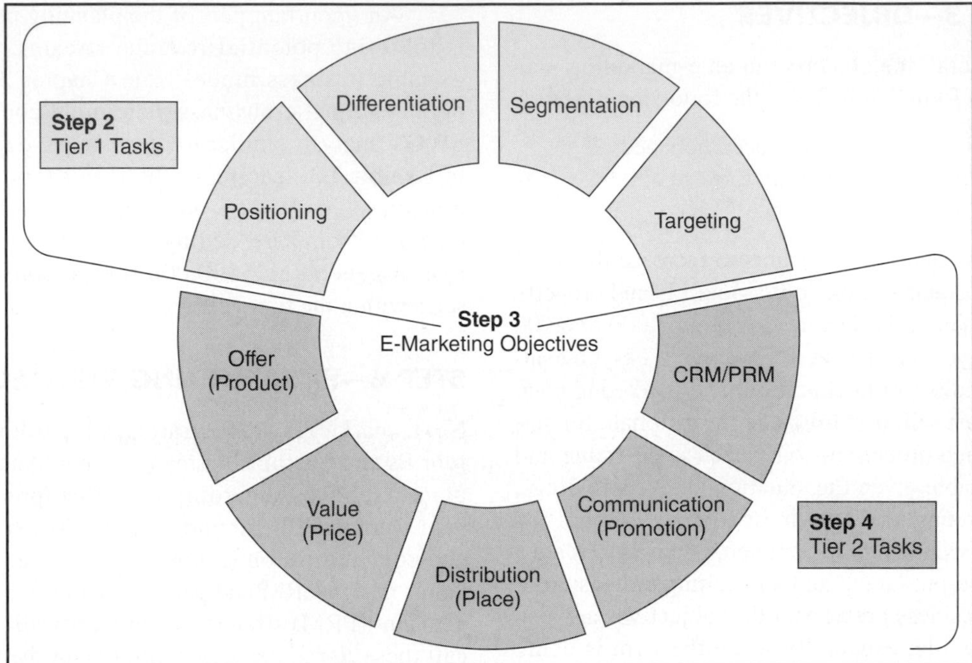

EXHIBIT 3.4 Steps 2, 3, and 4 of the E-Marketing Plan

firms take advantage of information technology capabilities to alter their online offerings. For example, Blue Nile allows product customization in a jiffy: Customers can select a diamond, jewelry type, and setting, and the database returns a page that includes current information about the finished ring or necklace and its price.

The Value: Pricing Strategies

A company must decide how online product prices will compare with offline equivalents. To make these decisions, firms consider the differing costs of sorting and delivering products to individuals through the online channel as well as competitive and market concerns. Two particularly important online pricing trends are the following:

- ***Dynamic pricing.*** This strategy applies different price levels for different customers or situations. For example, a first-time buyer or someone who hasn't purchased for many months may receive discounted prices to motivate purchase, or prices may drop during low-demand periods. The internet allows firms to price items automatically while users view pages.
- ***Online bidding.*** This approach presents a way to optimize inventory management. For instance, a few Seattle hotels allow guests to bid for hotel rooms on slow days, instructing their reservation agents to accept various minimum bid levels depending on occupancy rates for any given day. Priceline.com, eBay.com, and many B2B exchanges operate exclusively using this strategy.

Distribution Strategies

Many organizations use the internet to distribute products or create efficiencies among supply chain members in the distribution channel. Consider the following examples:

- ***Direct marketing.*** Many firms sell directly to customers, bypassing intermediaries in the traditional channel for some sales. In B2B markets, many firms realize tremendous cost reductions by using the internet to facilitate sales.

- ***Agent e-business models.*** Firms such as eBay and E*TRADE bring buyers and sellers together and earn a fee for the transaction.

Marketing Communication Strategies

The internet spawned a multitude of new marketing communication strategies, both to draw customers to a Web site and to interact with brick-and-mortar customers. Firms use Web pages, social media, and e-mail to communicate with their target markets and business partners. Companies build brand images, create awareness of new products, and position products using online content. Database marketing is key to maintaining records about the needs, preferences, and behavior of individual customers so companies can send relevant and personalized information and persuasive communication at strategic times.

Relationship Management Strategies

Many e-marketing communication strategies also help build relationships with a firm's partners, supply chain members, or customers. However, many firms up the ante by using CRM or partner relationship management PRM software to integrate customer communication and purchase behavior into a comprehensive database. They then use CRM software to retain customers and increase average order values and lifetime value. Social CRM is a recent development that uses social media conversation to engage and build relationships with prospects and customers. Other firms build extranets—two or more proprietary networks linked for better communication and more efficient transactions among partner companies.

One informative way to present the company's goals and accompanying e-marketing strategies is through an objective–strategy matrix. This graphical device helps marketers better understand their implementation requirements (Exhibit 3.5). Each cell contains a *yes* or *no*, depending on how the marketer will link particular goals and strategies.

STEP 5—IMPLEMENTATION PLAN

Now comes the part everyone enjoys: deciding how to accomplish the objectives through creative and effective tactics. Marketers select the marketing mix (4 Ps), relationship management tactics, and other tactics to achieve

	Online Strategies				
Online Goals	Online advertising	Online videos	E-Mail	Online sales	Social networking
Increase customer engagement	Yes	Yes	Yes	No	Yes
Increase customer database	Yes	No	No	Yes	Yes
Improve customer service	No	No	Yes	Yes	Yes
Build brand name awareness	Yes	Yes	Yes	No	Yes
Increase online sales	Yes	Possibly	Yes	Yes	Yes
Reposition brand	Yes	Yes	Yes	No	Yes
Increase Facebook "likes"	Yes	No	Yes	Yes	Yes
Generate sales leads	Yes	Yes	Yes	Yes	Yes

EXHIBIT 3.5 E-Marketing Objective–Strategy Matrix

the plan objectives and then devise detailed plans for implementation (the action plans). They also check to be sure the right marketing organization is in place for implementation (i.e., staff, department structure, application service providers, and other outside firms). The right combination of tactics will help the organization meet its objectives effectively and efficiently.

E-marketers pay special attention to information-gathering tactics because information technologies are especially adept at automating these processes. Web site forms, cookies, feedback e-mail, social media comments and likes, and online surveys are just some of the tactics firms use to collect information about customers, prospects, and other stakeholders. Other important tactics include the following:

- Web site log analysis software helps firms review user behavior at the site and make changes to better meet the needs of users.
- Business intelligence uses the internet for secondary research, assisting firms in understanding competitors and other market forces.

STEP 6—BUDGET

A key part of any strategic plan is to identify the expected returns from an investment. These returns can then be matched against costs to develop a cost/benefit analysis, for return on investment (ROI) calculation, or for calculating internal rate of return (IRR), which the management uses to determine whether the effort is worthwhile. Marketers today are especially concerned with adequate return on marketing investment (ROMI). During plan implementation, marketers will closely monitor actual revenues and costs to see that results are on track for accomplishing the objectives. The internet is terrific for monitoring results because technology records a visitor's every click. The following sections describe some of the revenues and costs associated with e-marketing initiatives.

Revenue Forecast

In this budget section, the firm uses an established sales forecasting method for estimating its site revenues in short, intermediate, and long terms. The firm's historical data, industry reports, and competitive actions serve as inputs for this process. An important part of forecasting is to estimate the level of Web site traffic over time, because this number affects the amount of revenue a firm can expect to generate from its site. Revenue streams that produce internet profits come mainly from Web site direct sales, advertising sales, subscription fees, affiliate referrals, sales at partner sites, commissions, and other fees. Companies usually summarize this analysis in a spreadsheet showing expected revenues over time and accompanying rationale.

INTANGIBLE BENEFITS The intangible benefits of e-marketing strategies are much more difficult to establish, as are intangible benefits in the brick-and-mortar world. How much brand equity is created, for example, through an American Airlines program in which customers receive periodic e-mail messages about their frequent-flyer account balances? What is the value of increased brand awareness from a Web site? Putting a financial figure on such benefits is challenging but essential for e-marketers.

COST SAVINGS Money saved through internet efficiencies is considered soft revenue for a firm. For example, if the distribution channel linking a producer with its customers contains a wholesaler, distributor, and retailer, each intermediary will take a profit. A typical markup scheme is 10 percent from manufacturer to the wholesaler, 100 percent or more from wholesaler to the retailer, and 50 percent to the consumer. Thus, if a producer sells the product to a wholesaler for \$50, the consumer ultimately pays \$165. Obviously, this revenue varies widely by industry. If the producer cuts out the intermediaries (disintermediation) and sells its product online directly to the consumer, it can price the product at $85 and increase revenue by $30. Whether this approach translates into profits depends on the cost of getting the product to the consumer. Other examples include the $5,000 a marketer might save in printing and postage for a direct-mail piece costing $1 per piece to 5,000 consumers, or the $270 million Cisco actually saved in one year on handling costs from its online computer system sales.

E-Marketing Costs

E-marketing entails many costs, including costs for employees, hardware, software, programming, and more. In addition, some traditional marketing costs may creep into the e-marketing budget—for example, the cost of offline advertising to draw traffic to the Web site (e.g., GoDaddy.com's Super Bowl ads). For simplicity, this section will discuss technology-related cost items only. See the "Let's Get Technical" box for the steps required to build a Web site. Consider that the cost of a Web site (except the most basic or a blog) can range from $5,000 to $50 million. Following are just a few of the costs site developers incur:

- ***Technology costs.*** These costs include software, hardware, internet access or hosting services, educational materials and training, and other site operation and maintenance costs.
- ***Site design.*** Web sites need graphic designers to create appealing page layouts, graphics, and photos.
- ***Salaries.*** The salaries for all personnel who work on Web site development and maintenance are included in the budget.
- ***Other site development expenses.*** Expenses not included in the technology or salary categories will fall here—things such as registering multiple domain names and hiring consultants to write content or perform other development and design activities.
- ***Marketing communication.*** All advertising, public relations, and promotional activities, both online and offline, that directly relate to drawing traffic to a site and enticing visitors to return and purchase are pegged here. Other costs include search engine optimization (SEO), online directory costs, e-mail list rental, prizes for contests, and more.
- ***Social media communication.*** Staff costs can really escalate when companies engage customers on Facebook, Twitter, or other social media pages. As well, organizations spend time monitoring their brands and other company mentions in social media so they can catch and respond to negative posts.
- ***Miscellaneous.*** Other typical project costs might fall here—expenses such as travel, telephone, stationery printing to add a new URL, and more.

STEP 7—EVALUATION PLAN

Once the e-marketing plan is implemented, its success depends on continuous evaluation. This type of evaluation means e-marketers must have tracking systems in place before the electronic doors open. What should be measured? The answer depends on the plan objectives. Review the Balanced Scorecard for e-business and social media metrics (in Chapter 2) to see how various metrics relate to specific plan goals.

In general, today's marketers are quite ROI driven. As a result, e-marketers must show how their intangible goals, such as brand building or CRM, will lead to higher revenue down the road. Also, they must present accurate and timely metrics to justify their initial and ongoing e-marketing expenditures throughout the period covered by the plan. For example, the huge German chemical company, BASF, must provide an ROI measure for its global search engine advertising. It is very difficult to follow lead activity because Web site leads are sent to sales people worldwide, who take many months to close the deals.

LET'S GET TECHNICAL

Building a Web Site

You have been added to the team charged with redesigning your company's Web site. You have heard that colleagues in graphic design and information systems will also be on the team. You are not quite sure who is responsible for what function or even what all the issues are. You would like to appear articulate and informed in the meetings.

How are Web sites actually built? The process is similar in some ways to building a home. In home building, an architect works with clients to determine their needs, draws up a design to meet those requirements, and then hands that design over to a developer who builds the home. The sequence moves from requirements to design to development. Similarly, the marketing department draws up a creative brief that specifies in detail the requirements for the site and specific design elements (e.g., fonts and colors that will go into the site). The next step is to create a mock-up of the homepage and a few interior pages in a design tool such as Adobe Photoshop. Mastery of Photoshop and of design theory in general requires training and practice. In a large shop, the marketing department would look to the visual communication or graphic design team to produce the design. The design is run past the client and adjustments are made. Once the design is finalized, the development team takes over. The development team takes the design and makes it functional. The development team has five major goals for the site. The site should be

1. ***Easy to update.*** Content changes should be easy to implement. Ideally, an input screen should allow an authorized user to type or paste content directly into the site without technical assistance. Any continuous updates such as stock feeds or weather updates should be programmed to take place automatically, without human intervention.
2. ***Optimized for quick download.*** Each page on the site should load on the user's computer within 10 seconds, even over a slow internet connection. Research shows that users will not wait longer than 10 seconds. Optimizing involves compressing the graphic elements on the page as GIF, JPEG, or PNG files. GIF files are used for line art that has areas of flat color (e.g., a corporate logo) and support having one-color transparent so that white backgrounds disappear. JPEG is used for continuous tone images such as photographs. PNG files do the best of both. Adobe Flash technology allows for animation and movies, but it rarely meets the 10-second threshold. Flash targets users who will be viewing over a high-speed connection. This is one reason why many sites offer the option to skip the Flash introduction. Text does not require compression because it loads quickly. Incidentally, Apple claimed that Flash was so inefficient that it discontinued support for Flash on its iPhone and iPad mobile devices.
3. ***Easy to find.*** The site should be easy for search engines to index and find. Among other things, this accessibility involves the careful placement of key word terms in locations that the search engines will rate highly.
4. ***Interactive.*** Simple interactivity is generated by including hyperlinks to link the pages together. However, more complex interactivity can require some sophisticated programming. Examples of complex interactivity include the following:
   - A search box on the site.
   - Validation of user input (e.g., checking to see that the e-mail address contains an "@" symbol or that a credit card number is valid).
   - Processing of transactions such as completing a purchase.
   - User login for sites requiring high security, such as bank or stock accounts.
   - Connection to backend databases, which could be public databases such as sports scores, news feeds, stock tickers, and weather updates. Databases could also be private, containing sensitive company or personal account information.

   Interactivity is accomplished using development tools such as Macromedia

Dreamweaver or Microsoft Visual Web Developer. These tools develop computer code in **HTML**, JavaScript, Java, Flash, and a variety of other computer languages. Mastery of these tools requires a considerable degree of training and practice.

5. ***Secure.*** In this age of hackers and viruses, the site needs to be protected against malicious attack. Often, organizations attempt to quantify the dollar value of their exposure to attack to determine whether to even continue with development.

Want to try it yourself? There are some great online site development tools that are free. One of the more impressive tools is Google Sites. If you have a Gmail account then you are already authorized to use Google Sites (find it under the "More > Even More" menu on the Google homepage). Google Sites integrates well with the other Google products such as YouTube, Google Docs, and Google Gadgets. Google's seamless integration makes it a fairly easy exercise to create an interactive site—something that only a few years ago would have required lots of coding expertise.

Chapter Summary

The e-marketing plan is a guiding, dynamic document for e-marketing strategy formulation and implementation. The purpose is to help the firm achieve its desired results as measured by performance metrics according to the specifications of the e-business model and e-business strategy. Although some entrepreneurs use a napkin plan to informally sketch out their ideas, an e-marketing plan will help show venture capital firms and banks that the e-business idea is solid and that the entrepreneur has an idea of how to run it.

Creating an e-marketing plan requires seven steps. The first is to conduct a situation analysis by reviewing environmental and SWOT analyses, existing marketing plans and company/brand information, and e-business objectives, strategies, and performance metrics. In the second step, e-marketers perform strategic planning, which includes a marketing opportunity analysis to develop segmentation, targeting, differentiation, and positioning strategies (tier 1 strategies). In the third step, e-marketers formulate objectives, usually setting multiple objectives; they may use an objective–strategy matrix to guide implementation. In the fourth step, e-marketers design e-marketing strategies for the four Ps and relationship management (tier 2 strategies).

In the fifth step, e-marketers develop an implementation plan with a suitable four Ps marketing mix, select appropriate relationship management tactics, design information-gathering tactics, and select other tactics to achieve their objectives. They must also devise detailed implementation plans during this step in the process. In the sixth step, e-marketers prepare a revenue forecast to estimate the expected returns from the plan's investment and detail the e-marketing costs to come up with a calculation that management can use to determine whether the effort is worthwhile. In the final and seventh step of the plan, e-marketers use tracking systems to measure results and evaluate the plan's success on a continuous basis.

Exercises

REVIEW QUESTIONS

1. What are the seven steps in an e-marketing plan?
2. Why do entrepreneurs seeking funding need a venture capital e-marketing plan rather than a napkin plan?
3. What is the purpose of the marketing opportunity analysis and the segment analysis?
4. What four elements in tier 1 and five elements in tier 2 are devised for e-marketing strategy?
5. What is the purpose of an e-marketing objective–strategy matrix?
6. How do managers use budgeting within the e-marketing planning process?
7. Why do e-marketing plans need an evaluation component?

DISCUSSION QUESTIONS

8. **Twitter story:** If you were a venture capitalist with millions to invest, what questions would you ask Jack Dorsey before investing in Twitter?
9. **Twitter story:** What other business models would you recommend to Twitter for generating profit, in addition to selling advertising (refer to the models in Chapter 2)?
10. What kinds of questions should a firm ask in developing an e-marketing plan to serve customers in current markets through an online channel?
11. Why is it important for e-marketers to specify not only the task but also the measurable quantity and time frame for accomplishing an objective?
12. Why would the management of American Airlines expect its e-marketers to estimate the financial impact of intangible benefits such as building brand equity through e-mail messages to frequent flyers?

WEB ACTIVITIES

13. Consider a local business with which you are familiar and sketch a bare-bones e-marketing plan for it.
14. Find the Web site of a firm that offers Web site building services. What steps does it recommend? What does it charge to develop a Web site?
15. Go to the Web site of your university and describe how well you think the site fulfills the marketing objectives of the university. Suggest improvements.

PART 2

E-Marketing Environment

CHAPTER 4

Global E-Markets 3.0*

The primary objective of this chapter is to help you gain an understanding of the main country-by-country differences in internet access and usage as a foundation for segmenting and targeting specific markets. You will learn about some of the barriers to internet adoption and e-commerce in emerging economies and see how these barriers are being addressed. You will learn how consumer behavior and attitudes, payment methods, technological issues, and both economic and technological disparities within nations can influence e-marketing in less developed countries.

After reading this chapter, you will be able to:

- Discuss overall trends in internet access, usage, and purchasing around the world.
- Define *emerging economies* and explain the vital role of information technology in economic development.
- Outline how e-marketers apply market similarity and analyze online purchase and payment behaviors in planning market entry opportunities.

---

* This chapter was contributed by Al Rosenbloom, Associate Professor of Marketing at Dominican University in Illinois (arosenbloom@dom.edu). In 2001, Rosenbloom was a Fulbright Scholar and taught internet marketing to MBA students in Nepal. This chapter is based on his experiences in a number of emerging economies with particular emphasis on Far Eastern nations, including Nepal, India, and China. Research for this chapter was conducted by Juan David Gomez.

- Describe how e-marketing strategy is influenced by computer and telephone access, credit card availability, attitudes toward internet use, slow connection speeds, Web site design, and electricity problems.
- Review the special challenges of e-marketing on the wireless internet in the context of emerging economies.
- Discuss the controversy related to the digital divide.
- Explain how e-marketing is being used with very low income or base of the pyramid consumers.

- The impact of the Great Firewall of China is well-documented, but China *is* connected, with over 513 million Internet users (www.worldinternetstats.com, December 2011). Driven by a massive online population and the censorship of key Western online brands, Chinese services are not simply imitating the Googles, Facebooks, and Twitters of the world. Instead they are often showing their better-known counterparts the way forward by integrating, if not adding to and enhancing, popular online services.

- September 2012 saw **Sina Weibo** unveil a feature which enables the social network's users to have their own personalized QR code for free. Scanning the QR code with a mobile device directs users to individual profile pages automatically, and via the service users can also opt to create a customized QR code.

Idol Goes Global

The names Randy Jackson and Paula Abdul, along with singers Carrie Underwood, Clay Aiken, Kelly Clarkson, and Jennifer Hudson, are well known in America. Even the name Sanjaya Malakar is known. These are all individuals connected with the American TV program *American Idol*. But what about Prashant Tamang, Jessica Mauboy, or Žanamari Lalić? These are also well-known names, but to TV viewers, internet surfers, and text messaging devotees in India, Australia, and Croatia, respectively. All these individuals are winners of local versions of the *American Idol* franchise in countries outside the United States or, as it is known in Germany, *Deutschland sucht den Superstar*. *American Idol* is broadcast in over 100 countries, often 48 hours after the original show has been aired in the United States. The success of *American Idol* spawned 39 national versions in countries like Ethiopia, the Philippines, Russia, and even Kazakhstan.

Georgians can follow the rise (or fall) of that season's music contestants by searching the YouTube key word: Geostari. Although the Georgian alphabet is distinctive, the blue logo with its curvy neon letters that greets each viewer on the homepage brands the Web page as connected with *American Idol*. Ethiopians living anywhere in the world can stay current by either logging onto Jump TV to see rebroadcasts of *Ethiopian Idol* or becoming an Ethiopian Idol fan on Facebook. *Ethiopian Idol* also has Feleke Hailu, a straightforward, sometimes rude, judge in the mold of Simon Cowell. Feleke alternates between his catch phrase "alta fakedem," or "you didn't make it" in Amharic, and blunt judgments like "You sing like a donkey."

SMS is very popular in India where Indian viewers not only vote for singers (30 million SMS messages were sent in the run-up to a final show) but can also apply to be a contestant on *Indian Idol* through SMS by typing the keyword *IDOL* into their handset when they call Sony Entertainment TV Asia, the cable system that carries *Indian Idol*. Avid *Idol* fans in India also have energetic debates on the all-India entertainment portal (india-forums.com), where contestants from season six are thoroughly critiqued. Tensions can run high in the Middle East, where the Arabic-language version is called *Arab Idol*. As a semifinal show drew near, for example, an ice cream shop in Amman, Jordan, offered free ice cream to anyone who voted for the Jordanian contestant, Diana Karzon. In Syria, a mobile phone company hung posters in the streets urging people to vote for the Syrian singer Rowaida Attiyeh as a way of tangibly showing country pride. When a popular Lebanese singer was eliminated in the semifinals, Lebanese audience members threw chairs and anything else they could find. In that mayhem, the two remaining singers fainted. In the end, free ice cream might have made the difference: Diana Karzon won.

From Israel to Indonesia (indonesianidol.com) and from Vietnam (vietnamidol.vtv.vn) to Nigeria (nigerianidol.com), the *American Idol* franchise is big business. In 2010, over 5 billion votes had been cast for *Idol* contestants worldwide (Lisanti, 2010). It is estimated that Freemantle Media, the company that markets *American Idol* abroad, generates over $1 billion a year from advertising, license fees, merchandising, co-branding, and recording in 110 different countries where some version of *Idol* is broadcast. The convergence of TV, internet, mobile phones, and short message services, when added to the unpredictability of what will happen on each show, keeps global and national audiences tuning in each week. As one cynic said, probably the only place in the world that *Idol* does not have a franchise is Antarctica—at least not yet.

OVERVIEW OF GLOBAL E-MARKETING ISSUES

Picture this Accenture ad in your mind: the silhouette of a Chinese fisherman as he sits atop his small boat at twilight. The ad's right-hand corner has a headline that looks like it had been torn from a daily newspaper: "Chinese to be the number one internet language by the year 2007." Beneath that are the words, "Now it gets interesting." This and the global *Idol* example are indications of how the online marketplace is changing—users from other countries, speaking languages other than English, will increasingly dominate the internet.

While Chinese is not yet the number one internet language, the gap between Chinese and English is rapidly closing. By May 2011, there were approximately 565 million English-speaking Web users, compared with 510 million Chinese-speaking Web users. Estimates are that if the current internet adoption rate continues, Chinese-speaking Internet users will overtake English-speaking Web users in 2015 (ITU, 2012). There are now more Chinese-speaking Web users than the total population of North America (Canada, the United States, and Mexico).

Geoffrey Ramsey, eMarketer statistician, envisioned the striking evolution of the Web as consumers in the twenty-first century have come to know it. In 2000, Ramsey saw that ultimately the internet would have significant amounts of local count, that languages other than English would dominate the Web, and that, because of the

Internet's extensive reach, a truly global marketplace would develop (New eGlobal Report, 2000). The Internet Corporation for Assigned Names and Numbers (ICANN), the official body that assigns internet domain names, has recognized the internet's changing language and usage patterns. Beginning in 2010, e-marketers could no longer create Web addresses that do not use the 26 letters of the Roman alphabet. Until now, Web users whose native language was written with non-Roman characters (e.g., Russian, Hindi, Japanese, Greek, Hebrew, and Arabic) had to use keyboards that could type both Roman and local characters. KIA Motors' Web address in Egypt, for example, is www.kia.com.eg. The final two letters, .eg., are part of the top-level domain address and stand for Egypt (مصر). With the ICANN change, KIA's Egyptian Web address could soon end in مصر. E-marketers living in Saudi Arabia (السعودية [AlSaudiah]) and the United Arab Emirates (امارات [Emarat]) have the same opportunities. As Paul Hoffman, the U.S.-based programmer who created these standards noted, these new domain names are not for the Web's current, 1-billion plus users, but for the next several billion users who are now not on the Web (Rhoads, 2007).

How can marketers capitalize on these changing dynamics when planning global e-marketing strategies? Foremost, global e-marketers must understand that a country's e-readiness profile significantly influences marketing strategy and tactics. It is important to differentiate between the industrialized nations of North America and Europe that held one-third of all internet users in 2011 and the emerging economies of India, China, Russia, and Brazil that provide great promise in the future. We briefly introduce the global market context in this chapter, but focus primarily on emerging economies. E-marketing strategies and internet usage in industrialized nations are generally similar to those in the United States (and will be discussed extensively in the rest of the text), while those in emerging markets are not. This chapter is about two paradoxes: (1) That although convergence may make global markets superficially look the same, there are still meaningful differences that e-marketers must understand and account for when working in emerging economies; and (2) that in some instances, emerging markets (which have traditionally been thought of as less advanced than fully industrialized markets) may be more advanced than Western, fully developed markets and thus require a different mix of e-marketing strategies.

Global Markets

Globalization has changed the way marketers conduct business. Market places that have been difficult to access, either because of their physical distance from company headquarters or because of a consumer buying profile that did not match the profile of the firm's core customer, are increasingly being targeted. Significant advances in telecommunications and computer technologies are driving this change, thus creating a whole world of opportunity for e-marketers. A company such as Haier illustrates this point. Haier is a Chinese company with one overriding ambition: It wants to be the first Chinese company to have a world-class global brand that is acknowledged as equal to (and Haier's CEO would say "better than") the best global brands from Japan, the United States, Germany, and South Korea. Indeed, some readers may already know the Haier brand name: Wal-Mart and other big box retailers sell Haier's popular mini-fridge, which has developed a cult following among college students living in campus dorms.

Haier is well on its way to achieving its goal of being a best-in-class global brand. Domestically, Haier is China's leading manufacturer of refrigerators, washing machines, and air conditioners. Globally, Haier has offices or production facilities in more than 100 countries (including a $15-million headquarters in Manhattan). Yet prominently displayed on its "About Haier" Web page is the announcement that Haier was ranked the number one appliance brand in the world by Euromonitor International in 2011 (haieramerica.com). Haier's internet presence supports its global ambition. Log on to Haier's English-language homepage (haier.com) to see a country list highlighting Haier's Web presence in China, Pakistan, Korea, Russia, Australia, the United Arab Emirates, Vietnam, Indonesia, and Poland.

Also, one can log on to Haier's North American Web site directly at haieramerica.com, where Haier presents the face of a contemporary online retailer. Consumers can shop and register for products, subscribe to a Haier newsletter, access warranty information, locate after-sales support, inquire about becoming a Haier distributor, and find tips and hints for maintaining Haier products. Haier is poised to become a fierce global competitor in the twenty-first century, and the continued development of its Web presence will help it achieve that goal.

E-marketing is flourishing all around the world. However, global e-marketers must be alert to the significant differences that influence e-marketing strategy wherever they occur. Savvy global e-marketers recognize that successful e-marketing strategies are dependent on a solid understanding of a country context. For example, mobile marketing campaigns are much more common—and successful—in Africa than they are in other parts of the world. In a country like Kenya, effective mobile campaigns can be text-based rather than graphics-based as in fully developed economies like the United States and Western Europe. Social media campaigns differ significantly by country as well. Would you be surprised to learn that Facebook is not the most popular social media site in Russia, or that Orkut (have you heard of it?) is the leading social media network in Brazil? While the globe is a world of opportunity for e-marketing, successful e-marketers know that what works in one's home market may not work as well in other markets.

Exhibit 4.1 shows that worldwide internet usage increased more than 82 percent between 2007 and 2011. In 2011, the number of internet users was over 2 billion. Yet absolute numbers and rates of growth vary considerably by continent. The Middle East saw the greatest growth in internet use, with an increase of 104.8 percent. Asia has the most internet users, with slightly more than 922 million users. This figure seems reasonable since Asia is home to China and India. Both countries have populations greater than 1 billion and both countries are experiencing

World Regions	2007 Internet Use (millions)	2011 Internet Use (millions)	User Growth (2007–2011) (percentage)	Percentage of Users Worldwide (2011)	Estimated 2011 Population (millions)	Internet Usage as Percentage of Population
North America	234.8	273.0	16.2	11.4	348.2	78.4
Europe	337.9	476.2	41.0	21.5	820.9	72.4
Asia	459.5	922.2	101	44.8	3,922.0	23.5
Latin America/ Caribbean	115.8	215.9	86.4	10.4	593.6	42.9
Africa	44.0	118.6	169.5	7.0	1,073.3	11.0
Middle East	33.5	68.6	104.8	3.7	223.6	30.7
Oceania	19.0	21.3	12.1	1.0	35.9	59.3
Worldwide Total	1,244.4	2,267.2	82.2	99.8	7,017.8	32.3

EXHIBIT 4.1 Worldwide Internet Usage and Population Statistics *Source*: Based on "Internet Usage Statistics—The Big Picture" at www.internetworldstats.com/stats.htm.

significant economic growth. Yet when internet penetration rates (internet use divided by population) are determined, a different global picture emerges. North America has the highest internet penetration rate, with more than three-fourths of all individuals (78.4%) having internet access. Europe is a close follower with 72.4 percent of its population using the internet. In Africa, the world's second most populous continent, internet penetration is just over 10 percent, even with its huge 170 percent increase between 2007 and 2011.

Most e-marketers prefer to evaluate individual countries for online-strategy profitability. Internet use varies greatly from country to country. A country's population, while always an important consideration for marketers, might not always directly correlate with internet penetration levels. This distinction is important because the countries with the highest internet usage may not contain a large population. For example, Chile has the largest internet penetration rate of all Latin American countries, with only 60 percent of its almost 17 million population being active internet users. Brazil, however, the largest country in Latin America, has an internet penetration rate of only 39 percent. (See Appendix A for a table of internet penetration and population estimates for all countries in 2011.)

Bhutan, a small country in the Himalayan Mountains, is a good example of how emerging markets can leapfrog fully developed economies and present new e-marketing opportunities in the process. Bhutan was literally excluded from the internet revolution until 1999. In June 1999, the king of Bhutan inaugurated DrukNet.com, the first and still only internet service provider (ISP) in the country (Long, 2000). The Bhutanese can now send e-mail, surf the Web, play online games, and establish online businesses just like citizens in other countries. With an internet penetration rate of 14 percent, internet access in Bhutan is still limited to major cities. Yet, the modern-day Bhutanese entrepreneur or farmer does not have to go to an internet café or have a computer in his or her home or work space for internet access. Mobile phones are the preferred way to access the internet in Bhutan. The total number of mobile subscribers was estimated to be 460,000 in 2009 ("Bhutan—Telecoms, Mobile and Internet," 2008)—this in a country of around 690,000 individuals. The Bank of Bhutan even has an active mobile banking division (bob.bt) for mobile-connected Bhutanese. While e-marketing is a demanding activity, we believe the greatest challenges for the global e-marketer lie in countries with emerging economies—countries such as Russia, India, Nepal, Egypt, and China—which present different and sometimes difficult e-marketing decisions.

Emerging Economies

Countries vary in their level of economic development. Some countries, such as the United States, Canada, Japan, Australia, Great Britain, and Germany, have high levels of economic development. Economists classify these countries as *developed*. Developed countries include all of Western Europe, North America, Japan, Australia, and New Zealand (Case and Fair, 2001). These countries are highly industrialized, use technology to increase their production efficiency, and, as a result, have a high gross domestic product (GDP) per capita. A high GDP means that citizens have enough discretionary income to buy items that will make their lives easier, richer, and fuller. Developed countries are, therefore, ideally suited for the broad range of e-marketing activities discussed throughout the text.

It is difficult to find a single label to describe the rest of the world's economies. Rapid economic growth has brought some countries, such as South Korea and Chile, much closer to developed economies. One term often used for countries with rapidly developing economies is *emerging*. The single most important characteristic of emerging economies is that they all have a rapidly developing middle class. A growing middle class in any country creates substantial demand for a broad range of products and services. Countries with large populations thus have the greatest potential for developing a vibrant middle class—all things being equal (ceteris paribus as an economist might say). Four countries, Brazil, Russia, India and China, represent the largest growth markets in the world. Collectively, these four countries are called BRIC countries or BEMs (big emerging markets). BRIC countries have more than 40 percent of the world's population and have received significant attention from many multinational corporations and entrepreneurs. IKEA, the Swedish furniture retailer, has a strong Web presence in Russia (ikea.com/ru/ru/) and China (ikea.com/cn/zh and ikea.com/hk/zh/), and will soon enter India.

The BRIC classification is useful, yet the dynamic, market potential of other countries in the world has led some individuals to describe the next group of emerging market economies as **CIVETS** (Colombia, Indonesia, Vietnam, Egypt, Turkey, and South Africa). E-marketers will see opportunity in a country such as Colombia, which has 25 million internet users. Over half of the population in Colombia (56%) is internet connected. A similar relationship exists for Vietnam, where over one-third of the population has internet access. E-marketers also see long-term opportunity in CIVETS because of the large number of youth in each country (Arno, 2012). Global youth markets are digitally connected in ways that their parents never were and present readymade markets for e-marketers.

Importance of Information Technology

Every country can improve its level of economic development through increased efficiencies in the production, distribution, and sale of goods and services. For countries with emerging economies, technology plays an especially important role. Although technology can, in general, boost a nation's overall production capacity and efficiency, it is through the application of information technology that countries with emerging economies can really open up new, exciting, global markets. Today, the internet, along with its supporting information technologies, can jump-start many national economies. India is a prime example of such efforts.

Bangalore, a city well known in India mainly for its wonderful gardens and mild temperatures, is now famous as the center of India's explosive growth in software and IT services. The epicenter of all this activity is a sprawling 330-acre industrial park called Electronic City. In Electronic City, one will find the corporate headquarters of Wipro and Infosys, two global giants that are leaders in this Indian information revolution. In addition, Electronic City is home to both well-known American companies (Motorola and Hewlett-Packard) and European companies (Siemens), which are outsourcing call center operations, medical transcription, and even income-tax processing to India.

The internet allows businesses in emerging economies to instantaneously tap a global marketplace. While this is true for all companies that use the internet to communicate and deliver products through the Web, businesses that are completely Web-based at their founding are given a distinctive name. They are called **born global firms**. Born global firms understand that the Web, along with e-mail, and Voice over Internet Protocol (VoIP) communications, such as Skype, enable them to tap global markets immediately. For example, Dewak is a company located in Medellin, Colombia, that offers customized helpdesk and chat services for businesses using an open source content management system called Joomla! As a born global firm, Dewak's Web presence focuses on business benefits (dewak.com) and dissociates itself completely from inaccurate perceptions that Medellin is still the center of Colombian drug-trafficking. As befits a born global firm, Dewak's revenues come from the United States, Great Britain, Australia, Denmark, Sweden, and even China. Interestingly, none of Dewak's revenues, to date, is from Colombia (Fuerst, 2010). Born global firms illustrate that successful marketing on the internet can leapfrog a company from nowhere to somewhere overnight.

E-marketers from countries with emerging economies still have many challenges. Not only must they confront all the marketing issues and decisions described throughout this text, but also they must address some unique challenges related to the conditions of operating within a still developing nation. Some of the internet marketing differences between developed and still developing countries are fewer computer users, limited credit card use, lack of secure online payment methods, and unexpected power failures. We will now look at these challenges in more detail.

COUNTRY AND MARKET OPPORTUNITY ANALYSIS

As noted in Chapter 3, an e-marketing plan guides the marketer through the process of identifying and analyzing potential markets. Market similarity is very powerful and the savvy e-marketer will understand and use it to her or his advantage. According to the concept of market similarity, marketers often choose foreign markets that have characteristics similar to their home market for initial market entry (Jeanette and Hennessy, 2002). Thus, a U.S.-based company would first target countries such as Canada, the United Kingdom, and Australia before targeting France, Japan, or Germany. The well-known global e-tailing giant, Amazon.com, used a market similarity strategy to begin its international expansion. After developing its domestic presence in the United States, Amazon first entered Canada, and then the United Kingdom. It then targeted France, Germany, and Japan. Three markets (the United States, Canada, and the United Kingdom) share a common language (English), but there are other market similarities across each foreign market: All these countries have high literacy rates, high internet usage rates, and clearly defined market segments willing to shop for books (and other products) online; in each country, credit cards are widely used for purchases; each country has secure, trusted online payment mechanisms; and each country has efficient package delivery services. For Amazon.com, market similarity not only reduces (without eliminating) the risk of entry into foreign markets but also helps to explain why the company targeted these countries in the first place. Similarly, the increasingly well-known Brazilian cosmetic company, Natura, began its international market expansion by first targeting Spanish-speaking countries within South America (Argentina, Chile, and Peru) before entering Mexico (McKern, Yamamoto, Bouissou, and Hoyt, 2010). Common language and geographic proximity, supported by a Web presence that is adapted to each country, helped Natura become a global cosmetic brand.

Yet both Amazon and Natura have continued to expand. In 2004, Amazon entered the Chinese marketplace, through its acquisition of a popular online bookstore, joyo.com. In 2007, joyo.com was co-branded with the amazon.cn name to further build its global brand equity. In 2012, Amazon announced that it would enter its second BRIC country: India. Through a partnership with Junglee.com, Amazon offers 14,000 global and domestic brands to consumers in this, the world's second most populace, country (Shani, 2012). Similarly, Natura products are available in France; the company has bypassed Spain for now and has expansion plans for Russia and the United States (Pearson, 2011).

Pankaj Ghemawat developed a framework called CAGE that helps explain the balancing act that e-marketers must engage in when they evaluate the similarities and differences between markets. Each letter stands for an important consideration that every global marketer, including e-marketers, must understand as they evaluate global markets: C stands for culture, A for administration, G for geography, and E for economic. Ghemawat suggests that the more similar two countries are in terms of CAGE, the more attractive they are for target market development (Ghemawat, 2007). The implication for e-marketers is simple: Target similar markets before targeting dissimilar ones. Both Amazon and Natura seem to have followed Ghemawat's advice.

Diaspora Communities

Globalization helps explain the increased migration of individuals from one country to another. When a large number of people leave their home country and live together in a common neighborhood or city abroad, they become part of a diaspora community. Diaspora communities often want to maintain a relationship with their homeland. E-businesses in countries with emerging markets use market similarity to target their own diaspora communities living abroad. For example, Tortas Peru (tortasperu.com.pe) specifically targets the Peruvian diaspora community who would like to surprise friends and family living in Peru with homemade, traditional Peruvian cakes. All of the cakes are made in Peru for delivery to a Peruvian home market. Peruvian homemakers who need a second income to help support their families do all the baking. A similar Web site, shop.muncha.com, offers a wide range of products that Nepalis living overseas can send to individuals back home. This site is presented online as a traditional retailer, which is appropriate because Muncha House is a famous department store in the main shopping center of Kathmandu. The January 2010 earthquake that destroyed the capital of Haiti, Port-au-Prince, also shows the connections between diaspora communities and the Web. As a collective effort to rebuild its homeland, the Haitian diaspora was galvanized into sending relief aid, including money. A leading conduit for those donations was Wyclef Jean's social action Web site, yele (yele-haiti.org). Jean is Haitian and played in the rock band, The Fugees, before beginning his solo career. *Yele* is a Creole word for *help*.

Market similarity can also be seen in the phenomenon called **market convergence**, in which markets that were once very different become more similar over time. The Czech Republic is an excellent example of how consumers have matured into accepting online marketing and appear to have online shopping preferences and attitudes mirroring those of consumers in developed countries. In 2001, one survey found that an astonishing 75 percent of Czech consumers said that it was more secure buying goods and services in a store than online. Sixty-five percent said it was both easier and more fun to buy goods and services in a store, and 61 percent said one of their prime concerns about online shopping was "You don't know what you get." Finally, 42 percent said they didn't trust online brands (Taylor Nelson Sofres, 2001). By 2007, however, 97 percent of Czech consumers who used the internet said they were aware of online shopping. Sixty-two percent said that they either "loved" or "liked" the online shopping experience. When asked what motivated their online shopping, respondents said that it saved them money (65%) and time (24%) (Gemius, 2009).

Similar to consumers in many developed countries, Czech consumers said the internet was their preferred way to obtain information about consumer electronics and domestic appliances, travel services, phones, and GSM (Global System for Mobile communications) accessories, along with computer hardware and software (Gemius, 2009). With a product list this long, it is not surprising that the Czech Republic has several mega online retailers, such as heureka.cz, obchodni-dum.cz (a specialist in appliances, consumer electronics, and mobile phones), vltava.cz (a site where users can buy music, books, videos, and software), alza.cz (where one can shop for consumer electronics in English and German, as well as in Czech), and finally, aukro.cz, the Czech version of eBay. Market convergence is also evident in Web sites that enable Czech consumers to buy sports equipment like "jumping stilts" online (apo-vystoupeni.cz), to feel the adrenaline rush of bungee jumping (bungee.cz) and to experience a similar rush from listening to music from independent metal and deadhead rock bands (czechcore.cz).

One area where emerging e-markets differ significantly from developed e-markets involves online purchasing. We turn to this topic next.

E-Commerce Payment and Trust Issues

E-commerce in emerging markets is often hampered by the limited use of credit cards and the lack of trust in safely conducting online transactions. In contrast to the prevalent ownership of credit cards in high-income countries, credit card ownership in low-income countries is quite different. In Egypt, Senegal and Pakistan, for example, less than 2 percent of the adult population in each country owns a credit card (Togan-Egrican, English, and Klapper, 2012). While entrepreneurs and corporations use the Web to communicate with customers in each of those countries, the limited use of credit cards makes online purchasing more difficult. In Nepal, credit cards are used primarily by young Nepali professionals, upper-income Nepalis, and tourists to Nepal.

When making a purchase on the Muncha site (shop.muncha.com), individuals living outside Nepal can use all major credit cards for their purchase. But for local Nepalis, only Visa, MasterCard, and Himalayan Bank cards are accepted (shop.muncha.com). Further, on the FAQ page about payment, the first method of payment is still cash.

An even more extreme example is Ethiopia. In this country of more than 90 million people, credit card use is virtually nonexistent. In fact, the World Bank database describing how individuals save, borrow, and make payments in countries around the world (Global Findex) does not even include Ethiopia. Cash and checks are the preferred payment methods between individuals, and a letter of credit is the preferred payment method for businesses. International visitors to Ethiopia with credit cards issued by foreign banks can use them only in a five-star hotel and a few selected stores in Addis Ababa, the capital. In May 2007, there was only one ATM machine in the entire country, and it was located in the lobby of the country's only five-star hotel. In 2012, many of the major hotel chains in Addis Ababa have ATMs, bringing the total up to 20 machines (dashenbanksc.com). Clearly, limited credit card use can severely restrict a target market's purchasing ability.

Marketers must also analyze relevant buyer behavior within a market. In addition to knowing how many credit cards are in circulation, e-marketers working in emerging economies should understand consumer attitudes toward online purchasing. In Lithuania, for example, research conducted in January 2007 found that 51 percent of current internet users had not made a purchase online because they thought it was too risky. When probed, 40 percent said they were afraid of sending their credit card information over the internet, while 39 percent were afraid of making personal information available.

Lithuanians are not alone in fearing that their credit card information might be stolen when buying online. When asked if they were either very concerned or extremely concerned about the security of credit card information while making online purchases, 89 percent of survey respondents in Chile said "yes"; 64 percent of survey respondents in Colombia said "yes"; 51 percent said "yes" in Macao; and 53 percent of all Mexican respondents said they also had serious concerns (World Internet Project, 2010). Exhibit 4.2 summarizes what consumers in other countries think about the safety of their credit card information.

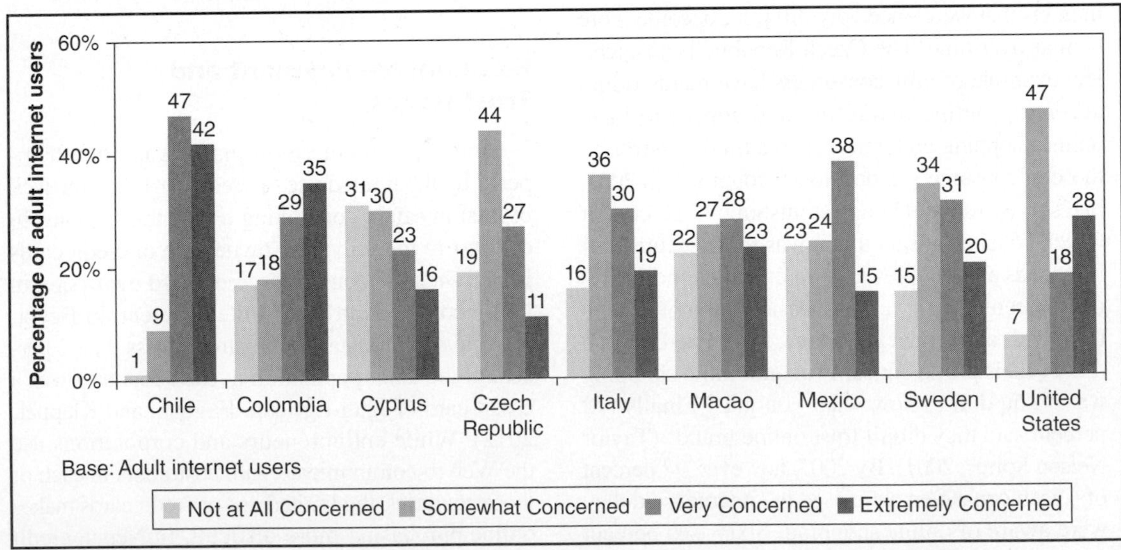

EXHIBIT 4.2 Strength of Consumer Concern About Online Use of Credit Cards in Selected Countries.
Source: World Internet Project: International Report, 2010. Reproduced with kind permission of the USC Annenberg School Center for the Digital Future.

Online security is essential for any e-commerce transaction. Some Brazilian Web sites have a unique security feature. Any individual who wants to make online purchases in Brazil must supply his or her CPF number. CPF stands for "Cadastro de Pessoas Fisicas" and is a unique number given to each individual who wishes to participate in the formal economy. A CPF is needed to open a bank account, make major purchases (such as a TV set), buy real estate, apply for a job, and shop online. Without a CPF, Brazilian consumers can only make major purchases from the informal gray and black markets. One author was prevented from purchasing online and activating a SIM card while traveling in Brazil because he did not have a CPF number. See the "Let's Get Technical" box for more details concerning online security.

One innovative solution to the credit card and online payment dilemma is eBanka (ebanka.com) in the Czech Republic. Established in 1998, eBanka is the oldest purely internet bank in Central and Eastern Europe. The bank issues credit cards (Eurocard, Visa, and MasterCard) and handles secure and efficient online money transfer accounts for online purchases. A customer simply opens an eBanka account, deposits money, uses that money to make online purchases, and deposits more money when the account balance is low. It is the Czech version of digital cash. Because of eBanka's success, in July 2006, Raiffeisen International (RI), an Austrian bank, bought eBanka for €30 million. Polish online shoppers stated that the second most frequently used payment method was through bank transfer, a la eBanka (or an electronic postal money transfer to the online business's bank account). The most preferred payment method for Polish online shoppers? Cash on delivery (Polasik and Fiszeder, 2010).

Infrastructure Considerations

A country's physical infrastructure also influences online marketing strategy. Unless the firm's product is completely digital, online retailers of tangible products still need to solve the logistics problems of physically moving the product from one location (a warehouse) to another (a retail outlet, consumer's home, or some other collection point). Road conditions in emerging market countries vary greatly including the roads in major cities. India is well known for congested city streets, with cars, autorickshaws, carts drawn by water buffalos, and cows all vying for space on many roads. Transaction costs increase as the length of transportation and time increase. This was exactly the situation DealDey.com found itself in when it began operation in Lagos, Nigeria. DealDey (dealdey.com/) is an online retailer selling everything from high-style fashion to cupcakes. (It seems that cupcakes are a status symbol in Lagos.) Traffic in Lagos, the largest city in Nigeria, is often quite literally at a standstill. DealDey uses couriers on motorcycles, who can zig and zag through grid-locked traffic, to deliver products to customers who will buy only using cash (Hinshaw, 2012). Trust is very low in Nigeria, where online fraud is rampant. The Nigerian e-mail from a "prince" asking for money is one of the best-known e-mail scams.

Countries with emerging economies are also prone to electricity blackouts. Nepal is a good example. One of the poorest countries in the world, with a gross national income per year of $540 per capita, Nepal is rich in many natural resources, including water. Through the efforts of the United Nations and other international aid organizations, Nepal has built a series of hydroelectric dams throughout the country. Nepal needs these dams because only 15 percent of all households in Nepal have electricity. Most people living in Nepal's major cities of Kathmandu, Pokhara, and Nepalgunj have electricity. Even so, households and businesses in these major cities are sometimes without electricity during the summer months, when frequent rolling blackouts occur across the entire country. In April 2010, consumers living in Kathmandu experienced 6 to 12 hours of blackout every day. The Nepal Electrical Authority (NEA) simply could not generate enough electricity for the entire country. A similar situation is common in Egypt, Brazil, and Vietnam. In 2008, several regions in China

LET'S GET TECHNICAL

Licensing Technology

Filename: LatestOperatingSystem.zip

Download Time: 10 hours and 34 minutes

Number of Files: 4,215 files, 78 folders

Price: $0.00

Legality: 100% ILLEGAL

The feud between music fans and the music industry over the illegal distribution of albums and songs has been all over the media. As many already know, computer users with high-speed connections can download a client to get in on the trading—illegal trading, that is. Software is distributed through this medium as well. Just like copying music files to shared folders, users are copying the contents of installation CDs for such software as Microsoft Office, Macromedia Flash, and Adobe Photoshop.

However, when a user purchases software, he or she is most often just purchasing one license, or the right to install and run the software on one computer. When purchasing and installing the software, the user agrees to the end user license agreement (EULA). He or she agrees by selecting "I agree" or "I accept" in the installation process. The EULA also protects the software company from liability in case the software causes damage to the user's computer.

Breaking the agreement used to be simple. The user simply had to copy the CD and the CD's product key and distribute it freely. Software companies then became more advanced in their quest to stop software piracy, or the illegal distribution of software, by instituting activation procedures. Upon installing the software, the computer user is allowed to either run the software for a certain number of days or open it a certain number of times. Once the user activates the software, either online or via telephone, the limitations are removed. The activation stops software piracy because it allows the software associated with the product key to be activated only once, and thus it can be installed on only one computer.

Also, this feature allows software companies to distribute trial versions of their software. Once the limit has been met, the software cannot be used without purchasing a full version. Other trial versions just offer limited features until a license is purchased.

Software piracy is often misunderstood, and it occurs in many different forms. Software piracy also includes illegal use of fonts. Licenses can be issued for fonts, and using copyrighted fonts without a license is illegal. Whether using the software or font for business or personal purposes, using it without a license is illegal and punishable by law. Forms of software piracy include the illegal use of a software program over a network, distributing specialized education versions to unauthorized markets, and reporting an inaccurate number of users using software at a site. Even the possession of software that has been illegally copied is piracy.

Many organizations have been created to monitor software piracy and the illegal duplication of all copyrighted material worldwide. Examples include the Software & Information Industry Association's (SIIA) Anti-Piracy Division (siia.net) and the Business Software Alliance (BSA) (bsa.org). The SIIA's anti-piracy division conducts proactive campaigns to educate users about software piracy. The BSA recently stated that software piracy cost the software industry nearly $64 billion in sales in 2011. The BSA ranks countries by their piracy rates. According to the BSA, piracy rates in the United States, Japan, New Zealand, and Luxembourg hover near 20 percent (a relatively low figure) while those in Armenia, Bangladesh, Georgia, and Zimbabwe all exceed 90 percent. Software manufacturers, such as Microsoft and Adobe, have also set up Web sites to help determine whether users' software is legal and to report software piracy.

Apple, always an innovator, takes a unique approach to piracy by acknowledging that some forms of copying are reasonable. Buy an app on your iPhone or iPad and you can install it on multiple devices that you own as long as all the devices are tied to your Apple ID.

In the professional world, it is tempting to hand a CD and product key to one's coworker to install. However, if an audit is conducted by an outside source, that simple act can get the company in hot water. Software manufacturers can take such actions as warning, fining, or suing the company. In a professional setting, it is best to pursue a site license agreement (SLA) for the organization to use the software. An SLA is simply a license to use the software within a certain facility. The license usually entails whether the software can be installed on all or specific computers or servers and if copies can be made and distributed within the facility.

experienced blackouts. But with major infrastructure improvements for the 2008 Summer Olympics, China seems to have resolved its electricity problem. When lack of electricity forces an e-business offline, the business is effectively closed. Running an e-business in countries with electricity shortages can be challenging, to say the least.

TECHNOLOGICAL TIPPING POINTS

Solving credit card payment and trust issues are only two of several marketing challenges in emerging economies. Equally important for global e-marketers is the need to understand the seismic changes occurring how consumers access online content. "Tipping point" is a phrase popularized by Malcolm Gladwell in a book with that title (Gladwell, 2000). A **tipping point** is that moment when an emerging trend or phenomenon becomes so big that it becomes irreversible. As the metaphor suggests, a tipping point changes the balance of things forever; there is no going back. Computer and mobile phone technology, along with the rapid development of broadband, are changing the way markets access and understand information, products, and services.

Legacy Technologies: Computers and Telephones

Clearly, customers need a mechanism for connecting to the internet. Historically, in every country, this has been through desktop computers and an ISP. For e-businesses operating in developed, high-income countries, connecting to the internet is generally not a problem. For consumers in emerging economies, however, owning a computer has been a significant barrier to access. For example, in a global survey done by the Pew Charitable Trust in 2007, the country with one of the lowest ownership rates was Bangladesh, with only 2 percent individual ownership. In Latin America, Venezuela had the highest computer ownership rate, with 43 percent, while Mexico had 22 percent. The Middle East also had striking contrasts. Seventy-seven percent of Israelis owned computers, while only 11 percent of Moroccans did. Africa had some of the lowest computer ownership rates: 27 percent in South Africa, 16 percent in Nigeria, 6 percent in Ivory Coast, 5 percent in Senegal, and 2 percent in Uganda.

E-marketers run the risk of being ethnocentric when they infer that because "I" don't access online content through a computer, the rest of the world does not as well. Access through desktops is still common in many countries. **Telecenters**—small shops with three to ten computers that offer internet connections to the general public in simply furnished settings—are the most popular means for accessing the Web in many countries. Peru, where the telecenters are called "cabinas publicas," has one of the highest usage rates of telecenters in the world. A 2005 study estimated that 6,000 cabinas were available in the capital city, Lima, with another 4,000 cabinas scattered throughout the rest of Peru (Exhibits 4.3) (cited in Curioso et al. 2007). The Peruvian Institute of Marketing found that 35 percent of cabinas users went there to check their e-mail, 25 percent went to do online chatting, and 20 percent went to surf the World Wide Web. This same study found that 62 percent of all cabinas users were online for two hours every time they logged on (Palacios, 2002).

China is a highly stratified society. Although luxury goods marketers, such as Gucci, Louis Vuitton, and Prada, find a growing market for their brands, the majority of Chinese consumers are in much lower-income categories. Cyber cafes in China are a significant access to the Internet, with a total of 140,000 operating in the country. All internet cafes provide access through desktop computers. Exhibit 4.4 shows a typical internet café in rural Guatemala with older model desktops for customer use.

Landline-connected telephones are, admittedly, entering the decline stage of their product life cycle. As wireless technology increases in its availability, landline telephones will become increasingly less useful and ultimately obsolete. When consumers depended only on landline connections to the internet, many consumers were

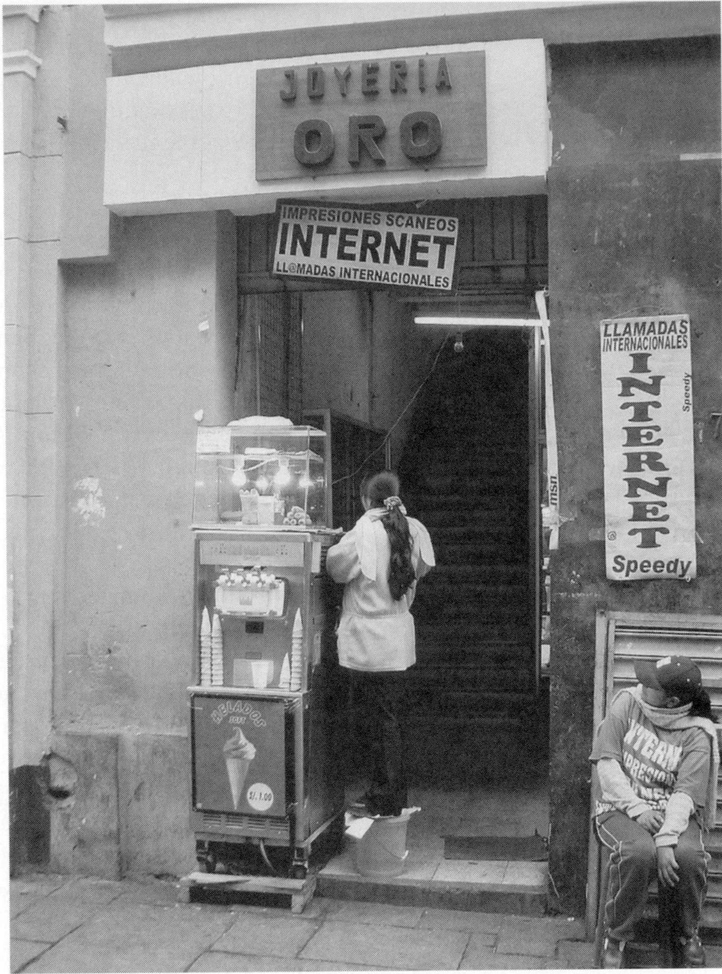

EXHIBIT 4.3 Entrance to a Typical Cabinas in Lima, Peru.

excluded from the market. Indonesia illustrates this point. As the world's largest Muslim country, most Indonesians pray in mosques five times a day. Devotion to their faith coupled with the lack of landline telephones in the country meant that most Indonesians were closer to a mosque than they were to a telephone (ITU, 2002). For example, eighty percent of all Indonesians were less than 1 kilometer (0.6 mile) away from a mosque; while slightly more than 20 percent were that close to a single telephone. Forty percent of all Indonesians were more than 5 kilometers (3 miles) from a telephone (ITU, 2000). The truly explosive growth of mobile technology has created a tipping point in Indonesia (and many other countries) and it is this phenomenon that we discuss next.

WIRELESS INTERNET ACCESS: MOBILE PHONES

The explosive growth and diffusion of cellular telephones throughout the world have dramatically changed online marketing. Indeed, it is the most significant tipping point in computer information technology—ever. Forrester Research expects the total number of mobile phone users in the world to

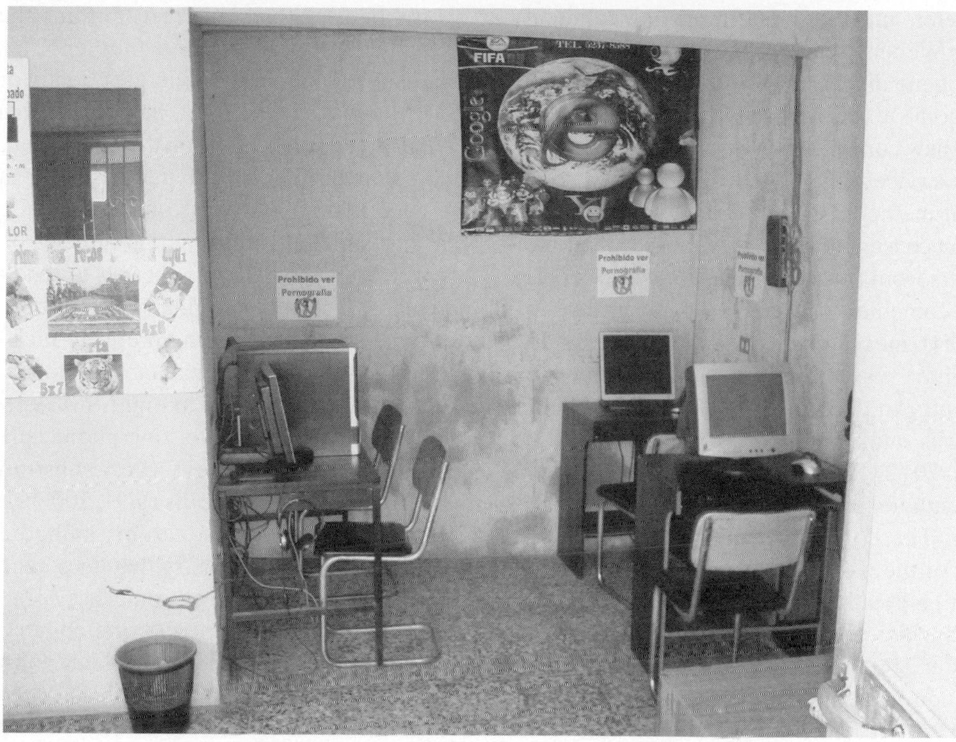

EXHIBIT 4.4 Inside an Internet Café in Guatemala.

exceed the number of PC-based internet users by 2016 (Huynh, 2012). Back in 2007, John Tysoe, cofounder of the British mobile phone company The Mobile World, made this statement, "[The cellular industry] took over 20 years to connect the first billion subscribers, but only 40 months to connect the second billion. The three billion milestone will be passed in July 2007" (Ridley, 2007). Tysoe was on target. In 2012, over half of the world's total population had at least one handset for a total of 4.3 billion users (Huynh, 2012). Other estimates suggested the number of total mobile subscriptions globally to be 6 billion (Bold and Davidson, 2012). Whatever the exact number, mobile phone usage is huge.

Nowhere is this great sea change more evident than in Africa, the most underserved—and underdeveloped—continent in the world by traditional measures of connectivity (number of landline phones and number of internet users). The number of African mobile phone subscribers skyrocketed from 11 million in 2000 to over 500 million in 2011, making Africa the second largest mobile phone market after Asia (Dutta, Bilbao-Osorio, and Geiger, 2012). Almost everyone in the tiny nation of Gabon had a cell phone. There were 96 cell phones for every 100 Gabonese. Similarly, the ratio of cell phones to every 100 inhabitants in South Africa was 92:100; in Botswana, 89:100; in the Gambia, 66:100; in Ghana, 48:100; and 42:100 in Kenya. Amazingly, in the small island nation of the Seychelles, there are more mobile phones than inhabitants, with a ratio of 101:100 (Maniewicz, 2009). Similar patterns are seen in Asia. As of May 2012, China alone had over 1 billion mobile subscribers, and it is estimated that by May 2013, India too will have a billion mobile subscribers (State of the Global Mobile Industry Annual Assessment, 2012).

Just having a cell phone, however, does not eliminate the challenges of wireless e-marketing.

E-marketers must still determine how to modify existing Web site content for the smaller screens of cell phone displays; how to resolve potentially cumbersome text entry using tiny keypads; how to develop new content that consumers will want; how to price services; and how to develop easy, secure payment methods. E-marketers must also understand that consumer behavior with the mobile internet differs from consumer behavior with stationary desktop computers or even laptop computers.

Text messaging is a good example. The Philippines was the number one text messaging country in the world—far surpassing China, which was ranked number 32 in the world (SMS Update, 2012). In 2012, the Philippines was the leader with about 1.8 billion SMS messages sent per day. The Philippines accounts for about 10 percent of the world's total SMS messaging, and this from a population of approximately 101 million and which has an internet penetration rate of just under 30 percent (see Appendix A). Zalora (zalora.com), an online retailer in the Philippines, used SMS messaging when it wanted to increase both brand awareness and online sales in the Philippines. Since SMS is a high-volume, quick response strategy, Zalora was able not only to find lower-income men and senior Pinoy consumers (*Pinoy* is the colloquial term for Filipinos), but also to further develop a marketing relationship with them through the responses to multiple SMS messages. Similarly, Pantene shampoo used SMS messaging as a strategy to increase its short-term sales with women living in Jakarta. Pantene sent women an SMS message offering them a discount on its shampoo. When interested women replied, they not only received a personalized message telling them the benefits of Pantene but were also sent a discount voucher redeemable at Carrefour, a well-known hypermarket. As a result, Pantene sales increased by 31 percent in two days.

Wise e-marketers, however, must not only look at the magnitude of these numbers but also at the consumer behavior that stands behind them. A comparison between the cell phone behavior of the mainland Chinese and Chinese living in Hong Kong SAR (Special Administrative Region) makes this point. Cell phone users in Hong Kong tend to be wealthy, sophisticated, and young. It would be easy (and incorrect) to think that they are constantly texting one another. The average Hong Kong cell phone user sends only 20 SMS messages a month. The average mainland Chinese cell phone user, on the other hand, sends more than 85. The underlying reason for this difference is that in Hong Kong many cell phone packages include around 1,000 minutes of usage per month, and while it is cheaper to send a short message, it is only marginally so. Mobile phone subscribers in Hong Kong prefer to pick up the phone and talk. On the mainland, a mobile phone subscriber can send up to eight SMS messages for the price of a minute-long phone call. Thus for the mainland Chinese, SMS substitutes for e-mail and some voice calls (ITU, 2006b).

Finally, a short note on Cambodian history. Cambodia is a country that does not receive much attention outside of Southeast Asia. But in 1993, Cambodia became the first country in the world to have more mobile telephone subscribers than fixed-line telephone subscribers. Why? Price is part of the answer. Even in 1993, cell phones and the accompanying technology for mobile networks were less expensive than fixed-line telephones. But the country's history also provides a clue. Cambodia's recent political history includes a long and violent civil war (the movie *The Killing Fields* is about this war). During this conflict, the Khmer Rouge, one of the warring political parties, planted 4 to 6 million land mines throughout the country (U.S. State Department, 1998). Digging up the ground to lay telephone cables is simply too risky in Cambodia. As a result, mobile phones and mobile phone networks found and satisfied a large, unmet need in Cambodia. E-marketers are served well when they place technology within a country's historical context.

Smartphones

Globally, smartphone use is on the rise. In fact, a recent study noted that smartphone adoption rates were the fastest of any technology innovation—ever. This study found that smartphones are being purchased and used ten times faster than the computer revolution of the 1980s, two times faster than the internet boom of the 1990s, and three times faster than recent social media adoption ("iOS and Android Adoption Explodes Internationally," 2012). The United Arab Emirates, the United Kingdom, Saudi Arabia, Sweden, Norway, Japan, and Australia have the highest rate of smartphone adoption, with over 50 percent of each country's population using a smartphone ("Leaders in Mobile Phone Adoption," 2012). Given the wide use of smartphones in the United Kingdom and United Arab Emirates, PizzaExpress, a London-based pizza restaurant, leveraged a successful domestic digital marketing campaign when it entered the United Arab Emirates. Downloads of a PizzaExpress app in the United Arab Emirates allowed not only fast and simple pizza ordering but also easy identification of the UK expatriates working in the United Arab Emirates. Identification of the UK citizens living outside the country is another example of diaspora marketing.

In addition to knowing that more and more consumers are using smartphones globally, marketers must understand how smartphones are actually influencing consumer purchase behavior in various countries. For example, 36 percent of Egyptian consumers who own a smartphone actually changed their minds about buying a product while they were in a store because of real-time, online research. In Brazil, about three-quarters of smartphone users who saw an offline ad did online research after seeing the ad, and in Argentina, 37 percent of smartphone users make a product purchase in a brick-and-mortar store after online research with their smartphone ("Leaders in Mobile Phone Adoption," 2012). The aware e-marketer understands that while mobile and smartphone devices may be fairly similar, consumer behavior in various countries is not.

Broadband

Broadband, or high-speed internet access, illustrates another significant tipping point. The rapid adoption of broadband networks from 1999 to 2011 can be seen at the interactive graphic at news.bbc.co.uk. Point Topic, a UK-based research firm specializing in broadband communication services, estimates that by 2014, there will be over 740 million broadband lines worldwide. The largest percentage growth, it predicts, will come from emerging markets. Point Topic estimates a 14 percent annual growth in broadband lines from BRIC countries and the emerging markets of South East Asia, Eastern Europe, and South America ("Emerging Countries Lead Broadband," 2009). Exhibits 4.5 and 4.6 illustrate

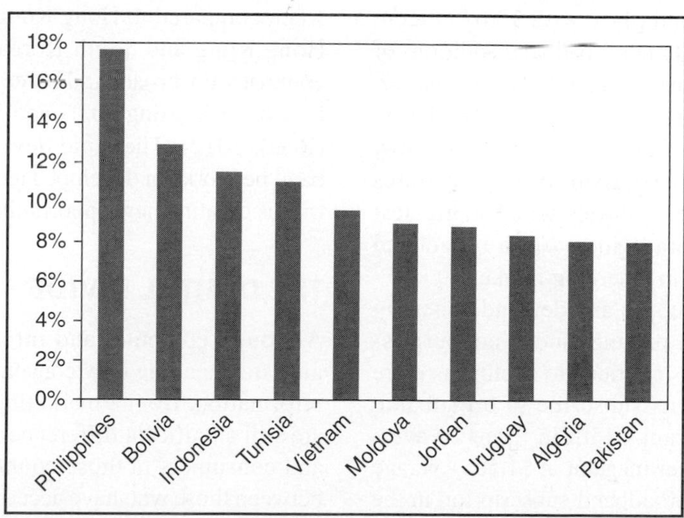

EXHIBIT 4.5 Top Ten Countries with New Broadband Subscribers by Quarterly Growth in Fourth Quarter 2009
Source: World Broadband Statistics, Q4 2009. Reproduced with kind permission from PointTopic.

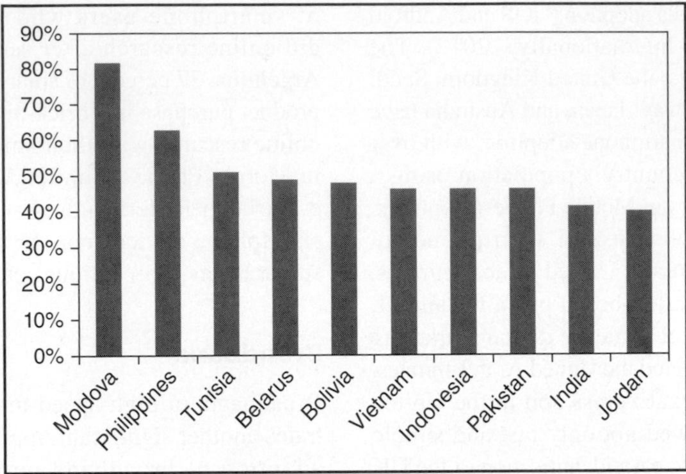

EXHIBIT 4.6 Top 10 Countries with Greatest Percentage of Annual Growth in Broadband Subscribers Q4 2008 to Q4 2009
Source: World Broadband Statistics, Q4 2009. Reproduced with kind permission from PointTopic.

the "top ten" countries in terms of quarterly and yearly broadband subscriber growth, respectively. Exhibit 4.5 shows that the Philippines had the highest single-quarter percentage growth at 17.46 percent in the final quarter of 2009. This represented 256,059 new broadband subscribers, up by 59 percent from the previous quarter. Bolivia was in second place with 12.67 percent quarterly growth, with net broadband additions of 11,500, up 57 percent from the previous quarter. Vietnam added the most new subscribers during the fourth quarter of 2009, with 259,000 new, broadband subscribers. Exhibit 4.6 illustrates a similar story: The countries with the greatest year-to-year percentage increase in broadband subscribers were all in emerging markets.

The laws of supply and demand generally apply to broadband pricing, and it not surprising that global prices continue to decline as more individuals and firms subscribe to broadband. The United States ranks 15th in terms of average download cost per megabit at $1.50. Average monthly cost for a broadband subscription in the United States is $75 (Reed, 2012). Consumers in other countries pay less for broadband not only on a per-month but also on a per-megabit basis. In the Czech Republic, Poland, and Bulgaria, for example, average per-megabit download costs are $0.36, $0.28, and $0.25, respectively, with consumers in Bulgaria and the Czech Republic paying on average $20/month and individuals in Poland paying $43/month for broadband service. However, even these costs can seem expensive when compared to Hong Kong and South Korea. Hong Kong and South Korea are two cheapest countries for broadband on a per-megabit download basis, costing $0.07 and $0.16, respectively (Reed, 2012). The rapid development of broadband networks in developed and developing countries is creating new opportunities for e-marketers.

THE DIGITAL DIVIDE

Although computer and information technologies are changing how consumers access and use information, from a marketing perspective there are still significant differences between countries and consumers in those countries. This division between those who have access to information and those who don't is termed the **digital divide**. Even in fast-developing China, there is a digital divide. It is the large gap between urban and rural internet users. In urban areas, internet penetration rate is around 50 percent, while in rural China, internet penetration rate is only 18 percent. CNNIC (China Internet Network Information Center), the Chinese government agency that reports internet statistics, reported that this gap was caused by a combination of high internet costs relative to rural income, less knowledge of the internet itself, and inadequate infrastructure (CNNIC, 2010). When surveyed in 2011, 58 percent of noninternet users living in rural China said they did not surf the internet because they did not know how to use a computer (CNNIC, 2012).

Although we have described the explosive growth of mobile phones in emerging market economies, a recent study found that gender creates a digital divide relative to cell phone ownership. "A woman is 21% less likely to own a phone than a man. The figure increases to 23% if she lives in Africa, 24% if she lives in the Middle East and 37% if she lives in South Asia" ("Women and Mobile: A Global Opportunity," 2009). In total, there are 300 million fewer women mobile subscribers than men. This translates into a $13 billion market waiting to be tapped.

The digital divide raises challenging questions for global policy makers, international businesses, and local entrepreneurs. What responsibilities, if any, do these different groups have for narrowing the gap between those that have and those that don't have access to technology? Should an e-business in Calcutta, India, be competitive with an e-business in Calumet City, Illinois? Numerous initiatives around the world are working to bring internet technology and e-commerce capabilities to LDCs (least developed countries). One such effort is the "One Laptop per Child" campaign spearheaded by Nicholas Negroponte. Negroponte's goal was to design a portable laptop that would cost around $100 for children living in LDCs. Some innovations in Negroponte's laptop were using Linux as the laptop's operating system, having a sunlight-readable screen so that children can use it outdoors, and building in a hand crank to generate power. The laptop does not need electricity to work. Exhibit 4.7 shows a picture of the bright green laptop, production of which began in November 2007. Further information can be found at laptop.org.

EXHIBIT 4.7 One Laptop per Child. Used with permission. One LapTop per Child Organization.

BUILDING INCLUSIVE E-MARKETS

Peter Drucker, perhaps the greatest management theorist of the twentieth century, said that business has only two core activities: marketing and innovation. Drucker's strategic insight is nowhere better illustrated than by the innovation that is occurring in the poorest of global markets—at the base of the world's economic pyramid. That phrase, *base of the pyramid*, has been used to describe the 4 billion people who live on less than $2 per day. The United Nations, the World Bank, the World Economic Forum, the Asian Development Bank, and the Inter-American Development Bank, among others, are working to reduce the income inequality that exists in many least developed and emerging market countries. Microfinance and microlending, both of which are clearly targeted at helping poor individuals develop economically sustainable businesses, are also part of this revolution. As noted earlier, the explosive growth of mobile phones throughout the developing world is enabling e-marketers to reach base of the pyramid consumer segments in interesting and creative ways.

Mobile banking is one of the most successful e-marketing efforts in countries that are the least economically developed. Low-income individuals around the world lack security for their money. Many of the world's "unbanked" (the shorthand phrase used to describe this market) live either in rural areas or in tightly packed slums. Slum life can be very violent and is often filled with material and financial theft. Banks generally do not operate in such environments. Poor individuals living in rural, remote areas face a different problem: There are simply not enough people living in any one village to make it profitable for a bank to have offices there. Mobile banking is the innovative, market-based solution that solves these problems.

Safaricom, the African subsidiary of the UK-based cell phone giant Vodafone, is a good example of m-banking. In 2007, Safaricom developed a new product called M-PESA (safaricom.co.ke). *Pesa* is the Swahili word for *money*. An agent, usually a dealer of a cell phone service authorized by both the bank and Safaricom, registers users and installs an application onto customers' phones. This application allows other users with the same application to send money to each other. Once installed, customers can pay bills, send money, and store money—all through their mobile phone. This means that a migrant worker, who lives in a remote, rural area but has traveled to Nairobi to find work, can easily send money back home. Of course, wives may see this as a dilemma. One the one hand, they certainly appreciate the money; on the other, they may miss visits from their husbands when the husband had to deliver the money himself! Taxi drivers also find benefit in mobile banking, since they now have less cash on hand for would-be bandits.

The success of M-PESA in Kenya has been impressive. From 2007 until early 2010, M-PESA had approximately 7 million m-banking customers—not too bad for a country that then had about 38 million inhabitants and 13 million cell phone users. Success has also brought competition. MTN, Africa's largest cell phone carrier, headquartered in South Africa, and Zain, a Kuwait-based, pan-African cell phone carrier, are also aggressively marketing mobile banking services throughout Africa (*Economist*, 2009). Banks and cell phone carriers profit from the resulting transaction fees.

LDCs have low annual per capita incomes, and one of their dominant characteristics is that many or most country inhabitants work in agriculture, sometimes subsistence agriculture. These farmers are often stereotyped as having no discretionary income. This is incorrect, and e-marketers are leading the way in breaking that myth. E-marketers know that creating value for target markets is essential for market success. In countries that are heavily agricultural, mobile applications for farmers are making them more productive. For example, Farmer's Friend in Uganda is a Web application that allows rural farmers to ask questions ("How can I get rid of tomato blight?" or "My chicken's eyes are bulging. What should I do?"), to receive answers to their questions through SMS, and to find out what the daily commodity prices are for their crops so that they can sell them at fair market prices. E-marketers have developed similar mobile apps for farmers in India: M-KRISHI® (*krishi* means *agriculture* or *farming* in Hindi). Often, farmers need specific information about weather as well as about pesticide and fertilizer use. M-KRISHI® allows rural Indian farmers to send questions about any of these items through a simple text, voice, or picture interface (see Exhibit 4.8). Farmers receive prompt responses and, most importantly, information tailored to *their* specific plots of land. Productivity and crops yields have increased. Rural Indian farmers pay 200 rupees (about $4.20) for a three-month subscription. The success of M-KRISHI® for farmers has recently led to the expansion of this service to fishermen (see Exhibit 4.9). E-marketers know that consumers will pay for services that create value.

E-marketers targeting rural consumers in India face another challenge. Many of these consumers live in media dark parts of the country. *Media dark* refers to those rural Indian communities that have no access to radio and television. A combination of factors may make a village media dark. A village, for example, may not have electricity; no one living in the village may actually own a television or radio; or no one in the village can afford the monthly subscription fee for a satellite connection. Hindustan Unilever, the Indian subsidiary of Unilever, developed an innovative way to reach media dark rural Indian consumers through its iShakti program. iShakti consists of electronic kiosks set up in rural villages through which local residents can obtain free health, hygiene, employment, agricultural, and legal information. Content is delivered through voice and streaming video, since many rural consumers, especially women, are illiterate. iShakti complements Hindustan Unilever's main Shakti project in which rural women are trained as Shakti-ammas to sell Unilever products in their villages. (*Amma* means *mother* in Hindi and is often used as a general term of respect for elder women in India). iShakti positions Hindustan Unilever as a socially responsible partner within the village, while it simultaneously co-brands Unilever products.

E-marketers targeting low-income consumers in urban areas can use a wider array of electronic strategies, since urban life incorporates all consumers within a rich media landscape. Casas Bahia, the largest retailer in Brazil selling electronics, appliances, and furniture, illustrates the

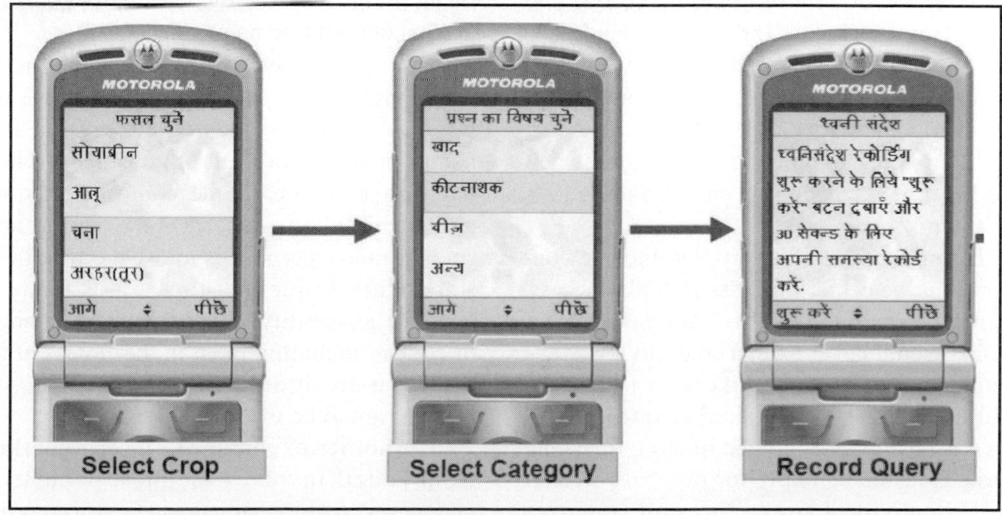

EXHIBIT 4.8 Screenshot of M-KRISHI® for Rural Indian Farmers.

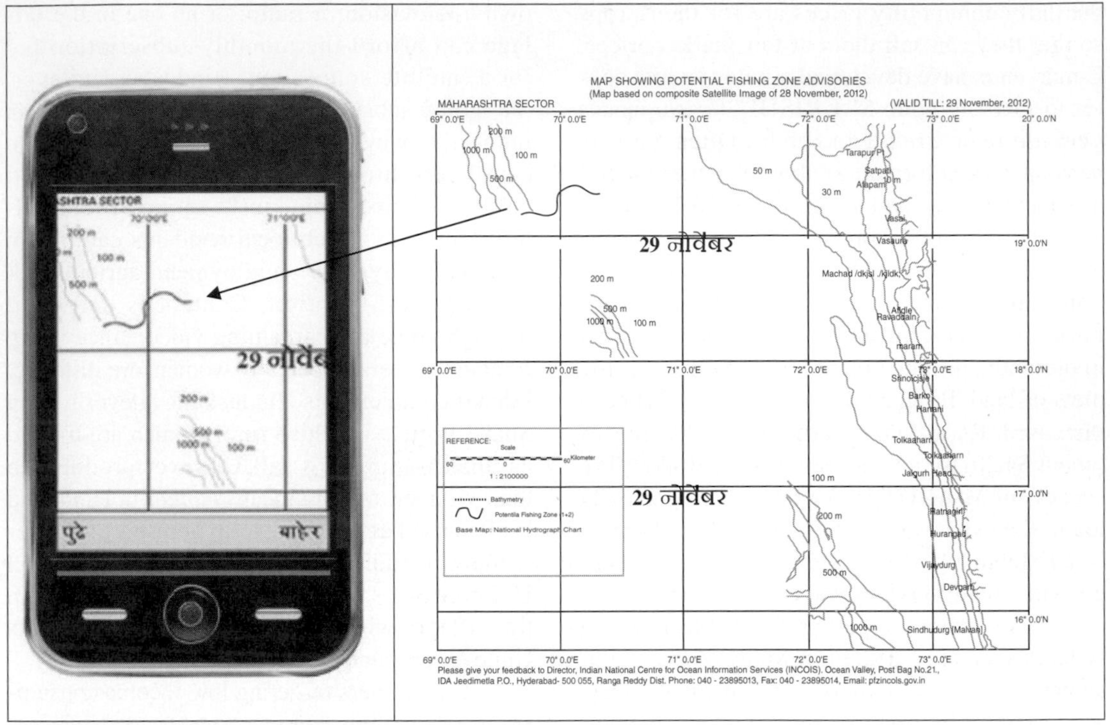

EXHIBIT 4.9 Demonstration of M-KRISHI® for Fishermen.

creative use of Web strategies with base of the pyramid consumers. Casas Bahia's core consumers are street vendors, maids, cooks, and construction workers—individuals who earn minimum wage and who often work several jobs. These individuals tend to live in the densely populated Brazilian slums called *favelas*. In 2008, Casas Bahia, in fact, opened a retail store right in the heart of Paraisópolis, one of São Paulo's largest slums.

Extending credit to very low-income consumers is at the center of Casas Bahia's success. In contrast to banks and other lending organizations that would never extend credit to low-wage consumers and seasonal workers, or if they did would charge very high interest rates, Casas Bahia has developed a unique in-store financing process. Consumers apply for purchase financing at an individual store. The store approves credit based on proof of address and not being blacklisted by a Brazilian credit rating agency. Seventy percent of all Casas Bahia purchases are financed this way and the store has less than a 10 percent default rate on payment.

In 2009, Casas Bahia developed its first online presence: casasbahia.com.br. Casas Bahia was clever in its e-marketing strategy. On the one hand, for the 10 percent of consumers who can pay with a credit card, the Web site functions as a standard online e-tailer. On the other hand, the site's primary purpose is to drive traffic into the store. Once inside the store, Casas Bahia staff have the possibility of upselling customers and, of course, including them in the store's branded consumer credit program—where higher profit margins are to be made.

Another example of clever e-marketing from Brazil involves the most popular soap opera ever to air on Brazilian television: Avenida Brasil (Brazil Avenue). Like all soap operas, the plot is complex, yet the main story line is about the romance between a single mother living in a favela and a solider sent into the favela to keep the peace because one of the main characters is seeking revenge for the death of her father in that same favela. The final episode brought all of Brazil to a halt—literally. Even the president of Brazil tuned in. The final episode had over 500 advertising deals. P&G alone had 10 commercials for brands such as Pampers (pampers.com.br/), Oral-B (oralb.com/brazil/), and Wella Koleston (koleston.com/pt-br/), all of which have localized Brazilian Web sites. Other global brands advertising on the final episode included Volkswagen (vw.com.br), Kia (kiamotors.com.br/), Trident chewing gum (tridentbrasil.com.br), and Mastercard (mastercard.com/br) (Chao, 2012). Additionally, one of the characters, Monalisa, operated a beauty shop in the soap opera, and now has her own line of branded beauty products in the home market, which are available on cosmetics's Web site, embelleze.com (embelleze.com) keyword search "monalisa."

SOCIAL NETWORKING

Perhaps nowhere is the convergence of new technology (the increased use of mobile and smartphones) and access to information (mobile broadband) more evident than in the increased importance of social media in the e-marketers integrated communications toolkit. As of late 2011, of the world's 1.2 billion online consumers, 82 percent reported using at least one social networking site when online. Interestingly, half of the world's most engaged markets for social networking are in Latin America: Argentina, Chile, Colombia, Peru, and Venezuela. Argentineans, for example, spend 10.7 hours/month just on social networking sites, while Chileans, Colombians, Peruvians, and Venezuelans spend 9.8 hrs./mo., 8.5 hrs./mo., 8.3 hrs./mo., and 7.9 hrs./mo., respectively, on social networking sites. Israel has the most engaged market for social networking, with Israelis spending 11.1 hrs./mo. on social networking sites (comScore, 2011).

Facebook is the social networking giant, and as Appendix A indicates, there are Facebook users in about every country in the world. Yet Facebook penetration varies by country, and, in fact, may not be the dominant social networking site in certain countries. VKontakte (vk.com/) dominates social networking in Russia. Hence, when the Clearasil brand of skin care and acne medication products wanted to increase its market share among Russian teens in 2010, the company created a brand page on Vkontakte that allowed users to post photos and exchange information on the site (vk.com). When integrated with Clearasil apps (one of which would allow users to remove blemishes and pimples from their photos), Clearasil experienced a 30 percent sales increase within one year. (To watch an English language video summarizing the campaign and use of Vkontakte, visit: vimeo.com.) Of course, if Clearasil was to launch a similar marketing program today, it would certainly add the social networking site, Odnoklassniki (odnoklassniki.ru/), which is the second most popular social networking site in Russia.

Global e-marketers understand that Russia is not unique in having strong, very popular local social networking sites. In South Korea, Japan, China, Brazil, and Vietnam, Facebook is a market follower rather than a market leader. In Vietnam, zing (news.zing.vn) is the most popular social network; in Poland, it is nk (nk.pl/); in South Korea, it is cyworld (cyworld.kr/); in Japan, it is mixi (mixi.jp/); and in Brazil, it is Orkut (orkut.com/), the social network owned by Google. Even the Baltic Republic of Latvia has a local, more popular network than Facebook: draugiem (draugiem.lv/).

Although the number of Facebook users varies widely by country (see Appendix A), forward-thinking e-marketers are integrating Facebook into their overall marketing strategy. Debenhams, a large mid-market retailer from the United Kingdom, is an example. Debenhams now targets consumers living in Armenia through its Armenian Facebook page (facebook.com/). Recent data indicate that Debenhams has the third most popular Facebook page in Armenia, with about 32,000 fans ("Social Media Report, 2012").

Only LightStyle clothing and Ashtakrak Kat, a local dairy, have more Facebook followers, with 53,000 and 40,000 fans, respectively. Debenhams was an early adopter of branded Facebook pages targeting consumers in emerging market countries. Marketing to Nigerian shoppers has been especially successful. The flagship store in London has a multilingual page that includes Hausa, one of the local languages in Nigeria. Nigerians spend £450 per transaction in Debenhams (Shannon, 2012). Through Debenhams's Facebook page in Armenian, Debenhams is now reaching shoppers in the Trans-Caucasus region with hoped for similar results.

Finally, Sproxil is a company that integrates many of this chapter's ideas. Sproxil is a born global firm that was founded in 2008 by Ashifi Gogo, a Ghanaian entrepreneur with a strong telecommunications background. Sproxil markets a mobile phone app specifically designed to combat the $200 billion trade in counterfeit drugs. Gogo had witnessed firsthand the consequences of taking counterfeit medications. Ghana had low internet access through desk and laptop computers, but had high mobile phone and mobile internet penetration rates. Consumers' ease-of-use, driven by a mobile product authentication (MPA) app that uses simple text messaging to tell a consumer whether the drug she or he has purchased is fake or not, has helped grow the company significantly. Sproxil's business model is to sell the printed labels with authentication numbers and SMS directions directly to pharmaceutical companies and distributors who, in turn, place the labels on their products to assure authenticity. For consumers, the authentication process is not only simple but also duplicates the process of recharging (i.e., adding money) to a SIM card. Sproxil first tested its mobile app in Nigeria and has since expanded into Ghana, India, and East Africa. Sproxil also uses Facebook and Twitter to leverage social networking to its advantage (Sproxil, 2012). Sproxil uses mobile phones and social media in emerging market countries to not only generate profit but also make the world a better, more humane place to live.

Chapter Summary

Within a worldwide business-to-consumer (B2C) market of 1.2 billion consumers, some countries have higher penetration rates of internet access, usage, and shopping. Among the many factors affecting internet penetration are income, infrastructure, computer ownership, telecommunication availability and pricing, social and cultural traditions, business attitudes, and wireless Web access. E-marketers must carefully research each country's current market conditions and environmental factors before selecting specific targets for entry.

Internet usage is growing so rapidly outside the United States that users from other countries will increasingly dominate the internet. This growth is creating opportunities and challenges for e-marketers to target or operate in countries that are less developed than the most highly industrialized nations. Emerging economies are those with low levels of GDP per capita that are experiencing rapid growth. Not only can technology generally boost a nation's overall production capacity and efficiency but also information technology can help countries with emerging economies open up promising global markets.

In the course of analyzing country and market opportunities, e-marketers in emerging economies that target markets in developed countries must understand market similarity. E-marketers in emerging economies that market within their own countries or those in developed economies that want to target groups in an emerging economy must understand market differences. In general, e-marketers that target emerging economies must deal with a variety of challenges, including limited credit card use, lack of secure online payment methods, consumer attitudes toward online purchasing and payment, limited computer and telephone access, slow connection speeds that affect Web page download rates, and unexpected power failures. Enterprising e-marketers have reacted to these challenges with innovative solutions.

Many countries, including those with emerging economies, have more mobile telephone subscribers than fixed-line telephone subscribers. As a result, e-marketers must consider how to modify Web site content for small cell phone displays, how to handle text entry using tiny keypads, how to develop appropriate content for wireless Web users, how to price services, and how to develop appropriate payment methods. E-marketers also must understand how consumers behave with the mobile internet.

Consumers living at the base of the world's economic pyramid are increasingly being targeted by e-marketers. Perceptions of low-income consumers as not being able to use technology, as not wanting quality products and services, and as not being able to afford such products are shown to be inaccurate. Low-income consumers provide significant marketing opportunity for e-marketers when products and services fulfil meaningful consumer needs. The extensive use of mobile phones by base of the pyramid consumers is providing a new platform for e-marketers to reach this new market.

Exercises

REVIEW QUESTIONS

1. What is an emerging economy?
2. How can countries with emerging economies make use of information technology?
3. What is the concept of market similarity and how does it apply to companies that target foreign markets?
4. Why is credit card payment a conundrum in emerging economies?
5. How do computer and telephone ownership affect e-marketing in emerging economies?
6. Why must Web site designers consider connection speeds in emerging economies?
7. What are some of the electricity problems faced by e-marketers in emerging economies?
8. How is wireless internet access likely to influence e-marketing around the world?
9. What is the digital divide, and what does it mean for e-marketers?

DISCUSSION QUESTIONS

10. ***American Idol* Story.** What differences do you see between the U.S. version of *American Idol* and the version in other countries? Use material from this chapter to explain the reason for those differences.
11. ***American Idol* Story.** Do you think that this brand needs to be consistent worldwide to maintain a desired brand image? Explain.
12. Do you agree with the observation that the global internet will drive styles, tastes, and products to converge and create a more homogenous global marketplace? Why or why not?
13. Knowing that many consumers in emerging economies are wary of buying online, what would you do, as an e-marketer, to encourage them to change their attitudes and behavior?
14. What are the advantages and disadvantages of e-marketers creating fast-loading, low-graphics versions of their Web sites to accommodate slower connection speeds in emerging economies?
15. What responsibility do you think e-marketers should assume for helping to close the digital divide? Do you think consumers and governments should assume some responsibility as well? Explain your answers.
16. How serious is the online threat from Chinese companies? Are Chinese companies more likely to succeed globally in some product or service categories than others? Explain your answer.

WEB ACTIVITIES

17. Visit Internet Usage Statistics at internetworldstats.com. According to this site, what percentage of the world is currently online? How has that changed since this book was written? Divided by region, which areas of the world show the highest percentage of online usage? In comparison to the United States, what are the usage patterns of those in Europe and Asia? What trends in internet adoption and usage do you think will occur as the internet continues to mature?
18. Visit the UPS Web site at ups.com. If you wanted to deliver a package to Paris, France, what steps would you have to take to complete the transaction? How has UPS made the process easier? What languages other than English are available to UPS customers? What difficulties might you run into when delivering to an address that doesn't use English characters? How does UPS address these issues?
19. More Web sites are providing pages in languages other than English. Visit Google.com and select language tools. What types of services does Google provide for specific languages and countries? Try translating an entire Web page into a different language and view the results. What languages are compatible with these feature sets? What efforts is Google making to translate sites from languages that are currently unavailable?

CHAPTER

5

Ethical and Legal Issues*

The main goal of this chapter is to help you explore the ethical and legal issues that e-businesses face in marketing online. You will learn about the current and emerging issues that have caused concern among a variety of stakeholders, including e-businesses and consumers.

After reading this chapter, you will be able to:

- Compare and contrast ethics and law.
- Discuss the implications of ethical codes and self-regulation.
- Identify some of the main privacy concerns within traditional and digital contexts.
- Explain some of the important patent, copyright, trademark, and data ownership issues related to the internet.
- Highlight key ethical and legal concerns related to online expression.

* This chapter was updated and augmented by Lara Pearson, Esq. and Inna S. Wood, Esq. Lara is a vice president and the Sustainability Steward at Exemplar Law and the Chief Pontificator at BrandGeek.net, a branding law blog where IP law and corporate social responsibility collide. Inna's expertise is primarily focused on Corporate and Business Law. She holds an LLM degree from the University of California, Berkeley, School of Law and a degree in Jurisprudence from the Moscow State Law Academy. Inna is admitted to practice law in the State of California as well as the Russian Federation.

- The benefits to both accessing and contributing to the wealth of information appear to have no end. Indeed, far from simply making life more efficient and enjoyable, there are now a whole host of products, services, and (especially) apps that help keep people *safe*, right when they might need it most.

- ***Softbank*** released the pantone 5 107SH in Japan, a smartphone with an inbuilt Geiger counter. The Android device can measure radiation in the surrounding air to within 20% accuracy, via a button adjacent to the LCD screen.

Software Infringement

Have you ever broken the law while sitting at your computer? Most people would probably say no—not recalling the times they installed computer software that they did not purchase (sometimes called software **piracy**). Infringement of copyright in software occurs when people download copyrighted software from the internet without a license, loan copyrighted software CDs to others, or install copyrighted software on more computers than is allowed under their software licenses. Counterfeiting occurs when copyrighted software is duplicated and distributed to others without the consent of the copyright owner. Both infringement and counterfeiting violate U.S. copyright laws and are illegal.

So what is the big deal? Suppose you spent months writing a best-selling novel and then learned that thousands of people were copying it instead of buying it. That copying would cut into your income and reduce your enthusiasm for writing more novels. Infringement of software copyrights creates a similar situation. The firms creating software use the income from their software sales to pay for innovative upgrades and new products, which they cannot do or do as much—if they lose income. Also, software makers must raise the price paid by legitimate buyers to replace income lost to infringement.

This cause and effect relationship between protection and innovation plays out around the globe. The United States, Japan, and most of the countries in Europe are examples of countries producing and protecting trillions of dollars worth of new software every year. In stark contrast, Asian-Pacific countries with very weak software copyright enforcement—like China, India, and Vietnam—produce little by way of valuable software, and tons of infringing software, which every year costs software owners billions of dollars in lost revenue. The United States has the lowest rate of software infringement in the world. Globally, however, over 40 percent of the software sold is an infringing version. Cutting this number by even a third would create millions of jobs and generate hundreds of billions of dollars in new economic growth around the world.

What can companies do? Microsoft, one of the main victims of software infringement, uses several methods: It proposes intellectual property legislation, files civil lawsuits, and creates non-infringement technologies such as digital rights management (DRM) security programs embedded in its software CDs. Critics have argued that security measures like DRM do little to stop sophisticated international counterfeiters, while making legal use of the software more difficult for the average user. A few years ago, Microsoft tried a system of sniffing out users' hard drives while they were online, but privacy advocates objected. In the end, Microsoft, and many companies like it, believes that education is the best weapon. Many people who use infringing software do not know they are stealing, and it is not against the law or against cultural norms in many countries. For example, executives in some countries believe that if they buy one copy of the software, they can use it as they please, as with other products. To support its educational goal, Microsoft created a Web site about software infringement that, like the campaigns of many other large copyright holders, refers to software infringement as *piracy* (click on "piracy" at microsoft.com). Infringement and counterfeiting remain huge problems for the software industry—problems that are unlikely to be solved for a long time.

OVERVIEW OF ETHICS AND LEGAL ISSUES

Scholars often treat ethical and legal issues as separate, even unrelated, subjects. In reality, ethics and law are integrally related. As we will see, **ethics** frequently concerns the values and practices of professionals and others who have expert knowledge of a specific field. Ethics is also a general endeavor that takes into account the concerns and values of society as a whole.

Law is similar to ethics in the sense that it, too, is an expression of values, but while ethics may be directed toward individual or group endeavors, laws are normally created for broader purposes, with the goal of addressing national, or sometimes international, populations. In the Anglo-American tradition, law is made by legislatures such as Congress or Parliament, enforced by executives or agencies, and interpreted by the courts. In all these instances, it is a public endeavor, which is reflected in the fact that law is often the result of political and social compromise. Additionally, law attempts to be consistent in both time and place, so that citizens will be familiar with their rights and obligations.

Because law results from combinations of interests, beliefs, and goals, the processes that lead up to the making of laws are often slow and complex. Unfair laws, a common by-product of one-sided lobbying efforts, overly generous political contributions, and other special influences have been the focus of criticism and call for reform. The problem has become so unwieldy that it prompted one of the world's premier copyright scholars, Lawrence Lessig, to consider a bid for Congress, running primarily on the platform of reducing political corruption. Groups seeking the reform of international copyright and patent laws are fielding political candidates under the Pirate Party affiliation. The Pirate Party platform also seeks to strengthen personal privacy rights and increase governmental transparency. Pirate Parties are currently active in over 30 countries.

Even in a perfect world of no political corruption, new laws cannot anticipate every nuance of how people and companies will push the proverbial legal envelope months, or years, down the road. New laws regulating the internet are at a particular disadvantage. Given the speed with which the internet landscape changes and the slowness with which laws are enacted, some laws are nearly obsolete by the time they are passed. Similarly troubling, even when Congress passes "good" laws, many questions remain concerning the meaning of the law itself or about how the law is to be enforced. Thus, aggrieved parties file lawsuits demanding courts to interpret these laws and to determine their impact on particular conflicts. Administrative agencies such as the **Federal Trade Commission (FTC)** also promulgate rules and opinions governing online activity. Given the complexity of the task, efforts to tame online transactions can be slow, particularly within the new and often unfamiliar context of digital communication.

Ethics make important contributions to legal developments, influencing lobbyists, legislators, and eventually judges. The filtering that takes place as an ethical tenet moves from idea to law and to **enforcement** interferes with what would ideally be a seamless legal enforcement of an ethical precept. As a result of this imperfect system, laws do not correlate directly with ethics. Ethics can be a casualty of the debates and compromises that end up dictating the metes and bounds of a resulting law. Problems like legislators' weak grasp of complex information technology issues, biased lobbying efforts, and the large time lag between online innovations and laws that govern them mandate that the law itself be merely the beginning, and not the end, of the ethical inquiry.

Laws lag far behind online innovations. Ethical debates surrounding these innovations, however, happen in real time. It is critical that lawmakers understand innovations clearly before trying to mold the laws governing them. Digital marketers play a crucial role in assisting legislators. Legislators seeking insight into the complex ethics of a particular online issue look to experts and real-world entities for guidance. Impressions from the trenches are lawmakers' most unvarnished source of information concerning the ongoing ethical debate.

Ethics and Ethical Codes

The study of ethics has been in existence for more than 2,500 years. The central focus of this study is the analysis and description of such basic concepts as right and wrong and how we judge the differences among them. An important dimension of this investigation concerns the types of conduct that comprise ethical behavior. These tasks necessarily involve the examination of rights, responsibilities, and obligations. Ethical inquiry is not limited to purely theoretical boundaries. Rather, questions are studied at all levels of human interaction and often appear as political, legal, and commercial issues. Consequently, the scope of ethics is virtually as wide as its subject matter. Similarly, many types of ethical positions compete against each other for acceptance.

A particularly important aspect of ethical inquiry involves the study of professional activities. Traditionally, groups of individuals possessing special skills or knowledge have established codes and systems of fair practice. A classic example is the Hippocratic Oath of physicians. Ethical standards work both externally and internally. They help to communicate consistency and trustworthiness to the community at large, while also assisting in maintaining stability and integrity within the profession. In these ways, ethics are both pragmatic tools and essential elements of professional identity.

Documents such as the American Marketing Association's (AMA) *Statement of Ethics*[1] (also referred to as the "AMA Code of Ethics") reflect the recognition of a commitment to the exercise of honesty, responsibility, transparency, respect, citizenship, and fairness within all professional transactions. In addition to articulating overall values, professional codes provide members with guidelines that are specific to their pursuits. They are often products of the combined experiences of practitioners, scholars, and the public that are passed along to the entire membership and eventually published. Historically, codes have been interpreted or revised to respond to changed circumstances and new issues. In the past, these processes have been relatively gradual, with modifications often coming in conservative degrees. Today, this situation has changed.

Modern technology presents a radical challenge to marketing ethics as well as to those of other professions. The extent of this demand is perhaps best reflected in the revolutionary features of the computer itself. When compared with other major technical advances such as the printing press, telephone, or automobile, digital media is arguably unique in its capacity for speed, ubiquity, and versatility. Computers serve as data collectors, compilers, and disseminators.

They represent the fastest-growing form of communication and, through the internet and similar systems, forge global links of unprecedented proportion.

These factors create vacuums in ethical policy. Although they do not directly challenge such general ideals as fairness or honesty, digital processes and potentialities are so new that ethics, like many other social endeavors, is only beginning to adapt itself to the computer revolution. Currently, a number of critical issues confront those who work within electronic environments, including the ownership of intangible data, often termed *intellectual property*; the role of privacy in a virtual world without walls, locks, or doors; the extent to which freedom of expression should be allowed; the uses of data, including methods of collection; and the special status of children who log on to digital networks.

Easy solutions are seldom achieved within ethics or law, and, in the electronic context, progress is complicated by a lack of comparative historical situations. Likewise, the ability to analogize computers to objects or institutions with which society has had greater experience is often questionable. Is the computer network more like a broadcasting station, a printing press, or a public library? Our current lack of experience in these matters makes it difficult to say for certain. Finally, the fact that electronic spaces are global in nature accentuates the earlier observation that ethical positions are by no means agreed upon. What is accepted in Europe may be rejected in Asia or America.

The seemingly limitless opportunities afforded by computers also suggest the need for the constant assessment of their implications. Each participant in electronic marketing is given not only the responsibility to adhere to professional codes but also, in a very real sense, the unique opportunity to contribute to these standards in a meaningful way.

The Problem of Self-Regulation

Although law and ethics are frequently directed toward the same goals and often provide mutual assistance in the examination of complex problems, one emerging area of conflict involves the role of formal law in the regulation of online conduct. Throughout their tenures, the Clinton, Bush, and Obama administrations have expressed the position that the development of the internet should be largely left to the free operation of the market. Within such a system, rather than mandate behavior through legislation, **ethical codes** developed by trade associations, commercial standards groups, and various professional organizations dictate appropriate behavior of participants.

Supporters of the self-regulation model point to the private sector's ability to rapidly identify and resolve problems specific to its areas of competence, particularly when compared to the seemingly confusing, contradictory, and lengthy processes of the law. According to this view, problems encountered within technological environments are particularly amenable to the expertise possessed by market actors. Once consensus is reached, uniformity is achieved through members' compliance with ethical codes, as well as by ongoing education of providers and consumers. Although the law cannot normally force anyone to adhere to these codes, many believe that improved consumer confidence resulting in enhanced economic opportunities will ensure voluntary compliance.

Critics of self-regulation argue that its incentives are insufficiently compelling. They note that perpetrators of fraud and deception frequently benefit from schemes of short duration and are rarely interested in the long-term gains offered by adherence to ethical codes. On a broader level, it has been suggested that commercial self-interest and pressures to maximize profits compromise the private sector's ability to police itself and that, absent the type of sanctions only the law can provide, true deterrence cannot be achieved.

Although the resolution of this debate is far from over, recent policy-making activities indicate that governments are asserting themselves more frequently in internet regulation and control. Issues of online privacy, data protection, and particularly internet crime and fraud prevention have been already addressed by many countries.

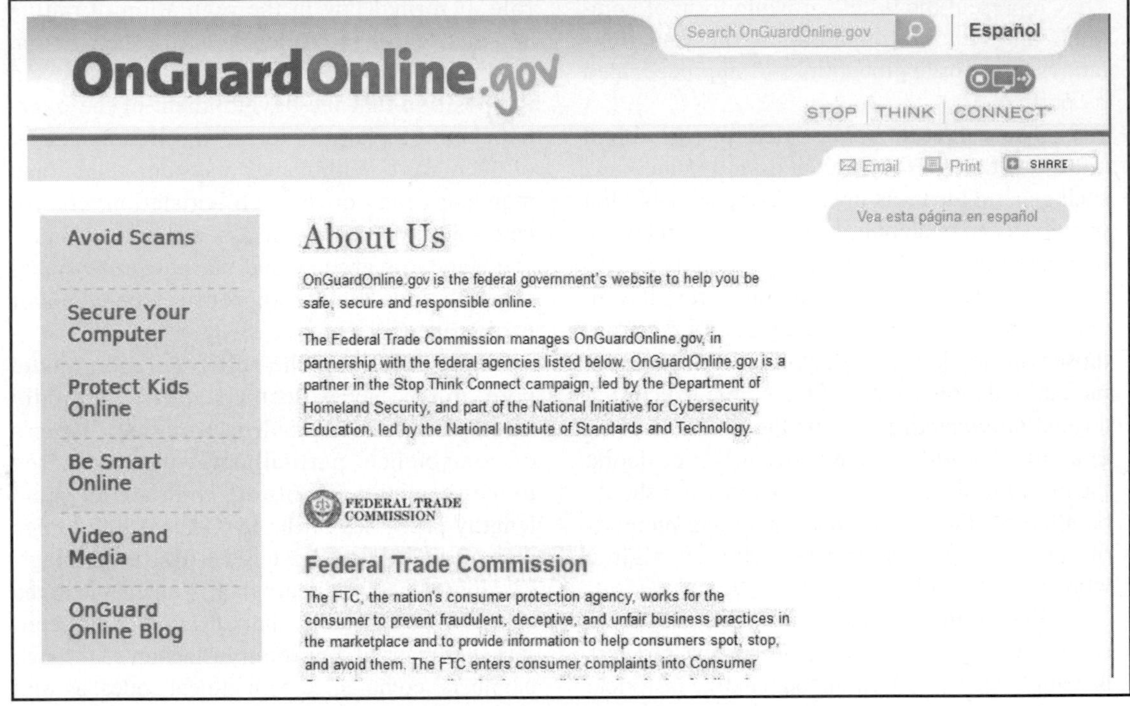

EXHIBIT 5.1 OnGuardOnline.gov Website *Source*: www.onguardonline.gov/

The Australian Competition and Consumer Commission (ACCC), the Office of Fair Trading in the UK, and the consumer protection agencies in several other countries, including the United States, have already implemented various programs aimed at decreasing the spread of online deception.

The International Consumer Protection and Enforcement Network (ICPEN), an organization uniting consumer protection authorities from almost 40 countries, conducts annual internet sweeps to detect online traders that defraud consumers. In 2001 the ICPEN created the "econsumer," a network Web site which gathers e-commerce consumer complaints and shares this information with the participating law enforcement agencies.

The FTC in the United States likewise considers detection and suppression of domestic and international fraud to be a priority. It regularly holds different seminars and trainings sessions for internet users as well as posts many useful tips and recommendations on OnGuardOnline.gov, the Web site developed specifically for the purpose of online fraud prevention (Exhibit 5.1).

The number of new governmental agencies, private and not-for-profit companies, and associations fighting online fraud keeps growing worldwide. As it was well noted by U.S. President Barack Obama: "Cybersecurity is not an end unto itself; it is instead an obligation that our governments and societies must take on willingly, to ensure that innovation continues to flourish, drive markets, and improve lives."[2]

In 2006 the UK government initiated the "Get Safe Online" campaign, which was meant to provide helpful information and practical guidance to internet users and prevent internet fraud.[3] The project, which was also broadly supported by major businesses, proved to be very successful and remains active today. On October 4, 2010, the National Cyber Security Division (NCSD), a division within the Department of Homeland

EXHIBIT 5.2 Stop.Think.Connect. Cyber tips *Source*: www.dhs.gov/

Security (DHS) launched the "Stop. Think. Connect," a similar campaign aimed at improving internet security awareness and educating the public about common methods to detect cyber threats (Exhibit 5.2).

Even though heightened governmental involvement appears to be an increasing response to many online issues, it is significant to note that lawmakers in the United States and elsewhere have entered into a close dialogue with private entrepreneurs, public interest groups, and commercial associations. Such arguably unprecedented instances of cooperation and sharing of resources suggest that future regulations will take the form of "networked responsibility" among many participants.

PRIVACY

The concept of **privacy** encompasses both ethical and legal aspects. It is also relatively new to both disciplines. Perhaps more than any other legal or ethical issue, privacy is a product of the twentieth century. Although many cultures follow established customs of social boundaries, detailed consideration of this subject did not come about until 1890 when Samuel Warren and future Supreme Court justice Louis Brandeis published an article that urged the recognition of a right to privacy within American law. This protection was defined as the "right to be left alone."[4] Significantly, many of the justifications for this new idea were reactions to the phenomena of a maturing industrial and technological age, including the mass distribution of newspapers, the development of listening devices, and the widespread use of photography. In essence, privacy's young tradition has always been about information and the means of its delivery.

Although it has been the subject of constant debate since the Warren and Brandeis article, privacy has proven to be an elusive concept, both ethically and legally. One reason for legal confusion is the lack of any specific privacy provision within the Constitution. This situation was recognized in the U.S. Supreme Court's 1965 decision of *Griswold v. Connecticut*,[5] which held that privacy in the use of contraceptives could be inferred from a number of enumerated Constitutional rights, including those of association, freedom from illegal searches and seizures, self-incrimination, and the quartering of soldiers. Later, in the 1973 opinion of *Roe v. Wade*,[6] the Court found a privacy right in a woman's reproductive decision making. Through the Fourth Amendment to the U.S. Constitution, the privacy of the home has been established against governmental agencies, which are required to obtain warrants before entering upon and searching a dwelling. This provision is, however, applicable only to officials or those acting on their behalf and not against private individuals.

In addition to Constitutional developments, privacy has been addressed in the common law. **Common law** refers to decisions, presumptions, and practices traditionally embraced by Anglo-American courts. The common law has established a series of privacy violations that, both individually and together, form the basis of invasion of privacy lawsuits. These are arranged into four categories: unreasonable intrusion into the **seclusion** of another, unreasonable publicity of another's private life, the appropriation of another's name or likeness, and the publication of another's personal information in a false light. These elements are codified in many state statutes and appear in the influential legal treatise, Restatement of Torts.[7]

Despite these developments, much disagreement remains as to what privacy entails. The identified central attributes of privacy fall into three general areas. The first is the Warren and Brandeis concept of a right to be left alone, often referred to as the *seclusion theory*. Privacy within this perspective is the ability to remain isolated from society. This model encourages laws and ethical standards that are oriented toward maintaining personal distance and punishing those who cross the limits set by individuals. A second intermediate theory, known as **access control**, does not presume isolation as a norm but places its emphasis upon laws and standards that enable persons to reasonably regulate the information that they are giving up. Expressions of this model can be found in laws and standards that empower individuals to protect personal material from unauthorized release.

Both seclusion and access control models provide measures of protection, but their focus is concerned more with how information is released and less with what actually constitutes private data. A third theory, known as the *autonomy model*, attempts to provide such a definition. It does so by identifying private matters as those necessary for a person to make life decisions. This model entails freedom from the coercive use of personal information as well as the ability to be alone when reflection is necessary.

In addition to presenting difficulties in definition and scope, privacy exists as one value among many. Within society, privacy interests routinely compete against concerns of personal and public safety, economics, and even the social and psychological need for association with others—a process that can require the divulging of sensitive information. The ways in which these interests are coordinated involve complex balances that can result in difficult choices. Often people are willing to give up personal information for benefits they perceive to be worthwhile—credit cards, frequent flyer mileage, and security precautions in airports are but a few examples. In such cases, ethics and law attempt to provide guidelines helpful in critically examining definitions, priorities, and implications.

Privacy Within Digital Contexts

Information plays a pivotal role in the concept of privacy, as well as that of marketing and electronic commerce. It is, therefore, not surprising that conflicts about how data should be collected and used have developed.

A starting point for this discussion is the American Marketing Association's *Statement of Ethics* (available at marketingpower.com). It states that the AMA and its members will "seek to protect the private information of customers, employees and partners." This principle is concise and straightforward in general terms, but it must be applied to the internet's many information-gathering mechanisms.

In the spring of 2000, the attention of the media, the government, and the public was captured by reports that DoubleClick, an online advertising firm, was engaged in an effort to collect and compile large amounts of personal consumer information. Within the relatively brief history of internet marketing, DoubleClick achieved success by establishing a system of more than 11,000 Web sites with advertising that, when clicked, enabled users to visit product sites. The system also recorded the responses, known as *clickstreams*, within its own databases. Clickstream information was then available to form a user profile, allowing the transmission of individually targeted advertising. Users were not required to give their active consent to this collection. At the time, DoubleClick had reportedly accumulated 100,000 online profiles.

Although privacy advocates had already voiced concern about the system's potential for abuse, the controversy reached a new height when DoubleClick acquired a second company, Abacus Direct, which specialized in the acquisition of offline consumer data. Abacus Direct had amassed an electronic list that included the names, addresses, and buying histories of a large percentage of American households. With the merger, plans were reportedly under way to integrate data, providing a premium subscription service that would, for the first time, link these real-life identities to DoubleClick's online personalities. Pursuant to this news, a coalition of privacy, civil rights, and consumer groups filed a complaint with the FTC in an effort to prevent the tying of the Abacus Direct information to online profile data and to enjoin the registration of users to the new database without first obtaining each subject's consent. Google purchased DoubleClick in 2008 and currently applies its privacy standards to the advertising subsidiary.

The most common means by which these types of data are obtained is through the use of cookies. Cookies are packets of data created within a user's hard drive in response to instructions received from a Web page. Once stored, cookies can be retransmitted from a user's computer to a pertinent Web site. Cookies serve many purposes. For example, they may handle online information, creating features like shopping baskets to hold purchases. They may recall stored sales information to remind users of items already ordered or to suggest new products. Significantly, cookies may collect other data, such as full name, e-mail and postal addresses, phone numbers, a computer's geographic location, and the time logged online.

Although cookies may be configured within a browser to run only with explicit permission, they are normally automatically executed without any user action. Cookie packets may be combined with other digital information and may be transferred between servers or sold on the open market. User tracking occurs when cookies are appended and examined in the course of a user's online travels. The result is an ability to pinpoint an individual's online behavior. With the integration of offline data, such tracking takes on a more encompassing, and more troubling, dimension.

The DoubleClick controversy illustrates several significant aspects of the online privacy controversy. Perhaps the most basic reflects the unsettled nature of privacy itself. Many people value privacy as a closely guarded right unto itself. According to this view, the ability to remain secluded from unwelcome intrusion as well as the capability to control the disclosure of personal data is presumed. This position advocates policies that require individuals to be explicitly informed of any data collection event and then to allow the individuals the opportunity to participate (opt in) or decline (opt out). Supporters of systems such as DoubleClick's argue an opposite presumption. They presume most users wish to receive the benefits of targeted advertising. This position reflects the view that privacy is only one of many values to be balanced. It generally supports an opt-out policy, which presumes that data collection will take place, but still allows users to withdraw consent by a variety of methods, including sending e-mail to collectors requesting removal from their databases.

Pro-privacy critics of opt-out presumptions point to the fact that most users have no significant knowledge of how computers operate or process data. They question whether the average person will take the steps necessary to withhold data and suggest that many opt-out routines are confusing and thus are unlikely to be successfully accomplished. Commercial proponents of opt-out solutions emphasize consumer surveys that reveal a preference for targeted advertising and argue that the data necessary to provide this service should be collected unless otherwise denied. Although several Congressional bills are pending, no law yet exists to resolve the debate. Similarly, industry has not developed a widely accepted solution to the challenge. Presently, many firms and associations are emphasizing notification as the best approach. Others, such as Real Media Corporation, have developed routines that do not allow the sharing of their visitors' information with other Web sites.

The DoubleClick matter was partially resolved by the withdrawing of the database integration plans within months of the initial announcement. Attention continued to be focused on the company until 2001, when, pursuant to an investigation, the FTC concluded that no privacy violations had been committed by the company. In the spring of 2002, a remaining group of state and federal class action privacy suits were settled. The preliminary terms of this agreement provide a template for contemporary industry standards in consumer privacy. They include the obligation to provide clear notice of data collection, a ban on combining existing data with personal information unless explicit (opt-in) permission is obtained. Moreover, data obtained from cookies must be routinely deleted and new cookies be programmed to deactivate at five-year intervals. Finally, DoubleClick was forced to initiate an extensive program of consumer privacy education and submit to regular, independent audits. Critics of the settlement point to the relative brevity of its two-year term of enforcement and to the overly generous lifespan given to cookies.

More recently, Web sites like Facebook have come under fire for using the personal information of their users. Facebook has been accused of using users' personal information in advertisements and sharing this information with third parties.

While Facebook provides methods for limiting the disclosure of personal information, critics argue these methods are intentionally complex and often misunderstood by users. While some users have deleted their Facebook accounts in response to the distribution of their personal information, deleting a Facebook account can be as difficult as trying to prevent disclosure of personal information in the first place. Users have even called for the creation of an "open source" alternative to Facebook, which gives users the ability to control all aspects of how their personal information is displayed and shared.

One of the most famous cases in this respect is *Lane v. Facebook*,[8] a class action lawsuit filed by one of Facebook's users whose personal information was disclosed by the Beacon application launched by Facebook. Beacon was based on targeting advertising and allowed users to share information about their online purchases with their Facebook "friends" or network. The plaintiff bought a diamond ring for his wife as a surprise gift. Unexpectedly and without his consent, this information was disclosed to everyone in his Facebook network, including his spouse. The plaintiff claimed that he did not give Facebook permission to publish such information on the Web site and that the company's actions intruded upon his privacy. The parties settled in 2010. One of the provisions of the settlement was termination of the Beacon program by Facebook.

Another remarkable privacy case involved Google and its e-mail users. In 2009 Google created a new messaging tool for its e-mail users, called "Buzz." The application was embedded into the Gmail program and allowed users to chat and share photos and other information more efficiently than by e-mail. In 2010, a class action lawsuit was filed against the company by a Harvard Law School student who claimed that Google violated privacy standards by failing to request prior consent from Gmail users for the new service. As it often happens with such notorious cases, the parties agreed to settle it.[9] This, however, was not the end of the story.

At the same time as the lawsuit was initiated, the Electronic Privacy Information Center (EPIC) filed a complaint with the FTC claiming similar violations. It argued that prior consent was necessary because the purpose of the new application, that is, social networking, was different from the purpose of general communication via e-mail. Following EPIC's logic, it was deceptive for Google to introduce such a service without providing their e-mail users with an option to opt out. Subsequently the FTC initiated an investigation of Google's privacy policy and issued an order to amend it. The FTC also required Google to abstain from misrepresenting their privacy practices, to receive prior consent before "any new or additional sharing" by the company of the user's personal information, and to develop a "comprehensive privacy program" to ensure better protection of personal information.[10]

To comply with these requirements, Google introduced new privacy policies and stronger safeguards for processing and maintaining personal data. As opposed to its previous practices, now all information about each user from various Google servers will be merged into one profile. This decision caused an immediate reaction from EPIC which filed a complaint in the district court for the District of Columbia stating that such consolidation would be detrimental to user privacy and compelling the FTC to prevent Google from acting this way. Although the court denied EPIC's motion, it is not yet known which position the FTC will take regarding the new developments in Google's privacy policy.[11]

While wholesale exploitation of personally identifiable information has decreased since the turn of the century, technology has increased the ways in which such information is collected. Accordingly, while the impact may not be as noticeable to consumers, the usage is more widespread. Adding to the problem is the confusion over what Web sites do with the information they collect. Nearly every major Web site collects some type of personally identifiable information. Just over half, however, specify on the Web site exactly how the information will be used. For several years, the industry has recognized that privacy is a significant consumer concern. This realization has prompted a greater use of privacy policies, including a more extensive use of opt-in routines.[12] It remains to be seen, however, whether these outward expressions will translate into greater protection of private information, or merely serve as a cover for greater, more widespread exploitation of personally identifiable information.

In addition to issues of data collection, the problem of access to data is of fundamental significance within the context of online privacy. In this area, the status of sensitive information is not only a matter of hardware security but also one of administrative policy. A clear example of the problem arose in 1998 when, with only an informal request, the U.S. Navy was able to obtain from America Online (AOL) the personal user data of a serviceman who was suspected of violating military rules concerning homosexual conduct. The resulting prosecution was later terminated after a court found that the Navy's request had likely violated federal privacy law.[13] An apology and compensation from AOL resulted, but the incident illustrates the risks involved after data leave the control of a user. The majority of privacy-related debates focus on traditional methods of data processing and the recently developed, but already well-established, use of cookies. Beyond these technologies, cutting-edge applications promise to gain popularity and to raise additional issues.

Java is a Web-friendly programming language that allows the downloading and running of programs or applets on individual computers. These applications are increasingly used to provide such enhancements as dynamic animation, Web-based simulations, and other useful additions to plain hypertext. Java may also be used to design programs known as **hostile applets**, which can be used to surreptitiously access and transmit data on hard drives, including e-mail addresses, credit card records, and other account information.

Intelligent agents are a growing topic of interest within Web marketing and computer science research. The products of developments in artificial intelligence agents are programs that, once released by a user, can function autonomously within the Web to make electronic decisions. Some potential tasks include the searching of sites or the buying of products that conform to an individual's tastes or interests. Critics of agents worry that the preferences they hold may be chosen or controlled by entities other than their "owner." Such a situation would limit the individual's ability to make autonomous decisions and could create an incentive to distribute personal information contained in the agent applications.

Cookies, Java applets, and intelligent agents are ubiquitous applications; that is, they are able to function in the course of nearly any online session, without a user's knowledge or control. The ease of their operation explains why some sites would not want to inform users that data are being collected. This objectionable attitude places technological ease above ethical principles. Similarly, because much of the information is not of an explicitly confidential character, it may be tempting to disregard privacy implications. This argument ignores the fact that even apparently innocuous data may, when combined, result in very specific information.

In addition to application-based collection, sites may gather information through online forms and e-mail, often in exchange for browsing privileges or other benefits with or without the full disclosure of the terms of use. Regardless of how it is elicited, the use of information as a form of currency has raised ethical questions, particularly when most average users (as well as information experts) are understandably uncertain of the ultimate value of the data. Although such valuation may indeed be undeterminable at this stage of internet development, consumer education about all uses of revealed data has been suggested as a solution to help users make informed judgments in this area. Information may also be gathered through explicitly fraudulent methods—an approach that has unambiguous ethical and legal implications.

A particularly active area of study involves the collection of material from children. In response to research, reports of abuses, and lobbying from parents and other advocates, Congress passed the **Children's Online Privacy Protection Act (COPPA)**.[14] In effect since 2000, the law requires that Web sites and other online media that knowingly collect information from children 12 years of age or under (1) provide notice to parents; (2) obtain verifiable parental consent prior to the collection, use, or disclosure of most information; (3) allow parents to view and correct this information; (4) enable parents to prevent further use or collection of data; (5) limit personal information collection for a child's participation in games, prize offers, or related activities; and (6) establish procedures that protect the "confidentiality, security, and integrity of the personal information collected." In addition, the FTC, as required by Congress, enacted specific rules to govern and enforce the act[15] and, in its second year of administration, instituted a total of six COPPA enforcement actions. One major change brought about by the act is the increasing presence of data collection policies on sites used by children and the provision of an active means, such as a click button, for parents to confirm their awareness of these practices. In some cases, sites previously open to children now restrict admission to users of certain ages.

While federal laws relating to internet privacy remain in debate, many explicit offenses can be addressed by conventional criminal statutes. Sanctions for misuse of consumer data are present in the **Fair Credit Reporting Act**[16] and the **Electronic Communication Privacy Act (ECPA)**.[17] Additionally, organizations such as the Direct Marketing Association (DMA) have developed comprehensive guidelines for Web privacy.[18] One troubling development within this area is a decision of a federal trial court to dismiss a class action suit that alleged breaches of privacy policies by an airline. The dismissal was based, in part, upon the court's finding that even though an allegedly violated privacy policy was posted on the airline's site, the plaintiffs did not claim to have read its contents and therefore had few actual privacy expectations.[19] Critics of this decision claim that requiring such a showing would impose an enormous burden upon those attempting to enforce Web privacy policies, essentially making those policies worthless.

The problem of privacy within e-mail remains an unsettled aspect of online interaction. Under U.S. law, users who operate e-mail accounts on private services (those that are not advertising supported) are generally assured of their legal privacy through service agreements with their internet service provider (ISP). In addition, the ECPA addresses the privacy of ISP clients, with certain exceptions that include situations in which e-mail is inadvertently discovered through system maintenance. The opposite condition applies to employees who use their organizations' computers or networks to communicate. Here, the current law generally extends no expectation of privacy to workers, particularly those employed by nongovernmental entities. Many companies emphasize this status in their memoranda of policies, but even when such notices are absent, the employee's wisest course of action is to assume that all material that passes through workplace facilities is monitored. Ethical questions remain as to whether strict surveillance policies adequately reflect reasonable expectations or values of personal autonomy and integrity. Compare this to laws that prohibit unlimited monitoring of employer-owned phone systems or dressing rooms.

In the beginning of 2012, the Obama administration came out with an official framework to improve protection of internet users' privacy rights (commonly referred to as the "**Consumer Privacy Bill of Rights**" or the "**Privacy Bill of Rights**")[20]. Through this initiative, the government instructed the National Telecommunications and Information Administration (NTIA) to work out a new set of rules for internet companies ("codes of ethics"), which will establish clear and fair standards for processing and safety of online personal information. These policies will be developed in close cooperation with the internet community and should address seven basic online privacy rights: individual control, transparency, respect for context, security, access and accuracy, focused collection, and accountability. Even though the document does not have the status of a law and many critics forecast its low efficiency, at least this initiative is a sign of governmental concern about online privacy, whether it is effective.

International Privacy Issues

On an international level, privacy issues have also received close attention. The most comprehensive privacy legislation so far has been developed by the European Union (EU).

The foundation stone in creating the current personal data protection system was the Privacy Guidelines prepared by the Organization for Economic Co-Operation and Development (OECD) on September 23, 1980.[21] These guidelines introduced basic principles for personal data protection and processing such as collection limitation, data quality, purpose specification, use limitation, security safeguards, openness, individual participation, and accountability. Although helpful, these guidelines were not mandatory for the member countries of the OECD.

In order to bring more clarity and enhance enforcement of data privacy rules, the EU developed the Data Protection Directive (95/46/EC), which became effective in October, 1998. According to this act, all member states of the EU were instructed to enact national laws to protect "fundamental rights and freedoms of natural persons, and in particular their right to privacy with respect to the processing of personal data."[22]

The directive's provisions require that:

- Subjects be apprised of how their data are used and be given opportunities to review and correct information.
- Data use be restricted to the announced purpose.
- The origin of data be disclosed, if known.
- Procedures to punish illegal activities be established.
- Consumer data collection procedures contain opt-out capabilities.
- Sensitive data collection cannot be accomplished without explicit permission.

- Any international transfer of data be executed only with countries possessing adequate privacy protection laws.

In March 2000, after extensive negotiation, the U.S. Department of Commerce and the European Commission reached an agreement that U.S. organizations would submit to a series of **safe harbor** provisions for the protection of EU citizens' data. These provisions essentially reflect the directive's emphasis on notice about collection, purpose, and use; choice in ability to opt out of disclosure and third-party dissemination—including a requirement of affirmative permission in matters involving sensitive personal data; third-party transfer protection; and provisions for security, data integrity, redress, and enforcement.[23] Companies participating in data transactions with the EU can fulfill the safe harbor provisions by allowing the U.S. government to monitor compliance, by affiliating with a self-regulatory group under FTC supervision, by reporting directly to EU data protection agencies, or, if not currently online, by promising to work with an EU privacy panel. A criticism of this plan focuses on its reliance on private compliance. Critics are particularly worried that without active governmental supervision, the aims of the safe harbor plan may largely be unfulfilled. The European Commission issued several reports on the safe harbor agreement process, affirming the establishment of required procedures, but expressing concern that some U.S. corporate policies and dispute resolution processes failed to meet expectations.[24]

Another important EU privacy act is the DirectiveonPrivacyandElectronicCommunications (2002/58/EC)[25] which was introduced in July 2002 and amended in 2006 and 2009. The act supplements the Data Protection Directive of 1995 and covers questions related to computer data privacy such as spam, cookies, and confidentiality of online information.

In light of various developments in rapidly growing computer technology, in 2012 the European Commission proposed the Data Protection Regulation,[26] a new single set of privacy rules which will consolidate, modify, and extend its prior privacy guidelines to address the current technology challenges facing the union. As opposed to the industry-based approach for privacy policy implemented in the United States, the EU leans to a more universal regulation which will apply to the public as a whole irrespective of their business focus. The new regulation sets forth stricter rules for personal data processing and greater responsibility for those personal data operators which violate legislative requirements. According to the European Commission this reform will end fragmental data privacy legislation and lift bureaucratic and administrative barriers for businesses by establishing clear and concise data protection principles. The financial gain from the proposed regulation is estimated at 2.3 billion euro for businesses per year.[27] The new regulation is expected to take effect in two years following its adoption by the European Parliament and EU member states.

There is also growing attention being paid to the issues of personal data protection in Asia. The increasing popularity of this region among international businesses and overall globalization call for data privacy standards and legislation in this region as well. Particularly responsive to the new challenges in this field are Hong Kong, Japan, South Korea, and Singapore.

The Personal Data (Privacy) Ordinance[28] adopted in Hong Kong in 1996 contains a set of basic requirements for personal data operators, which are broadly defined as any private or public organization that collects or processes personal data. The law protects any personal information that could reveal the identity of the individual. The other Hong Kong law in the area of data privacy is the Code on Access to Information,[29] which governs how those governmental agencies, that by the nature of their service have access to private information of individuals, manage and protect that information.

The Personal Information Protection Act of Japan (PIPA)[30] became effective in April 2005. It is based on the same principles of data privacy as the EU Data Protection Directive but has more limited coverage; that is, it applies only to those businesses which process the information of more than 5,000 individuals. In March 2011, a similar Personal Information Protection Act was passed in South Korea.[31] The law has a very broad scope, applies to all companies and organizations, and replaces various fragmented regulations that existed prior to its enactment.

The Singapore government is also becoming proactive in its development of a data privacy framework. Although the country does not currently have overarching data privacy legislation, in 2012 aiming to meet the heightened demands of the country's consumers for protection of their personal information, the Singapore Ministry of Information, Communications and the Arts (MICA) initiated a draft of the Personal Data Protection Act.[32] Besides the commonly known principles of data protection (e.g., prior consent for personal data collection and processing, free access by individuals to their personal data) the bill contains several additional requirements for those who collect personal data, aka personal data operators. For example, it requires any such organization to appoint at least one individual who will ensure the organization's compliance with the rules of the Act and other applicable privacy legislation along with implementing internal data protection policies. It also has wide coverage; that is, its application is not limited to Singapore-located personal data operators only but extends to any foreign organizations that process personal data in Singapore.

There is an expectation that other Asian countries will follow these initiatives and introduce similar data privacy laws. At the moment most Asian countries, including the People's Republic of China (PRC), Thailand, and others, have no overarching data privacy laws with the data privacy issues being regulated instead by industry-specific acts and regulations.

Although there is much debate over which privacy policies most evenly balance corporate and individual interests, the following norms identified by the FTC[33] represent a consensus regarding the minimum requirements in the ethical use of consumer information (Exhibit 5.3):

1. ***Notice:*** Users should be aware of a site's information policy *before* data are collected.
2. ***Consent:*** Users should be allowed to choose participation or exclusion from the collection.
3. ***Access:*** Users should have the ability to access their data and correct them if erroneous.

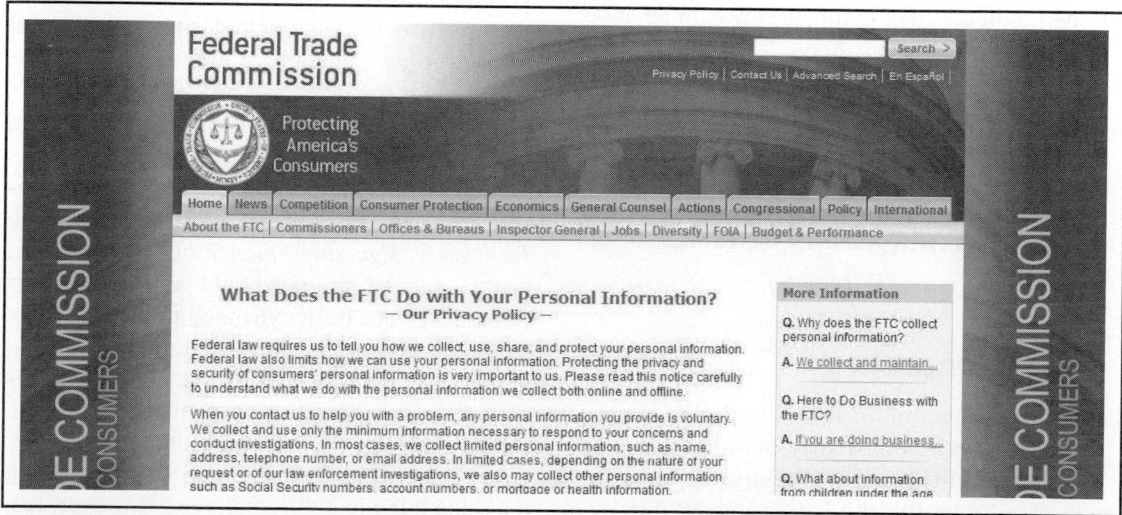

EXHIBIT 5.3 FTC Online Privacy Policy *Source*: www.ftc.gov/

4. ***Security:*** Policies to ensure the integrity of data and the prevention of misuse should be in place.
5. ***Enforcement:*** Users should have effective means to hold data collectors to their policies.

The FTC has been actively involved in the development of additional recommendations for the internet community which would help to improve personal data protection. Likewise, in March 2012 the FTC issued a detailed report which clarified the agency's position on privacy issues and established an extensive framework for companies involved in collection and processing of personal data.[34]

The framework basically repeats the key privacy standards outlined in the proposed EU Data Privacy Regulation. It expresses concerns about the methods used by large ISPs to process personal data of online users. It also encourages personal data operators: to promote consumer privacy; introduce reasonable safety measures for personal data protection, retention, and disposal; limit collection of personal data only to such information which is specifically necessary for their business purposes; and ensure accuracy of personal data and implement procedural protections (e.g., internal policies and regulations) in order to enforce the data protection principles. It also indicates that companies should develop clear and transparent privacy guidelines for consumers and provide them with an adequate mechanism to access, modify, and control their personal data and its collection. The FTC report demonstrates a current global trend that even though the government allows self-regulation in data collection, it is gradually increasing its control over it.

DIGITAL PROPERTY

A primary function of law is to define ownership, but this is constantly being challenged by the mercurial nature of digital technology. Traditionally, the law protected intangible or intellectual property through three basic mechanisms—patent, trademark, and copyright law. It is important to note that none of these areas of law protect ideas. Rather, they protect inventions, expression, and brands.

Patent law is centered upon inventions and the ability to reproduce or manufacture an inventor's product. **Copyright** addresses the realm of creative expression—specifically, the right to publish, duplicate, or alter expressions of ideas. **Trademark** is concerned with brands—source identifiers that consumers use to identify and distinguish products and services in the marketplace. It is important to note that these categories have been flexible and often the boundaries between them have been modified by legislation and the courts. In addition, international treaties can redefine both distinctions and protections.

Computer-based communication poses particularly difficult problems for intellectual property. These communications may incorporate elements of patent, copyright, and trademark or any combination thereof. A single communication may contain: (1) a novel way of communicating covered by a patent; (2) text and pictures protected by copyright; and (3) proprietary branding covered by trademark law.

Patents

The application of patent law to computing is a continually developing field. Under conventional American law, patents are granted by the U.S. government for inventive processes or steps.[35] Grounded in English legal foundations and the heritage of conventional invention, the law is tailored toward industrial or mechanical concerns. In 1998, the case of *State Street Bank & Trust Co. v. Signature Financial Group, Inc.* held that a computer program could be patented. This ruling has since been expanded to include other methods of doing business. Since *State Street*, online businesses have been making use of this type of patent protection. A primary motivation for this may lie in the fact that, unlike copyrights, patents prevent competitors from doing the same thing in a different way. However, like copyright, American patent powers derive from

Constitutional concerns. Thus, public access to patented material is assured after the term of the patent has expired and the patent itself is always on file with the government.

The inclusion of software under patent law is largely based upon the assertion that programs describe inventive processes. A contrary opinion holds that software at its root consists of algorithms—formulas that are generic in nature and, therefore, cannot be owned by anyone. A similar criticism states that programs are merely schemes or plans that machines actually execute. The details of both sides' arguments are complex and promise to be the subject of much future debate, litigation and, perhaps, Congressional action. An area of current internet focus centers on the use of *business patents* that describe such activities as marketing approaches and methods for conducting commerce. Patent protection has been claimed for reverse online auctions, secure credit card processing, and incentive-based methods for reading Web site advertising. When the Patent Office first started granting patents on business methods, the review process was less than vigorous. Many overly broad patents were issued in a short period of time. Opportunistic companies bought large numbers of these patents and began filing infringement lawsuits around the country. These patent trolls are still around, reaping millions of dollars in royalties every year for doing nothing but threatening to sue on somewhat suspect patents.

An example of the attempted enforcement of a software patent is found in the claim that secure digital time-stamping is a unique and protected process. Critics fear that if this assertion is upheld, the majority of online encryption routines will be affected. Similarly, in *Amazon.com v. Barnesandnoble.com*, the plaintiff (Amazon.com) relied upon a patent to allege that it alone had the ability to use *1-Click* ordering routines—a now common practice within the internet.[36] The matter was settled in 2002, without final judicial resolution and the details of the settlement have not been disclosed.

The U.S. Patent Office recently decided to increase the rigor with which it reviews applications for software-related protection. Likewise, both courts and Congress are being called upon to carefully examine whether historical data support the inclusion of software and business practices within a patent's ambit. Advocates of inclusion argue that the granting of patents in these areas will encourage productivity and innovation. Critics argue the opposite, stating that both the encryption matter and the unanswered issues of the *Amazon* case point to the potentially stifling and monopolistic effects of patent law's strong protections.

In 2010 the U.S. Supreme Court ruled on the biggest "business method" patent case since *State Street*. The issue in *In re Bilski* was the allowable scope of business method patents.[37] In particular, the court considered whether an invention had to be tied to a machine or transform something from one state to another to become patentable. The plaintiff in this case appealed the U.S. Patent and Trademark Office's refusal to patent his risk-management business method, which was further affirmed in court. The U.S. Court of Appeals for the Federal Circuit held that the business method was not patentable because it did not meet the "machine-or-transformation test." This decision placed under risk all other business methods which would have been deprived of patentability if the Supreme Court affirmed as well. While the Supreme Court affirmed the decision of the lower court that the specific risk hedging method was unpatentable, it completely disagreed that business methods as a whole were unpatentable. It also found that the "machine-or-transformation test" was not the only basis for determining the patent eligibility, but rather a helpful tool that could be used to resolve disputes.[38] The main outcome of this case is that business method patents will be very carefully scrutinized and depend on the circumstances of each situation. They also are likely to be heavily litigated.

Copyright

At this comparatively early stage of online legal development, copyright appears to be established as the primary means of protecting most expression on the internet, including text and other data. In the conventional world, copyright has protected expressions of ideas in such formats as books, recordings, and film. Under American law, copyright law is derived from the Constitution as a protection established for the benefit of the public. Chief among these protections are the doctrines of fair use and of first sale.[39] Fair use consists of the ability to copy—without cost—reasonable portions of protected material for purposes of such public activities as education, news reporting, and editorial comment. The doctrine of first sale limits the ability of a copyright holder to obtain profit from the sale of his or her work after the initial time at which the material is sold. Purchasers are subsequently given the ability to transfer or otherwise dispose of their copy. The first sale doctrine is viewed as benefiting such institutions as public libraries and can also increase access to intellectual material through discounts such as those offered by used bookstores. The issue is unsettled when it comes to digital property, like music downloads.

In 1997, President Clinton signed the **No Electronic Theft (NET) Act**[40] into law. The NET Act confers copyright protection for computer content and imposes sanctions when infringement is committed for commercial or private financial gain, or by the reproduction or distribution, either commercial or noncommercial, of one or more copies of copyrighted works having $1,000 or more in retail value. Punishment under this provision may include criminal prosecution. While proponents believe that the NET Act will encourage innovation by protecting material placed on the internet, critics believe that the definition of *infringement* has been made problematically broad by shifting its traditional meaning, which is normally associated with permanent or semipermanent reproduction (known as fixing), to now include electronic distribution without reproduction. It is argued that such acts could include the mere perusal of digital material through a Web browser and, thus, make criminal activities of what has been previously protected by the First Amendment. Additional criticism has been directed to the use of criminal sanctions, particularly at a time when there is great debate about the economic value of electronic material.

A related law, enacted in 1998, is the **Digital Millennium Copyright (DMCA) Act**.[41] The DMCA is a complex piece of legislation that contains several provisions. It grants ISPs protection from acts of user infringement as long as certain procedures are followed, including the prompt reporting and disabling of infringing material. Supporters of this legislation claim that the DMCA will free ISPs from liability for their users' illegal actions and, thus, encourage industry growth. Critics believe that the reporting and disabling requirements may cause innocent behavior to be presumed infringing and wrongfully censored.

The DMCA also criminalizes the circumvention of software protections and the development or distribution of circumvention products.[42] As with the NET Act, DMCA supporters believe that this law will increase commercial willingness to place material on the internet by deterring online infringement. Although some exceptions exist for educational and scientific activities, critics maintain that the DMCA goes well beyond this goal by banning the development of innocent and useful applications that may have minor circumvention capabilities, giving copyright holders a veto over any development that they perceive as a challenge to their profits.[43]

The DMCA was enacted in part to comply with the World Intellectual Property Organization's (WIPO) Copyright Treaty and the WIPO Performances and Phonograms Treaty.[44] These documents set forth international standards for copyrighted material and were recently ratified by the United States. Treaty proponents argue that, in a global networked environment, international consensus regarding ownership, protection, and transfer of digital property is essential. As with the DMCA, critics argue that the specific laws required by the treaties unfairly favor copyright owners.

In 2011, there were serious efforts made in Congress to pass the two legislative acts aimed at establishing stricter guidelines for internet companies operating Web sites involved in copyright infringement. The **Stop Online Piracy ACT (SOPA)**[45] and the **PROTECT IP (Preventing Real Online Threats to Economic Creativity and Theft of Intellectual Property, or PIPA) Act**[46] called for enhanced enforcement against individuals and companies engaged in copyright infringement.

The introduction of these bills caused a great storm of protests among the internet community and its supporters. Google, Mozilla, Facebook, Twitter, Yahoo!, and many other internet companies started a petition against the proposed legislation which reportedly collected approximately 4.5 million signatures.[47] Wikipedia, Google, Craigslist, Mozilla, Flickr, Reddit, Peter Gabriel, and other Web sites performed a 24-hour blackout on January 18–19, 2012.[48]

On the black background of its English page, Wikipedia placed a mourning message warning its online users against the fatal consequences of the proposed legislation to the open internet. Several other internet Web sites took similar actions and eventually, due to the enormous pressure caused by numerous boycotts and picketing, the bills were rejected. The Obama administration spoke against the bills stating that it would not support such legislation. However, it also indicated that the issues of online copyright infringement remain very important and called for an open dialogue between the ISPs and those lobbying for stricter regulation.[49] Thus, there remains a strong likelihood that the government's attempts to increase control over the internet will continue and similar bills will be proposed in the future.

Trademarks

Trademark law is the area of intellectual property that governs source identifiers for goods or services. At its heart, trademark law is a consumer protection law. Under the federal **Lanham Act**,[50] trademarks may be registered with the government. Registered or not, however, they may still be protected under the Act. To pursue an infringement case, claimants must prove that the trademark is *protectable*. Generally, the more distinctive (unique) the mark, the greater is the strength of this claim. The Act also prohibits **dilution**—the unauthorized use of famous trademarks in association with goods or services that is likely to lead to a lessening of the uniqueness of the trademark.

In 1995, the U.S. Congress passed the **Federal Trademark Dilution Act (FTDA)**[51] which established guidelines on how to determine whether a particular trademark has been diluted. Dilution protects the substantial investment made by owners of famous marks—those widely recognized by the general consuming public of the United States in those marks.

There are two types of dilution: **blurring** and **tarnishment**. Blurring results from activities that reduce the "distinctiveness" (uniqueness or brand recognition) of the famous mark. Tarnishment occurs when the famous mark is cast in an unflattering light.

In response to the Supreme Court's ruling in *Moseley v. V Secret Catalogue, Inc.*, 537 U.S. 418 (2003)—which interpreted the FTDA to require actual dilution—the **Trademark Dilution Revision Act of 2006 (TDRA)**[52] was enacted on October 6, 2006, to substantially revise the FTDA. Under the TDRA, if a famous brand is *likely* to be diluted, then the brand owner has grounds to file suit.

Trademark law has recently been applied to the internet-naming system. Domain names (aka domains) are unique configurations of letters or numbers that are used to route data. The most familiar examples of domains are addresses of Web sites, for example, someplace.com. In addition to designating Web sites, domain names are used in e-mail addresses. As the primary means to reach commercial destinations, the significance of these identifiers is obvious.

Although the creative application of language provides for many distinctive names, it is inevitable that some similarity will occur. For example, "General Signpost" can plausibly be thought to resemble "General Sign," but traditionally, trademark law has been able to allow such similarities because trademark protection is typically limited to a particular class or classes of goods or services. When enough dissimilarity of goods or services exists, overlap in the similarity of brands is permitted.

Another type of trademark violation is known as **cybersquatting**. This activity involves the registration of domain names that resemble or duplicate the names of existing corporations or other entities. The initial registrants are typically unrelated to the institution at issue. The domain name is then offered for sale at a price far greater than that originally paid. On November 29, 1999, President Clinton signed the **Anticybersquatting Consumer Protection Act (ACPA)**.[53] Under this law, a person is liable if, in bad faith, he or she registers, traffics, or sells a domain bearing a name that is identical or confusingly similar to a protected trademark, or which would dilute the worth of the trademark. As a national law, the Act makes it easier to place notoriously elusive cybersquatters under the control of the court system and allows for swift possession by a successful complainant of the disputed domain name. Heralded by trademark holders, the Act has received criticism similar to that lodged against the DCMA, specifically, that the swiftness of the transfer of contested domain names may unfairly deprive a defendant of a proper hearing and due process.

Metatags are HTML statements that describe a Web site's contents. They are not normally displayed by browsers. They allow search engines to identify sites relevant to topics of their inquiries. Accordingly, these tags can provide a valuable means of attracting users to a site. Because metatags are defined by HTML authors, it is possible to insert words or phrases that are calculated to provide optimal attractiveness, including material protected by trademark. In a matter involving Playboy Enterprises, Inc., the defendant included in its metatags the protected words *Playboy* and *Playmate*. In the subsequent suit, the court found that the intent of the site was to profit from a false association with Playboy and prohibited the inclusion, stating that dilution of the trademarks had occurred as a result.[54] This outcome should be contrasted with a more recent matter in which a former Playmate of the Year included similar terms within her site, albeit repeatedly noting that she was not presently associated with Playboy Enterprises. Here, the use was upheld as applied to the metatags, with the court holding that their presence was "nominative," meaning that the terms were simply descriptive and did not inaccurately imply an endorsement or make other misrepresentations. Significantly, the court did find that the repeated use of a trademarked term on the site's wallpaper did constitute an infringement and was unnecessary for the purposes of simple description.[55]

A variation of the metatag problem is found in the practice of assigning **keywords** within search engines. In one case, the cosmetic manufacturer, Estée Lauder, sued Excite and others, alleging that the entry of its trademarked name at the Excite Shopping Channel would direct users to the site of a specific, unlicensed dealer.[56] In addition to deception, Estée Lauder claimed that the practice diluted its trademark. The case was subsequently settled with Estée Lauder reacquiring control over its name. The selling of trademark-protected keywords has also been claimed to occur at other Web portals where these words or phrases trigger banner advertising that is not sanctioned by or directed to the trademark holder.

In addition to word appropriation, trademark law has been implicated in matters involving use of hyperlinks. Although the Web has flourished with its abilities to seamlessly transfer information from site to site, some entities have become concerned that links that take users to areas other than their introductory page may cause confusion or deprive the target sites of revenue obtained through the selling of advertising. Such *deep linking* was the subject of litigation when Microsoft's Seattle Sidewalk created deep links to city-specific event sales within a site run by Ticketmaster. Here, Ticketmaster claimed that the practice diluted Ticketmaster's trademarks and constituted unfair competition. Microsoft countered that the placement of any material within public areas of the Web would make it open to access. These contrasting theoretical positions were never subjected to a final court ruling because the case was ultimately settled with Microsoft agreeing to link only to Ticketmaster's primary entry page.[57]

Related to linking is the practice of **framing**, a process in which a Web browser is instructed to divide itself into two or more partitions and load within a section material obtained from another Web site through the execution of an automatic link. In *Washington Post v. TotalNEWS, Inc.*, a suit was filed over the use of a collage of frames, some linked to the *Post*, within a page dedicated to a sampling of news on the Web. Among other things, the *Post* alleged that the unattributed displays diluted trademarks, appropriated copyrighted material, and deprived the *Post* of advertising revenue.[58] The matter was settled before decision with TotalNEWS agreeing to use only nonframed, attributed textual links to the *Post.*

Several court cases about linking and framing have been decided in California. Most of these lawsuits were initiated by holders of copyrighted images against various search engines that used linking and framing to display such images in their search results. As a rule, the courts were supportive of the defendant if they used such images only as "thumbnail" pictures linked to the Web sites of their copyright owners and not as genuine images. For example, in *Kelly v. Arriba Soft Corp.* the court ruled for Arriba's search engine, which used thumbnail images of Kelly's photographs in order to catalogue them for searching purposes. Stating that its use of Kelly's images was a "fair use," the court found that Arriba's use served a new purpose of a "transformative nature" of the images and created a significant value for the public.[59] The creativity of Arriba's product outweighed any slight economic harm caused to the plaintiff under the circumstances.

The same approach was taken by the court in *Perfect 10 v. Amazon* which involved Google. In this case the court determined that framing of copyrighted images by Google could not be considered as "display" of such images under the meaning of the applicable copyright law. Taking into account that such pictures were not stored on Google's computers but simply provided a link to the Web sites of their owners, such activity of the search engine was not illegal.[60] Considering the fact that Google's product was highly transformative, the court ruled against Perfect 10.

Licenses

An increasingly popular method of intellectual property protection involves the use of **licenses**—contractual agreements made between consumers and software vendors, which allow the buyer to use the product but restrict duplication or distribution. Because laws related to licenses are derived from the commercially oriented law of contract, rather than through the constitutionally related realm of copyright or patent, public policy exceptions have traditionally played a less important role in its development. Moreover, because it is assumed that parties to contractual agreements bargain under conditions of informed self-interest, licenses may contain waivers of many protections normally found in consumer transactions (see the "Let's Get Technical" box).

Within the computer environment, a great deal of attention has been paid to the validity of licenses appearing upon or within software. Variations of this format are often known as shrinkwrap or *break-the-seal* licenses (when appearing outside of software) and clickwrap licenses when a user is required to click a button online or within a program to acknowledge acceptance of terms. Although common to conventional business situations, the extent to which licenses with noncommercial purchasers will be enforced by the courts is not entirely clear, primarily due to the lack of bargaining that takes place between the user and the seller. Normally, a contract requires that an agreement can be demonstrated and it is uncertain that average buyers agree to or even read the fine print in the software licenses that appear on their diskettes, boxes, installation routines, or software manuals.

The legal trend seems to favor enforcement of software licenses. Courts have upheld a shrinkwrap term that limited the vendor's liability for errors within the program.[61] At least one

LET'S GET TECHNICAL

Licensing Technology

Filename: LatestOperatingSystem.zip

Download Time: 10 hours and 34 minutes

Number of Files: 4215 files, 78 folders

Price: $0.00

Legality: 100% ILLEGAL

The feud between music fans and the music industry over the illegal distribution of albums and songs has been all over the media. As many already know, computer users with high-speed connections can download a client to get in on the trading—illegal trading, that is. Software is distributed through this medium as well. Just like copying music files to shared folders, users are copying the contents of installation CDs for such software as Microsoft Office, Macromedia Flash, and Adobe Photoshop.

However, when a user purchases software, he or she is most often just purchasing one license, or the right to install and run the software on one computer. When purchasing and installing the software, the user agrees to the end user license agreement (EULA). He or she agrees by selecting "I agree" or "I accept" in the installation process. The EULA also protects the software company from liability in case the software causes damage to the user's computer.

Breaking the agreement used to be simple. The user simply had to copy the CD and the CD's product key and distribute it freely. Software companies then became more advanced in their quest to stop software piracy, or the illegal distribution of software, by instituting activation procedures. Upon installing the software, the computer user is allowed to either run the software for a certain number of days or open it a certain number of times. Once the user activates the software, either online or via telephone, the limitations are removed. The activation stops software piracy because it allows the software associated with the product key to be activated only once, and thus it can be installed on only one computer.

Also, this feature allows software companies to distribute trial versions of their software. Once the limit has been met, the software cannot be used without purchasing a full version. Other trial versions just offer limited features until a license is purchased.

Software piracy is often misunderstood, and it occurs in many different forms. Software piracy also includes illegal use of fonts. Licenses can be issued for fonts, and using copyrighted fonts without a license is illegal. Whether using the software or font for business or personal purposes, using it without a license is illegal and is punishable by law. Forms of software piracy include the illegal use of a software program over a network, distributing specialized education versions to unauthorized markets, and reporting an inaccurate number of users using software at a site. Even the possession of software that has been illegally copied is piracy.

Many organizations have been created to monitor software piracy and the illegal duplication of all copyrighted material worldwide. Examples include the Software & Information Industry Association's Anti-Piracy Division (siia.net/piracy) and the Business Software Alliance (bsa.org). The SIIA's Anti-Piracy Division conducts proactive campaigns to educate users about software piracy. The Business Software Alliance (BSA) recently stated that software piracy cost the software industry nearly $64 billion in sales in 2011. The BSA ranks countries by their piracy rates. According to the BSA, piracy rates in the United States, Japan, New Zealand, and Luxembourg hover near 20 percent (a relatively low figure) while those in Armenia, Bangladesh, Georgia, and Zimbabwe all exceed 90 percent. Software manufacturers, such as Microsoft and Adobe, have also set up Web sites to help determine whether users' software is legal and to report software piracy.

Apple, always an innovator, takes a unique approach to piracy by acknowledging that some forms of copying are reasonable. Buy an app on your iPhone or iPad and you can install it on multiple devices that you own as long as all the devices are tied to your Apple ID. This works especially well for families that have multiple devices and do not wish to buy separate apps for all the devices. Buy a movie on iTunes and you can watch it streamed from the cloud, or download it to your iPad or computer. All of the permissions are keyed to your Apple ID.

In the professional world, it is tempting to hand a CD and product key to one's coworker to install. However, if an audit is conducted by an outside source, that simple act can get the company in hot water. Software manufacturers can take such actions as warning, fining, or suing the company. In a professional setting, it is best to pursue a site license agreement (SLA) for the organization to use the software. An SLA, or site license, is simply a license to use the software within a certain facility. The license usually entails whether the software can be installed on all or specific computers or servers and if copies can be made and distributed within the facility.

court also found enforceable a clickwrap term that dictated the state in which a suit against the vendor could be brought.[62] Whether a particular language in a clickwrap license will be legally enforceable will often depend upon the reasonableness of the language, as it is in contract law in general. Language prohibiting unauthorized copying and distribution of copyrighted material likely will be enforceable; language mandating $300,000 for each infraction likely will not.

A broad effort to enforce the terms of software licenses comes in the form of the **Uniform Computer Information Transactions Act (UCITA)**. In the two states which have adopted it (Virginia and Maryland), the UCITA governs all legal agreements pertaining to software transactions, including sales. Supported by the majority of software manufacturers and publishers as a measure of legal uniformity, critics argue that the UCITA will enforce license provisions, including those restricting copying and resale of material, liability for damages incurred from defective software, and possibly the ability to criticize software performance. Because the UCITA applies to any material in computer-readable form, including electronic books and other reading materials, librarians and educators fear it will effectively remove the public policy protections of copyright and patent, making online information expensive and restricted. In 2001, the attorneys general of 32 states and 2 territories stated their opposition to the act, and in 2002 a task force of the American Bar Association issued a call for its redrafting. As the debate on intellectual property continues, it will be important to consider that, although intellectual property laws can act as incentives to create useful material, they can also work to restrict the data exchange that has contributed to the internet's popularity. The achieving of a balance between both concerns will be an important and a continuing task for digital law and ethics.

Trade Secrets

The field of trade secrecy has taken on new proportions with the advent of online technology. A trade secret is an economically valuable business secret that is not generally known or readily ascertainable. The federal **Economic Espionage Act** of 1996[63] was enacted in part to address digital advances and now makes it a criminal offense to divulge trade secrets, which are broadly defined to include such areas as commercial, scientific, and technical endeavors. Trade secrets can include, but are not restricted to, formulas, market data, algorithms, programs, codes, and models. They may be stored online or in tangible formats. Significantly, computer based disclosures such as e-mails, downloads, Web publications, and similar means are within the scope of the act.

Employees with access to trade secrets may be prohibited from engaging in similar businesses for a period of time—so long as the time and geographic scope of the restriction are reasonable given the nature of employment. In one notable case, a court determined that an employee's particular skills in Web marketing were sufficiently protected under a noncompetition agreement with a former employer to prevent him from working for a competitor within a one-year period following his departure from a company.[64]

Another important Act in trade secrets law is the **Uniform Trade Secrets (UTSA) Act** that was introduced by the Uniform Law Commission in 1979 and amended in 1985. So far 47 states have adopted it.[65] The main purposes of the UTSA is to unify the existing trade secrets legislation across all 50 states and, consequently, to provide certainty to U.S. businesses that their confidential information will be protected uniformly throughout the whole country.

Data Ownership

It is not an overstatement to say that the online world runs on data. Not surprisingly, access and ownership questions relating to data and databases abound in current legal and ethical debate. As the electronic market becomes more competitive, attempts to obtain the advantages provided by control of information become more numerous.

Until recently, data relating to such technical issues as Web site usage was easy to access and were often shared among site owners, marketing professionals, advertisers, and consumers. Currently, a new technology is being introduced that would make information collected from banner advertisements invisible to site owners and their clients. These *click data* have been important in determining such factors as site content and marketing strategy. Such protective technologies raise new issues concerning the ownership of information that is both a necessary element of online interaction and of extreme value in itself. A particularly significant question is whether the *fencing in* of data will achieve the same status as the more formal application of copyright, patent, trademark, or licensing laws. This process will challenge the model of cooperation that has been a characteristic of online dynamics and, arguably, a primary reason for the success of the interactive digital medium.

Another complex issue involving online data is an activity known as spidering. This process involves the use of software applications called robots to enter targeted Web sites and obtain data for the use of its owner. In a recent matter, the online auction site eBay instituted an action against Bidder's Edge, which operated a service that presented comparative auction information through spidering. The information collected from eBay was unprotected by copyright. Advocates of eBay's position that it has proprietary rights in its auction data claim that another's use of the data constitutes unfair competition and dilutes the worth of eBay's business. They also maintain that the spidering activity constituted a trespass of property, potentially impairing the eBay system. Supporters of Bidder's Edge expressed concern that if data are cordoned off from the rest of the online community, the presently information-rich internet will increasingly become a gated community where actions in trespass will become the predominant means of enforcing boundaries. The matter was settled before judgment on the merits, after the court sustained eBay's request for a preliminary injunction of Bidder's Edge's activity based upon the trespass claim.[66]

A final area of consideration is that of the special protection of data relating to facts. As previously noted, U.S. copyright law protects *expressions* of ideas but not the ideas themselves. This distinction is owing to the public policy emphasis of protecting the raw material of free expression and national learning. For similar reasons, copyright cannot be used to protect facts. Because electronic databases often contain arrangements of facts, a movement is growing within the law to protect specially compiled or sui generis data.

The Agreement on **Trade Related Aspects of Intellectual Property Rights (TRIPs)** of 1995 is part of the World Trade Organization's (WTO) program of international treaties. Provisions within this agreement set forth sui generis protection. The EU's Database Directive[67] also includes protection for compiled facts. Currently, the U.S. Congress has not adopted a sui generis law.

Arguments favoring sui generis protection revolve around the belief that this type of protection will afford an incentive for database vendors to create more of their products by assuring them of potential return on their investments and that their product will not be copied or diluted. In the long run, society will benefit from the increase in the number of databases, which would in turn help decrease the price of information.

Critics of these laws argue that no economic proof indicates that such incentives would produce an increase in databases or that, with an increase, prices would necessarily come down. Instead, they state that worries about copying and dilution can be addressed through encryption and similar methodologies. In the balance, they claim that sui generis protection could erect legal barriers that stifle innovation and lead to a monopolization of the basis of all education and learning. Another troubling fact is that many current proposals allow a virtually infinite term under which data could be kept out of the public domain. Under U.S. law, settling these issues will involve a close examination of the reasons underlying the constitutional aversion to the ownership of facts, and it will raise ethical questions about whether facts are merely commodities or are so valuable that exclusive control can never be granted to one individual.

ONLINE EXPRESSION

The mass distribution of unsolicited e-mail or spam has been the subject of much complaint within the online world. The practice has been criticized on many levels. ISPs point to the burdens that spamming places upon networks' resources. Spam is, by definition, unrequested, and users complain of the unwanted intrusion into their affairs. Privacy-related worries are not restricted to transmission alone. Much spam is derived from mailing lists that are collected from e-mail addresses posted on such locations as Web bulletin boards or **newsgroups** without any intention to participate in mass mailings. Similarly, many users are disturbed to find that information given to individuals or entities for one purpose may be collected and sold for mass distribution. The frustration with spam is further compounded by the fact that often these messages are sent without valid return addresses or unsubscribe links, making it nearly impossible to stop receiving them.

Although spam has been the subject of much-justified criticism, its regulation must be approached with some caution. First, the topic implicates freedom of expression, which is a right protected under the First Amendment in the United States. Disagreement remains between those who believe that participation in mass e-mails should be restricted to those who voluntarily agree to receive mailings and those who advocate an opt-out-only approach. The DMA has established such an opt-out list for those who seek to avoid mass e-mail messages. Although it is certainly a progressive step, critics point out that only DMA members are obligated to respect this list and also worry that, like other opt-out systems, complexity and difficulty will prevent many average users from participating.

Within the law, spam has become a major issue. In the case of *Cyber Promotions, Inc. v. America Online, Inc.*,[68] the court held that a spam producer had no First Amendment right to send its product to AOL subscribers and that consequently the ISP could block its messaging activity. Similarly, a court ruled that spamming activity violated the federal Computer Fraud and Abuse Act.[69] Additionally, Congress passed, and President Bush signed, the **Controlling the Assault of Non-Solicited Pornography and Marketing Act** of 2003, better known as the CAN-SPAM Act.[70] The act creates a comprehensive, national framework for the use of marketing-directed e-mail. Although criticized by some consumer organizations as being more lenient than many state laws, the act permits federal and state authorities as well as ISPs to initiate both civil and criminal actions against advertising deemed to be conducted through spamming activities. Currently, the task of precise definition of illicit spamming is being determined by the FTC, but will include communications containing deceptive information, misleading statements, and false representations of an e-mail's content as displayed on the subject line. It will also require that e-mail headings reveal their commercial nature and that, in most circumstances, recipients are provided with clear instructions on how to terminate further contact. Finally, the use of autonomous data collection applications (e.g., spidering) will be prohibited. To many critics, a significant deficiency of the legislation is the absence of a private right to pursue actions against spammers.

Criticism of products or industries has also been addressed within and outside the spam context. In one case, a court prohibited an individual from sending mass e-mails to a corporation's employees complaining of employment violations. The trial court reasoned that corporate e-mail does not resemble traditional places of commentary and should, therefore, not be treated as a public forum, but instead, constituted private property, subject to trespass allegations. The decision was appealed to the California Supreme Court, which reversed the ruling, finding that because no impairment of the computer system or network occurred as a result of the mailings, a trespass action could not be maintained.[71] Less-specific mailings may also be restricted through terms of service agreements. A Canadian decision enforced such a contract that prohibited spam activity by an ISP's users.[72]

The inception of ISPs gave rise to a question about the liability of network owners for defamatory messages posted on bulletin boards or other public areas. Although most courts adopt the view that like publishers, ISPs are not normally susceptible to suit, Congress resolved the problem by placing this immunity within federal law.[73] The primary reason for this provision is a fear that if liability were at issue, a provider would be required to actively monitor and censor activity within its service, thus decreasing the level of free expression. The significance of this policy was demonstrated when a court determined that an ISP could not be held liable for negligently publishing anonymous, allegedly false, and defamatory statements concerning an individual's profiteering from the Oklahoma City bombings.[74]

The issue of expression directed to children remains a highly visible issue within online law and ethics. In 1996, the federal Telecommunications Act of 1934 was amended to include the **Computer Decency Act (CDA)**, which in relevant part made it a criminal act to send an "obscene or indecent" communication to a recipient who was known to the sender to be under 18 years of age. An additional provision made it an offense to use an interactive computer service to present material that "depicts or describes, in terms patently offensive, as measured by contemporary community standards, sexual or excretory organs" in a context available to minors. In 1997, in the case of *Reno v. American Civil Liberties Union*,[75] the U.S. Supreme Court found that these provisions were unconstitutionally vague, prohibiting, among other things, the exchange of information about such subjects as AIDS and reproductive decision making. It further noted that the provisions would hinder or *chill* adult speech through the placement of undue burdens.

Although the broad regulatory attempts of the CDA failed, a number of efforts are under way to provide more narrowly defined regulations for children's content. In addition, the use of filtering models has been considered. Perhaps the best-known program is the **Platform for Internet Content Selection Rules (PICS)**. This application allows the filtering of sites that are deemed inappropriate for minors. Advocates claim that PICS will place control into the hands of parents and schools. Some civil rights groups are concerned that this device, which works behind the scenes, presents a subtle but powerful means of censorship.

In December 2000, Congress passed the Children's Internet Protection Act (CIPA). The legislation links federal funding to libraries with the use of filtering software in public internet terminals. In May 2002, after hearing extensive evidence, a federal judicial panel invalidated the Act, stating that blocking software cannot adequately guarantee that only material harmful to minors would be screened. The decision was appealed to the U.S. Supreme Court, and on June 23, 2003, a plurality opinion reversed the lower court, holding that public funding can be made contingent upon the use of filters. Significantly, this declaration was effectively limited for, in the course of the proceedings, the government stated that libraries would retain the ability to remove filtering software if simply requested to do so by a patron. This concession was cited by two individual concurrences and likely played a determinative role in the outcome.[76]

These examples strongly suggest that the boundaries of expression will continue to be challenged by the internet. Although specific outcomes remain open to question, it appears that expression will be protected when the courts and the legislatures realize the purpose and importance of electronic communication. Education of all parties involved may prove to be the best security for the continued flourishing of online speech.

EMERGING ISSUES

Along with the more conventional problems of online dynamics, additional challenges are particularly unique to the internet at its current stage of development. The responses to these challenges will require the same levels of imagination and creativity demonstrated in the internet's creation.

Online Governance and ICANN

In 1998, the U.S. Department of Commerce called for the creation of a private, nonprofit regulatory body that would be responsible for the administration of the internet name and address system. In response, the **Internet Corporation for Assigned Names and Numbers (ICANN)** was formed. Ideally, the purpose of ICANN is to govern the assignment and possession of domains and resolve the conflicts that arise in relation thereto. Today, ICANN is comprised of a governing board that currently faces substantial criticism for operating under secrecy and for failing to represent the broad range of online users. Many of these problems may be attributed to the newness of this endeavor, but other questions concern the ability of any private regulatory organization to enforce its decisions within the online community. Along these lines, parties to serious disputes may attempt to bypass ICANN or other arbitration arrangements in favor of the conventional enforcement abilities of legal forums, through trademark infringement suits and cybersquatting claims.

Jurisdiction

The establishment of ICANN reflects the growing awareness that online controversies transcend physical boundaries. **Jurisdiction** is the legal term that describes the authority of a court over a given party. Jurisdiction is traditionally based upon physical presence, which becomes an issue in the nonphysical nature of the online world. Similarly, attempts to exercise jurisdiction within the geographic territories of other nations or states will most likely be rebuffed.

The majority of cases decided within the United States have focused upon the character and quality of contacts with the forum's state; generally, the more active the involvement, the more likely that jurisdiction will be conferred. Thus, jurisdiction over online activity was found where the court determined that an out-of-state defendant had knowingly and purposefully done business within the state of suit.[77] In contrast, another court found that mere advertising within a state (i.e., via a Web site) will not subject the advertiser to the jurisdiction.[78] A similar decision held that the ability to access a Web site within a particular state does not subject the site owner to jurisdiction.[79] As previously mentioned, digital licensing agreements that defined the jurisdiction in which a suit may be brought have been upheld. Similarly, a recent state court decision indicated that such a selection may be contractually specified by digital means. In upholding the vendor's choice of forum, as disclosed through an internet hyperlink, the court noted that the use of hyperlinks to convey information has become an increasingly accepted practice and can validly designate a forum's choice.[80]

In addition to conventional legal tribunals, such mediation-oriented programs as **Virtual Magistrate**[81] have been developed to resolve online disputes. These programs often attempt to tailor their procedures toward the special circumstances of the internet. Advocates of these approaches argue that their online orientation will encourage users to work out difficulties within a non-confrontational framework. Critics voice concerns that online arbitration cannot adequately ensure enforcement or recognition of judgments.

The previously mentioned cases dealt exclusively with U.S. jurisdictional questions. Although difficult problems are presented, they are arguably less complex than those involving international disputes. One method aimed at achieving international cooperation is through the mediation of organizations. For example, the WIPO Arbitration and Mediation Center[82] exists to resolve commercial disputes relating to intellectual property.

Supranational organizations such as the EU may also regulate disputes between their members. Likewise, treaties may provide for international resolution and enforcement. The **Model Law on Electronic Commerce**[83] by the **United Nations Commission of International Trade Law (UNCITRAL)** has been established to provide for global uniformity in digital commerce. This developing collection of laws addresses such matters as digital signatures, electronic documentation, sales of digital goods, contracts, exchanges of information, and credit records. The force of such model laws comes through their actual adoption or through the pressure that they can exert upon national legislatures and other organizations to conform to international standards. Although acceptance of jurisdiction cannot be forced upon non-cooperating countries, the weight of international agreements concerning key questions favors the mutual enforcement of obligations.

Fraud

The use of deception and false claims to obtain profit is, of course, not unique to the internet. However, the nature of online dynamics introduces several factors that affect prevention efforts. The first general factor relates to the technical nature of networked communication. The average person is not in a position to understand exactly how information is displayed, transferred, or stored, and this lack of knowledge provides opportunities for novel deceptions. Included within this category is the use of e-mail or Web sites to impersonate individuals or corporations. This activity, known as **spoofing**, is often used to extract sensitive information by leading a user to believe that a request is coming from a reputable source, such as an ISP or a credit card company. Other common swindles involve the use of programs that secretly dial long-distance locations for which the unknowing user pays the fees, or false login pages that record account information.

A second factor involves the psychology of digital environments. The media is full of stories concerning technological advances and opportunities for profit. Unfortunately, many people are unable to differentiate genuinely worthwhile endeavors from those presented by mere opportunists. Messages originating from the online world are likely to be viewed by some as having an air of authority, solely due to their association with the digital revolution. Many investment opportunities make use of this rhetoric, often promoting breakthrough technologies and applications.

The problem of consumer **fraud** is being addressed on several dimensions. Federal agencies such as the FTC and the FBI have increased their efforts to track and prosecute fraudulent conduct (Exhibit 5.4). Likewise, many state agencies have begun to prosecute criminal activity within their borders. The range of sanctions available includes stipulated lifetime bans in the conduct of internet commerce, civil judgments, forfeiture of property, and referrals for criminal prosecution. In 2009, the FTC issued new guidelines prohibiting online reviews that do not disclose the relationship between the reviewer and the owner of the product reviewed. Similar initiatives have been undertaken by authorities of other countries.

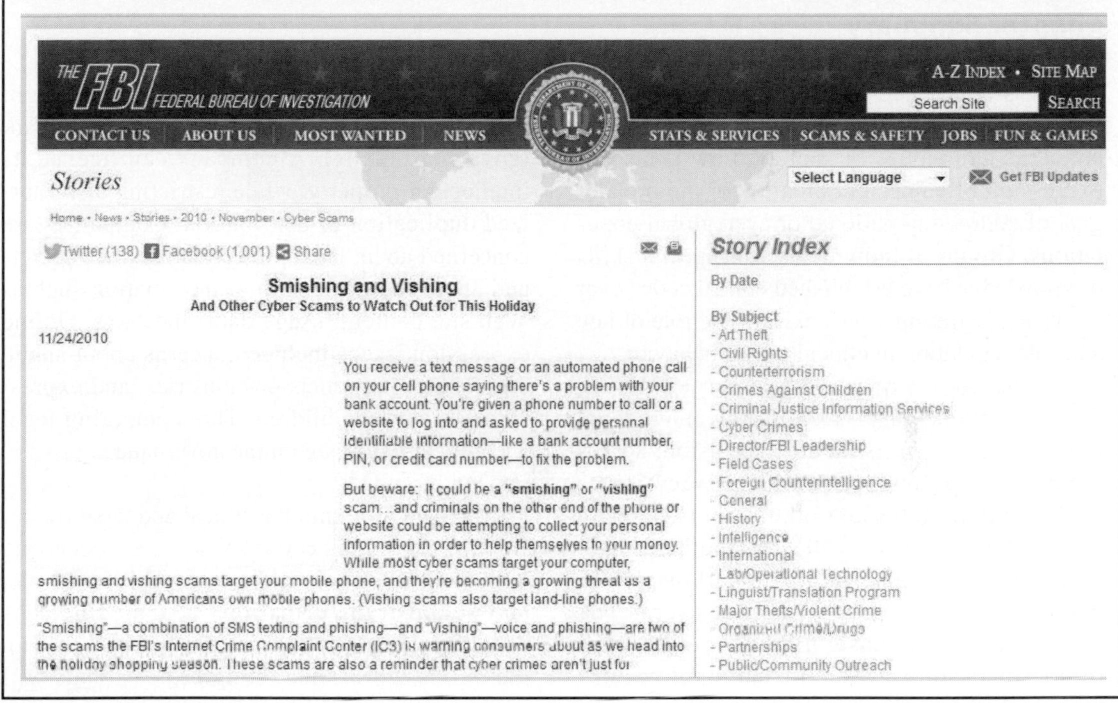

THE FBI FEDERAL BUREAU OF INVESTIGATION

A-Z INDEX • SITE MAP

Search Site SEARCH

CONTACT US | ABOUT US | MOST WANTED | NEWS | STATS & SERVICES | SCAMS & SAFETY | JOBS | FUN & GAMES

Stories

Select Language Get FBI Updates

Home • News • Stories • 2010 • November • Cyber Scams

Twitter (138) Facebook (1,001) Share

Smishing and Vishing

And Other Cyber Scams to Watch Out for This Holiday

11/24/2010

You receive a text message or an automated phone call on your cell phone saying there's a problem with your bank account. You're given a phone number to call or a website to log into and asked to provide personal identifiable information—like a bank account number, PIN, or credit card number—to fix the problem.

But beware: It could be a **"smishing"** or **"vishing"** scam…and criminals on the other end of the phone or website could be attempting to collect your personal information in order to help themselves to your money. While most cyber scams target your computer, smishing and vishing scams target your mobile phone, and they're becoming a growing threat as a growing number of Americans own mobile phones. (Vishing scams also target land-line phones.)

"Smishing"—a combination of SMS texting and phishing—and "Vishing"—voice and phishing—are two of the scams the FBI's Internet Crime Complaint Center (IC3) is warning consumers about as we head into the holiday shopping season. These scams are also a reminder that cyber crimes aren't just for

Story Index

By Date

By Subject
- Art Theft
- Civil Rights
- Counterterrorism
- Crimes Against Children
- Criminal Justice Information Services
- Cyber Crimes
- Director/FBI Leadership
- Field Cases
- Foreign Counterintelligence
- General
- History
- Intelligence
- International
- Lab/Operational Technology
- Linguist/Translation Program
- Major Thefts/Violent Crime
- Organized Crime/Drugs
- Partnerships
- Public/Community Outreach

EXHIBIT 5.4 FBI Warns against Cyber Scams *Source*: www.fbi.gov/

The basis of fraud is usually incomplete or false information. Thus, a consumer's ability to evaluate online material is essential. Promotion and adherence to codes of ethics, such as those promulgated by the AMA, are one means of inspiring consumer confidence. Codes may include requirements that members refrain from doing business with questionable clients or third parties. Many online and real-world businesses, particularly those within the finance and credit industry, require that their licensees follow strict legal and ethical protocols and may withdraw affiliation in cases of violation.

Although the establishment and enforcement of laws are necessary responses to the problem of fraud, the internet's global reach continues to frustrate even the most comprehensive of enforcement plans. On the other hand, a weakness of purely private regulation is the potential for conflicts of interest or less than rigorous enforcement of rules. Recent revelations of unpunished violations by members of eTrust,[84] the internet's largest nongovernmental privacy watchdog, have caused many to wonder whether industry-based enforcement is truly possible.

Even though law must frequently play a reactive role, the conditions of the online environment create unique opportunities for marketing professionals to educate potential victims of fraud. Professional associations have particular abilities to establish sites that outline and explain minimum standards and consumer protections. They may also serve as clearinghouses, reporting unethical or illegal conduct. Even within the information-rich environment of the internet, online knowledge continues to be a need without limits.

Chapter Summary

Ethics is concerned with the values and practices of professionals and experts, as well as the concerns and values of society. Law is also an expression of values but created for the broader goal of addressing national or even global populations. Groups of individuals with special skills or knowledge have established ethical codes over the years. Differing views exist of the role of law and self-regulation in ethical online behavior.

The notion of privacy emerged during the twentieth century as a key ethical and legal concern. Key aspects include seclusion, access control, and autonomy. Online privacy issues in the United States and other countries relate to how data should be collected and used. U.S. firms can participate in a safe harbor plan to protect data from EU's internet users. The FTC set forth five basic norms for ethical use of consumer information, including provisions for user notice, consent, access, security, and enforcement.

Intangible or intellectual property is protected through three basic legal mechanisms: patent law (covering inventions), copyright (covering the expression of ideas), and trademark (covering brands). A company can license its intellectual property, while restricting unauthorized duplication or distribution. Companies are concerned about legal protection for trade secrets and about the ownership of information such as Web site content, usage data, and facts. Online expression issues include concerns about spam, criticisms of products or industries, and expression directed to children. Three emerging legal and ethical issues are online governance, jurisdiction, and fraud.

Changes within the ethical and legal framework of networked communication are occurring with swiftness equal to the technical, economic, and social transformations this medium has brought about. As critical participants within the online world, marketing professionals will not only be required to remain well informed of regulations and accepted practices but will also be increasingly called upon to contribute to the global dialogue on electronic spaces.

Exercises

REVIEW QUESTIONS

1. Define ethics and law and show how they are different and similar.
2. What are some of the threats to internet user privacy?
3. According to the FTC, what are the minimum requirements for ethical use of consumer information?
4. Evaluate the current trend and direction in copyright law.
5. How does copyright differ from patent and trademark law?
6. Which types of trademark dilution exist and how do they differ from each other?
7. What does it mean to clickwrap a license?
8. What are the NET Act and the DMCA?
9. What is the doctrine of first sale? How should it be applied online?
10. What is the doctrine of fair use and how should it be applied online?
11. What are the EU safe harbor provisions and why are they important for U.S. companies doing business in Europe?

DISCUSSION QUESTIONS

12. **Copyright Infringement.** Do you think education is the answer for stopping copyright infringements in other countries? Why or why not? If yes, what type of education might work?
13. **Copyright Infringement.** If you were a famous recording artist what would you do to protect your income from piracy in the United States (illegal sharing and downloading of your music)?
14. Is it better to regulate industry via laws or let industry self-regulate? Support your claim.
15. Which is more ethically problematic: attacking a former employer via online discussion or making the same attack by e-mailing current employees?
16. Deep linking takes place regularly over the internet. Anytime a Web page links to another site and bypasses the homepage of that site, deep linking occurs. Should this practice be allowed? Explain your position.
17. Framing takes place regularly over the internet. To see an example of framing, look up information at AskJeeves (ask.com). Should framing be allowed? Support your claim.
18. The CEO of Amazon.com publicly questioned the advisability of granting patents for business processes such as his company's 1-Click ordering process. Do such patents put a chilling effect on the expansion of e-commerce? Justify your position.
19. Which court should have jurisdiction over the internet? Why?

WEB ACTIVITIES

20. Visit google.com/doubleclick/. Do you find any of its services ethically objectionable? Why or why not?
21. Visit the FTC site at ftc.gov. What cases is it currently reviewing that relate to the internet? Describe several and give your opinion about how the agency should rule.
22. The World Wide Web is a borderless medium that spans the globe. Check out the Internet Law and Policy Forum at ilpf.org. What attempts have been made to regulate the internet both domestically and overseas? What kind of problems may arise concerning jurisdiction and enforcement in a medium that spans the globe? Jurisdiction is typically based on the location of Web servers. What recourse do users have if they are wronged in activities such as gambling and if the servers are physically located outside the United States? What about spam outside the United States?
23. Visit epinions.com and amazon.com and review privacy policies of epinion and Amazon. What sorts of things do they cover? Which one has a better policy in your opinion?

Notes*

*Notes: See Appendix C for the footnoted references in this chapter.

PART 3

E-Marketing Strategy

CHAPTER

6

E-Marketing Research

The main objective of this chapter is to help you develop an understanding of why and how e-marketers conduct online marketing research and how they turn data into marketing knowledge that provides insight into marketing activities. You will learn about the three categories of internet data sources, consider the ethics of online research, look at key database analysis techniques, and explore the use of knowledge management metrics.

After reading this chapter, you will be able to:

- Identify the three main sources of data that e-marketers use to address research problems.
- Discuss how and why e-marketers need to check the quality of research data gathered online.
- Explain why the internet is used as a contact method for primary research and describe the main internet-based approaches to primary research.
- Describe several ways to monitor the Web for gathering desired information.
- Contrast client-side data collection, server-side data collection, and real-space approaches to data collection.
- Explain the concepts of big data and cloud computing.
- Highlight four important methods of analysis that e-marketers can apply to information in the data warehouse.

trend

- In a world that is completely dependent on being connected, with ever-more powerful and exciting devices, it's now actually extended battery life and charging options that are the holy grail for anyone addicted to an online lifestyle.

trend watching .com

impact

- ***Power Felt*** (not yet in mass production) is a flexible thermoelectric fabric that can be attached to a smartphone. The device is then able to convert body heat into power, and charge the battery whilst inside its owner's pocket.

The Purina Story

Nestlé Purina PetCare Company knows with certainty that Purina Web sites and online advertising increase offline buying. How? Through a carefully conducted study that integrated online and offline behavioral data.

Switzerland-based Nestlé S.A. purchased the Ralston Purina Company in December 2001, gaining a full line of dog- and cat-care brands such as Friskies, Alpo, Purina Dog Chow, and Fancy Feast. The firm manages more than 30 branded Web sites, serving the following markets: consumers, veterinarians/veterinary schools, nutritionists/food scientists, and breeders/other enthusiasts. Nestlé started its inquiry with the following three research questions:

1. Are our buyers using our branded Web sites?
2. Should we invest beyond these branded Web sites in online advertising?
3. If so, where do we place that advertising?

Combining comScore Media Metrix's representative panel of 1.5 million internet consumers and the Knowledge Networks, Inc.'s frequent grocery shopper panel of 20 million households revealed 50,000 consumers belonging to both panels. Researchers created three experimental cells from survey panel members, with two of the cells receiving Purina O.N.E. banner advertising as they naturally surfed the internet: a control cell (no ads), a low-exposure test cell (1 to 5 exposures), and a high-exposure test cell (6 to 20 exposures). Banner ads were randomly sent as exposure-cell subjects viewed Web pages anywhere on the internet. Next, the firm surveyed all cell members to assess the brand awareness of Purina, purchase intent, and advertising awareness. Finally, the researchers compared survey results with offline buying, as measured in the Knowledge Networks panel.

Nestlé's marketers were very interested in the study's findings. First, banner click-through was low (0.06% on average). Second, when study participants were asked, "When thinking of dog food, what brand first comes to mind?" 31 percent of both exposure-cell subjects mentioned Purina. In contrast, only 22 percent of the no-exposure subjects mentioned the brand; this result clearly showed an advertising effect. Further, 7 percent more of the subjects in the high-exposure group mentioned the brand compared with those in the low-exposure group. Next, researchers reviewed the internet panel's Web site-viewing habits of those who purchased Purina products and determined that home/health and living sites receive the most visits from these customers. This information helped the firm decide where to place banner ads. Among the sites frequented by Purina's market, petsmart.com and about.com enjoyed heavy usage and were thought to be great ad buys.

Source: "Does Online Marketing Really Lead to Offline Buying?" 2002.

DATA DRIVE STRATEGY

U.S. marketers spend $6.7 billion annually on marketing research and global spend is about $18.9 billion, according to the Council of American Survey Research. This will buy a lot of data. Information overload is a reality for most consumers and marketers alike. It is an especially difficult problem for marketing decision makers as they gather survey results, Web analytics, call center data, product sales information, secondary data about competitors, social media conversations, and much more. The problem is compounded by automated data gathering at Web sites, brick-and-mortar points of purchase, and all other customer touch points. For example, if Susan is following a brand on Twitter, the company can send her a message: "click here and get $10 off your next purchase." When she clicks, she will be prompted to enter her e-mail address and other information prior to receiving the coupon. At this point, her Twitter response and data go into a database. If she purchases on the Web site, this information as well is recorded and thus the database grows with her address and other information. If she calls to ask a question about the product, then that becomes part of her record in a database. This cycle continues as the company gathers more information about Susan and her behaviors. Multiply this by the number of all the other customers and there is a lot of actionable data, ready to help marketers achieve their objectives of building or retaining a relationship and increasing customer value.

What to do with all the data? Purina marketers sorted through lots of consumer data to build a road map for their internet advertising strategy. As you read this chapter, keep one important thing in mind: Data without insight or application to inform marketing strategy are worthless.

Exhibit 6.1 displays an overview of this process. Data are collected from a myriad of sources, filtered into databases, and turned into marketing knowledge that is then used to create marketing strategy. This chapter discusses internet data sources, describes important database analysis techniques, and, most importantly, examines the purposes and payoffs for all this work. Most of these techniques are well grounded in marketing practice; however, new technology brings new applications that are both helpful and confusing for market researchers. Web analytics and performance metrics permeate each of these processes—these were discussed in Chapter 2 and are described in subsequent chapters as they relate to discussions of specific marketing tactics.

Marketing insight occurs somewhere between information and knowledge. Knowledge is more than a collection of information but something that resides in the marketer, not the computer. It can be compared to the difference between teaching and learning. A professor might spout information in a lecture or from a textbook, but it is not usable unless the student ponders over it, relates it to other pieces of information,

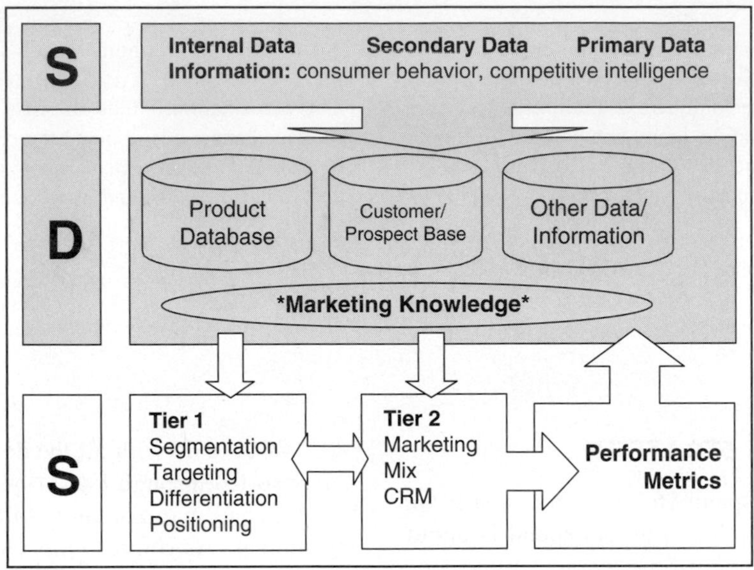

EXHIBIT 6.1 From Sources to Databases to Strategy (SDS Model)

and adds insights that result in acquired and useful knowledge. People, not the internet or computers, create knowledge; computers are simply learning enablers.

BIG DATA

In 2011 a book was published with the title: *Drinking from the Fire Hose: Making Smarter Decisions without Drowning in Information.* We've said it before: Marketers are drowning in data. IBM maintains that every day the world creates 2.5 quintillion bytes of data, and much of this is from the online environment. **Big data** refers to data sets that are so big that they are difficult to manage with currently available software. For example, how can a marketer turn 15 terabytes of Tweets a day into actionable brand tactics?

Data growth rates are astounding, at over 30 percent a year, necessitating an increasing amount of storage hardware space which is only growing at 20 percent a year according to **market intelligence** firm IDC. This presents a problem for information technology managers, and e-marketers must determine how to glean insights from these billions of bytes. In 2012, the capacity of disk storage systems sold came to 6,037 petabytes, according to IDC (1 petabyte is 1,000,000 gigabytes). What does this mean? At about 1GB per feature length movie, it would be enough storage capacity to hold over 6 billion movies. At about 1MB per compressed photograph, it would be enough storage capacity to hold over 6 trillion pictures.

IBM maintains that businesses must manage four aspects of big data: volume (the quantity), velocity (handling time-sensitive data quickly), variety (ranging from social media conversation to customer click patterns and census data), and veracity (is the information reliable and trustworthy?) ("What Is Big Data?" 2012). Several studies about big data in early 2012 found the following ("Marketers Struggle to Link Digital Data to 'Big Data' Picture," 2012):

- 31 percent of marketers would like to collect Web data daily.
- 74 percent of U.S. marketers collect customer demographic data, 64 percent collect

transaction data, and 35 percent monitor social media content.

- 42 percent of marketers said they are not able to link their data to individual customers. This finding shows one difficulty of big data. If the customer relationship management (CRM) systems are not designed with data analysis in mind, then adding the analysis after the fact is difficult, time consuming, and expensive. Therefore, marketers should clearly define their reporting needs before buying into a CRM system.

Amazon makes wonderful use of big data. It tracks page views and purchases history of individual customers and uses that information in real time to offer buying suggestions—see the "Let's Get Technical" box.

The Purina research vignette is a good example of how a firm sorts through hundreds of millions of pieces of data from about 21.5 million consumers, collects even more data, and makes decisions (Exhibit 6.2). Organizations must go through this process with all the data they collect, or their data will simply be an overwhelming bunch of facts and numbers.

MARKETING KNOWLEDGE MANAGEMENT

Knowledge management is the process of managing the creation, use, and dissemination of knowledge. Thus, data, information, and knowledge can be shared with internal marketing decision makers, partners, distribution channel members, and sometimes customers. When other stakeholders can access selected knowledge, the firm becomes a learning organization and is better able to reach the desired ROI and other performance goals.

Marketing knowledge is the digitized "group mind" or "collective memory" of the marketing personnel and sometimes of consultants, partners, and former employees as well. Sometimes the knowledge management technology even allows marketing staff to chat in real time for problem solving, which is why the system also includes contact information. For example, a Context Integration, Inc. consultant working on an e-commerce problem at the client's offices can enter a "911" help call into the Web page and immediately chat with other internal experts to solve the problem. A complete marketing knowledge database includes all the data about customers, prospects, and competitors, the analyses and

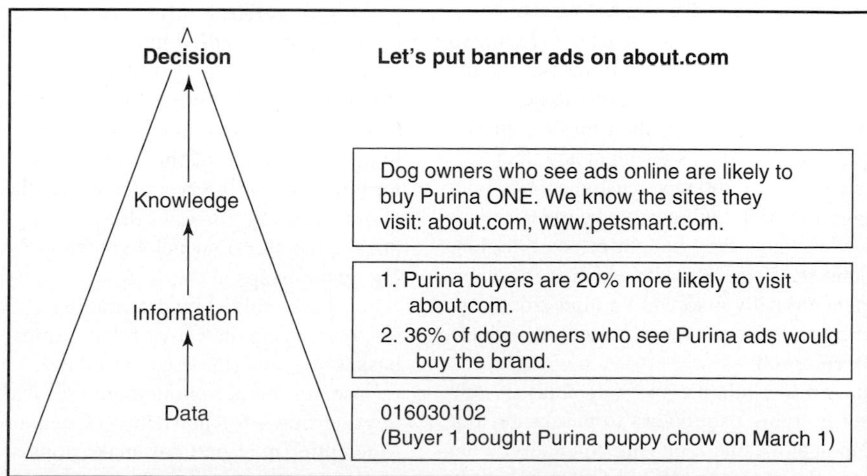

EXHIBIT 6.2 From Data to Decision at Nestlé Purina PetCare Company
Source: "Does Online Marketing Really Lead to Offline Buying?" 2002

LET'S GET TECHNICAL

Data Mining

You've just been hired to an entry-level position in marketing research. Your boss has asked you to find interesting cross-sell opportunities for the new iXT widget. He asks you to base your findings on the database of early adopters. You get the feeling that messing up this assignment could be bad, but you have no idea where to start. A friendly colleague suggests that you contact the data mining guru down the hall and recommends that you earn her good favor with a can of Coke. Rushing to the Coke machine you head off with a smile.

Data mining is the search for information hidden in large databases. It is much like scientific inquiry except that the subject of study is human-made data rather than nature. The larger the database, the more the need for specialized data mining tools to spot patterns and relationships in the data. The tools themselves are quite sophisticated and data miners tend to have advanced degrees—with special emphasis on statistical training.

A common form of data mining familiar to online shoppers is cross sell data. Based on past sales patterns, marketers can predict which products sell well together. They then present this information to the shopper with a friendly note saying something like, "customers who bought the iXT widget also bought…" The larger the database of customers, the more accurate the predictions are likely to be.

Here is how cross sell data mining works. Imagine that Joe buys the iXT widget and the alpha widget. As it turns out 200 other customers buy both widgets together. For each customer, the database examines what items they bought in combination. Then it counts the frequency with which each combination appears. Finally it sorts the counts from largest to smallest and presents future customers with the most likely cross sell.

Amazon has taken cross sell analysis one step further by tying page **views** to purchases. For example, look at a camera on Amazon and you are likely to see the message, "What Other Items Do Customers Buy After **Viewing** This Item?" (emphasis added). Maybe you are on the fence between two camera models. Amazon will tell you what others on the fence ultimately purchased! Amazon does this by counting page views of every customer and correlating those views with purchase behaviour. So as you click around Amazon's Web site, you are creating a massive amount of data which is automatically mined.

Note that the cross sell data is process of fishing for relationships. We are looking at the strength of correlation between *every* combination of variables in the database, which is sometimes called *factor analysis*. However, factor analysis does not show the direction of dependence—which variable causes which. Nor does factor analysis incorporate subtle hypothesis variations to find just the right fit with the data.

But data mining can be more directed—a form of hypothesis testing. The investigator forms a hypothesis (e.g., advertising dollars are best spent on existing customers) and then uses a statistical technique such as regression to test the hypothesis. This process is the foundation of most academic research. However, it is somewhat slow and requires inventive hypothesis formation. Typically tools to carry out this analysis include SPSS and SAS.

More sophisticated still is a data mining technique called evolutionary programming. A computer program adopts the role of a scientific investigator and it forms and tests hypotheses. When it finds a hypothesis that looks promising, it varies it slightly, forming a series of daughter hypotheses. Each of these hypotheses is tested in turn looking for the best match with the data. After churning away for a while, the program reports back to the user on which hypotheses show interesting relationships in the data.

Tasks solved by data mining include predicting, classifying, detecting relationships, and market basket analysis (the cross sell data). The packages themselves are becoming more user friendly, which is good news for marketers. Companies such as Megaputer may one day make sophisticated data mining commonplace.

outputs based on the data, and access to marketing experts, all available 24/7 through a number of digital receiving appliances. Consider the following examples:

- An international technology firm uses Salesforce.com to manage the sales pipeline. When someone downloads a white paper from the Web site, registers online, or sends an e-mail inquiry, it goes into the Salesforce.com software for all salespeople and managers to view—and pick up contact information for e-mail or phone follow-up. The CEO gets a text message for each new lead.
- An insurance firm with 200 independent agents allows them access to claim data from more than 1 million customers. This access allows the agents to avoid high-risk customers as well as to compare claim data with their own database of customers.
- i-Go, a catalog marketer and online retailer, integrates incoming customer service calls with Web purchases, e-mail inquiries, and fax and postal orders, allowing customer service representatives to have up-to-date information when talking with customers.
- Johnson and Johnson, the pharmaceutical company, learned through survey research that contact lens wearers communicate with frequent text messages, so it created a game for mobile phones featuring its ACUVUE brand of contact lenses.

The Electronic Marketing Information System

A **marketing information system (MIS)** is the process by which marketers manage knowledge. The MIS is a system of assessing information needs, gathering information, analyzing it, and disseminating it to marketing decision makers. The process begins when marketing managers have a problem that requires data to solve. The next step is to gather the data from internal sources and from secondary sources, or by conducting primary marketing research. The process is complete when these managers receive the needed information in a timely manner and usable form. For example, Web advertisers need audience statistics prior to deciding where to purchase online display ad space (the problem). They want to know how many people in their target market view various Web or social media sites to evaluate the value of Web ads versus TV and other media ads (information need). One way to get this information is through secondary sources such as comScore or Nielsen//NetRatings. Such companies rate Web sites and monitor traffic statistics by researching the internet usage habits of large panels of consumers. Web advertisers use the data to make effective and efficient Web media buys.

In the past, marketers needing answers asked information technology or information systems personnel what software they had on the shelf. Today, however, e-marketing actually drives technology change. E-marketing changed the MIS landscape in several ways. First, many firms store electronic marketing data in databases and data warehouses. These data warehouses enable marketers to obtain valuable, appropriate, and tailored information anytime—day or night. Second, marketers can receive database information in Web pages and e-mail on a number of appliances in addition to the desktop computer: pagers, fax machines, smartphones, and even basic cell phones. Third, customers also have access to portions of the database. For example, when consumers visit Amazon.com, they can query the product database for book titles and also receive information about their account status and past book purchases. Business customers, channel members, and partners often have access to customer sales data to facilitate product planning. Customer inquiries are usually automated, with personalized Web pages created instantaneously from customer databases. Finally, most firms recognize that data and information are useless unless turned into knowledge to increase profits. Therefore, cutting-edge firms make each employee's project reports, proposals, and data analyses available to other stakeholders in the MIS network. In sum, all the data, the output from their use, and stakeholders' contact information that are gathered via an MIS comprise a firm's marketing knowledge.

The internet and other technologies greatly facilitate marketing data collection. Internal records give marketing planners excellent insights about sales and inventory movement. Secondary data help marketers understand competitors, consumers, the economic environment, political and legal factors, technological forces, and other factors in the **macroenvironment** affecting an organization. Marketing planners use the internet, the telephone, product bar code scanners, and other technologies to collect primary data about consumers. Through online e-mail and Web surveys, online experiments, focus groups, and observation of internet user discussions, marketers learn about both current and prospective customers.

Exhibit 6.3 displays the most commonly used primary data-collection methods, according to a MarketResearchCareers.com survey. Syndicated research involves data collected regularly using a systematic process, such as the Nielsen Company's Television and NetRatings. Companies purchase syndicated research as a part of their secondary data-gathering efforts. Scanner data are collected at the point of sale, such as a grocery store cash register with a universal product code (UPC) scanner—you'll learn more about this in the "Real-Space Approaches" section later in this chapter. All of the approaches in this exhibit benefit from online methods, except for focus group research.

Source 1: Internal Records

Internal records, such as sales data (Exhibit 6.3), comprise one important source of marketing knowledge. Accounting, finance, and production personnel collect and analyze data that provide valuable information for marketing planning. The marketing department itself collects and maintains much relevant information about customer characteristics and activities. For example, logistics personnel use the internet to track product shipment through distribution channels—information that can help marketers improve the order-to-delivery and payment cycles.

SALES DATA Sales data come from accounting systems and the company **Web site log**, retrieved via the Web analytics discussed in

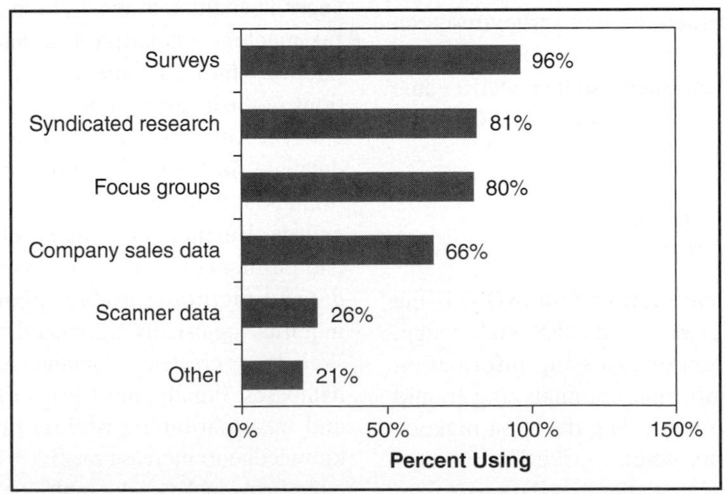

EXHIBIT 6.3 Most Commonly Used Data-Collection Methods
Source: Data from MarketingResearchCareers.com "2011 Annual Survey of Market Research Professionals," 2011.

Chapter 2. When a customer purchases online, the transaction is recorded in a database for access. Marketing managers review and analyze these data to determine conversion rates (proportion of visitors who purchase online) and to see if online ads and other communication are driving sales.

Sales information systems, often using sales force automation software (such as Salesforce.com), allow representatives to input results of sales calls to both prospective and current customers into the MIS. Many sales reps use their laptop or tablet computers to access the product and customer databases both for input and review of customer records while on the road. For example, one office products firm has salespeople from different divisions calling on the same large customer. When the customer has a complaint, the sales rep must enter it into the database and other reps review the customer record prior to making a visit to the same customer. This firm has a rule: If four reps record the same complaint, a warning is issued and they must immediately visit the customer as a team and solve the problem. Sales reps are also instrumental in entering competitive and industry information gained in the field. For cutting-edge firms, marketers enter proposals, reports, and papers written on various topics into the knowledge database.

CUSTOMER CHARACTERISTICS AND BEHAVIOR Perhaps the most important internal marketing data involve individual customer activity. Exhibit 6.4 gives a hypothetical scenario for a computer company that collects data from its customers online and by telephone and uses the information to improve its products. At a minimum, database entries include an electronic list of prospective and existing customers, along with their addresses, phone numbers, and purchase behavior. Firms have used this technique for many years, but new storage and retrieval technologies, and the availability of large amounts of electronic information, recently escalated its growth. For example, visitors to Expedia are asked to register before using its services. This firm has a large database that includes e-mail addresses, customer characteristics, and Web viewing and purchase behavior. Each customer file in a database might

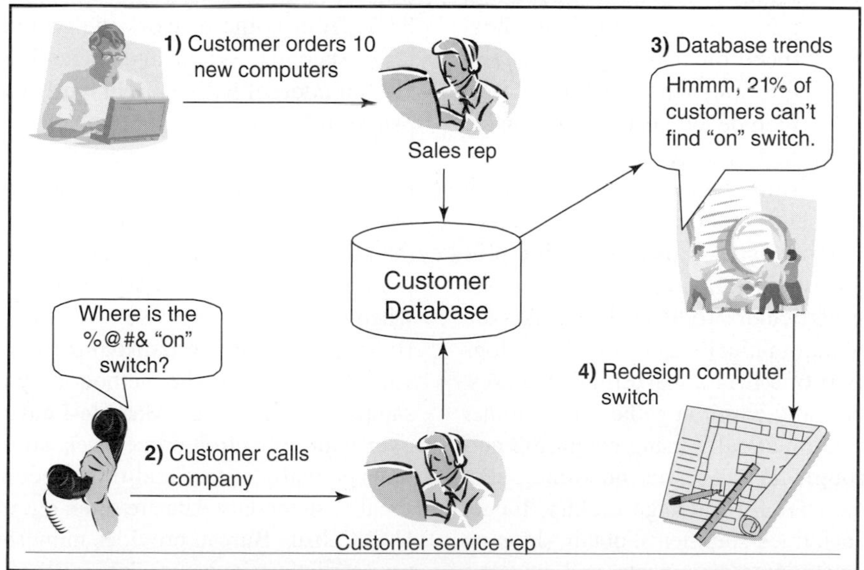

EXHIBIT 6.4 E-Marketers Learn from Customers *Source*: Adaptation of ideas from "Facing up to CRM" at business2.com, Brian Caulfied, 2001.

also include a record of calls made to customer service reps, product service records, specific problems or questions related to various products, and other data such as coupon and other promotional offer redemption. A complete customer record will include data from every customer touch point (contact with the company), including internet orders and e-mail interaction, and product purchases and coupon redemption at the retail store. Data on in-store behavior are gathered through scanning UPCs (bar codes) on products. Firms use the data in customer databases to improve sales rep effectiveness, refine the product mix, identify optimum pricing for individual products, assess promotion effectiveness, and signal distribution opportunities. For example, have you ever wondered why your local retailer asks for a ZIP code when you make a purchase? The retailer adds this information to the marketing database and uses it to decide whether a new store location might be profitable.

Many organizations with Web sites track user movement through the pages and use these data to improve their site effectiveness. They also track how users found the site (via Google or other search engine or from a link on another site). By knowing how users find the site, how much time they spend on each page, how long they are at the site, and what path they take through the site, Web developers can reorganize pages and content frequently and in a timely manner. In addition, companies can identify the Web site users visited immediately before and after the firm's site. This information provides competitive insights, especially if a user is reviewing particular products. These data are all generated automatically in the Web site logs and can be part of a firm's marketing databases. FedEx is especially adroit at gathering customer information automatically using electronic networks. Through its Web site, customers can dispatch a courier for package pickup, locate drop-off points, track shipments, obtain shipping rates, prepare shipping documents, and request a signature proof of delivery in many different languages. All this information can be analyzed by FedEx's marketers for planning purposes. FedEx maintains an extranet for frequent shippers, providing them with individualized rate books and other special services. In addition, FedEx maintains an intranet hub that serves over 20,000 visitors a month for human resources management and workplace and marketplace integration—a thorough system of internal data input for effective marketing knowledge management.

This said, integrating internal and external data is a difficult task because the data are quite different in type, timing, and quantity. In a 2012 survey of global marketers, 43 percent said that integrating internal and external customer data was a top digital challenge ("Global Marketers Say Management Keen on Customer Data Insights," 2012).

Source 2: Secondary Data

When faced with a need for specific information not available in company or partner databases, the e-marketer first looks for secondary data, which can be collected more quickly and less expensively than primary data—especially on the internet, where up-to-date information from more than 200 countries is available 24/7, from home or work, delivered in a matter of seconds. Syndicated research is available via the internet with a credit card sign-up and a password entry.

On the other hand, secondary data may not meet the e-marketer's information needs, because they were usually gathered for a different purpose than the one at hand. Another common problem is the quality of secondary data. For example, when writing this book we often find many conflicting statistics on particular topics—results vary depending on the methodology and survey sample characteristics. Marketers have no control over data-collection procedures, so they should always evaluate the quality of secondary data. Finally, secondary data are often out of date. The U.S. Census Bureau provides numerous population statistics; its heavy data-collection periods occur only every 10 years, and most results will not appear on the Web site until a year or two later. A marketer using data from census.gov

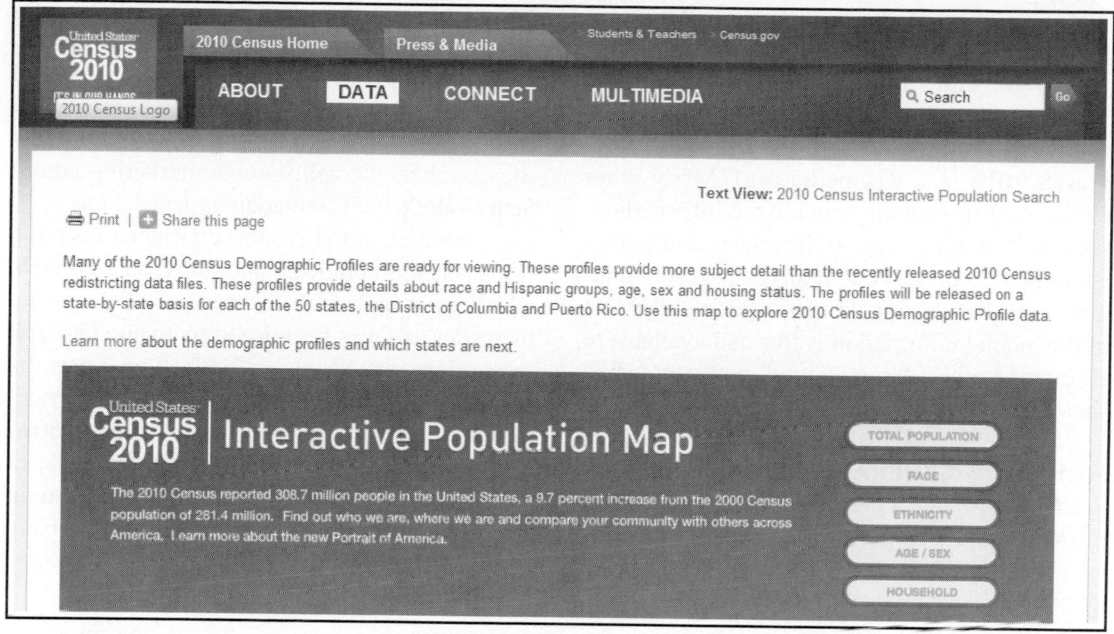

EXHIBIT 6.5 The Biggest Database of All: The U.S. Census Bureau *Source*: census.gov

must read the fine print to see when and where the data were collected (Exhibit 6.5).

Marketers continually scan the company's macroenvironment for threats and opportunities. This procedure is commonly called **business intelligence**. What type of information do marketing managers need? An environmental scan seeks market information about the following:

- Demographic trends
- Competitors
- Technological forces
- Natural resources
- Social and cultural trends
- World and local economies
- Legal and political environments

For example, an organization wanting to understand the characteristics and behavior of the Millennial demographic group can visit the U.S. Census Bureau site, read appropriate articles in online magazines and newspapers, and monitor general research Web sites such as Clickz or sites that target this group (MillennialMedia.com and gurl.com). The following sections present examples of public and private sources of data about the firm's macroenvironment. We then move to secondary sources of data for understanding consumer behavior.

PUBLICLY GENERATED DATA Most U.S. agencies provide online information in their respective areas. The U.S. Patent Office's homepage can explain how to apply for a patent and research pending trademarks. Many global organizations, such as the International Monetary Fund (imf .org), are also good sources of data for environmental scans involving countries other than the United States. Generally speaking, however, U.S. agencies collect and disseminate a great deal more data than do governments in other countries. For example, the CIA's *The World Factbook* is an excellent source of information on internet adoption and telecommunications in every country. In the not-for-profit category, most universities provide extensive information through their libraries, and many faculty post their research results online. Finally, industry- or profession-specific information is available at the sites of professional associations such as the American Marketing Association (marketingpower.com).

Wikipedia, a social media database with over 29 million articles, is edited by over 77,000 anonymous contributors in 285 languages as of March 2013 (see wikipedia.org). Many other wikis exist to provide specialized information, such as Wikihow.com, with articles and videos about how to do just about anything from building a workbench to making a voodoo doll. Most of this public information is free and available to all internet users. A sampling of important public sites is displayed in Exhibit 6.6.

PRIVATELY GENERATED DATA Company Web sites provide a great overview of the firm's mission, products, partners, and current events. Individuals often maintain sites with useful information about companies as well. Politicians and other public figures create sites containing commentary about political issues. An important source of current information and commentary comes from leading bloggers in various industries, such as the well-known marketing author Seth Godin's blog (sethgodin.typepad.com).

Another good resource is large research firms, such as comScore and Forrester Research, which put sample statistics and press releases on their sites as a way to entice users to purchase full research reports. Nielsen//NetRatings posts the top Web sites and advertisers in a survey period. Several large research firms now also offer e-mail newsletters that are sent automatically to subscriber desktops. For e-business information, free newsletters from the Interactive Advertising Bureau (iab.net) and eMarketer (eMarketer.com)

Web Site	Information
U.S. Patent Office uspto.gov	Provides trademark and patent data for businesses.
World Trade Organization wto.org	World trade data.
International Monetary Fund imf.org	Provides information on many monetary issues and projects.
Mohanbir Sawhney and Dave Chaffey mohansawhney.com davechaffey.com	Academicians who generously publish many e-marketing articles on their Web sites.
Securities and Exchange Commission sec.gov	Edgar database provides financial data on U.S. public corporations.
Small Business Administration sba.gov	Features information and links for small business owners.
University of Texas at Austin advertising.utexas.edu/world	Ad world with lots of links in the ad industry.
Federal Trade Commission ftc.gov	Shows regulations and decisions related to consumer protection and antitrust laws.
U.S. Census census.gov	Provides statistics and trends about the U.S. population.

EXHIBIT 6.6 Sample of Public Online Data Sources in the United States

are especially helpful. Although often incomplete, these titbits of information are generally useful in an environmental scan and help marketers decide whether to purchase the full report.

Commercial online databases contain publicly available information that can be accessed via the internet. Thousands of databases are available online covering news, industry data, encyclopedias, airline routes and fares, Yellow Page directories, e-mail addresses, and much more. Marketers increasingly access syndicated data via the internet from well-respected firms such as the Nielsen Media television ratings, the Simmons annual survey of over 20,000 consumers, and the Standard Rate and Data Service (SRDS) listings of media advertising rates and specifications. Students and faculty often access articles from a number of respected media via the university library databases from home—using the internet.

Note that many of these databases are not available on Web pages but are simply electronic versions of articles and other information ordinarily found in the library. Some databases are free but others charge a fee for access.

See Exhibit 6.7 for a sample of privately generated data sites.

COMPETITIVE INTELLIGENCE EXAMPLE

Competitive intelligence (CI) involves analyzing the industries in which a firm operates as an input to the firm's strategic positioning and to understand competitor vulnerabilities. It is a legal activity conducted by many companies. It can be very difficult because companies know others are watching and put out information that can lead competitors astray. Specialists at Fuld & Co. suggest the following intelligence cycle (fuld.com):

1. Planning and direction
2. Published information collection
3. Primary source (human intelligence) collection
4. Analysis and production
5. Report and inform

Web Site	Information
ACNielsen Corporation acnielsen.com	Television audience, supermarket scanner data, and more.
The Gartner Group gartnergroup.com	Specializes in e-business and usually presents highlights of its latest findings on the Web site.
Symphony IRI Group symphonyiri.com	Supermarket scanner data and new-product purchasing data.
Arbitron arbitron.com	Local market and internet radio audience data.
Commerce Business Daily cbd-net.com	Lists of government requests for proposals online.
Simmons Market Research Bureau ExperianSimmons.com	Consumer behavior data.
Dun & Bradstreet dnb.com	Database on more than 195 million companies worldwide.
LEXIS-NEXIS lexis-nexis.com	Articles from business, consumer, and marketing publications.
Hoovers hoovers.com	Business descriptions, financial overviews, and news about major companies worldwide.

EXHIBIT 6.7 Sampling of Privately Generated Data Sources in the United States

The Fuld & Co.'s Web site includes a thorough review of software to aid in CI activities as well as seminars on the topic. Astutely they note that companies should not invest in technical CI software tools unless they have the right processes in place, or it is a waste of money. Just like everything else internet related!

A few sources of CI include competitor press releases, new products, alliances and co-brands, trade show activity, and social media conversations. The internet simplified CI. Companies can observe competitive marketing strategies right on competitors' Web sites and can sometimes catch announcements of new products or price changes prior to media reports about them.

Marketers should be sure to check the Web sites linked to competitors' pages. For this activity, simply type link:companyname.com in Yahoo!, Google, or other search tools offering this protocol. The result is a list of links that may provide insight: Why are these sites linking to the competitor? Another technology-enabled CI activity involves analyzing a firm's Web site log to see which Web page users visited immediately prior to and after visiting the company's site. If, for example, Honda marketing managers noticed that a user visited the Toyota Matrix Web page prior to checking out Honda models, they would gain a consumer's perspective on competitive shopping behavior. In a later section, we discuss online monitoring techniques in more detail.

Third-party, industry-specific sites can also provide timely information about competitive activities. An airline will monitor online travel agents to watch competitive pricing and route changes (e.g., Expedia and Travelocity) and social media sites such as Tripadvisor.com (where travelers post hotel reviews). Company profiles for public firms are available in the Securities and Exchange Commission's (SEC) online EDGAR database as well as at many investment firm sites (e.g., E*TRADE).

Another valuable source of CI comes from user conversation in the social media, as will be discussed in the primary data-collection section later—Facebook has over 900 million registered users, and they each have something to say about brands they like and dislike. Companies can often find consumer conversation about competitive product strengths and weaknesses via keyword searches; but much more sophisticated monitoring is now available with social media dashboards.

FACEBOOK EXAMPLE Anyone can track Facebook engagement metrics using the free Page Data application owned by Inside Network (pagedata.appdata.com). This company updates page statistics daily for the most popular Facebook sites and provides lists of the following:

- Sites with highest total page likes
- Top gainers in likes over one day and over the past week
- Sites with most comments posted, most shares, and most posts

In addition, users can enter any Facebook page and find these metrics. This helps marketers compare their Facebook page with those of competitors and get a quick update on these important metrics for their own site.

INFORMATION QUALITY Secondary and primary data are subject to many limitations; thus, marketers should use all information with caution and with a full understanding of how the data were collected. It is advisable to be as objective as possible when reviewing data prior to using it for making marketing decisions—especially before using information on Web pages. Why? The reason is that anyone can easily publish on the Web without being reviewed by a publisher or being screened for accuracy or appropriateness and because so many different methods are used to generate research data. Special care is needed when dealing with secondary data from international sources because of cultural and data-collection differences.

E-marketers should not be seduced by good design: The best-designed sites may not be the most accurate or credible, and vice versa.

For example, the SEC publishes reports filed by public companies in simple text, spending little of the taxpayers' money to make them look pretty. Two librarians at the University at Albany, SUNY (library.albany.edu), created a fake Web page to show just how easy it is to get fooled (Exhibit 6.8). Interestingly, this site was online for nearly 10 years before the authors had to take it down because so many people "misunderstood" its purpose, thinking it was a real site. The following steps can be taken to evaluate the quality of secondary data collected online (much of this information is from the Albany site):

- ***Discover the Web site's author.*** A site published by a government agency or a well-known corporation has more credibility than one by an unknown author. Sometimes discerning the difference is quite tricky: For example, the same musical group usually has a number of sites—some official and some published by individual fans. A search in Google for *Justin Bieber* yielded more than 600 million results in 2012. Which of these sites are authorized by the singer?
- ***Try to determine whether the site author is an authority on the Web site topic.*** For example, an economist from Harvard University or Merrill Lynch might have more credible information about interest rates than a politician. Furthermore, the university's Web site may be more objective than the financial firm's site.
- ***Check to see when the site was last updated.*** Many Web sites change every day, but some have not been maintained for years. Obviously, the more current the information is, the more useful it will be for decision making. Check the hyperlinks. Although many sites contain occasional broken links, a site with many inoperative links is a site that has not been updated recently.
- ***Determine how comprehensive the site is.*** Does it cover only one aspect of a topic, or does it consider the broader context?
- ***Try to validate the research data by finding similar information at other sources on the internet or in hard copy at the library.*** If the same statistics are not available elsewhere, look for other ways to validate the data. For example, one validation of the number of people using the internet might be to check the number of people with computers (the latter should be larger).

UNIVERSITY AT ALBANY
STATE UNIVERSITY OF NEW YORK

Psychosocial Parameters of Internet Addiction

Rudolph G. Briggs, Ph.D.
Department of Psychotechnology

- Internet Addiction Disorder (IAD) is characterized by seven basic diagnostic criteria, among them increasing tolerance of long online hours, withdrawal, and unsuccessful efforts to control Internet use.
  Ferris, Jennifer R. *Internet Addiction Disorders: Causes, Symptoms, and Consequences.* http://www.chem.vt.edu/chem-dept/dessy/honors/papers/ferris.html
- College officials are increasingly concerned about the growing number of students who are unable to control and amount of time they spend with their computers. These students are being called 'Internet vampires' because they emerge from computer laboratories often at dawn.
  DeLoughry, Thomas J. "Snared by the Internet: College Officials Debate Whether Students Spend Too Much Time On Line." *The Chronicle of Higher Education,* March 1, 1996, 42 (25), A25.
- Alcoholics Anonymous is considering setting up a separate division of their organization to work with people addicted to browsing the Internet.
  Press Release.

EXHIBIT 6.8 A Real Web Page? *Source*: Laura B. Cohen and Trudi E. Jacobson at library.albany.edu/briggs/addiction.html.

In general, it is also a good idea to compare sites that cover the same topic.

- ***Check the site content for accuracy.*** If a site has lots of errors or if the numbers don't add up properly, it is a sign that the data cannot be trusted.

Don't stop looking when the first good screen full of hyperlinks appears. Remember that this site is only one of many potential sites to research, and the list of related hyperlinks is provided as a service—so these sites are not necessarily the best sources for the topic.

What about Wikipedia—is it accurate? Students like to use this site in their research, and many professors believe it is not accurate because all content is created and edited by citizen journalists—anonymous internet users who contribute their perspectives by posting content to online blogs, forums, and Web sites, usually without editorial review. *Nature*, an international science and medicine journal, conducted a study that compared articles from both *Wikipedia* and *Encyclopedia Britannica* for accuracy. *Nature* received 42 peer reviews from a preselected field of science experts and found that Britannica had 2.92 mistakes per article and Wikipedia had 3.86. However, Wikipedia's articles were on an average 2.6 times longer than the Britannica's articles, indicating a lower error per word ratio in Wikipedia (Terdiman, 2005). Wikipedia is fairly accurate partially because there are so many citizen journalists editing the articles and they keep each other from making too many errors. As with all Web pages, however, it is always better to check Wikipedia's original sources and validate the information by looking for similar work by other authors.

Source 3: Primary Data

When secondary data are not available to assist in planning, marketing managers may decide to collect their own information. Primary data are information gathered for the first time to solve a particular problem. Gathering primary data is usually more expensive and time consuming than it is to gather secondary data; on the other hand, the data are current and more relevant to the marketer's specific problem. In addition, primary data have the benefit of being proprietary and, thus, unavailable to competitors.

This section describes traditional approaches to primary data collection enhanced by the internet: experiments, focus groups, observation, content analysis, and survey research. **In-depth interviews (IDIs)** are another important form of primary data collection, but they are better done offline because the questions tend to be less structured and more open ended (of course, the researcher could use a Skype phone call online for this). A subsequent section discusses several other nontraditional primary data-collection techniques only made possible by internet technologies. Whether collected on the internet or offline, all electronic data gathered at any customer touch point (e.g., e-mail, telephone, Web site, grocery store purchase, social network site, and store kiosk) end up in a marketing database and become part of the marketing knowledge to be used for effective planning.

Each primary data-collection method can provide important information, as long as e-marketers understand the limitations—one of which is that internet research can collect information only from people who use the internet, which leaves out nearly 20 percent of the U.S. population, and many more in other countries. As a review, we present the steps for conducting primary research and then discuss each approach along with its particular uses, strengths, and weaknesses.

PRIMARY RESEARCH STEPS A primary data-collection project includes five steps (Exhibit 6.9).

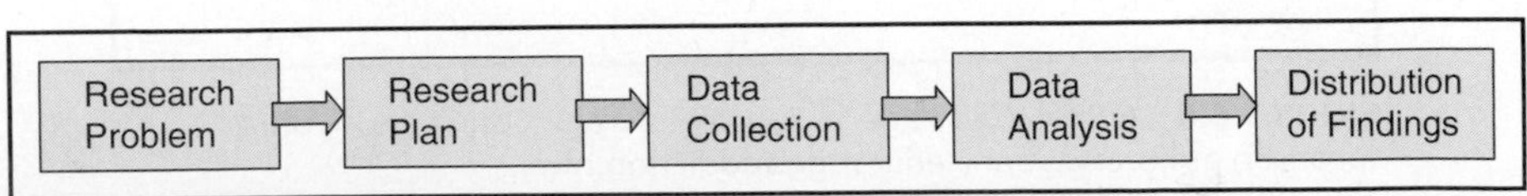

EXHIBIT 6.9 Primary Research Steps

Online Retailers	Web and Social Media Sites
Improve online merchandising	Pages viewed most often
Forecast product demand	Increase customer engagement
Test new products	Increase number of comments posted to a blog
Test various price points	Path users take through the site
Test co-branding and partnership effectiveness	Site visit overall satisfaction efficient?
Measure affiliate program effectiveness	Social media conversation sentiment
Customers and Prospects	**Marketing Communication**
Identify new market segments	Test social network application
Measure loyalty among registered users	Test new promotions
Profile current customers	Optimize site usability and revenue
Test site-customization techniques	Measure display ad clickthrough

EXHIBIT 6.10 Typical Research Problems for E-Marketers

1. ***Research problem.*** As with secondary data, specificity is vital. Exhibit 6.10 shows some typical internet marketing research problems that electronic data can help solve.
2. ***Research plan.***
   - ***Research approach.*** On the basis of the information needed, researchers choose from among experiments, focus groups, observation techniques, and survey research, or Web conversation monitoring, real-time, and real-space techniques.
   - ***Sample design.*** At this stage, researchers select the sample source and the number of desired respondents.
   - ***Contact method.*** Ways to contact the sample include traditional methods such as the telephone, mail, and in person, as well as the internet and other technology-enabled approaches.
   - ***Instrument design.*** If a survey is planned, researchers develop a questionnaire. For other methods, researchers develop a protocol to guide the data collection.
3. ***Data collection.*** Researchers gather the information according to plan.
4. ***Data analysis.*** Researchers analyze the results in light of the original problem. For quantitative research, this step includes using statistical software packages for traditional survey data analysis or data mining and other approaches to find patterns and test hypotheses in databases.
5. ***Distribution of findings/Addition to the database.*** Research data might be placed in the marketing knowledge database and be presented in a written or oral form to marketing managers.

INTERNET-BASED RESEARCH APPROACHES

The internet is a fertile ground for primary data collection. One reason is declining cooperation from consumers when using traditional research approaches. Telephone survey refusal rates are between 40 and 60 percent, and 28 percent didn't even answer the mailed 2010 U.S. Census form. It is difficult to obtain a representative sample of respondents when survey research response rates are so low. Although it is also difficult to obtain a representative sample online, with a large number of consumers online, conducting research using this inexpensive and quick method makes sense. According to a survey conducted by MarketResearchCareers.com, 95 percent of marketers use online research methodologies and 71 percent are worried by the low response rates ("2011 Annual Survey of Market Research Professionals," 2011). Here are four examples of successful online research:

- ***Creative test.*** Leo Burnett, the advertising agency, built a panel of 50 elementary schools for the purpose of testing advertising directed to the "kid" market. Burnett put some advertising posters online and sent e-mails directing students to the Web pages displaying the posters. After viewing the posters, students completed a survey to select the best one. In this test, more than 800 kids helped decide the best creative approach for the poster.
- ***Customer satisfaction.*** British Airways posted a questionnaire on its Web site to gather opinions of company services among Executive Club members. More than 9,000 people completed the questionnaire within nine months.
- ***Product development.*** The University of Nevada, Reno, posted a questionnaire on the marketing program Web site, inviting practitioners and academics to give opinions about what should be included in e-commerce programs at the university level; 140 respondents helped to shape new courses.
- ***Reputation management.*** A large manufacturing company made a small mistake and shortly afterward found negative comments in 90 percent of the first page and 80 percent of the second page of Google search results for the company. These included bloggers talking about the incident and YouTube visitors posting negative comments under the company's videos. Primary research data collection takes on a new meaning when companies, brands, and executives must monitor for internet conversation.

Marketers combine online and offline data effectively and efficiently, as in the Purina example and as done by some brick-and-mortar retailers that also conduct e-commerce. This task involves merging data from older legacy systems, incoming call centers, retailer bar code scanners, government statistics, and many other places that are difficult to integrate. In one example, comScore Media Metrix installed PC meters on the computers of several thousand Information Resources, Inc. (IRI), Shoppers Hotline panel members. Web data include exposure to ads, sites visited, and purchasing frequency and patterns. These data are combined with offline panel data: actual packaged goods purchased at brick-and-mortar grocery stores, as well as the volume purchased, timing of purchases, promotional effectiveness, and brand loyalty.

In addition, primary data are collected online using experiments, focus groups, observations, in depth interviews, and survey research, many of which are discussed in the following sections.

Online Experiments Experimental research attempts to test cause-and-effect relationships, as in the Purina example. Offline, a researcher will select subjects, randomly put them into two or more groups, and then expose each group to different stimuli. The researcher then measures responses to the stimuli, usually in the form of a questionnaire, to determine whether differences exist among the groups. If the experiment has been carefully controlled (i.e., only the experimental stimuli have been varied), group differences can be attributed to the stimuli (cause and effect). Of course, these effects must be tested in other situations and with other subjects to determine their degree of generalizability.

Online, marketers tend to use experiments to test alternative Web pages, display ads, and promotional offers. This is commonly called "A/B" testing: One group sees a particular ad or Web page and another group sees a different version (A page or offer and B page). Marketers use this quite successfully for improving response rates and sales online. For example, a company might send an e-mail notification of two different pricing offers, each to one half of its customer database. If a hyperlink to two different

Web pages at the sponsoring firm's site is included in the e-mail, it will be quickly apparent which offer "pulls better." In another example, when a consumer searches for a particular product on Google the company might randomly link to one landing Web page for half the group and another page for the other half and see which results in better sales.

In one study of 71 companies that conduct online testing, Forrester Research found that 73 percent of respondents experienced increased orders or visits from A/B testing. Forrester also found the top challenges for marketers who used all types of online testing included (1) 71 percent test Web site usability (design/navigation), (2) 58 percent test Web site revenue generation (from promotional offers), (3) 42 percent use testing for customer satisfaction and engagement, and (4) 42 percent test for visitor segmentation and targeting (Stanhope, 2011). Further, 100 percent tested fixed Web sites and 23 percent their mobile Web sites. The internet is fantastic for this kind of testing because it can be done quickly and cheaply and produces measurable results.

Online Focus Groups Focus group research is a qualitative methodology that attempts to collect in-depth information from a small number of participants. Focus groups are often used to help marketers understand important feelings and behaviors prior to designing survey research. This type of qualitative research has grown considerably in the past five years such that 40 percent of market researchers conducted online focus groups in 2011 (versus 81 percent who conduct in-person groups) ("2011 Annual Survey of Market Research Professionals," 2011).

This contact method provides some advantages over traditional focus groups, where all participants are in one room. First, the internet can bring together people who do not live in the same geographic area, such as a focus group with consumers from five different countries discussing online shopping experiences. Second, because participants type their answers at the same time, they are not influenced as much by what others say (known as *groupthink*). Finally, by using the Web, researchers can show participants animated ads, demonstrate software, or use other multimedia stimuli to prompt group discussion.

Conversely, online focus groups can accommodate only 4 to 8 participants at a time while traditional groups generally host 10 to 12. The reason behind the small group size is the difficulty in managing simultaneous, overlapping conversation online. Some researchers avoid this problem by using online bulletin boards and keeping focus groups going on for weeks. Also, nonverbal communication is lost online—in offline groups, facial expressions can be revealing in a way that typed smiley faces do not match. Another disadvantage of online groups is the authenticity problem. Without seeing people in person, it is difficult to be sure they are who they say they are. For example, it is quite common for children to pose as adults online. This dilemma can be solved by verifying **respondent authenticity** and requiring password entry to the group. Technical problems can also stall an online group. Finally, one study compared face-to-face, telephone, and online focus groups and found that subjects used stronger positive and negative words online than in other modalities—typing is different from speaking (Ponnaiya and Ponnaiya, 1999).

In a crowdsourcing example, the Belgium research firm Synthetron conducts simultaneous online focus groups with up to 200 participants each (synthetron.com). Participants type their opinions in response to questions, then everyone votes on the best responses, and collaborative filtering software sends these high-consensus views to another group working at the same time. The voting continues until the most agreed-with opinions percolate to the top and end up in the final report. The following is the user four-step process:

1. Input your idea.
2. Read and evaluate the ideas of others (click on "level of agreement").
3. React, bring nuance, depth, and sharpness to the ideas you like by adding more opinion.
4. Click on a summary tab to reflect on all the best ideas generated thus far in the session.

In a similar example, TechSmith, the company that created the Snagit software for taking high-quality screen shots, used crowd sourcing for research during the beta testing stage of software development. Over a 10-month beta test period, over 400,000 people joined the TechSmith community to discuss and comment on the software (Barker, 2012). TechSmith estimated that it saved $300,000 to $500,000 by conducting research this way. We think it is safe to say that the internet has expanded the definition of a focus group to include an increasingly large number of participants over a specified time period that is longer than the few hours for face-to-face groups.

Online Observation Observation research monitors people's behavior by watching them in relevant situations. For example, retailers videotape shoppers to see the pattern they choose in moving through the store and to monitor other shopping behaviors. Some researchers believe that actions speak louder than words, making customer observation stronger than surveys that record people's statements from memory about what they believe and do. Of course, as a qualitative approach, observations of a small number of people cannot be used to describe how all people might act.

An interesting and important form of observational research, available only on the internet, involves monitoring consumers' conversation in social networks, bulletin boards, and other social media. To get an idea of the value of consumer observation, see Exhibit 6.11 for part of a discussion about the Apple products. There are 1,280 groups on this topic. Such information is extremely important for both Apple Computer and its competitors. Other ways to monitor customers' chat are to provide space on the firm's Web site or to subscribe to e-mail lists on product-related topics.

The citizen journalists post multimedia all over the social media, and companies must now observe to see which of the 181 million individual or company blogs or 6 billion photos at Flickr.com (in 2012) concern their brands, company, or executives. This has become a

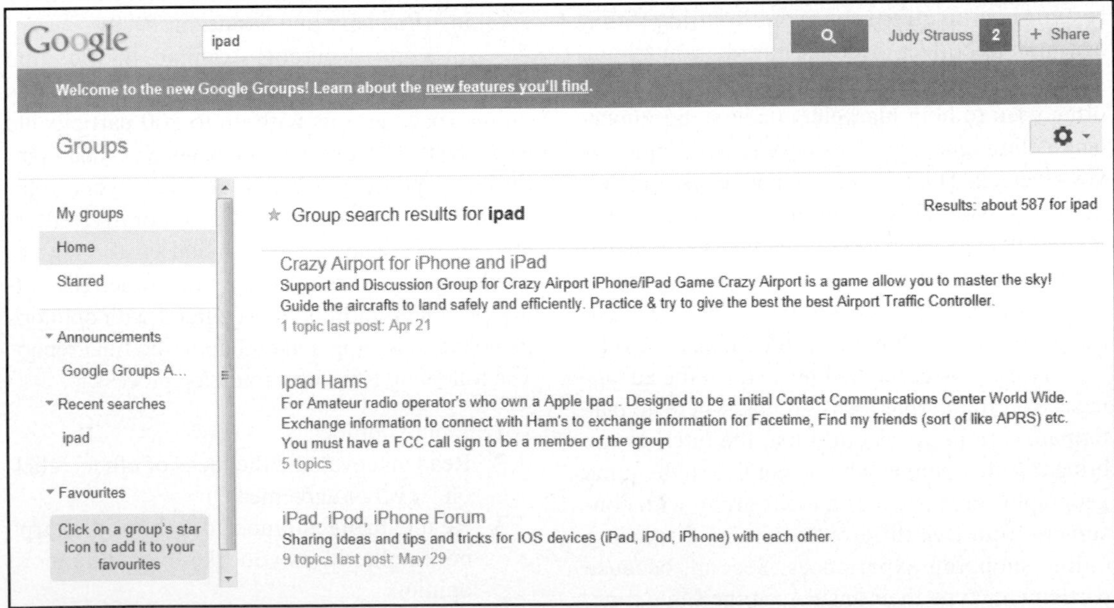

EXHIBIT 6.11 Consumers Discussing Apple Products in Google Groups (formerly the USENET)
Source: groups.google.com.

huge problem because a quick Google search is no longer enough to catch a potentially damaging rumor or competitive announcement as it breaks. For example, an MSN.com reporter posted a story "Is Home Depot Shafting Shoppers?" and within one day he received 10,000 e-mails and 4,000 posts on MSN.com that told tales of poor customer service at Home Depot. The company needed automated tracking to catch something like this in time to make a response and control the crisis. This rapid spread of citizen journalists' content is part of the reason that companies are losing control of their brand images. Sometimes they pay public relations firms or online reputation management firms to help (such as Weber Shandwick or ReputationDefender.com). However, companies can easily set up an automated monitoring system on their own, using e-mail, RSS feeds, or special software.

Google offers e-mail alerts for any keywords of the user's choice—such as a person's name, a brand name, or a competitor's brand name, and so forth. Exhibit 6.12 shows a Google alert in the weekly incoming e-mail for one of the author's names. Users can set up an alert e-mail for the entire Web, blogs, news, videos, or groups and have them sent automatically as they happen, daily, or weekly. Technorati, a search engine that monitors blogs, will also send e-mail alerts. YouTube and other social media sites will send e-mail notifications when users make a comment on the owner's posted media. It also helps marketers to subscribe to e-mail newsletters in their industry so they can watch for competitive and market announcements. This is observation aided by technology.

Really Simple Syndication (RSS) feeds are an **extensible markup language (XML)** format designed for sharing headlines and other Web

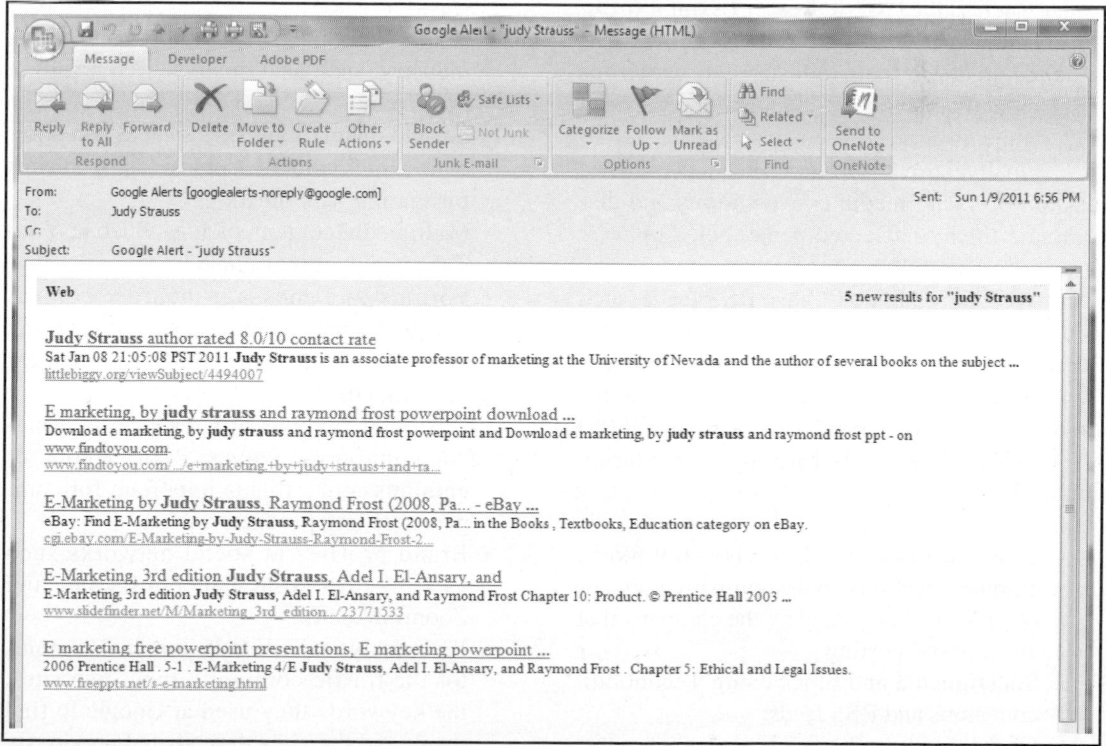

EXHIBIT 6.12 Google Alert for the Author's Name *Source*: Author's e-mail.

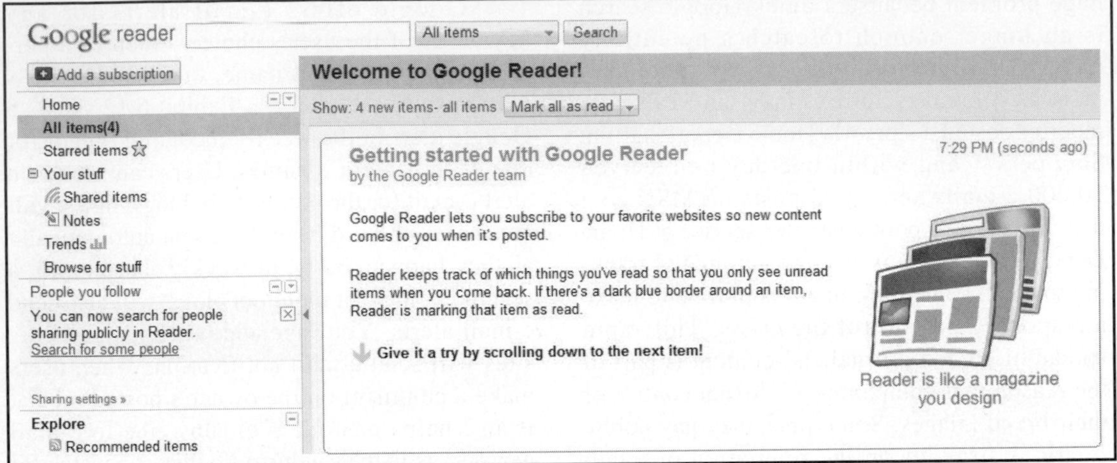

EXHIBIT 6.13 Google Reader Aggregates RSS Feeds *Source*: Courtesy of Google (google.com/reader).

content. When individuals subscribe to a blog or other social media site via RSS, the content goes to readers' desktops as it is published. Customers can read the RSS feeds by downloading a free reader, such as the Google Reader (Exhibit 6.13). This is the way that most companies follow influential bloggers in their industry and watch for posts about their company and brands so they can add comments or react when crises hit.

Finally, special software allows companies to monitor social media conversations and disseminate them to affected personnel. *Copernic Tracker* is especially strong because it will track many Web sites that don't have RSS feeds, such as business profiles (e.g., at the Better Business Bureau), online forums, and competitor Web sites.

Where should companies look online for such conversation? Beal and Strauss (2008) offer these 12 channels for online reputation monitoring:

- Your own content channels—any blogs, comment sections on the company's site, or other Web sites owned by the company that allow users' posting.
- Social media and blogs using Technorati.com alerts and RSS feeds.
- Google's network of video, news, groups, and more.
- Industry news via e-mail newsletters or competitive site monitoring.
- Stakeholder conversations that occur at any other Web site not monitored in other ways.
- Social communities in the company's industry, such as Tripadvisor.com for the travel industry.
- Social bookmarking sites such as delicious.com, which allows users to tag Web sites for sharing with others.
- Multimedia content such as video at YouTube and photos at Flickr.
- Forums and message boards, both in Google Groups and in Yahoo! Groups, and at any Web site in the company's industry that hosts them.
- Customer reviews at sites such as Amazon.com book reviews, BizRate.com, or epinions.com—this is important for companies selling products online.
- Brand profiles at social networks such as LinkedIn.com, Facebook.com, and ZoomInfo.com.
- Web analytics will help companies monitor the traffic coming to their own sites, the keywords they used at Google to find them, and the sites they visited previously to landing at the company's site.

We categorize this nearly real-time monitoring as observational research, but it can also be considered content analysis when social media conversation is analyzed at a later date.

CONTENT ANALYSIS This is the examination of text or images in order to evaluate the communication content. Market researchers have used this technique for evaluating press releases or other text and for examining advertising models or their settings (e.g., what roles do men play in advertisements?). Researchers have used content analysis for a long time to understand the communication context, antecedents, trends, persuasive techniques, and much more. This research method can be quantitative or qualitative in nature and fits somewhere between secondary and primary research depending on the project's goals, but usually researchers will count words or concepts and report quantitative results.

The river of social media conversation online has opened a flood gate of opportunities for market researchers. They can learn many things about internet users through content analysis, such as:

- Consumer characteristics (e.g., Facebook profiles)
- Customer preferences (e.g., company and competitor site traffic and Twitter streams)
- Brand images (e.g., product review and rating sites and Google group discussions)

Solve Media's Brand Tags provides content that helps thousands of marketers to understand their brand images, in what it calls "the world's first brand sentiment network." Exhibit 6.14 displays a word cloud based on a free association qualitative research technique from over 3,000 consumer participants: "describe this brand with any word(s) . . . Purina." Consumers simply register at the site (brandtags.com) and describe any brands of choice in their own words. This is a great way for companies to understand the current image and sentiment of their brands, using qualitative research collected for free by another company.

Social networks, such as Twitter, product review and ratings sites, and message boards, such as Google Groups, are the best places to conduct market research and monitor conversation about competitors, according to Raab Associates. This can be done after the fact in a content analysis or in real time as observation research.

ONLINE SURVEY RESEARCH According to MarketResearchCareers.com, online survey research is now the most used methodology—used by 95 percent of market research professionals and found to be an extremely valuable decision-making tool by 35 percent (see Exhibit 6.15). E-marketers conduct surveys online in several ways:

- Intercept sampling is used when Web site users are browsing or shopping on a Web site and get a pop-up window asking them to participate in a survey. This is a form of self-selection that marketers sometimes call "river" sampling. This is parallel to offline intercept surveys when interviewers stop potential respondents in a public place asking them to answer survey questions. BizRate is a good example of a firm that has built its business using intercept survey research. BizRate presents Web questionnaires to a random sample of shoppers at client sites for the purpose of helping the sites improve their marketing efforts.
- Direct targeting occurs when organizations send invitations to individuals via e-mail with a link to a survey form on the Web. Organizations either draw a probability sample of e-mail addresses or contact specific people from their databases. They can also purchase a list of e-mail addresses of a specific demographic, geographic, or professional group from a vendor (and addresses based on many other segmentation variables).
- Panels are opt-in communities with a large number of people who have agreed to respond to surveys, usually for some incentive (discussed in a subsequent section).

SOLVE media BETA brand tags

My Account / Log out

Tag Brands Explore Brands Guess Brands Search Tags About

Brand: Purina

amazing animal animal food animals awesome
bad beautiful best black car cat cat chow cat food
catchow catfood cats cheap chow clean cool crap crunchy
cute delicious dependable describe describe this describe this
brand describethis brand dog dog and cat food dog chow
dog food dog gone good dog's food dogchow dogfood
doggie doggies doggone good doggy dogs dogs food dogs love it dogs3
don't know dont know dontknow drink dunno eat epic error
excellent expensive famous fantastic feed feeds fine fish
flour food food dog food for animals for cats for dogs for the dogs fresh
fun funny gay god good good brand good dog food good food good
for dogs good for pets good for your dog good pet food good petfood good quality good stuff
goog great great dog food great dogfood great food gross ha ha haha health healthy
healthy pet food hello hi horrible horse feed hot i don't know i dont know i dunno
idk idontknow lame lol love media media error mediaerror meow my dog loves it nasty never
heard of it nice no no idea nutrition nutritious ok okay penis perfect pet
pet food pet foods pet's food petfood pets pets food pig pizza poo poop
popular puppy puppy chow pure purina describe purina describe this
brand wit quality red reliable retarded shit solve stupid sucks sweet
tasty the best thebest trusted trustworthy ugly unknown very good water
well known what wonderful word wow yes your answer youranswer yum
yummy

EXHIBIT 6.14 Solve Media's Brand Tags Word Cloud for Purina *Source*: Courtesy of Solve Media's Brand tags (brandtags.com)

- Bulletin board/groups are sometimes asked to complete surveys or respond to new products, such as in the Snagit example previously mentioned although that was mostly based on pure discussion, versus a structured questionnaire.

Web Surveys Many companies post questionnaires on their Web pages. Respondents type answers into automated response mechanisms in the form of radio buttons (users click to indicate the response), drop-down menus, or blank areas for open-ended questions. One such Web survey was conducted to determine what beverages students consumed, as the basis of a positioning assignment. Exhibit 6.16 displays question types from the Web survey. Sometimes the purpose of these questionnaires is to gather

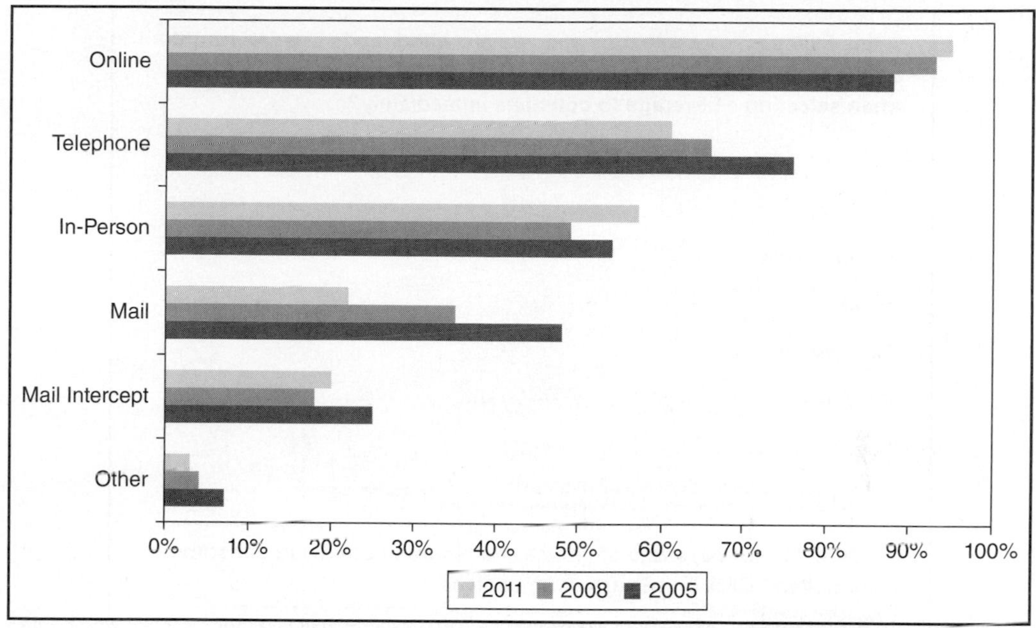

EXHIBIT 6.15 Proportion of Marketing Research Professionals Using Various Methodologies
Source: Based on "2011 Annual Survey of Market Research Professionals," 2011.

opinions from a site's visitors (e.g., Web site registration); sometimes it is a more formal survey research. For example, New Balance asks random Web site visitors to rate the importance and performance of various site features: customer service, navigation ease, product selection and prices, site security, and shopping. Through this process it learned that customers are willing to pay for shipping, which is why the firm added that element to the pricing structure.

As previously mentioned, researchers often create a Web survey and then send e-mail and use other forms of publicity to direct respondents to the Web site. The best response rates come from members of e-mail lists, such as customers and prospects, because they usually have a special interest in the topic. Advertising in the social media (or using poll widgets), or via banner ads and links from other Web sites, will also drive a small amount of traffic to a Web survey. For example, one company placed a display ad on Yahoo! and received 1 percent click-through, which totaled 826 respondents. In general, response rates to online surveys are as good as or better than surveys using traditional approaches, sometimes reaching as much as 40 percent.

Online survey research has many advantages and disadvantages over traditional contact methods. Some are discussed in the next paragraphs; Exhibit 6.17 contains a more extensive list.

Online survey research is fast and inexpensive, especially when compared with traditional survey methodologies, perhaps its most important advantage. Questionnaires are delivered nearly instantaneously worldwide over the internet without paying for postage or an interviewer. Web surveys are created as HTML files and do not need lengthy printing, collating, and mailing time. Those who complete the questionnaires generally do so in the first three days, making the entire process very quick. It is also easy to send multiple reminders if using e-mail invitations.

Some researchers believe that Web surveys reduce errors. For example, contingency questions are those that the computer automatically presents depending upon responses to previous questions. If a respondent answers "c" to question 9,

1. It is 5:00 p.m. on a weekday and you are with friends at a restaurant selecting a beverage. How important are each of the following to you when selecting a beverage to consume immediately?

	Extremely unimportant	Somewhat unimportant	Somewhat important	Extremely important
Low price	○	○	○	○
Energy - boosting	○	○	○	○
Healthy	○	○	○	○
Thirst-quenching	○	○	○	○
Good taste	○	○	○	○
Good social drink	○	○	○	○

Radio button "choose all that apply"

1. What is your beverage of choice at a restaurant/that you consume most often? Click on the arrow for choices.

drop down menu of choices

2. Gender

○ Male

○ Female

Radio button "choose one"

3. Age (please use number, not a word)

Open-ended

EXHIBIT 6.16 Web Survey Question Types

Advantages	Disadvantages
Fast and inexpensive	Sample selection/generalizability
Diverse, large group of internet users worldwide to small specialized niche	Measurement validity/self-selection bias
Reduced researcher data entry errors because of respondent data entry	Respondent authenticity uncertain
Honest responses to sensitive questions	Frivolous or dishonest responses
Anyone-can-answer, invitation-only, or password protected	Duplicate submissions
Easy tabulation of electronic data	Declining response rates
Less interviewer bias	Perception that research solicitation is spam

EXHIBIT 6.17 Advantages and Disadvantages of Online Survey Research

the software can immediately skip three questions and present question 12. This technique reduces the complexity and time involved for respondents. In addition, respondents enter their answers, which eliminate data entry errors found in traditional methods when converting answers from paper questionnaires. In addition, some researchers have discovered that respondents will answer questions more honestly and openly on a computer than when an interviewer is present—and will answer sensitive questions about private matters over the internet. The reason may be that the computer is impersonal and no one is watching what the respondent types.

Sample representativeness and measurement validity are the biggest disadvantages of online surveys over their offline counterparts; however, some researchers think the idea of sample representativeness is no longer possible for any type of market research. Marketers cannot draw a scientific **probability sample** because no list of internet users currently exists—unless the sample is only from a firm's customer list, they all use the internet, and the firm has all the e-mail addresses. In contrast, researchers employing in-person or mail contact methods have population lists and can draw probability samples. Although no public lists of all telephone numbers exists, random-digit-dialing technology solved the probability problem for this contact method—at least until great numbers of the population cut the cables on their land lines and now only have mobile phones. Without the ability to draw a random sample, researchers cannot generalize results to the entire population being studied. Therefore, researchers can send e-mail questionnaires to samples of respondents or put a Web survey online, but they must be careful when interpreting the results. What does it mean when 15,000 online survey participants click off the products they've shopped for online? How does the result relate to all Web users? This problem is one of generalizability. Some firms, such as BizRate.com, compensate for **sampling** problems by offering the questionnaire to every *n*th visitor at a Web site. This technique works well if the firm wants information from a good sample of site visitors.

Online research entails several measurement issues. First, because of many different browsers, computer/tablet/mobile screen sizes, and resolution settings, researchers worry that colors will look different and measurement scales will not display properly online.

A majority of researchers are concerned about declining online research response rates and the quality of online survey data. In one study 71 percent of market research professionals are concerned about low response rates to online surveys ("2011 Annual Survey of Market Research Professionals," 2011). In this survey, the majority of MarketResearchCareers.com survey respondents noted that declining response rates were due to questionnaires being too lengthy and respondents getting invitations too frequently. Their suggested solutions were to shorten the questionnaires and make them more engaging to respondents. As previously mentioned, it also helps when respondents have a special interest in the topic (e.g., you would be more likely to respond to a survey about your favorite music band than one about politics in some other country).

Weighting is one way of handling survey sampling problems—the responses of underrepresented groups in the survey are multiplied by a specific number to bring it closer to the number in the overall population.

Another problem with Web surveys and questionnaires that are not password protected is that the firm has no control over who responds. Whereas the person receiving an e-mail generally keeps it private and responds personally, anyone can answer a Web survey if the address is published. This possibility creates a self-selection bias that is difficult to measure.

A closely related concern is respondent authenticity. This problem affects any self-administered survey methodology, but it seems particularly acute on the internet. Surveys found that anywhere from 20 percent to 50 percent of Web users posed as the opposite sex on the internet, and children often pose as adults online. This situation is not easy to correct and obviously biases survey results. Many researchers are attempting to screen out illegitimate or flippant respondents. One way is to watch for frivolous results such as responses that form a pattern (e.g., each response is increased by one: 1, 2, 3, 4, and so on).

Another problem concerns duplicate responses to online surveys. However, it is easy to remove duplicate responses from a database by just checking for identical responses submitted near the same time.

Finally, when researchers use e-mail to solicit responses to Web-based questionnaires, it may be perceived as spam unless the sample consists of a firm's customers.

Note that survey forms are not nearly as easy to create as most other types of Web pages. Also, in order to make the form interactive, developers must place a special program on the Web server (CGI or Perl script) that "tells" the server what to do with the respondent information. A few enterprising firms created software to assist in this process, such as the Web-based surveymonkey.com. Google Forms software allows researchers to create a free Web form survey nearly as simply as other Web page authoring tools or word-processing software. Researchers then put the Web page on their site, and all the interactive work is done on the Google server. Survey responses can be downloaded by the researcher as tables or data appropriate for analysis in spreadsheet or statistical software.

ONLINE PANELS Most researchers are using online panels to combat sampling and response problems. Also called **opt-in** communities, **online panels** include a group of people who have agreed to be the subject of marketing research. Usually they are paid and often receive free products as well. Panel participants complete extensive questionnaires after being accepted, so that researchers have information about their characteristics and behavior. This way, when panel members are asked to test a product, are given questionnaires to complete, or are sent coupons and other promotions, researchers can correlate results with already collected demographic data. In turn, the research firms can use shorter questionnaires, thus increasing response rates (i.e., no need for demographic questions). An advantage of large panels such as those in the Purina opening story is that smaller groups of members can be targeted based on their behavior or demographics.

Firms with large online panels include America Consumer Opinion, Nielsen//NetRatings, NPD Group, Harris Interactive, and Digital Marketing Services (DMS). For example, Harris Interactive has over 40 specialty panels, from affluent people to physicians, wireless users, and those with chronic illnesses.

In one interesting use of its 100,000-member panel, Nielsen//NetRatings tracked panel viewership of online advertising. This was achieved by asking the ad agency to place a tracking pixel in the ad. A pixel is one dot of light on a computer or television screen, so this was invisible to the ad viewer. Nielsen put a cookie on each panel member's computer that indicated when the pixel was viewed—that is, who was viewing the ad. After correlating the cookie information with panel demographics, Nielsen was able to build a complete profile of the online ad viewers (Bruner and Koegel, 2005).

On the downside, panel access is often more expensive for client firms than traditional methods of sample generation. Also, because research firms sometimes recruit panel members in nonscientific ways, the generalizability of survey results from panels is questionable. Large numbers of respondents and high response rates minimize this problem, however. One other problem with panels is that they are paid for their participation and sometimes cheat to get the participation money in three different ways:

1. Cheat by answering "yes" to questions they think will keep them from getting terminated mid-survey because of not using particular products or other screening criteria (they don't want to be terminated because they don't get paid).
2. Inattentive behavior so they can get through it quickly—for example, just clicking random answers without reading carefully, or

"straight lining" (clicking all of one number for several questions in a row). Researchers check this by setting traps, such as oppositely worded questions that respondents must closely read to avoid giving inconsistent responses.

3. Closely related to inattention is speeding. Researchers detect this by timing how long it takes respondents to answer a survey, and if they took 5 minutes on a 15-minute questionnaire, their responses are not counted.

ETHICS OF ONLINE RESEARCH Many companies conducting marketing research on the Web have considered its "gift culture" and decided to give something to respondents as appreciation for participating. With traditional research, respondents are sometimes offered a nominal fee (e.g., $5) to complete a questionnaire, which increases the response rate. Some researchers draw names from those who submit responses, offering them free products or cash. Others donate money to charities selected by respondents (e.g., $3 to one of three charities listed on the Web page for each questionnaire submitted). Many post the entire results in downloadable form, and most provide at least some results on the Web sites after the survey period is completed.

Marketers face several other ethical concerns regarding survey research on the internet.

1. Respondents are increasingly upset at getting unsolicited e-mail requesting survey participation.
2. Some researchers "harvest" e-mail addresses from internet forums and groups without permission. Perhaps, this practice is analogous to gathering names from a telephone book, but some people object because consumers are not posting with the idea of being contacted by marketers.
3. Some companies conduct "surveys" for the purpose of building a database for later solicitation. Ethical marketers clearly mark the difference between marketing research and marketing promotion and do not sell under the guise of research.
4. Privacy of user data is a huge issue in this medium, because it is relatively easy and profitable to send electronic data to others via the internet. Farhad Mohit, CEO at BizRate, notes that many others want the data they collect. According to Mohit, guarding respondents' data privacy is central to the success of BizRate.

These and other concerns prompted ESOMAR, the European Society for Opinion and Marketing Research, to include guidelines for internet research in its International Code of Marketing and Social Research Practice. ESOMAR had more than 4,900 members in over 130 countries in 2012 (esomar.org).

In spite of serious shortcomings, the internet is critical for conducting primary research and is an important tool for marketers. However, when using any primary or secondary data, marketers must evaluate their quality carefully and apply it accordingly.

OTHER TECHNOLOGY-ENABLED APPROACHES

The internet is an excellent place to observe user behavior because the technology automatically records actions in a format that can be easily, quickly, and mathematically manipulated for analysis. Computer client-side and server-side automated data collection are two technology-enabled approaches deserving special emphasis. Real-time profiling at Web sites is one particularly powerful server-side approach. These techniques are especially interesting and unusual because they did not exist prior to the internet, and because they allow marketers to make quick and responsive changes in Web pages, promotions, and pricing.

Client-Side Data Collection

Client-side data collection refers to collecting information about consumer click behavior right at the user's PC. One approach is to use cookies when a user visits a Web site. Cookie files are quite helpful, and even necessary, for e-commerce and other internet activities. Some cookies help marketers present appropriate promotions and Web pages to individual users using database information. Exhibit 6.18 displays an example of the sales funnel. It shows how cookie files and Web site logs can identify the number of visitors to a Web site that view desired pages and eventually purchase the product. As discussed in Chapter 2, these numbers are a result of Web analytics software.

One important client-side data-collection method involves measuring user patterns by installing a PC meter on the computers of a panel of users and tracking the user clickstream. This approach is similar to the ACNielsen "people meter" used on TV sets to determine ratings for various programs.

Server-Side Data Collection

Web analytics uses site log software to generate reports on numbers of users who view each page, the location of the site visited prior to the firm's site, and what users buy at a site—fundamental elements in **server-side data collection**. For example, because of its online registration requirement, Expedia can track visitors' ticket purchases, browsing patterns, and how often they visit the site. It uses this information to send special offers to customers as well as to offer services such as the fare watcher. Amazon.com, through collaborative filtering software, keeps track of books ordered by customers and makes recommendations based on customers' trends in its database. These observational data help firms improve online marketing strategies, sell advertising, and produce more effective Web sites. See Exhibit 6.19 for an example of the clickstream at FTC.gov that Web analytics software would help analyze. Armed with these data, the FTC can determine which pages are the most relevant to citizens and should remain as prominent banner links from its homepage.

Increasingly, firms use server-side data to make frequent changes in Web pages and promotional offers. **Real-time profiling** occurs when special software tracks a user's movements through a Web site, and then compiles and reports on the data at a moment's notice. Also known as "tracking user clickstream in real time," this approach allows marketers to analyze consumer online behavior and make instantaneous adjustments to a site's promotional offers and Web pages. Real-time profiling is not cheap—one estimate puts the software at $150,000 to start and $10,000 a month thereafter. The ability to predict future behavior based on past behavior and, thus, offer customized Web pages to appropriate customers while they are visiting a Web site can, however, pay off handsomely.

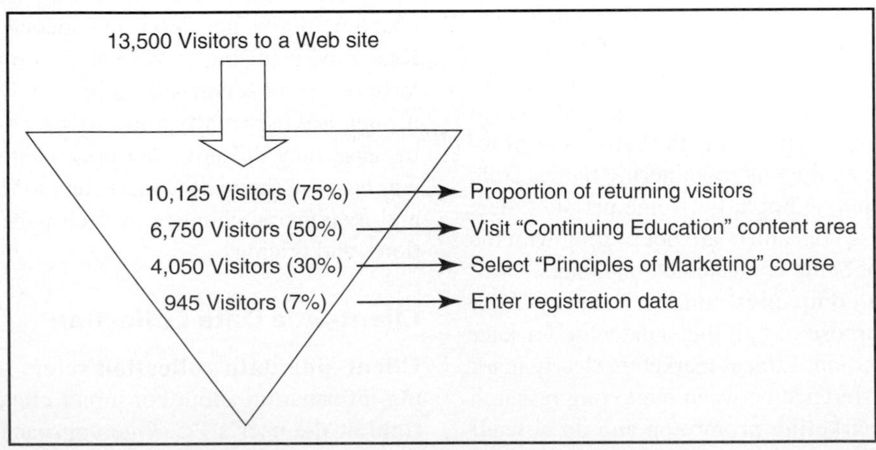

EXHIBIT 6.18 Web Site Logs Assist in Sales Funnel Analysis

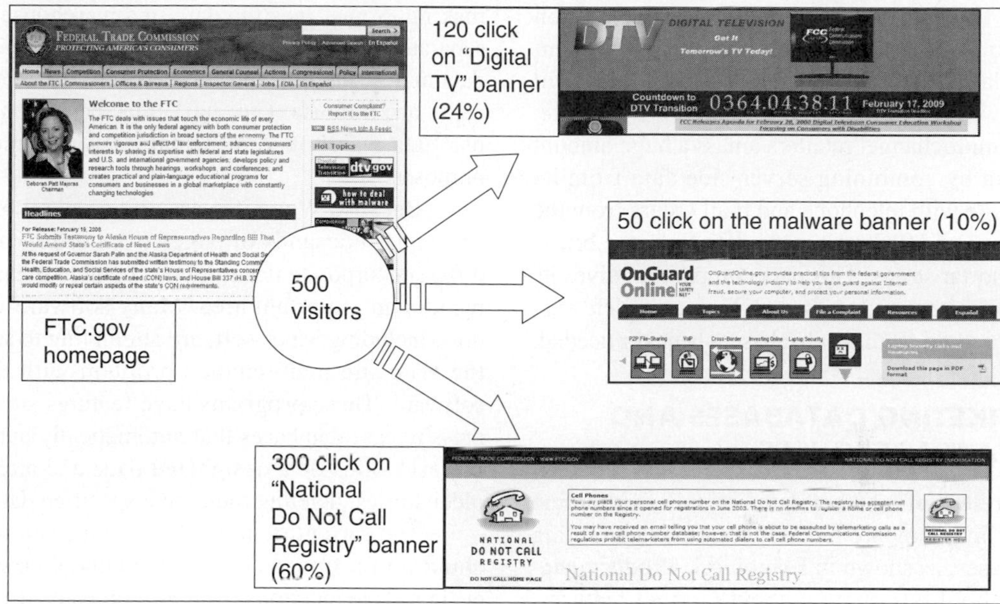

EXHIBIT 6.19 Following the Clickstream at FTC.gov *Source*: ftc.gov.

REAL-SPACE APPROACHES

Real-space primary data collection refers to technology-enabled approaches to gather information offline that is subsequently stored and used in marketing databases. The most important real-space techniques are bar code scanners and credit card terminals at brick-and-mortar retail stores, although computer entry by customer service reps while talking on the telephone with customers might also be included here.

Real-space primary data collection occurs at offline points of purchase. Offline data collection is important for e-marketing because these data, when combined with online data, paint a complete picture of consumer behavior for individual retail firms. Smart card and credit card readers, interactive point of sale (iPOS) machines, and bar code scanners are mechanisms for collecting real-space consumer data. Even though the UPC, also known as the bar code, has been in grocery stores since 1974, its use has grown to the point where such codes are now scanned billions of times a day. Product sales data gathered by scanning the UPC at retail stores are currently used primarily for inventory management. As UPC data go from the cash register into the computer, the software reduces accounting inventory levels automatically and sends communication to suppliers for replenishment of physical goods. This immediate inventory updating is quite efficient for retailers, wholesalers, and manufacturers. It is also an example of the big data problem discussed earlier in this chapter—how to store, analyze, and take action on that much data?

Catalina Marketing uses the UPC for promotional purposes. This firm places small machines next to the cash registers of grocery stores to generate coupons based on each customer's purchase. For example, if a customer buys Smucker's jam, the machine might spit out a $0.50 coupon for Knott's Berry jam. When the consumer redeems the Knott's coupon, the bar code scanner records it. In the process, Catalina Marketing and the retailer are building huge databases of customer purchases and responses to various offers. If consumers redeem only a small proportion of the Knott's coupons, Knott's

Berry Farm might choose to increase the coupon size to $0.75. Marketers always attempt to combine data collected at the brick-and-mortar retail store with that of the online version of the store. Most multichannel retailers amass a huge amount of data by combining server-side data from its Web site with telephone and mail orders from the catalog and UPC real-space data from the brick-and-mortar stores. This data compilation gives its customer service representatives a complete customer record from the database whenever needed.

MARKETING DATABASES AND DATA WAREHOUSES

Regardless of whether data are collected online or offline, they are moved to various marketing databases, as shown in Exhibit 6.1. Product databases hold information about product features, prices, and inventory levels; customer databases hold information about customer characteristics and behavior. Transaction processing databases are periodically copied into a data warehouse (Exhibit 6.20). Data warehouses are repositories for the entire organization's historical data (not just marketing data). They are designed specifically to support analyses necessary for decision making. Sometimes the data in a warehouse are separated into more specific subject areas (called data marts) and indexed for easy use. These concepts are important to marketers because they use data warehouse information for planning purposes.

Because Web sites are so complex, often including thousands of pages from or for many different corporate departments, content management is an important area. Many software vendors, including Microsoft, are attempting to solve the Web site maintenance problem with their software. These programs have features such as press release databases that automatically put the newest stories on a designated page and archive older stories, deleting them on a specified date.

The current trend in data storage is toward **cloud computing**: a network of online Web servers in remote locations from the company, used to store and manage data (Exhibit 6.21). Authorized employees can access or upload data from any internet connected device. The advantages to companies include no investment cost for server space, no software investment to manage the data, and access to free applications such as those offered by the U.S. Post Office or Google Earth. Of course, the company pays to use the cloud

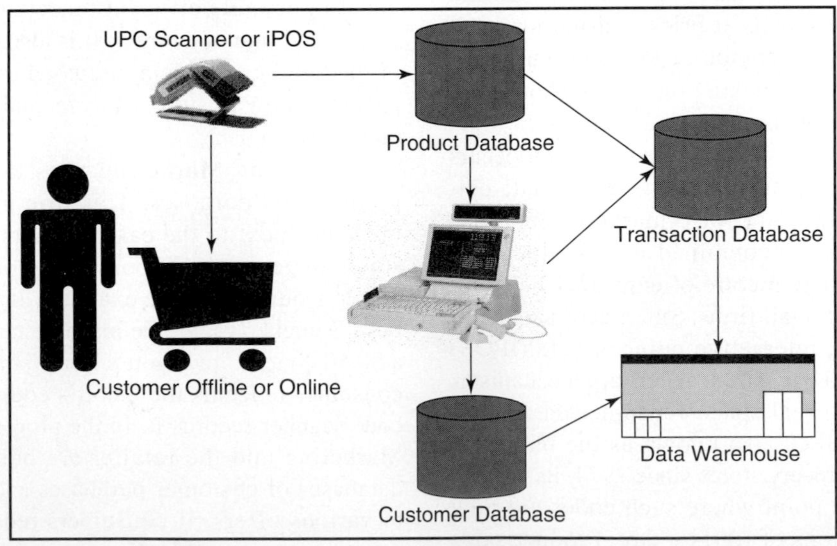

EXHIBIT 6.20 Real-Space Data Collection and Storage Example

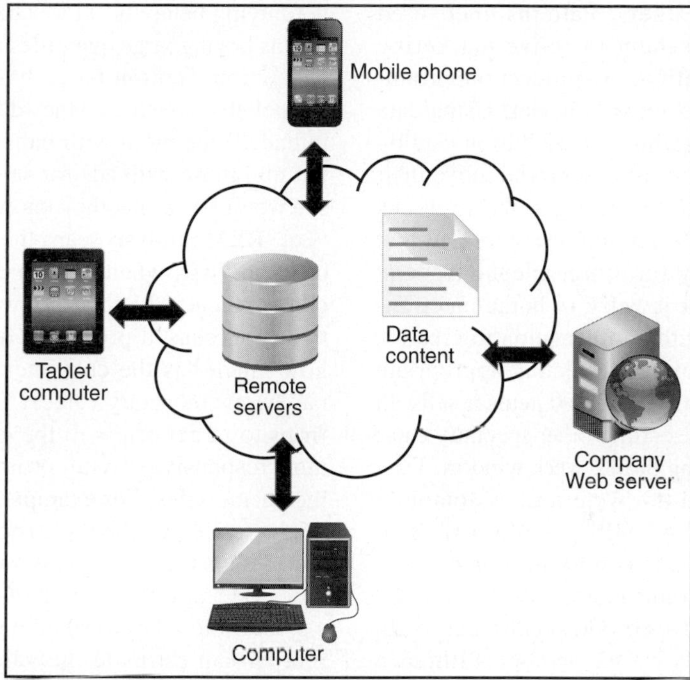

EXHIBIT 6.21 Cloud Computing Allows Internet Data Access Anytime, Anywhere With Any Device

computing service. Amazon.com and Salesforce.com are two of the most well-known cloud computing options for companies.

Individuals can also access cloud computing, such as the iCloud for storing all the data on an Apple device (photos, contacts, calendar, and so forth) and retrieving it on any Apple phone, computer, or tablet. Dropbox.com is another great application for individuals who want to store data on a server and have it automatically synch to any computer. The authors used Dropbox to write this book sharing files from thousands of miles away. When one author updates a chapter, it automatically saves to the other author's computer, via Dropbox.

Note that cloud computing is not just for data storage. Data processing can also take place in the cloud. For example, Facebook and all its many apps live in the cloud, as do Twitter, Gmail, YouTube, and a host of other services. Many multiplayer games similarly live in the cloud.

DATA ANALYSIS AND DISTRIBUTION

Data collected from all customer touch points are stored in the data warehouse or cloud knowledge management system, ready for analysis and distribution to marketing decision makers. Four important types of analysis for marketing decision making include data mining, **customer profiling**, RFM analysis (recency, frequency, monetary value), and report generating.

Data mining involves the extraction of hidden predictive information in large databases through statistical analysis (see the "Let's Get Technical" box). Here, marketers don't need to approach the database with any hypotheses other than an interest in finding patterns among the data. For example, a marketer might want to know whether a product's heaviest users tend to purchase more during particular months, or how many people in a social network share applications with others. Patterns uncovered by marketers help them to refine marketing mix strategies, identify new-product opportunities, and predict consumer behavior. Using data mining helped Fingerhut, the $2 billion catalog retailer, discover that customers who move their residence triple their purchasing in the 12 weeks after the move. Data mining also revealed that movers tend to buy furniture, telephones, and decorations but not jewelry or home electronics. Fingerhut used this information to create a special Mover's Catalog, selecting appropriate products from among the 15,000 items it sells. In addition, it stopped sending other specialty catalogs to movers during the 12-week window. Data mining also helped the American Automobile Association's (AAA) Mid-Atlantic office to streamline its marketing communication process, decreasing the amount mailed by 96 percent, from 1.2 million to 40,000 pieces per year. This reduced costs by 92 percent without a membership-enrolment decline.

Customer profiling uses data warehouse information to help marketers understand the characteristics and behavior of specific target groups. Through this process, marketers can really understand who buys particular products and how they react to promotional offers and pricing changes. Some additional uses of customer profiling include the following:

- Selecting target groups for promotional appeals.
- Discovering the best way to engage customers in social media.
- Finding and keeping customers with a higher lifetime value to the firm.
- Understanding the important characteristics of heavy product users.
- Directing cross-selling activities to appropriate customers.
- Reducing direct-mailing costs by targeting high-response customers.

Sometimes the predictive nature of data mining can cross the line of invasion of privacy. For example, Target is able to predict when a woman is pregnant by looking at changes in her buying behavior. For example, she suddenly begins buying large quantities of unscented soaps and lotions, cotton balls, hand sanitizers, and washcloths. So what do they do? They target (pun intended) the mom with baby product coupons, but mix those with ads for say a lawn mower so she won't know that they know.

RFM analysis scans the database for three criteria. First, when did the customer last purchase (recency)? Second, how often has the customer purchased products (frequency)? Third, how much has the customer spent on product purchases (monetary value)? This process allows firms to target offers to the customers who are most responsive, saving promotional costs, and increasing sales. For example, an online retailer might notice that the top customer segment generated 32 percent of the sales with a $69 average order value (AOV), or $22 of sales per thousand exposures to a keyword ad on Google. Now the retailer can estimate the value of this type of advertising and take steps to reach the top customer segment as directly as possible.

Individual marketing personnel can perform data mining, customer profiling, and RFM analyses at any time through access to the data warehouse and distribute the results to other staff members involved in a particular decision. Report generators, on the other hand, automatically create easy-to-read, high-quality reports from data warehouse or cloud information on a regular basis. These reports may be placed in the marketing knowledge database on an intranet or extranet for all to access. Marketers can specify the particular information that should appear in these automatic reports and the time intervals for distribution, as in the earlier example of a retailer that sends online weekly sales reports to all its managers. Back Web Technologies (backweb.com), HotOffice (hotoffice.com), and many similar firms provide collaborative software that automatically integrates data from both the firm's macroenvironment and its **microenvironment**. For example, when a marketing manager working on a marketing plan saves the data, the system can automatically put the file on the server for other managers to access. Internal data are seamlessly integrated with the firm's Web site, external Web sites, newsgroups, and databases—all with search capabilities. Such software helps firms distribute the results of database analyses. Cloud computing vendors also have this capability.

KNOWLEDGE MANAGEMENT METRICS

Marketing research is not cheap. Marketers often weigh the cost of gaining additional information against the value of potential opportunities or the risk of possible errors from decisions made with incomplete information. They are also concerned about the storage cost of all those terabytes of data coming from Web site logs, social media conversations, online surveys, Web registrations, and other real-time and real-space approaches. The good news is that data storage costs have declined steadily since 1998, and marketers can now buy disk drives for a dollar per gigabyte or online storage for anywhere from $10 to $23 per gigabyte. Online storage has many additional benefits, such as duplicate storage and fast recovery on demand, and more. Two metrics are currently in widespread use:

- ***ROI.*** Companies want to know why they should save all those data. How will they be used, and will the benefits in additional revenues or lowered costs return an acceptable rate on the storage space investment? For hardware storage space (either on site or in the cloud), ROI usually means total cost savings divided by total cost of the installation (Gruener, 2001). Notably, companies use ROI to justify the value of other knowledge management systems as well.
- ***Total Cost of Ownership (TCO).*** Largely a metric used by information technology managers, TCO includes not only the cost of hardware, software, and labor for data storage but also other items such as cost savings by reducing Web server downtime and labor requirements.

For example, Galileo International offers travel reservations and maintains 102 terabytes of data—schedule, fare, and reservation information for 500 airlines, 47,000 hotels, and 37 car rental companies (Radding, 2001). The company booked 345 million reservations in 2000, sometimes handling 10,000 requests a second! Galileo's ROI is simple: According to its owner, Frank Auer, every bit of the firm's $1.6 billion in revenue is a return on its data storage system.

In another example, trucking company Schneider National had enough data to fill ten 53-foot trailers with data disks. But it still could not easily figure out why it cost $0.20 a pound to deliver cars to a Ford dealership in Texas and only $0.17 elsewhere. The firm spent an estimated $2 million to purchase business intelligence software that allowed employees to get quick answers to marketing problems and realized a $2.5 million return on that investment within two years (25% ROI) (Brown, 2002).

Chapter Summary

E-marketers need data to guide decisions about creating and changing marketing mix elements. These data are collected from a myriad of sources, filtered into databases, and turned into marketing knowledge that is then used to develop marketing strategy. Knowledge management is the process of managing the creation, use, and dissemination of knowledge. A marketing information system is the process by which marketers manage knowledge, using a system of assessing information needs, gathering information, analyzing it, and disseminating it to decision makers.

Marketers can tap three sources of marketing knowledge: (1) internal records (such as cash flow, sales force data, and customer data), (2) secondary data (publicly and privately generated, from online databases, and for competitive intelligence), and (3) primary data (gathered for the first time to solve a particular problem). Competitive intelligence (CI) involves analyzing the industries in which a firm operates as input to the firm's strategic positioning and to understand competitor vulnerabilities. Marketers must evaluate the quality of data before relying on them to solve research problems.

Primary data are collected on the internet by nearly all companies. The steps to conduct primary research are as follows: (1) define the research problem, (2) develop a research plan, (3) collect data, (4) analyze the data, and (5) distribute findings. Internet-based research may include any of the following activities conducted online: experiments, focus groups, observations, and surveys. Surveys may be conducted by e-mail invitation to a Web site. Advantages of online surveys are that they are fast and inexpensive, have a broad reach, reduce errors, elicit honest responses, can be restricted to authorized participants, and are easy to tabulate. Disadvantages include poor generalizability of results due to poor sample selection, self-selection bias, inability to confirm the respondent's authenticity, frivolous or dishonest responses, and duplicate submissions.

Online panels are increasingly being used to combat sampling and response problems of online surveys. Although some of these panels are small, others contain millions of participants. Some ethical concerns of online research include unsolicited e-mail, harvesting e-mail addresses from newsgroups, selling under the guise of research, and lack of privacy of user data.

Companies must constantly monitor the social media and other Web sites to identify content about their brands and personnel that are posted by citizen journalists and other stakeholders. New technologies such as e-mail alerts, RSS feeds, and special software make this an easy and automated process.

Marketers use technology to observe user behavior on the user's computer (client side) via cookies and PC meters or the server (server side) via the use of log files and real-time profiling. Real-space data collection takes place at offline points of purchase such as smart card and credit card readers, iPOS machines, and bar code scanners. The data can be used for inventory control and to target promotions.

Data warehouses are repositories for the organization's historical data. Data marts are subsections of the warehouse categorized by subject area. Data from all customer touch points are stored in the warehouse. Four types of analysis are conducted with the data: data mining, customer profiling, RFM (recency, frequency, monetary value) analysis, and report generation. Data mining extracts hidden predictive information from the warehouse via statistical analysis. Customer profiling helps marketers understand the characteristics and behavior of specific target groups. RFM analysis allows firms to target offers to customers who might be most responsive. Sophisticated report generation tools can automatically schedule and publish reports.

Exercises

REVIEW QUESTIONS

1. What are the three main sources of data for solving marketing research problems?
2. Contrast primary with secondary data and explain the advantages and disadvantages of each.
3. Why is big data a problem for marketers?
4. What is competitive intelligence, and what are some sources of online CI data?
5. Why and how do e-marketers evaluate the quality of information on a Web site?
6. What are the strengths and weaknesses of the internet for primary and secondary data collection?
7. Identify the key primary research methods and the appropriate use of each one.
8. What is A/B testing and why is this important?
9. How do marketers turn marketing data into marketing knowledge?

10. What are the 12 channels for online reputation monitoring? Why are they important to a company?
11. What is real-space data collection? Why is it important?
12. Is data mining possible without a data warehouse? Why or why not?
13. What is cloud computing and how does it help marketers?
14. Give an example of how data mining uncovers new knowledge.
15. Identify the steps in a primary marketing research project.

DISCUSSION QUESTIONS

16. **Purina story:** Review Exhibits 6.2 and 6.14. What conclusions can you make about Purina's customers and brand based on these and the opening story?
17. **Purina story:** classify each of the research methods used by Purina, using concepts from the chapter.
18. What online research method(s) would you use to test a new-product concept? Why?
19. What online research method(s) would you use to test the brand image of an existing product? Why?
20. What combination of techniques would you recommend for conducting competitive intelligence?
21. Of the ethical issues mentioned in the chapter, which are you most concerned about as a consumer? Why?
22. Can you think of a marketing research technique that could not be supported online? Explain your answer.
23. What are the current limitations for undertaking market research on the general population on the internet? How might these be overcome now and in the future?
24. Given that the cost of sending an e-mail questionnaire to 10,000 people is no higher than the cost of sending it to 10 people, why would market researchers bother devising samples if they were planning to undertake some research online?
25. What do you think a company should do if it receives a Google Alert or RSS feed showing that customers are speaking poorly about its products?
26. What are the pros and cons of cloud computing?
27. How would you monitor a brand image in the social media?

WEB ACTIVITIES

28. Join the American Consumer Opinion online panel and take a survey (acop.com). Did they screen for a particular type of respondent? What observations can you make about the client and research problem?
29. Look for the cookies file(s) on your hard drive (on a Microsoft PC, use the *find file* function and search for *cookie*). Do you see sites there that you have never visited? Is DoubleClick on the list? If so, visit the DoubleClick site to see why. If not, visit another site that you don't recognize.
30. Find information on the U.S. Census and Nielsen TV ratings, either online or in the library. What methodology does each use? Evaluate their strengths and weaknesses based on what you've learned about research methods in this chapter.
31. Watch a friend surf for 10 minutes and record the clickstream. (Internet Explorer records sites visited using the drop-down arrow by the back button.) List each site, page within, and how long your friend spends on each page. Can you make any determination about your friend's attitudes, interests, and opinions based on the clickstream?
32. Toyota has asked you to test the effectiveness of its new banner ad using four primary research techniques. Design these tests.
33. Visit allfacebook.com and report on the top pages. What statistics does this site provide and how can it help marketers?
34. Visit brandtags.com, register, and check out two competitive brands (like Coke and Pepsi). What are the differences in their brand images?

CHAPTER

7

Connected Consumers Online

The primary objective of this chapter is to help you develop a general understanding of the online consumer population. You will explore the context in which online consumer behavior occurs, the characteristics and resources of online consumers, and the outcomes of the online exchange process.

After reading this chapter, you will be able to:

- Discuss general statistics about the internet population.
- Describe the internet exchange process and the technological, social/cultural, and legal context in which consumers participate in this process.
- Outline the broad individual characteristics, psychology, and consumer resources that consumers bring to the online exchange.
- Highlight the five main categories of outcomes that consumers seek from online exchanges.

• Consumers will welcome products, apps, or services that (constantly) monitor, remind, prod, and even force them to behave and perform "better."

• ***Audi's*** e-bike ***Wörthersee*** features an onboard computer that connects to a smartphone, offering challenges and tips on how to improve performance. An online point-rewarding platform enables users to keep track of successes and compare their achievements with fellow cyclists.

The Customer's Story

This is the story of a typical one-hour adventure on a weekend afternoon in the life of a 25-year-old professional, Justin. It begins when he tunes his iPod to the latest Diggnation podcast, downloaded automatically via his WiFi network at home. Diggnation's Alex Albrecht and Kevin Rose chat about the weekly top stories on Digg.com, a social media site where users submit interesting news headlines and then the site's visitors vote by clicking that they "digg it." As our consumer watches the video podcast, he also has the television tuned to a soccer game and his smartphone and iPad tablet are within reach.

Part way through the podcast, Kevin Rose mentions his blog on Tumblr.com: kevinhasablogg. Tumblr is a social networking site—a Web site that holds small bits of quickly posted, user-generated content (tumblr.com). Justin looks away from the podcast and picks up his iPad to find the blog. He is still listening to Rose and Albrecht but not watching them on the iPod. He is captivated by a video on the blog "Lip Dub Flagpole Sitta by Harvey Danger," so he tunes it in on his television set, also via the WiFi connection in his home. This video contains a bunch of employees in hip clothes having fun by lip-synching to the song and dancing around the office doing silly stuff. While watching it, Justin picks up his smartphone to text a friend who lives in a different time zone: "You gotta see this video."

Justin wonders who created this hot video. He searches the title on Google and finds Vimeo, an online video-posting site predating YouTube. The text explaining the video notes that Connected Ventures' employees created the video at work and that the company is currently hiring (see connectedventures.com/jobs.php). Justin follows the link to see that there are no more jobs available because the company got several hundred résumés just based on the Lip Dub video posting. Justin wasn't the first to arrive, but he really wants to work for a company like this.

During Justin's last few minutes of the one-hour stretch, he shares the video with his

(*continued*)

Facebook friends and posts a link to the video and Vimeo site on his Twitter stream. Twitter.com is another micromedia site that his friends and colleagues follow, and pretty soon other messages about the video and company appear. The buzz quickly spreads.

This is the new consumer. Justin is a multitasker, attending to many different electronic media simultaneously. He is difficult to catch online and won't stick around one Web site or smartphone application for long. His connections with friends and colleagues are enhanced by the internet, where they like to share their online treasures and conversation in a myriad of ways from e-mail to text to social media sites. They don't pay much attention to traditional Web sites, preferring to connect with others and view fresh content in the social media. Justin is an important consumer because if brands can't attract the young demographic, they will eventually head into the decline stage and die. Justin did not pay anything for this travel through online content and communication with friends (except for the WiFi and cell phone services). How can a marketer capture dollars from this—advertising online, selling music downloads and other products, charging fees for premium social media subscriptions? That is a problem marketers are trying to solve as you read this. Oh, and by the way, if you are doing this kind of content consumption and conversation in class, you might want to tear yourself away from your smartphone ☺.

CONSUMERS IN THE TWENTY-FIRST CENTURY

This chapter is about the 85 percent of U.S. consumers who used the internet in 2012. Before we delve into understanding them and their behavior, it is important to think about the 15 percent of Americans who don't use the internet. It would not benefit a company to build a Web presence if its market were mostly in that minority percentage. The less-connected groups tend to be older, less educated, Hispanic, and have a lower income or a disability (according to Pew Internet & American Life Project data from 2012 research). These demographics are not likely to change quickly, and this is why internet adoption has matured, hovering between 75 and 80 percent for the past five years (Exhibit 7.1).

Globally, internet use is still growing, but very slowly. On December 31, 2011, 2.3 billion people had access to the internet, representing 32.7 percent of the global population (up 528 percent since 2000). As can be seen in Appendix A, 65 countries have a penetration rate of at least 50 percent. The top 10 countries, in terms of absolute number of users, account for nearly 60 percent of all internet users. In these countries, adoption rates range from 10 percent (India) to 84 percent (United Kingdom). Note that these numbers have obviously grown from December 2011 to mid-2012, when the United States was measured at 85 percent adoption.

Where are the world's other 4.7 billion people? Not online. Chapter 4 describes many social, cultural, technological, legal, and political issues as the main reasons that consumers do not use the internet in emerging economies. Without major shifts, some countries may not ever achieve high levels of internet adoption among individual consumers, although high cell phone adoption may change this picture eventually. This is important to know as marketers chase international markets.

Internet usage in developed nations has reached a critical mass, and marketers now ask practical questions such as whether a company's target market is online, what these customers do online, what determines whether they'll buy from a site, and how much of the marketing effort should be devoted to online channels. This chapter addresses typical consumer behavior among internet users in the United States in order to discover the answers to some of these questions. One thing is certain: Technology is growing in importance for most citizens of industrialized nations.

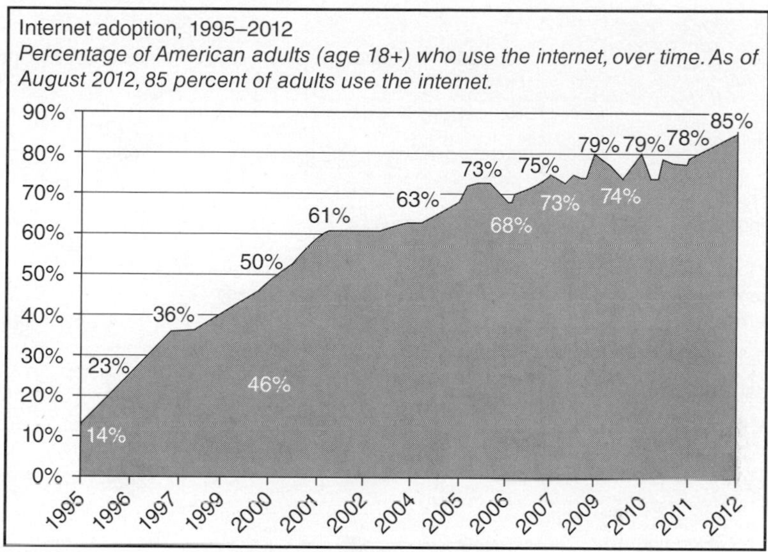

EXHIBIT 7.1 Internet Reaches Maturity: Penetration from 1995 to 2012
Source: Pew Internet & American Life Project (accessed September 8, 2012, from pewinternet.org)

CONSUMER BEHAVIOR ONLINE

Many consumer behavior principles that describe offline buying behavior also apply to online marketing. For example, the following consumer behavior models apply to all buying decisions (basic marketing review for you here):

1. Consumers experience all or many of the buying process steps: need identification, information search, alternative evaluation, purchase and postpurchase activities.
2. Consumers also go through a hierarchy of effects model—from first becoming aware of the product or brand, then developing an attitude as positive or negative, and possibly concluding with some behavior, such as registering online or purchasing the product.
3. Marketers often use an AIDA model to entice buyers: attention, interest, desire, and action. Japan's top ad agency, Dentsu, Inc., modified this model in 2004 for the social media environment by replacing "desire" with "search" and adding "share" with others: attention, interest, search, action, and share (see dentsu.com).
4. Word of mouth has been used forever when people share their product experiences with friends and family; however, an online share can quickly reach the entire connected world: word of mouth on steroids!

These processes vary based on whether the purchase situation is high or low involvement (amount of social, financial, and self-esteem risk). This also holds true for both online and offline buying situations.

Consumer online buying behavior has many additional characteristics that differ from offline behavior, as discussed in this chapter. Dr. Paul Marsden, Editor of Social Commerce Today, devised an interesting explanation of social commerce buying behavior based on consumer psychology (Exhibit 7.2). Marsden starts with the classic work of Robert Cialdini (*Influence: Science and Practice*), extended by Daniel Goleman in *Social Intelligence: The New Science of Human Relationships*. Key theories follow:

- Scarcity: When a product is scarce, it will create more demand, such as a discount offered for a "limited time only." Groupon

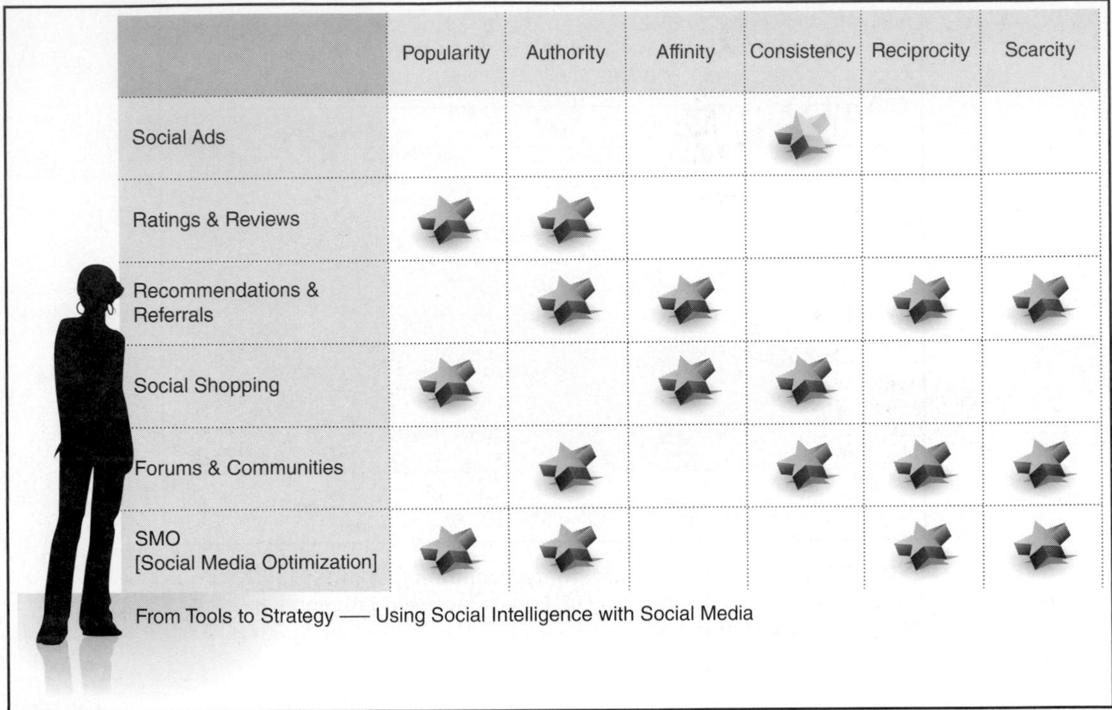

Popularity
Authority
Affinity
Consistency
Reciprocity
Scarcity
Social Ads
Ratings & Reviews
Recommendations & Referrals
Social Shopping
Forums & Communities
SMO [Social Media Optimization]
From Tools to Strategy — Using Social Intelligence with Social Media

EXHIBIT 7.2 Social Psychology of Social Shopping *Source*: SocialCommerceToday.com/ Syzygy Group

and Gilt use this principle when offering the "deal of the day."

- Popularity: Formerly called the bandwagon effect, consumers are more likely to purchase a brand that their friends or many others like and use (the most popular brand in its category gathers more buyers). This is why many people send requests to "Like" their Facebook pages and why Amazon five-star product reviews lead people to believe it is a great book or CD.
- Affinity: Consumers are persuaded by friends and family because they like and trust them. Viral marketing is based on this principle—you are likely to watch a YouTube video when someone you trust sends the link to you or purchase something that your social network friends highly recommend.
- Authority: If a celebrity or other famous figure uses and recommends a particular brand, social network, or Web site, it will become more popular. If you like Lady Gaga and she recommends a new artist, you are more likely to purchase a CD from that artist.
- Consistency: When individuals hold particular beliefs and attitudes about a product, it is hard to change them. Also called cognitive consistency, this explains habitual buying patterns or consistently using the same online news or weather site for information. It also explains why you take a chance on Lady Gaga's recommendation if you like her, and don't if you dislike her music.
- Reciprocity: Do me a favor and I owe you. This is why free product samples in grocery stores or 30-day free software trial downloads tend to increase product sales of that item around the sampling period.

Dr. Marsden connects this basic theory with social media consumer behavior and social shopping marketing tactics, such as (1) ads placed in social media, (2) product ratings and reviews online (such as Amazon or ePinions), (3) recommendations and referrals (such as on Facebook), (4) social shopping (when online friends become involved in the shopping process), (5) forums and communities (such as brand discussions on Google Groups or on an online travel site), and (6) social media optimization—a component of search engine optimization that uses an optimal variety of social media sites for building awareness of a product, brand, event, or Web site. Exhibit 7.2 suggests the social media tactics that evoke various underlying social psychology principles.

INSIDE THE INTERNET EXCHANGE PROCESS

Many additional stimuli, characteristics, and processes explain consumer buying behavior. Stimuli that can motivate consumers to purchase one product rather than another include marketing mix tactics and cultural, political, economic, and technological factors. Individual buyer's characteristics such as income level and personality also come into play, along with other psychological, social, and personal aspects (as previously mentioned). Finally, consumers move through a variety of decision processes based on situational and product attributes. Marketing knowledge about consumer behavior theory is quite complex, and although we make many generalizations, individual differences are also important—especially because internet technology allows for effective and efficient customization to target markets as small as one person.

To create effective marketing strategies, e-marketers need to understand what motivates people to buy goods and services, both in the short term and in the long term (i.e., develop brand loyalty). Exchange is a basic marketing concept that refers to the act of obtaining a valued object from someone by offering something in return. When consumers purchase a product, they are exchanging money for desired goods or services. However, many other types of marketing exchanges can be made, such as when a politician asks citizens to exchange their votes for his or her services.

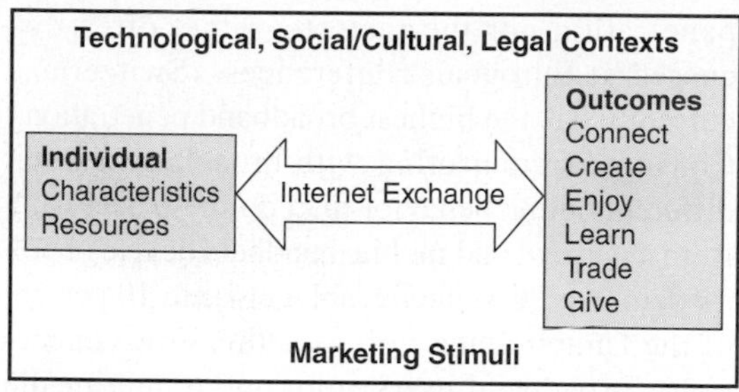

EXHIBIT 7.3 The Online Exchange Process

Exhibit 7.3 summarizes the basic internet exchange process—a graphical representation to help focus this discussion. Individuals bring their own characteristics and personal resources to the process as they seek specific outcomes from an exchange. This process occurs within a technological, social/cultural, and legal context. The exchange is often motivated by marketing stimuli—the topic of Part IV of this book.

Technological Context

The internet moved from novelty to utility in the United States and most developed nations (see Appendix A). Arranging for ISP services is like getting cell phone services and a postal address: Most U.S. consumers consider this activity routine. It is critical for e-marketers to understand the current state of ever-changing internet technology if they want to entice consumer exchanges. "Let's Get Technical" boxes within this text assist in this process, and the Semantic Web and other innovations mentioned in Chapter 1 bear watching. Here we focus upon three important developments affecting online consumer behavior today—home connection speeds; the changing landscape of digital-content receiving devices such as smartphones, televisions, and many more; and Web 2.0 technologies.

HOME CONNECTION SPEEDS Estimates ranged from 66 to 77 percent of online Americans connected to the internet at home with broadband (fast) internet service in 2012. Incidentally, the United States has neither the highest broadband penetration nor the fastest—a fact often discussed at European conferences. (Switzerland currently has the highest broadband penetration.) Consumers connecting with broadband exhibit different online behavior than do those accessing from a narrowband mobile handheld device or 56k modem in a PC (unbelievably, close to 10 percent of the United States still uses this slow connection). Broadband users enjoy more multimedia games, music, and entertainment because these download quickly (see the "Let's Get Technical" boxes on broadband options and bandwidth and marketing issues). At the other extreme, those accessing with handheld devices such as small-screen smartphones tend to focus on texting, Facebook, news, weather, stock quotes, and other data services that are low in graphics. Although YouTube videos and other large files will play well if the smartphone is connected to WiFi, many still find it better to view them on a larger screen. From a marketing perspective, Travelocity (and an increasing number of companies) has a large, user-friendly Web site for making travel arrangements, and also a mobile site that allows travelers to access the information they need, with mostly text and simple graphics, from a smartphone.

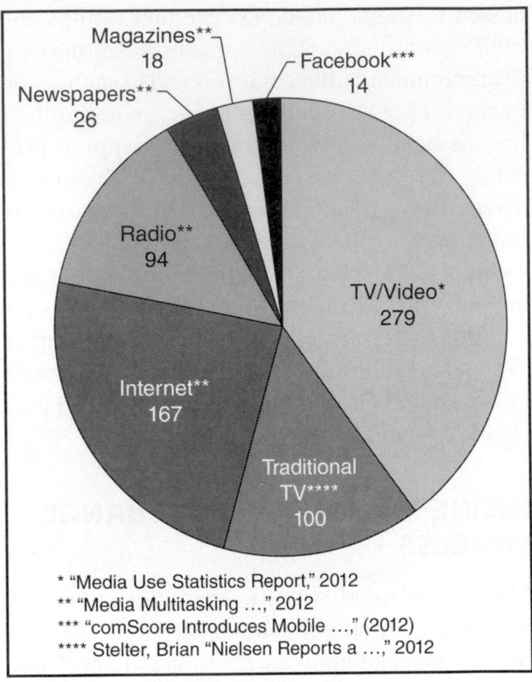

EXHIBIT 7.4 U.S. Daily Media Use (Minutes per Day)

RECEIVING DEVICES The typical U.S. home has 26 different electronic devices for media and communication, according to the Consumer Electronics Association. Traditional paper newspaper and magazine readership is still on the decline. Television appliances are no longer the killer receiving device and, in fact, the number of TV households connected to satellite services declined slightly in 2012, as was television programming viewership, according to the Nielsen Company. Exhibit 7.4 displays U.S. technology device ownership statistics for 2012. Further, marketers are very interested in viewing habits on the "three screens" in the United States (Exhibits 7.4 and 7.5). Some examples follow:

- On average, Americans watch 1 hour and 40 minutes of television per month at home on a standard, old-fashioned TV set. Conversely, other individuals watch about 4.5 hours of live or recorded TV/video programming each month on some combination of a standard television set or internet-connected device (smartphone, tablet, desktop/laptop computer).
- American consumers spend over two hours a day on the internet.
- Consumers spend over an hour a day on a mobile device.
- With 52 percent of cell phone owners using the device while watching television, about 23 percent send text messages, 11 percent post comments online about the show they are watching, and 38 percent use the phones during TV commercials (according to Pew Internet & American Life).
- From another perspective, the number of people who watch television or video from each device follows: 30 million on a mobile phone, 143 million on the internet, 288 million on a traditional television, and 111 million time shift with a DVR or Video on Demand (VOD) ("State of Media . . .," 2012).

U.S. Technology Penetration Stats in 2012	
234 million	Use a mobile phone (88 percent of population)[1]
58 percent	Have a desktop computer (61 percent have a laptop)[5]
101.3 million	Use a smartphone (Android has 48.6 percent share and iOS 29.5 percent)[1]
44 percent	Have an mp3 player[5]
29 percent	Of internet users have a tablet computer[2]
18 percent	Have an eBook reader[5]
Three screen usage sample stats in 2012: TV, PC, mobile device (smartphone, tablet)	
52 percent	Of adult cell owners use the phone while watching television[3]
20–35 percent	Of cell users visit a Web site mentioned on television with e-mail, apps, or a browser on their phone[3]
65 percent	Of internet users start shopping using their cell phones and half continue on a PC[4]
25 percent	Of internet users start shopping on a PC/laptop[4]
11 percent	Start shopping on a tablet computer[4]

EXHIBIT 7.5 Adult Internet Users on Three Screens

Sources:

[1] "Smartphones Account for Half ...," 2012
[2] "iPad Use ...," 2012
[3] Smith, Aaron and Jan Boyles, "The Rise of the "Connected Viewer," 2012.
[4] "Smartphones Launch 65% ...," 2012
[5] "Adult Gadget Ownership..." (these figures are 2010–2012 from this chart), 2012.

Time shifting is also of interest: DVR (digital video recorder) adoption grew in 2012 to 44 percent of all households (from 1 percent in 2000), according to the Nielsen Company. The TiVo and other DVRs offered by cable companies allow owners to record digital programs and send to their PCs over the in-home wireless network. DVR use hasn't affected consumer shopping behavior or purchase of advertised products, according to Carl Mela, a professor at Duke's Fuqua School of Business. In a three-year study that ended in 2010, Mela found that 95 percent of people still watch live television, thus being exposed to commercials, and that only 70 percent of viewers with DVRs fast-forward through commercials (Gallagher, 2010).

Finally, streaming music, television, and video are gaining ground as people "cut the cables" and expand the use of cloud computing. In one example, Netflix had 23 million streaming subscribers in 2012. Of these, 50 percent watched via a game console, 42 percent on a computer, and 6 percent on their smartphone (see statisticbrain.com). In another example, a study cited by eMarketer found that 38 percent of U.S. households have at least one television set connected to the internet. Consumers can control music in the house from their iTunes library or Pandora streaming radio using a Sonos wireless WiFi box or other receiving appliance via their smartphone. The possibilities for media consumption are endless, and this makes marketing very complex. Where to find these consumers for sending marketing messages?

WEB 2.0 TECHNOLOGIES The term *Web 2.0* is often used synonymously with social media and refers to second-generation internet technologies

LET'S GET TECHNICAL

Bandwidth and Market Opportunities

You are asked to help design a Web site with some eye-catching graphics. Your manager wants you to report on the bandwidth implications. You are not quite sure what bandwidth is and would rather not look like a fool at the meeting. You need to know about bandwidth and how it affects Web site design.

The online world is divided between those with a slow-speed and those with a high-speed connection to the internet. If you have experienced the difference, then you know just how dramatic it can be. At work most people have a high-speed connection to the internet through their corporate network, which is sometimes called a broadband or high bandwidth connection. At home some people still have slow-speed modem connections over their phone lines, though more and more home users are purchasing high bandwidth connections from their cable or phone companies. Cell phones are also relatively slow. Many users will modify their online behavior based on the speed of the connection (e.g., shopping at work because the pages load so much faster).

The speed divide is a tremendous challenge for marketers. Rich multimedia content flows effortlessly over a high-speed connection but is almost unbearable to wait for over a slow modem connection. What's a marketer to do?

Three possible strategies deal with a mixed bandwidth audience.

1. ***Design for the slowest user:*** The safest bet is to design content for a slow-speed connection so as to avoid alienating any group of users. This technique is adopted by some internet giants, including Amazon.com and Yahoo! Their sites tend to be light on graphics and heavy on text content that loads quickly.
2. ***Design for the fastest user:*** Ignore the slow-speed users and design for the higher bandwidth and generally more affluent audience. Some services (e.g., streaming HD video) are viable only over a high-speed connection.
3. ***Create fast and slow versions of the site:*** Customize content for the speed of the user's connection by using an auto detect feature or just by asking the user what her connection speed is. News sites providing video clips will routinely adopt this approach, as will sites for music downloads.

The bandwidth issue is similar to the move from broadcast to cable and satellite TV. Cable and satellite TV subscribers incurred a higher cost to receive content in their homes. In return they got both more channels (more bandwidth) and a higher definition picture. In the United States, consumers opted for these alternatives. (The United States later required broadcasting HD video over the airwaves.) Growing evidence indicates that U.S. consumers are similarly willing to pay for high-speed internet access. In return they receive access to the following services:

- Personal selling and customer service via the computer as a videoconferencing device. Conferencing services are most important for products requiring explanation to close the sale such as the plumbing fixtures offered by FaucetDepot.com.
- Phone calls delivered over the internet using Voice over Internet Protocol (VoIP) services such as Skype.
- Delivery of music over the Web such as those offered by Apple iTunes, Rhapsody, and Pandora.
- Delivery of movies over the Web such as those offered by Apple TV and Netflix.
- Virtual reality such as Google Earth.

Bandwidth (speed) is measured in bits per second (bps). It takes about 10 bits to code a single letter. It takes about 500,000 bits to code a photograph. With such big numbers, it is easier to speak about kilobits per second (Kbps). So the question is how long is the user willing to wait on a slow-speed connection? Research shows the maximum waiting time is about 10 seconds. Using this number as a guide, rough minimums for tolerable bandwidth to transmit different media are shown in the following table:

Media Type	Minimum Tolerable Bandwidth (kilobits per second)
Text	25
Graphics (pictures)	50
Sound	100
Video	1,000

Today's fastest phone line modems operate at 56 Kbps—fast enough for text and graphics. However, today's phone line modems are not fast enough for acceptable quality multimedia (sound and video). High-speed internet access can be purchased at a premium through cable, phone, and satellite companies. And consumers are increasingly opting for these services.

LET'S GET TECHNICAL

Broadband Options

You are trying to decide whether to get a high-speed internet connection for your apartment. You know of the different options—cable modems, DSL, and satellite—you are not quite sure how they are different and would rather not buy more than you need. You need to know about broadband connections to the home and their options.

The information channels that form the internet backbone have amazing carrying capacities and are constantly being upgraded by firms such as Cisco, Sprint, and AT&T. However, consumers pay for the last mile along the path to the internet, the connection to the consumer's home. Various wired and wireless alternatives are available.

The wired alternatives make use of two wires that are already connected to the user's home—the phone line and the cable TV line. These wires can do double duty to carry internet content on one channel while they perform their normal functions on the other channels.

Digital Subscriber Line

Digital subscriber line (DSL) technology refers to a family of methods for transmitting at speeds up to 8 Mbps (8 million bits per second) over a standard phone line. DSL uses the phone line already installed in consumer homes, allowing users to simultaneously make phone calls and surf the Web because the data travel outside of the audible voice band. Users must install a DSL modem; some computer manufacturers offer these modems as a pre-installed item, and some phone companies supply them. The major phone companies have deployed the infrastructure to support DSL technology, but they were a bit late to the game and have been playing catch-up with cable modems. As a result, phone companies aggressively price DSL service to attract cable subscribers.

Cable Modems

The cable companies have banded together into two consortiums. In one example, Time Warner, Time Warner/Advance-Newhouse, and Media One Group, Inc. formed a consortium called Road Runner. These consortiums help to set standards and share development costs.

The consortiums attracted venture capital. As an example, Compaq Computer (now HP) and Microsoft each invested $212.5 million in Road Runner years ago. Clearly, the personal computer industry has a stake in selling computer upgrades to consumers who need beefed up machines to handle the additional bandwidth.

Cable modems allow transmission of internet traffic over the cable TV wire connected to the home. The speed of transmission over a cable modem ranges between 500 Kbps and 10 Mbps. The major problem cable companies may face is having too many subscribers! This problem arises because subscribers in

(*continued*)

a cable neighborhood share bandwidth. The more the subscribers who share, the less bandwidth is available to repartition. Therefore, if a neighborhood becomes saturated with subscribers, each subscriber will experience delays.

Cable companies have two big advantages—early market penetration and a much bigger information pipe. The early adopters opted for cable modems because they were the first technology available. This early usage also gives cable modems the advantage of diffusion via word of mouth. The cable companies solved their infrastructure issues early and can now focus on establishing value-added services such as the following:

- Video-on-demand
- CD-quality audio
- Online games available for download and purchase

Each value-added service provides a barrier to entry for the phone companies. Why purchase a service with fewer features? And because providing each service requires a learning curve, phone companies will experience difficulty catching up.

Cable also has a higher theoretical maximum speed than DSL. Nonetheless, phone companies such as AT&T continue to question the actual versus advertised speed of cable. However, if both networks are properly supported, cable still wins the battle.

One way the phone companies are competing is through price. DSL typically undercuts cable, though there are regional variations in price. In some cases, the companies will waive the installation fee if the user signs up for an extended period of service.

Wireless Broadband Options

Three smaller competitors in the broadband game are satellite, fixed wireless, and mobile wireless. Satellite broadband is offered through HughesNet. The major limitation is limited bandwidth that does not scale well with the increase in the number of subscribers.

Fixed wireless access is best categorized by distance and bandwidth. Some systems are designed to work over a range of miles, effectively replacing wired access to the home. Other systems operate over a range of up to hundreds of feet, providing local connectivity within the home or office. In either scenario, the bandwidth of the system determines its suitability as a broadband connection.

Mobile wireless is available over the cell phone network. With cell phone towers already in place in many areas, Web access via cell phone would seem to be a natural outgrowth. The cell phone network is reliable and in many areas the communication is already digital. The problem is bandwidth. The cell phone network was designed to handle low-bandwidth voice communications. As a result, data communication over the network is relatively slow. Third-generation (3G) cell phone networks help solve the bandwidth problem, by transferring data at 0.2 Mbps and sometimes faster. Fourth-generation (4G) networks will eventually deliver from 100 Mbps up to 1 Gbps! This phenomenally fast rate would surpass even cable modems. It will be interesting to see if home owners abandon their cable modems and transfer all data through their cell phones, in the same way that many abandoned their voice land lines when cell phones became available. Smartphone users and laptop road warriors are leading the charge to popularize 3G and 4G services. Ultimately, users want access to anything, anytime, anywhere, and from any device.

behind blogs, wikis, social networks, product review sites, image and video upload sites, and folksonomies (the technology behind classification techniques for online media, such as collaborative tagging or social bookmarking). The term *Web 2.0* was coined by O'Reilly Media in 2004. We could write an entire book on the technology behind Web 2.0 and the future projections. We simply mention it here because of its importance for driving marketing strategies and tactics.

The key is to learn which devices and technology applications an organization's customers and prospects own and prefer to use for connecting. Companies send data to customers' digital-content receiving devices such as the PC/laptop, electronic pager, fax machine, TV, game console box, smartphone, and many other devices such as the connected refrigerator. Users access stock prices, extranet FedEx package tracking information, airline schedule changes, weather, and more over their smartphones while in a taxi on the way to a client meeting or the airport. Don't overlook telematics—a communication system in an automobile that uses a global positioning system (GPS) for interactive communication between companies and drivers. This system allows drivers to receive directions and internet content or send for emergency help. It allows marketers to send information and entertainment to automobiles. And some of this may be obsolete by the time you read this book because things change so quickly in the technology context! It is a world of new opportunity for marketers.

Social and Cultural Contexts

The days of marketers holding consumers captive for the 30 seconds of a TV commercial are quickly coming to a close, and captivity in front of a display ad online is virtually nonexistent. As well, traditional media don't have the same ability to reach the masses of consumers who have fragmented into increasingly smaller markets, down to a market of one person. The internet allows individuals and organizations to discuss products with each other online and to help themselves to information, products, and practically everything they want when and where they please. For example, consumers walk into brick-and-mortar car dealerships after chatting online with strangers about options and carrying printed information sheets on automobile options and pricing.

Thus, power is shifting to consumers, and marketers are not as successful with interrupt communications (such as television commercials) as they are when they draw consumers and engage them with relevant content, as mentioned in Chapter 1. Three cornerstones for attracting today's customers online are reputation, relevance, and engagement (Exhibit 7.6).

REPUTATION Brand image and reputation are based on the market's perception. Companies with good reputations are authentic, are honest, apologize for errors, and follow through on brand promises. In reward, they receive more recommendations from customers, enjoy longer and more profitable relationships, and sell more products and services. One of the most important social trends is that oftentimes consumers trust each other more than they trust advertising or companies, and when the product conversation turns negative it can hurt a company's reputation. The increase in user-generated content in online communities from Facebook, Amazon, YouTube, and Twitter to the Google Groups has consumers looking to each other for advice. For example, Askapatient (askapatient.com) hosts thousands of posts about side effects of various medicines. Consumers visit the site to see

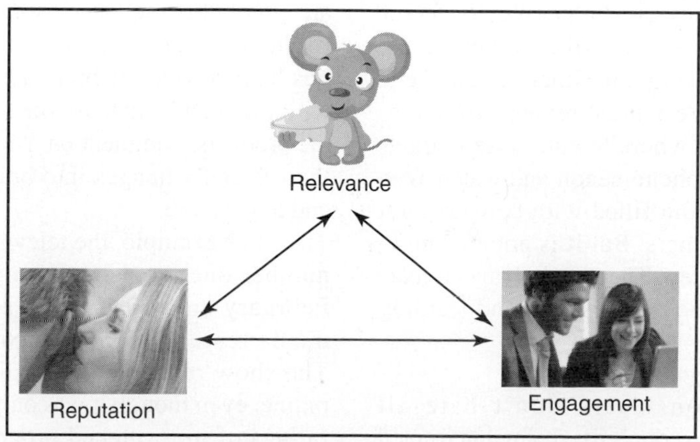

EXHIBIT 7.6 Engaging Customers with Tasty, Relevant Content

if other people experience the side effects that they experience, and what to expect from a new drug—this information seems more reliable than the corporate spin from pharmaceutical companies and even the lack of knowledge of some medical doctors. The social PR firm, Edelman, asks this question each year in its Global Trust Barometer: "If you heard information from each of these sources, how credible would the information be?" Here are the sources consumers said they trusted in 2012 (see trust.edelman.com for the annual survey):

- 68 percent: an academic or expert.
- 66 percent: a technical expert in the company.
- 65 percent: a person like yourself. (Note that in 2011 the Nielsen Company found that 92 percent of consumers trust people they know and 70 percent trust consumer reviews posted online.)
- 50 percent: a regular employee.
- 50 percent: nongovernment organization (NGO) representative.
- 46 percent: a financial or industry analyst.
- 38 percent: the CEO or leader of a company.
- 29 percent: a government official or regulator.

A person like yourself is someone who shares your interests, such as other patients, movie goers, travelers, or sports fans. Often called twinsumers, these taste "twin consumers" share similar opinions, buying patterns, entertainment, and other behaviors. They can be people you know in the physical world or online connections. For example, travelling consumers often check Yelp.com for local restaurant reviews from others before deciding where to eat. Wise marketers understand this phenomenon and watch Web sites and social media filled with conversation among target customers. But it is not enough to just observe and listen. The truly advanced marketers are joining the conversation and learning from customers.

RELEVANCE Consumers don't hate all advertising—they just don't like being interrupted with irrelevant communication. This is why the national telephone "do not call" registry has been such a success for consumers, who report receiving fewer telemarketing calls since registering. Conversely, the large number of online users who opt in to receive e-mail messages from companies they patronize enjoy and welcome relevant communication. As you'll learn in later chapters, marketers use many methods, such as behavioral targeting and keyword advertising, to present relevant offers to potential customers. It takes research, insight, two-way communication, and presenting the right product to the right customer at the right time.

ENGAGEMENT The key to drawing internet users is to provide relevant content or entertainment. According to Time, Inc., the three pillars of customer engagement are content engagement, media engagement, and engagement marketing activities. The consumer story that opened this chapter is an example of interesting content that engaged the user into following the path to learn more and share with friends. The more relevant, entertaining, and emotion-laden the content, the more likely it will be to involve the audience. Media engagement is the context for the content. Social media venues such as Twitter, Facebook, and applications for the iPhone provide a compelling environment for attracting and engaging customers. These sites are also outstanding because they allow for easy recommendations to friends—a powerful form of brand communication. Engagement marketing activities are simply the sequence used to draw users to the medium and through the content. The best activities help consumers build a personal association with the brand, such as when they can customize the products, comment on YouTube videos, insert their friend's images into brand-related content, and much more.

For example, the television show *Lost* was number one in customer engagement between February and April 2010, according to social media research company Networked Insights. The show ranked #1 in audience conversation online, even though it was only #10 in the Nielsen ratings of top-watched programs. In mid-2012, the Discovery Channel's *Shark Week* became the most talked about show in social networks, with 34 percent discussing their love for the show and 29 percent talking about playing drinking games during the show. Networked Insights analyzes the sentiment and content from over 800 million viewers who either posted comments or read conversations in the social media after watching specific media programs (networkedinsights.com). These are engaged consumers and this engagement analysis adds another important dimension to the pure audience viewership statistics. We'll say it again: the social media are like word of mouth on steroids.

OTHER KEY TRENDS The following general social/cultural trends also have a huge affect on online exchanges:

- ***Information overload.*** Too much information overwhelms consumers. It creates an attention economy—the idea that information may be infinite, but the demand for it is limited by human capacity. This serious problem is compounded by the internet and is one reason why consumers have little tolerance for spam (unsolicited e-mail) and look to twinsumer recommendations for great content in videos and social media.
- ***Multitasking.*** Multitasking speeds up normal processes and lowers attention to each task. By example, the Millenials, a consumer segment born between 1974 and 1994 (also called Generation Y), are great multitaskers, likely to watch a television screen at home, text a friend on the cell phone, and check sports scores via the internet on their iPad at the same time. Notably, 52 percent of adults with cell phones use the internet while watching television, according to Pew Internet & American Life.
- ***Home and work.*** The boundaries between home and work are dissolving. Many U.S. internet users have access to the internet both at home and at work. Fourteen percent report spending more time working at home because of the internet (see pewinternet.org). Also, comScore Media Metrix found that many U.S. workers make travel arrangements, purchase products, and handle other personal tasks online while at work. The home has become more like a center of life and home office for many; this trend will increase as more Americans telecommute (work and live in different cities and rarely visit the physical office).
- ***I want what I want when I want it.*** Anywhere, anytime convenience is critical for busy people. They want to view online content, shop, or pay bills anytime of the day or night from any geographic location whether online or not, and receive deliveries when convenient for them, not for the firm or package delivery service. Online users access the internet from mobile devices, sending e-mail, text messages, photos, and searching the Web for maps and other things. Consumers have high expectations that firms will answer e-mails within 48 hours and generally perform as expected—otherwise they will post a complaint on a blog or social network, or at epinions.com and tell a few thousand "friends" about the underperforming company. One example of a company meeting these needs is Dubai's Red Tomato Pizza that provides a free magnet that looks like a pizza with the words: "Push for hunger." Customers push the button, and Bluetooth technology via smartphone notifies the company, who immediately delivers the customer's favorite pizza to the registered address (see redtomato.biz).
- ***Online oxygen.*** This term, coined at trendwatching.com, means that an increasing number of consumers cannot do without their internet access—they crave it. As an example, when Canadian internet users were asked what they would want with them if stranded on a desert island, 51 percent said the PC, 21 percent mentioned telephone, and only 12 percent said their television. Anyone who is addicted to e-mail or particular Web sites certainly understands this trend!

- ***Connectivity.*** Being connected means everything in this social media world. It is all about who you are connected to in social networks, how many friends you have or how many of them liked what you posted, how many people looked at and rated your photos or YouTube video, and how many Twitter followers you have. Marketers who develop applications to help customers build their connections in an entertaining way will win positive brand recognition.
- ***"In the Know."*** This is another term coined by trendwatching.com. People in the know have access to information that others don't, such as the coolest iPhone application or which band is playing at that joint near campus. These consumers are seen as insiders when they can whip out a mobile device, find something quickly, and show that they are experts and are at the cutting edge. Marketers creating applications and search/GPS combinations appeal to this trend.
- ***Self-service.*** This feature is required. Empowered customers want to log on, find information, make purchases, track package shipments, check their accounts, and make inquiries anytime, 24/7. Furthermore, they want to do these tasks on a computer via e-mail, on the Web or on a smartphone—and they want all these methods to produce identical information. It is an interesting contradiction: Consumers want to help themselves when they feel like it and be pampered by firms at other times.
- ***Privacy and data security.*** These are paramount, especially in Europe. Customers want marketers to keep their data confidential. They also want to safeguard children from Web sites they find objectionable. Consumers want marketers to ask permission before sending commercial e-mail messages. In one report, only 13 percent of consumers said they'd be willing to exchange personal data for free entertainment online (according to an Edelman study). Conversely, consumers are putting personal data in social network profiles all over the internet, perhaps without realizing or caring about the public nature of this information. A recent development is that an increasing number of consumers are abandoning smartphone apps due to privacy concerns (especially those using GPS for location detection).

Legal Context

Chapter 5 presents a thorough discussion of legal factors affecting e-marketers, so we mention only two factors here. First, in spite of the Can-Spam act in the United States, the number of unsolicited e-mails was 71.9 percent in June 2012, according to the Kaspersky Lab (kaspersky.com). Called SPAM, this type of mail is not in the best interest of consumers who want relevant, engaging content. Second, in spite of piracy laws, illegally used software abounds. However, when the Recording Industry Association of America (RIAA) sued thousands of illegal music file downloaders, legal factors actually had a huge affect on online consumer behavior. In 2002, 37 percent of online consumers shared music files with others, which dropped over time (pewinternet.org). Yet, in 2012 the RIAA claimed that the music industry still realizes $12.5 billion in losses from music piracy a year, as well as 71,060 lost jobs and $422 million in lost government tax revenues (riaa.com). This is important because all digital products face this problem (e.g., movies, software), and many consumers feel no hesitation about obtaining illegal copies. If the RIAA's success is any indication, the law may indeed change consumer behavior such that products can be offered over the internet without losing profits—as experienced by Apple's iTunes.

Individual Characteristics and Resources

Beyond general social and cultural environmental trends, obviously, individuals vary in their online behavior. Some of this variance is based on differences in characteristics, such as demographics and attitudes, and some is based on the resources consumers bring to the exchange process.

INDIVIDUAL DIFFERENCES Internet users have several characteristics that differentiate them from nonusers, and similarly, users differ in their needs and desires. The first variable involves demographics. Age, income, education, ethnicity, and gender all affect internet use, as previously mentioned. For example, 96 percent of 18- to 29-year-olds use the internet, as compared with about 85 percent of the general population and 58 percent of those over 65 (Pew Internet & American. . ., 2012).

Second is a positive attitude toward technology. Internet users who purchase products online tend to hold the attitude that technology helps make their lives richer and easier. (Forrester Research created a market segmentation scheme using this variable, as described in Chapter 8.) Third, online skill and experience play an important role in the exchange process. Consumers who have been online for more than three years or have broadband connections tend to be more adept than new users at finding information and products quickly, resulting in less frustration and less shopping cart abandonment. Finally, social media veterans tend to use Twitter, while beginners start with Facebook, according to eMarketer.

Next, two researchers found that online shoppers tend to be more goal oriented than experience oriented while shopping (Wolfinbarger and Gilly, 2001). Goal-oriented behavior often includes going to a specific Web site with a purpose in mind, or searching for the lowest price for a particular product. Experience orientation relates to having fun, bargain hunting, or just surfing to find something new. Goal-oriented individuals like the idea that they don't have to deal with salespeople or crowds in the online environment, and they appreciate the online product selection, convenience, and information availability. When consumers are looking for experiential shopping, it makes sense that they would find this element more often in brick-and-mortar stores than online. While this finding is quite old, we think it still applies. However, social shopping and sharing sites, such as Polyvore, and Pinterest may increase the experience orientation for many online shoppers.

Now that the internet has matured in terms of usage patterns, we could write an entire book on individual differences in online behavior, but with 85 percent online it is starting to look like the offline consumer population. Instead, marketers thoroughly explore the differences in online behavior for their target markets and then design marketing mixes accordingly. It is especially important to provide options as markets continue to fragment to increasingly smaller target groups.

CONSUMER RESOURCES Chapter 2 introduced the value equation showing that consumers perceive value as benefits minus costs. These costs constitute a consumer's resources for exchange: money, time, energy, and psychic costs.

Monetary Cost: Clearly, consumers need enough discretionary income to exchange for the goods and services they want—and to afford a computer, smartphone, tablet, and ISP connection for internet access. What makes the internet exchange different, however, is that consumers usually can't pay cash or don't write paper checks for online transactions. Instead, consumers pay by credit card, debit card, electronic check, or smart card. Most consumers in developed nations use credit cards. However, not everyone is able to acquire or wants a credit card. This problem is big for e-marketers targeting the huge teen market online and for those targeting consumers in countries with low credit card availability.

Consumers with bank accounts can use debit cards or pay by electronic check. Electronic checks (also called digital money) work this way: The consumer sets up an account and authorizes a third party's Web site (such as PayPal) to pay a specified amount and withdraw funds from the user's checking account. This method is now so popular that PayPal, the market leader (purchased by eBay in 2002), had over 113 million customer accounts in 190 markets and in 25 different currencies in 2012. Finally, smart cards are used in many countries and are becoming popular in the United Kingdom. Also called splash plastic, smart cards have an electronic chip that can be coded to hold a certain amount of funds, payable by the bank or by a depository company. The advantages are that anyone with the cash can get one, and the limit of potential fraud is the amount of money coded into the card.

A few innovative forms of digital money appear in other countries (Farivar, 2004). In South Korea, some mobile phones include special electronic chips that allow consumers to charge vending machine purchases with their phones. In Japan, a Casio watch can be read by a retail scanner to debit the user's bank account. In Hong Kong, smart cards use radio frequency chips that store up to the equivalent of US$128 for ATM-type use. Finally, in Spain 38 important guests at a beach club had radio frequency identification (RFID) chips (the size of a grain of rice) implanted in their arms. They simply move their arms over the bar to run a tab.

Time Cost: Time poverty is a problem for today's consumers, so they want to receive appropriate benefits for the time they spend online. Exhibit 7.7 shows that in April 2011, the average U.S. user went online 56 times in a month, visiting over 2,500 different Web pages at an average of 57 seconds per page. Did this average user get what he or she wanted for the time invested? The burden is on internet firms to be sure their sites are well organized and are easy to navigate so users can quickly find what they want.

The internet's property of time moderator, discussed in Chapter 1, helps consumers manage their scarce time. Users can shop, e-mail, chat, or perform other activities anytime, 24/7—a big advantage for anyone without enough time.

Time resource is a critical topic because online attention from consumers is a desirable and scarce commodity. The clutter of Web sites and social media, when combined with mobile phone activities and applications, now parallels that of other media—with some differences. Some believe that consumers pay more focused attention to Web sites than to the content in any other medium, except perhaps e-mail and text messages. When in front of a television, consumers are easily distracted by other people or activities in the environment. The same holds true for the passivity of radio listening. Consumers seem to pay more attention to print media but may still flip pages quickly.

However, consumers are 100 percent involved and are not easily distracted when they are online. Whether they are in a goal-oriented or experiential shopping trip online, they are focused and in the "flow." Therefore, once e-marketers can capture a pair of consumer eyeballs or earlobes, they can make a big impression in a short time as long as the Web site is enjoyable, self-reinforcing, and engaging. It was certainly the case for BMWfilms.com when it drew 30 million viewers in three years to watch 8- to 10-minute films online that were created by famous directors and also for the most watched YouTube video "PSY- Gangnam Style" with 1.5 billion views as of March 2013 (in only 8 months after its July 15, 2012, upload).

Metric	April 2011
Sessions/visits per person	56
Number of domains visited per person	80
Web pages per person	2,573
PC time spent per person	56 hour, 20 minutes, 54 seconds
Duration of time spent per page	57 seconds

EXHIBIT 7.7 U.S. Combined Home and Work Internet Usage *Source*: Nielsen. July 2012. Available at http://blog.nielsen.com/nielsenwire/online_mobile/may-2011-top-u-s-web-brands/

Energy and Psychic Costs: Closely related to time are energy and psychic resources. Sometimes it is just too much trouble to turn on the computer, log on to the internet, and check e-mail, especially for dial-up users. This factor accounts for the rising popularity of short text messaging (SMS) via cell phones and other handheld mobile devices. Smartphones, such as the Android and iPhone, allow users to browse the Web or e-mail anywhere, anytime—however, international standards are not yet consistent enough for travelers to count on this type of cell connectivity at reasonable prices so they must find a WiFi hotspot.

Consumers apply psychic resources when Web pages are hard to figure out or when facing technological glitches. Such may be the case with some of the up to 75 percent of all online shoppers who abandon online shopping carts (Goldwyn, 2012). This is akin to three quarters of the shoppers at a brick-and-mortar store arriving at the checkout stand, leaving the full cart there and walking away with no purchase. At one time or another, all users abandon carts due to technical problems and other issues—buying just gets to be too much trouble to figure out at some sites. However, much of the hassle for today's online shopper involves unexpectedly high shipping or other transaction costs. Other reasons for shopping cart abandonment are reluctance to input credit card and other personal information and unanswered questions about the product or return policies. Some consumers are willing to trade energy searching online for higher prices—managing their resources based on which are plentiful and which are scarce. For example, some very busy professionals may purchase a book on Amazon.com just because it is easy and the total cost, including shipping, doesn't matter.

Internet Exchange

Now comes the actual moment when exchange occurs. Browser favorites and social bookmarks (e.g., delicious.com) help consumers quickly jump to their favorite online retailer when looking for a product or making a purchase. In addition, e-mail messages or social network widgets often contain hyperlinks to bring consumers directly to specific information, news reports, or advertised specials. The internet has the added feature of automation to facilitate exchange. For example, CNN.com sends one-sentence e-mails with breaking news several times a day or week for those who sign up for the service—the full story is a click away. CNN also offers this as a Twitter feed. Also, Amazon.com sends consumers a link to a new book by a previously purchased author. These automated e-mails facilitate the exchange process.

Exchange Outcomes

Just what benefits do consumers get by exchanging all that money, time, and energy? The Pew Research Center conducts continuing research entitled Pew Internet & American Life. Along with comScore Media Metrix, Nielsen//NetRatings, the ClickZ network, and information from many other sources, we now have a rich understanding of what American consumers do online and how the internet has changed the way people behave. Using these generalizations, marketers look for differences in their target markets and then build online and offline strategies to meet their needs.

People do only six basic things online—connect, create, enjoy, learn, trade, and give. Each is ripe with marketing opportunity. In the following sections, we categorize the myriad of online activities into these areas of consumer need and desire. Looking at it this way helps marketers remember that profits come from focusing on the customer.

CONNECT Unlike any other medium, the internet allows consumers to interact with individuals and organizations using multimedia in two-way communication. Nearly all internet users send e-mail (91 percent). E-mail is still the internet's "killer app" worldwide, in spite of spam and social media—although 66 percent of all consumers use social networking sites for communication. Consumers communicate online with e-mail, text messages, Tweets, and Facebook wall posts because it is an inexpensive and convenient way to keep in touch, and because it is usually text based so it can be easily accomplished with a slow modem or over a wireless handheld device. In addition, consumers make new connections with people and business partners they meet online that sometimes carry over to the physical world.

Why do consumers connect with companies on social sites? In one recent study, the key reason was to obtain discounts (61 percent), followed by purchasing (55 percent), reviews and product rankings (53 percent), gain general information (53 percent), get exclusive information (51 percent), learn about new products (51 percent), and to feel connected to the company (33 percent), among other reasons (as cited in "The Elegance of Simplicity. . .," 2012).

Consumers also spend time instant messaging (IM), use the internet to make phone calls (Skype), and find people to date online (Exhibit 7.8). Some of this communication takes place in dedicated sites such as online dating sites, book reviews at Amazon, blog sites, social networks, Flickr, and many more. Consumers exchange time and energy to build relationships with friends and family, and even to work out problems with companies.

E-mail's popularity explains the success of Web-based e-mail services, such as Hotmail (Microsoft), Gmail (Google), and Yahoo! These sites consistently get a huge number of visitors, and the late introduction of Gmail serves as a reminder that many new business opportunities still exist around online consumer needs, even in crowded competitive fields.

Appliance convergence created a new form of connecting. Most internet users send and receive digital pictures, some from a smartphone. Connecting allows users to send virtual greeting cards, Jib Jab video greeting cards (jibjab.com), and much more.

CREATE This need to connect was one springboard for the Web's social networking sites, where users can create profiles and connect with friends, businesses, and colleagues. Content creation occurs when these users upload pictures and other content on these sites. It is the highest form of user engagement because users are participating by adding to the Web's offerings. Facebook is the most popular social networking site with 62.7 percent share of the social network market in June 2012, followed by YouTube with 20.1 percent share (according to dreamgrow.com). In this same analysis, Twitter had 1.8 percent share and Google+, Pinterest, and MySpace all scored less than 1 percent share. For professionals, LinkedIn sets the standard, with over 200 million members in 200 countries (with 64 percent being outside the United States) (see linkedin.com). LinkedIn's members include executives from all Fortune 500 companies.

Outcome	Percentage	Outcome	Percentage
Send or read e-mail	91	Read a blog	32
Send or receive text messages from cell phone	74	Make internet phone call	25
Support for specific situation	58	Share files (P2P)	15
Use social networking site	66	Use Twitter	15
Send instant messages	46	Visit dating Web site	8
Post or review a comment online	32		

EXHIBIT 7.8 Proportion Connecting Online in the United States *Source*: Data from 2009 to 2012 studies at pewinternet.org

Outcome	Percentage	Outcome	Percentage
Upload photos to share	46	Create content and post	30
Rate a product, person, service using online rating system	37	Create webpages	14
Post comments to blog or other site	32	Create an avatar for virtual world	6

EXHIBIT 7.9 Proportion Creating and Uploading Content in the United States *Source*: Data from 2009 to 2012 studies at pewinternet.org

User-content creation for uploading has grown so quickly and is so vast that we put it in a separate category. Exhibit 7.9 shows that 30 percent of all internet users create and post content. The biggest activity involves sharing digital photos at sites such as Flickr.com (46 percent). Users also create or post comments to blogs and create videos for YouTube and for a myriad of online contests for user-created television commercials (e.g., the Doritos Super Bowl Contest). It is no wonder that users create all these videos for uploading—over half of all internet users enjoy watching videos on social media sites. Finally, 6 percent create avatars for virtual worlds, such as Second Life and Webkinz (for kids). You'll find social media strategies to capitalize on this content creation trend in later chapters.

ENJOY Many consumers use the internet to enjoy entertainment (Exhibit 7.10). Seventy-four percent browse for fun. One of the internet's big promises, however, is audio and visual entertainment. Nearly three-quarters of U.S users currently watch video online (71 percent), and 37 percent download music, largely due to high broadband connectivity adoption rates. We believe these numbers will continue to increase in the future for the following reasons: First, all television content is now transmitted digitally. Second, devices such as the DVR allow TV programs to be delivered on demand. In addition, services such as Netflix and Hulu store programming for internet delivery to either television or PC anytime. Third, consumers are cutting the cable and using WiFi for their TV service, as previously mentioned. As more do this, online entertainment content will grow considerably and become just one of the choices for consumers deciding how to spend time online. In the meantime, streaming media and improved compression techniques give more consumers access to online entertainment.

One way for marketers to keep their fingers on the pulse of internet users is to monitor search terms entered at Google, Yahoo!,

Outcome	Percentage	Outcome	Percentage
Surf for fun	74	Play a game	36
Watch video on social media site	71	Download video	27
Sports scores	52	Download podcast	21
Download music	37	Visit adult Web site	13

EXHIBIT 7.10 Proportion Enjoying Entertainment Online in the United States *Source*: Data from 2009 to 2012 studies at pewinternet.org

Google		Yahoo!		Bing	
Rank	Term	Rank	Term	Rank	Term
1	Rebecca Black	1	iPhone	1	Fauja Singh
2	Google+	2	Casey Anthony	2	Katy Perry
3	Ryan Dunn	3	Kim Kardashian	3	The cardinals
4	Casey Anthony	4	Katy Perry	4	Harry Potter
5	Battlefield 3	5	Jennifer Lopez	5	Adele
6	iPhone 5	6	Lindsay Lohan	6	Rory McIlroy
7	Adele	7	American Idol	7	Japan Earthquake
8	Tepco	8	Jennifer Aniston	8	Job crisis
9	Steve Jobs	9	Japan Earthquake	9	Foreclosures
10	iPad2	10	Osama Bin Laded	10	Weather disasters

EXHIBIT 7.11 Top 10 Search Terms for 2011 *Source*: Data reported by Google, Yahoo!, and Bing

and other search engines. Popular search items tend to change every month with breaking news events or holidays; however, a glance at the most-entered terms in 2011 validates the high use of the internet for entertainment, celebrity news, and sports (Exhibit 7.11).

LEARN Consumers access information to learn things online such as news, driving directions, travel information, jobs, weather, sports scores, and radio broadcasts over the internet (Exhibit 7.12). Thirteen percent of all users take a class online, just for fun. In fact, 72 percent of respondents in a Harris Poll said the internet made them more resourceful, and 46 percent said it made them smarter (see redefineyourworld.com). This is good because of the trend to be in the know and to be cool.

E-marketers have known for some time that consumers have only a limited amount of time to exchange for media consumption and that the internet takes away from offline media time. For instance, 76 percent of internet users access news online, and 81 percent of online users check the weather online.

How do internet users find information for learning? Many are loyal to particular media sites, often prompted by breaking news e-mails. Ninety-one percent use search engines and 53 percent use Wikipedia for information. Queries range from the vanity search ("How many times does my name come up on Google?") to the soul searching ("Who is God?") and ridiculous ("what is what") to the heartbreaking ("My mom has breast cancer—what should I do?").

TRADE Most consumers shop, buy, or conduct other transaction-oriented activities online. Seventy-one percent purchased products online and a majority make travel reservations online (Exhibit 7.13). Further, online classifieds are thriving, largely led by Craigslist. Online auctions are also declining a bit, with 15 percent of internet users selling something online either via classified or by auction. Consider eBay, with 100 million active, registered global users and $68.6 billion in product value sold in 2011 (see ebay .com). Due to its popularity, several firms offer special software to assist bidders in finding value at eBay. Conversely, online grocery shopping has dropped from the list in the past due to its lack of viability as an online model for most U.S. grocers.

It is important to note that 78 percent of all internet users seek information online prior to buying products. Sometimes they use

Outcome	Percentage	Outcome	Percentage
Use search engine for information	91	Research for school/training	57
Map or driving directions	84	Info about a job	56
Hobby information	84	Find phone number/address	54
Check the weather	81	Use Wikipedia	53
Health/medical	80	Virtual tour of location	52
Get news	76	Financial	37
Search for info about a person	69	Look for religious/spiritual info	32
Find "how-to" or repair info	68	Listen to/see a live event online	29
Government site	67	Research family genealogy	27
Buy/make travel reservation	65	View live images of places or of a person	17
Political news/information	61	Take a class online for fun	13

EXHIBIT 7.12 Proportion Learning and Getting Information Online in the United States *Source*: Data from 2009 to 2012 studies at pewinternet.org

this information to purchase online, and sometimes they purchase at a local brick-and-mortar store—many consumers purchase outside of the internet based on information they get online. A 2012 Nielsen Company study discovered that 59 percent of consumers favored online purchasing and 68 percent said it was the most convenient method. However, in-store purchasing was perceived as the safest (77 percent) and only 27 percent said mobile shopping was the easiest ("Shopper Sentiment: How Consumers Feel. . .," 2012).

A typical internet consumer spends an hour per day shopping online, makes 21 online purchases a year, and 57 percent of them say the internet has made them better consumers (see redefineyourworld.com).

Consumers also sell their ideas and work online. They can upload photos via the Foap app and receive 50 percent of the $10 selling price if someone buys the photo (foap.com). Travelers can receive goods or cash for bringing desired items from their home countries by making arrangements with people who want those items

Outcome	Percentage	Outcome	Percentage
Research product before buying	78	Pay bills online	38
Buy a product	71	Participate in online auction	26
Buy/make travel reservation	65	Sell something online	15
Bank online	61	Take class for college credit	13
Use online classifieds (Craigslist)	53	Buy/sell stocks, bonds, mutual funds	11

EXHIBIT 7.13 Proportion Trading Online in the United States *Source*: Data from 2009 to 2012 studies at pewinternet.org

via pleasebringme.com and bistip.com. There are also many sites available for selling your labor online, such as cloudfactory.com and guru.com.

GIVE As previously mentioned, many people create art, text, and other things purely for the benefit of others. Trendwatcher.com mentions "Generation Generosity" as one of the top global consumer trends in 2011. This includes financial donations as well as conversation gifts of care and sympathy online. As evidence, Trendwatcher notes that 86 percent of consumers worldwide want businesses to focus on society's interests as well as on their own business interests, and nowhere is this generosity greater than in China, India, and Brazil. At least a quarter of American consumers donates to causes via the internet or helps others in need online (according to Pew Internet & American. . .):

- 25 percent made an online donation to charity in 2011. These largely occur on political or nonprofit Web sites, who usually offer a contribution page. Also, consumers often send e-mail to friends enticing them to donate to a cause (e.g., American Heart Association when a family member had died of a stroke), or to sponsor them in an event to raise money for charity (e.g., a run- or sit-in to help inner-city children buy books). These e-mails have a link to the nonprofit page for easy contribution.
- 22 percent participated in an online conversation to help people with personal or health problems in 2006. This occurs in many venues from Google Groups on specific health issues to the four Facebook pages on depression (in 2012). As well, many sites offer space for question and answer advice with everything from lonely people to simply those who want to learn how to get someone to return a loaned book.

Kickstarter.com is a standout in this area because it offers a Web platform purely for individuals wanting funding for their creative projects. New project ideas range from art to fashion, film, food, music, publishing, technology, and many more. For example, Pebble is a proposed new customizable wrist watch that gained $10.3 million from over 68 thousand backers in 37 days—that computes to an average of $148.95 per donor (data from kickstarter.com).

Chapter Summary

The internet has grown more quickly than any other medium in history. In 2011, 2.3 billion people had access to the internet, representing 32.7 percent of the global population. Yet 4.7 billion other people are not online, due to social and cultural, technological, and legal and political issues, as well as the idea that many activities cannot be replaced by the internet.

Underlying consumer behavior and psychology is similar online as offline in most cases; however, the online environment drives many new behaviors. Technology allows marketers to apply traditional theories in interesting ways to consumers as they use social media and other internet venues.

The basic marketing concept of exchange refers to the act of obtaining a desired object from someone by offering something in return. Individual consumers bring their own characteristics and personal resources to the process as they seek specific outcomes from an exchange. All of this interaction occurs within a technological, social/cultural, and legal context. The cornerstones for attracting customers online are reputation, relevance, and engagement. The technological context is quite complex, including receiving device ownership, connection speed and usage, along with time shifting through DVRs and VOD. Among the U.S. social/cultural trends affecting online exchanges are information overload, multitasking, home and work boundary blur, I want what I want when I want it, online oxygen, connectivity, in the know, self-service, and concerns about privacy and data security.

Internet users tend to have a more positive attitude toward technology and be more adept and experienced with computer usage. Many demographics affect internet usage. Online shoppers tend to be more goal oriented and be either convenience or price oriented. Finally, broadband connectivity means the ability to watch videos and listen to music online.

The four main costs that consumers exchange for benefits are money, time/energy, and psychic costs. The internet exchange can be facilitated by browser and social bookmarks, e-mail messages with hyperlinks, and automated e-mails from Web sites seeking to attract visitors. The main consumer activities online can be categorized by these general outcomes: connect, create, enjoy, learn, trade, and give. Each outcome represents a marketing opportunity for savvy e-marketers.

Exercises

REVIEW QUESTIONS

1. Name several consumer behavior theories that apply both online and offline.
2. Identify and describe the six consumer behavior theories described in Dr. Marsden's work.
3. What is an exchange?
4. What are some of the trends affecting online exchanges in the United States?
5. What are Web 2.0 technologies?
6. What does customer engagement mean?
7. What individual characteristics influence online behavior?
8. What are twinsumers and how can marketers use this concept?
9. What are the three costs that constitute a consumer's resources for exchange?
10. How can e-marketers facilitate internet exchange?
11. What are the five main categories of outcomes sought by internet users?
12. In what ways do consumers create content for the Web?

DISCUSSION QUESTIONS

13. **The Customer's Story.** Relate Dr. Marsden's six consumer behavior theories to Justin's behavior in this hypothetical situation.
14. **The Customer's Story.** Which of the five exchange outcome categories is Justin using? Give specific examples.
15. Using the six consumer behavior theories (Marsden), name one online tactic for each that might motivate consumers to purchase.
16. How can a marketer use the electronic device and consumer viewing patterns displayed in the exhibits and described in this chapter? Why should marketers be concerned with device ownership?
17. How has cloud computing and streaming media changed the content consumption landscape?
18. Do you use music for which you did not pay? How do you justify this in terms of the losses mentioned in the chapter?
19. Why would a consumer go to the library instead of using the internet for research?
20. Describe two recent online and offline purchases (one each) and describe how the three resources/costs played out for each. What were the differences online and offline?
21. Can an attention economy exist in countries where internet penetration is low? Explain your answer.
22. What might e-marketers do to accommodate consumers who are experiential shoppers?
23. How might e-marketers capitalize on consumer interest in relationships as an internet strategy?

24. What are the reasons for the growth in social networking online?
25. Why do you think that consumers trust each other more than they trust companies? What can marketers do about this?
26. What are some of the ways marketers can engage customers in content?
27. Do you "like" any businesses or brands on Facebook? Why or why not?

WEB ACTIVITIES

28. Search for a good movie to rent on Netflix, Whattorent.com, and Rottentomatoes.com. Compare the reviews on each site for one movie and explain the differences and similarities.
29. Customers face many barriers when purchasing online. Many purchases are abandoned midstream. Working in groups, try to develop ways that online retailers can help more site visitors be converted to buyers.
30. Visit your local newspaper classified ads online, and then examine Craigslist for your local area. Why do you think that Craigslist and eBay have taken a part of the share from newspaper classifieds? What advice do you have for newspapers to regain customers?
31. Assume you wanted to buy an iPhone. Go online and shop for the right model and store. Relate your process to the consumer behavior theories in this chapter.
32. Visit Tripadvisor.com and search for a hotel room in San Francisco, California. Read the reviews. To what extent can you trust the reviewers, and why?

CHAPTER

8

Segmentation, Targeting, Differentiation, and Positioning Strategies

The main goal of this chapter is to help you examine the various bases for market segmentation and the classifications and characteristics of several important e-marketing segments. It also provides examples of product differentiation and positioning strategies for e-marketing.

After reading this chapter, you will be able to:

- Outline the characteristics of three major markets for e-business.
- Explain why and how e-marketers use market segmentation to reach online customers.
- List the most commonly used market segmentation bases and variables.
- Outline several types of internet usage segments and their characteristics.
- Describe two important coverage strategies e-marketers can use to target online customers.
- Define differentiation and positioning and give examples of online companies using them.

- Consumers make money from selling their insights to corporations, hawking their creative output to fellow consumers, or renting out unused assets. This trend has steadily evolved since we started tracking it five years ago, with more ways for consumers to make money, we're now seeing rapid growth of consumers who make money from carrying out small tasks, for other individuals or corporations.

- Launched in May 2012, ***EasyShift*** is a smartphone app from San Francisco that rewards users for completing 'Shifts' (tasks for other businesses). Shifts are mapped out so that users can find the nearest available one, whether it's answering a few questions, or taking a picture of a promotion at a shopping mall. Payments are made daily via PayPal, and regular users can build on their reputation to reach opportunities for higher pay.

The 1-800-Flowers Story

Jim McCann is a guy who keeps up with technology. He started with 14 retail flower shops in New York City in 1976 and is now a multichannel retailer who understands his target customers. Ten years later, he acquired the incoming toll-free number 1-800-Flowers so that customers could order flowers over the telephone from any location for delivery in New York. In 1995, McCann was quick to jump onto e-commerce with an early Web site to extend the brand (1-800-flowers.com) and offer 24/7 worldwide delivery. By this point, the company had expanded to plants, gourmet food, gift baskets, and other gift-related merchandise.

The Web site worked well and the company generated much data about prospects and customers who registered and purchased online. How to sort it all out and use it for increasing profits? McCann used data mining software from SAS® to identify customer segments for better targeting. The software sifted through Web site clickstreams and purchasing patterns of the firm's 21 million customers and spit out some interesting findings. According to Aaron Cano, Vice President of Enterprise Customer Knowledge, "Not every customer wants the same relationship. Some want you to be more involved with them than others; some will give you different levels of permission on how to contact them. At the end of the day, you have many different customers . . . [information about] who they are and how they would like to be treated." 1-800-Flowers can respond to the segment of one person who purchases every year only on Valentine's Day, or the larger segment of people who want several birthday reminders a year so they don't forget to honor their friends and family. All of this individual attention is possible at McCann's place. As a result, 1-800-flowers .com has appeared for seven years on the Internet Retailer's "Best of the Web Top 50 Retail Sites" and has been a *Forbes Magazine* "Best of the Web" site (according to 1-800-flowers.com site information).

1-800-Flowers also has an active Facebook page with nearly 500,000 likes and 13,829 people were talking about the site in September 2012. This page engages users with its frequent posts of very creative floral bouquets and other ideas for upcoming holidays. Its Twitter account has over 20,000 followers.

1-800-flowers.com currently uses SAS business analytics to compete by managing customer relationships and building customer value. This process resulted in millions of dollars of additional revenue, partially due to increased customer satisfaction—customer problems dropped by 40 percent after implementation (according to sas.com success stories). As well, the company discovered and developed Mother's Day flower offers targeting the female customer segment because they are the biggest buyers of flowers for their mothers and mothers-in-law. The company can analyze multichannel sales data in real time and make adjustments to its Web site offers based on retail demands in various geographic zip code (geographic) segments.

This focus on customer service by using business analytics and narrow customer segment targeting works well for 1-800-Flowers. Revenues grew 7.6 percent to $716.3 million in 2012 with a gross profit of 41 percent (1-800-Flowers.com, Inc. . ., 2012). The company had 4.6 million e-commerce customers, over half of whom were repeat buyers. Founder McCann attributes this to the company's leadership in its three business segments (Consumer Floral, BloomNet Wire Service, and Gourmet Food and Gift Baskets) and success in the rapidly growing social and mobile channels.

SEGMENTATION AND TARGETING OVERVIEW

1-800-Flowers clearly understands the needs and behaviors of its various target markets. A company must have in-depth market knowledge to devise a savvy segmentation and targeting strategy, especially in today's multichannel commerce environment. As explained in Chapter 3, e-marketing strategic planning occurs in two highly interrelated tiers. The first involves segmentation, targeting, differentiation, and positioning, topics covered in this chapter. Second-tier strategies involving the 4 Ps and customer relationship management (CRM) are discussed in Chapters 9 through 15.

Marketers make informed decisions about segmentation and targeting based on internal, secondary, and primary data sources (see Exhibit 8.1). **Marketing segmentation** is the process of aggregating individuals or businesses along similar characteristics that pertain to the use, consumption, or benefits of a product or service. The result of market segmentation is groups of customers called market segments. We use the word *groups* loosely here. A market segment can actually be of any size from one person to millions of people—an important point because the technology of internet marketing allows companies to easily tailor market mixes for targeting individuals. It is also important to note that segments are worth targeting separately only when they have bigger differences between them than within them. For example, if internet users behave differently at work than at home, marketers can capitalize on these differences by targeting each as a separate segment—otherwise why bother separating these users into two targets with different marketing mix offerings?

Market targeting is the process of selecting the market segments that are most attractive to the company. Some criteria companies use to select segments for targeting include accessibility, profitability, and growth potential.

THREE MARKETS

Sergio Zyman, formerly chief marketing officer of Coca-Cola, has been quoted as saying, "Marketing is supposed to sell stuff." One way information technology helps sell stuff is by facilitating relationships before, during, and after the transaction with prospects, customers, partners, and supply chain members. Yet all

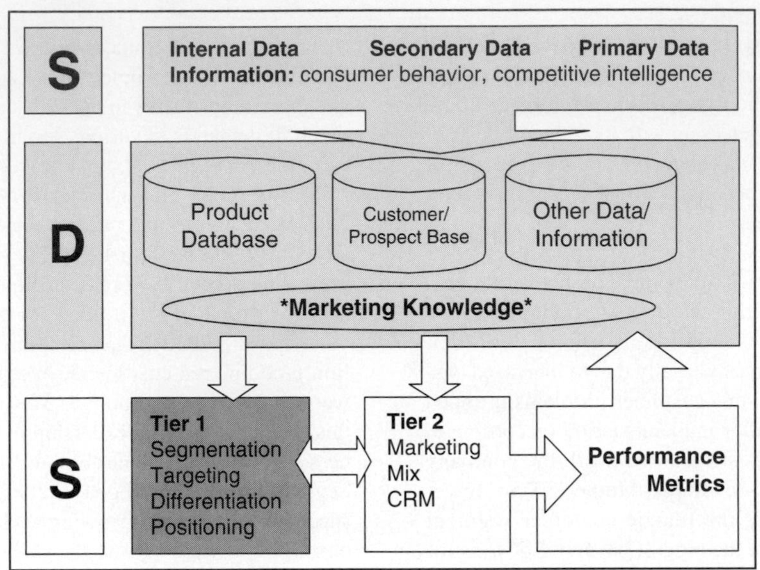

EXHIBIT 8.1 Sources and Databases Inform Tier 1 Strategies

the latest technology can't help marketers sell stuff if they don't identify appropriate markets. Exhibit 8.2 highlights three important markets that both sell to and buy from each other: businesses, consumers, and governments. Although this book focuses on the **business-to-consumer (B2C)** market with some coverage of **business-to-business (B2B)** activities, all three markets are important. Note that after B2C and B2B markets, the **business-to-government (B2G)** and **consumer-to-consumer (C2C)** markets are where most e-business activity occurs.

Business Market

The business market involves the marketing of products to businesses, governments, and institutions for use in the business operation, as components in the business products, or for resale. The online B2B marketing is huge because a higher

	To Business	To Consumer	To Government
Initiated by business	Business-to-business **(B2B)** *The Idea Factory* ideafactory.com	Business-to-consumer **(B2C)** *Classmates* classmates.com	Business-to-government **(B2G)** *State Supply Commission* ssc.wa.gov.au
Initiated by consumer	Consumer-to-business **(C2B)** *Better Business Bureau* bbb.org	Consumer-to-consumer **(C2C)** *eBay* ebay.com	Consumer-to-government **(C2G)**, *U.S. Department of The Interior* govworks.gov
Initiated by government	Government-to-business **(G2B)** *U.S. Small Business Administration* sba.gov	Government-to-consumer **(G2C)** *State of California* state.ca.us	Government-to-government **(G2G)** USA.gov usa.gov

EXHIBIT 8.2 Three Basic Markets *Source*: Updated in 2012 from Wood, Marian. (2001). *Prentice Hall's Guide to E-Commerce and E-Business.* Upper Saddle River, NJ: Prentice Hall

proportion of companies are connected to the internet than consumers, especially in developing countries. Much of the B2B online activity is transparent to consumers because it involves proprietary networks that allow information and database sharing (e.g., extranets). Consider FedEx, the package delivery company. This company maintains huge databases of business customers' shipping behavior and account information. FedEx's customers can schedule a package pickup using its Web site, track the package using a PC or smartphone, and pay the shipping bill online. Sometimes the shipping order is automatically triggered when a consumer buys something online from a FedEx client; then FedEx sends an e-mail notification of its delivery progress to the retailer.

Information technology created tremendous efficiencies in the B2B market, yet businesses that sell online face increasing competition due to globalization and lower market entry barriers brought about by the internet. As well, many companies are changing their entire supply chain structures, which often results in conflict between different marketing channels. This conflict is especially problematic when manufacturers sell directly to consumers online, thus taking business away from their retail partners. On the other hand, many companies experience greater interdependence in their value chain due to electronic collaboration practices. Many challenges and opportunities exist for companies in the B2B market.

Finally, the internet allows for strange bedfellows. Companies in unlikely industries find it relatively easy to forge partnerships that supply value to customers. Consider, for example, the joint venture that created MSNBC (Microsoft and the NBC television network). In this environment, companies compete not only for customers but also for partners and sometimes even for partnerships with rivals. As an example, the major airlines came together to form an airline reservations hub—thus undercutting online travel agents (e.g., Star Alliance with United Airlines and 26 others). As another example, the major U.S. auto manufacturers have a shared procurement hub to link to their suppliers.

Government Market

The U.S. Federal government is the world's largest buyer. Add to this the purchasing power of U.S. states, counties, cities, and other municipal agencies, which makes for huge markets. The governments of other countries are also major purchasers. The state government of Western Australia, for instance, buys $6 billion in goods and services annually and authorizes more than 40,000 work contracts.

Businesses wishing to sell to governments face challenges unique to this market. Government agencies have many rules for suppliers to follow regarding qualifications, paperwork, and so on. Additionally, companies often must compete to be on the government list of approved suppliers, and then compete yet again for specific work contracts through a bidding process. Government agencies are generally very particular about timely delivery of quality products at reasonable prices.

The good news is that small and large businesses usually have an equal chance of selling to governments, and government Web sites announce their buying needs in advance of the bidding process. The U.S. government maintains a searchable Web site displaying nearly 40,000 opportunities in September 2012 (FedBizOpps .gov in Exhibit 8.3). Internet technology has helped businesses to be more effective when selling to government markets because they can upload proposals at the site and handle much of the bidding process online.

Consumer Market

The consumer market involves marketing goods and services to the end consumer. This chapter describes many consumer market segments, and most of this text is dedicated to e-marketing in the consumer market.

MARKET SEGMENTATION BASES AND VARIABLES

Marketers can base their segmentation of consumer markets on demographics, geographic location, psychographics, behavior, and many

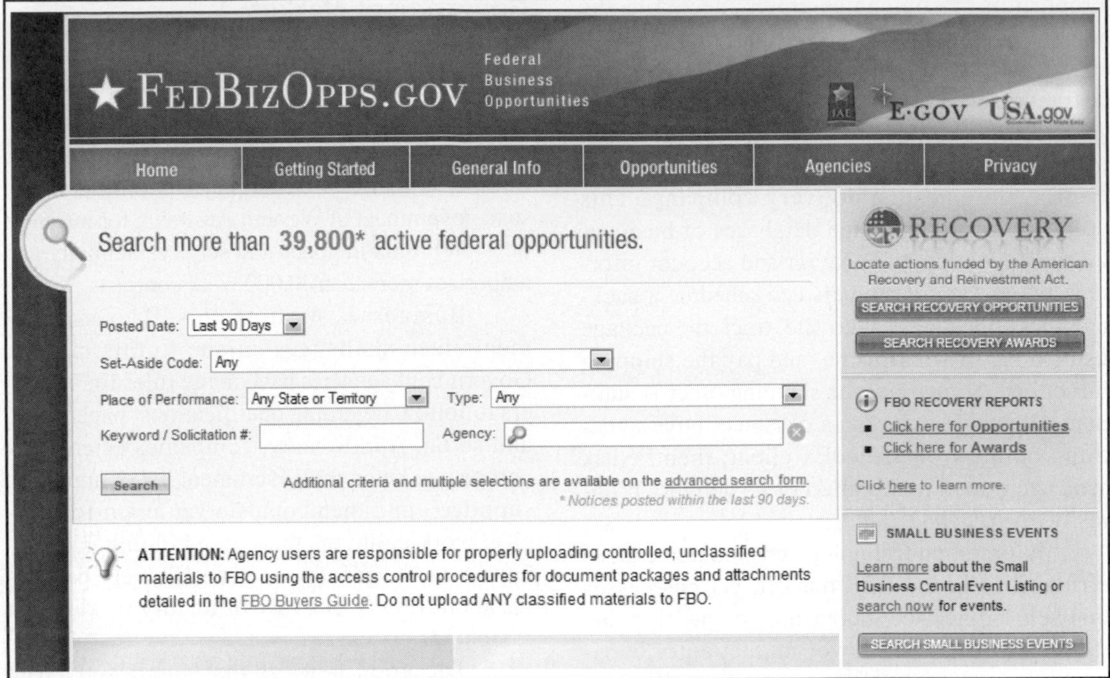

EXHIBIT 8.3 U.S. Government Federal Business Opportunities *Source*: fbo.gov

combinations of these. Within each base, many **segmentation variables** come into play (see Exhibit 8.4). For example, McDonald's demographic segmentation uses the variables of age and family life cycle to target adults, children, senior citizens, and families. One way to understand segmentation bases is to consider these as a few general organizing categories and segmentation variables as numerous subcategories.

Companies often combine bases and focus on categories such as **geodemographics** (geography and demographics). For example, the Claritas PRIZM system, owned by the Nielsen company, contains 62 geodemographic segments (with segment names such as Blue Blood Estates and Young Digerati). Similarly, marketers can build segments using any combination of variables that make sense for their industry. The important thing to remember is that marketers create segments based on variables that can be used to identify, enumerate, and reach the right people at the right time.

Bases	Geographics	Demographics	Psychographics	Behavior
Identifying	City	Age	Activities	Benefits sought
Profiling	County	Income	Interests	Usage level
Variable	State	Gender	Opinions	Online engagement level
Examples	Region	Education	Personality	User status
	Country	Ethnicity	Values	

EXHIBIT 8.4 Segmentation Bases and Examples of Related Variables

After using any of these four bases alone or in combination, marketers profile segment members using many other variables. For example, a Web site such as iVillage.com uses demographic segmentation, targeting women. It can create a list of mothers who register at the site, and then use Web analytics and other online research to develop profiles that describe these mothers (such as, how old are their children and what activities the family enjoys). These profiles might indicate that 30 percent of mothers like to search for places to take their children for a family excursion. iVillage can then determine which other Web and social media sites reach this target market (for advertising) and what content and products to display on its own site and in email communication to this market. It is much more difficult to figure out how to reach these women when they are offline and want to find places to take their children. Thus, marketers use profile variables to refine the marketing mix, including Web site content and advertising. 1-800-Flowers also does this type of segmentation analysis, as discussed in the chapter opening story.

The next sections describe geographic, demographic, psychographic, and behavior segments on the internet.

Geographic Segments

Most companies target specific cities, regions, states, or countries with their product offerings. Even the largest global companies usually develop multisegment strategies based on geographics.

Product distribution strategy is a driving force behind geographic segmentation. A consumer goods online retailer, such as rakuten.com, will want to reach only customers in countries where it distributes its products. Similarly, companies offering services online will only sell to geographic areas where they can provide this service and follow-up customer assistance in the appropriate language. Before an organization decides to use the internet channel, it must examine the proportion of internet users in its selected geographic targets. For example, would it make sense to build a Web site that serves citizens of Samoa, where the internet adoption rate is only 6.6 percent (or the 40 countries with lower rates than that as seen in Appendix A)?

Important Geographic Segments for E-Marketing

China boasts the largest internet usage in the world with 513 million users, although this represents only 38.4 percent of the population. The United States is the second largest geographic segment with 245 million users and a higher penetration rate (78.3 percent of population—although other studies show 85 percent, as previously mentioned). In contrast, Iceland boasts the highest proportion of internet usage among its population. In total, 67 country markets now have at least 50 percent internet penetration. These countries represent good markets for new technology because they are quite internet savvy. Appendix A lists all countries in the world with available statistics on internet usage, and this would be a good starting point for geographic segmentation. Bear in mind that these figures represent one point in time during 2011 and that internet usage statistics vary widely depending on who conducts the study. Marketers using geographic variables for segmentation also evaluate online markets by region, city, urban area, and so forth. For instance, the entire North American and Scandinavian regions contain attractive markets, and most urban areas, such as Mexico City, Mexico, are more wired than are rural areas. Many factors indicate market viability for e-commerce and other e-business activities in countries outside of the United States, as explained in Chapter 4.

GLOBAL FACEBOOK AND SEARCH ENGINE ADOPTION While China is the big bang in internet adoption, it is very low with Facebook adoption (3.3 percent of the population). It is important to realize that Google and Facebook are international but other countries have their own similar search engines and social networks that gain many local adopters. For example, China's Sina Weibo is similar to Twitter and has 22 percent adoption in China (Mei, 2012). And Renren is China's Facebook look-alike, with 147 million registered users (11 percent of the population). In the search engine market, Google pales in China, with only 6.6 percent share of the market compared to industry giant Baidu (with 78.6 percent market share) (CIW Team Staff, 2012). Obviously, a global e-marketer must study geographic markets carefully before planning internet strategies and tactics.

LANGUAGES ON WEB PAGES English has not been the language of most Web pages and online bulletin boards for many years, yet it has seen a slight increase in the past two years. In 2011, the top internet languages included English (33 percent), Chinese (29 percent), Spanish (9 percent), Japanese (6 percent), and Portuguese (5 percent), according to internetworldstats.com data (Exhibit 8.5). These findings obviously have huge implications for e-marketers desiring to reach global markets via the internet; until more online text appears in local languages, users in those countries will not be able to participate in e-commerce or other online activities. Unfortunately, Web developers in many Asian and Middle Eastern countries face technical challenges because local languages require double-byte character sets (versus single byte for Romance languages) and, therefore, need more database and transaction customization and complicated search algorithms.

Another factor is that many countries recognize more than one national language, such as Canada, which has both English- and French-speaking citizens. Consider the U.S. Small Business Administration (SBA) (Exhibit 8.6). This government agency serves citizens speaking both Spanish and English, and, like many companies and nonprofits, the agency has created Web site content in different languages.

LOCAL MARKETING Finally, local marketing efforts work well online, thanks to Google and Yahoo! local searches and company review sites, such as Yelp and Foursquare. Small companies, such as the local physician or car repair shop, can be listed in these searches even if they don't have Web sites. Google offers amazing applications for smartphones, allowing owners to get from

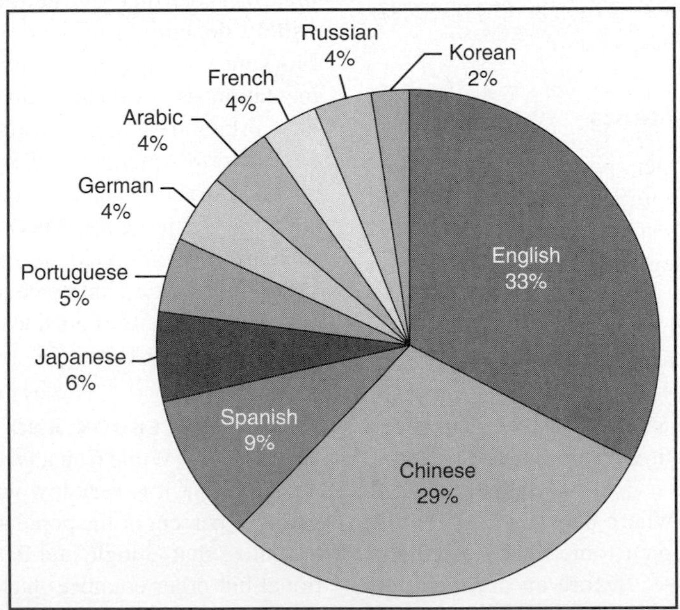

EXHIBIT 8.5 One-Third of Web Users in 2011 Use English Online
Source: Data from internetworldstats.com

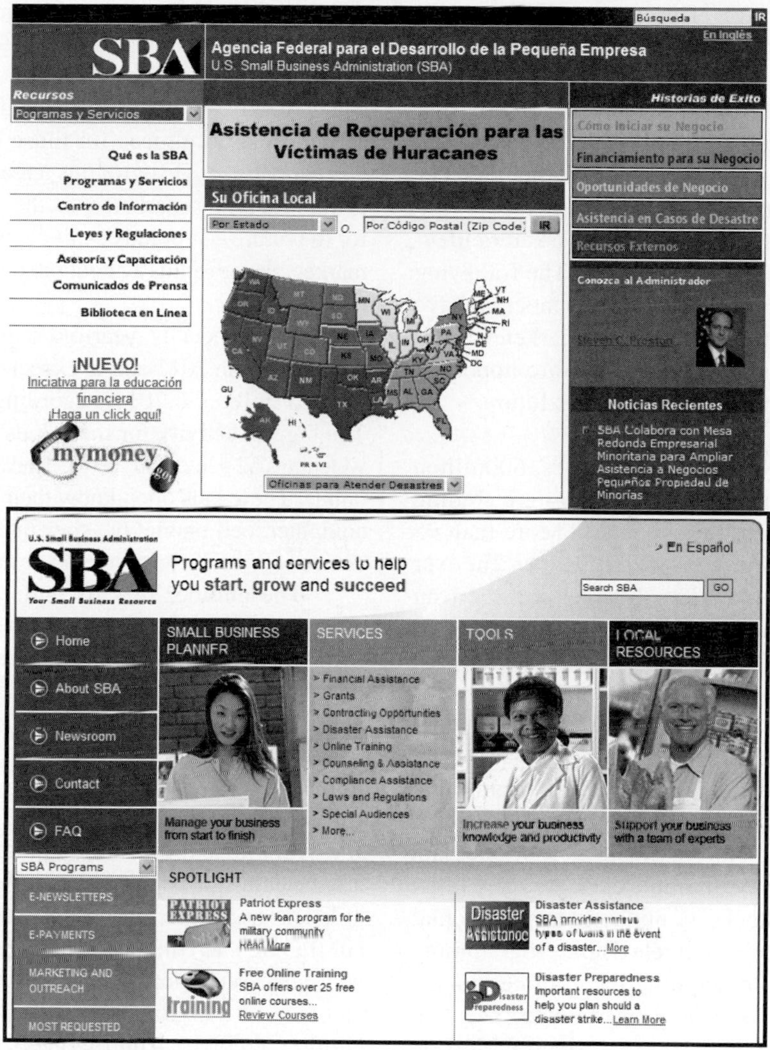

EXHIBIT 8.6 U.S. Small Business Administration Site in Spanish and English *Source*: sba.gov

where they are to any local business. In 2012, 61 percent of smartphone owners used a smartphone to search for a local business, resulting in 72 percent who purchased from that business (versus 86 percent who purchased after searching on a tablet computer), according to the 5th Annual Local Search Usage Study conducted by comScore.com. As well, comScore found that over half of mobile device searchers used consumer reviews on social networks and 45 percent posted a review. Other important local marketing efforts include eBay classifieds (with over 100 million visitors exchanging $68.6 billion worth of goods in 2011) and the hugely popular Craigslist.

Demographic Segments

In the internet's early years, the typical user was a young male, college educated, with a high income—except for gender, the description of a typical innovator. This picture is generally repeated in countries with low levels of internet adoption and in most social media adoption rates at this point. In developed nations, users look more like the mainstream population with a slight skew toward younger people with higher incomes and more education.

To reach these segments, marketers identify attractive demographic niches. The following sections describe two market segments that have recently caught the attention of e-marketers: millennials and kids. Obviously, these are important because they represent the internet's future.

MILLENNIALS In the United States, 60 million people born between 1979 and 1994 are coming of age in the twenty-first century. More than 95 percent use the internet—nearly 10 percent over the national average. Pew Internet & American Life calls millennials "confident, connected, and open to change." They are the hyper connected generation. Millennials are able to handle multitasking and information overload better than older internet users because they grew up with the internet. They are the folks who can easily operate any receiving appliance and see information, communication, and entertainment as just one data stream available on multiple devices. They often use pop-up ad blockers online and use the digital video recorder to watch television programming on their schedule, zapping the commercials—unless these are especially entertaining. They are heavy social networking users, sleep with their cell phones, and live on text messages.

Millennials are an important market segment because they are the first generation to control information quickly, use many technology gadgets at once, and totally ignore marketers. More than half of the millennials watch television and use the internet at the same time, sometimes voting online while watching *American Idol* or other television programs. They use many media channels, such as instant messaging, e-mail, Facebook chat, iPods or other MP3 players, P2P networks, online virtual games, and virtual worlds.

If marketers can get their attention and entertain them, they will listen and spread the news through online word-of-mouth (viral marketing) and social networks. However, marketers must attend to the millennial's thirst for instant gratification by responding to their Tweets instantly and generally mimicking millennial behavior—an especially difficult task for those marketers over 35 years of age. This group is a real challenge and is important to e-marketers as the proving ground for the future—if brands can't capture the younger markets they eventually become obsolete.

KIDS The under 11-year-old segment jumped to 20.2 million in 2011 and is expected to increase to over 25 million in 2015, according to eMarketer. The biggest activity for these kids is online video watching (62 percent in 2012). They also play games online. These kids often know their way around the computer, cell phone, or other internet-connected device before they learn to read or ride a bike.

The number of kids under the age of 17 online is increasing. What do kids between 12 and 17 do online? According to Forrester Research, Inc., boys play 6.1 hours of video games a week. As well, 41 percent of girls and 32 percent of boys post on a social networking site every day (see Reineke Reitsma's blog on blogs.forrester.com). Young kids also hang out at social networking site Webkinz.com for hours at a time. Webkinz are the cute stuffed animals that sell for $10–$20 at brick-and-mortar retailers. Once home, kids cut the tag and find an eight-digit code that can be used at Webkinz.com to register their new toy and receive a digital look-alike pet. Once there, children receive virtual money (KinzCash) and can spend it to build things or to buy clothes and other items for their virtual pet unicorn, cat, or tie dye frogs. Kids can play games to earn more money and, naturally, parents can add money to their children's accounts. Webkinz provides safe connections and chats with other pet owners, allows members to have virtual jobs that earn money, and also provides creative outlets, such as allowing children to create TV shows.

Many parents worry about the security and privacy of their kids online but they can't stop marketers from targeting this huge potential new market. Instead, many parents censor Web content for children (see the "Let's Get Technical" box on content filtering). Kids are

LET'S GET TECHNICAL

Content Filtering

Somehow, you were sucked into babysitting your seven-year-old cousin. He asks you if he can go online while you are making his dinner—macaroni and cheese with hot dog chunks, of course. However, you think, "How am I going to monitor him while I am downstairs cooking?" You know that you, or his parents, would never want him to experience inappropriate material online. As you pause to mull over this dilemma, your cousin says, "Don't worry! My mom and dad made the computer safe for me."

One growing segment of Web users is children under the age of 18. Children often have their own personal e-mail accounts and online nicknames. Many families are concerned that their children will be exposed to unwanted material online, such as pornography or violence, which can be considered objectionable. Even children not seeking such material may be exposed when conducting innocent searches. For example, a simple search for "girls' sites" using one of the top search engines resulted in numerous objectionable links to sex sites, such as a link titled "Naked Girls Sites Teenager Drunk and Naked."

Many solutions are available to serve the needs of user segments that do not want exposure to this type of material. One group of solutions aims to curb exposure to offensive material through education or legislation. Another group of solutions aims to limit exposure by the use of technology. Education- and legislation-based solutions include the following:

- Educate children not to pursue offensive online material.
- Ban offensive material through legislative means.
- Require or encourage providers of offensive material to put age warnings on their sites (i.e., "if you are under 18 do not enter here").
- Require or encourage providers of offensive material to run an age verification system. Such systems require users to purchase a password using a credit card or require a valid credit card number to verify age. The presumption is that minors do not have access to credit cards.
- Require or encourage providers of offensive material to rate their material using industry-standard ratings similar to those used by the television or film industries.

Technology-based solutions include the following:

- Ask the internet service provider (ISP) to filter the content coming to the user.
- Filter the content right on the user's own computer using specialized software.
- Use search engines that filter the results based on user preferences.

All solutions mentioned have pros and cons, and they have been the subject of lively debates. This section focuses only on solutions that are technology based.

The internet is comprised of many different types of computers, and, when users access Web pages, they are metaphorically hopping from computer to computer until their destination is reached. At any one of these hops, the content can be scanned and filtered for appropriateness. In the corporate world, employees are typically barred from objectionable sites by software running on a corporate computer that serves as the gatekeeper to the internet. This computer is called a **proxy server**. All communication between any corporate computer and the internet passes through the proxy server. It is an efficient solution and even allows employers to record attempted accesses to objectionable sites and to take disciplinary action when desired. Proxy servers have also been used to reduce employees' leisure-surfing while at work. For example, some corporations have chosen to block sports-oriented sites, such as espn.com or social networking sites such as Facebook.

The home Web user typically does not have access to a similar service; ISPs are reluctant to filter content because many users want to access this type of material. Some countries, such as China and Vietnam, filter content at the ISP level for everyone (adults as well as children). Incidentally, censorship is at the heart of the ethics debate on this issue.

Normally, the home user installs software on his or her computer to filter content. A number of products can perform this task, including Net Nanny,

(*continued*)

CYBERsitter, and CyberPatrol. As their names indicate, these products are intended to impede children's access to the objectionable sites. Many provide password overrides so other household members can have full internet access if they wish. Filters are also customizable, allowing users to set the strength of the filter for each user.

One way the products operate is by maintaining a "can't go" or "can go" list. Under the "can't go" scenario, the products maintain a list of banned sites—tens of thousands of these.

Each time a child attempts to access a site, the software checks the site address against the list of banned sites. If it matches, the software can take one of the following actions:

1. Allow access to the site and silently make a record of the access for the parent to see later.
2. Allow access to the site and mask out objectionable words or images.
3. Block any access to the banned site.
4. Shut down the browser completely.

Under the "can go" scenario, the child can visit only sites that are on an approved list and nothing else. These sites might include G-rated sites such as disney.com or toysrus.com. The parents can always add to this list according to requests from the children. The same series of actions would be available should a child try to access a site not on the "can go" list.

Most products provide free updates as the list of objectionable sites grows. Updates are a major concern due to the constant production of new adult sites. However, filters that block access to sites based on words in the site name (e.g., cybersextalk.com) or the words in the Web page itself (e.g., "this site contains graphic sex") provide increased protection against the new sites. Even incoming e-mail or Microsoft Word documents can be scanned. In all cases, the same list of foregoing action options is available.

The products can also monitor outgoing e-mail messages to ensure that children do not give away private information such as name, phone number, or address to a cyber pedophile. To accomplish this monitoring, the software is programmed to recognize the name, phone number, and address of household members and then scan for these keywords in any outgoing message. ISPs have also begun to offer e-mail filtering. Users are drawn to the e-mail filtering services, but still reject the idea of ISPs filtering their Web content. America Online's (AOL) filtering service is based on its customers' input. When a specific number of customers report an e-mail to be objectionable, AOL begins filtering it out of all subscribers' incoming e-mail.

Leading search engines, such as Google and Bing, also offer content filtering. Both have a default setting of a moderate filter, and users can permanently set their preferences to a higher or lower filter. Another type of service available is a search engine designed specifically for children, such as Ask Jeeves for Kids (ajkids.com) and Yahoo! Kids.

Apple builds parental controls right into its operating system. In addition to limiting the sites visited, the controls can also limit the overall amount of time that a child spends on the computer each day. One can even limit the time of day that a child is on the computer. So late night surfing when the parents are asleep can be eliminated. The time limits are a welcome feature for parents who tire of nagging their children to get off the machine.

Many feel that **content filtering** products do provide the level of protection that families need. Some communities also install content filtering software in public libraries. These products are an example of a unique marketing mix that is tailored to a target market based on both demographics (age) and **psychographics** (beliefs). However, none of these products is completely foolproof, because Web sites change too quickly and determined kids are very clever.

responsive to marketing messages; however, e-marketers must be careful not to irritate their parents who might perceive promotional messages as manipulation. Nonetheless, this is a hugely important demographic segment following in the footsteps of millennials and definitely worth watching.

Psychographic Segments

User psychographics include personality, values, lifestyle, activities, interests, and opinions (**AIO**). *Personality* characteristics are traits such as other-oriented versus self-oriented and habits such as procrastination. *Values* are deeply held convictions such as religious and green environment beliefs. *Lifestyles* and *activities* as psychographics refer to nonproduct-specific behavior such as playing sports, writing product reviews online, or eating out. For example, users say that their internet time takes time away from these other activities: reading (39 percent), sleeping (23 percent), socializing (14 percent), and working (12 percent) (intelliquest.com). *Interests* and *opinions* are attitudes and beliefs people hold. As an example, some people believe that Facebook is a waste of time, and others think they could not exist without e-mail.

INTEREST COMMUNITIES The internet is ideal for gathering people from all corners of the globe into communities with similar interests and tasks. Social media and other online communities attract users, who then post their comments and profiles and upload content for others to see—sometimes paying a subscription price for the benefit. Communities can form around social media or other Web sites and forums, or via e-mails to the entire group membership. We've identified 10 important types of online communities ripe with marketing opportunity (Exhibit 8.7).

Perhaps the most important type is **social networking**—the practice of expanding the number of one's business and social contacts by making connections through individuals online. It is based on the idea of *six degrees of separation* (that any two people are connected through contacts with no more than five others). LinkedIn is a great example of a professional network with over 175 million professionals worldwide, representing 200 countries (Exhibit 8.8). Recall that people trust others like them more than many company professionals, so social networking and other communities will continue to grow in importance.

Three ways can be used to target online communities. First, a company can build a community at its own Web site through online discussion groups, bulletin boards, and online events or through company-owned social network pages. When folks with similar interests gather at the virtual watering hole to discuss issues, the value they receive in both information and **social bonding** keeps them returning. Second, companies can advertise on another company's community site or via blog comments and e-mails to community members. Finally, many companies actually join the communities and listen and learn from others who are talking about their industry. For example, Scott O'Leary, Managing Director, Customer Experience, at Continental Airlines spends several hours each day to find customer problems posted on travel sites such as Flyertalk (flyertalk.com). This network has nearly 500,000 members, who post their air travel problems and tips for readers. O'Leary reportedly posted over 500 comments one recent year on Flyertalk and similar sites, answering questions and stopping rumors, according to *The Cincinnati Post*.

Several advantages and disadvantages characterize community targeting online. When an organization builds and maintains the community, it can present products and controlled messages customized to the group's interests, such as at Amazon.com. These communities are good targets for products of interest to them. For example, online gamers are always interested in hearing about the latest subscription-based game, and members of the Harley Owner's Group enjoy hearing about Harley-Davidson-branded products. Perhaps, most importantly, communities are good places for companies to learn about customer problems and suggestions, such as O'Leary and Dell experienced. Conversely, online community conversation will often gather negative product postings and offensive language. When companies sponsor a community, they must watch the content; however, if they edit it too heavily they will discourage future postings. Besides, if a company removes negative posts, users will just post elsewhere online and discuss it all over the Web in blogs and on Facebook, so it is better to host the conversation at the company's own Web site. Next, Web sites based on communities, such as Yahoo! Groups, experience some difficulty in drawing advertisers because of the unpredictable content and its possible effects on brand image. Finally, it takes a lot of time to participate in and monitor social media and other online communities.

Community Type	Description and Example
1. Entertainment communities	People join for multiplayer online gaming such as Second Life at secondlife.com or chess at Games.Yahoo.com.
2. Social networking communities	Users join and visit these communities to meet others, such as for dating (Match.com), getting a job (Monster.com), or finding a business connection (LinkedIn.com). Users are willing to pay a fee to join these communities, especially if they are large. Some sites exist purely for connecting to meet and make friends with like-minded people. These include Twitter.com, Facebook.com, and many others.
3. Trading communities	These communities exist so that users can exchange goods and services. Examples include online auctions in the consumer market (eBay.com) and business market (Guru.com), and music-sharing sites (Kazaa.com).
4. Education communities	These communities form around particular education disciplines, such as Elmar for marketing educators (marketingpower.com), educational software, or students participating in class or university discussion groups.
5. Scheduled events communities	When *American Idol,* the televised competition, invites viewers to vote and chat online, or businesses hold online conferences, they form a community for a one-time event.
6. Advocacy communities	Nonprofit communities form to influence public opinion. MoveOn.org formed to make a change in politics and used its community to create and pay for television ads. According to its founder, the internet is about listening to users, not talking to them.
7. Brand communities	Firms create CRM communities around their brands on Web sites by allowing user posting. Examples include product reviews (Amazon.com), travel experiences (Tripadvisor.com), and tips for using your electronic gadget (engadget.com) or SAP software (Sap.com). Many companies also create branded social network pages.
8. Consumer communities	Consumers post product reviews on epinions.com and discuss their product experiences on Google Groups. What differentiates these from CRM communities is their lack of brand sponsorship, and thus, they are basically unedited opinions.
9. Employee communities	One example is the large network of former Microsoft employees who use e-mail and a private bulletin board to discuss Microsoft gossip and to network for professional purposes. LinkedIn.com and Xing.com are two important professional networks.
10. Special topics communities	In addition to the others on this list, some sites exist purely for user chat and bulletin board posting on a narrow topic of interest, such as movies, a particular automobile brand/model, various religions, and so forth. Leading this category are Google Groups (the former UseNet) and Yahoo Groups.

EXHIBIT 8.7 Ten Important Types of Online Communities

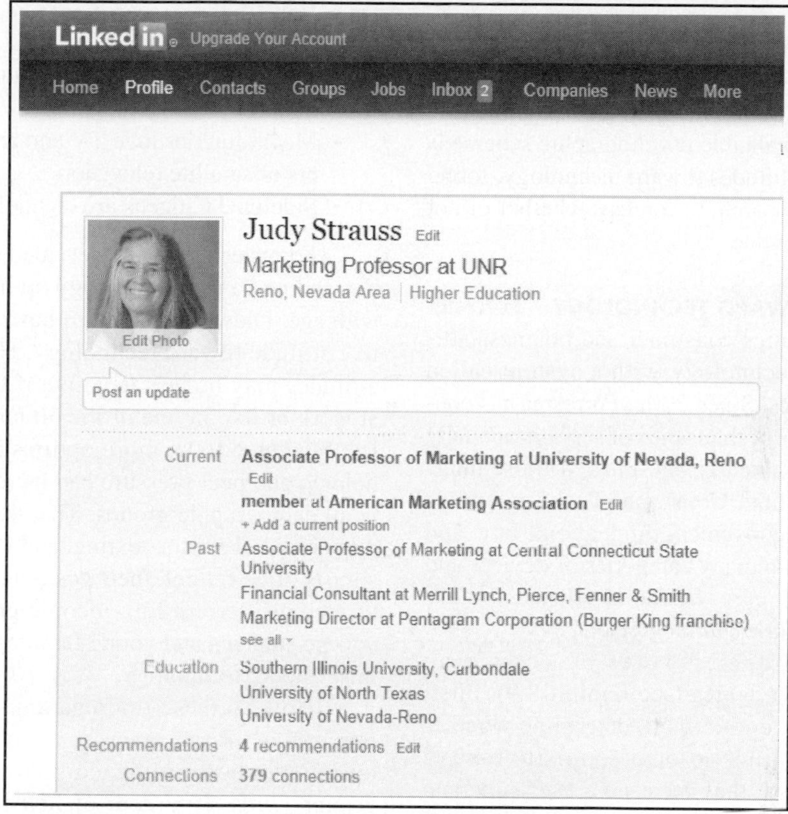

EXHIBIT 8.8 Social Networking Community for Professionals
Source: linkedin.com

ATTITUDES AND BEHAVIORS How do attitudes and behavior differ? Attitudes are internal evaluations about people, products, and other objects. They can be either positive or negative, but the evaluation process occurs inside a person's head. Behavior refers to what a person physically does, such as talking, eating, registering at a Web site, posting a comment on a blog, "Liking" a Facebook page, or visiting a Web site to shop or purchase a product. However, marketers do not include product-related behaviors in psychographic segmentation. Product behaviors are such a vital segment descriptor that they form an entirely separate category (see the next section). Thus, when marketers discuss psychographics, they mean the general ways that consumers spend time and when they discuss "behavior" it is usually about product-specific behaviors.

Psychographic information helps e-marketers define and describe market segments so they can better meet consumer needs. It is especially important for Web page design and deciding what social media to use for connecting with prospects and customers. For example, Japanese users do not like the flippant and irreverent tone at some U.S. sites. Japan's Web sites are more serious and do not include content such as political satire. Baby boomers prefer earth tone colors and positive, well-worded conversation on Web and social media sites and the millennials prefer more hip, bright colors, and authentic talk. This type of attitudinal information is increasingly available about Web users.

Most marketers believe that demographics are not helpful in predicting whether a person will purchase online or offline. Demographics help marketers find target markets for communication, but other variables are more valuable for prediction, so marketers try to find a balance between both types of variables to identify and then profile segments. One valuable psychographic scheme is the segment's attitudes toward technology, found by Forrester Research, to forecast whether or not users will buy online.

ATTITUDES TOWARD TECHNOLOGY Forrester Research measures consumer and business attitudes toward technology with a system called **Technographics**. Since 2002, Forrester has conducted hundreds of thousands of surveys annually worldwide, with nearly one-third of those interviews held offline. Consumer Technographics discovers how consumers think about, buy, and use technology in many categories of devices and media in health care, financial services, retail, and travel industries, among others.

Technographics works by combining three specific variables (see Exhibit 8.9). First, researchers ask questions to determine whether a person is optimistic or pessimistic toward technology. Next, they measure a user's income level because it is an important determinant of online shopping behavior. Finally, they query users about their primary motivation for going online. After over many years of collecting data, Forrester identified 10 consumer Technographics segments in the United States. Exhibit 8.9 displays these segments along with their descriptions. According to Forrester, the following is an example of how each segment uses technology:

- Fast Forwards are the biggest users of business software.
- New Age Nurturers are the most ignored group of technology consumers.
- Mouse Potatoes love interactive entertainment on the PC.
- Of all low-income groups, Techno-Strivers have the highest proportion of PC ownership.
- Digital Hopefuls are a strong potential market for low-cost PCs.
- Gadget Grabbers buy low-cost, high-tech toys such as Nintendo.
- Handshakers aren't into technology for their business dealings.
- Traditionalists use VCRs but not anything more.
- Media Junkies love TV and are early adopters of satellite television.
- Sidelined Citizens are technology laggards.

Forrester's research revealed some interesting findings. First, technology optimism declines with age. Older users tend to have a more negative attitude toward technology. However, their attitudes may be less negative if they use a PC at work or live in one of the 50 largest U.S. cities. Men tend to be more optimistic about technology, and peer pressure can increase optimism in all demographic groups. That is, when friends discuss social media, texting, and Web sites, pessimists often rethink their positions. With regard to income, certain low-income groups such as college students and young families are also optimistic about technology.

How do these findings translate to online purchasing? First, twice as many high-income optimists shop online compared with other groups. Only 2 percent of low-income pessimists shop online, and therefore they are not a good target for e-commerce companies. Second, combining Technographics with adopter categories, Forrester found that early adopters are high-income technology optimists, thus identifying the first consumers to shop online. Conversely, **laggards** are low-income pessimists who will be last to shop online. Finally, companies can use Technographics segments to profile customers who shop online and to determine where to allocate resources to attract more of the same. Starbucks used Technographics and discovered that 47 percent of its customers are early adopters (Fast Forwards, New Age Nurturers, and Mouse Potatoes). It further found that 22 percent are career oriented, with Fast Forwards using the internet for self-advancement. These findings prompted Starbucks to begin selling merchandise online many years ago.

Forrester also maintains a database for its business Technographics. It conducts more than

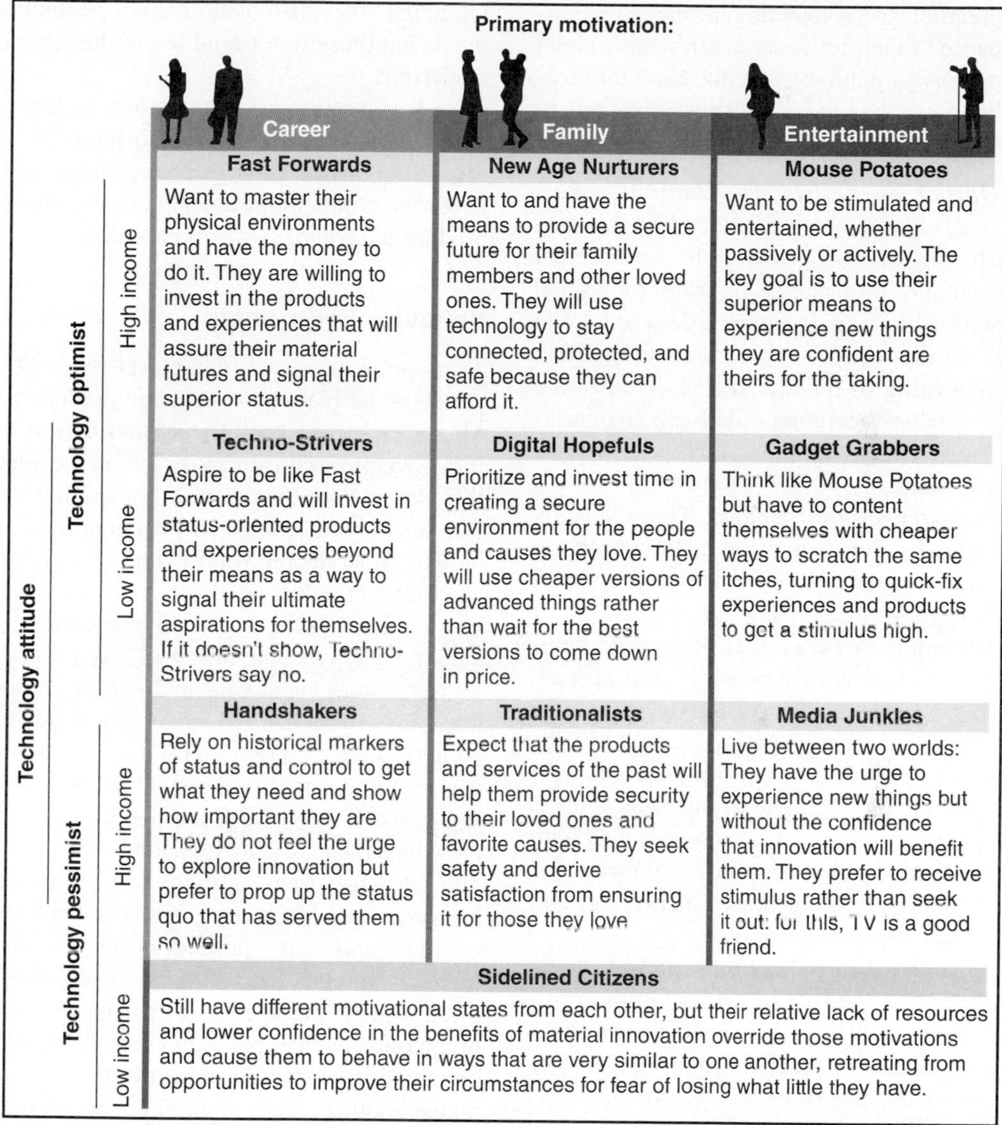

Primary motivation:

Technology attitude		Career	Family	Entertainment
Technology optimist	High income	**Fast Forwards** Want to master their physical environments and have the money to do it. They are willing to invest in the products and experiences that will assure their material futures and signal their superior status.	**New Age Nurturers** Want to and have the means to provide a secure future for their family members and other loved ones. They will use technology to stay connected, protected, and safe because they can afford it.	**Mouse Potatoes** Want to be stimulated and entertained, whether passively or actively. The key goal is to use their superior means to experience new things they are confident are theirs for the taking.
Technology optimist	Low income	**Techno-Strivers** Aspire to be like Fast Forwards and will invest in status-oriented products and experiences beyond their means as a way to signal their ultimate aspirations for themselves. If it doesn't show, Techno-Strivers say no.	**Digital Hopefuls** Prioritize and invest time in creating a secure environment for the people and causes they love. They will use cheaper versions of advanced things rather than wait for the best versions to come down in price.	**Gadget Grabbers** Think like Mouse Potatoes but have to content themselves with cheaper ways to scratch the same itches, turning to quick-fix experiences and products to get a stimulus high.
Technology pessimist	High income	**Handshakers** Rely on historical markers of status and control to get what they need and show how important they are They do not feel the urge to explore innovation but prefer to prop up the status quo that has served them so well.	**Traditionalists** Expect that the products and services of the past will help them provide security to their loved ones and favorite causes. They seek safety and derive satisfaction from ensuring it for those they love	**Media Junkies** Live between two worlds: They have the urge to experience new things but without the confidence that innovation will benefit them. They prefer to receive stimulus rather than seek it out: for this, TV is a good friend.
Technology pessimist	Low income	**Sidelined Citizens** Still have different motivational states from each other, but their relative lack of resources and lower confidence in the benefits of material innovation override those motivations and cause them to behave in ways that are very similar to one another, retreating from opportunities to improve their circumstances for fear of losing what little they have.		

EXHIBIT 8.9 Customer Technographics Segmentation *Source*: "Segmenting Customers by Technology Preference," 2012. Forrester Research , Inc. Reprinted with permission

2,500 interviews with senior managers of North American companies with more than $1 billion in annual revenues. In sum, Technographics survey results assist businesses with product development and launches, lead generation, cross-selling opportunities, customer service, and brand building.

INFLUENTIALS Many online marketers target influential people who are opinion leaders online. These could be company stakeholders who are passionate about the brands and have big social network followings or others who hold some type of status that is instrumental in influencing purchase behavior. In traditional marketing, public relations personnel targeted media reporters because of their influence when writing about the company in published media. Now the field of influencers has considerably expanded to include the following (and more):

- ***Online journalists.*** *The Huffington Post* (huffingtonpost.com), started by Arianna Huffington, has grown to be a prominent source of information on many topics and with many expert authors. Between 4 and 6 million people visited the site in 2012, according to quantcast.com. Traditional journalists operating online can also influence readers with their articles (such as on cnn.com).
- ***Industry opinion leaders.*** These vary by industry, but commonly include industry analysts, traditional journalists, prominent bloggers, thought leaders, and CEOs of leading firms. It is difficult to seed opinion leaders with new ideas that spread, but if an idea rides the tide of an emerging social trend, opinion leaders will be quick to create a buzz when given the right information. Example: Brian Solis, author, speaker, and analyst, maintains a blog with the latest developments in social media and their effects on business, marketing, and culture (briansolis.com).
- ***Influential social network authors.*** Lady Gaga was the first to gain 20 million followers on Twitter. When she tweets about a restaurant or hotel she likes, readers pay attention. Many consumers or business customers are also opinion leaders in their social networks and when marketers locate those customers with big networks they want to befriend and chat with them.

We shouldn't ignore the influential citizen journalists. Even a relatively unknown person can post something negative about a company that will spread all over the internet in a "blogstorm." Jeff Jarvis's complaining post about Dell computer had a huge impact in 2005, in what is known as "Dell's Hell." Individuals often post videos or images of product malfunctions online. Of course, they also post positive product comments but those don't tend to get the same high readership.

It is important for marketers to determine who the influentials are in their industry. They must also decide how to entice them to write about the company/products and to monitor for product and company mentions online.

Behavior Segments

Two commonly used behavioral segmentation variables are benefits sought and product usage. Marketers using **benefit segmentation** often form groups of consumers based on the benefits they desire from the product. For example, what benefits do you seek when searching travel sites online? Most people want to check flight prices and routes at airline or travel agent sites (such as Expedia.com), some want to find hotels ratings by other travelers (people like "me"), and some look for discussions about what to do or see at specific locations. These desired benefits help travel site owners, such as Travelocity and TripAdvisor, design content that will appeal to these benefit segments. If done well, the people looking for these benefits may actually purchase as well.

Product usage is applied to segmentation in many ways. Marketers often segment by light, medium, and heavy product usage. As a hypothetical example, heavy internet users might be those who go online constantly using either a PC or a mobile device; medium users, those who go online using a PC only while at work and a smartphone at other times; and light users, those who connect only once every day or two. Companies must research to determine actual usage and decide how to split their target into appropriate user categories. For example, Amazon.com offers free shipping for users in an effort to move them from light to medium use: those who purchase at least $25 in one order. Another approach is to categorize consumers as brand loyal, loyal to the competitive product, **switchers** (who don't care which site they use), and nonusers of the product. Next, we discuss some of these variables as they apply to the internet.

BENEFIT SEGMENTS Clearly, the internet offers something for everyone. If marketers can form segments based on the benefits sought by users, they can design products and services to meet those needs. This approach is often more practical than simply forming demographic segments and trying to figure out what, say, professional women in Peoria want from the Web. Marketers will use all segmentation bases to define, measure, and identify target markets, but "benefits sought" is the key driver of marketing mix strategy.

What better way to determine benefits sought than to look at what people actually do online? Marketers can evaluate online activities, such as those presented in Chapter 7. (Recall that the six basic online activities are connect, create, learn, enjoy, trade and give.) Marketers also check which Web sites are the most popular. Several sites report each month on the top online properties. Listed next are the top Web site parent companies for May 2012, according to nielsen.com. Microsoft, Google, and Yahoo! are consistently among the top sites in most (but not all) countries and Facebook was not even in the top 10 a couple of years ago. The list demonstrates that many people search, use social networks, use Microsoft for downloads, read news, and purchase from Yahoo! These figures have grown considerably in the past year. Comparing these data with activities in Chapter 7 presents a rich picture of current and emerging benefits desired by internet users.

1. Google sites (413.7 million visitors and 91.5 percent reach)
2. Microsoft sites (350.9 million visitors and 77.6 percent reach)
3. Facebook.com (323.2 million visitors and 71.5 percent reach)
4. Yahoo! sites (246.7 million visitors and 54.6 percent reach)
5. Wikimedia Foundation (175.3 million visitors and 38.8 percent reach)

USAGE SEGMENTS Marketers also segment internet users according to many technology-use characteristics such as smartphone, tablet, or PC access and which browser they use. Following are two important internet usage segments: mobile access and online engagement level. Many others are worth exploring, such as video watchers, social network users, and online gamers.

Mobile Access Clearly, the type of internet connection and the information-receiving appliance affect usage behavior. Fifty-five percent of cell phone owners connect to the internet using smartphones, according to Pew Internet & American Life. Mobile internet use is paralleling the early days of internet adoption, with the younger, better-educated, and higher-income consumers using their smartphones online more than the reverse demographics. However, Caucasians remain the lowest users of all ethnic groups. The main two reasons cell owners use the internet are because it is convenient and the cell is always with them, according to the Pew study.

Obviously, wireless users do a lot more than just talk on their cell phones and receive e-mail. They send and receive all kinds of voice, text, video, music, and graphic data—anyplace, anytime. Wireless users also track information on package shipment, stock quotes, airline schedules and changes, and news. As we've already mentioned, smartphone users multitask, using their phone while watching television, on a PC, reading, listening to music, and more. Next are some recent statistics about smartphone use among their owners (Voskresensky, 2011):

- Use smartphone at home (93 percent)
- Browse the internet (81 percent), with search engines being the most frequented (77 percent)
- Access a social networking site (89 percent)
- Read news and research (82 percent)
- Conduct shopping-related activity (79 percent)
- Use downloaded apps (68 percent)
- Look for more information after seeing a mobile ad (49 percent)
- Watch videos (48 percent)
- Purchase on a mobile Web site (27 percent)

Perhaps the most meaningful statistic is that 90 percent of smartphone users have taken some sort of action after searching via a smartphone (like book a hotel or purchase).

What about tablet use? According to one study of tablet owners, 84 percent play games, 74 percent search the internet, 72 percent e-mail, 56 percent access social networks on their tablet computers, 51 percent consume entertainment, and 42 percent shop (AdMob by Google, 2011).

Pew Internet & American Life studied mobile users versus "the Stationary Media Majority," and devised five segments in each category (Exhibit 8.10). It is very interesting to review these segments and devise product opportunities, especially when combined with the usage statistic previously mentioned. Note that these statistics are several years old but the segments still apply.

The mobile wireless segment creates huge opportunities for companies wanting to produce wireless portals: a customized point of entry to the internet where subscribers can access Web sites and information in a low bandwidth format. Big technical problems face global e-marketers, so marketers must be clever to provide both wireless and wired users with desired services. At the same time, the wireless market is unstoppable

Mobile User Segments (39 percent)	Stationary Media Majority (61 percent)
• **Digital Collaborators** (8 percent of the population) are very much concerned about continual information exchange with others, as they frequently mix it up with online collaborators to create and share content or express themselves.	• **Desktop Veterans** (13 percent) are tech-oriented, but in a "year 2004" kind of way. They consume online information and connect with others using traditional tools such as e-mail on a home high-speed connection. They are not heavy users of cell phones for much beyond a voice call.
• **Ambivalent Networkers** (7 percent) are extremely active in using social networking sites and accessing digital resources "on the go" yet aren't always thrilled to be contacted by others. They sometimes yearn for a break from online use and pervasive connectivity.	• **Drifting Surfers** (14 percent) have the tools for connectivity, but are relatively infrequent users of them. They say they could give up their internet and cell phones. In spite of years of online experience, they seem to have checked out of the digital revolution.
• **Media Movers** (7 percent) are the accelerants of user-generated content as they use their ICT assets to send material (say, a photo or video they've taken) out onto the Web.	• **Information Encumbered** (10 percent) have average amounts of connectivity, but suffer from information overload and have a tough time getting their gadgets to work without help from others.
• **Roving Nodes** (9 percent) are active managers of their social lives using basic applications—texting and e-mailing—to connect with others, pass along information, and bolster personal productivity.	• **Tech Indifferent** (10 percent) have limited online capability at home, and, even though most have cell phones, they bristle at the intrusiveness cell phones can foster.
• **Mobile Newbies** (8 percent) are occasional internet users, but many in this group are recent cell phone adopters and very enthusiastic about how mobile service makes them more available to others. They would be hard-pressed to give up their cell phones.	• **Off the Network** (14 percent) lack the tools for digital connectivity, as they have neither online access nor cell phones.

EXHIBIT 8.10 Mobile and Stationary User Segments *Source*: ("The Mobile Difference. . .," 2009) Pew Internet & American Life Project

and will grow considerably. Further, expect huge changes when consumers access the internet from their refrigerators, cars, and other appliances. At that time we think it will be about distinctly desired data, not Web pages.

ONLINE ENGAGEMENT LEVEL Chapter 1 introduced the concept of customer engagement online—the idea that many users actively participate by adding content for others to view. In Chapter 7, we discussed several forms of content creation, as measured by Pew Internet & American Life: uploading photos, rating products, tagging online content, posting comments to a blog, creating a blog, and creating an avatar for a virtual world. Because this is an important new concept born from social media use, Forrester Research devised a very descriptive typology for engagement segments (Exhibit 8.11) using its Social Technographics questionnaire. This exhibit displays the proportions of internet users in each category in 2011 for both the United States and the European Union (a combination of behavioral and geographic segmentation).

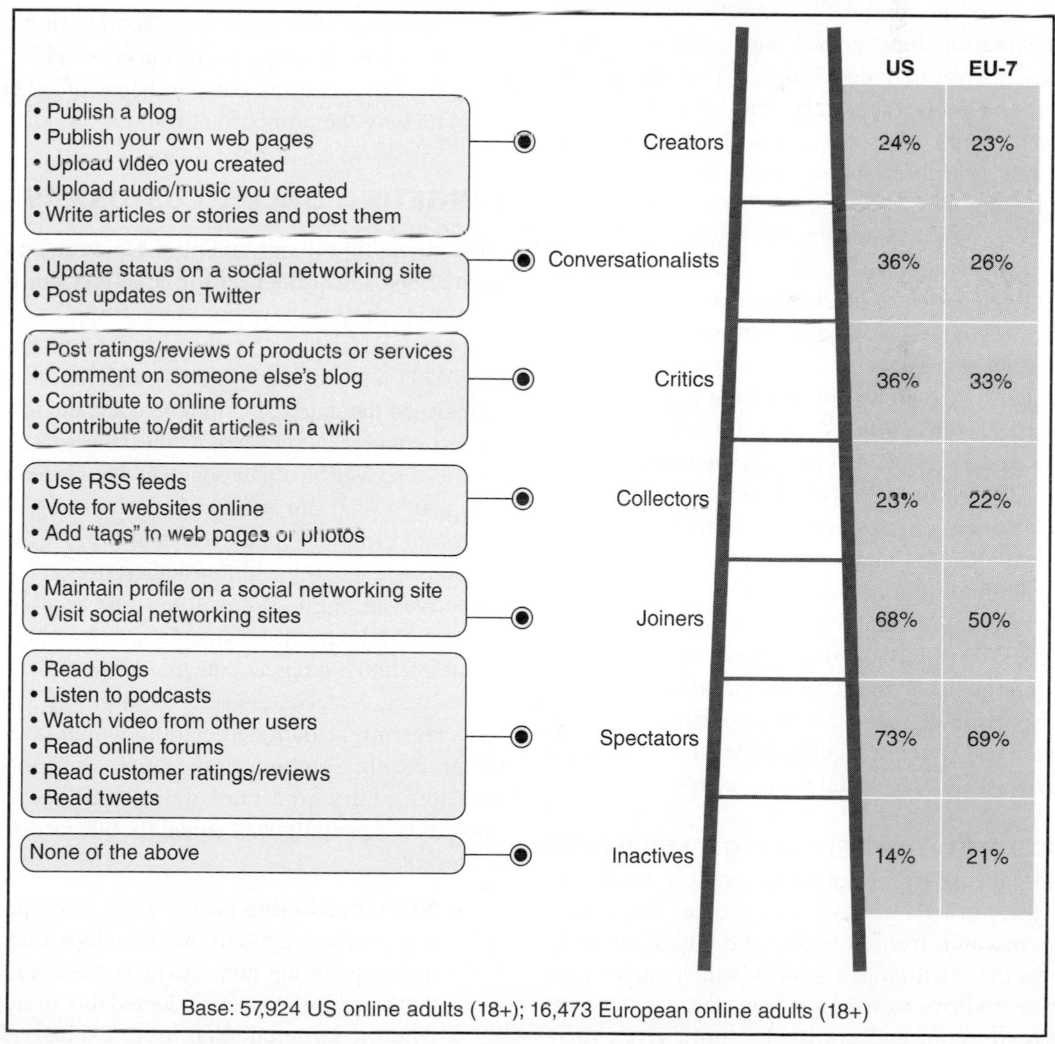

EXHIBIT 8.11 Social Media Engagement Segments Based on Participation Level in 2011
Source: Forrester Research, Inc

Forrester asks questions that categorize social media users according to usage segments such as creators, conversationalists, and critics—the three most highly engaged segments online. Curators are one important segment not in this typology (although collectors are closely related to this concept). Curators traditionally are people who handle the art and other collections in museums and galleries. Online, curators gather other people's content and upload or share it on their social media sites. Pinterest is one image-sharing site that is completely populated by curators. Incidentally, one reason that a large number of online users perform these four activities (creators, conversationalists, critics, and curators) is that many are trying to develop their personal brands online. This is especially true for consultants, entrepreneurs, and speakers but also holds true for many upwardly mobile employees and students soon entering the job market. "What you find on my Web and social media sites is who I am."

If a company uses Forrester's services, it will learn which of its customers are in these and other segments. If the company's customers are not content creators, then a contest asking them to create a video commercial for the company will not be effective (unless they are able to attract new customers). Conversely, if the company follows the norm and has nearly three quarters of spectators in its customer base, it knows that they will still read its blogs and other social media content without uploading content or commenting. Marketers are scrambling to figure out how deeply to get involved in social media initiatives and how to communicate with customers, influencers, and prospects in these venues. Segmentation by social media engagement level provides data that helps drive e-marketing social media tactics.

INDUSTRY-SPECIFIC USAGE SEGMENTS

Segmenting by usage varies widely from one industry or business type to the other. For example, research from Forrester and comScore indicates that visitors to car sites behave differently from visitors to other e-commerce sites (see forrester.com and comscore.com). Even serious car buyers tend to visit car sites only a few times—64 percent of all buyers complete their online research in five sessions or fewer. Further, about 25 percent buy a car within three months of visiting a car site. Forrester identified these three visitor segments for car Web sites:

- *Explorers* are the smallest group, but almost half buy their new vehicle within two months of visiting a car site. They want a convenient, explicit buying process.
- *Off-roaders* tend to do a lot of research online and, subsequently, are likely to purchase in an offline showroom.
- *Cruisers* visit car sites frequently, but only 15 percent buy a car in the short term. Still, they have a strong interest in cars and heavily influence the car purchases of others, making them important visitors.

TARGETING ONLINE CUSTOMERS

After reviewing many potential segments, marketers must select the best for targeting. For this selection, they review the market opportunity analysis (see Chapter 3), consider findings from the SWOT analysis, and generally look for the best fit between the market environment and the firm's expertise and resources. Sometimes, this task is as easy as discovering a new segment that visited the company's Web site and then experimenting with offers that might appeal to this group. At other times, it is a lengthy and thorough process. To be attractive, an online segment must be accessible through the internet, be sizable and growing (if possible), and hold great potential for profit.

Next, e-marketers select a targeting strategy. This might include deciding which targets to serve online, which in the brick-and-mortar location, and which via catalog mailing. The internet is especially well suited for two targeting strategies:

- **Niche marketing** occurs when a company selects one segment and develops one or more marketing mixes to meet the needs of that segment. Amazon adopted this strategy when it targeted Web users exclusively. Cyberdialogue/findsvp (now Fulcrum) calls the internet "a niche in time," indicating its ripeness for niche marketing. This strategy has real benefits but can be risky because competitors are often drawn into lucrative markets and because markets can suddenly decline, leaving the company with all its eggs in one falling basket.

- **Micromarketing**, also known as **individualized targeting**, occurs when a company tailors all or part of its marketing mix to a small number of people. Taken to its extreme, it can be a target market of one person.

The internet's big promise, one that is currently being realized by many companies, is individualized targeting. Exhibit 8.12 shows a sales funnel that allows marketers to follow users as they go through the Web site registration and purchase processes. Each step creates a user segment that can be targeted with persuasive communication based on behavior, such as e-mailing those who completed registration but did not purchase.

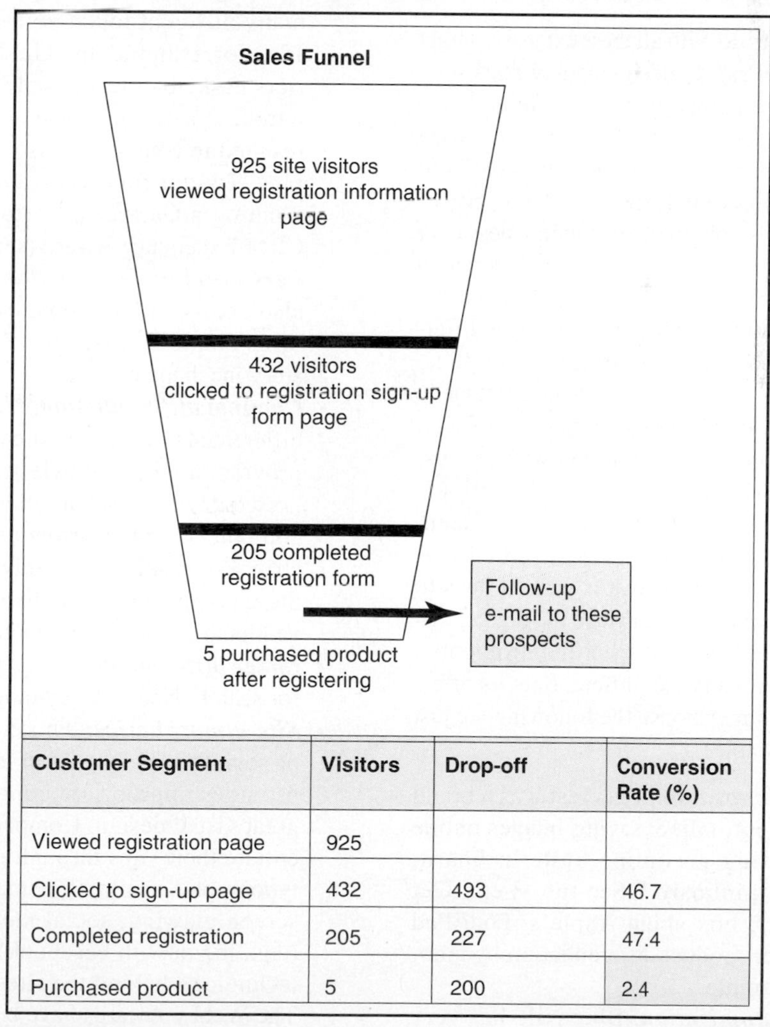

Customer Segment	Visitors	Drop-off	Conversion Rate (%)
Viewed registration page	925		
Clicked to sign-up page	432	493	46.7
Completed registration	205	227	47.4
Purchased product	5	200	2.4

EXHIBIT 8.12 Targeting the Right Customers

Amazon.com builds a profile of each user who browses or buys books at its site. It tracks the books that its customers read and makes recommendations based on their past purchases. Amazon also sends e-mail notifications about products that might interest particular individuals. This approach is the marketing concept at its finest: giving individual consumers exactly what they want at the right time and right place. The internet technology makes this mass customization possible in ways that were unimaginable prior to the internet.

DIFFERENTIATION ONLINE

What do marketers do with all these extensive target market profiles? Prior to designing any marketing mix strategies, the company makes differentiation and positioning decisions based on target market needs and competitive offerings. The goal is to obtain a **differential advantage**: (1) A property of any product that is able to claim a uniqueness over other products in its category. To be a differential advantage, the uniqueness must be communicable to customers and have value for them. The differential advantage of a firm is often called its distinctive competencies, and (2) An advantage unique to an organization; an advantage extremely difficult to match by a competitor (reprinted with permission from American Marketing Association's Online Marketing Dictionary). In short, differentiation is what a company does to the product, as opposed to positioning, which is what it does to the mind by attempting to convince the market that the product indeed has the specified differential advantage. A company can differentiate its offering along many dimensions. The following are just a few online examples:

- ***Product innovation.*** Pinterest was a brand new concept online: saving images online and creating an online bulletin board, called a "pinboard." See the "Let's Get Technical" box about Apple's iPod/iPad for another product differentiation by innovation example.
- ***Mass customization.*** Blue Nile has very different features compared to other similar jewelry sites because visitors can customize diamond rings and other jewelry online.
- ***Service differentiation.*** Amazon.com excels in customer service. It is part of the company's mission and it delivers. Amazon received over 80 percent positive reviews for its customer service in the 2011 MSN Money-Zogby customer service survey, giving it the top 10 company Hall of Fame status (Aho, 2011).
- ***Customer relationship management (CRM).*** CRM is closely related to service differentiation and involves gaining a 360-degree view of the customer through many different touch points (see Chapter 15). For example, the Golden State Warriors basketball team used social media to introduce a new logo and branding and this resulted in a huge increase in its Facebook fans, Twitter followers, and the honor of winning a Gartner and 1to1 Media 2011 CRM Excellence Award (see gartner.com).
- ***Personnel differentiation.*** Zappos.com also excels with customer service because of its employees (see the Zappos opening story in Chapter 11).
- ***Channel differentiation.*** Netflix and Hulu differentiate by offering streaming television programming and movies to internet-connected devices, such as televisions, tablets, computers, and smartphones. This digital channel created a competitive advantage for these companies when disrupting the conventional television distribution model.
- ***Image differentiation.*** Google versus AOL for search: Need we say more?
- ***Site atmospherics.*** This involves a Web or social media page that is user-friendly, provides appropriate content, and has a great visual design. Companies can differentiate their sites through graphic design, typography, scaling for smartphone/small-screen viewing, social media integration (e.g., log in with Facebook), and advanced technology behind the sites. For example, The Webby Awards have been in existence since 1996 to honor the leading international internet sites in many categories. See

LET'S GET TECHNICAL

iTunes, iPod, iPhone, iPad

You are making a cross-country trip in your late model Mini Cooper. For 200 miles you have driven through what appears to be an unbroken string of corn fields and flat earth. Though your car has a great sound system, for the last four hours you have been listening to country stations and talk radio. Right about now you are really wishing that you had remembered to pack at least one CD. Suddenly you remember that your iPod is sitting in the glove compartment. Plugging it in to your Mini Connected dock, you bathe the car in rock and roll. Before you know it, the hours melt away and the Rocky Mountains loom gracefully in the distance.

Apple Computer has long been the master of the simple and stylish user interface. With iTunes and the devices that connect to it they continue that long tradition. iTunes is a digital media organizer and playback mechanism for the Macintosh and Windows computers. iTunes can digitize and store music, videos, books and applications, and then allows users to download that content to their iPods, iPhones, and iPads. Apple gives away iTunes but makes its revenue by selling content and portable devices on which to consume that content. Apple earns commissions on digital content sales from the iTunes store as well as profit on sales of iPods, iPhones, and iPads.

To enable this process, three principal technologies are required: compressed digital media (music, video, apps, and books), high-speed data transfer, and really small storage devices.

Files stored on a music CD are not compressed. Therefore they take up a lot of space—about 600 MB for an album. That's too much space for a computer. After 50 albums, your hard drive might be completely filled. Those same albums can be compressed into tracks one-tenth their original size when digitized on a computer. You have probably heard of MP3 files, which are just compressed music files. MP3 is one compression standard; others, such as Apple Computer's advanced audio coding (AAC), are also available. Compression results in a very small loss of audio quality—undetectable by many users. iTunes and iPod can play music digitized in either MP3 or AAC format.

However, even a compressed collection of music and video can be pretty large. Moving all that content from the computer to the iPod could take hours—and reduce the appeal of the product. To speed up data transfer, a USB cable is used with the iPod. The iPod synchronizes to a computer over the USB connection. Just a few minutes later, the contents of hundreds of CDs and videos can be transmitted to the iPod.

The final enabling technologies deal with storage. All that music and video must fit in a tiny lightweight package. Tiny hard drives up to 160 GB are used on the high-end iPods. But hard drives, even small ones, drain battery life. The iPod touch, iPod nano, iPhone, and iPad store the music instead in a flash drive—basically a large memory chip—which is the same technology used for the popular USB pen drives. Because it requires no moving parts, the gadgets' battery life is enhanced.

With iTunes and its associated devices, Apple has a winning formula. But the game does not end there. Another product line extension, Apple TV, bypasses the computer altogether and lets users download content (movies, music, and pictures) from the internet directly to a box attached to the TV. Using Apple TV, users could subscribe to their cable company's internet service and listen to music and watch movies without subscribing to even **basic cable**. Clever indeed!

the Web sites and mobile apps that won a recent Webby Award (webbyawards.com).

- ***User-Generated Content (UGC).*** A company can differentiate by using effective crowdsourcing to generate content or simply by providing an active online space for users to post comments and ideas. Starbucks.com did an excellent job with My Starbucks Idea, inviting customers to propose new products, experience, and service or store improvements and vote for the best ideas on a dedicated Web page.
- ***Efficient and timely order processing.*** Some companies excel at this in their

industries. When you order something online, sometimes it arrives in a very short time and the company sends several confirmation e-mails to update the delivery status. The following are automated e-mail addresses sent from airlines and agencies, for which consumers receive an e-mail after buying an air ticket. Which are most descriptive, trust-generating, and effective (Beal and Strauss, 2008)?

- Member@p21.travelocity.com (Travelocity),
- pgtktg@bangkokairwaysna.com (Bangkok Airways),
- SouthwestAirlines@mail.southwest.com (Southwest Airlines),
- notify@aa.globalnotifications.com (American Airlines),
- itinerary@pcsoffice02.de (Lufthansa),
- travelercare@orbitz.com (Orbitz),
- confirmation@uasupport.com (United Airlines), or
- travel@expedia.com (Expedia).

ONLINE POSITIONING BASES

Positioning is a strategy to create a desired image for a company and its products in the minds of a chosen user segment (consumers, business or government buyers, and so forth). The first step in positioning is to determine the product category in which the brand competes. For example, when tablet computers were first introduced, it was unclear whether they were competing with laptops or smartphones. Does bottled water compete with soft drinks? This is a tough question that must be answered. Once the company decides who the direct competition is, then it determines whether or not the brand is differentiated in that product category and thus has a competitive advantage to form the basis for competitive positioning.

The previous discussion on differentiation provided many examples of companies who do have a competitive edge for creating their product's position. E-marketers often position based on technology (the new iPad tablet or the smartphone with the most apps), benefits (fastest product delivery from a Web site order), user category (Nick.com is one of the most popular sites for kids), or competitive position (the Android is less expensive than an iPhone). Some internet marketers position as an integrator: TheKnot.com offers everything to do with weddings, from gift registry to wedding planners and other consultants.

Regardless of the selected positioning basis, the brand story must be told from the customer's viewpoint—otherwise it is considered as self-aggrandizing and chest thumping. E-marketers only have a short time to capture and engage their market's attention and this is accomplished with interesting content that reaches the right consumers and business prospects, resonating and engaging them.

Chapter Summary

E-business occurs primarily in three markets: business-to-business (B2B), business-to-consumer (B2C), and business-to-government (B2G), although businesses also become involved in the consumer-to-consumer (C2C) market. The majority of dollars change hands in the B2B market, with many companies connected to the internet. Information technology is creating efficiencies while increasing competition. The consumer market is huge and active online. The government market consists of numerous states, cities, counties, municipal agencies, and countries buying goods and services. Businesses must pay close attention to the rules for selling to this market. A number of trends are affecting the ability of marketers to tap new growth areas and become successful e-marketers.

Marketing segmentation is the process of aggregating individuals or businesses along similar characteristics that pertain to the use, consumption, or benefits of a product or service, which results in groups of customers called market segments. Targeting is the process of selecting market segments that are most attractive to the company and choosing an appropriate segment coverage strategy.

The four consumer market **segmentation bases** are demographics, geographic location, psychographics, and behavior with respect to the product. Each basis is further refined into segmentation variables—such as age and gender variables within demographics. Currently, e-marketers are targeting a number of demographic niches and look forward to newly important segments: millennials and kids. Different strategies are used to target each segment.

User psychographics include personality, values, lifestyle, attitudes, interests, and opinions. The internet is an excellent way to gather people with similar interests and tasks into online communities for effective targeting. An important segmenting variable to predict online purchase behavior is attitude toward technology. Important behavioral segmentation variables commonly used by e-marketers are benefits sought (based on the benefits customers desire from the product), product usage (based on how customers behave on the internet), and influentials (journalists and others who influence opinions). Forrester's Social Technographics is an important social media engagement segmentation scheme.

User segments can be divided according to home or work access, mobile access, online engagement level, and industry-specific usage segments.

Marketers use two important coverage strategies to reach the segments: (1) niche marketing and (2) micromarketing (individualized targeting). The internet holds tremendous promise, especially for effective micromarketing.

Differentiation is what a company does to the product. Positioning is what it does to the customer's mind. The proliferation of information, products, and services available on the internet means companies must find ways of differentiating their products and services in order to attract customers and build long-term relationships. Many traditional differentiation strategies can be applied to an e-marketing strategy, such as product, service, personnel, channel, and image differentiation. These require some additional and unique differentiation strategies for e-marketing, focusing on site/environment atmospherics, trust, efficiency, pricing, customer relationship marketing, and inviting user-generated content.

Traditional offline positioning strategies also apply to the internet. However, e-marketers can use internet-specific strategies such as positioning on the basis of technology, benefit, competitor, or integrator.

Exercises

REVIEW QUESTIONS

1. What are the three main markets of e-business, and how do they differ?
2. Define the four main segmentation bases and list at least two segmentation variables for each.
3. Why are millennials and kids important market segments for e-marketers?
4. Why do e-marketers need to measure attitude toward technology? What measures are available?
5. What benefits do consumers seek online?
6. How do benefit segments differ from usage segments?
7. What are the three most important online engagement segmentation levels? Describe Forrester's Social Technographics segmentation scheme.
8. How does micromarketing differ from niche marketing?
9. Why would an e-marketer want to create or nurture a Web site for building a community?
10. How does differentiation differ from positioning?

DISCUSSION QUESTIONS

11. **The 1-800-Flowers Story.** Identify the types of consumer segments used by this company to build revenue. What other segments might be profitable?
12. **The 1-800-Flowers Story.** What is this company's competitive advantage, and thus its differentiation and positioning bases?
13. Underdeveloped countries tend to have sharper class divisions than those that exist in the United States. It is not uncommon for 2 percent of the population to control 80 percent of the wealth. As a marketer, how would you use this knowledge to develop a segmentation strategy for targeting consumers in these countries?
14. Many parents are upset that some Web sites specifically target children and young teens. Outline the arguments for and against a company using this segmentation and targeting strategy. Which side do you support, and why?
15. Some company managers forbid employees from using the internet for nonwork-related activities. What are the implications for e-marketers that segment their markets using the variable of home and work access?
16. Forrester Research suggests a segmentation scheme for online engagement. Interview some of your classmates to see what proportion falls into each segment.
17. Looking at the list of 10 community types in Exhibit 8.7, name one Web company that capitalizes on each for marketing purposes.
18. How can a company identify influentials that might affect its product sales or branding efforts?
19. How can marketers use the data about smartphone use to build profitable target market segments?
20. Why would an e-marketer choose to use competitor positioning? Integrator positioning?
21. Which mobile or stationary market segment fits you the best? What kinds of products would succeed in this segment?
22. How might an online company react if a rival embarks on competitor positioning in an unflattering way?
23. Are customers likely to be confused by an integrator positioning that suggests a Web site sells anything and everything? What are the advantages and disadvantages of this positioning?

WEB ACTIVITIES

24. SRI Consulting, through the Business Intelligence Center online, features the Values and Lifestyles Program (VALS). Many marketers who wish to understand the psychographics of both existing and potential customers use this market segmentation program. Companies and advertisers on the Web can use this information to develop their sites. Visit strategicbusinessinsights.com and follow the links to the VALS questionnaire. Take the survey to determine your type and then read all about your type. What is your VALS type? Does it describe you well? Why or why not? How can marketers use information from the VALS surveys?
25. Visit iVillage and write a profile of a typical female user based on the site content.
26. Visit Yahoo! and Google Local searches and look for a grocer in your area. Then text Google to find all grocers in your zip code. Compare the results of these searches based on the effectiveness of their results and how easy these were to use.
27. Amazon.com is a site trusted by millions of customers. Visit the site and identify what makes the site trustworthy.
28. Find one Web site that caters to kids, one to teens, one to millennials, and one to older adults. Evaluate the site atmospherics for each and report on their differences.

PART

4

E-Marketing Management

CHAPTER

9

Product: The Online Offer

The primary goal of this chapter is to help you analyze the development of consumer and business products that capitalize on the internet's properties and technology by delivering online benefits through product attributes, branding, support services, and labeling. You will become familiar with the challenges and opportunities of e-marketing–enhanced product development.

After reading this chapter, you will be able to:

- Define *product* and describe how it contributes to customer value.
- Discuss how attributes, branding, support services, and labeling apply to online products.
- Outline some of the key factors in e-marketing-enhanced product development.

• Status has always been the driver deep at the heart of all consumer behavior. When consumers connect with a pre-launch product or service, and support that project towards launch, it makes for a great status story to tell, tweet, post, and otherwise share.

• In April 2012 **Nike** launched a number of highly collectible limited edition sneakers using a Twitter reservation system. Stores would randomly tweet specific product hashtags during the day of release, and the first followers to include this in a direct message to the store would reserve a pair of the sneakers.

The Google Story

What performs over a billion searches a day in 181 countries; speaks 146 languages including Xhosa, Māori, and Zulu; and is the most-visited U.S. Web site? The answer is Google.com, the fastest-growing and fourth highest-value Global Brand of the Year in 2011, according to Interbrand. It was the top Web brand in April 2012, with 171.3 million visitors who spent an average of one hour and 56 minutes on Google in April, according to the Nielsen Company. Google is so popular that it has changed the English language—the verb *to google* has been added by two dictionaries. Google's 2011 revenues were $37.9 billion, while it earned an admirable 25.7 percent in net income. The firm continues to grow in sales, new markets, number of employees, and new products offered.

This success is particularly remarkable because Google entered the market in 1998, well after other search engines were firmly entrenched with loyal customers. How did Google do it? First, it got the technology right at a low cost. Co-founders Sergey Brin and Larry Page figured out how to pack eight times as much server power in the same amount of space as competitors by building their own system from commodity hardware parts. Second, they invented an innovative new search strategy: ranking search query page results based not only on keywords but also on popularity—as measured, in part, by the number of sites that link to each Web page. These criteria meant that users' search results were packed with relevant Web sites. Finally, the founders maintained a customer focus, used simple graphics, allowed no advertising on the homepage, and allowed only text ads (without graphics) so search result pages download faster and are easier to read.

Google continues to excel through rapid and continuous product innovation. It makes new products available on Google Labs, moves them to beta testing when they seem useful to customers, and finally adds them to the suite of products—a process sometimes lasting up to a year. Through this process, Google learns from customers and incorporates improvements based on their feedback. Google is constantly revising its search algorithm, which contains over 200 variables used to present the most relevant search results based on the user's selected key words. Exhibit 9.1 displays the idea generation and external testing process used to improve user searches. Google's product mix includes 24 search products (Web, blog, Earth, Maps, alerts, and more), 3 advertising products (AdSense, AdWords, and Analytics), 20 applications (e.g., Google Docs, Picasa, YouTube, Blogger, and mobile products), and many enterprise products to maximize revenue from Web content, increase marketing ROI, reach new customers, enhance a Web site, and increase productivity. All products adhere to Google's philosophies of simplicity, customer focus, speed of service, and product excellence.

Google primarily uses a media e-business model, connecting users with information and selling eyeballs to advertisers. In 2011, 96 percent of Google's revenues came from advertising. It generates revenues from several B2B markets. It licenses search services to companies, powering a majority of all searches worldwide; it sells enterprise services; it also sells advertising to Web advertisers, sharing risk with the advertisers by using a pay-per-click model (advertisers only pay when users click on an ad). Google's advertising revenues continue to rise at its own site and on customer sites, including Google ads, because it delivers narrowly targeted relevant ads based on keyword searches.

In a firm where many employees hold a PhD, the innovation continues. This fact plus a monomaniacal customer focus is why the company is always right on target with new services. The profitability is likely to continue as well, because Google pays close attention to user value, keeps costs low, and delivers eyeballs to advertisers. Google does everything extremely well.

Sources: Google.com and the 2011 Annual Report.

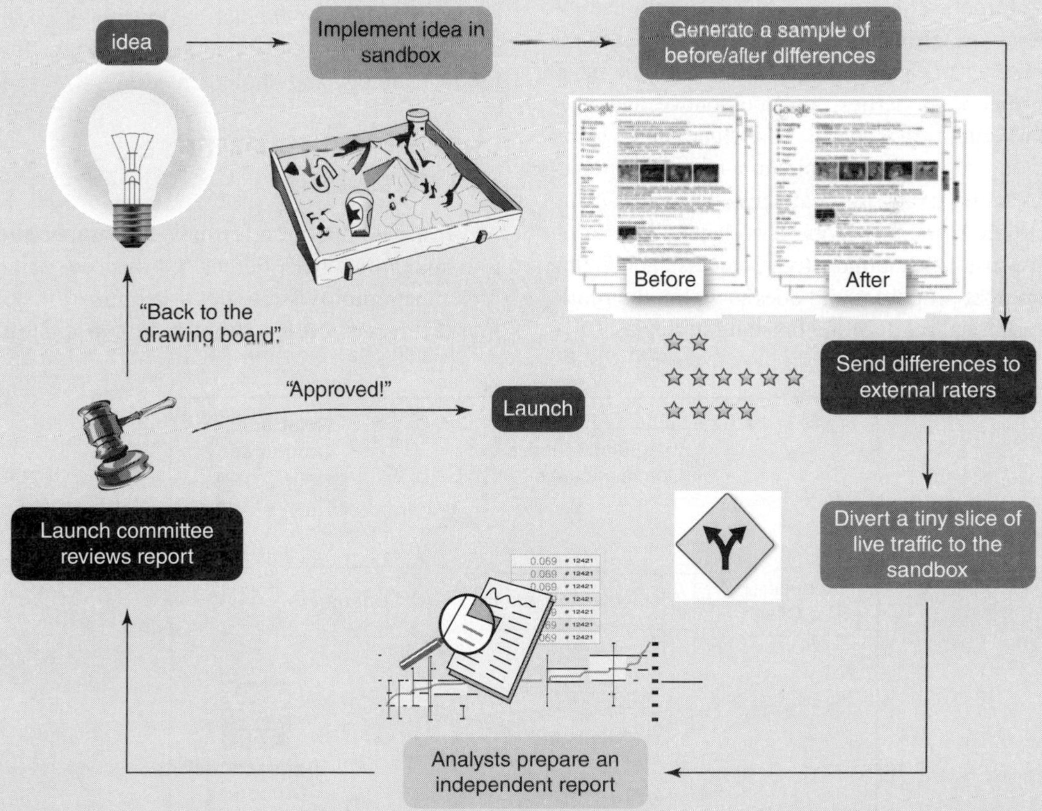

EXHIBIT 9.1 Google Process for Testing Changes to its Search Algorithm *Source*: Courtesy of Google (google.com)

MANY PRODUCTS CAPITALIZE ON INTERNET PROPERTIES

The success of Google demonstrates how a new and purely online product can use the internet's properties to build a successful brand. And now Microsoft's Bing engine is nipping at Google's heels, showing that innovative online products continue to enter even a crowded marketplace. A product is a bundle of benefits that satisfies the needs of organizations or consumers and for which they are willing to exchange money or other items of value. The term *product* includes items such as tangible goods, services, ideas, people, and places. All of these can be marketed on the internet (people? Yes, politicians, sports figures, movie and music stars, and dating services).

Some new products such as search engines, smartphone apps, and social networks are unique to the internet, others such as music simply use the internet as a distribution channel, and some use the internet as an electronic storefront. With the internet's unique properties, customer control, and other e-marketing trends, product developers face many challenges and enjoy a plethora of new opportunities while trying to create customer value using electronic marketing tools. This chapter focuses on both consumer and industrial products capitalizing on internet properties and does so within the rubric of traditional product and branding strategies.

To create new products, organizations begin with research to determine what is important to customers and proceed by designing strategies to deliver more value than do competitors. In line with the sources-databases-strategy model discussed in Part III, tier 2 strategies involve the marketing mix 4 Ps and customer relationship management (CRM). Because the process of designing these strategies is closely tied to the tactics used to implement them, strategies and tactics together are presented in the chapters of Part IV. As shown in Exhibit 9.2, the marketing mix (product, price, distribution, and marketing communication) and CRM work together to produce relational and transactional outcomes with consumers. Assumed in the model is the parallel idea that this activity occurs in all markets—that is, marketers want the same outcomes with government and business customers (especially those in the supply chain). The present chapter begins this discussion by describing how information technology affects product strategy and implementation.

CREATING CUSTOMER VALUE ONLINE

Never has competition for online customer attention and dollars been fiercer. To succeed, companies must employ strategies—grounded in solid marketing principles—that result in customer

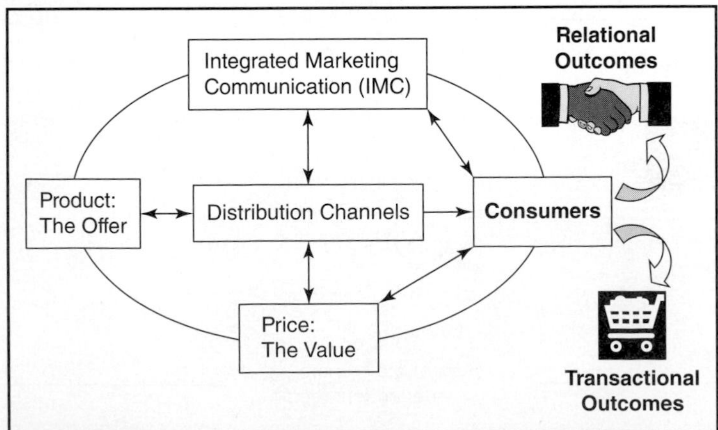

EXHIBIT 9.2 Marketing Mix and CRM Strategies and Tactics for Relational and Transactional Outcomes

value. Recall from Chapter 2 that Customer Value = Benefits – Costs. But what exactly is value? First, it is the entire product experience. It starts with a customer's first awareness of a product, continues at all customer touch points (including things such as the Web site experience and e-mail from a firm), and ends with the actual product usage and postpurchase customer service. It even includes the compliments a consumer gets from friends while whipping out that iPad, or the fun he or she has when messaging friends on Skype or Facebook. Second, value is defined wholly by the mental beliefs and attitudes held by customers. Regardless of how hard the company works to develop the right value proposition, it is the customers' perceptions that count. Third, value involves customer expectations; if the actual product experience falls short of their expectations, customers will be disappointed. Fourth, value is applied at all price levels. Both a $0.05 micropayment for an online article in a newspaper archive and a $2 million e-commerce computer application can provide value.

The internet can increase benefits and lower costs, but it can also work in reverse. The next sections explore the value proposition online.

PRODUCT BENEFITS

Along with internet technology came a new set of desired benefits. In Chapters 7 and 8, we discussed many of the benefits customers seek online while connecting, creating, enjoying, learning, trading, and giving. Web users also want effective Web navigation (thank you Google), quick download speed, clear site organization, attractive and useful site design, secure transactions, privacy, free information or services, and user-friendly Web browsing and e-mail reading. Today's connected consumers also want a place to join conversations, curate images, videos, and more, and create and upload content. Mobile users want useful and fun applications, location services, fast Web site downloading, and much more. Thousands of new products and Web and social media sites were quickly created to fill these and many other user needs. As internet technology evolves, user needs change, and the opportunities continue to expand. Astute marketers are ready to capitalize on these opportunities.

To capitalize on these opportunities, marketers must make five general product decisions that comprise its bundle of benefits to meet customer needs: attributes, branding, support services, labeling, and packaging. Except for physical packaging, all of these can be converted from atoms to bits for online delivery. Here we will discuss the first four in terms of the online benefits they provide to customers and their associated e-marketing strategies.

Attributes

Product attributes include overall quality and specific features. With quality, most customers know "you get what you pay for." That is, higher and consistent quality generally means higher prices, thus maintaining the value proposition. Product features include such elements as color, taste, style, size, and online speed of service, or the ability to connect and personalize. Benefits, on the other hand, are the same features from a user perspective. (That is, what will the attribute do to solve problems or meet needs and wants?) For example, Facebook hosts a lot of page profiles (attribute) that help users connect with old and new friends quickly online (benefit). Product benefits are key components in the value proposition.

The internet increases customer benefits in many remarkable ways that have revolutionized marketing practice. The most basic is the move from atoms to bits, one of the internet's key properties. This capability opened the door for media, music, software, and other digital products to be presented on the Web. Mass customization is a very important benefit. Tangible products such as laptop computers can be sold alone at rock-bottom prices online or bundled by individual buyers with many additional hardware and software items or services to provide additional benefits at a higher price. The same is true for intangible products, some offering tremendous flexibility for individual benefit bundling. For example, online research firms can offer many different business services in a variety of combinations; similarly, Pandora radio combines songs from many different artists as desired by customers. It is important to realize that information products can be reconfigured and personalized easily, quickly, and cheaply, as compared to manufactured products. Consider that changing an auto design takes years, and one model may be offered in only a few versions. In contrast, changing and customizing smartphone apps is much easier and faster—consider how many update notices you receive for your apps.

Even though this type of benefit bundling occurs offline as well as online, the internet offers users the unique opportunity to customize products automatically without leaving their keyboards. For example, Blue Nile, the profitable online jewelry retailer (bluenile.com), allows Web users to select from among many gemstone features (e.g., stone type, clarity, and size) and pick a ring setting to match (mass customization).

User personalization is another form of customization. Through Web site registration and other techniques, Web sites greet users by name and suggest product offerings of interest based on previous purchases. For instance, a returning customer to Amazon.com gets an item with his name on it: "Hello Sam. We have recommendations for you." Clicking on the link reveals a list of items that Sam might be interested in examining, based on his previous purchases from Amazon or those of similar buyers. Going one step further, Amazon allows individuals to create "wish lists," thus shifting this data storage function from the customer to the retailer: more benefits. Another form of personalization occurs when sites allow registration via a visitor's Facebook or other social network membership. One big benefit is about making it convenient for the customer.

Branding

A brand includes a name (McDonald's), a symbol (golden arches), or other identifying information. When a firm registers that information with the U.S. Patent Office, it becomes a trademark and is legally protected from imitation. According to the U.S. government, "A trademark is a brand name. A trademark or service mark includes any word, name, symbol, device, or any combination, used or intended to be used to identify and distinguish the goods/services of one seller or provider from those of others, and to indicate the source of the goods/services. Although federal registration of a mark is not mandatory, it has several advantages, including notice to the public of the registrant's claim of ownership of the mark, legal presumption of ownership nationwide, and exclusive right to use the mark on or in connection with the goods/services listed in the registration" (definition from.uspto.gov).

It is notable that dictionary words can't be trademarked for Web site use—companies can own books.com or music.com but can't trademark the word *book* for a company name.

A brand is much more than its graphic and verbal representation in marketing materials, however. Many marketers have noted that a brand is also the following:

- A promise to customers.
- Beliefs in the market's mind about what the brand delivers.
- Innovation to the product that continues to improve on the brand promise.
- Generates trust in customers that the brand will deliver on the promise.
- The sum of all customer touch point experiences.
- A relationship between buyer and brand.

Delivering on this promise builds trust, lowers risk, and helps customers by reducing the stress of making product switching decisions. Reducing stress is especially important online because of concern over security and privacy issues and because firms and customers are often separated by large distances. Brand names such as Amazon and Apple generate consumer trust, add to customer-perceived benefits and, thus, can command higher prices from consumers. See the "Let's Get Technical" box for McAfee and Symantec's Norton AntiVirus products, brands that also generate

LET'S GET TECHNICAL

Computer Viruses and Protection

The day has finally come for your presentation to the company's largest client. You have been working on the new marketing campaign for over a year, and you were at the office until 10 P.M. every night for the past week agonizing over final changes. Wearing your best suit, you walk into work, grab a cup of coffee, and turn on your computer. You notice out of the corner of your eye that the familiar screens are not flashing while your computer starts up; there is simply a message that says, "No hard disk found." You immediately call the company's helpdesk, only to learn that someone in the Human Resources Department opened a virus-infected e-mail attachment that has wiped out many computers across the company's network. After hanging up, you calmly reach into your briefcase and pull out the flash drive you made last night with the campaign and presentation on it. Not even an annoying virus can stop you from giving this presentation today.

Computer Viruses and Spam

Computer viruses are an e-marketer's worst nightmare. They reinforce consumer perceptions that the internet and computers in general are not secure. Computer viruses are intrusive pieces of computer code that secretly attach to existing files. Viruses are often self-reproducing and have the potential to wreak havoc on data. Harmful viruses can spread throughout a computer network, overwriting data files with nonsense. On the other hand, prank-like viruses might be as small as making the computer beep on a certain day of the month when the user strikes a particular keyboard letter or opening the CD-ROM drive every so many minutes. In addition, some viruses, known as dormant viruses, can infect a computer and not cause problems until a specified date or time.

Three common types of viruses are macro viruses, worms, and Trojan horses. **Macro viruses** attach to data files and infect common desktop applications when users open the infected data file. For example, the NightShade macro virus infected Microsoft Word 97 documents. When the user closed the infected document, the Word Assistant displayed a message with the word *NightShade* in it and password-protected the file with the same word.

Worms reproduce rapidly throughout a computer's memory, destroying the stored information and eating up resources. In 2004, multiple variations of the Sasser Worm infected computers worldwide. German teenager Sven Jaschan is the alleged author, and he was arrested following the incident. Additional viruses posed as cures for the virus, causing even more chaos.

Trojan horses do not replicate and often appear as legitimate programs. The virus-like program can do damage to the computer and open doors to let hackers enter the computer to do damage. The common CodeRed worm dropped a Trojan horse that facilitated remote access to computers' drives, allowing hackers to run a program on the computer.

Computer viruses can appear in data, e-mail, or software from any source. In 2000, the I Love You virus and its variants made the rounds of the world's computers and caused billions of dollars worth of damage in a matter of days. The virus, which was transmitted via e-mail, mostly affected users of Microsoft Outlook, a common e-mail program. Old, unpatched versions of Outlook allowed small programs, called scripts, to run on the user's computer in order to automate tasks. Although this means that users can customize the program to their needs, it also means that the scripts can run almost any Windows command—including the delete command. In this case, the virus writers sent a script as a file attachment that deleted files on the user's computer. The virus also looked up addresses in the Outlook address book and sent all of the user's contacts a copy of the virus as well. The result was rapid dissemination of a destructive virus. Variants that followed were even more sophisticated and destructive. Knowing that users would be on the lookout for "I Love You" in the subject line, one variant randomly generated a new subject line on each transmittal. Also knowing that antivirus programs would be scanning messages in search of the virus script, that same variant modified the script slightly on each transmittal to escape detection. Malicious programmers often target Outlook, which is tightly integrated with Windows, and other Microsoft applications because of their popularity. However, with the release of Windows 7, Microsoft offers free antivirus protection with Windows Security Essentials.

Even though viruses most commonly affect computers, they are also beginning to infect mobile devices, such as cell phones and PDAs. A worm named Cabir infected mobile phones running the Symbian OS operating system in 2004 and spread by detecting and infecting Bluetooth-enabled devices in proximity to the infected phone.

What can e-marketers do? The best place to stop a computer virus is before it reaches the end user. All e-mail messages pass through a mail server that stores the messages on a disk drive in users' mailboxes. Software can be installed on the mail server to scan all incoming messages for known viruses and destroy them if identified as containing a virus or quarantine them if suspected. In this way, the virus never reaches the end user and infection is avoided. Patch all programs regularly. Security updates from Microsoft and other vendors are often designed to thwart viruses. You should have your system set to auto update. Antiviral software can also be installed on each individual computer. One robust antiviral program is McAfee Anti-Virus (mcafee.com). Also popular is Symantec's Norton AntiVirus (symantec.com). The market share of these products may be threatened now that Microsoft is giving away Windows Security Essentials. Virus activity is reported to and recorded by the WildList Organization International, and information about viruses is available at its Web site: wildlist.org.

There are far fewer viruses that attack Apple computers. Much of that is due to protections built into Apple's operating system and distribution system. Much of Mac software is distributed online through the Mac App store. Before allowing the software into the store, Apple checks it for viruses. But what about software that you buy outside of the Mac App Store? The Mountain Lion operating system includes a feature called Gatekeeper. Gatekeeper checks to see if software is code signed by Apple. If not, then it won't install the software. The developer needs to register with Apple in order to get a code key. If it turns out that the developer is producing infected software, Apple will simply revoke the key.

Almost as annoying and frustrating as viruses, spam has taken over hundreds of users' e-mail inboxes. Spam is unwanted e-mail that is sent to many e-mail addresses at one time. Spam often has subject lines such as "Get rich quick!!!!" or "Cheap prescriptions." According to a report published by Nucleus Research in 2004, spam costs employers $1,934 a year per employee in loss of productivity. The business advisory firm did note that the figure does not include the dollars spent on software, hardware, IT personnel, and wasted bandwidth related to spam.

Although most spam messages are harmless, viruses often mask themselves as spam. Users often increase the amount of spam they receive by signing up for services online that subsequently sell user addresses. Many ISPs and e-mail providers offer spam or junk mail filters. These filters attempt to separate the spam messages from the important messages. Software similar to antivirus software scan incoming messages and either separate or delete them from the user's inbox.

Both antivirus and antispam detection are a boon for marketers because they keep the internet clear of destructive or unwanted content, helping to focus user attention on the desired content.

a lot of trust. Of course, some brands, such as Wal-Mart in the United States or Aldi food stores in Germany and Australia, have a brand name synonymous with low prices and fairly good quality. The value proposition is preserved in these cases with some buyers because the products provide fewer benefits for lower costs (e.g., a smaller set of features or fewer services).

Customers and prospects become aware of brands and develop beliefs and attitudes based on every brand contact, also called touch points. Some contacts are through one-way media such as advertising and packaging, and others are through two-way communication such as conversations with the firm's customer service or salespeople on the phone, at trade shows, on Web sites, or in company-initiated e-mail.

BRAND EQUITY **Brand equity** is the intangible value of a brand, measured in dollars. Exhibit 9.3 displays rankings for some of the top 100 U.S. brands in 2011. Google took the fastest-growing Global Brand of the Year award with a huge increase in brand value from 2008, putting it in the top 10 of all brands—and it continued to grow substantially in 2011. Note that Google is fourth on the Interbrand list but first on the Brand Finance list and second in Brand Z's evaluation. These differences arise because each company uses different criteria to evaluate brand value. It is not a perfect science because it involves an estimate of future revenues.

Beyond its rapid value growth, Google was praised by Interbrand for its rapid product expansion beyond search while maintaining a consistent feel to everything it does. Yahoo! and AOL had the same potential but did not realize the same results, while newcomer Bing quickly rose in 2011 to second place in the search market. Dell, Amazon, and eBay did not exist prior to the internet, yet appear on this list. How did they accomplish their equity rankings? See Exhibit 9.4 for suggestions, gleaned from many brand experts and marketers.

We add the idea that a great brand taps into the popular culture and touches consumers, as shown in Exhibit 9.5. Popular culture trends in music, entertainment, sports, and more help the brand touch consumers and remain current. For this reason, many firms use celebrities as spokespeople and sponsor sporting events that interest their target markets. For example, the iPad found

2011 Ranking and (Estimated Value in $ millions)			Brand
Interbrand	**Brand Z**	**Brand Finance**	
1 (71.9)	6 (73.8)	16 (25.8)	Coca-Cola
2 (69.9)	3 (100.8)	4 (36.2)	IBM
3 (59.1)	5 (78.2)	2 (42.8)	Microsoft
4 (55.3)	2 (111.5)	1 (44.3)	Google
5 (42.8)	10 (50.3)	7 (30.5)	General Electric
6 (35.6)	4 (81.0)	17 (21.8)	McDonald's
7 (35.2)	58 (13.9)	27 (19.1)	Intel
8 (33.5)	1 (153.3)	8 (29.5)	Apple
9 (29.0)	38 (17.3)	47 (15.4)	Disney
10 (28.5)	18 (35.4)	13 (26.8)	Hewlett Packard

Additional Internet Pure Play Companies, according to Interbrand (most business done online)		
2011 Interbrand Rank	**Brand**	**Value in $ millions**
26	Amazon.com	12.8
36	eBay	9.8
43	Dell	8.3
76	Yahoo!	4.4

EXHIBIT 9.3 Highest Value Global Brands in 2011 *Sources*: Interbrand (2011). *Best Global Brands.* Available at interbrand.com *BrandZ Top 100 Most Valuable Brands (2011).* Available at millwardbrown.com *Brand Finance Global 500* (2011). Available at brandfinance.com

Interbrand	BrandZ	Brand Channel
• Internal clarity • Internal commitment to the brand • Responsive to market changes • Legal protection • Customer relevance • Authenticity • Differentiation from other brands • Touch point consistency • Positive presence in social media • Deep customer understanding	• Appealing value proposition • Renewability when things change • Relevancy to consumers • Positive reputation and trust • Reimagining to be present in both physical and virtual reality • Financial contribution of the brand itself • Consistent brand personality • Perpetual innovation and experimentation • Technology is key • Digital omnipresence	• Built from a great idea • Holds true to core purpose and values • Employs brand as the central organizing principle • Continuously delivers on the brand promise • Possesses superior products, services, and technologies • Owns a distinct position and delivers a unique customer experience • Focuses on "internal" branding • Improves and innovates

EXHIBIT 9.4 What Makes a Great Global Brand? *Sources*: Interbrand (2011). *Best Global Brands.* Available at interbrand.com *BrandZ Top 100 Most Valuable Brands (2011).* Available at millwardbrown.com "What Makes Brands Great." Available at brandchannel.com

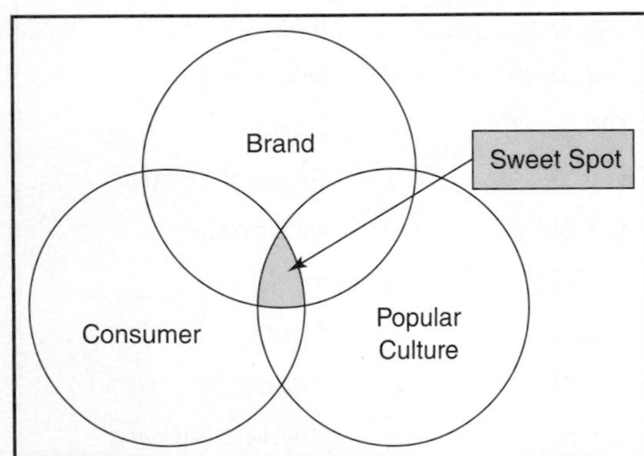

EXHIBIT 9.5 A Great Brand Intersects with Popular Culture and Touches Consumers

the branding sweet spot when it gave customers the ability to flip magazine pages and enjoy many other forms of entertainment and personal connection while on the move. This strategy capitalized on consumer desires to have products and communication tailored to their individual needs, and popular culture trends involving increased use of the internet for 24/7 entertainment and connection with others. Skype found the sweet spot when it brought **internet telephony** to the global masses, and LinkedIn hit the spot for business networking.

BRAND RELATIONSHIPS AND SOCIAL MEDIA Yahoo! has been so successful that individual customers actually created the Yahoo! yodel, subsequently used in the firm's commercials. This response is every brand marketer's dream—to build a following of cult-like customers who live, breathe, wear, and talk about their brand. Such is the case for Harley-Davidson motorcycle owners, Saab automobile owners, Apple computer and iPod fans, Craigslist, Google searches, and others. Such is the case for Amazon users who vie to become a top reviewer. How does a firm go from an unknown to this high level of acceptance?

Duncan, 2002 discusses five possible levels of brand relationship intensity:

- ***Advocacy***—customers tell others about their favorite brands, both online and offline.

- ***Community***—customers in communities, such as Facebook, communicate about brands with each other.
- ***Connection***—customers communicate with the company between purchase events.
- ***Identity***—customers proudly display the brand name of products they use.
- ***Awareness***—consumers include the brand in their list of possible purchases.

The fewest customers are at the highest level, where they have become advocates who tell everyone how great *their* brand is—YouTube and Twitter are fortunate to be in that spot today.

The explosion of social media sites escalated this process with peer-to-peer communication about brands. Yahoo! began its Life Engine repositioning by promoting an employee contest, with 800 entries describing why Yahoo! was their life engine. This type of internal marketing helps firms communicate a consistent message at all points where customers interact with employees. (Refer to Exhibit 9.4 regarding the importance of internal commitment to the brand.)

When using the internet, a company must be sure that its online messages and employee e-mails convey a positive brand image that is consistent with messages from all other contact points. One writer coined the term *smash test* to refer to the idea that when a Coca-Cola bottle is smashed, an individual can identify the brand from any little piece of the bottle. Web sites should pass the smash test as well—after removing logos and other identifying information, users ought to be able to identify the brand from any piece of the site. This type of identification means that the colors, font style and size, writing tone and voice, image size and appearance, and more should communicate the desired brand image.

Although the internet can assist organizations in moving customers up the pyramid, it is particularly difficult to control brand images because internet users often receive brand messages about the brand from sources that the company has not planned and managed, such as blogs, social networks, consumer e-mail among friends, or a customer burning a faulty product in a homemade video posted on YouTube. The internet provides information—good, bad, and ugly—about brands. Marketers must monitor the Web for brand information, as discussed in previous chapters, and do their best to shape brand images using every available tool, including internet technology. See the marketing communications and media chapters for more details about managing brand reputation crises online.

Ernst & Young surveyed entertainment and media CEOs in September 2012 and found that 63 percent used social media for brand building ("Media CEOs Look...," 2012). Forrester Research, Inc, agrees. Their study found that brand building and social media are intertwined. Forrester's research revealed that 92 percent of surveyed marketing leaders believe that social media has fundamentally changed the way consumers relate to brands (Stokes, 2012). Forrester summarizes with three roles for social media in branding: (1) build trust through social media relationships with consumers, (2) differentiate the brand in social media to enhance the emotional connections, and (3) nurture consumers in social media to build brand loyalty. It is also important to note that the marketing leaders in this study said that in the B2C market the Web and internet are first in importance for brand building, social media are second, search marketing third, followed by content development and e-mail marketing (and in the B2B market, social media are fourth, after Web, content, and e-mail). Yes, Web sites are still important for brand building.

BRANDING DECISIONS FOR WEB PRODUCTS Companies with products for online sale face several branding decisions: whether to apply existing brand names or to create new brand names for new products; whether to lend their brand name as a co-brand with other firms; and what domain name to use for the Web site.

Using Existing Brand Names on the Web An existing brand name can be used for any product extensions, and it makes sense when the brand is well known and has strong brand equity. For example, Amazon added music CDs, videos, software, electronics, and nearly everything else to its product mix. It is beneficial for Amazon to use its well-established online brand name for these other offerings rather than launch a new electronic storefront with another name for different product categories. Similarly, when products with offline sales introduce **online extensions**, many choose to use the same brand name (e.g., *The New York Times* became nytimes.com online). In fact, the dot-com crash showed that the strength of brick-and-mortar brands carried over to the internet, which is what gave many Web sites their staying power.

Some companies may not want to use the same brand name online and offline, for several reasons. First, if the new product or channel is risky, the firm would run the risk of jeopardizing the brand's good name by having it associated with a possible product failure. Entering the online publishing business tentatively, *Sports Illustrated* did not want to use its brand online and instead created an extension, naming it *Thrive* (thriveonline.com). The *Sports Illustrated* affiliation was not mentioned online. The thriveonline name was subsequently sold to Oxygen Media.

Also, a powerful internet success might inadvertently reposition the offline brand. Most internet products carry a high-tech, cool, and young image, which will carry over to offline branded products. For example, NBC (the television network) serves an older market than does MSNBC online. Because the network hoped to bring younger viewers from MSNBC on the internet to its television network, it made a decision to stick with the brand name—thus intending to reposition the offline brand image. In such situations, firms must ensure that online brand images will have the desired effect on the offline versions and that overextended product lines do not create fuzzy brand images. Finally, sometimes the firm wants to change the name slightly for the new market or channel, as a way of differentiating the online brand from the offline brand. For example, *Wired* magazine changed the name of its online version to *HotWired* to convey a high-tech image and perhaps to position the two publications differently. Perhaps due to its success, it has since reverted to the well-known *Wired* brand name.

Creating New Brands for Internet Marketing If an organization wants to create a new internet brand, it is critical to select a good name. Good brand names should suggest something about the product (e.g., WebPromote.com and MySpace.com), should differentiate the product from competitors (e.g., gURL.com), and should be suitable for legal protection. On the internet, a brand name should be short, memorable, easy to spell, and translate well into other languages. For example, Dell Computer at dell.com is much easier than Hammacher Schlemmer (hammacher.com), the gift retailer. As another example, consider the appropriateness of these search tool names: Yahoo!, Excite, Lycos, Ask, AltaVista, AOL Search, DogPile, AllTheWeb, InfoSeek, HotBot, WebCrawler, Google, Technorati, GigaBlast, iWon, LiveSearch, About, and LookSmart. Which ones fit the preceding criteria?

Co-branding This occurs when two different companies form an alliance to work together and put their brand names on the same product or service. This practice is quite common on the internet and is a good way for firms to build synergy through expertise and brand recognition, as long as their target markets are similar. For example, *Sports Illustrated* co-brands with CNN as CNNSI. Even the Web site address displays the co-brand: sportsillustrated.cnn.com. Yahoo! is a good place to look for co-branded services. In the past, it has joined with *TV Guide* and then Gist to provide TV listings; it has also offered the Yahoo! Visa Shopping pages. As a second example, EarthLink, the sixth largest ISP, joined forces in early 1998 with Sprint, the telephone company, to form a co-branded business with a new EarthLink–Sprint name and logo. They used the co-brand to provide ISP services to Sprint customers and to pursue AOL customers.

Internet Domain Names Organizations spend a lot of time and money developing powerful, unique brand names for strong brand equity.

According to Netcraft, in March 2012 there were 9.4 billion indexed Web pages and 644 million Web sites. With 201.5 million hosts for .com sites how can a company find a unique Web site name (Exhibit 9.6)? Of course, it could be worse—Royal Pingdom counts 380 million abandoned site names. Using the company trademark or one of its brand names in the Web address helps consumers find the site quickly. For example, coca-cola.com adds power to Coca-Cola brands (Exhibit 9.3). Note that most of the top global brands use their brand names in the Web site name. Disney's address is disney.go.com to let people know they should visit Disney, but typing disney.com in the browser immediately redirects to the same place. Disney owns both of these names and many more. This parallel name usage is not always possible, however. Many factors must be considered when it comes to domain names.

A **URL (uniform resource locator)** is a Web site address. It is also called an **IP address (internet protocol)** and a **domain name**. This categorization scheme is clever; it is similar to telephone area codes in the way it helps computer users find other computers on the internet network.

http://www.support.dell.com

http://	**www.**	**support.**	**dell.**	***com***
hypertext protocol	World Wide Web subdomain	third-level domain	second-level domain	top-level domain

URLs are actually numbers, but because users can more easily remember names, a domain name server translates back and forth. Without this system you'd be saying to a friend: "Check out this awesome site at 71.24.607.304." A domain name contains several levels as depicted in the following table:

The *http://* indicates that the browser should expect data using the hypertext protocol—meaning documents that are linked together using hyperlinks. Sometimes URLs start with *ftp://* (file transfer protocol), which means that an **FTP** server will send a data file to the user (most likely a document that is not an HTML page). The *www* is no longer necessary and most commercial sites register their name both with and without it and then direct one to the other using an automated re-direct command. Sometimes a URL is for Web-based mail and the word *mail* will replace the "www" subdomain (e.g., http://mail.yahoo.com).

When organizations purchase a domain name, they must first decide in which top-level domain to register. Most businesses in the United States and other English-speaking countries want

Domain Designation	Top-Level Domain Name	Number of Hosts (millions)
net	Networks	332.7
com	Commercial	201.5
jp	Japan	63.6
it	Italy	25.5
de	Germany	20.6
br	Brazil	24.3
cn	China	20.2

EXHIBIT 9.6 Largest Top-Level Domain Names in January 2012 *Source*: Data from Network Wizards. Available at isc.org

.com, because users usually type in the firm name. com as a best guess at the site's location. Other countries have top-level domains such as .mx, for Mexico, or .uk for the United Kingdom and .de for Germany. Thus, Amazon in the United Kingdom is amazon.co.uk. Exhibit 9.6 displays the largest top-level domains, ranked by number of hosts. A *host* is a computer connected to the internet and may contain multiple IP addresses. For this and other technical reasons, these numbers represent the minimum number of possible IP addresses in each domain.

An interesting wrinkle on the country domains designation is that marketers outside those nations sometimes want the name. For example, many doctors registered in Moldavia may want to obtain the .md country extension. Another interesting example comes from the Pacific Island nation of Tuvalu (.tv). DotTV agreed to pay Tuvalu $50 million in revenues for the right to sell .tv extensions—a big offer for a country with only $20 million gross national product. However, cbs.tv or nypdblue.tv did not materialize. Since the 1998 deal, the new owner of the .tv deal, VeriSign, had spent $60 million promoting the extension to yield 400,000 registrations in 2001, with only half of that remaining by the end of 2003 ("False Hopes…," 2003). So far, most of the networks have chosen to brand through their .com Web sites. However, many other possible top-level domains remain as choices. The Internet Corporation for Assigned Names and Numbers (ICANN) is a nonprofit corporation that operates like a committee of experts to make decisions about protocol and names such as the latest: .xxx, and .post. Incidentally, .edu and .com were introduced in 1985. At last count, in 2012, there were:

- Seven generic top-level domain names that must be used by the type of organization indicated in the name (.com, .edu, .gov, .int, .mil, .net, and .org).
- 250 two-letter country top-level domain names (e.g., .de, .mx. and pn, for the Pitcairn Islands with a population of 50 residents).
- Many other general names, such as .biz, .info, .pro, .name, .coop, .aero, .museum, .asia, .cat, .jobs, .mobi, .tel, and .travel (see icann.org).

GoDaddy, along with many other sites, provides domain registering services for a mere $12.99 a year, including an e-mail address (godaddy.com). For this low price, students can leave less professional yahoo.com and other Web-based e-mail addresses behind and get a more professional address to impress recruiters (such as firstname.lastname@lastname.com).

One problem is that with more than 97 percent of words in the dictionary already registered as domain names, the desired online name may not be available. A dictionary name is not necessarily the best option because it already has a meaning attached to it, which is generic for the product category, making it difficult to build a competitive advantage and impossible to trademark. Thus, it is more difficult to build a unique brand identity for a wine firm called wine.com than for gallo.com, a well-known brand name. Consider the brilliance of Amazon.com when it selected a unique name and avoided the soon-to-come crowd of online booksellers using "book" in their names. The similarities in the following brand names make it very difficult to find a competitive positioning online (some now out of business, not surprisingly). See the list of online booksellers using the word *book* in their brand names on the next page.

What happens if the firm name has been registered by someone else? For example, DeltaComm, a software developer and ISP in North Carolina, was the first to register delta.com, preempting Delta Airlines (originally delta-air.com) and Delta Faucet (deltafaucet.com). These firms were forced to come up with alternative names. Another solution is to buy the name from the currently registered holder, and that is what Delta Airlines eventually did. In another example, Grupo Posadas, the large Mexican hotel chain owner, negotiated for 18 months to buy posadas.com.mx from a local family with the same last name. The company paid for the name with a

1bookstreet	BooksAMillion	gobookshopping
A1Books	BookSense	Gobookshopping
Abebooks	books-forsale	HalfPriceBooks
allbooks4less	BooksNow	Nwbooks
AllBookstores	Bookspot	Textbooks
Alotofbooks	Bookwire	Textbooksatcost
BestBookBuys	CheapyBook	Textbooksource
BookCloseOuts	Classbook	Textbookx
Bookland	CoolBooks	TheBookPeople
BookNetUSA	Ebooks	TrueBooks
BookPool	eSuccessBooks	VarsityBooks

free condo, many nights of free hotel stays, and *mucho dinero.* Many creative internet users register lots of popular names and offer them for sale at prices of up to millions of dollars. GoDaddy offers second-level domain name auctions, and GreatDomains.com allows users to buy and sell popular domain names. Insure.com went for $16 million in 2009. If you have an extra $25,000 to spare, you can buy the name "heroine.com" or participate in an auction for shoppingbuzz.com. As you read in Chapter 5, cybersquatting—which occurs when a domain name registrant takes an already trademarked brand name—is illegal. The same is not true, however, for dictionary or personal names. A "whois" search at GoDaddy.com reveals domain name owners. One of this book's authors contacted a domain name owner directly through this process and was able to obtain the name from him at no cost (pathtobliss.com).

Incidentally, when registering a name, organizations would be well advised to also purchase related names for several reasons. First, this keeps them out of the hands of others. Many individuals publish Web sites that include criticisms and comments from disgruntled customers about a company, calling them companynamesucks.com (e.g., paypalsucks.com). To combat this issue, some companies have begun buying their own companynamesucks.com to preempt their detractors.

Second, users don't always know what URL to type to find a company. Posadas, the Mexican hotel firm, purchased domain names for more than 17 different spellings of its various hotels to make things easier for customers. Coca-Cola owns cocacola.com, coca-cola.com, and coke.com; cocacolacompany.com, the cocacolacompany.com, and cocacola.net, .info, .us., .org, .me, and many more.

Bently Nevada wishes that it could own both bently.com and bentley.com due to this common misspelling of its name. We recently noted that netmanners.com was accidentally hyphenated at the end of a line in a book to become net-manners.com—a site written entirely in an Asian language. Also, Compaq Computer Company paid $3 million to develop the AltaVista search engine site (altavista.com) only to find that alta-vista.com was already in operation as an adult site with sexual material. Fortunately, the search engine outlasted the adult site, and Compaq's oversight has been remedied.

Picking the right domain name can make a huge difference when trying to entice users to the site and to build consistency in the firm's marketing communications. For example, Time Warner's Pathfinder.com was the firm's first Web site, containing online versions of its many successful magazines: *People*, *Time*, *Fortune*, *Money*, and *Entertainment Weekly.* Dan Okrent, editor of *New Media* for Pathfinder, claims that the biggest error the firm initially made with the online division was selecting the name *Pathfinder* for the site. *Pathfinder* lacks the name recognition of its well-established magazine brands, and, thus, the firm failed to capitalize on the value of its brands. Furthermore, according to Okrent, *Pathfinder* has little meaning to users. Type pathfinder.com today and you will be immediately presented with a page that links to all the firm's magazines.

Support Services

Customer support—during and after purchases—is a critical component in the value proposition. Customer service representatives should be knowledgeable and concerned about customer experiences. Sites that care about developing relationships with their customers, such as Amazon.com, place some of their best people in customer support. In the early days, Amazon's billionaire founder and CEO Jeff Bezos even answered some of the e-mail messages himself. Some products need extra customer support. For example, when a user purchases software such as Constant Comment to design e-mail newsletters and maintain e-mail databases, technical support becomes important. Customer service reps help customers with installation, maintenance problems, product guarantees, and service warranties, and in general work to increase customer satisfaction with the firm's products.

CompUSA, Inc., the largest U.S. computer retailer, astutely combines online and offline channels to increase support services. At compusa.com, customers can enter their ZIP code to check the availability and pricing of any product at the five nearest brick-and-mortar stores. Customers can also check the status of items left for repair at the store, searching the Web site by status or product serial number. Customer service as a product benefit is an important part of CRM; however, it has now become more of a necessity than a competitive edge.

Online chat bots are an important and growing part of customer service. Live chat online occurs when a user is at a site and types into a box to communicate in real time with a company customer service representative—either during the purchase process or as postpurchase customer service. While fewer than 2 percent of internet users participate in online chat, a person who chats on a site is 7.5 times more likely to purchase than another site visitor who doesn't use the chat feature ("Live Chat…," 2012).

The topic of customer service online is such an important part of product design that we dedicate much of Chapter 15 to it (as part of CRM).

Labeling

Product labels identify brands, sponsoring firms, and product ingredients, and often provide instructions for use and promotional materials. Labels on tangible products create product recognition and influence decision behavior at the point of purchase. Labeling has digital equivalents in the online world. For online services, terms of product usage, product features, and other information comprise online labeling at Web sites. For example, when users download iTunes software for organizing their iPod music, they can first read the "label" to discover how to install and use the software.

In addition, many companies have extensive legal information about copyright use on their Web pages. Microsoft, for instance, allows firms to reproduce product images without permission, but any images on its former Expedia.com site must receive special permission before being copied and used in printed materials such as this book. Like many organizations, the Federal Trade Commission has a "label" page discussing its privacy policy (see Exhibit 9.7). Online labeling can serve many of the same purposes on the Web as offline. Many brick-and-mortar businesses display the Better Business Bureau logo on their doors to give the customer a sense of confidence and trust. Similarly, the BBB offers the BBBOnLine logo to its members. Another validating label is the TRUSTe privacy shield. If firms agree to certain terms of use regarding

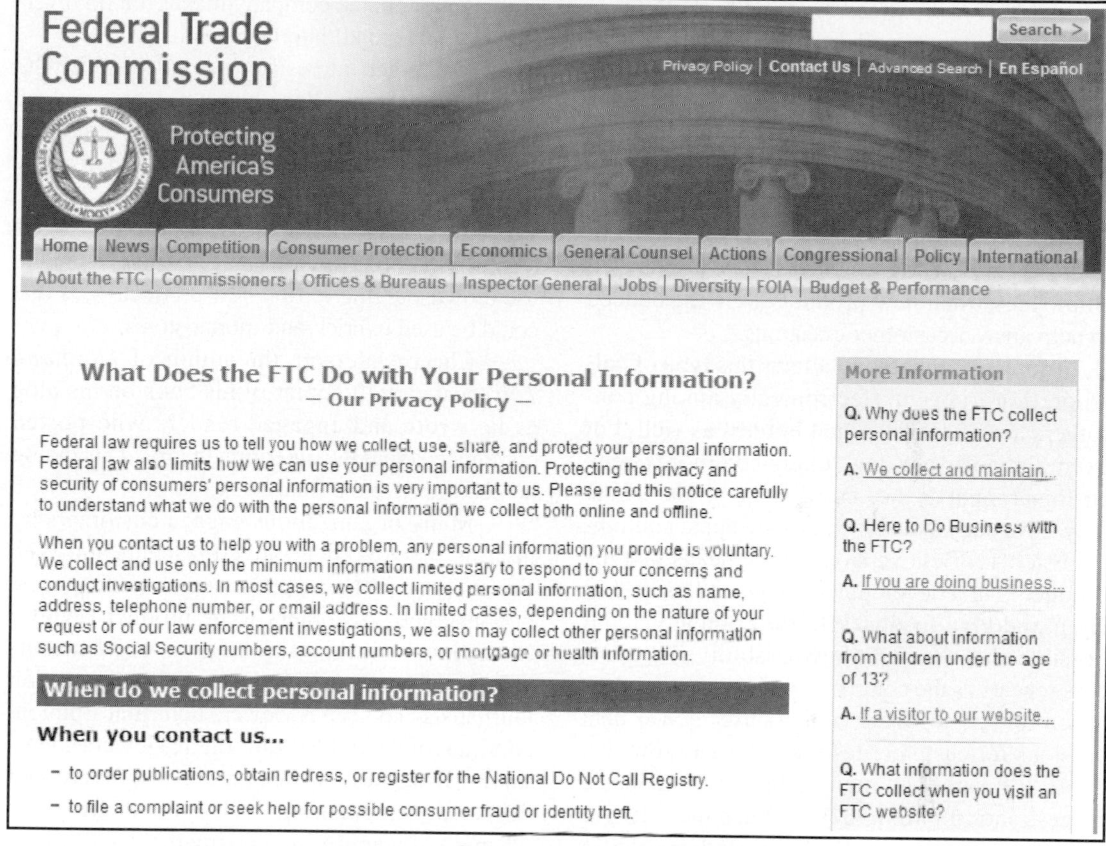

EXHIBIT 9.7 U.S. Federal Trade Commission Privacy Policy *Source*: ftc.gov/

privacy of customer information collected at their site, they may register at TRUSTe, download the TRUSTe seal, and affix it to their Web sites as part of a label.

Finally, many sites present social media logos as labels on their pages. The purpose is to allow sharing, commenting, or registering via Facebook and others. These logos add to the credibility and technology competence of the original company.

E-MARKETING-ENHANCED PRODUCT DEVELOPMENT

The move from atoms to bits adds complexity to online product offers. Developers must now combine digital text, graphics, video, and audio and use new internet delivery systems (see Chapter 11 for a discussion of how to monetize digital products). They must integrate front-end customer service operations with back-end data collection and fulfillment methods to deliver product. These requirements create steep learning curves for traditional companies as they work these factors into the product value proposition. E-marketers, therefore, need to consider several factors that affect product development and product mix strategies with new technologies (and other marketing mix factors in the following chapters).

Customer Codesign via Crowdsourcing

The power shift to buyers, when combined with the internet's global reach, allows for many unusual business partnerships and for both business and consumer collaboration. Partners form synergistic clusters to help design customer products that deliver value. For example, after Dell Computer contractually gave one supplier 25 percent of its volume requirement for computer monitors, the supplier assigned engineers to work with Dell's product development team (Ghosh, 1998). These engineers stood beside Dell employees when new products were introduced to help answer customer questions.

Internet technology allows this type of collaboration to occur electronically among consumers across international borders as well. For example, software developers commonly seek customer input as they develop the product. You may have seen Web sites, mobile apps, and others listed as "Beta version." This means that the product is in a development stage and users will try it and give feedback to the company about possible changes to improve usability. This process repeats as the company improves the product based on this feedback and releases newer beta versions for customer testing. Internet browsers, CRM software, and many others use this basic process shown in Exhibit 9.8. When the software is good enough, the company makes the final version available to all internet users.

In another interesting example, the LEGO Group, a toy maker, allows consumers to download software for creating virtual LEGO designs (see ldd.lego.com). Consumers then upload their fancy palaces and robots to the LEGO gallery online, where others can view their great designs. This is a great way for LEGO to engage customers and to use crowdsourcing to find new product ideas that could be used in brick-and-mortar stores.

Chris Anderson, the author of *The Long Tail*, posted draft copies of his book on his blog as he wrote and engaged readers who posted comments about the emerging theory. This dialog helped improve the final book.

Many organizations engage customers by inviting them to create advertisements and Web site content on their sites or social media pages. For instance, customers write product reviews and authors write blogs at Amazon. CNN encourages breaking news video uploads by citizen journalists. To keep reviewers honest at Epinion.com, anyone can also rate the reviewers themselves. Blogs are one technology that increased this co-development of Web content. Bloggers

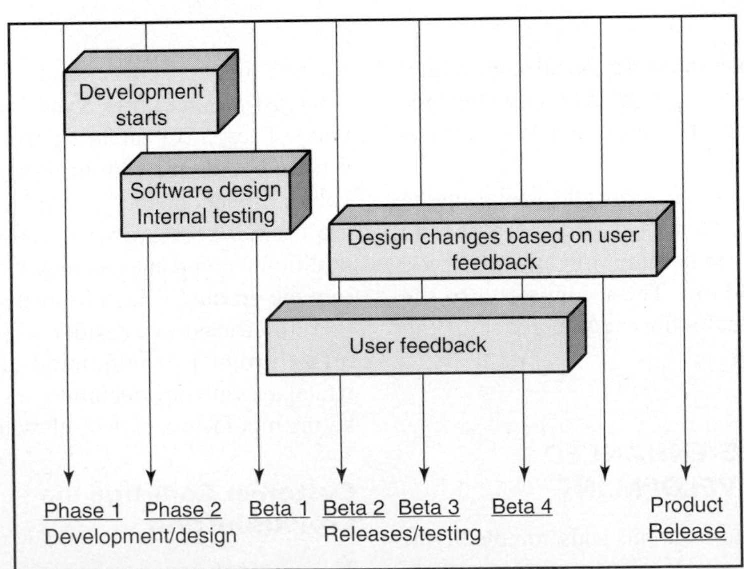

EXHIBIT 9.8 Customer Codesign of Software Products

invite comments to their posts, thus increasing the content value for readers.

Good marketers look everywhere for customer feedback to improve products, even setting up blogs for the sole purpose of gathering customer ideas and input. One great example is Starbucks' mystarbucksidea.com, mentioned in Chapter 2. Also Dell's ideastorm.com invites product suggestions from users and had received over 17,808 ideas with 738,740 votes by September 2012. Dell implemented over 500 of these product suggestions.

However, sometimes this feedback comes uninvited. With the proliferation of video posting sites and e-mail "word of mouse," the speed and reach of the internet, and the fact that consumers trust people like them more than they trust companies, customers are quick to spread the word about product strengths and weaknesses. In this environment, savvy firms monitor customer input electronically (as discussed in Chapter 6). Using an online monitoring service, Mrs. Field's Cookies caught wind of false rumors spreading on the internet that had caused offline sales to drop 1 percent in a short time period.

Internet Properties Spawn Other Opportunities

The internet's unique properties, discussed in Chapter 1, generated unusual new products and companies. Location-based services (LBS) are one such example. Global positioning devices (GPS) in smartphones and other mobile online devices track user locations and send to friends via "check-ins" while at restaurants, retailers, and many other locations. This has created many marketing opportunities, discussed in later chapters.

The AutoMall Online and Lending Tree are two companies that aggregate services for users. The Lending Tree is a firm that offers online searches for the best prices for mortgages and other types of loans. These firms provide bundles of benefits difficult to achieve before the advent of internet. Because they also represent a new type of intermediary, these services are discussed more thoroughly in Chapter 11.

The internet is a great information equalizer, which means fierce competition, lots of product imitation, and short product life cycles. Online auctions are a perfect example. Not long after eBay came online, Amazon.com and others began offering auctions; now one restaurant in San Francisco is even auctioning meals to draw patrons during slow times. Also, Groupon and other "deal of the day" sites bring a new type of competition to the masses. Many search engines are starting to look similar. In this environment, product differentiation is key because if consumers cannot find meaningful product differences they will purchase based solely on price.

Taking short product life cycles to an extreme, Direct Hit Technologies, Inc., the firm that sells internet search engine software, was known to launch six new product versions within a few days (King and Hoffman, 1999). Imagine how much more quickly that happens, now, in 2012! In another example, when Frank Sinatra died, BMG's five-person new-product development team created a lifetime tribute and a series of product offerings for the Web site in six short hours. The firm would have needed four months to produce this in a paper catalog. CNN and other news sites refresh stories every minute, 24/7. While all of this may sound like normal business activity to readers, it is the internet that made it possible. Organizations must respond quickly to new technology or lose. As one astute pundit said, "Eat lunch or be lunch." Despite the internet adoption flattening at maturity, innovation online is still rewarded.

New-Product Strategies for E-Marketing

Many new products, such as YouTube, Yahoo!, and Twitter.com, were introduced by "one-pony" firms, built around the company's first successful product. Other organizations, such as Microsoft, added internet products to an already successful product mix (e.g., the Internet Explorer Web browser). This section explores product mix strategies to aid marketers in integrating offline and online offerings.

PRODUCT MIX STRATEGIES How can marketers integrate hot product ideas for the internet into current product mixes? Companies can choose among six categories of new-product strategies. Discontinuous innovation is the highest-risk strategy, while **me-too lower-cost products** are the least risky ones. Companies will select one or more of these strategies based on marketing objectives and other factors such as risk appetite, strength of current brand names, resource availability, and competitive entries.

Discontinuous Innovations These are new-to-the-world products never seen before. Hula hoops and computers were discontinuous innovations when introduced. On the internet, the first Web page design software, shopping agent, and search engine fall into this category. Levi's Personal Pair product body scanning hardware and software is another. This idea is great for customers who can't find clothing with a proper fit and who want more influence on its design. It also helps manufacturers and retailers increase customer loyalty, lower inventory costs, and avoid seasonal cost reductions. Social networking is another discontinuous innovation—the idea that each internet user has a rich array of contacts for fun and profit when tapped. And, let's not forget the 675,000 crazy, interesting, entertaining, and educational Google Android applications in 2012. Many discontinuous innovations are yet to come on the internet. Want to keep up? Just read the most popular technology blog online Engadget (engadget.com).

A **disruptive innovation** is a special category of discontinuous innovation that changes the existing market in a drastic way. Sometimes called disruptive technologies, examples include digital music downloads disrupted the CD market, desktop publishing disrupted the magazine and newspaper markets, GPS devices disrupted the physical paper map market, and Facebook and Twitter disrupted the market for how people communicate and share ideas. This is another reason that marketers must carefully watch new technologies.

Although a discontinuous innovation strategy is quite risky, the potential rewards for success are great. E-marketers planning discontinuous innovations must remember that their customers will have to learn and adopt new behaviors—things they have not done before. The company faces the risk that customers will not change unless the new behavior is easy and they perceive that the benefits are worthwhile. However, if the target group is under age 35, the risk is lower because the technologically savvy among this group yearn for cool new technologies.

New-Product Lines These are introduced when companies take an existing brand name and create new products in a completely different category. For example, Microsoft created a new line when it introduced its Internet Explorer Web browser. Because the Netscape browser was already available at that time, Microsoft's entry was not a discontinuous innovation. And Netscape is history now.

Additions to Existing Product Lines This occurs when organizations add a new flavor, size, or other variation to a current product line. *USA Today* (usatoday.com) is a slightly different version of the hard copy edition, adapted for online delivery. It is yet another product in *USA Today's* line. At the beginning of this chapter, we mentioned that Google has many different product lines (search, advertising, applications, enterprise, and more)—all leveraging the great brand name and helping to increase brand equity.

Improvements or Revisions of Existing Products These products are introduced as "new and improved" and, thus, replace the old product. For example, Web-based e-mail systems improved on client-based e-mail systems such as Eudora or Outlook because users could check and send e-mail from any Web-connected computer. One provider, Web2Mail.com, allows users to pick up e-mail from any existing account, say at a computer lab in Thailand (from Gmail, Hotmail, or Yahoo! Web mail). On the internet, firms are continually improving their brands to add value and remain competitive.

Repositioned Products These are current products that are either targeted to different markets or promoted for new uses. As previously mentioned, Yahoo! began as a search directory on the Web and then repositioned itself as a portal (an internet entry point with many services), and then as a Life Engine. By doing so, Yahoo! first positioned itself against the early leader, America Online, and is now positioning away from prime competitor, Google. MSNBC repositioned its news organization for younger viewers.

Me-Too Lower-Cost Products These are introduced to compete with existing brands by offering a price advantage. For example, MailChimp competes with Constant Contact by offering absolutely free e-mail marketing services for companies, and an evaluation of paid services shows $10 for up to 500 e-mail contacts (versus $15 for Constant Contact). The internet spawned a multitude of free products with the idea of building market share so the firm would have a customer base for marketing its other products. For example, Eudora Light, the e-mail reader software, and WS_FTP LE, the file transfer software, were two early entries with this strategy. This strategy can also be considered promotional sampling.

Although the B2C market gets most of the attention, many cutting-edge technology products and trends in the B2B markets are discussed in the many "Let's Get Technical" boxes throughout this book.

A WORD ABOUT ROI Part I of this book discussed the need for performance metrics as feedback so firms can assess the success of their e-marketing strategies and tactics. This type of assessment is especially important when introducing new products, online or offline. Marketers generally forecast the expected product revenue over time, deduct marketing and other expenses, and generate a break-even point and return on investment estimate for new products prior to their launch. Usually, brand managers compete for the firm's resources by showing that their products will generate either a higher ROI or a break even in a shorter time frame. By *break even* we mean that the R&D and other initial costs will be recovered at a particular date based on projected sales. In the process, they calculate a break-even date when the product is projected to start making a profit. How long is acceptable? Ten years ago, some managers were saying that internet projects had to break even within three months or they would not get funded. Of course, the exact timing varies by industry—Boeing does not expect most new aircraft to pay out for 20 years! And Twitter is just now trying to figure out how to fully monetize its successful service. Nonetheless, ROI and break-even point are important metrics for selling new-product ideas internally and for measuring their success in the market.

Chapter Summary

A product is a bundle of benefits that satisfies the needs of organizations or consumers and for which they are willing to exchange money or other items of value. A product can be a tangible good, a service, an idea, a person, a place, or something else. The entire product experience provides value to the customer, is defined by the customer, involves customer expectations, and applies at all price levels.

Of the five general product decisions that comprise a bundle of benefits for meeting customer needs, four (attributes, branding, support services, and labeling) apply to online products. Companies creating new products for online sale must decide whether to use existing brand names or create new brand names for new products; whether to co-brand; and what domain name to choose. Customer support—during and after purchases—is a critical component in the value proposition. Online labeling is the digital equivalent of product labeling and can serve many of the same purposes as offline labeling.

When branding products, marketers consider popular culture, the brand, and the consumer. Firms attempt to move consumers to higher levels of relationship intensity from awareness to advocacy.

When developing new online products, e-marketers can turn to customer codesign and use internet properties to spark other opportunities. They can choose among six categories of new-product strategies (discontinuous innovations, new-product lines, additions to existing product lines, improvements/revisions of existing products, product repositionings, and me-too lower-cost products) and are generally required to estimate revenues, costs, and ROI or payout for management review and approval.

Exercises

REVIEW QUESTIONS

1. What are the arguments for and against using existing brand names on the Web?
2. List six new-product strategy categories and provide internet examples of each.
3. Why is value tied to the entire product experience?
4. What are some important criteria for naming internet domains?
5. How does labeling work on the internet?
6. What techniques can e-marketers employ to enhance new-product development?
7. Why do e-marketers need to forecast revenue, expenses, ROI, and break even for new products under consideration?

DISCUSSION QUESTIONS

8. **The Google Story.** Describe Google's strategy for creating value: attributes, branding, support services, and labeling.
9. **The Google Story.** Why do you think Google's primary revenue comes from advertising? What other products do you think Google could monetize?
10. What similarities do you see in Exhibit 9.4 that makes for great brands? Do you have other ideas?
11. Under what circumstances would it make sense to take an existing brand name online? When would it not make sense?
12. Given the list of online booksellers in this chapter, what name would you pick for a new bookstore selling both new and used books online?
13. How would you use social media to build the brand of your university?
14. What discontinuous innovations have you seen since this book was written? What's next in your opinion?
15. Why do e-marketers often have difficulty estimating the revenues, costs, and payout or ROI of a new product under development?

WEB ACTIVITIES

16. Visit GreatDomains at greatdomains.com. Do you see any names represented there that could be interpreted as cybersquatting?
17. Visit the Country-Code Top-Level Domain database at icann.org. Notice how Web sites originating in the United States do not have to append the ".us" root to the end of URLs. Which root names owned by these countries could be used for commercial purposes rather than differentiating country of origin? If you wanted to register a Web site ending in one of these country root names, what requirements do you have to meet? What country root names are already being offered through registrations sites like GoDaddy.com?
18. Visit godaddy.com and do a "whois" search for your own name.com. Is it available? If so, what would it cost to get and what services are available for that fee? If it is not available, how can you attempt to obtain it using GoDaddy's services?
19. Many companies use a new-product development process called scenario planning. For example, Microsoft executives wonder what it would be like if you could search your computer for phone numbers, e-mail addresses, and both file names and document content all at once with one search word. Think of five scenarios that would make your life easier while using the internet.

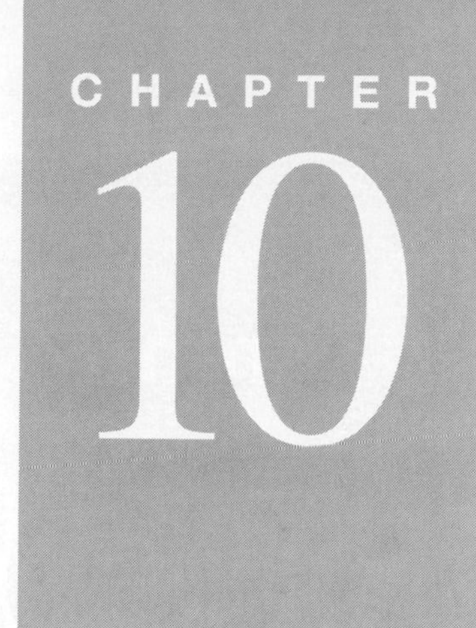

Price: The Online Value

The primary goal of this chapter is to help you examine how internet technology influences pricing strategies. You will gain an understanding of both the buyer's and the seller's perspectives of pricing online and consider whether the internet is an efficient market. You will also read about fixed pricing as well as the return to dynamic pricing, such as online auctions, and many other strategies and tactics.

After reading this chapter, you will be able to:

- Identify the main fixed and dynamic pricing strategies used for selling online.
- Discuss the buyer's view of pricing online in relation to real costs and buyer control.
- Highlight the seller's view of pricing online in relation to internal and external factors.
- Outline the arguments for and against the internet as an efficient market.
- Describe several types of online payment systems and their benefits to online retailers.

- For truly time starved consumers, nothing beats the simplicity and convenience of ordering or paying with a single touch, swipe, tap, or button press.

- ***Ushuaïa Ibiza Beach Hotel*** teamed up with Barcelona-based biometric payment provider ***PayTouch*** so that guests (who register upon arrival) can make payments with their fingerprints.

The Price of an iPhone App

Instapaper is an award-winning app for the iPhone, iPad, and iPod Touch (Exhibit 10.1). It allows users to download up to 500 Web page articles using WiFi or 3G/4G coverage and then read them later when not connected to the internet. Users can change the font size, save articles in folders in the app, and even browse to see what others are downloading. The app received stellar reviews by reporters from *The New York Times*, *Wired*, *Mac World*, *PCMag*, and more (see instapaper.com).

How much would you pay for an app like this, if anything? Mobile apps have several different pricing and revenue models:

- Freemium is a combination of "free" and "premium," where companies offer a basic product for free and then provide upgraded versions for a fee. For example, *Angry Birds Free*.
- Lite versions of apps are sold at low prices and do not include all the features of the full app versions. For example, *Angry Birds Lite*.
- Full price versions include many more features. For example, *Doodle Jump* sold for $0.99 and netted $2.08 million in one year ("iPhone App Business. . .," 2012).

In June 2011, 52 percent of the revenue for the top game app producers came from freemium games (Perez, 2011). How to monetize freemium or lite apps? Some marketers expect users to upgrade to versions containing more advanced features after they've enjoyed the free version. Others sell advertising in the freemium apps and get paid for each click-through (such as *FreeTheApps*, which brings in $800,000 a year in ad revenue), and still others sell products within the apps themselves. Companies like Netflix use freemium apps to move users to their paid Web services.

Instapaper was introduced in 2008 with a freemium version plus a full app at the price of $9.99. In June 2009, the company lowered the price to $4.99, receiving the standard 70 percent cut from Apple ($3.50). At that point, the freemium version was downloaded three times as often as the paid version. Then in fall 2010, the company removed the freemium version as an experiment and sales of the paid app increased incrementally (see marco.org).

The removal of the free app not only drove sales higher for the paid app but also reduced costs, according to owner Marco Arment. First, it costs more in development time to maintain, upgrade, and support more than one version of an app. Second, Instapaper uses a Web service to handle the Web page download technology for app users, and that was an unreimbursed cost to support freemium users. Instapaper sold advertising space in the freemium app; however, not many users clicked on it to generate revenue for Instapaper. The paid app generated much more revenue. As well, the reviews in the iTunes store for the paid app were much better than those for the free app (probably because the paid app had more features).

Using Web analytics, Arment noticed that few people upgraded from the freemium version to the paid version. According to owner, Arment, "I'm primarily in the business of selling a product for money. How much effort do I really want to devote to satisfying people who are unable or extremely unlikely to pay for anything?"

EXHIBIT 10.1 Instapaper, the Popular Mobile App *Source:* Used with permission from www.marco.org

THE INTERNET CHANGES PRICING STRATEGIES

In the narrowest sense, **price** is the amount of money charged for a product or service. More broadly, price is the sum of all the values (such as money, time, energy, and psychic cost) that buyers exchange for the benefits of having or using a good or service. Throughout most of history, prices were set by negotiation between buyers and sellers, and that remains the dominant model in many emerging economies. Fixed price policies—setting one price for all buyers—is a relatively modern idea that arose with the development of large-scale retailing and mass production at the end of the nineteenth century. Now, 100 years later, the internet is taking us back to an era of **dynamic pricing**—varying prices for individuals.

Information technology complicated pricing strategies and changed the way marketers use this tool, especially in online markets. In addition, the increasing power of buyers means control over pricing in some instances—such as with online product bidding. The internet's properties, especially in the role of information equalizer, allow for **price transparency**—the idea that both buyers and sellers can view competitive prices for items sold online. This feature would tend to commoditize products sold online, making the internet an efficient market. But is it?

We explore the internet as an efficient market in this chapter, using the economist's view as a guide. We also discuss both the buyer's and the seller's views of price and explain why some pricing strategies are more effective online than others.

BUYER AND SELLER PERSPECTIVES

The meaning of *price* depends on the viewpoint of the buyer and the seller. Each party to the exchange brings different needs and objectives that help describe a *fair* price. In the end, both parties must agree or no sale takes place.

Buyer View

Recall that buyers define value as benefits minus costs. In Chapter 9, we discussed the benefit variable, explaining that the internet creates many benefits important to consumers and business buyers alike. Here we explore the cost side of the formula: money, time, energy, and psychic costs.

THE REAL COSTS Today's buyer must be quite sophisticated to understand even the simple dollar cost of a product sold online. The seller's price may or may not include shipping, tax, and other seemingly hidden elements—hidden in the sense that these costs often are not revealed online until the last screen of a shopping experience. For example, Exhibit 10.2 displays the different prices for the book, *The Hunger Games* (book one in the series), as displayed by several different online booksellers. These prices are fairly clear yet complex to understand, and the burden is on the consumer to understand his or her needs and translate those into the best price. Note that tax is not included because it varies by state or country—another complexity. The lowest price bookseller, Biblio, does not have the highest rating, so is it better to pay an additional few

Bookseller	Stars/ Reviewers	Price ($)	Shipping ($)	Price with Shipping ($)
DeepDiscount.com	Not rated	10.39	0.99	11.38
Alibris.com	*****/17	5.13	3.99	9.12
Books-A-Million	****/102	9.98	2.99 +0.99/item	13.96
Biblio.com	*/1	3.74	4.00	7.74
Tower.com	Not rated	5.74	3.99	9.73
Barnes & Noble	*****/44012 (4.66/5)	9.98	3.00 +0.99/item	13.97
Ecampus.com	*****/1	$7.03	$2.98 +0.99/ item	$11.00
Amazon.com	*****/6783	$5.82	$3.00 +0.99/item	$9.81

EXHIBIT 10.2 Online Search, *The Hunger Games*: book by Suzanne Collins *Source*: Booksellers in column one

dollars to use a more highly rated store with more reviewers and a better-known brand name? Also note how there is quite a range in shipping prices from most sellers. Finally, why is there an 80.5 percent price dispersion from the lowest to the highest price?

This example is what is meant by the time, energy, and psychic costs that add to a buyer's monetary costs. As well, sometimes the internet is slow, information is hard to find, and other technological problems cause users to spend more time and energy, thus becoming frustrated (psychic cost). Shopping agents will find the lowest prices online, but the search adds to the time cost. For example, when buyers search for the lowest airfare at online travel agents Orbitz.com or Travelocity.com, the search time is minimal compared to the dollar savings, but users need to know that these sites don't represent all airlines (e.g., Expedia.com doesn't include Southwest Airlines). The same nonmonetary savings may not be true for a book-price search—it all depends on the time it takes to search, the savings as a percentage of the item cost, and how much familiarity and experience the buyer has with the search engine (making an easier search process). The internet technologies and content are far from perfect, but as broadband adoption continues to increase, technology evolves, and firms develop better online strategies, some of these costs will decline.

In contrast, buyers often enjoy many online cost savings:

- ***The internet is convenient.*** It is open 24/7 so that users can research, shop, consume entertainment, or otherwise use the Web's offerings anytime, anywhere, and on any stationary or mobile receiving appliance. E-mail allows asynchronous communication among buyers and sellers at any location and prevents "telephone tag" (both parties need not be online simultaneously to communicate). Shopping bots (automated chat and animated help programs on Web sites) provide synchronous help as a customer is shopping online.
- ***The internet is fast.*** Although it might take more time to download a Web page than the few remaining dial-up users would like, anyone can visit a site such as iGo.com, order a laptop battery, and receive it the following day—even while on a foreign business trip.
- ***Self-service saves time.*** Customers can track shipments, pay bills, trade securities, check account balances, and handle many other activities without waiting for sales reps. In addition, technology allows users to request product information at Web sites and receive it immediately. Of course, all these activities take time to perform.
- ***One-stop shopping saves time.*** The internet opened the door for companies to increase customer convenience through one-stop shopping. AutoMall Online has partnered with a number of firms to provide automobile price comparisons, research about various models and manufacturers, financing and insurance information, and service options. This firm also offers instant online pricing from a large network of auto dealerships and gives customers a *purchase certificate* guaranteeing that the price quote will be honored at the dealership. AutoMall Online's track record proves that customers receive value: More than 50 percent of its users purchase a car within 45 days of using the service, and 90 percent do so within six months.
- ***Integration saves time.*** Web portals such as Yahoo! and Google Mobile allow users to quickly find many things they want online from any device. Even Pinterest could now be considered a Web portal. Some sites allow users to create individualized Web pages with news, stock quotes, weather, and other customized information. For example, one consumer purchased a unique backpack online only to find out, via e-mail, that the firm was out of business. No problem—it forwarded the order to a partner e-commerce company, which filled the order in a day.

- ***Automation saves energy.*** Customers value simplicity and ease; because the internet makes some activities more complex, technology can help. For example, Web browsers, sites, and companies that allow customer computers to keep track of passwords for Web sites (such as RoboForm) and to track previous purchases at Web sites save time and energy.

Note that not everyone wants to save money in online transactions. Customer needs and their views of the value proposition vary as each individual weighs the desired and perceived benefits against all the costs. For example, some people prefer to order books from Amazon.com with overnight delivery, knowing well that Amazon prices are often higher than other online booksellers, that the book is in stock at a local bookstore, and that overnight delivery costs quite a bit more and saves only a few days from the delivery time. Nevertheless, the Amazon brand name is trustworthy, these customers have had excellent previous experiences with Amazon, and they are familiar with the site, quickly finding what they need. And they don't have to leave their house or business to get the book they want. Thus, those benefits and time/energy-saving features overcome the higher expense.

BUYER CONTROL The shift in power from seller to buyer affects many e-marketing strategies, including pricing. For instance, in what is known as a **reverse auction**, buyers set prices for products, and sellers decide whether to accept these prices. A good example is Priceline.com, where you name the price you want to pay for hotels, flights, cars, vacations, and cruises. In the B2B market, buyers bid for excess inventory at exchanges and for products at firms such as General Electric and Caterpillar. In the B2G market, government buyers put out a request for proposal for materials and labor needed for a particular project, and businesses bid for the work (see Exhibit 10.3). The government buyer selects the lowest price, in effect having control over the exchange.

Online sellers are more willing to negotiate than their offline counterparts in most industrialized nations, thus giving power to buyers in the exchange. Perhaps it is easier for U.S. consumers to negotiate from behind an impersonal computer, as compared with standing face to face with the

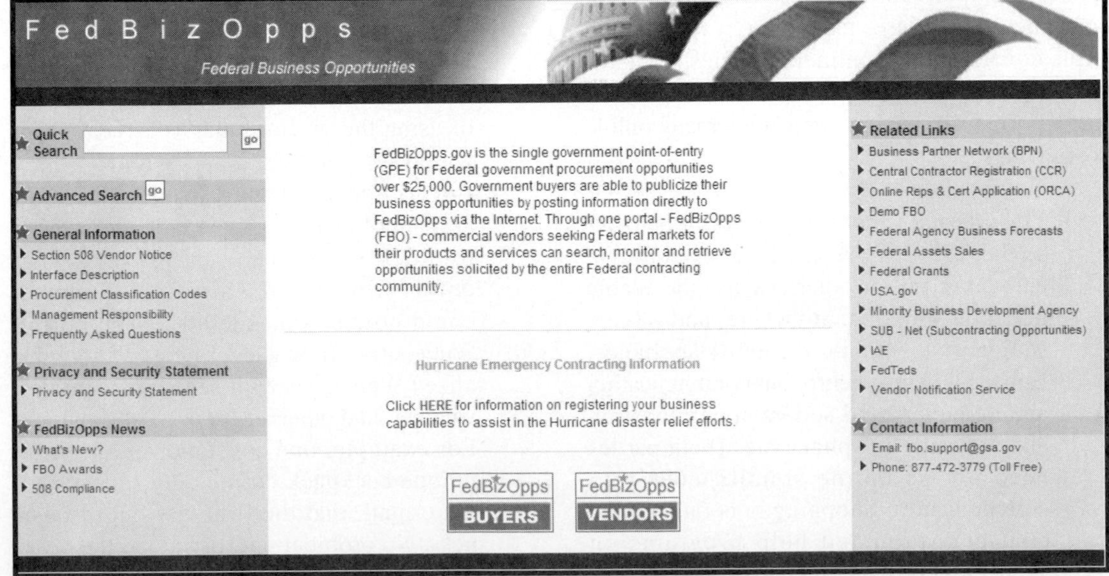

EXHIBIT 10.3 Government Portal for Vendors Seeking Government Buyers *Source*: fedbizopps.gov

seller. Also, sellers realize that information technology can help them better manage inventories and automate frequent price changes.

Buyer power online is also based on the huge quantity of information and product availability on the Web. As a result, online buyers are becoming more sophisticated—as they must be, considering the example of the *Hunger Games* book pricing options. This was put well by Erik Brynjolfsson, codirector of the E-business Center at MIT: "We're moving toward a very sophisticated economy. It's kind of an arms race between merchant technology and consumer technology (in the form of shopbots). If consumers are not sophisticated they can be soaked. If managed intelligently, the tools are there to create a revolution."

Also, the social media save time and money when consumers can look at online reviews written by "people like them." For instance, it saves time to search for the highest rated tires at epinions.com or the highest recommended books in a category at Amazon. This is much faster than facing the alphabetized books on shelves at the brick-and-mortar bookseller. Social networks such as Facebook and Twitter, as well as many other sites, give consumers the power to find the best products without even consulting company sites. Also, consider the social media cooperative buying sites, such as Groupon.com, where consumers can purchase an item and watch the price drop as other individuals elect to purchase the same item.

With power comes risk. Consider what happens to a substantial number of bidders in online auctions. In what has been called "the winner's curse," some people actually pay a higher price for auctioned products than they would pay an online retailer. In the B2B market, one study found that car dealers pay significantly more for used automobiles online than they do offline. In the B2C market, researchers evaluated the winning bids for new surplus computer items at Egghead.com and compared prices for the exact items sold on the retail portion of the Egghead site (Pellegrino, Amyx, and Pellegrino, 2002). They found that 20 percent of winning bidders overpaid. This holds true today. One eBay seller reported placing video games on eBay for the "buy it now" price of $10 (his cost), and they all sold for an average of $15 each plus $4 shipping ("Why do People Overpay. . .," 2011). Perhaps the entertainment benefit of an online auction keeps the value equation in balance, but just as likely, buyers do not realize they've overpaid.

Seller View

Sellers view price as the amount of money they receive from buyers, unless they are making a **barter** exchange. Seller costs for producing the good or service represent the pricing floor, under which no profit is made. Above that floor, marketers have the freedom to set a price that will draw buyers from competing offers. Between cost and price is profit.

The seller's perspective on pricing includes both internal and external factors. Internal factors are the firm's strengths and weaknesses from its SWOT analysis, its overall pricing objectives, its marketing mix strategy, and the costs involved in producing and marketing the product. External factors that affect online pricing in particular include the market structure, competition, and the buyer's perspective, as discussed earlier.

INTERNAL FACTORS: PRICING OBJECTIVES

Marketers begin by setting overall pricing objectives from among those that are profit oriented, market oriented, or competition oriented. The most common profit-oriented objective for pricing is current profit maximization. Online research firms such as Forrester and Gartner Group are using a profit-oriented approach when they charge $1,500 to $4,500 and more to download current e-business research reports.

Companies can also select among various market-oriented objectives. Building a larger customer base may lead to lower costs and higher long-run profit. Low prices generally build market share. For example, Survey Monkey, a Web-based survey software program, offers its basic level software at a low price to build share (compared to competition), and then upsells to annual maintenance fees and programs with more functionality. Negotiation and bidding are also market-oriented approaches. For example, consumers can bid for hotel room nights on priceline .com, hotwire.com, roomauction.com, and many individual hotel Web sites.

The objective of competition-based pricing is to price according to what competitors charge for similar products, paying less attention to the company's own costs or to demand. The internet's pricing transparency gives firms quicker access to competitive price changes and increases the number and speed of online price changes.

INTERNAL FACTORS: MARKETING MIX STRATEGY Successful companies use an integrated and consistent marketing mix strategy. For example, a study of over 4,000 U.S. consumers discovered that more than 70 percent of both new and used automobile buyers spent 18–19 hours shopping online first ("Online Vehicle Shopping. . .," 2011). In this study, 58 percent said the internet research was the most influential of all sources, with half of the respondents rating referrals from friends and family as "extremely helpful" and traditional media (television, radio, direct mail) as much less helpful. However, only 3 percent said social media influenced their purchases. A whopping 42 percent used Google and other search engines to find promotional deals on cars of interest. Marketers pay careful attention to this type of research so they know how to integrate promotional channels (e.g., the Web, social media, offline media and other marketing communication) with pricing tactics and offline retailing.

The internet is only one sales channel and must be used in concert with other marketing mix elements. Marketing managers carefully consider how to price the same product for sale in both online and offline channels. For instance, you can subscribe to *The New York Times* via smartphone for $0.99 (promotion for first 4 weeks and then $7.50 to $10 each 4 weeks thereafter) or get mail delivery of the physical paper to your home for $7.70 a week (prices as of October 2012). There are also different pricing schemes for education and business market segments. No proven rules or standard practices have emerged at this point—practices vary widely by product and industry.

INTERNAL FACTORS: INFORMATION TECHNOLOGY AFFECTS COSTS Information technology can be expensive, but once it is running smoothly it can create tremendous cost efficiencies—putting both upward and downward pressure on prices.

The Internet Puts Upward Pressure on Prices Many companies fail with expensive customer relationship management software or other software that does not help to generate enough new revenue to cover the sites' costs due to competitive pricing constraints. Following are some of the factors that put upward pressure on internet pricing:

- ***Online customer service.*** In the past, customer service online provided a competitive edge for firms such as Dell Computer and Amazon. Conversely, customers now expect firms to return e-mail promptly, provide thorough help and FAQ functions online (or even Twitter), and provide telephone and other contact information. Online customer service is no longer a competitive edge, but an expensive competitive necessity.
- ***Distribution.*** Online retailers face hefty distribution costs for their products: Each product must be shipped separately to its destination rather than by the case to brick-and-mortar retailers or centrally located warehouses. This is similar to the catalog marketer's cost structure. Retailers pass shipping costs on to their customers, thus raising prices. Not surprisingly, some customers are offended by the shipping costs if they are higher than expected and if the shipping cost is presented in the shopping cart only at the last minute. High shipping costs are one reason for shopping cart abandonment.
- ***Affiliate programs.*** Many Web sites pay a commission on referrals through affiliate

programs. Affiliate sponsors reward the referring Web sites by paying a 7 percent to 15 percent commission on each reference that leads to a sale. This commission, like all channel intermediary costs, has the effect of inflating the price of the item or lowering company profits if referral fees are absorbed.

- ***Site development and maintenance.*** Web site development and maintenance are not cheap. Forrester Research estimates the cost for a "conservative" site to be $10,000 to $100,000, while an "aggressive" site costs $1 million or more—and that is just to develop the site. Maintenance can be quite expensive, especially with hardware, software, and data storage costs.
- ***Social media maintenance.*** Companies spend a lot of staff time monitoring and responding to consumer posts in Facebook, Twitter, and other social media. It is important for businesses to identify which social media are key to customer development and engagement and to focus on those (more on this in later chapters).
- ***Customer acquisition costs (CAC).*** The cost of acquiring new customers online is quite high; this factor caused the downfall of many dot-com firms in 2000. For example, the average CAC for early online retailers was $82. How many orders must a firm receive to recoup that cost, and at what price? In addition, many customers are not nearly as brand loyal online as they are offline.

The Internet Puts Downward Pressure on Prices The internet also allows marketers to save costs, translating into lower prices and ultimately higher value for customers. When lower costs lead to higher prices, profit increases—a win for the company. The following are a few ways firms can save costs using internet technology for internal processes:

- ***Order processing—self-service.*** Because customers fill out their own order forms, firms save the expense of order entry personnel and paper processing. These expenses can be considerable. The average cost of producing and processing an invoice electronically is $10, compared with $100 in offline transactions. An average retail banking transaction costs $0.15 to $0.20 online versus $1.50 offline. Cisco Systems, the world's largest manufacturer of networking equipment, invites Web-based orders from customers. The paperwork reduction it reaps from its Web site saves hundreds of millions of dollars each year.
- ***Just-in-time inventory.*** Some manufacturers use electronic data interchange (EDI) to drive down costs in the digital channel by coordinating value-chain activities and allowing for just-in-time (JIT) delivery of parts and reduced inventories. Some online and offline retailers do not even hold inventory, saving considerably on financing costs. Instead, they acquire the inventory in response to customer orders or have partners drop-ship products directly to customers.
- ***Overhead.*** Online storefronts can lower their overhead costs because companies do not have to rent and staff expensive retail space. Amazon's physical warehouses are considerably less expensive to rent and staff than the retail space of a trendy shopping mall. Furthermore, these warehouses can be located in areas with low rents, low wages, low taxes, and quick access to shipping hubs, such as northern Nevada.
- ***Customer service.*** Although customer service can initially add to an organization's costs, companies save by automating some customer service functions that were formerly performed by employees. Animated shop bots are just one of the newest ways companies automate customer service. Companies also save money by posting FAQs and video instructions online, as well as providing automated e-mail responses to questions. Customer service requests an average $15 to $20 in an offline call center

versus $3 to $5 when customers help themselves on the internet.

- ***Printing and mailing.*** Online sellers do not incur mail distribution and printing costs for their product catalogs. Once the catalog is placed online, access carries little or no incremental costs. The same holds true for e-mail and social media promotions. As you'll read later in this book, the U.S. Postal Service is in serious trouble financially due to the decline in direct mail (what consumers call "junk mail").
- ***Digital product distribution costs.*** Distribution costs for digital products are extremely low in the internet channel, such as when a customer downloads a purchased music file from iTunes or reads articles with Instapaper. Conversely, the internet channel has high distribution costs for tangible products because they are sent to individuals in small quantities instead of in larger lots to brick-and-mortar intermediaries.

These efficiencies usually result in lower prices for consumers online; technology enables buyers to evaluate and demand appealing prices. For example, online stock trades cost as low as $10, while broker-assisted offline trades often cost hundreds of dollars. One older study found internet-only retailers to price 6.42 percent lower than multichannel retailers (equivalent to 3 percent after shipping costs) (Tang and Xing, 2003). Deviating from the norm, Circuit City announced its "One Price Promise" strategy in 2008, which meant consumers could pay the same price online or offline. This was prompted by the SPSS, Inc. research that showed 47 percent of consumers believe that retailers charge different prices online and offline for the same product and that more than half of the consumers would trust a company more if its pricing was the same in both channels. Does this mean that all prices online are lower? A recent study found that 45 percent of retailers offer the same prices in all channels, and 49 percent sometimes price differently, as appropriate ("Retailers Experiment with…," 2012). Because of the economy, 85 percent of consumers named price as the key criterion for deciding where to shop, so this fact is also guiding marketers.

EXTERNAL FACTORS AFFECTING ONLINE PRICING The competition, market factors, price-demand relationship (i.e., elastic or inelastic), and customer behavior all affect a firm's pricing strategies online and offline. The buyer's viewpoint was covered earlier; online behavior affecting pricing was covered in Chapter 7. In this section, we examine two important market factors affecting pricing in the online environment: market structure and market efficiency.

Market Structure The seller's leeway to set prices varies with different types of markets. Economists recognize four types of markets, each presenting a different pricing challenge:

1. ***Pure competition.*** This market consists of many buyers and sellers trading in a uniform commodity such as corn. Product differentiation and marketing communication play little or no role, so sellers in these markets do not spend much time on marketing strategy. Many online products could be seen as pure competition, such as MP3 music downloads; however, the retailers offering the products can differentiate based on customer service.
2. ***Monopolistic competition.*** This market consists of many buyers and sellers who trade over a range of prices rather than a single market price. A range of prices occurs because sellers can differentiate their offers to buyers. Online university courses are one product delivered over the internet that falls in this category.
3. ***Oligopolistic competition.*** This market consists of a few sellers who are highly sensitive to each other's pricing and marketing strategies. If a company drops its price by 5 percent, buyers will quickly switch over to this supplier. Online travel agents, such

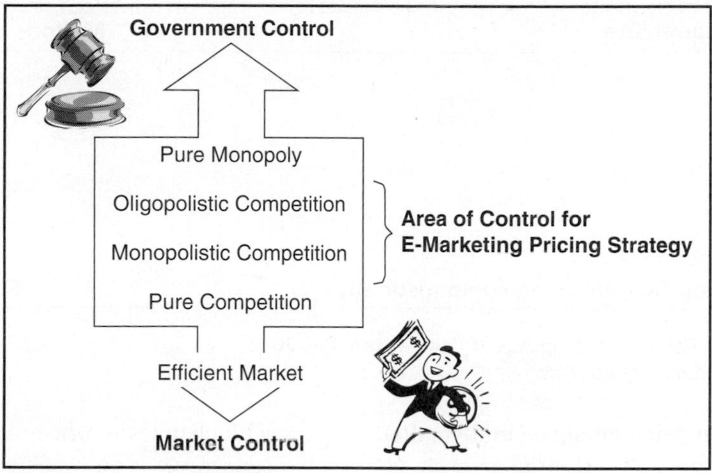

EXHIBIT 10.4 Efficient Markets Mean Loss of Pricing Control

as Expedia and Travelocity, fall into this category.

4. ***Pure monopoly.*** This market consists of one seller whose prices are usually regulated by the government. If you are in a smaller town, your internet service provider could fall into this category.

This market structure distinction is extremely important for online sellers because if *price transparency* eventually results in a completely efficient market for some products, sellers will have no control over online prices—the result will be pure competition as depicted in Exhibit 10.4. One example of a nearly efficient market is the stock market. Note that online stock trading firms operate in a monopolistic competition because they compete based on trade commission prices and customer service, not actual security selling prices. If other products follow suit, the internet will have a profound effect on pricing strategy. This probably won't happen, however, for reasons mentioned in the next section. Next, we examine what comprises an efficient market and discuss whether the online market is approaching efficiency.

Market Efficiency Economists have long theorized about consumer behavior in **efficient markets**. Such markets would experience perfect price competition. A market is efficient when customers have equal access to information about products, prices, and distribution. In an efficient market, one would expect to find lower prices, high **price elasticity**, frequent price changes, smaller price changes, and narrow **price dispersion**—the observed spread between the highest and lowest price for a given product. As previously mentioned, the closest example of an efficient market is the stock market. Commodity markets came close to being efficient until the government intervened with controls. However, the internet is probably as close to a test ground for efficient markets as has ever existed because it exhibits so many of the appropriate characteristics. Interestingly, the behavior of consumers on the internet does not bear out all of the economists' predictions.

Is the Internet an Efficient Market? Many people believe that the internet is an efficient market because of access to information through corporate Web sites, shopping agents, and distribution channels. For instance, a search for a flight to Bangkok at Kayak .com or Travelocity.com will display a complete array of airlines and prices. Products sold online generally exhibit lower prices, high price

Shopping Agent Site	Millions of Visitors
BizRate.com	18.4
NexTag.com	17.5
Shopzilla.com	8.9
Shopping.com	8.3
PriceGrabber.com	3.8
Visitors to top five shopping comparison sites	**57.1**

EXHIBIT 10.5 Retail Shopping Agent Comparison, July 2012
Source: Data from compete.com

elasticity, frequent price changes, and smaller price changes: all symptoms of efficient markets. But do these factors actually make the internet an efficient market? The following external market factors place a downward pressure on internet prices, contributing to efficiency:

- ***Shopping agents.*** Shopping agents, also called comparison shopping agents, such as BizRate (bizrate.com) facilitate consumer searches for low prices by displaying the results in a comparative format. Exhibit 10.5 displays the top shopping agents in 2012. Many people use shopping agents. Did you price shop online for this textbook in your hands? See Exhibit 10.6 for an example of a search for an earlier edition of *E-Marketing* at Shopzilla.com. The prices range from $79.96 to $119.75—quite a price dispersion and quite a valuable service for consumers.
- ***Flash sales.*** **Flash sales** are limited-time offers for site members to purchase a product at a deep discount. Gilt and Rue La La were among the first to offer flash sales, such as a 20 percent discount, good for only 4 hours. The primary way of announcing these sales is via e-mail marketing to members and some question the viability of this business model due to the interrupt nature of the marketing communication (i.e., the e-mails create overload and are easy to ignore).
- ***High price elasticity.*** Price elasticity refers to the variability of purchase behavior with changes in price. As an example, leisure travel is an especially elastic market: When the airlines engage in fare wars, consumers snap up ticket inventories creating huge demand. For many products such as books and CDs, the online market is more elastic than the offline market, so we would expect internet users to be sensitive to price changes.
- ***Reverse auctions.*** Reverse auctions allow buyers to name their price and have sellers try to match that price (such as Priceline.com). This format pits sellers against one another and usually drives prices down.
- ***Tax-free zones.*** Most online retailing takes place across state lines, so buyers often pay no sales taxes on purchases, reducing total out-of-pocket expenditures by as much as 5 percent to 8 percent per transaction. Although states and foreign governments have challenged the internet tax-free zone, the U.S. government continues to support a moratorium on taxes for internet purchases.
- ***Venture capital.*** Many internet companies are financed through venture capital or angel investors. Many investors take a long-term view and are willing to sustain short-term losses to let those companies grow by establishing brand equity and grabbing market share. These companies can price lower because they do not have a profit-maximization pricing objective.

Price	Condition	Seller
Textbooks.com (35 comparisons)		
$122.25	*New*	*Textbooks.com*
$81.25	*Very Good*	*Textbookcenter.com*
$73.65	*Very Good*	*Bookbyte-OR*
$78.00	*Good*	*Firstclassbooks.com*
Shopzilla.com (Three comparisons)		
$142.74	*New*	*eCampus.com*
$121.22	*New*	*Amazon.com*
$11.95	*Used*	*Alibris.com*
Nextag.com (Eight Comparisons)		
$100.74	*Acceptable*	*Skyo*
$84.92	*New*	*Amazon.com*
$72.82	*Pre-Owned*	*BigPlanetBooks.com*

EXHIBIT 10.6 E-Marketing, 6th Edition Shopping Agent Search Results
Source: Data from Textbooks.com, Shopzilla.com, and Nextag.com

- ***Competition.*** The competition online is fierce and highly visible. Furthermore, some competitors are willing to set prices that return little or no short-term profits to gain brand equity and market share.
- ***Frequent price changes.*** The online market experiences more frequent price changes than the offline market because (1) online suppliers must jockey with competitors to attract price-sensitive consumers; (2) shopping agents give consumers excellent comparative information about prices, and vendors may frequently alter their pricing to place themselves higher on the results; (3) sellers can easily change prices using databases to drive Web page content; (4) in a computerized environment firms can offer volume discounts in smaller increments than in an offline environment (e.g., FedEx creates millions of different rate books based on shipping volume for posting on Web pages for individual clients); and (5) experimentation is easy online, allowing firms to change prices frequently, see how demand changes, and then adjust as competition and other factors emerge.
- ***Smaller price change increments.*** In one study, the smallest offline price change was \$0.35, whereas the smallest online price change was \$0.01. Some of the same factors that encourage frequent price changes may play a role here as well. First, price-sensitive consumers may respond to even a small price advantage with respect to the competition. Second, shopping agents rank their results by price—even a

$0.01 advantage will earn a higher ranking than the competition. Third, because it is difficult to change prices offline, retailers may wait until the need for a price change is even greater.

Is the Net an Inefficient Market? Even though the Web exhibits many characteristics of an efficient market, it does not act like an efficient market with respect to narrow price dispersion. Prices tend to equalize in commodities markets, because sellers cannot easily differentiate one bushel of peas from another. With perfect information for all, one would expect narrow price dispersion online—for example, because buyers can search many Web sellers for this book, we might expect the prices to gravitate to the same level.

Interestingly, this expectation does not hold on the internet, due to the strength of a firm's brand, the way goods are priced online as well as delivery options, time-sensitive shoppers, differentiation, switching costs, and second-generation shopping agents:

- ***Branding.*** In spite of the proliferation of products, a brand is still a sought-after benefit. The most highly recognized and preferred branded Web sites get most of the traffic. Consumers will show a preference for brand when using online services, such as search engines. Many consumers will pick a well-known merchant brand from the search results even if that brand does not offer the lowest price. Because of the importance of brand, the best-branded Web sites spend millions of dollars to attract customers. Amazon spent $1.6 billion on marketing expenses in 2011 (nearly 4 percent of sales). The brand-loyal customer base allows Amazon to charge more than bargain online retailers.
- ***Differentiation.*** One result of strong branding is perceived or real product differentiation, which enables marketers to price their products differently.
- ***How products are priced online.*** Most goods are offered at fixed prices offline in industrialized nations. By contrast, marketers use many more strategies on the Web. The same product is often available for a fixed, a dynamically updated, or an auction price on different sites at the same time—and the prices among them may vary widely. In addition, products are bundled with shipping and special services in different ways, confusing shoppers who want to compare similar products.
- ***Delivery options.*** The same product delivered under differing conditions (time and place) may have considerably different value to the consumer. For example, a beer served at a bar has more value than one bought at a supermarket. Similarly, a product delivered to the door may have considerably more value for some consumers than one that is bought at the store (convenience). Online grocery shopping follows this value model. Some marketers would argue that groceries delivered to the door are not the same product as the same groceries picked up at the store. By this argument, the additional benefits actually differentiate the product. Normally, the consumer has to wait longer for a product delivered to the door, but that may be changing. Amazon offers one-hour delivery of popular books and music in some metropolitan areas and other firms may follow suit.
- ***Time-sensitive shoppers.*** Time-sensitive shoppers may not wish to invest the time and energy required to track down the best price. Also, some sites may be so complex that consumers need more time to navigate and complete the transaction.
- ***Switching costs.*** Customers face switching costs when they choose a different online retailer. Some customers are not willing to incur those costs and, thus, stick with a familiar online retailer. If an Amazon customer shops at another retailer, he or she loses access to a familiar interface,

personalized book recommendations, and the 1-Click ordering that Amazon has patented. Switching costs are even higher in the B2B market. Many organizations have found that it is more effective to build relationships with a limited number of suppliers rather than offer all items out for bid. These organizations readily pay a slight premium to enjoy better service and support.

- ***Second-generation shopping agents.*** **Second-generation shopping agents** guide the consumer through the process of quantifying benefits and evaluating the value equation. If a consumer ranks certain benefits highly, that consumer may be willing to pay more to receive those benefits. BizRate allows consumers to evaluate merchants based on ratings compiled from previous customers. PriceScan and DealTime allow consumers to set filters so that merchants delivering the desired benefits will rise in the rankings. See the "Let's Get Technical" box for more information on shopping agents.

Is the internet an efficient market? The answer is no, not now. However, it has all the features to move toward efficiency in the future. This shift would have devastating effects for e-marketers wanting control over pricing strategies; thus, marketers will watch this trend closely.

PAYMENT OPTIONS

Electronic money, also called e-money or digital cash, is a system that uses the internet and computers to exchange payments electronically. It can be used in offline or online transactions, using the internet to transfer money between buyer and seller accounts. In the United States, the only well-known offline e-money transactions occur at toll booths when autos with transponders drive through them—and drivers receive a monthly invoice. Conversely, digital cash has widespread adoption in other countries. In Hong Kong, there are 20 million Octopus cards—nearly three times the number of Hong Kong's population. These are smart cards with a computer chip that is charged with cash for users to spend. Octopus cards are used in 12 million daily transactions from the ferry system to convenience stores, according to octopus.com.uk. BART in San Francisco also uses the Clipper Card for smart card ticketing. Other interesting offline e-money payment systems include the following:

- ***Payment by smart chip.*** MZOOP, created by Harex InfoTech in South Korea, is a chip inserted in a cell phone that can be pointed at a vending machine or other point of purchase reader for purchasing items. The transaction is charged to the owner's debit or credit bank card. Similarly, Offica Watch, made in Japan by Casio, allows wearers to pay by e-money via the chip in the watch itself. Buyers just wave the watch near a scanner and the purchase is done. If you'd like to get rid of all gadgets, you can even have an RFID chip planted in your arm for payment at the Baja Beach Club in Barcelona or use your fingerprint to pay at Barcelona's Ushuaïa Ibiza Beach Hotel!
- ***Mobile wallets.*** Japan and Finland already allow offline payments via cell phone at vending machines and elsewhere. Google recently introduced a mobile wallet application that stores all credit cards in the mobile phone. Owners simply swipe the phone at participating retailers and can remotely disable the function from the Web if the phone is lost. Various research findings indicate that between 41 percent and 60 percent of U.S. consumers are not interested in using mobile wallets, primarily due to security fears ("Mobile Wallets Have. . .," 2012).

Online, 61 percent of U.S. consumers pay bills with a bank's online banking service, showing the huge adoption of e-money systems (as mentioned in Chapter 7). Payment systems in other countries vary, and marketers must learn what technologies to offer for facilitating

LET'S GET TECHNICAL

Unwrapping Online Shopping's Secrets

Five days before the holidays . . . and you have not even started shopping for gifts. By the time you get home from work, it is after 7 P.M. and you are tired. Because you were so busy with your new job this year, you forgot everyone's birthday, and only remembered to send a card a month late. If things weren't bad enough, you are strapped for cash because your old clunker of a car died last month, and you were forced to get a new one. Your sister wants a digital camera, and your mom wants a new TV for her bedroom. The convenience of online shopping is appealing, and you might just score some coupons on RetailMeNot.com. After a couple of hours of clicking and shipping, your holiday shopping is finished and you saved a bunch of dough.... Now it's time for some holiday cookies!

A majority of the large retailers in the United States and shoppers worldwide have all caught the bug—the online shopping bug, that is. While the Saturday trip to the mall used to be commonplace, many households are now doing a majority of their shopping online. Whether it is the latest consumer electronic or a new bedspread, consumers are more than happy to shop from the comfort of their homes—wearing who knows what. Most consumers say they are lured by the convenience of online shopping. Retailers are certainly used to attracting consumers to their stores using circulars, commercials, and coupons, and similar concepts are being deployed online to get consumers to their Web sites.

Since the onset of online shopping, consumers' perceptions have been that better "deals" can be found online. Of course, a "deal" is based on the individual consumer's values. However, Web sites are cropping up to help frugal consumers find the best deals online. So, instead of clipping the coupons and flipping through circulars, savvy online shoppers are giving shopping agents and coupon Web sites a try. It is important for e-marketers to understand the technologies employed by consumers—and for e-marketers to properly utilize them.

A *shopping agent* is a Web site that collects product and price information from online retail sites and displays all of the information together. For example, many Web sites sell digital cameras. If consumers are looking for a certain digital camera, such as the Sony DSC-RX100, they would be able to enter that information into the shopping agent's search box and receive prices from all over the Web. Many shopping agents display Web sites' advertised prices, but some also ask for the consumer's ZIP code to calculate tax and shipping costs. The final result is a list of the sites on which the item is available at the cost of the item on that site. Links are also available to go directly to the Web sites or the product pages. In addition to providing prices, some shopping agents review products and retailers. Consumers are invited to rate retailers and record comments about their buying experience on the site.

From an e-marketing standpoint, shopping agents are beneficial because they are attracting to the retailers' Web sites the consumers who are ready to buy—what more could an e-marketer ask for? The answer is that e-marketers want to attract more consumers to their sites using the shopping agents, of course. Although consumers believe that shopping agents are providing unbiased results to their queries, the truth is that most are not. Some agents list only retailers that have registered with them, and other agents list sites based on who has paid for the top spot on the results list.

Shopping agents are popular, and consumers can find hundreds of products using common search engines. When marketing products using shopping agents, it is essential to understand how to register a product and select one that is appropriate for the e-marketing campaign.

When registering a product with a shopping agent, marketers are usually required to pay a fee and give the Web site a product feed. Most agents have a pay-per-click (PPC) policy. Prices range from a few cents to more than $1.00 for each time a consumer clicks on the link to the product. Some sites also require a deposit of $100 to $200 when registering, which would be applied to the PPC account.

A product feed contains information about the product that is being featured, such as its name, description, category, price, and availability. Agents also ask that a URL to the product be included for linking purposes. Product feeds are fairly simple to create and give marketers an opportunity to compel consumers to purchase the product from their Web sites. Expert e-marketers recommend that clear and concise language be used when writing product feeds, and industry abbreviations should never be used. For example, the abbreviation *DJ* may seem reasonable when marketing a Hewlett-Packard DeskJet printer, but it is better to write out the term. Agents ask that product feeds be submitted in one of a variety of ways, such as online forms or file uploading.

When choosing which shopping agent to register with, one should definitely do one's homework. Some sites are known for their ability to provide information on a wide variety of products, while others are more specialized. Also, registering with one shopping agent can have the product listed on multiple sites due to the agent's affiliation with other agents. An example of this affiliation is Shopping.com, which shares information with DealTime and eBay.

Shopping agents that are known for their high volume of visitors include BizRate, NexTag, and DealTime. Each offers a slightly different service. BizRate, which like most agents lets retailers pay for top spots on results lists, is known for its high traffic rates and unique consumer survey information. BizRate's original business model included providing consumer research and added product comparison services only in 2000.

Consumers' use of online coupons is also increasing. Many retailers with Web sites also offer free coupons on their own sites, especially when introducing new products. For example, when Veet debuted its Bladeless Razor Hair Removal Kit in the summer of 2004, it offered a $2.00 off coupon on its Web site when consumers filled out a form asking for contact information.

However, coupon sites are another story. These sites offer a variety of services for the penny-pinching consumer:

- Links to company Web sites that offer free coupons.
- Printable coupons for use in brick-and-mortar stores.
- Coupon codes for online retailers.
- Links to sites that will automatically give a percentage off an order.
- Information about sale and clearance-priced items at online retailers.

Some sites require consumer input to get the coupon or information listed on the site. E-marketers can submit their coupons, promotional codes, and sales to these sites usually via e-mail. Coupon sites include retailmenot.com, couponcabin.com, and couponmountain.com. Traditional paper coupon distributors, such as SmartSource and ValPak, are also offering online coupons. Industry experts say that the circulation of coupons and promotional codes online is high and that the best way to get noticed is to offer two deals in one, such as free shipping and $10 off an order.

e-commerce. Exhibit 10.7 displays the preferred payment systems for e-commerce transactions in 12 countries.

For one-time payments, PayPal has become the industry standard, with over 113 million accounts worldwide. This eBay-owned company allows users to pay for online purchases via credit card or bank debit. Exhibit 10.8 shows the various accounts and fees online merchants pay for the service—which are comparable to the fees credit card companies charge merchants. Competing with PayPal, Western Union offers MoneyZap for buying online products from merchants offering the option. Western Union targets the 29 percent of Americans without credit cards.

One important e-money service uses a model quite different from PayPal's—so much so that eBay purchased the company to add to PayPal's product mix. Called Bill Me Later, this model allows buyers to pay for online goods and services without a credit card. They must be approved by Bill Me Later and are billed after making the purchase. This service is growing quickly, having signed up merchants such as Walmart, the Apple Store, Office Max, and

	Credit Card (Percent)	Debit Card (Percent)	Debit and Credit Cards (Percent)	PayPal (Percent)	Cash on Delivery (Percent)	Online or Offline Bank Transfer (Percent)	Invoices (Percent)
Brazil	75					13	
Canada	79			47			
China	10	31			43		
Denmark			89				
Finland			21		19	44	21
France		80		14			
Germany	10	30				51	
Japan*	52				18	10	
Mexico	73					12	
Norway			61			18	12
Sweden			35			30	28
U.K.	75			21			

*Ten percent of Japanese pay by Konbini (payment at convenience stores).

EXHIBIT 10.7 Preferred Payment Systems for E-Commerce Transactions in Various Countries
Source: "Global Payment Options" (2012)

Overstock.com. It is especially good for small businesses that purchase online because it costs them less than their credit card fees and interest.

Electronic money has distinct advantages for online retailers. It is more efficient, with lower transaction fees, and draws new customers without credit risk fears. Also, these services allow online merchants to sell to internet users who don't have credit cards or who don't want to input their credit cards on a new Web site. Finally, offering multiple payment options can actually entice more people to buy online. A Quality Research Associates study of 147 leading online retailers found that those offering only one type of payment (such as a credit card) convert 60 percent of shoppers on average, while those offering multiple payment options convert up to 72 percent of their site visitors (see ecommercetimes.com). Conversely, potential downsides include large economic issues involving all e-commerce, such as less taxes for states when transactions occur out of state, the possibilities of exchange rate fluctuations with high levels of international e-commerce, and the criminal use of the systems for money laundering and other fraudulent or illegal activities.

Electronic cash is an important pricing component for two reasons. First, when merchants use PayPal or other systems, their costs increase and this is reflected in the product's price. Second, when online purchasing is easier for customers, this balances the higher price—recall that the costs for consumers include money, time, energy, and psychic costs.

PRICING STRATEGIES

Price setting is full of contradictions. It has become nearly as much art as science, with lots of data needing insightful interpretation for best application. If the price is too low, profits will suffer, yet if it is too high, sales may decline. And that is just the short-term view. In the long run, an initial low price that builds market share can create economies of scale to lower costs and, thus, increase profits. Also, how marketers apply pricing strategy is as important as *how much* they charge. PayPal's merchant pricing

	E-mail Payments	Web Site Payments Standard	Web Site Payments Pro	Payflow Gateway	PayPal Express Checkout
Customer Experience					
Where customers shop	Varies by business	Shop on your Web site	Shop on your Web site	Shop on your Web site	Shop on your Web site
Where customers check out	PayPal	PayPal	Your Web site or PayPal	Your Web site or PayPal	PayPal
Customers need PayPal account	No	No	No	No	Yes
Integration					
Internet merchant acct.	Not needed	Not needed	Included	Required	Required
Shopping cart support	Not required	Yes	Yes	Yes	Yes
Technical skills	Not required	HTML	APIs	APIs or HTML	APIs or HTML
Pricing					
Setup	Free	Free	Free	$14.95 –$249	Free
Monthly	Free	Free	$30	$9.95–$59.95	Free
Per transaction	1.9 %–2.9% + $0.30	2.2%–2.9% + $0.30	2.2%–2.9% + $0.30	Depends	2.2%–2.9% + $0.30
For phone, fax, mail orders	$30 per month	$30 per month	Included	Included	$30 per month

EXHIBIT 10.8 PayPal Account Options *Source*: Data from paypal.com on September 2012

system demonstrates the skill that goes into pricing strategy.

Another contradiction is that information technology complicates pricing in some ways while making it simpler in other ways. Sellers easily change prices at a moment's notice or vary them according to each individual buyer's previous behavior. Next, buyer value perceptions vary between rational and emotional, and not everyone reacts the same way. For example, some high-income customers enjoy walking into the Volvo dealership with a printed Web page detailing what they want and how much it should cost, while others enjoy the emotional relationship with a favorite salesperson and return every 3 years for the latest model, trusting that "Joe will take care of me." Finally, firms using multichannel delivery systems must consider the varying costs of each channel and buyers' differing value perceptions about purchasing on the internet versus at the brick-and-mortar store. Pricing is a tricky business, guided by data, experience, and experimentation.

In general, marketers can employ all traditional pricing strategies to the online environment. Here we focus on four types of pricing strategies particularly important to online sellers: fixed pricing, dynamic pricing, renting instead of buying, and price placement on Web pages.

Fixed Pricing

Fixed pricing (also called *menu pricing*) occurs when sellers set the price and buyers must take it or leave it. With fixed pricing, everyone pays the same price. Most U.S. brick-and-mortar retailers use this model. Even when wholesalers and manufacturers offer quantity discounts, the price levels apply to all businesses that purchase the required amount. The basic pricing principles every marketer uses offline also apply online. Three common fixed pricing strategies used online are price leadership, promotional pricing, and freemium pricing:

- ***Price leadership.*** A **price leader** is the lowest-priced product entry in a particular category. Both online and offline, Walmart is a price leader, setting the pace for other retailers. With shopping agents on the Web, a price leader strategy is sweet indeed. To implement this strategy, however, marketers must keep costs to a minimum. Reducing costs can be done through internet marketing cost efficiencies previously described, but a firm must do it better than the competition. Often the largest producer becomes the price leader because of economies of scale, but on the internet an entrepreneur building mobile phone apps out of a basement constantly challenges the large producer. This strategy is productive for the internet, although competition is fierce and price leadership is often fleeting. Of course, the second-lowest-priced item will also gain sales, especially if it offers benefits perceived as better than those of the price leader. On the internet, Buy.com is a price leader in many different categories, selling many items below market value and recouping losses through advertising revenue from its Web site.
- ***Promotional pricing.*** Many online retailers have turned to **promotional pricing** to encourage a first purchase, encourage repeat business, and close a sale. Most promotions carry an expiration date that helps create a sense of urgency. For example, Amazon offered free shipping with any order over $25 with such success that it became standard. It didn't arrive at that order amount, however, without trying several other price points first to find the optimum promotional offer to motivate sales. Promotional pricing on the internet can be highly targeted through e-mail messages.
- ***Freemium pricing.*** Many companies offer free versions of products, as mentioned in the Instapaper opening story. Skype is one of the first to successfully use a freemium pricing model. Individuals can call each other for free worldwide from computer to computer (or mobile to mobile via the Skype app). The premium part of this model is the calls from computer to land line—a minimal charge, but not free. Skype adds lots of other related products for a fee, such as voice mail and call forwarding. Do not confuse this with free promotional pricing, where free product is offered for a limited time. For example, a free 30-day software download that expires and users must purchase the full software package.

Dynamic Pricing

Dynamic pricing is the strategy of offering different prices to different customers. According to one study, personalized pricing and promotions are the number-one way that retailers are combating price transparency online ("Retailers Experiment with…," 2012). This was followed by improved monitoring of competitive prices. **Yield management** is a strategy used most often by the travel industry to optimize inventory management through frequent price changes. Airlines have long used dynamic pricing software for yield management when pricing air travel—dropping prices when traffic is light. Dynamic Web pages allow travel companies to make quick and frequent changes in order to rent cars and fill seats or hotel beds.

Dynamic pricing can be initiated by the seller or the buyer (as compared with fixed pricing, which is always initiated by sellers). Two types of dynamic pricing are **segmented pricing**, where the company sells a good or service at two or more prices, based on segment differentiation rather than cost alone, and **price negotiation**, where the company negotiates prices with individual customers, who comprise segments of one. Negotiation is more often initiated by the buyer, while segmented pricing is usually set by the seller.

SEGMENTED PRICING Segmented pricing uses the internet properties for mass customization, automatically devising pricing based on order size and timing, demand and supply levels, and other preset decision factors. With segmented pricing online, the company uses decision rules to set pricing levels for segments of customers all the way to a segment of one person—that is, any customer who is X or does X gets Y price. For example, any person who books a flight within 7 days of departure is quoted the full price (no discount), whereas advance purchasers may receive a discounted price. Segmented pricing has its roots in traditional marketing, as when theaters lower prices for consumers attending afternoon movies. Pricing according to customer behavior segments is becoming more common as firms collect an increasing amount of electronic behavioral information. See Exhibit 10.9 for an example of dynamic pricing by customer type, showing how Constantcontact.com practices segmented pricing based on the size of the customer's e-mail database. Note that Constant Contact also offers discounts for paying in advance and to the nonprofit organization customer segment.

Segmented pricing at the individual level is easier online because sophisticated software and large databases permit firms to set rules and make price changes in a *nano*second—even as a buyer is clicking on a Web page. This capability has marketers quite excited—the internet's ability to customize prices, marketing communication, and products to the individual level. Using cookie files, online sellers recognize individuals and experiment with offers and prices to motivate transactions. Sometimes these individuals are particular customers, as when Amazon.com recognizes the customer and presents customized recommendations. Other times, individuals are part of a larger segment, such as those logging in from a particular geographic location or those exhibiting a behavior such as abandoning a shopping cart. Sellers define the segment and then customize prices following preset decision rules when an individual member of the segment visits the site. For example, an online retailer can lower the price by small increments on each subsequent visit to see whether the buyer will buy. Also, online firms can build loyalty programs, like frequent flyer programs, to offer special prices to individuals who return and purchase often.

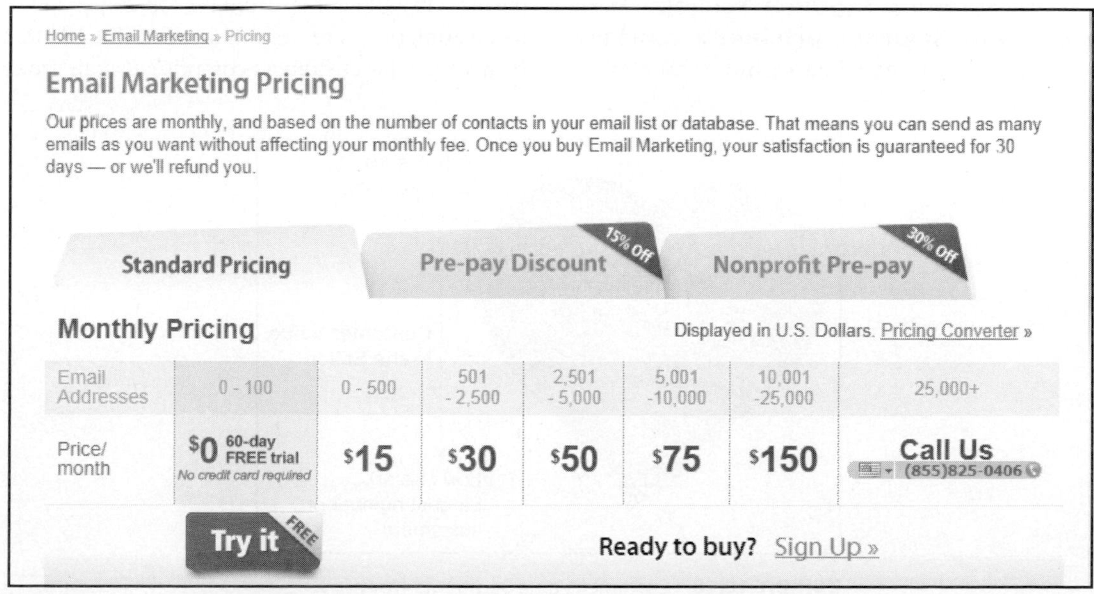

EXHIBIT 10.9 Constant Contact Segmented Pricing for Services (as of August 2012)
Source: constantcontact.com

Segmented pricing can be effective when the market is segmentable, the different prices reflect real differences in each segment's perceptions of the product's value, and the segments show different degrees of demand. It is also appropriate when the costs of segmentation and segmented pricing do not exceed the extra revenue obtained from the price difference. In addition, the company must be sure that its segmented pricing meets legal and regulatory guidelines. Finally, the firm must take care not to upset customers who learn they are getting prices different from their neighbors. Amazon.com created uproar when customers learned of its segmented pricing for individual customers; for some reason, airline passengers have accepted this practice but not book buyers. Thus, e-marketers employing segmentation must use customer-accepted reasons such as giving discounts to new or loyal customers or adjusting shipping fees for purchases sent to outlying locations.

Internet users can be segmented using many variables, as discussed in Chapter 8. Two variables that are particularly important to online pricing strategies are geographic and value segmentation.

Geographic Segment Pricing With **geographic segment pricing**, a company sets different prices when selling a product in different geographic areas. An online seller often knows where the user resides because server logs register the user's IP address, and the top-level domain name typically indicates country of residence (e.g., a Japanese user will have a .jp designation). Geographic pricing can help a company better relate its pricing to country-by-country or regional factors such as competitive pressure, local costs, economic conditions, legal or regulatory guidelines, and distribution opportunities. For example, a Dell computer priced at $1,000 in Los Angeles may be priced at £839 in London (US $1,303 in May 2013). This difference is because the manufacturer faces price escalation and therefore must price to reflect the higher costs of transportation, tariffs, and importer margins, among other costs involved in selling in another country. Increased transportation costs also affect product prices within a country.

Value Segment Pricing With **value segment pricing**, the seller recognizes that not all customers provide equal value to the firm, segmenting by high, medium, and low value—and pricing accordingly. The well-known **Pareto principle** states that 80 percent of a firm's business usually comes from the top 20 percent of its customers. As represented in Exhibit 10.10, a firm's five-star customers comprise a small group

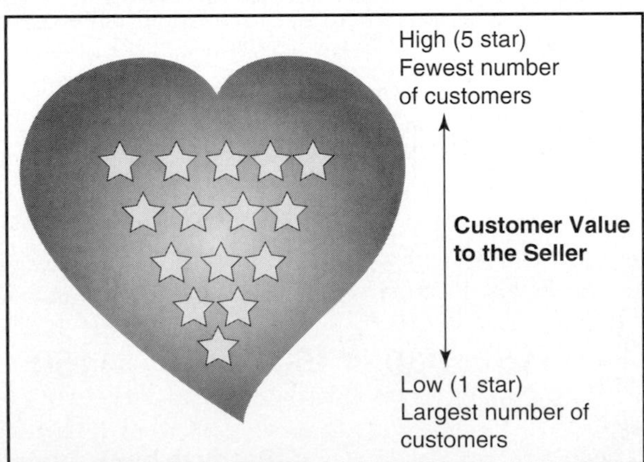

EXHIBIT 10.10 Customer Value Segments from Low (One Star) to High (Five Star) *Source*: clip art courtesy of openclipart.org

that contributes disproportionately to the firm's revenues and profits. These customers tend to be the most loyal and may become brand advocates to their friends and acquaintances: the frequent flyers who always go first class, the casino high rollers who return repeatedly, or the high-volume package shippers who use the FedEx Web site to automate all services. These customers are also brand-loyal frequent customers who provide significant value to the seller. When four- or five-star customers appear at the Web site, they will be recognized and receive special attention. These customers may not be price sensitive because they perceive that the brand or firm offers greater benefits (e.g., free upgrades and special treatment) and has earned their loyalty.

The large group of three-star customers may be price shoppers or infrequent users of the product category, not accounting for much of the seller's revenue. Two-star customers are also price sensitive and probably use the product category more than do one-star customers.

Market factors tend to drive customers to the one-star level, whereas moves such as competitive offerings and price cuts attempt to lure five- and four-star customers away. The seller's goal is to keep five-star customers brand loyal and to move all groups up to a higher level of value. Pricing strategies can help. For example, five-star customers might be allowed to bid on surplus inventory before others get a chance. Giving high-value customers the first shot at new products or promotions (e.g., Amazon's free shipping) will reinforce their loyalty. Conversely, one- and two-star customers most often seek the lowest price, so discounts are not likely to create brand loyalty—they will continue being price-shopping brand switchers. These customers might enjoy e-mail blasts with fixed prices so they can be informed of the firm's prices and competitive benefits of the brand. The seller can use this technique to build a database for moving customers up in value. Incidentally, the heart shape in this exhibit refers to the fact that companies love all their customers; however, they spend more time satisfying the high-value segment. See Chapter 15 for more about value segmentation and marketing communication techniques for building customer relationships.

NEGOTIATED PRICING AND AUCTIONS Sellers usually set pricing levels when using segmented pricing, and buyers usually initiate pricing when bidding for items online. Through negotiation, the price is set more than once in a back-and-forth discussion—a major difference from all other pricing strategies. Haggling over price is common in many countries; however, with a few exceptions, U.S. consumers have shied away from such bargaining. The internet is changing this reluctance, as evidenced by the spectacular growth of online auctions. Many consumers enjoy the sport and community of an auction, while others are just looking for a good deal.

In the C2C market, trust between buyers and sellers is an issue because the transaction happens among strangers—there is no brand name to generate trust. To assist buyers, eBay uses a feedback system consisting of one, zero, or minus one points for positive, neutral, or negative comments and ratings, respectively. Points build to the star and shooting star levels and are placed near seller profiles on eBay Web pages. The red shooting star is reserved for a seller with 100,000 or more points. This system works: Highly rated eBay sellers are more likely to make a sale and do it at a higher price. In one study of 861 golf club auctions, when sellers increased their feedback scores by zero to 25 points, they had a 3.4 percent higher probability of selling the clubs and received 5 percent higher prices (according to researcher Jeffrey Livingston).

While it seems that high levels of positive feedback mean higher prices, there are eBay scams that allow sellers to buy positive feedback. Academic researchers Jennifer Brown and John Morgan found an entire market for feedback itself at eBay, with an average value of at least $0.61 per feedback point (compiled with over 5,000 feedback market transactions) (Beal and Strauss, 2008).

Auctions in the B2B market are an effective way to unload surplus inventory at a price set by the market. For example, uBid has worked with over 7,000 businesses to sell more than $2 billion of excess inventory.

Renting Software

Companies developing software sometimes decide to rent rather than sell it to customers. Buyers want to purchase software they use on a regular basis, such as Microsoft Office, but if organizations want to use software for a short-term project or don't want to go to the expense of installing and maintaining it on their servers, renting makes sense. For example, Salesforce.com offers an incredibly complex and rich, leading CRM software system. Its customers don't want to purchase and install the system internally and watch hidden costs emerge (estimated by Salesforce.com at 90 percent above the purchase price of CRM software). Salesforce rents its software instead, pricing in a range from $65 per month per user to $1,200 a year for five users (based on a minimum annual commitment). Renting software is analogous to leasing cars. When leasing, the driver doesn't have to pay for maintenance and many other costs that purchasers must bear.

Price Placement on Web Pages

Many physical world retailers have found that if they first offer customers a higher-priced product overall sales will be higher than if they first offer a lower-priced product. For example, if similar tables sell at prices from $400 to $4,000 (with several priced in the middle), it is best to offer the $4,000 version first. The customer will often look at lower-cost versions, but fewer offered the $400 table will look at much higher-cost versions. Robert Cialdini discussed this "larger and then smaller request" principle in his famous book, *Influence*. This principle may also hold true online; thus, marketers might arrange online pricing pages as shown in Exhibit 10.11B, not Exhibit 10.11A as a way to increase the average sales price, and thus, overall sales (see sixteenventures.com for more commentary on this still unproven concept).

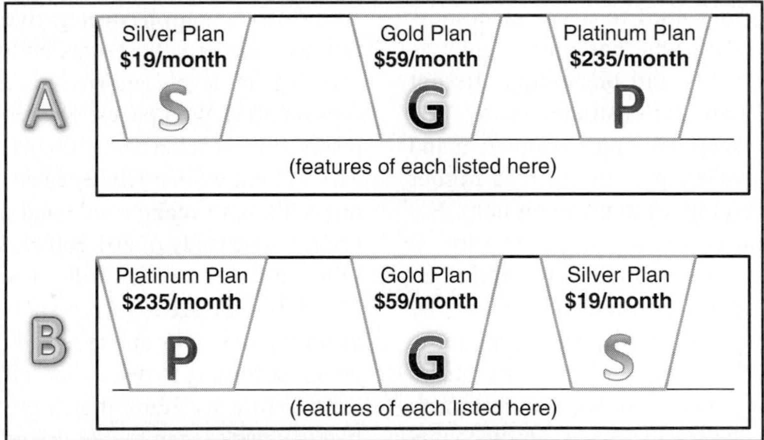

EXHIBIT 10.11 Price Placement on a Web page

Chapter Summary

Price is the amount of money charged for a product or service. More broadly, it covers the sum of all the values (i.e., money, time, energy, and psychic cost) that buyers exchange for the benefits of having or using a good or service. Fixed price refers to one price set for all buyers. Dynamic pricing means varying prices for individual customers. Internet technology has prompted mass customization and a return to dynamic pricing—especially negotiation and pricing for segments as small as a single buyer. This capability is creating huge opportunities for marketers to optimize pricing strategies, including changing them daily or more often. However, the internet is also facilitating price transparency, the idea that both buyers and sellers can view all competitive prices for items sold online.

From the buyer's perspective, the cost of a product purchased online may be higher than that offline (due to seemingly hidden elements such as shipping costs and the time and effort needed to search out and compare prices). Yet buyers may also enjoy online cost savings due to the internet's convenience, speed, self-service capability, one-stop shopping, integration, and automation. Moreover, online buyers have more control through strategies such as reverse auctions, the availability of information and products, and negotiation opportunities.

From the seller's perspective, any price above the cost of producing the good or service has the potential to return profit. The seller's perspective on pricing covers internal factors such as pricing objectives, the marketing mix strategy, and information technology. Beyond the buyer's perspective, the market structure and the efficiency of the market are key external elements affecting online pricing.

A market is efficient when customers have equal access to information about products, prices, and distribution. Efficient markets are characterized by lower prices, high price elasticity, frequent and smaller price changes, and narrow price dispersion. The Web exhibits many characteristics of an efficient market except narrow price dispersion. Because the internet could become a more efficient market in the future, marketers who want to maintain control over pricing should differentiate their products on bases other than price, create unique product bundles of benefits, and consider the role of customer perceptions of value when determining pricing levels.

Exercises

REVIEW QUESTIONS

1. How does fixed pricing differ from dynamic pricing?
2. What is price transparency, and why is it an important concept for e-marketers to understand?
3. List the main factors that put downward pressure on prices in the internet channel.
4. List the main factors that put upward pressure on prices in the internet channel.
5. From the buyer's perspective, how does the internet affect costs?
6. What is an efficient market? What makes the internet an efficient market, and what indicates that it is not an efficient market?
7. How do e-marketers use geographic, value segment, and negotiated pricing online?
8. Why is PayPal a good idea for merchants?
9. What are the advantages of electronic money for online retailers?

DISCUSSION QUESTIONS

10. **The Price of an iPhone App Story.** If you created a cool new app, which pricing model would you use and why? Consider all the important pricing variables in this chapter when answering.
11. **The Price of an iPhone App Story.** What is the difference among the three versions of *Angry Birds* (free, light, and full versions)? Do the product differences justify the pricing strategies?
12. Near-perfect access to pricing information is a problem that airlines have faced for years. How have airlines responded to this problem? Should internet businesses adopt similar strategies?
13. Which of the online cost-saving factors do you think has the greatest effect on price? Why?
14. Which pricing strategy would you use to introduce a new product for wireless Web access? Why?
15. Internet technology allows a company to price the same product differently for different customers. What do you think would be the advantages and disadvantages of Amazon offering the same book at one price to a professor and at a different price to a student?
16. As a buyer, how do you think price transparency affects your ability to develop an appropriate bidding strategy for new products auctioned by companies through eBay?

17. As a seller, how do you think price transparency affects your ability to obtain as high a price as possible for used products you auction through eBay?
18. Would you like to use your cell phone to pay for goods and services? Why or why not?

WEB ACTIVITIES

19. Using a shopping agent such as mySimon, what is the very lowest price that you can find for a bare-bones notebook computer sold online? How is it configured? What is the highest price for the same computer?
20. Clip an ad for electronic products from the newspaper. Pick a specific electronic product and look up the product online using a shopping agent such as bizrate.com or pricegrabber.com. Create a table showing how the online prices compare with the local ad.
21. Visit PayPal, MoneyZap (Western Union), and Bill Me Later. Review the prices and options for a new online bookseller and report on the pros and cons of each service. Which one(s) do you recommend?

The Internet for Distribution

The key objective of this chapter is to help you develop an understanding of the internet as a distribution channel, identify online channel members, and analyze the functions they perform in the channel. You will learn how the internet presents opportunities to alter channel length, restructure channel intermediaries, improve the performance of channel functions, streamline channel management, and measure channel performance. Special emphasis is on e-commerce, m-commerce, and social commerce.

After reading this chapter, you will be able to:

- Describe the three major functions of a distribution channel.
- Explain how the internet is affecting distribution channel length.
- Discuss the trends in supply chain management and power relationships among channel players.
- Outline the major models used by online channel members.
- Distinguish among e-commerce, m-commerce, social commerce, and F-commerce.
- Highlight how companies can use distribution channel metrics.

- Exactly as predicted by e-gurus 15 years ago, **e-commerce is hotter than ever.** Whether in mature markets, where consumer spending is shifting online, or in growth markets where rapid urbanization and increasing (mobile) internet penetration are unlocking new shopping habits, shoppers are "e-commercing" it up.

- In May 2012, ***Hyundai Home Shopping*** introduced its new mobile application, ***"H-Codi."*** It is a "virtual fashion coordination" program with Augmented Reality Technology. Via this application customers can virtually try on or test most products from Hyundai Home Shopping. For example, the camera on smartphones scans customer's face or body and shows pictures with coordinated fashion products such as earrings, neckties, and handbags.

The Zappos Story

How did Zappos go from concept to the world's largest online shoe store worth $1.2 billion in a short 10 years? Founder Nick Swinmurn, with early investor and former CEO Tony Hsieh, built a strong brand based on customer service and produced stellar revenue growth from day one. The company started at zero in 1999 and grossed over $1 billion in 2009. In November 2009, Amazon.com bought Zappos for a hefty $1.2 billion. Even the great online retailer, Amazon.com, knows better than to change a good thing—Zappos continues with the same management team and operates as a wholly owned subsidiary with headquarters in Henderson, NV. With the online shoe market expected to reach $7.8 billion in 2012, Zappos is in a position to remain a quickly growing e-commerce business ("Running Smoothly: Online…," 2012).

Founder Nick was initially turned down by most venture capitalists in 1999 because they doubted that anyone would buy shoes online, without the chance to try them on first. But Nick knew that $2 billion of the then $40 billion shoe market happened via catalog, so they ought to sell online, too. And he showed he was right by surviving the dot-com crash and copy-cat competitors. Key success factors in this astounding e-commerce story all centered on the company culture of customer service. Zappos wants every customer to say "That was the best customer service I've ever had," and the company even publishes a "culture book" where employees write about what this culture means to them. The customer service policies include free shipping both ways, a 365-day return policy, and a call center that is open 24/7. In the first 9 years Zappos offered a 110 percent price protection policy. Other success factors include:

- ***Great search engine marketing.*** People search for shoes by brand, so Zappos didn't need to build the company name, but simply optimize the site for searches for Rockport or Vans and capitalize on the strength of shoe branding. Search marketing was unheard of in 1999, so this was very forward-thinking.
- ***Word of mouth.*** An estimated 20 percent of new customers are referrals from current customers, who serve as brand advocates.

- ***Astute competitiveness.*** When the management realized that online and catalog competitors were taking an average of 6 days to deliver shoes to customers, Zappos surprised its repeat customers with free overnight or 2-day shipping. The customer got an e-mail saying that they were upgraded to overnight shipping because they are valued.
- ***Repeat customers.*** This strong customer service orientation resulted in 60 percent repeat customers in 2005, according to the CEO of Zappos.

Great customer service starts with great employees. Zappos requires a 2-week customer service training to every new employee, regardless of level. This includes 2 weeks of working in the call center and talking with customers. At the end of 2 weeks, employees are offered $2,000 to "quit now." The 97 percent who stay do it because they fit the customer service "wow" culture, not for the money.

All of this reminds us of the marketing adage: underpromise and overdeliver. Zappos continually shows that it cares about customers and this translates to the top line revenue. It is inspiring to know that this value, when coupled with employee happiness, translates to business success. The company has since expanded to clothing and handbags and continues to grow and delight its customers. You can read all about this formula for online retailing success in Tony's book: *Delivering Happiness: A Path to Profits, Passion, and Purpose*.

DISTRIBUTION CHANNEL OVERVIEW

Marketers are concerned about distribution because it involves point of purchase decisions and whether or not the customer receives a product or service satisfactorily. A **distribution channel** is a group of interdependent firms that work together to transfer product and information from the supplier to the consumer. It is composed of the following participants:

- ***Producers:*** Manufacturers and their suppliers, or originators of the product or service.
- ***Intermediaries:*** Firms that match buyers and sellers and mediate the transactions among them (e.g., wholesalers and retailers).
- ***Buyers:*** Consumers or users of the product or service.

A customer's experience in gaining access to the product often colors his or her satisfaction with the product, brand image, and brand loyalty. This often results in online product reviews and social media conversation about the brand.

The structure of the distribution channel can either make or impede possible opportunities for marketing on the internet. If the transaction is automated, the consumer could save money. Conversely, a consumer who purchases online must perform the search function personally that is normally performed by retailers—if you've ever searched for the lowest cost flight at online travel agents, you'll realize the additional time spent versus simply calling a brick-and-mortar agent. Four major elements combine to form a company's channel structure, and all affect internet marketing strategy as shown in the sections that follow:

1. Types of online channel intermediaries.
2. Length of the online channel.
3. Functions performed by members of the channel.
4. Physical and informational systems that link the channel members and provide for coordination and management of their collective effort to deliver the product or service.

ONLINE CHANNEL INTERMEDIARIES

A good way to understand online intermediaries is according to their business models. Many e-business models have new names, but how many of them are really new? On closer

1. Content sponsorship	
2. Infomediary	
3. Intermediaries	
Broker:	Online exchange
	Online auction
Agent:	Agent models representing sellers
	Selling agent (affiliate program)
	Manufacturer's agent (catalog aggregator)
	Agent models representing buyers (purchasing agent)
	Shopping agent
	Reverse auction
	Buyer cooperative
Online retailer (e-commerce, m-commerce, social commerce):	Digital products
	Tangible products
	Direct distribution

EXHIBIT 11.1 E-Business Models

inspection, most e-business models turn out to be variations on existing marketing concepts, but technology makes them more effective or efficient. For some digital products, such as software or music, the entire distribution channel may be internet based. When a consumer buys software online, the supplier often delivers it over the internet to the buyer's computer. In most cases, however, only some of the firms in the channel are wholly or partially Web enabled. For example, nondigital products such as flowers and wine may be purchased online but must be delivered via truck. Nonetheless, the exact location of that shipment can be tracked using a Web-based interface (the informational role of distribution). Exhibit 11.1 shows the overall classification scheme for the discussion that follows.

Channel intermediaries include wholesalers, retailers, brokers, and agents.

- **Wholesalers** buy products from the manufacturer and resell them to retailers.
- Both brick-and-mortar and online **retailers** buy products from manufacturers or wholesalers and sell them to consumers.
- **Brokers** facilitate transactions between buyers and sellers without representing either party. They are market makers and typically do not take title to the goods.
- **Agents** usually represent either the buyer or seller, depending upon who hires and pays them. They facilitate transactions between buyers and sellers but do not take title to the goods. **Manufacturer's agents** represent the seller, whereas **purchasing agents** represent the buyer.

Content Sponsorship

Chapter 1 discussed the many ways companies use content to increase revenues. In this chapter, we discuss selling content (e-commerce) and content sponsorship: Companies create Web sites, attract a lot of traffic, and sell advertising. Some firms use a niche strategy and draw a special interest audience (e.g., iVillage.com for women), and others draw a general audience (e.g., CNN .com or YouTube.com). Web properties using the content sponsorship model include all the major portals: Google, Yahoo!, MSN, and so on. Many online magazines and newspapers also use this model; indeed, much content on the internet is ad supported. Pandora Radio provides streaming radio based on user preferences. Listeners enter a song or artist they like and Pandora creates an individual radio station with similar music. Pandora delivers content to computers, smartphones, cars, and WiFi-enabled televisions and radio receivers. Pandora monetizes its e-business model by presenting ads on the Web page that is open while users listen to music. Pandora limits free, ad-supported listening to 40 hours a month and charges a subscription fee for its content beyond 40 hours. According to Pandora, there were 1.15 billion listeners in September 2012, an increase of 67 percent from the previous year. This high number of users creates great content sponsorship opportunities.

Many Web sites desire to sell advertising space, but it is difficult to get enough traffic to compete with the portals and news sites. See Exhibit 11.2 for some facts about advertising impressions to Web users (impressions are the number of times an ad can be viewed). Google is the king of content sponsorship, serving online ads to an estimated 410.2 million users in August 2012, and holding an ad revenue share of 74.4 percent.

We include this model in the e-commerce chapter because content sponsorship generates revenues in the business-to-business (B2B) market (Web companies selling ad space to other companies). In fact, content sponsorship grew from $72 to $1.56 billion in the 2 years ending mid-2012 (according to eMarketer). The product, of course, is ad space on a Web site, and the price for it usually increases with audience size. This model has its roots in traditional media, where television, magazines, and other media sell space and airtime. In Chapter 14, we discuss the other side: companies that buy advertising space as a way to communicate with stakeholders.

Craigslist uses the content sponsorship model because in 2012 it provided free listings to the tune of 60 million ads a month that draw 50 billion page views a month. These are sponsored by paid classified ad listings from companies, such as brokered apartment listings in New York City and job listings.

The **content sponsorship** model is often used in combination with other models to generate multiple revenue streams. For example, Buy.com, an online retailer, sells ads on its site to generate additional revenue, which in turn allows it to lower prices. Similarly, while most online newspapers offer their current edition for free, they often charge a small amount to retrieve an archived article.

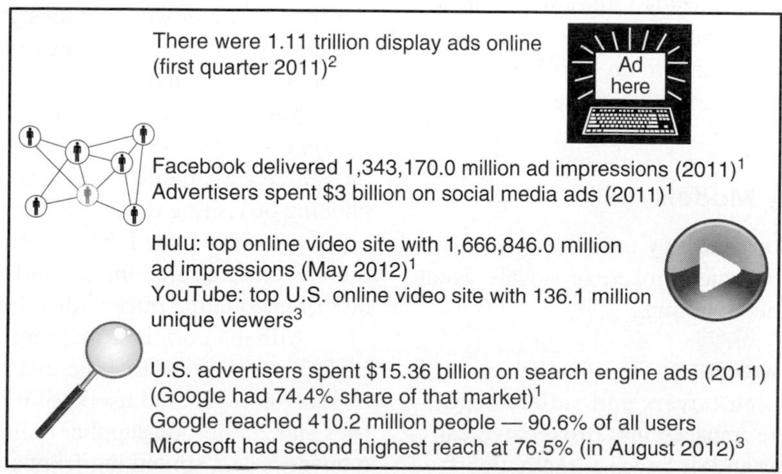

There were 1.11 trillion display ads online (first quarter 2011)[2]
Ad here
Facebook delivered 1,343,170.0 million ad impressions (2011)[1]
Advertisers spent $3 billion on social media ads (2011)[1]
Hulu: top online video site with 1,666,846.0 million ad impressions (May 2012)[1]
YouTube: top U.S. online video site with 136.1 million unique viewers[3]
U.S. advertisers spent $15.36 billion on search engine ads (2011) (Google had 74.4% share of that market)[1]
Google reached 410.2 million people — 90.6% of all users
Microsoft had second highest reach at 76.5% (in August 2012)[3]

EXHIBIT 11.2 Facts About the Web Content Sponsorship Model
Sources: [1](khalid 2012) [2]("U.S. Online Display. . .2011) [3]("Top 10 Global. . ." 2012) clip art courtesy of openclipart.org

Infomediary

An **infomediary** is an online organization that aggregates and distributes information, acting as a personal agent for Web users. One form of infomediary is a market research firm. Sometimes, the infomediary compensates the consumer for sharing information. For example, a comScore Media Metrix research panel member is paid; however, some intermediaries cull the information covertly and without compensation (e.g., Google's DoubleClick uses cookies to track users as they surf the Web). Web sites that require registration for downloading white papers and then provide the user data to authors and others also fall into this category.

Product review sites, such as ePinions.com, are another type of infomediary. These sites accumulate ratings and written reviews on Web pages that provide information to other consumers and the reviewed companies. They often receive revenue through commissions by providing click-throughs to online retailers where consumers can purchase the products.

The original idea behind the infomediary model was to give consumers more control over how they receive marketing messages. The benefit to the infomediary is that the consumer information increases the value of its ad inventory. The benefit to advertisers is that they can market to a highly targeted audience that has expressly opted into the system. Permission marketing allows advertisers to do something never before possible—advertise while the consumer is on a competitor's site!

Intermediary Models

Three main **intermediary** models are in common use on the internet: brokerage models, agent models, and online retailing.

BROKERAGE MODELS The broker creates a market in which buyers and sellers negotiate and complete transactions. Brokers typically charge the seller and/or buyer a transaction fee, but they don't represent either party for providing exchange and negotiation services. Some brokers also charge listing fees. Brokers provide many value-added services to help attract customers and facilitate transactions. Brokerage models operate Web site exchanges in B2B, business-to-customer (B2C), and customer-to-customer (C2C) markets. The best example in the offline world is a stockbroker who brings buyers and sellers together at the NYSE or other exchanges. Exchanges and auctions are the most popular online brokerage models.

The primary benefits to the buyer are convenience, speed of order execution, and transaction processing. Cost savings to the buyer come in the form of lower prices, decreased search time, and savings of energy and frustration in locating the appropriate seller. The primary benefit to the seller is the creation of a pool of interested buyers. Cost savings to the seller come in the form of lowered customer acquisition costs and transaction costs.

Online Exchange E*TRADE, Ameritrade, Schwab, and a host of other online brokerages allow customers to place equity and other trades from their computers without phoning or visiting a broker. These brokerages pass along the cost savings to the buyer in the form of lower transaction fees. They also provide the benefits of executing trades quickly, providing reference resources, and allowing for program trading. Some newer services catering to day traders bypass the Web entirely and connect traders straight to the market.

Autobytel and other online brokers allow customers to receive bids from qualified dealers on vehicles available in their area without first phoning or visiting the dealer. The dealers offer a no-hassle price quoted through the service. Thus, the customer avoids the potentially unpleasant task of negotiating price with a dealer.

Alibaba.com is a marketplace for global buyers and sellers. In June 2012, it had nearly 30 million registered users from over 240 countries and 2.5 million supplier online stores. When a buyer orders something from another country, the money goes to Alibaba and is held in escrow until the goods are delivered in good shape. After the buyer completes a form as such, the money is released to the seller.

The B2B market has spawned a number of successful brokerages. Converge is the leading anonymous exchange for the global electronics market (converge.com), aggregating supply and demand from thousands of component, original equipment and contract manufacturers, distributors, and resellers. The model is similar to a stock exchange. Customers contact a Converge trader on the floor of the exchange with their request (e.g., an order for 100,000 transistors). The trader locates a supplier, completes the purchase, and pockets the spread between the buying and selling price. Additional revenue comes from other fixed fees. The exchange is anonymous: Suppliers ship to a Converge quality control warehouse where the goods are inspected and then forwarded to the buyer. Converge guarantees the quality of the products and has a no-questions-asked return policy. Converge online services include personal buy-and-sell portfolios, chat communication with traders, and multiple methods for issuing requests, including uploading a list of items or searching for items individually.

Guru.com is an exchange for talent. Employers can find freelancers in this large global marketplace with over 1 million freelancers in the database and 8,000 projects posted monthly. Guru.com employers can locate consultants in 220 professional categories, including Web site design, programming, graphic design, business consulting, and administrative support. When a match is made, Guru.com collects a fee, just as do stock broker companies.

Online Auction Online auctions are challenging the fixed price model, which has been the norm for the past 100 years in most industrialize nations. Auctions are available in the B2B (uBid.com), B2C (priceline.com), and C2C (eBay.com) markets. Even though some merchants choose to host their own auctions, many more auction their surplus through auction brokers such as uBid. When merchants auction items on their own Web sites, they become direct sellers using dynamic pricing. Third-party auctioneers are broker intermediaries.

Sellers benefit by obtaining the market price for goods and unloading surplus inventory. Buyers benefit by obtaining a good price and, in many cases, enjoying the sport of the auction. The downside is that the buyer can waste a lot of time monitoring the auction and sometimes overpay (the "winner's curse" discussed in previous chapters). Although buyers can use services to automatically proxy bid, studies show that many repeatedly visit auction sites to check on bids.

Some auction houses offer a broad range of products. uBid hosts a B2C auction for products ranging from computers to travel. Other auction houses specialize in niche markets. Industry giant eBay hosts C2C auctions in thousands of product categories. eBay has rolled out a number of innovative services to benefit the customer and facilitate the auction process, including escrow, electronic payment via its PayPal company, and appraisal services.

AGENT MODELS Unlike brokers, agents *do* represent either the buyer or the seller, depending on who pays their fee. In some cases, they are legally obligated to represent the interests of the party that hires them. In the brick-and-mortar world, real estate agents who are hired to list a property must represent the interests of the seller.

Agent Models Representing Sellers Selling agents, manufacturer's agents, metamediaries, and **virtual malls** are all agents that represent the seller.

Selling agents represent a single organization, helping it sell its products; these agents normally work for a commission. For example, **affiliate programs** pay commissions to Web site owners for customer referrals. Normally the referral must result in a sale in order to qualify for the commission (Exhibit 11.3). For example, KarstadtQuelle AG, a large holding company for European department stores, pays a commission of €2 to its more than 4,000 selling agent affiliates for referring each new customer. Some affiliates demand a share of the lifetime

EXHIBIT 11.3 Affiliate Program Mechanics

value of the customer as opposed to just a piece of the first sale.

Amazon.com pioneered one of the first affiliate programs in 1996, calling it Amazon Associates. Every Web site displaying an Amazon logo graphic that links to Amazon .com is an affiliate selling agent. It has hundreds of thousands of associates—each a point of sale for Amazon products. And when an affiliate site sends a customer to Amazon.com, that affiliate will earn up to 10 percent of the transaction price.

Manufacturer's agents represent more than one seller. In traditional marketing, they generally represent only firms that sell complementary products to avoid conflicts of interest, but in the virtual world they often create Web sites to help an entire industry sell its products. In e-marketing, manufacturer's agents are often called seller aggregators because they represent many sellers on one Web site.

Almost all of the travel reservations Web sites qualify as manufacturer's agents since their commissions are paid by the airlines and hotels they represent. Expedia, CheapOAir, Orbitz, and many other travel agent sites allow customers to make online travel reservations. In some cases the traveler can get a better deal online but often the greatest benefit is simply convenience.

In the B2B market, manufacturer's agents are sometimes called *catalog aggregators*. Each of the sellers these firms represent generally has a broad catalog of product offerings. Picture a purchasing manager in a small room surrounded by hundreds of catalogs, which suggest the origin of the term. The challenge for the aggregator is to gather the information from all of these catalogs into a database for presentation on the Web site. Normally, the catalog aggregator offers software that seamlessly interfaces with the suppliers' internal database systems. The task is made significantly easier when the suppliers use industry standard software such as Arriba, CommerceOne, Concur, or Alliance to manage their catalogs. Furthermore, the catalogs must be constantly maintained as product availability and prices change.

The more advanced manufacturer's agents support catalog customization and integration with the buyer's enterprise resource planning (ERP) systems. The customized catalogs display prenegotiated product offerings and prices. Some will even maintain spending limits for particular employees and automatically forward big-ticket orders to the appropriate officer for approval. Additional services include recommending substitutions, notifying buyers of production lead times, processing orders, and tracking orders.

With this model, the buyer gains substantial benefits, including shorter order cycles, reduced inventories, and increased control. Order processing costs are lowered through paperless transactions, automated request for proposal (RFP) and request for quote (RFQ), and integration with ERP systems.

The College Source (collegesource.org) is a catalog aggregator for the college market where students can search 66,958 college catalogs at one site. Another player is Catalogs.com.

There are two other intermediaries that act like agents but defy easy categorization. One represents a cluster of manufacturers, online retailers, and content providers organized around a life event or major asset purchase. They solve four major consumer problems—reducing search times, providing quality assurance about vendors, facilitating transactions for a group of related purchases, and providing relevant and unbiased content information about the purchase. These Web site companies receive commissions for referrals or completed transactions. Edmunds.com is a good example in the car-buying market, providing information about new and used automobiles and advice on negotiating deals. It also refers interested customers to a car-buying service, financing information, aftermarket parts, and insurance alternatives. The Knot represents the bridal market, offering information about planning, fashion, beauty, grooms, bridesmaids and moms, and so forth. It also has tools such as a gown finder, registry, checklist, and guest list. In addition, *TheKnot.com* provides sponsored content such as the guide to invitations by OurBeginning.com or the guide to bridal showers by GiftCertificates.com.

The other intermediary hosts multiple online merchants in a model similar to a shopping mall. Hosted merchants gain exposure from traffic coming to the virtual mall. The mall gains through a variety of fees: listing fees, transaction fees, and setup fees. Although brick-and-mortar malls provide a desirable collection of stores in one location, are easily accessible from major highways, and have ample free parking, none of these benefits apply online. Nonetheless, virtual malls may provide six customer benefits. The first is branding—consumers may be more comfortable buying from a store listed on the Yahoo! Shopping pages than buying from one that is not. The second benefit is availability of electronic money, allowing customers to register their shipping and billing information just once, and retrieve that information when purchasing at any participating store, thus simplifying the order process. The third benefit is availability of frequent shopper programs that reward consumers for shopping within the mall. The fourth is a gift registry that operates across multiple stores. The fifth benefit is a search facility to locate products in mall stores. The sixth is a recommendation service such as suggestions for Mother's Day gifts.

Yahoo! Shopping hosts a number of large merchants, including Best Buy and Target, as well as a number of other well-known retailers. It offers e-money that can be used to shop at many of its listed merchants; it also has a frequent shopper program, a gift registry, product recommendations, and a search facility. Amazon.com could be considered a virtual mall now that it offers such a huge variety of products and second-party retailers.

Agent Models Representing Buyers

Purchasing agents represent buyers. In traditional marketing, they often forge long-term relationships with one or more firms; however, on the internet they represent any number of buyers, anonymously in many cases. Shopping agents and reverse auctions help individual buyers obtain the prices they want, while buyer cooperatives pool buyers for larger volume buys and, thus, lower prices.

As discussed in Chapter 10, when shopping agents were first developed, many feared that they would drive prices on the internet down to impossible margins. That scenario has not happened because price is not the only factor consumers consider when making a purchase.

Newer, second-generation shopping agents can now measure value and not just price. PriceScan and CNET Shopper are two firms offering this service.

Consumers who desire a quantitative performance evaluation of a merchant can shop through Shopzilla's BizRate.com. BizRate links customers with over a million products and retailers online. BizRate Insights rates online merchants based on customer feedback. BizRate posts a report card of past consumer experiences with the merchant (generated from customer surveys) and shows the merchant's stated business policies. BizRate also offers a rebate program for customers who buy from participating merchants.

A **reverse auction** occurs at a Web site serving as purchasing agent for individual buyers. In a reverse auction, the buyer specifies a price and sellers bid for the buyer's business. The buyer commits to buying at a specified price, and the seller either meets the price or tries to get close enough to make the sale. Priceline was the first major player in reverse auctions.

The benefit to the seller is in unloading excess inventory without unduly upsetting existing channels—a valuable benefit for sellers with perishable inventory such as airline seats or hotel rooms. The benefit for the buyer comes in the form of lower prices and the satisfaction of being able to name one's price. However, buyers have fewer choices of brand, suppliers, and product features. The reduced choice feature sufficiently differentiates the product in most cases to avoid conflict with the supplier's existing channel partners.

The **buyer cooperative** (also known as a buyer aggregator) pools many buyers together to drive down the price of selected items. The individual buyer, thus, receives the price benefit of volume buying. The more buyers that join the pool, the lower the price drops, usually in a step function. For example, 1 to 5 buyers pay $69 each; 6 to 10 buyers pay $58 each, and so on. The step function encourages buyers to recruit their friends to help push the price down to the next step. Buyers can make their bid contingent on the product reaching a specified price point.

MobShop, Mercata, and other promising buyer's cooperatives closed as they were not able to build profitable business models online. The remaining online co-ops represent more traditional brick-and-mortar buyer's co-ops such as the Solar and Renewable Energy Cooperative (soarenergy.org) and Wasatch Rendezvous for small businesses. Nonetheless, we believe that the internet is capable of supporting this model as evidenced by the emergence of new co-ops on a regular basis.

Groupon and LivingSocial are two leading buyer cooperative sites in the United States (there are many in other countries as well). They offer discounts on merchandise for a limited amount of time. Users sign up for the deal and if the minimum required number is reached, all get the discount. The advantage to sellers is that they gain a large number of new customers, often from many different locations. Another interesting example is a homeschooling cooperative buying program representing over 57,000 families (homeschoolbuyersco-op.org).

ONLINE RETAILING: E-COMMERCE

E-commerce is one of the most visible e-business models. In this business model, merchants set up online storefronts and sell to businesses and consumers (refer to the Zappos story).

What sells well online? Exhibit 11.4 displays the results of the U.S. Department of Commerce's retailer survey with 11,000 merchants. Leading the pack is the nearly $25 billion spent on clothing and accessories. A private study found the top-selling products in the fourth quarter of 2011 to be digital content/subscriptions, jewelry/watches, consumer electronics, toys, and software (see. comscore.com). In contrast, the proportion of consumers purchasing various online items paints a different picture: 81 percent buy books; 74 percent buy apparel; 65 percent purchase music, TV shows, or movies; and 59 percent buy beauty/personal care items online—followed by footwear, consumer electronics, services, jewelry, furniture, and more ("Multichannel Is a Must. . .," 2012). Incidentally, the shoppers in several other countries represent

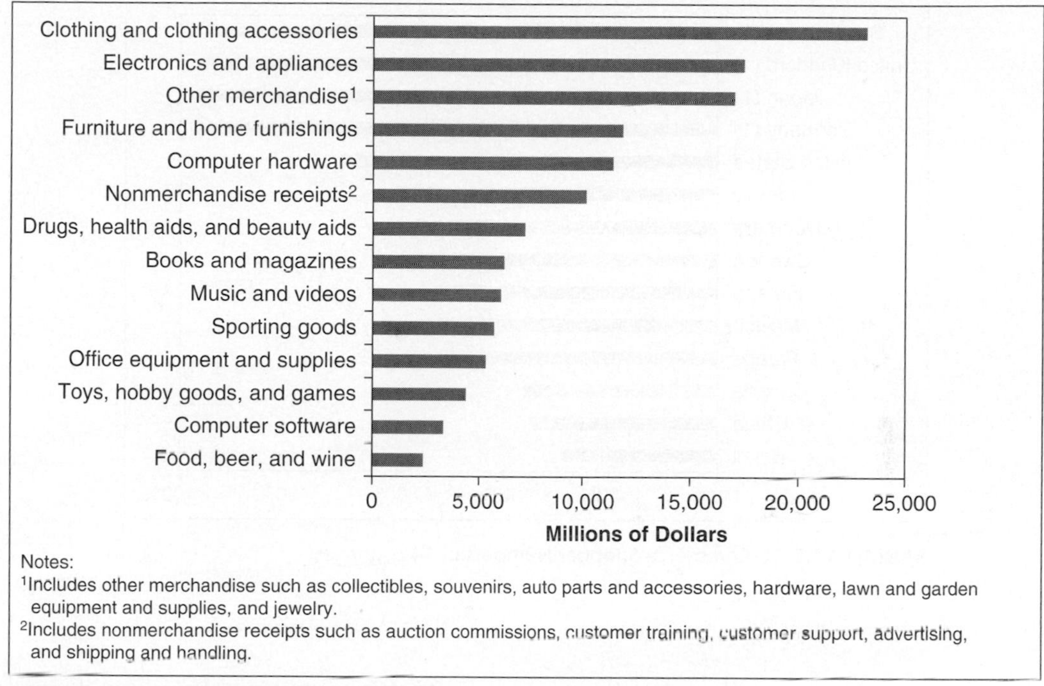

EXHIBIT 11.4 What Do U.S. Consumers Buy Online? *Source*: census.gov

a higher proportion of online users—99 percent in South Korea, 97 percent in the United Kingdom and 97 percent in both Germany and Japan (according to imarketingmag.com).

Digital goods may be delivered directly over the internet while physical goods are shipped via a **logistics** provider such as UPS, USPS (U.S. Postal Service), or FedEx. Companies selling physical products online can make any level of commitment from pure play to barely dabbling; however, most reasonably sized brick-and-mortar retailers offer at least some products online.

Although a pre-internet presence carries brand equity, it does not guarantee online success. Often the pure plays are free from the cultural constraints of the established businesses and can innovate more quickly in response to customer needs. Some internet pure plays established brick-and-mortar operations to enhance branding through additional exposure and an additional channel for customers to experience their products. E*TRADE is one of the more prominent examples, extending its brick-and-mortar presence in recent years.

An advantage of online retailing is that companies can sell a wider and deeper assortment of products in smaller quantities than in offline stores, because they are not bound by the space constraints in malls and free-standing buildings located in expensive areas. Instead, they can use warehouses on cheap land and ship from there. Named "the long tail" by Chris Anderson, editor of *Wired* magazine, this refers to the reason it is possible to increase revenue by selling small quantities of a large number of products online. For example, Netflix is reported to have about 75,000 DVDs in inventory as compared to 3,000 at a typical Blockbuster brick-and-mortar store and the gap has continued to widen. Netflix is able to sell a large variety of hard-to-find DVDs in smaller quantities, and the product not available in offline rental stores comprises 20 percent of Netflix's total sales. As well, in 2012 Netflix .com had 23 million streaming subscribers and

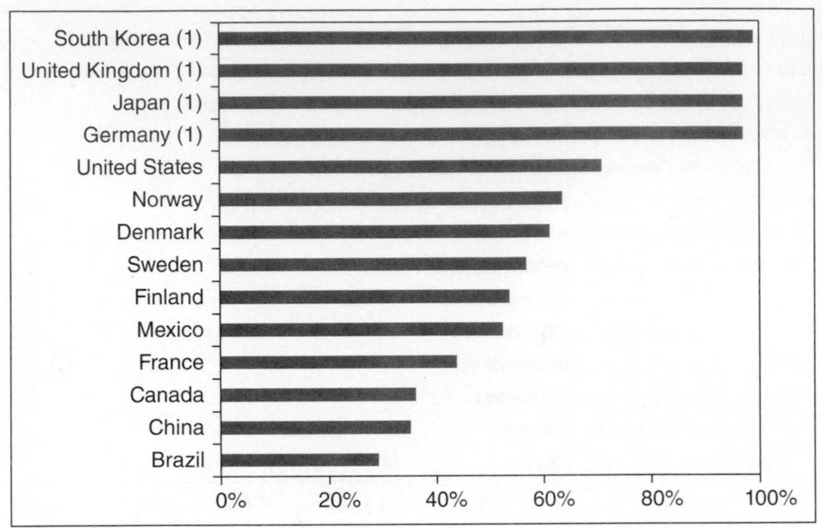

EXHIBIT 11.5 E-Commerce Shopper Numbers in 14 countries

35 percent of the customers still used snail-mail for DVD rental (see the Netflix annual report).

Some of the friction consumers have regarding online shopping still needs to be addressed by e-commerce firms. In order to purchase online, a consumer needs a bank account, credit card, and computer access, so this cuts out some consumers, especially in lesser developed countries. Nonetheless, 71 percent of the 85 percent using the internet in the United States has purchased a product online and 78 percent have done research for an offline purchase (see Chapter 7). However, four other countries have higher penetrations of online shoppers (Exhibit 11.5). There are 639.7 million online shoppers in the 14 countries in this exhibit. Nice opportunities for international marketers.

One of the biggest problems for online retailers is shopping cart abandonment part way through the purchasing process. The goal is to convert site visitors to purchasers, and that only happens about 2.2 percent of the time, on average—although the top 10 e-commerce sites experience a 12 percent conversion (according to invesp.com). Exhibit 11.6 displays statistics and reasons for shopping cart abandonment.

Multichannel marketing is the use of more than one sales channel, such as Web, mobile, brick-and-mortar, and catalog. Most large traditional retailers are multichannel marketers because they also sell products online. Most catalog retailers also use multichannel marketing. Among catalog retailers, 78 percent said their return of investment (ROI) is better when both channels are used—possibly partially because they can reach different customers through each channel. Important decisions involve product selections and appropriate pricing in each channel.

Omni-channel shopping is the shopper's perspective of multichannel marketing, describing the way consumers move seamlessly through many shopping channels: Web, brick-and-mortar store, computer, mobile device, catalog, and so forth. For example consumers (1) are in a physical store using a smartphone to research a product and do price comparisons (maybe by scanning a QR code), (2) purchase online and pick up the product in a physical store, (3) research online before visiting a physical store, or (4) seek opinions about a product in social media while in a physical store. This

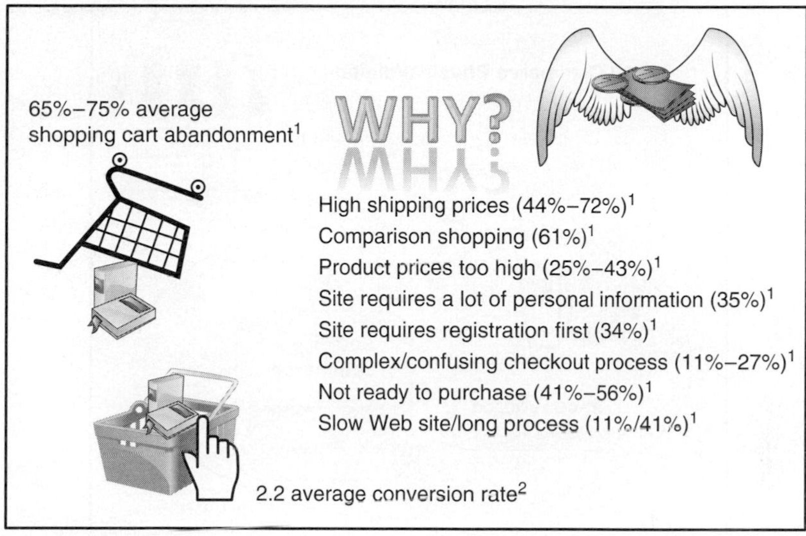

EXHIBIT 11.6 Reasons for Shopping Cart Abandonment *Sources:* [1]Various studies (e.g., visibility.tv and invesp.com) [2]Shop.org clip art courtesy of openclipart.org

type of customer has been known to purchase more often, spend more money, and be more loyal to specific retailers. One study found that 45 percent of online shoppers combine this with brick-and-mortar and mobile shopping channels ("2012 Shopping Outlook," 2012). With this in mind, we now move to the mobile commerce experience.

M-COMMERCE **Mobile commerce** (m-commerce) occurs when consumers make a transaction with a smartphone or other mobile device (e.g., iPhone, iPad, Android). M-commerce is a subset of e-commerce, as shown in Exhibit 11.7. Nearly 77 percent of the U.S. population has a mobile phone, and half of these are smartphones (enabling m-commerce), according to eMarketer.com. Although estimates vary, comScore found that 38 percent of U.S. smartphone users had made a purchase with the device during 2011 (other estimates range up to 63 percent). You read in Chapter 8 that 90 percent of smartphone users have taken some sort of action after searching via a smartphone (like book a hotel or purchase). Mobile user purchases include ordering products from Web sites (including tickets, services, and more), paying for online content (such as apps or music), online banking, and more. Following are some facts about m-commerce:

- M-commerce sales in 2012 were predicted to reach $11.6 billion, growing to $31 billion by 2015 ("Smartphones Turn Millions...," 2012). The 2012 projection amounts to 5.9 percent of all e-commerce sales (based on the Department of Commerce figures). Small, but growing rapidly.
- $8.52 billion was spent on mobile apps in 2011. This is 54 percent of all m-commerce (Meeker, 2012). Forester Research predicts that by 2015 the mobile application market will reach $54 billion.
- There were 46 million music and app downloads a day from iTunes store in 2011 (Meeker, 2012).
- 62 percent of U.S. tablet owners paid for music download, 51 percent for movies, 41 percent for TV shows, and 19 percent for news (Lunden, 2012).

M-commerce is a rapidly growing area of e-commerce, which involves not only the ultimate act of online purchasing but also all the

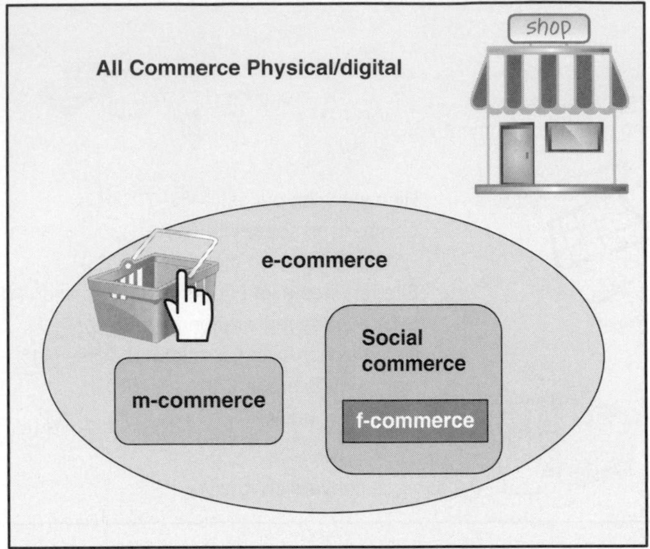

EXHIBIT 11.7 Relationship among Commerce, E-Commerce, M-Commerce, Social Commerce, and F-Commerce

related e-marketing activities (most of which are discussed elsewhere in this book):

- Mobile search (e.g., company store locators),
- Location-based services (such as Foursquare),
- QR code scanning (for more product information or promotions),
- Two-dimensional bar code scanning (for building a shopping list or comparing products),
- Image recognition (for linking to online content),
- Voice and text message offers from businesses (e.g., airline flight delays and breaking news alerts),
- Social networking (e.g., answering product questions via Twitter) and
- Marketing-related apps (Clorox has three apps, including "MyStain").

Near-field communication (NFC) is another tactic involving two smartphones or a smartphone and another device that communicate by touching each other or being in very close proximity. This is how the Google wallet works, as discussed in Chapter 10. NFC can also be used for checking in at hotels and conferences or downloading content.

In one interesting mobile example, Sonos is a wireless music system that uses WiFi for controlling a user's music from a smartphone (or computer) as it plays through the stereo speakers in a house. The Sonos app can access Pandora stations, iTunes library, Sirius radio, and many other digital music services.

Some companies predict that mobile internet access will soon overtake computer access. This is a huge market for companies, who must add mobile tactics to their e-marketing strategies, including creating mobile Web portals (with fewer big graphics so they download in a few seconds). In a 2012 global survey of marketing executives, 45 percent said they were currently using mobile as a marketing channel, and of the 55 percent not involved, 43 percent planned to incorporate mobile within the year ("eMarketer Mobile Roundup," 2012). As marketers integrate mobile tactics into e-marketing plans, they focus on customer convenience and engagement at many touch points as customers travel through the purchase funnel stages (from awareness to purchase and brand loyalty).

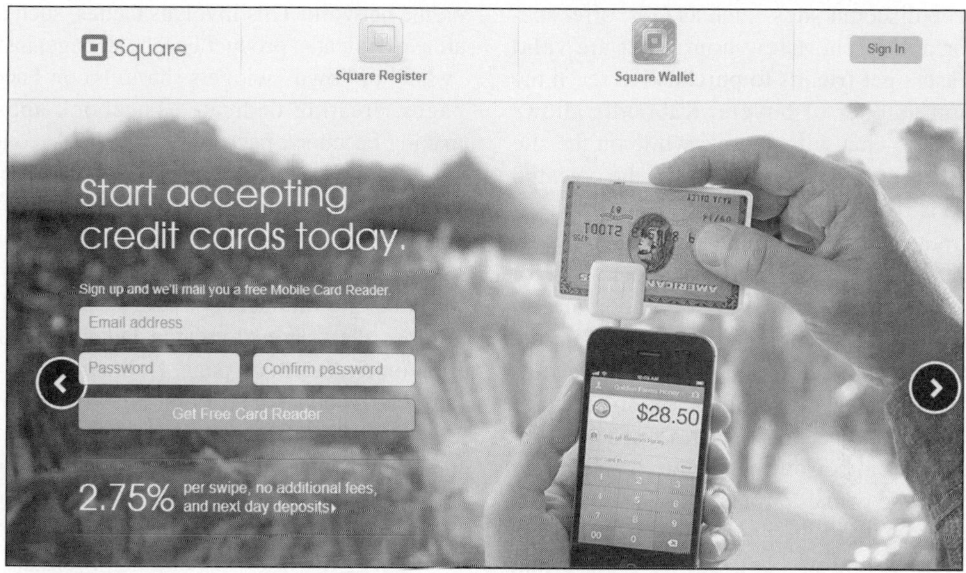

EXHIBIT 11.8 Square Card Reader Facilitates M-Commerce *Source:* © 2012 Square, Inc.

As an example, Exhibit 11.8 displays an iPhone with a small, square plastic device that plugs into the audio jack of the phone. This allows businesses to swipe credit and debit cards for purchases on the go at trade fairs and events, and e-mail the receipt to the customer. The company, Square, charges businesses a small fee and deposits the money into the user's bank account. This is quite convenient both for customers and for businesses.

SOCIAL COMMERCE **Social commerce** is a piece of e-commerce that uses social media and consumer interactions to facilitate online sales. See the infographic at the end of this chapter for the history of social commerce. Social media demonstrate a move from corporate to user control, yet these same social media conversations provide great opportunities for building revenue, cutting costs, and increasing customer satisfaction through social commerce. For example, over half of social media users prefer to use Facebook to sign into a Web site, followed by Google and Yahoo!: This is called **social sign-in** ("Facebook Solidifies Hold. . .," 2012).

In one social commerce example, Best Buy, the consumer electronic retailer, answers product and service questions via its Twitter account. Another example is when Blendtec, the blender company, created a number of "will it blend" videos that users shared with each other and this increased blender sales (e.g., the video blending an iPad had 14.6 million views 46,358 "likes" and numerous comments in October 2012, just 2 years after the video release).

Social shopping is one aspect of social commerce. Polyvore has 17 million visitors who create fashion ensembles by mixing and matching clothing and accessories, share with others, and click/purchase based on what they see on the site. Pinterest allows users to create digital bulletin boards ("pinboards") with everything from fashion to decorated living rooms that others can click, visit, and purchase from the sites selling featured products. In late 2012, ComScore found that between 18 and 23 percent of Pinterest users also visited online retailers selling jewelry, luxury goods, flowers, cosmetics, food, books, and travel sites ("More Than One. . .," 2012). This is one clue about Pinterest's social commerce effectiveness.

Group buying sites, such as Groupon and Living Social, are also in this category. Flash sales/deep discount sites, such as Gilt, offer specials for a very short few hours that are valid only if users get friends to purchase to reach the minimum number of buyers. Kaboodle allows consumers to chat with friends while on the site and get their opinions about whether the potential purchase is right for the person.

Product rating, recommendation, and review sites that provide space for users to post allow for the sharing aspect critical to social commerce. Examples include ePinions, Tripadvisor, Amazon, and many others. Online marketplaces, such as Craigslist and eBay, also allow for social commerce activities. Peer-to-peer sites, such as Zopa, bring lenders and borrowers together for a transaction. This type of marketplace also occurs in the B2B market, with auction and exchange sites.

By now you are getting the picture that social commerce is initiated by customers via online spaces provided by businesses. Some of the tactics used by social commerce companies include widgets on social media sites ("buy now"), crowdsourcing that entices users to help companies develop new products, location-based commerce that offers discounts when customers share their location with friends, and many other collaboration models as seen on blogs, wikis, and other Web sites. Following are some examples of profitable social commerce tactics:

- Dell computer claims to have made a $6.5 million profit by selling computers on Twitter in 2 years (Nutley, 2010).
- PepsiCo gives a live notification when its customers are close to physical stores that sell Pepsi products (supermarkets, restaurants, and gas stations). Then PepsiCo sends them coupons and discount information using Foursquare.
- Starbucks, Mountain Dew, and Dell all improved products and services through crowdsourcing on dedicated sites.

F-commerce (Facebook commerce) is a subset of social commerce, where companies use Facebook to facilitate e-commerce. Because of Facebook's huge number of users and activity, many companies have attempted to sell products on the network. This involves tactics, such as creating a dedicated product Facebook page, installing "want" or "own" widgets (buttons) on Facebook pages, creating dedicated Facebook apps, and making Facebook pages with searchable content.

For example, Disney sells tickets on Facebook, Levis allows auto population of shopping cart on Facebook based on what friends might like, Wendy's awards $50 gift cards for funny responses to challenges on Facebook and Twitter, and Delta Airlines allows users to search and purchase tickets right on its Facebook page. Hallmark has a popular social calendar app (for birthday reminders) and Heinz Ketchup has an app that allows users to write the name of a friend on the soup can label and send it to them (such as a "get well" with this can of soup message) (Chowney, 2012).

Does it work? Yes and no. There are many successful stories, such as when a user buys a ticket from the Ticketmaster Facebook page and shares this in the newsfeed, friends also purchase tickets to the tune of an additional average of $5.30 in ticket purchases (Chowney, 2012). In contrast, the Gap, Banana Republic, Old Navy, JC Penney, Nordstrom, and Gamestop all closed their dedicated Facebook storefronts for lack of business (Lutz, 2012). Facebook recently added a photo posting app that allows users to "like," "want," "collect," and "buy." In conclusion, Facebook is for communicating, not selling, so the storefronts don't work as well as the product apps and pages that create fun apps and other ways of communicating with friends on the network.

TANGIBLE PRODUCTS All tangible products sold online, such as books and furniture, are distributed through conventional channels. This type of distribution is relatively inefficient: Rather than deliver 100 copies of a book to a brick-and-mortar store in a single shipment, the UPS truck must make deliveries to 100 individual customers. Consumers pay a premium for this service, which may outweigh the cost savings of purchasing online. Furthermore, local regulations sometimes impede the direct distribution of a product. For example, Wine.com (the former Virtual Vineyards at wine.com), a wine distributor, has been forced by some state regulations to operate through local intermediaries rather than mail wine across state lines—which lengthens its distribution channel.

Digital Products/Content Sales The internet serves as the actual distribution channel itself for digital goods and services such as news, music, software, movies, education (online classes), and so forth. This is an important part of the growing field of content marketing, as discussed in Chapter 1 and in the previous m-commerce section. Clearly, distribution costs are significantly lower for digital products, compared with physical distribution. *The New York Times* (nytimes.com) was one of the first to make the online subscription model pay off—it attracted several hundred thousands of new customers to its Web site who were not reading the printed paper. Classmates.com, iTunes, and the *Wall Street Journal Online* are also successful at selling content online. The Amazon Kindle e-book reader and many competitors, such as the iPad, have boosted sales of online content.

One interesting tactic involves the content subscription **paywall**: Some Web content is hidden and only available to users who pay a fee for access. Many studies found that users expect free content prior to being asked to pay for content. Some companies include a notice on the home page that the user can read five or so articles within a month and then must pay for more. Others allow users to read part of an article and then require subscription fees for the remainder. Marketers are experimenting to see which system delivers the most revenue. For example, the *Wall Street Journal* allows nonsubscribers to read some stories in their entirety, but cuts others off after a few paragraphs. Interestingly, the paper sometimes posts stories on its Facebook page that anyone can access. Yearly subscription prices to the paper in October 2012 were $259.48 (digital only), $311.48 (digital and selected print for home delivery), and $119.08 (print only).

Consumers purchase a large amount of online content (Exhibit 11.9). Leading the pack are music, magazines, and movies. In a global

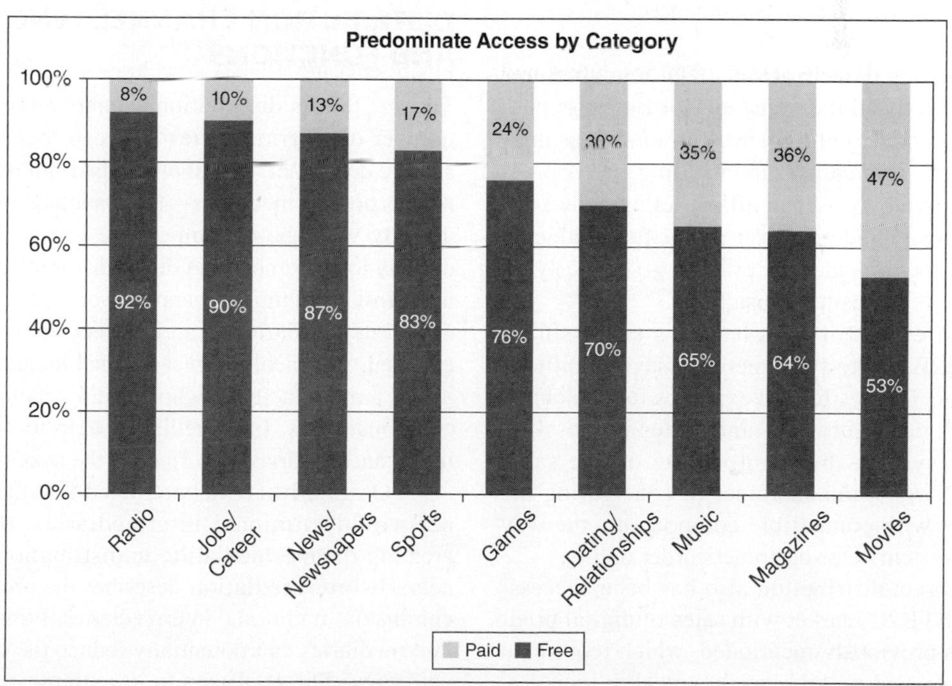

EXHIBIT 11.9 Online U.S. Content Spending *Source:* MarketResearchCareers/DigiCareers

study, Nielsen asked 27,000 consumers if they would buy content online and 85 percent said they preferred it to be free. This is definitely the internet culture as seen in the exhibit; however, online content sales continue to grow—both because of the huge tablet use and in the B2B market, where companies purchase online research reports and database access.

Want to become an e-commerce vendor and sell your original content online? Artists sell their artwork on deviantArt and Zaarly. Crafters sell vintage and handmade items on Etsy.com. YouTube will pay for indie videos by splitting ad revenue with the video creator. Scribd and Amazon will let you sell your digital book online and split the proceeds (one young author reportedly made several hundred thousand dollars via her $1.99 teen age paranormal novels on Amazon). CD Baby and iTunes will sell your music and split the proceeds. Demotix gives you cash and recognition for selling photojournalist stories on the site (e.g., breaking news with images). Gumroad lets you use its site for selling and link to your products on your own site. It also provides dynamic pricing so you can change the price as demand increases.

Direct Distribution The manufacturer sells directly to the consumer or business customer in the **direct distribution** model, as does Dell, Inc. (also called direct selling). This practice is commonly used in offline selling; however, the internet made it much easier for producers to bypass intermediaries and go directly to consumers or business customers.

Direct distribution has been successful in some B2B markets—sometimes saving millions of dollars in sales-related expenses for personnel, product configuration, and order processing. Expert systems built into some online sales systems assist the customer in configuring the product with compatible components, the way Dell's system helps customers order online.

Direct distribution also has been successful in the B2C market with sales of digital products, as previously mentioned, which require no inventory and no pick, pack, and ship logistics. Perishable products such as flowers and fresh food are also well served by direct channels. As one example, Proflowers.com delivers flowers fresh from the grower. Flowers that don't pass through an intermediary tend to be fresher and last longer, and are in many cases less expensive.

Direct distribution saves customers money by avoiding intermediaries; sometimes it leads to more rapid delivery of the product. For example, Fresh Direct calls itself a "private online farmer's market." It processes and delivers Web orders of fresh produce and meat everyday to its New York and Philadelphia customers. By cutting out the intermediaries and using databases to keep inventory at a minimum, Fresh Direct is able to make profits unseen by other online grocers (see freshdirect.com).

Benefits to the manufacturer include the ability to claim a piece of the intermediary's margin, but, of course, someone has to perform the functions of those intermediaries. The major costs of direct distribution for the customer include higher search costs to locate individual manufacturers, the time costs of transacting with each manufacturer, and delivery costs (e.g., Fresh Direct charges $6.99–$8.99 for a minimum $30 order).

DISTRIBUTION CHANNEL LENGTH AND FUNCTIONS

The length of a distribution channel refers to the number of intermediaries between the supplier and the consumer. The shortest distribution channel has no intermediaries—the manufacturer deals directly with the consumer, the way Dell sells directly to customers in a direct distribution channel. Most distribution channels incorporate one or more intermediaries in an **indirect distribution channel**. A typical indirect channel includes suppliers, a manufacturer, wholesalers, retailers, and end consumers. Intermediaries help to perform important functions (described in the next section).

Originally, it was predicted that the internet would eliminate intermediaries, thereby creating disintermediation in distribution channels. **Disintermediation** describes the process of eliminating traditional intermediaries. Eliminating intermediaries can potentially reduce the costs as with Fresh Direct. Taken to its extreme, disintermediation allows the supplier to transfer goods and services directly to the consumer in a direct channel. Complete disintermediation tends to be the exception because intermediaries can often handle channel functions more efficiently than producers. An intermediary that specializes in one function, such as product promotion, tends to become more proficient in that function than a nonspecialist.

Much of the initial hype surrounding the internet focused on disintermediation and the possibility that prices would plummet as the internet eliminated costly intermediaries. This line of reasoning failed to recognize some important facts. First, the U.S. distribution system is very efficient. Second, using intermediaries allows manufacturing companies to focus on what they do best. Third, many traditional intermediaries have been replaced with internet equivalents. In many cases, the online intermediaries are more efficient than their brick-and-mortar counterparts. Consider the online storefront. Online retailers do not have to rent, maintain, and staff expensive retail space in desirable shopping areas. An inexpensive warehouse provides an acceptable storage location for goods sold online. On the other hand, online stores incur the costs of setting up and maintaining their e-commerce sites. Although these charges can be significant, they do not outweigh the savings realized by eliminating the physical store.

The internet has added new intermediaries that did not exist previously. For example, Yahoo! Launch aggregates multimedia content. Yahoo! and Yahoo! Launch together are like a record store, audio bookstore, radio broadcaster, and TV broadcaster all rolled into one. Other new intermediaries include shopping agents and buyer cooperatives.

Functions of a Distribution Channel

Many functions must be performed in moving products from producer to consumer, regardless of which intermediary performs them. For example, online retailers normally hold inventory and perform the pick, pack, and ship functions in response to a customer order. In an alternative scenario, the retailer might **outsource** the pick, pack, and ship functions to a logistics provider such as UPS. Here, the retailer forwards the order to a UPS warehouse where the product waits in storage. UPS picks, packs, and ships the product to the consumer. Distributors perform many value-added functions. The functions can be broadly characterized as transactional, logistical, and facilitating.

TRANSACTIONAL FUNCTIONS **Transactional functions** refer to making contact with buyers and using marketing communication strategies to make buyers aware of products. They also include matching products to buyer needs, negotiating price, and processing transactions.

Contact with Buyers The internet provides a new channel for making contact with buyers. Forrester Research calls the internet the fourth channel after personal selling, mail, and the telephone; retailers see it as the third channel after brick-and-mortar stores and catalogs. The internet channel adds value to the contact process in several ways. First, contact can be customized to the buyer's needs. For example, the Honda site (honda.com) allows customers to find a dealer in their area where they can buy Honda vehicles. Second, the internet provides a wide range of referral sources such as search engines, shopping agents, social networks, e-mail, Web pages, and affiliate programs. Third, the internet is always open for business, 24 hours a day, 7 days a week.

Marketing Communications Marketing communication encompasses advertising and other types of product promotion (discussed in Chapters 12 through 14). This function is often shared among channel players. For example, a manufacturer may launch an ad campaign while its retailers offer coupons. Cooperative advertising is another example, with manufacturers sharing advertising costs with retailers. These communications are most effective when they represent a coordinated effort among channel players.

The internet adds value to the marketing communications function in several ways. First, functions that previously required manual labor can be automated. When American Airlines sends out a promotional message to millions of its registered users, it requires no papers to fold, no envelopes to stuff, no postage to imprint—its marketers simply click "Send" to distribute the message. As another example, promoting a Web site to the search engines can be automated by services such as Submission Pro (submission-pro.com) and MoreVisibility (morevisibility.com). These firms study how the search engines rank Web sites and then optimize their clients' Web sites to achieve a higher ranking.

Second, communications can be closely monitored and altered minute by minute. Google's AdWords program, for instance, allows its clients to monitor the click-through rates of their online ads in real time and quickly make substitutions for poorly performing ads. Third, Web analytics software for tracking a user's behavior can be used to direct highly targeted communications to individuals.

Finally, the internet enhances promotional coordination among intermediaries. Companies e-mail ads and other material to each other, and all firms may view current promotions on a Web site at any time. It is still all too common for brick-and-mortar headquarter firms to run promotions that retailers don't know about until consumers begin asking for the special deals—internet communication helps prevent this kind of surprise from occurring.

Matching Product to Buyer's Needs The Web excels at matching products to buyer's needs. Given a general description of the buyer's requirements, shopping agents can produce a list of relevant products. Online retailers can also help consumers match products to needs. Polyvore, Pinterest, and Gap (gap.com) let consumers mix and match clothes to create outfits. Most automobile sites allow consumers to custom-configure vehicles. Of particular interest are **collaborative filtering** agents, which can predict consumer preferences based on past purchase behavior. Amazon uses a collaborative filtering agent to recommend books and music to customers. Once the system is in place, it can handle millions of users at little incremental cost. The effectiveness of the collaborative filtering agent actually increases as consumers are added to the database. Note that all of these services scale well because they are automated. By contrast, efforts to match product to buyer needs in the brick-and-mortar world can be labor intensive and are quickly overwhelmed as volume increases. Salespeople in retail outlets attempt this chore, but the internet improves on this function by being on call anytime and by matching buyers with products across retailers. Of course, this capability puts a burden on electronic retailers to compete on the basis of price or to differentiate their products in a way that is meaningful to the market.

Negotiating Price True price negotiation involves offers and counteroffers between buyer and seller such as might be conducted in person, over the phone, or via e-mail—a two-way dialog. Even so, shopping agents implicitly negotiate prices downward on behalf of the consumer by listing companies in order of best price first. Bidding, on the other hand, is a form of dynamic or flexible pricing in which the buyer gives suppliers an equal opportunity to bid (see Chapter 10). Many businesses currently conduct bidding online. Consumer market auctions include those held by eBay and Amazon. Businesses such as General Electric also solicit online bids from their suppliers. Online bidding effectively widens the supplier pool, thereby increasing competition and lowering prices. Many auction houses allow buyers to program an agent to represent them in bidding against other buyers or their agents.

Process Transactions Studies show that electronic channels lower the cost to process transactions dramatically. The National Association of Purchasing Management places the cost of manually processing an average purchase order at $79—mainly due to labor costs.

LOGISTICAL FUNCTIONS Logistical functions include physical distribution activities such as transportation and inventory storage, as well as the function of aggregating product. Logistical functions are often outsourced to third-party logistics specialists. RFID tags are an important development for tracking products through the distribution channel (see the "Let's Get Technical" box). **Radio frequency identification (RFID)** tags are used to transmit a signal to scanners, which detect the presence of the RFID tag in products, credit cards, or even under a person or animal's skin.

LET'S GET TECHNICAL

RFID Technology

Tired of waiting in long lines at the grocery store? Never again want to hear the phrase, "I'll have to send someone to check that price" when you just want to buy a carton of milk? Many customers become frustrated when making trips to supermarkets or large discount retailers. No matter when they choose to shop, the lines are often long, wasting valuable time. With the onset of RFID technology solutions, the supermarket of the future may not have lines at all. All customers might have to do is swipe their credit card and walk out the door.

Radio frequency identification (RFID) technology is an old technology in the field of automatic identification, but it has recently been getting lots of attention. Common forms of automatic identification include the classic bar codes, used on millions of consumer products, and magnetic strips, commonly found on credit cards. Automatic identification replaced manual entry, drastically decreasing error rates, and saving companies millions of dollars. Nonetheless, some action is required: cashiers run the UPC bar codes over the scanner and customers swipe their credit cards in the readers. However, RFIDs, which were originally developed during World War II, do not require manual intervention. As their price continues to fall, RFIDs may well revolutionize the field of automatic identification.

As the technology's name indicates, radio frequencies are used to communicate between the RFID tag and a scanner. This technology requires three components: an RFID tag, an RFID scanner, and a recording device (i.e., a computer). The RFID tag is attached to the product that is being tracked. The tag is made up of an RFID chip and a mini-antenna. The simplest tags can cost anywhere between $0.07 and $0.15. As the popularity of RFID tags has increased, their prices have declined. The goal of EPCglobal, an industry standards group, is to have the price drop to $0.05 per tag.

The RFID scanner, which can also be called a reader, is connected to the computer. The RFID scanner constantly sends out a low frequency electromagnetic signal (100 kHz to 5.8 GHz). The signal powers the RFID chip and antenna to transmit data back to the scanner. When the scanner receives the information, it sends this data to the computer to store and analyze. As the technology matures, increasing amounts of information can be stored in the RFID chip and transmitted to the scanner.

The distance between the RFID tag and the scanner depends on the size of the RFID chip and mini-antenna. The more sophisticated the chip and the larger the antenna, the farther the tag and scanner can be from each other.

RFID technology has many applications in the distribution and retail industries. RFIDs are already being used to track palettes of products at large distribution centers. As shipments of products enter and exit the distribution center, the movement is automatically tracked with intense accuracy.

RFIDs are also being used at gas and toll stations. Specific gas companies have distributed a small plastic key chain to consumers, which holds the consumer's credit card information. When the consumer purchases gas, he waves the keychain in front of a small reader at the pump. The reader receives the credit card information, authorizes the pumping of the gas, and subsequently charges the credit card. The gas company's intent in providing this service was to increase customer loyalty because the key chains work only at their stations.

Many commuters pass through tollbooths each day on their way to and from work, and they painstakingly wait in lines at busy booths. Local and state governments, such as Pennsylvania, Virginia, and Florida, have implemented RFID solutions. For little or no fee, commuters can purchase a small box that sits near the windshield of the vehicle. The number of the box and a credit card to pay tolls are registered with the transit authority. When the commuter comes to a tollbooth, he or she is allowed to enter a "Fast Pass" lane equipped with the RFID scanner. The scanner obtains the box number and bills the credit card on file. Some booths do not even require the traveler to drop their speed below 55 miles per hour. Another example of RFID in a similar application is with keyless entry systems.

Walmart uses RFID to manage the supply chain with hundreds of its suppliers. The benefits

(*continued*)

include a 16 percent reduction in out-of-stocks as well as 63 percent more effective restocking. RFID also ensures proof of delivery and eases reconciliation of purchase orders.

The goal is to eventually replace bar codes company wide and to increase efficiency within the supply chain process.

Although the RFID solution will benefit Walmart, the large retailer also promises benefits for its suppliers. These benefits include notifications when goods arrive at stores and when they enter the sales floor, which allow suppliers to better track demand. Walmart also places RFID tags on point-of-purchase displays used as end caps and other displays for in-store promotions. These displays are often costly to produce, according to suppliers, and end up left in the back room. With the RFID tags, suppliers can track the deployment of the displays. As a result, new products reach the shelves three times faster.

With the world's largest retailer backing RFID technology, it appears poised for success. Distribution networks worldwide may need to adopt RFID standards as part of the cost of doing business.

Physical Distribution Most products sold online are still distributed through conventional channels. Yet digital content can be transmitted less expensively from producer to consumer over the internet: text, graphics, audio, and video content. The alternative step, physical distribution of digital product, is comparatively expensive. Trisenx experimented with transmitting digital smells and tastes over the Web, and Professor Bob Stone of Birmingham University attaches smells to video games (such as napalm, raw sewage, and more lovely scents)! This is done with a computer peripheral device.

Aggregating Product In general, suppliers operate more efficiently when they produce a high volume of a narrow range of products. Consumers, on the other hand, prefer to purchase small quantities of a wide range of products. Channel intermediaries perform the essential function of aggregating product from multiple suppliers so that the consumer can have more choices in one location. Examples of this traditional form of **aggregation** include online category killers such as Amazon.com, with a broad product mix. In other cases, the internet follows a model of virtual aggregation, bringing together products from multiple manufacturers and organizing the display on the user's computer (e.g., Pinterest using social commerce). In the case of shopping agents, the unit of aggregation is the product page at the online store. A search for a particular product will produce a neatly arranged table with comparative product information and direct links to the vendor pages.

Third-Party Logistics—Outsourced Logistics A major logistics problem in the B2B market is reconciling the conflicting goals of timely delivery and minimal inventory. One solution for many companies is to place inventory with a **third-party logistics** provider such as UPS or FedEx. Taking logistics one step further, third parties can also manage the company's supply chain and provide value-added services such as product configuration and subassembly. The logistics providers will even handle the order processes, replenish stock when needed, and assign tracking numbers so customers can find their orders. Alcatel, for example, uses UPS to manage orders and distribute cellular phones in Europe.

In the B2C market, a major logistics problem is product returns (reverse logistics), which can run as high as 15 percent. Customers frequently complain about the difficulty and expense of returns. Some Web sites offer to pay return shipping. But even with a credit for return shipping, the customer still has to weigh the package, pay shipping fees up front, and schedule pickup (or deliver to a shipping location).

The United States Postal Service (USPS) has introduced a clever program to ease the return process. Merchants can install software on a site that allows them to authorize customers to download and print postage-paid return labels. The customer simply boxes the item, slaps on the label, and leaves it by the door for the letter carrier. Even if a Web site does not participate in the USPS program, customers can still weigh their packages at home and download appropriate postage onto a laser-printed label using a service from eStamps.

In the C2C market, eBay has formed a partnership with brick-and-mortar Mail Boxes Etc. After auctions close, sellers take their items to Mail Boxes Etc. to be packaged and shipped.

The Last Mile Problem One big problem facing online retailers and logistics managers is the added expense of delivering small quantities to individual homes and businesses. It is much less expensive to send cases of products to wholesalers and retailers and let them break the quantities into smaller units for sale. Two other problems arise: 25 percent of deliveries require multiple delivery attempts, thus increasing costs, and 30 percent of packages are left on doorsteps when no one is home, opening the way for possible theft (Laseter, Torres, and Chung, 2001). With billions of packages delivered in the United States, e-marketers are looking for ways to save costs and solve this last mile problem.

Innovative firms have tried four solutions; however, none have solved the problem thus far. First is a smart box. The consumer buys a small steel box that comes with a numeric keypad connected to the internet via a two-way modem. Delivery people, such as FedEx or the USPS, receive a special code for each delivery and use it to open the box and leave the shipment. This activity is sent via the internet and recorded in a database. The consumer uses his or her own code to open the box and receives the delivery—also recorded in the database. This solution is efficient and secure for consumers who are willing to pay the hefty box fee. Brivo introduced this technology but no longer offers this product.

A second solution involves a retail aggregator model. Consumers can have packages shipped to participating retailers, such as local convenience stores or service stations; then, consumers pick up the package—not as convenient as the current method. In Japan, NTT DoCoMo customers can use their Web-enabled cell phones to order goods for shipment to local 7-Eleven stores. The third solution calls for special *e-stops*, storefronts that exist solely for customer drive-through and package pickup.

Finally, many multichannel retailers allow customers to order online for offline retail delivery. Recreational Equipment, Inc. (REI), the outdoor apparel and gear retailer, began offering this service in its 67 U.S. retail stores in mid-2003. Within one month 25 percent of Web sales were picked up in the offline store with the added bonus of $32 of impulse buying during the same visit (Budis, 2004). Today, many retailers offer this option, including Walmart.

FACILITATING FUNCTIONS Facilitating functions performed by channel members include market research and financing.

Market Research Market research is a major function of the distribution channel. The benefits include an accurate assessment of the size and characteristics of the target audience. Information gathered by intermediaries helps manufacturers plan product development and marketing communications. Chapter 6 explored market research in detail, and Chapter 7 examined internet user behavior. This section will look at the costs and benefits of internet-based market research.

The internet affects the value of market research in five ways. First, some of the information on the internet, especially government reports, is available for free. Second, managers and employees can conduct research from their desks rather than making expensive trips to libraries and other resource sites. Third, information from the internet tends to be timelier, as when advertisers monitor banner ad click-through. Fourth, Web-based information is already in digital form, so e-marketers can easily load it into a spreadsheet or other software. Finally, because so much consumer behavior data can be captured online, e-marketers can receive detailed reports. For example, comScore (comscore.com) produces a site interaction report that details to what extent a site shares audience with another site—showing exclusive and duplicated audience.

Nonetheless, little market research is free. Even free government reports require a significant investment of human resources to distill the material into a useful form for making decisions. Furthermore, many firms need access to costly commercial information such as comScore reports, which sell for about $50,000 each.

Financing Financing purchases is an important facilitating function in both consumer and business markets. Intermediaries want to make it easy for customers to pay in order to close the sale. Most online consumer purchases are financed through credit cards or special financing plans, similar to traditional store purchases. However, some consumers are understandably concerned about divulging credit card information online—resulting in safeguards that probably make online purchasing the most secure channel for consumers.

Online merchants have a major concern as well: How do they know that they are dealing with a valid consumer using a legitimate credit card? The major credit card companies have, therefore, formed **Secure Electronic Transaction (SET)** as a vehicle for legitimizing both the merchant and the consumer as well as protecting the consumer's credit card number. Under SET, the card number goes not to the merchant but to a third party with whom the merchant and consumer communicate to validate one another as well as the transaction. The communication occurs automatically in the background and places no technical burdens on the consumer. However, SET is so technical that most consumers do not appreciate its subtleties. Furthermore, most merchants do not want to pay for costly upgrades to a SET system.

Still, SET has been successful inside the United States, in part because of legislative protections: U.S. consumers have a maximum $50 liability for purchases made with a stolen card. The card issuer usually waives the $50 in order to retain customers, and some issuers now advertise $0 liability for online purchases. However, that legal protection does not exist in some countries, and consumers may be liable for all charges on their card up to the time they report it stolen.

In the B2B market, brokers and agents often extend lines of credit to buyers to facilitate purchases. These lines of credit significantly speed the buying process and make the online channel more attractive.

Distribution System

The distribution channel is actually a system, when viewed by the flow of products, information, and finances along the channel—a unified system of interdependent organizations working together to build value as products proceed through the channel to the consumer. This perspective recognizes that a channel system is stronger when its participants compete in a unified way with other channel systems.

Defining the scope of the channel as a system can be done in three ways:

1. The first is to consider only distribution functions that are downstream from the manufacturer to the consumer, the traditional definition of the distribution channel.
2. The second is to consider only the supply chain upstream from the manufacturer working backward to the raw materials, the traditional definition of the supply chain.
3. The third view is to consider the supply chain, the manufacturer, and the distribution channel as an integrated system called the **value chain** (a more recent name for the value chain is *integrated logistics*). Many refer to the supply chain *as* the value chain. By this definition, the supply chain includes upstream and downstream activities as well as processes internal to the firm. See Exhibit 11.10 in which the circles represent firms in a network of suppliers, manufacturers, and intermediaries.

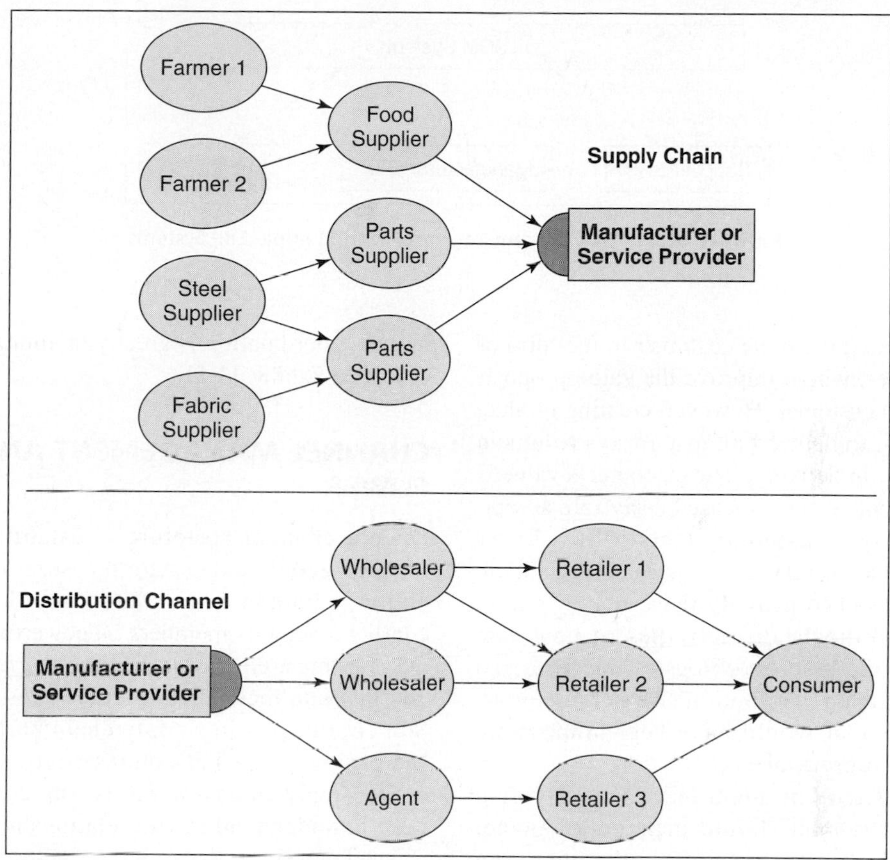

EXHIBIT 11.10 Supply Chain + Distribution Channel = New Definition of Supply Chain

Redefining the supply chain to include the entire value chain is now mainstream, reflecting what a great number of practitioners mean when they talk about supply chain management. Thus, value chain, integrated logistics, and supply chain are equivalent terms.

This definition of the supply chain is used to describe the field of **supply chain management (SCM)**. SCM refers to the coordination of flows in three categories: material (e.g., physical product), information (e.g., demand forecast), and financial (e.g., credit terms). The word *flow* evokes the image of a continuous stream of products, information, and finances flowing among the channel members much as blood and nerve impulses flow through an organism. The most important flow is that of information because creation of the physical product and the financing depend on the information.

The Holy Grail in supply chain management is "scan one, make one—and deliver it fast." This process is known as **continuous replenishment**. For more complex products such as computers, the goal is to build to order and deliver quickly. Both continuous replenishment and **build to order** help to eliminate inventory. In turn, this practice reduces costs because inventory is expensive to finance; it also increases profits by avoiding unsold inventory going stale and being sold at a discount. The cost savings

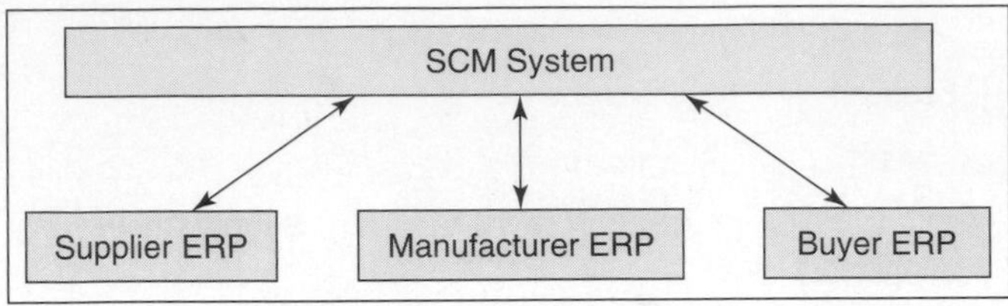

EXHIBIT 11.11 SCM System Interfaces with Multiple ERP Systems

may be passed on to the customer in the form of lower prices, which improve the value proposition for the customer. However, creating product in response to demand almost always results in some delay in delivery. The customer's value is increased only if the increased delays are acceptable. Today's customer wants it all—lower prices, quick delivery, and custom configuration. The only way to provide these benefits is to tightly coordinate the activities of upstream suppliers, the inner workings of the firm, and the downstream distribution channel—a formidable task that would have been impossible before the information age.

A difficult problem in SCM is deciding which participant should manage a channel composed of many firms. For example, Sun Microsystems designs computers but doesn't build any of them—yet Sun manages the entire supply chain, even the suppliers, of its contract manufacturers. The coordination is made possible by sophisticated SCM software from i2, which operates over the internet. Interestingly, the coordination is cooperative rather than dictatorial. Sun makes customer demand information visible to the suppliers, who then indicate what portion of the demand they can handle. Supply chain management allows for coordination of all supply chain functions into a seamless system, made possible by internet technologies.

Interoperability is especially important in SCM because many of the participants in modern supply chains have **enterprise resource planning (ERP)** systems to manage their in-house inventory and processes. If the individual ERP systems can seamlessly share information with the SCM system, coordination is greatly facilitated in real time. See Exhibit 11.11.

CHANNEL MANAGEMENT AND POWER

Once a channel structure is established, its viability requires a certain measure of coordination, communication, and control to avoid conflict among its members. A powerful channel member must emerge to assume the leadership and institute these required measures, the way Sun coordinates its supply chain participants. Increasingly, market competition is between entire supply chains, which is why e-marketers need to understand power relationships among channel players.

Whenever new information technology is introduced into a distribution channel, it can potentially alter the power relationships among existing channel players. Nowhere has this effect been more evident than with the internet. In many cases, buyer power significantly increased at the expense of the supplier. In other cases, the power of the supplier has come out on top. Walmart gained power over its channels when it introduced electronic systems to notify suppliers of a needed product. This shift caused a major power upheaval in channels where giant manufacturers such as Procter & Gamble had previously been in control. A classic source of power for retailers and distributors has been geographic location. Retailers have built power on the place (location), utility, and restricted access to manufacturers. The internet neutralizes the importance of location and offers new sources of supply for purchasing.

Just as the internet increased the power of buyers by providing access to more information and to more suppliers, it increased the power of suppliers, as well. First, the supplier that takes the early lead online will receive business from consumers and firms eager to shop in this channel. But even in cases when multiple firms are online, suppliers can gain power by establishing structural relationships with buyers. For example, Amazon establishes structural relationships with its customers using its 1-Click ordering and collaborative filtering technologies. Amazon customers switching to another site would have to reenter their billing information and, more important, they would lose access to Amazon's recommendations.

A type of business-to-business (B2B) commerce known as **electronic data interchange (EDI)** is particularly effective for establishing structural relationships between businesses. Electronic data interchange is the computerized exchange of information between organizations, typically used to eliminate paperwork. A buyer logs onto the supplier's computer system and types in an order. The order is electronically conveyed to the supplier and the buyer receives an electronic bill.

The internet puts a new face on EDI with the advent of open standards and interoperable systems. First, the internet replaces expensive proprietary networks, yielding tremendous cost savings. Second, business can use the same computer to interface with multiple suppliers. Third, networks of suppliers and buyers can more easily exchange data using a Web-based interface.

Thus, EDI is based on three key variables: the openness of the system, the transport method (internet or noninternet), and the type of technology used for implementation. Combining these variables in different ways results in many types of EDI most commonly used today, such as Application Program Interface (API) and Extensible Markup Language (XML).

The goal is to create a standards-based open system that runs over the internet so all suppliers and buyers can seamlessly integrate their systems.

DISTRIBUTION CHANNEL METRICS

Does online commerce work? To answer this question, a company must consider its effectiveness in terms of reaching target market segments efficiently and enticing them to purchase online.

B2C Market

E-commerce has grown consistently since its inception; however, the $194.3 billion spent online in 2011 only represents 4.6 percent of all retail sales (Exhibit 11.12). The internet influences offline sales, as previously mentioned (e.g., mobile search while in a brick-and-mortar store). Forrester predicted that cross-channel commerce will increase to five times the dollars currently

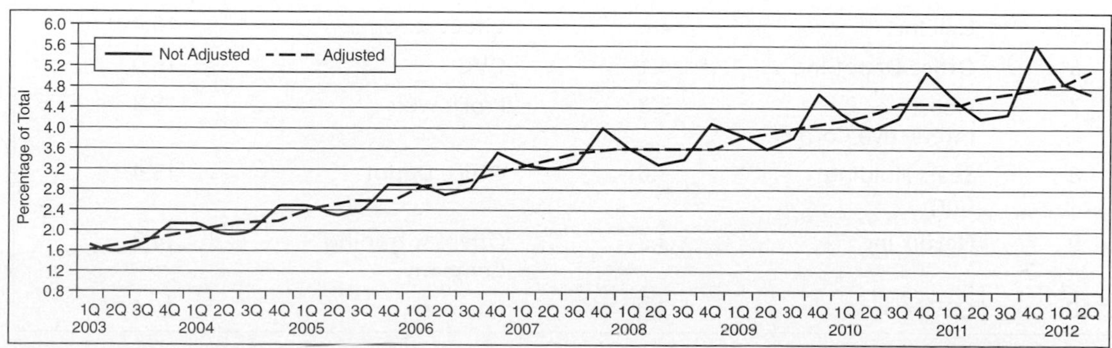

EXHIBIT 11.12 U.S. Retail E-commerce Sales 1st Quarter 2003–2nd Quarter 2012 *Source:* census.gov.
Note: Adjusted for seasonal variation and holiday and trading-day differences, but not for price changes

spent on e-commerce (Abraham, 2011). In what is called "Web-influenced" sales (sales in stores, influenced by online research and marketing), Forrester predicted that these would increase to $1.23 trillion in 2012.

These statistics show general spending levels; however, individual retailer sales vary based on how well their online strategies work. Companies track sales from all channels (online, retail, mobile, social, and catalog) on a daily basis to determine whether they are meeting their objectives and to refine Web sites, cross-channel promotion, and both online and offline communication to achieve better results.

In one global study of online retailers, McKinsey and Company researchers found that two strategies are particularly effective online:

- A high-reach strategy of accumulating large numbers of customers with cost-effective conversion rates (visit the site and buy) for high-frequency purchases of low-margin products and services such as CDs and books (e.g., Amazon.com).
- A niche strategy with narrow focus on a particular product or service category, such as luxury items or apparel (e.g., Dell.com).

For all others, the best use of online retailing is as a complement to offline channels. As you've read repeatedly, it is all about the customer and marketers track every detail to identify winning tactics.

Chapter 2 presented many performance metrics to aid e-marketers in evaluating online retailing and supply chain management. A few of the more important include revenues (as just mentioned), ROI, customer satisfaction levels, customer acquisition costs, conversion rates, and average order values. Conversion refers to the proportion of all Web site visitors who actually purchase on that visit. Exhibit 11.13 displays the top 10 online retailers in terms of both sales and conversion rates in 2011. Interestingly, the top 10 in terms of dollars were not as successful at converting visitors to customers, with the exception of Office Depot. Both dollars sold and conversion rates are good benchmark metrics for e-commerce companies.

Rank	Top Companies Revenues[1]	2011 Web Sales (in billions of $)	Top Companies Conversion[2]	Percentage of Visitors in March 2010
1	Amazon.com	48.1	Schwan's	40.6
2	Staples Inc.	10.6	Woman Within	25.3
3	Apple Inc.	6.7	Blair.com	20.4
4	Walmart.com	4.9	1800petmeds.com	17.7
5	Dell Inc.	4.6	VitaCost.com	16.4
6	Office Depot Inc.	4.1	QVC	16.0
7	Liberty Interactive Corp*	3.8	ProFlowers	15.8
8	Sears Holding Corp.	3.6	Office Depot	15.4
9	Netflix Inc.	3.2	Oriental Trading Company	14.9
10	CDW Corp.*	3.0	Roamans	14.4

EXHIBIT 11.13 Top Ten Online Retailers in 2011 *Source*: [1]Data from Internet Retailer (available at internetretailer.com/ [2]Data from Nielsen Online (available at marketingcharts.com)
* indicates the only companies without a Pinterest account

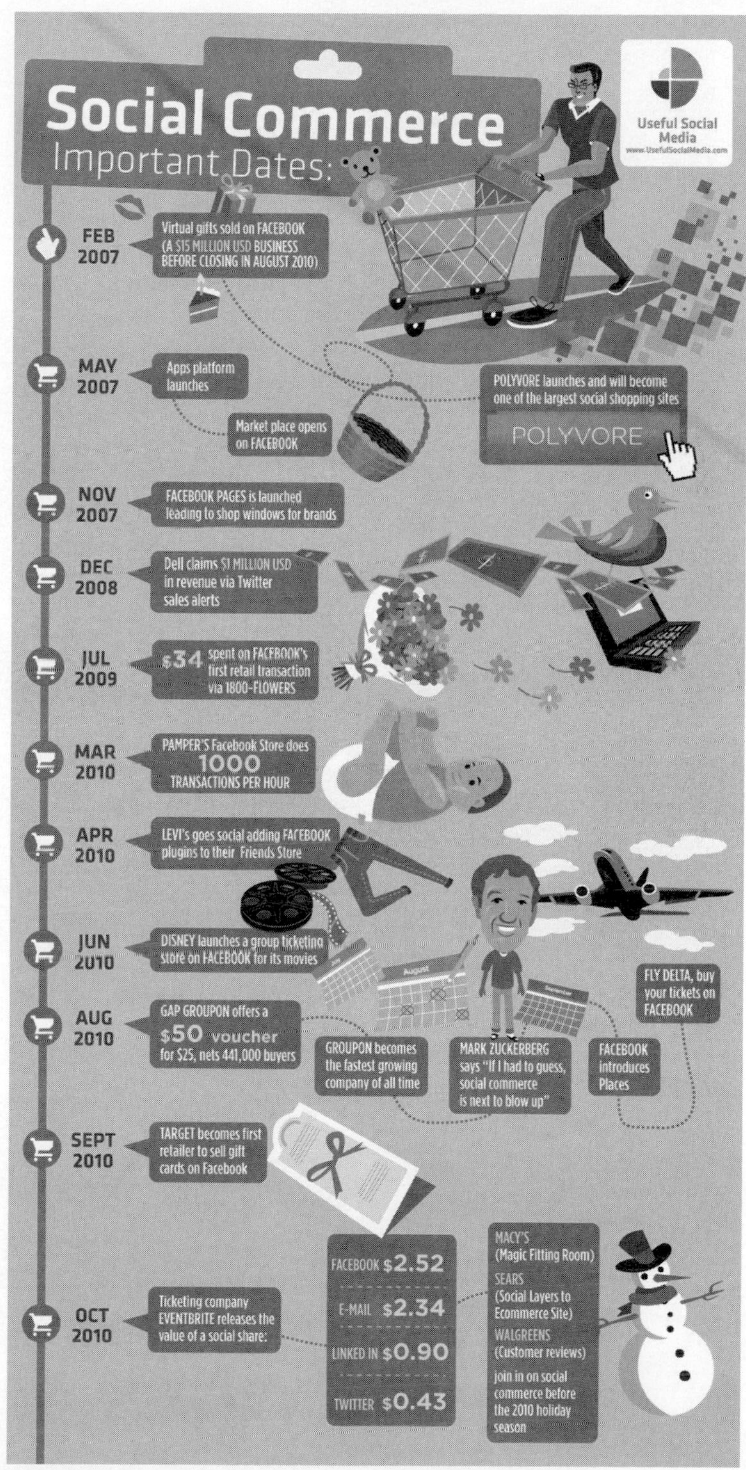

Reproduced with permission from Useful Social Media (usefulsocialmedia.com/)

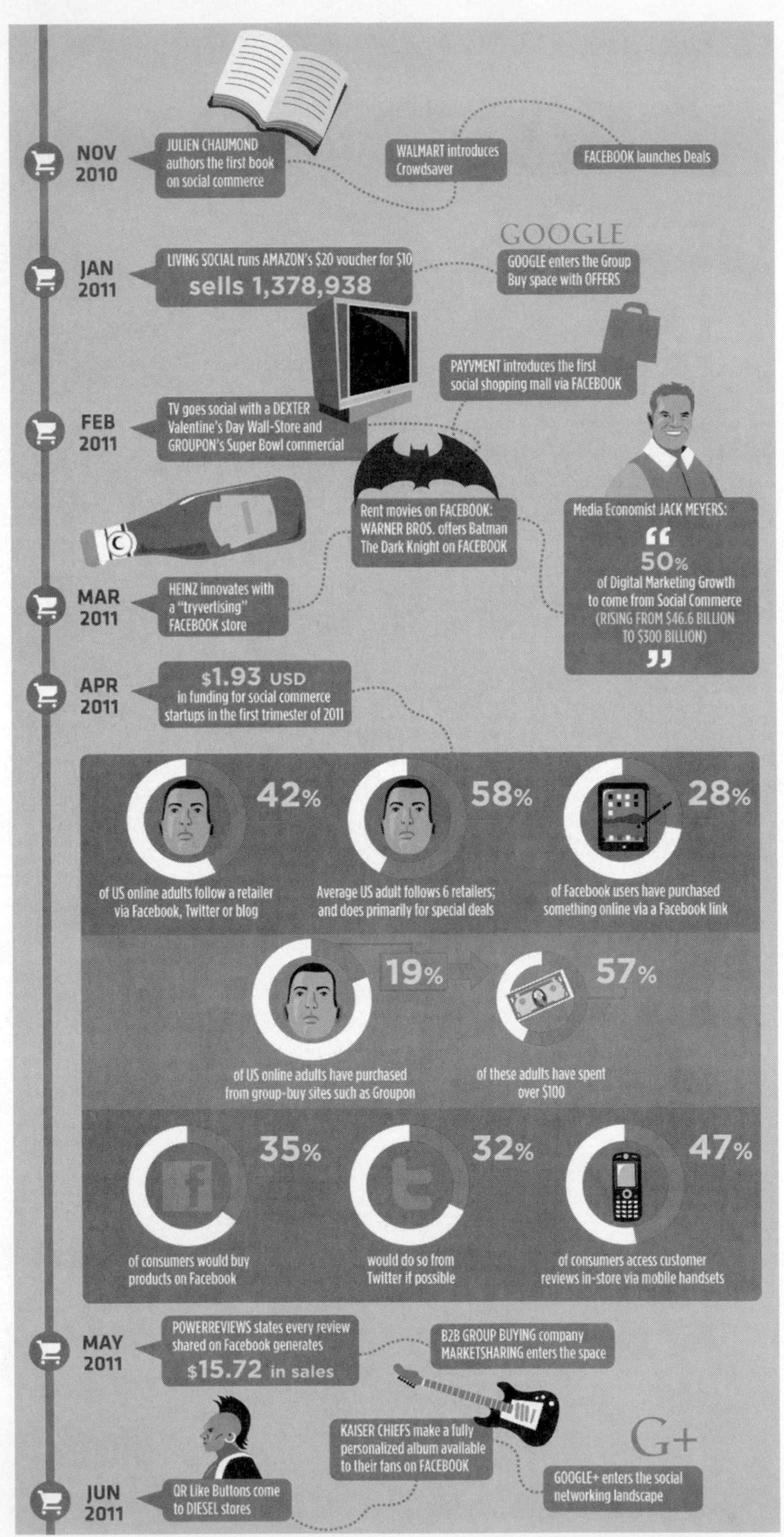
NOV 2010
JULIEN CHAUMOND authors the first book on social commerce
WALMART introduces Crowdsaver
FACEBOOK launches Deals
GOOGLE
JAN 2011
LIVING SOCIAL runs AMAZON's $20 voucher for $10 sells 1,378,938
GOOGLE enters the Group Buy space with OFFERS
PAYVMENT introduces the first social shopping mall via FACEBOOK
FEB 2011
TV goes social with a DEXTER Valentine's Day Wall-Store and GROUPON's Super Bowl commercial
Rent movies on FACEBOOK: WARNER BROS. offers Batman The Dark Knight on FACEBOOK
Media Economist JACK MEYERS:
" 50% of Digital Marketing Growth to come from Social Commerce (RISING FROM $46.6 BILLION TO $300 BILLION) "
MAR 2011
HEINZ innovates with a "tryvertising" FACEBOOK store
APR 2011
$1.93 USD in funding for social commerce startups in the first trimester of 2011
42% of US online adults follow a retailer via Facebook, Twitter or blog
58% Average US adult follows 6 retailers; and does primarily for special deals
28% of Facebook users have purchased something online via a Facebook link
19% of US online adults have purchased from group-buy sites such as Groupon
57% of these adults have spent over $100
35% of consumers would buy products on Facebook
32% would do so from Twitter if possible
47% of consumers access customer reviews in-store via mobile handsets
MAY 2011
POWERREVIEWS states every review shared on Facebook generates $15.72 in sales
B2B GROUP BUYING company MARKETSHARING enters the space
KAISER CHIEFS make a fully personalized album available to their fans on FACEBOOK
G+
GOOGLE+ enters the social networking landscape
JUN 2011
QR Like Buttons come to DIESEL stores

JUL 2011
FACEBOOK requires all game developers to process payments via Facebook Credits
AMERICAN EXPRESS introduces Link, Like, Love
JUL 2011
FACEBOOK stops running Deals- can't match up to other players in the Group Buying Space
SEP 2011
8TH BRIDGE
releases a complex Social Commerce IQ report analyzing 200 of the top US retailers on FACEBOOK.
TOP 5 BRAND IQ'S:
GameStop
Walmart
VICTORIA'S SECRET
CLINIQUE
SEPHORA
KABOODLE merges with StyleSpot to bring together powerful content, commerce, and online communities for women who shop online
TODAY
MORE THAN 800 MILLION PEOPLE ON FACEBOOK AVAILABLE IN OVER 70 LANGUAGES
MORE THAN 200 MILLION PEOPLE ON TWITTER
MORE THAN 10 MILLION PEOPLE ON FOURSQUARE
TOP 3 BRANDS BY FANS
COCA-COLA 34M
WALT DISNEY 28M
STARBUCKS 25M
ARE SELLING ON FACEBOOK
ARE YOU ENGAGING YOUR CUSTOMERS ON THE PLATFORMS THEY USE THE MOST?
DATA COLLECTED FROM SOCIAL COMMERCE TODAY / SOCIAL MEDIA INFLUENCE.
Useful Social Media
http://usefulsocialmedia.com/socialcommerce

Additional important measures relate to affiliate sites and how many customers they refer to the e-commerce site. Also, what proportion of these customers purchase at the site? Online sellers also want to know what sites their customers visit immediately prior to arriving. These measures help marketers evaluate affiliate and other partner effectiveness.

Other important metric priorities reported in a 2012 PulsePoint study include: Optimizing within channels (45), attributing results across channels (28.8), gaining a unified customer view (23.8), consistent branding across channels (13.1), and applying cross channel lessons (13.1) ("Are Marketers Missing. . .," 2012). These reflect the move to more multichannel marketing to attract the omni-channel customer.

M-commerce presents another set of metric opportunities, such as click-to-call rate, secondary actions (what users do after viewing a mobile site/promotional message), click-through rate, search for store directions, text response, time spent with an app, click to social network, and many others. F-commerce also has its own metrics, discussed in later chapters. But above all, marketers want to know click-through rates, conversions to sales, and average order value (including marketing/promotional costs).

B2B Market

The B2B market is big business. It is impossible to measure the amount of dollars that exchanges hands in supply chains because it happens behind company walls. Most B2B business deals still happen via the telephone, fax, and salespeople. The internet has proven to be a much more efficient way for firms to improve the quality, efficiency, and timeliness of orders from each other, spurring growth in e-procurement and process improvement. Businesses use the Web to search for suppliers, but more often they simply facilitate current relationships throughout online ordering, shipment tracking, and more.

In the B2B market, as in B2C, e-marketers should select metrics that relate to their e-marketing goals. It is critical to understand how e-commerce fits into the overall marketing strategy, what the firm expects to accomplish through it, and whether it is working. For B2B, metrics may look at time from order to delivery, order fill levels, and other activities that reflect functions performed by channel participants.

Chapter Summary

The internet increased the power of buyers and suppliers. It also changed the way electronic data interchange is used to establish structural relationships between suppliers and buyers. The major business models used by online intermediaries can be categorized as content sponsorship, direct distribution, infomediary, brokerage models (online exchange and online auction), and agent models (selling agents, manufacturer's agents, shopping agents, and buyer's cooperative). Online retailing (e-commerce, social commerce, m-commerce, and F-commerce) is another important model, including online sales of digital or tangible products, which is done by direct distribution, with intermediaries, or by using multichannel marketing (to attract the omni-channel customer).

A distribution channel is a group of interdependent firms that work together to transfer product and information from the supplier to the consumer. The transfer may be either direct or through a number of intermediaries that perform certain marketing functions in the channel between suppliers and customers. By specializing, intermediaries are able to perform functions more efficiently than a supplier could.

Channel intermediaries include wholesalers, retailers, brokers, and agents. The length of a distribution channel refers to the number of intermediaries between the supplier and the consumer. The shortest distribution channel has no intermediaries; the producer deals directly with customers. Indirect channels include one or more intermediaries. Disintermediation describes the process of eliminating traditional intermediaries. Eliminating intermediaries can potentially reduce costs but functions must be performed by someone. Although the internet was expected to lead to disintermediation and lower prices, new intermediaries are emerging instead.

Three broad types of value-added functions performed in the channel are transactional, logistical, and facilitating functions. Transactional functions refer to making contact with buyers, using marketing communication strategies to raise awareness of products, matching product to buyer needs, negotiating price, and processing transactions. Logistical functions include physical distribution such as transportation and storing inventory and aggregating product; e-marketers often outsource these to third-party logistics providers. Facilitating functions include providing marketing research about buyers and providing financing. The last mile problem is the added expense of delivering small quantities to individual homes or businesses.

The distribution channel is a unified system of interdependent organizations working together to build value as products proceed through the channel from producer to consumer. This perspective recognizes that channels are stronger when they compete in a unified way with other channels. Supply chain management is the coordination of flow of material (e.g., physical product), information (e.g., demand forecast), and financial (e.g., credit terms). Marketers measure the success of their distribution strategies and tactics through a number of important performance metrics.

Exercises

REVIEW QUESTIONS

1. What is a distribution channel?
2. What are the types of intermediaries in a distribution channel?
3. What are the three major functions of a distribution channel?
4. What is supply chain management (SCM) and why is it important?
5. Why are e-marketers concerned with the last mile problem?
6. What is disintermediation? Give an example.
7. What is an infomediary? Give an example.
8. What is multichannel marketing? Omni-channel marketing? Give examples.
9. How do brokers and agents differ?
10. What types of distribution channel metrics are used in the B2C market?
11. Name five reasons consumers abandon online shopping carts.
12. Compare and contrast social commerce, m-commerce, and F-commerce.

DISCUSSION QUESTIONS

13. **The Zappos Story.** Do you think it is viable for Zappos to move to m-commerce, social commerce, and F-commerce? If yes, how could they do this? If no, why not?
14. **The Zappos Story.** This company uses a direct marketing distribution model, selling to customers directly. Review the functions channel intermediaries perform and explain what extra tasks Zappos has undertaken by eliminating intermediaries.
15. How does the value of distribution channel functions change when they become internet based?
16. Do you agree with the more inclusive definition of the supply chain to include the entire value chain? Support your position.

17. Although direct distribution often results in lower prices, what disadvantages does it have for buyers?
18. Each intermediary in the channel has to mark up a product's price to make a profit. Some retailers sell products for almost double the wholesale cost. What would a retailer have to do to add enough value to justify such a markup?
19. How would you suggest e-marketers solve the last mile problem?
20. What is the future of e-commerce, in your opinion? Will it continue to increase? Will it ever become larger in terms of sales than offline retailing? Explain your answers.
21. Which social commerce tactics are the best, from a user perspective? Explain.
22. What is your opinion of F-commerce? Do you think it is appropriate for companies to sell on Facebook? Why or why not and what tactics are appropriate, if any?
23. What digital content do you think will bring the most revenue online in 5 years?

WEB ACTIVITIES

24. Survey 20 people. Ask them to rate their online purchase experience on a scale of 1 to 10, with 10 as the best. If they have never purchased online, try to find out what stops them. Summarize the results.
25. Working in small groups, discuss online shopping experiences and what companies did to meet group members' needs, including follow-up e-mail/customer service.
26. Survey 10 people. Ask them to recall a time when they abandoned a shopping cart online while in the middle of a purchase. Query them about what the online retailer could have done to prevent that from happening. Summarize the results.
27. Visit Polyvore.com and Kaboodle.com. Report on how they are using the social commerce strategy and what are their business models.

CHAPTER 12

E-Marketing Communication: Owned Media

This chapter discusses how marketers use communication media and social media to connect with customers and prospects. After reading an overview of integrated marketing communication (IMC), you will learn about selecting, applying, and evaluating tools for messages in owned media, one of the three main elements of content strategy. You will also gain an understanding of the complex art and science of search engine optimization.

After reading this chapter, you will be able to:

- Define integrated marketing communication (IMC).
- Explain how marketers use the AIDA model and the hierarchy of effects model when making communication decisions.
- List the five traditional marketing communication tools and distinguish between traditional media and social media.
- Identify the differences in control and reach between owned, paid, and earned media.
- Discuss why companies use content marketing.
- Describe the most commonly used owned media and their benefits for marketing.
- Explain how and why marketers use search engine optimization.
- Highlight some of the metrics marketers can use to evaluate owned media performance.

- Datamonitor found that 44% of consumers across 14 countries now say that it's difficult to manage their daily obligations and find time to relax. They expect **the best of the online world** – instant information and immediate gratification – to be built-in to their offline experiences.

- Marks & Spencer's ***Virtual Manicure*** is a free online and in-store service that enables customers to test the U.K. retailer's nail polish range on their own fingers. Shoppers upload an image of their hands and then click on a nail color to see what it would look like before they purchase it.

Will It Blend?

"Will It Blend? That is the question." Thus opens a video starring Blendtec's CEO, Tom Dickson. Wearing a white lab coat and safety glasses, and appearing very scientific yet amused, Dickson stands next to an ordinary-looking blender on a table. The things he blends are anything but ordinary—a wood handled garden rake, a golf club, light bulbs, glow sticks, marbles, and even the sacred iPad and iPhone. The latter received 3.9 million views on YouTube in an 8-month period—and continues to draw eyeballs, with 8.2 million views nearly 3 years after launch in 2010. This was only surpassed by an iPod blending video, which received over 5 million views in a year. Viewing the destruction of these objects in the blender is like watching a train wreck—irresistible. Sending the links to friends is also irresistible. This is viral marketing at its best.

Blendtec is well known in the business market for supplying commercial blenders to Starbucks and others. The goal of the hilarious videos was to build awareness of a new high-quality blender for the consumer market. Dickson is famous for saying that before the videos, "Great products + Weak branding = Weak sales." The videos changed this equation for Blendtec. Retail sales for the $400 blender increased substantially in the first year after the video series began, and 186 videos later in 2008, sales have reportedly increased by 700 percent. Not bad for an initial $100 investment in the first video. Blendtec posts videos both on YouTube and on its microsite WillItBlend.com, and the latter has prompted ancillary revenue streams. Visitors can purchase "Tom Dickson is My Homeboy" T-shirts and the videos themselves.

The brainchild of Dickson, the *Will it Blend?* campaign clearly shows the product benefits in a relevant, humorous, and engaging way. This campaign shows the value of connecting with consumers versus interrupting them with unwanted advertising. It also shows the strength of consumer conversation because over 12,000 viewers posted responses to the iPhone-blending YouTube video, including five video responses prior to YouTube disabling the comment feature. The video was marked as a favorite by nearly 10,000 registered YouTube visitors. It helped that Blendtec added search engine optimization and keyword advertising purchases to draw more traffic to the videos. Brilliant job, Blendtec!

E-MARKETING COMMUNICATION

As the opening example of *Will it Blend?* demonstrates, internet marketing is a powerful way to build brands and start and strengthen relation ships with customers. However, online marketers must be increasingly clever to design and deliver brand messages that capture and hold audience attention—because on the internet, users are in control. They can delete unwanted incoming e-mail and impatiently click away when Web sites don't quickly deliver desired information. Also, the internet allows consumers to widely disseminate their own views and brand experiences via e-mail and social media, shifting the balance of control over brand images from companies to consumers. In this environment, the keys to success include (1) providing relevant, interesting messages when and where target customers want them and (2) engaging internet users by enticing them to upload content, make comments, share content, or simply play with a game or other fun content.

Marketing communication (MarCom) tools that use technology to build brands, in conjunction with value-added product experiences, are important in capturing attention and winning long-term customer relationships. Advertising online still works for building brands, but there are many other innovative techniques that are often more successful—discussed here and in Chapters 13 and 14. And as a bonus, technology lowers the costs of communicating with customers and prospects. For example, companies spend about $33 to serve a customer over the phone, $9.99 through e-mail, and $1.17 using automated Web-based support, according to Forrester Research.

Integrated Marketing Communication (IMC)

Integrated marketing communication (IMC) is a cross-functional process for planning, executing, and monitoring brand communications designed to profitably acquire, retain, and grow customers. IMC is cross-functional because every touch point that a customer has with a firm or its agents helps to form brand images. For example, a Home Depot retail customer might buy and use a product from the Web site, then e-mail or call 1-800 to complain about a problem, write about the problem on a product review site or on her Facebook wall, and finally return the product to the brick-and-mortar retail store. Every contact with an employee, a Web site, a blog comment about the product, a YouTube video, a magazine ad, a mobile app, a catalog, the physical store facilities, and so forth helps the customer form an image of the company. In addition, the product experience, its pricing level, and its distribution channels enhance the firm's marketing communication in a variety of online and offline media to present a strong brand image. The best marketing communication can be undermined if these online and offline contact experiences do not communicate in a unified way to create and support positive brand relationships with customers.

Profitable customer relationships are key to a firm's existence. Successful firms recognize that not all customers are equally valuable—some, such as frequent flyers or buyers, are more important than others. Using technology, firms can monitor profits customer by customer and, based on this analysis, pay more attention to high-value customers both online and offline. Databases and the analysis techniques described in Chapter 6 allow firms to differentiate customers by value, send them appropriate e-mail offers and Web site landing pages, and track the results of company MarCom campaigns. You'll find more about online customer relationship management in Chapter 15.

IMC strategy begins with a thorough understanding of target markets, the brand, its competition, and many other internal and external factors. The Interactive Advertising Bureau suggests a four-step process, good for any marketing communication campaign:

1. Set clear and measurable objectives and strategies.
2. Understand your audience motivations and behavior, especially in social media.
3. Develop a creative approach appropriate for the brand in one or more platforms (earned, paid, or owned media).
4. Define success metrics.

Many IMC experts agree that it should "(1) be more strategic than executional (i.e., more than just about 'one voice, one look'), (2) be about more than just advertising and sales promotion messages, (3) include two-way as well as one-way communication, and (4) be results driven" (Duncan and Mulhern, 2004, p. 9).

IMC Goals and Strategies

Marketers create marketing communication objectives based on overall marketing goals and the desired effects within selected target markets. For instance, Mitsubishi Motors desired to sell more automobiles, so it identified marketing communication goals of (1) driving prospects to the Web site, (2) increasing Web site registrations, and (3) increasing test drive appointments. Sales were the primary goal, and the three communications objectives helped Mitsubishi reach it.

The traditional **AIDA model** (awareness, interest, desire, and action) or the "think, feel, do" **hierarchy of effects** model is part of what guides marketers' selection of online and offline MarCom tools to meet their goals. Both the AIDA and hierarchy of effects models suggest that consumers first become aware of and learn about a new product (think), then develop a positive or negative attitude about it (feel), and ultimately move to purchasing it (do) (Ray, 1973). The thinking, or cognitive, steps are awareness and knowledge. The feeling, or attitude, steps are liking and preference.

Following are examples of social media campaigns at each level, from awareness to behavior:

- **Product awareness:** Sick Puppies is an Australian band that posted a YouTube video entitled "Free Hugs Campaign" and received over 73 million views in the 6 years since its 2006 upload.
- **Interest and Desire:** Dunkin' Donuts used a Facebook crowdsourcing campaign that invited followers to design a new donut, with a prize of $1,200 in free donuts and a promise that the winning entry would go on sale at the stores. It received 90,000 entries in 2010, tripling the Facebook fan base and gathering 53,000 Twitter followers. WaveMetrix measured the conversation sentiment and discovered a substantial amount of positive conversation: 44 percent regarding the promotion, 38 percent discussing the great taste, and nearly 20 percent expressing love for the brand. The negative comments centered on lack of product availability or inconvenient store locations (Harrison, 2010).
- **Behavior/Purchase:** Mazda Motors UK ran a Facebook location "check-in" deal, offering a limited number of 20 percent discounts on the Mazda Mx-5s automobile. Sales increased 34 percent during the February 2011 campaign, selling out of 100 in stock Mx-5s model within 2 weeks of launching the campaign. The check-in promotion motivated 742 people to visit Mazda dealerships so that they could check in with their mobile phones and compete for the discount (see Facebook Success Stories for more information).

Consequently, e-marketers must select the appropriate IMC tools, which may vary depending on the desired results. For example, e-marketers may opt to use traditional IMC tools of sales promotion, such as giving away free iPads, to create awareness and entice recipients to visit a blog; television advertising to create interest and desire; and direct selling by mailed catalog to get the desired action (purchasing). They might combine these with online tools of sales promotion (free music sampling at iTunes), keyword advertising on search engines, or direct selling via e-commerce at the online store.

If an organization wants to build its brands and inform customers, it will operate at the cognitive and attitude levels of the hierarchy of effects, perhaps using blogs, white papers (as PDF files) on Web sites, Web advertising, e-mail campaigns, social network fan pages, and other promotional techniques. When Ourbeginnings.com spent more than $4 million on Super Bowl XXXIV TV ads, it was trying to build awareness of the Web site—and it was so eager to achieve this goal that it spent four times its annual revenue on the campaign. This strategy turned out to be a poor one, which is why now only the strongest internet firms purchase Super Bowl advertising, such as E*TRADE in 2002 and 2008, and Careerbuilder.com in 2010. If a company wants to encourage online transactions (behavior), it needs persuasive communication messages that tell how to complete the transaction on the Web site, over the telephone, and so forth. Postpurchase behavior doesn't appear on the commonly accepted hierarchy, yet many IMC strategies seek to build customer satisfaction after the purchase. E-mail is especially well suited for this goal.

The hierarchy of effects model is important because it helps marketers understand where consumers stand in relation to the purchase cycle so the company can select appropriate communication objectives and strategies that will move consumers closer to purchase and loyalty. Bear in mind that some traditional IMC tools are more appropriate for building awareness and brand attitudes (advertising, public relations), and others are more suited for encouraging transactional behavior (direct marketing, sales promotions, personal selling). Nevertheless, all can be used at each level.

Obviously, businesses want to be sure they find the right social media tactics to achieve their objectives and ROI requirements in this uncharted territory. The best place to start is with the company's objectives. Exhibit 12.1 displays

	Hierarchy Stage	Social Media Strategy
Strategic	awareness	Raise brand awareness
↑	attitude	Improve favorable perception of a brand/product/service
	behavior	Increase customer acquisition
	behavior	Maintain customer loyalty
	attitude	Create user advocacy and/or advocates
		Gather nonscientific/informal research
		Develop new target market insights
	awareness	Develop/create word-of-mouth and viral opportunities
	awareness	Create buzz on branded experience
	awareness	Build incremental reach
	behavior	Increase marketing ROI
	awareness	Increase consumer conversation about brand
	behavior	Drive qualified registrations (newsletter, contests, etc.)
	awareness	Support a new product launch
↓	behavior	Drive site traffic
Tactical	behavior	Increase sales

EXHIBIT 12.1 Social Media Strategies and Tactics
Source: Adapted from "IAB Social Media Buyer's Guide" (2010)

a continuum of social media goals, from broad business strategies to specific brand tactics. We've indicated in which level of the hierarchy of effects each goal falls. The social media are especially well suited at raising brand awareness and creating a buzz, but they can also result in sales when customers read about the brand and either purchase at the Web site or offline. Note that many other IMC tools can achieve these goals and that an integrated marketing communication effort will be the most effective over time.

Traditional Marketing Communication Tools

Consumers tend to think that everything with a company name on it, from a Facebook contest, Web site or YouTube video to an iPhone application, is "advertising." In contrast, marketers have specific definitions of the five key marketing communication tools they use (often called the "promotion mix"). These definitions help when selecting the appropriate tool(s) to create the desired effect in the target market. Following are marketing tool definitions, along with social media platform examples that the company controls (versus user-generated content [UGC]):

- **Advertising: Advertising** is defined as "Any paid form of non-personal presentation and promotion of ideas, goods, or services by an identified sponsor" (Kotler and Armstrong, 2011). Social media examples: Paid message placed in a YouTube video, Facebook or LinkedIn ad, Google AdWords, promoted Tweets, paid product placement in virtual worlds or online games, and ad sponsored content delivered to mobile phones.
- **Public relations: Public relations** involves "Building good relations with the company's various publics by obtaining favorable publicity, building up a good corporate image, and handling or heading off unfavorable rumors, stories, and events" (Kotler and Armstrong, 2011). Social media examples: company- created multimedia content (e.g., online videos, blogs, wikis, photos, book/product reviews, podcasts, answering questions on sites such as eHow and Yahoo! Answers), social media press releases, viral videos and other content, social media events, participation in virtual worlds, social bookmarking and tagging, conversation/commenting on other people's content about brands, and social media apps for mobile phones.
- **Sales promotion: Sales promotion** consists of "Short-term incentives to encourage the purchase or sale of a product or service" (Kotler and Armstrong, 2011). Social media examples: Groupon shared discounts, free sampling of digital products (e.g., music, software, and research or news stories), contests/sweepstakes, games (e.g., advergames, where the product is featured in the game, can be a combination of advertising and sales promotion).
- **Direct marketing: "Direct marketing** is an interactive process of addressable communication that uses one or more. . . media to effect, at any location, a measurable sale, lead, retail purchase, or charitable donation, with this activity analyzed on a database for the development of ongoing mutually beneficial relationships between marketers and customers, prospects, or donors" ("The Power of. . .," 2011–2012). Social media examples: The entire internet and social media might be considered direct marketing; however, specific examples falling only in this category include e-mail and text messaging with offers from companies, behavioral targeting (displaying ads based on user behavior online), location-based systems (such as Foursquare), and RSS feeds of content to individuals opting for it.
- **Personal selling: Personal selling** is defined as "Personal interactions between a customer's and the firm's sales force for the purpose of making sales and building customer relationships" (Kotler and Armstrong, 2011). We extend this definition to the internet by noting that the

1:1 interaction can also be done online and not only in person. Social media examples: Chat bots that allow for conversation on a Web site (also called virtual agents/assistants) and sales lead generation tools.

In general, marketers have the least control over the advertising tool because they are placing messages in someone else's media platform, and the medium will have technical, legal, content, and ad size requirements. In addition, companies must develop the advertising content and also pay for the space, whereas the other tools only require staff time or technology costs to develop the content. Also, note that marketers combine many of these tools for increased e-marketing effectiveness, such as when an advertisement carries a sales promotion discount offer or link to a public relations content (such as a video). For example, an ad intended to build awareness of a new product will more likely compel users to purchase if the ad also carries a link to the product page and a limited time discount offer.

These tools have been used for decades in traditional media (such as television, radio, magazines, newspapers, and outdoor spaces), but social media opportunities are really pushing marketers to redefine the tools. They still constantly use these tools; however this way of organizing marketing communication no longer works well due to the incredible amount of digital media available that use creative technologies. Thus, marketers often discuss IMC in one of the following ways:

- **Senders and recipients.** "**1 to 1**" is communication from a single marketer to a single recipient, as can occur with personal selling, database marketing, and some direct marketing tactics. "**1 to many**" occurs when a single marketer sends communication to many people at once, such as with traditional television advertising, sales promotion coupons, or public relations events. "**Many to many**" occurs when consumers talk in social media to each other.
- **Media type.** Marketers speak of traditional media (television, radio, newspapers, outdoor, and so forth), new media (internet), and social media (such as social networks).
- **Owned, paid, and earned media.** This system depends on who is communicating and who owns the medium (the company owns the medium and pays for space elsewhere or others talk about the company in social media and elsewhere). A recent Google search shows that many marketers are moving to this way of organizing, understanding, and selecting marketing communication goals and tactics. Therefore, we follow suit and organize this and the next two chapters using this system.

One difficulty now facing marketers is how to retain control over brand images in light of the social media, the amount of user control online, and the degree of trust consumers have in one another (and not in companies). The answer is that they can't. Instead, companies can use the brand Web site, blogs (owned media), display ads on Web sites (paid media), and many social media to tell the company story; then they must monitor the internet for conversations about their brands (earned media), responding when appropriate. See Exhibit 12.2 for the varying degrees of control and audience reach marketers have over messages using various communication models and example tactics, previously discussed.

Owned, Paid, and Earned Media

The term *media* formerly meant only traditional media. Now the definition is more general: **Communications media** are communication channels used to disseminate news, information, entertainment, and promotional messages. Digital media can take many different forms including text, images, audio, or video. Examples include online video, product review site, the online newspaper, a mobile phone app, and e-mail. Even word-of-mouth communication can be considered media (yes, your mouth or fingers on the keyboard). **Social media** are one media type with one differentiating characteristic: They blend technology and social interactions for the

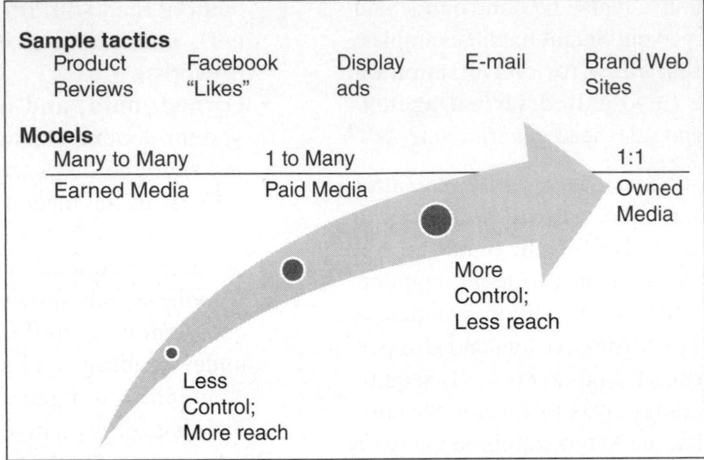

EXHIBIT 12.2 Marketer's Control and Reach with Sample IMC Tactics and Models

co-creation of content and value. That is, people use them for social interactions and conversations. In this definition, "people" collectively refers to organizations, their employees, customers and prospects, and the general population of internet users.

For disseminating content, media can be either paid or free. By "free," we mean that marketers do not have to pay for the space to run their message, but they do often have to pay for technology software and hardware, and employee and other costs related to producing or distributing the communication piece.

Forrester's Industry Analyst Sean Corcoran developed a rubric to explain the roles, definitions, benefits, and challenges of three categories of all media (traditional, internet, and social) (Kim, 2010). Many others have subsequently revised this rubric to classify all digital media into three categories, as previously mentioned (Exhibit 12.3):

- **Owned media** carry communication messages from the organization to internet users on channels that are owned and, thus, at least partially controlled by, the company. Owned media offline include company brochures, catalogs, signs, promotional items (e.g., branded pens), and more.
- **Paid media** are properties owned by others who are paid by the organization to carry its promotional messages (e.g., advertising). The company controls the content; however, the media have content and technical requirements to which the advertisers must adhere (thus, less control than owned media). Paid media offline include traditional advertising in magazines, newspapers, television, radio, outdoor, cinema, in stores, and more.
- **Earned media** are when individual conversations become the channel: messages about a company that are generated by social media authors (such as bloggers), traditional journalists on media Web sites and by internet users who share opinions, experiences, insights, and perceptions on Web sites and mobile applications. This is sometimes also called user-generated media (UGM) or user-generated content (UGC). Offline, earned media includes word-of-mouth and stories about the company or brands in traditional media. Companies have the least amount of control over this media channel; however, they respond to customer conversation and try to guide it toward their positive brand messages.

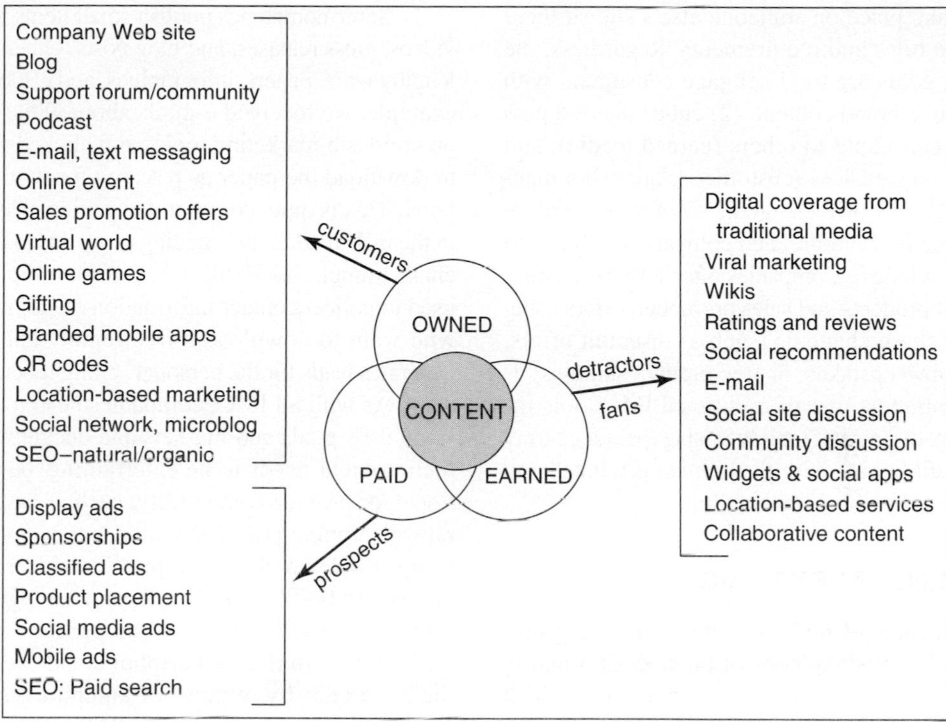

EXHIBIT 12.3 Owned, Paid, and Earned Media Are All Content Driven

IMC campaigns will have both owned and paid media components as their foundation in order to achieve earned media objectives—such as a YouTube video it creates (owned) and an ad on Facebook (paid). These, in turn, will help motivate earned media components, such as when consumers comment on the videos or pass the video link along on their Facebook walls and other media (earned). If the video becomes hugely popular, bloggers and traditional journalists might discuss it (earned). Exhibit 12.4 displays this phenomenon.

You will read about owned media in this chapter, paid in Chapter 13 and earned in Chapter 14. Note that many new social and other high tech media techniques do not fit well into the traditional marketing communication tools; thus, this is a more inclusive way to organize the IMC field. Also, many of the traditional IMC tools are used in more than one of the three types of media.

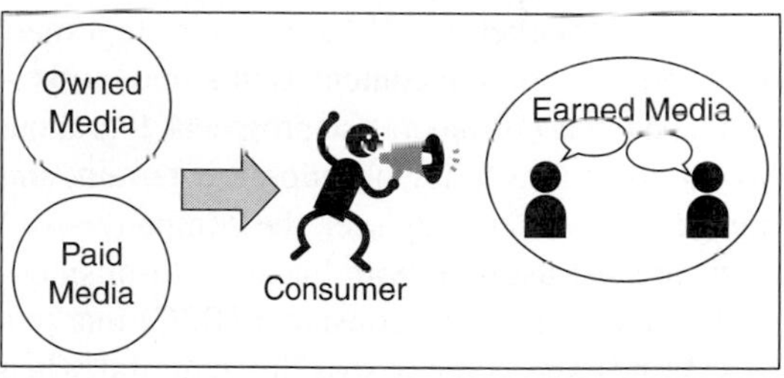

EXHIBIT 12.4 Owned and Paid Media Drive Earned Media

OWNED MEDIA

In this chapter, we will discuss some of the e-marketing media channels that are fully or partially controlled by the organizations who create the lion's share of the multimedia content. For example, a company's Web site and e-mail are totally controlled by the company, but its Facebook page and many other tactics are conducted on "borrowed space." This means that some company-owned media take place on someone else's site so there are more rules and requirements. Regardless, the primary goals are to (1) engage consumers with the positive brand content; (2) entice them to pass this content along to others (earned media); and (3) to exercise CRM (customer relationship management)—all of these goals attempt to increase commerce for brand-related companies (initial and repeat purchases). Companies often inform consumers about products and sales promotion offers using some of these channels (such as discount offers, contests/sweepstakes, or free product samples) as well. Marketers use all traditional IMC tools for owned media, except for advertising (paid media).

It all begins with the content produced and distributed by companies online.

CONTENT MARKETING

Content marketing is a strategy involving creating and publishing content on Web sites and in social media. This is an interesting trend, in which companies are organizing themselves as media publishers online. Marketers have long created content offline when they create paper flyers, newsletters, brochures, catalogs, infomercials, and DVDs ("interrupt" marketing). What is new is that marketers now use digital content as inbound marketing that attracts customers and prospects. It is about having content available to inform, entertain, and engage users when they seek the company—and most internet users in both business-to-business (B2B) and business-to-consumer (B2C) markets do searches and come across this material when shopping. For example, instead of placing a banner ad that might receive as little as 0.5 percent click-through, *Will it Blend?* created video content that entertained, engaged, and enticed users to visit the company Web site to learn more.

All owned media can be considered content marketing. However, now many marketers see themselves as publishers online and organize internally to include a content manager and staff with journalism or multimedia production experience. This is important and the largest expense, because content needs to be fresh online. There are way too many companies with out-of-date Web sites, Facebook pages, and infrequent posts on blogs and Twitter.

Some companies publish small items, such as videos, press releases, and blog posts. Others create lengthy white papers, infographics, and eBooks. For example, we received e-mails about white papers on various e-marketing topics and clicked through to download the paper as research for writing this book. This is quite common for getting sales leads in the B2B market, thus adding prospects to the purchase funnel. See Exhibit 12.5 for a sample form used to collect contact information from prospects who want to download a free report. This tactic generates leads for the personal selling function.

As with all IMC, companies need to understand their goals and markets and decide whether their content needs to be entertaining, be educational, or provide some utility, such as an interest rate or shipping price calculator. For example, the Camp Finder mobile app provides information on over 15,000 U.S. RV parks and campgrounds. Users can find the nearest campground via the GPS feature in their smartphone and then filter their searches by reviews or amenities, such as showers (see camp-finder.com). It surely took a lot of staff time to gather all this information for publishing in the app database.

Note that companies can monetize their owned media content in three important ways. First, they can sell digital content on their media properties, such as white papers, music, software, or online Webinars (or many other products). Second, they can accept Google's Ad Sense or other types of ads and receive payment when users click on

Please fill out this form to receive your free white paper

First name*
Last name*
E-mail*
Company*
Title
Zip code*
Industry* --None--
Area of interest* --None--
Number of employees* --None--
Contact me ☐ Yes

EXHIBIT 12.5 Example Lead Generation Form

these ads. These ads can appear on a company's own Web site or blog, and also in multimedia content it uploads elsewhere, such as ads shown in their own YouTube videos (in this case, the company shares revenue with the site owner, YouTube). The third way is to become an affiliate of another Web site, such as Amazon. Companies receive revenue when users click on a book or other product featured on its blog or other social media property and subsequently purchase it on Amazon. The business models discussed in previous chapters outline many other ways to monetize owned media.

Next, we present some of the most used owned media.

Web Site

Marketing public relations (MPR) includes brand-related activities and nonpaid, third-party media coverage to positively influence target markets. Thus, MPR is the marketing department's portion of PR directed to the firm's customers and prospects in order to build awareness and positive attitudes about its brands. Blendtec's *Will it Blend?* videos did a brilliant job using MPR with its owned content. MPR activities using internet technology include the Web site content itself, online events, and many other online tactics discussed in this chapter.

According to one estimate, there were 555 million Web sites at the end of 2011 (royal .pingdom.com). Every organization, company, individual, or brand Web site is an MPR tool because it serves primarily as an electronic brochure, including current product and company information. In Chapter 7, you learned that most internet users purchase online and even more use the internet to gather information before shopping either online or offline. This underlines the importance of the company Web site and its tactics to be found via search engines. The Web site is far from dead, as some suggest. For example, Butterball's site (butterball.com), which features cooking and carving tips, received 550,000 visitors in one day during Thanksgiving week. Although it costs the firm money to create such a Web site, it is not considered advertising (paid-for space on another firm's site).

Several advantages come with using the Web for publishing product information. First, the Web is a low-cost alternative to paper brochures or press releases sent in overnight mail. Second, product information is often updated in company databases, so Web page content can be updated more easily. Finally, the Web can reach new prospects who are searching for particular products (inbound marketing). Many books discuss how to create effective Web sites—thus, the topic is beyond the scope of this book. The most important point is to create a site that satisfies the firm's target audiences better than the competition and to keep populating it with current content. Web sites can entertain (games and electronic postcards), build communities (online events and social media), provide a communication channel with the customer (customer feedback, forums, and customer service), provide information (product selection and purchase, product recommendation, and retailer referrals), and assist in many other ways.

The Web site is a door into a company, and must provide inviting, organized, and relevant content. Exhibit 12.6 shows the U.S. Census Bureau front door (home page) with a good navigation system to find population statistics. It also now offers a mobile phone app for monitoring economic indicators. During Census years, running population clocks display its key "product"—population data. It is difficult to make a simple Web doorway when there is such an abundance of data and tens of thousands of Web pages on the site, and we think the Census site is clear, user friendly, and easy to navigate.

Microsites are Web sites designed for a narrow purpose, with only three to five pages. For example, WillitBlend.com is a microsite containing only the *Will it Blend* videos. It also contains many social media hooks (such as an RSS subscription button). The company's main site is blendtec.com, and the microsite links to a store for blender purchase on the main site. However, many marketers have noticed that linking a microsite to the company's main site dilutes its efforts to build a large presence on search engines (because Google sees them all as related and not separate sites warranting separate

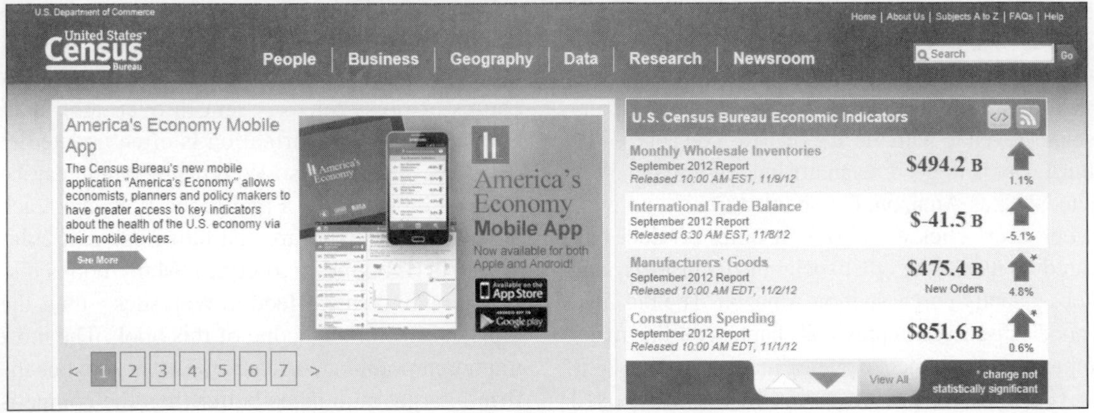

EXHIBIT 12.6 U.S. Census Bureau Web Site Home Page *Source:* census.gov

links on a search results page). Other examples of microsites include one for a specific model of automobile, specific television program, or contest site (such as "In an Absolut World").

Web Site Landing Pages

Landing pages are closely related to Microsites because they are often stand-alone Web pages. Unless headed to a particular Web site, most people begin their internet experience by typing key words at Google or another search engine. Internet users also click on ads, links in social media, e-mail links, and many other places seeded with links to company Web sites. A **landing page** is a unique page that appears after a user clicks on a link associated with a Web site. For example, if a user does a branded search for something like "Dell laptops," they will likely see the link to Dell.com/laptops, not the home page. And below that in the Google search engine results page will be a series of other links, such as "Official Dell Coupons," "Bookmark Our Black Friday Site," "Small Office Laptop Deals," and more. Each of these links takes the user to a specific landing page appropriate to the headline. Similarly, if a user clicks on a Facebook ad for a special event, the page promoting that event will appear instead of the company home page.

The trend is for companies to create many different landing pages that match key words, current special offers, ads, and more. These pages have attention getting headlines that match the offer or key words from the referring link. They also have specific images and copy on the page to match the source link and compelling words to move users to action (such as purchase). This makes the page more relevant to the user, versus linking to the generic home page.

A/B testing is when there are two versions of a Web page with similar content and images for testing which performs better. Companies conduct A/B tests on landing pages to be sure they optimize click-through rates and conversion to purchase. Some of the variations might include amount of text (heavy/light), animation versus static content, and various images (such as only the product or a person using the product). Sometimes companies only change one element on the page so they will know for certain what caused the performance difference. When marketers use several different elements on the two pages they will use multivariate testing to find statistical significance in the page differences (recall that multivariate testing is a comprehensive statistical test of more than one variable).

Companies often track landing pages at a much more detailed level, such as putting tracking links within the page to identify many other metrics. For example, they want to learn which page the customers came from prior to the landing page and where they go next (e.g., Expedia.com knows when you leave the site to check a specific airline site directly). Companies can also tell which areas of the page get more readership and how long people stay in a certain section before scrolling down. Interestingly, marketers can also gather data from mobile users, such as, where they swipe or double finger to enlarge text and whether the user is viewing in portrait or landscape orientation.

CustomInk started selling custom t-shirts and hats in 2000. They are pros at landing pages, offering many different ones. They also change their home page quite often to optimize conversions, considering it a type of landing page. Exhibit 12.7 displays the CustomInk home page. Above the "fold" indicates the portion of content a

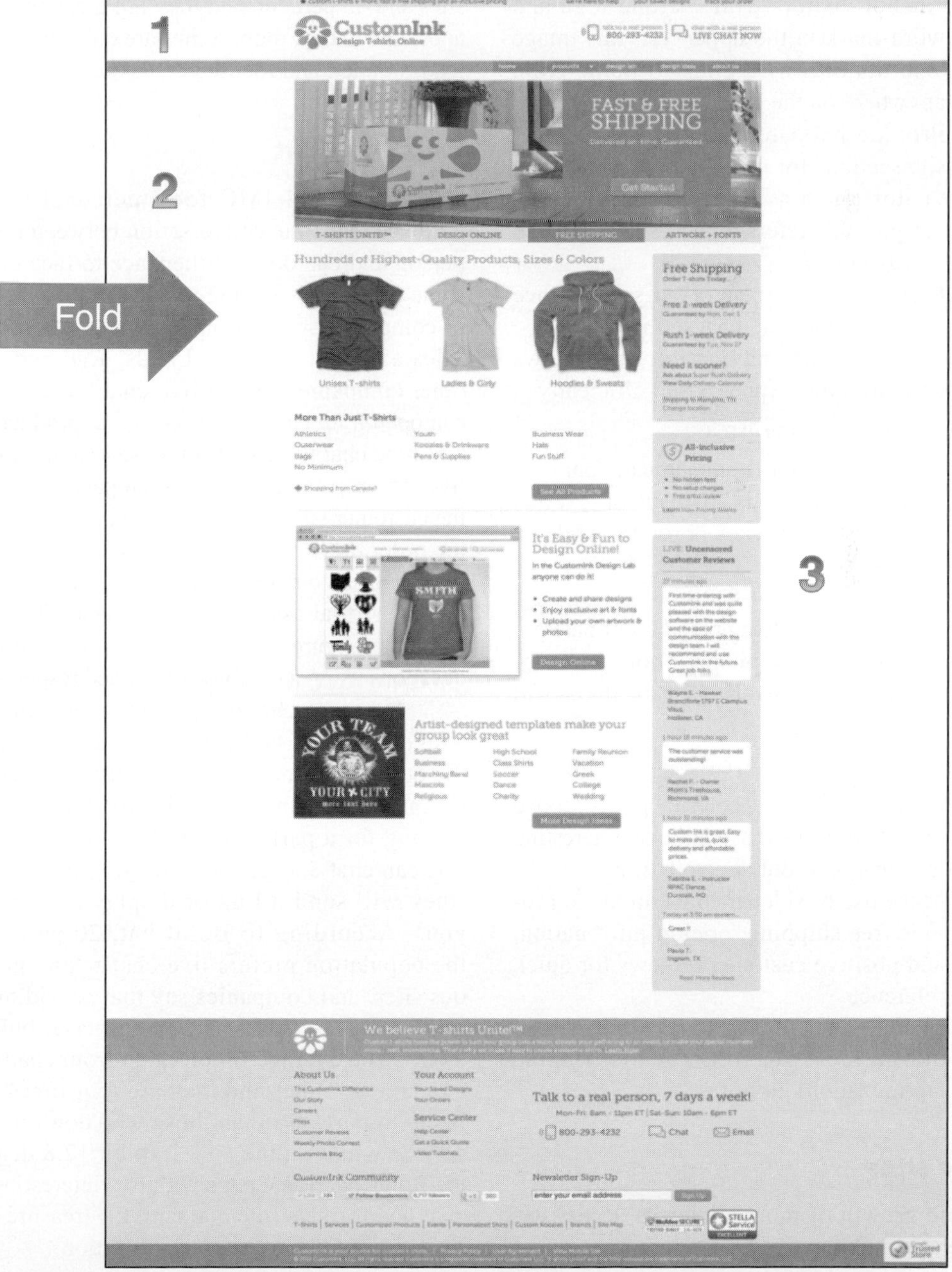

EXHIBIT 12.7 CustomInk Home Page Optimized for Best Results *Source:* customink.com

user sees without scrolling down. The most important and compelling information should appear above the fold. Following is CustomInk's description of the various areas (1, 2, 3 in Exhibit 12.7) and how it optimizes them:

1. "Header
   - Anchor visitors with a strong logo and word-mark in the upper left; this image also doubles as a click-to-home from anywhere on the site.
   - Provide persistent links to functional site sections for returning customers and visitors such as, 'Retrieve your saved design' (this refers to the t-shirt designed by customers).
   - Prominent placement of our sales service phone number and chat service.
   - Persistent site navigation that allows users to browse quickly and efficiently.
2. Primary Messaging Area
   - Use of a rotator to communicate four core messages (rotator is an image or text that changes on each view or rotates while on the page).
   - Persistent strong Call-To-Action in a stand-out color from brand color palate.
   - Complimentary imagery/copy to communicate the offering in an impactful way.
3. Secondary Content Areas
   - Ensure that product content "peeks" above the fold as a cue that additional interesting information is only a scroll away
   - Make use of sidebar conventions to provide free shipping, pricing information, and positive customer reviews for quick reference.
   - Include links to additional products and design ideas for SEO (Search Engine Optimization) purposes."

Mobile sites

The rapid growth of mobile internet access has marketers scrambling to create mobile versions of their Web sites. In fact, in a 2012 study by IBM, 41 percent of global marketers said that their biggest challenge over the next few years is the growth of marketing channels and device choices ("Marketers Challenged to Keep. . .," 2012). In response to this challenge, 46 percent noted that they are currently creating mobile versions of Web sites and 45 percent said they are creating mobile apps. Obviously, mobile sites are quicker to download, simpler, and focused on the key content.

Web Site Chat

One traditional IMC tool, personal selling, involves real-time conversation between a salesperson and customer, either face to face or with some technology mediator, such as the telephone or computer. Some companies provide real-time sales assistance online. Lands' End and many other companies have a live chat feature. Users can open it and ask questions about products in a real-time chat with a customer service representative. The rep can also push Web pages directly to the customer so she can view the product and take the order during the chat session. Then there are the robots: automated **chat bots**, also called virtual agents, virtual assistants, and avatars. These are automated figures that will answer many customer questions using a database of canned responses.

If you are having problems downloading a digital book at audible.com, you can chat with the customer service representative and get her technical assistance immediately. Or, if you are looking for a particular clothing item on a site, you can chat and get help locating it on the site (they will send a link or display the page for you). According to BoldChat, 20 percent of the population prefers live chat while on various sites, and companies say that providing this service increases sales by 20 percent (see boldchat.com). The average order value from chatters is 25 percent higher and they are four times more likely to purchase than those who don't use this service while on the site. Exhibit 12.8 displays the BoldChat home page with two interesting live chat box formats (the one with the treasure chest floats across the page to gain attention).

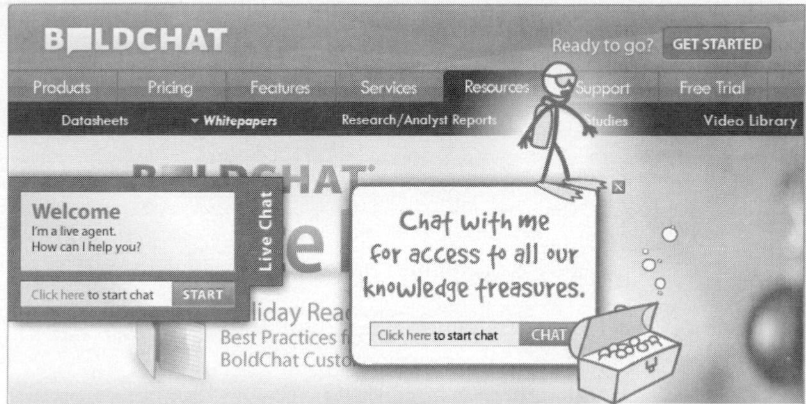

EXHIBIT 12.8 Live Chat Boxes for Web Sites from Boldchat
Source: boldchat.com

Blogs

Blogs (from the term *Web logs*) are Web sites where entries are listed in reverse chronological order and readers can comment on any entry. There were more than 181 million blogs at the end of 2011 (an increase from 35 million in 2006), according to DazeInfo.com. Examples: WordPress, Blogger, and the millions of blogs on company Web sites. According to Nielsen, about 6.7 million people publish on blogging sites, another 12 million blog in social networks, and the remainder on their own sites using blogging technology. When blogs first emerged in 1999, it appeared that they contained irrelevant scribbling about miscellaneous personal topics and would probably not work their way into marketing strategy. How did this change? Marketers began paying attention to blogs because many people writing them had valuable things to say. For instance, Robert Scoble in the Microsoft marketing department wrote about his views on Microsoft's role in the industry—and competitors surely read his musings. Blogs are considered social media because of all the commenting done by blog readers (earned media).

Sometimes blogs are authored by many employees. For example, Engadget, a technology blog, offers many daily posts about new technologies, most by different authors. This blog is always listed in the top three of all blogs on Technorati because of its high readership and activity (with each post generating lots of comments) and high confidence ratings by users. It is helpful to have multiple blog authors to keep the posts frequent, as long as they all follow the goals and style of the blog. The Huffington Post is another extremely popular multiauthor blog.

There are many types of blogs. Many CEOs blog to put a personal face on their companies. When JetBlue had its huge crisis in February 2007, its then-CEO David Neeleman posted blog apologies and introduced the new company Bill of Rights. The Eastman Kodak Company produces a brilliant company blog that is populated by employee stories and photos (1000words .kodak.com).

Many consultants and thought leaders create blogs to disseminate their views and gain clients, promote books, and more. Exhibit 12.9 displays the personal profile of Andy Beal on his blog. Note the user-friendly format for an online resume. Beal has been quite successful with his MarketingPilgrim. com blog, gaining over 3,000 subscribers who follow his fresh commentary on SEO, reputation management, and all things related to e-marketing. Why does he blog? Besides being fun, it keeps him current on his industry and helps him gain paid speaking and consulting jobs.

EXHIBIT 12.9 Consultant Andy Beal's Business Profile Blog
Source: andybeal.com

Marketers also use blogs to draw users to their Web sites. For example, in 2004 Dr. Pepper/Seven-Up introduced the new flavored milk product with a blog written by a cow: Raging Cow Blog. Ghostwritten by six teenagers under the supervision of marketing staff, it sounded like a cow discussing her adventures as she traveled across country. It read like a travelogue written with a Generation Y attitude based on the product positioning: ". . . a milk-based drink 'gone wild' because there are outrageous, intriguing, and delicious flavor combinations." Within 3 weeks of the launch, 20,800 users logged on each day to read the crazy cow ramblings such as (Arnold, 2004):

> Ho hee, we did it! Fate was on our side that night—the moon was in its final quarter (I hear a number of you asking, "How would a cow know diddly about the phases of the moon?" Good question, but ever since that whole jumping over the moon incident, we cows and yonder moon have been TIGHT.)

This type of strategy can backfire, however. When Jim and Laura took their RV across country and camped in Wal-Mart parking lots, they wrote a blog about it (any RV or trailer owner can spend the night for free at any Wal-Mart). The blog gained many readers, but then a few questioned why all the reports of interactions with Wal-Mart employees were so glowing—where were the criticisms? Finally, Laura was exposed as a freelance writer hired with Wal-Mart funds to do the blog. This hurt Wal-Mart's reputation. Online, transparency, authenticity, and consistency rule the day because if other bloggers discover corporate dishonesty, the entire blogosphere will be buzzing about it. Laura and Jim ended up returning the money they were paid and making a public apology.

EXHIBIT 12.10 Consultant Debbie Weil's Blog about Corporate Blogging *Source:* debbieweil.com/

The *Wall Street Journal* helps bloggers by sending an e-mail each day offering a link to a free online article (versus the normal subscription rate). It encourages bloggers to write their reactions to the article and link the blog to the *WSJ* Web site (earned media). The newspaper reports that the number of visits from blog sites is often as high as those from search engines.

There are many things to consider when companies want to start blogging, such as which platform to use, who will do the writing, how often will they post, and what is the purpose of the blog. For more details on starting a blog, we recommend *The Corporate Blogging Book* by Debbie Weil (Exhibit 12.10).

Finally, companies can become involved in blogs without starting their own. It is important to find influential bloggers in one's industry, follow their posts using RSS feeds, and add occasional comments. This keeps companies engaged in important conversations and projects them as experts in the industry. It is equally important because when they follow blogs through some automated monitoring system, as discussed in Chapter 6, they will discover potentially reputation-damaging discussion when it breaks and can become involved in the discussion by telling their side of the story.

Support Forums/Communities

Companies create spaces for consumers, prospects, and business customers to discuss topics of interest, provide new product ideas, or seek company support with technical or product issues (among other goals). The discussion itself is earned media (Chapter 14), so here we just present a few principles for building a successful online community on a company Web site (such as Tripadvisor.com) or on Google or Facebook Groups. It is not as simple as making a Facebook page and hoping folks will drop by—after all, marketers are competing with billions of other pages, groups, or events for viewer attention. As with most e-business strategies, research and planning precede success. Larry Weber (2007) suggests a seven-step program that works to this day:

1. ***Observe.*** Visit social media hangouts for Web users on the topics of interest in the industry of the company that wants to start a social media community. For example, the Saturn automobile brand managers would track conversations among users and industry analysts at blogs and Web sites to find the largest and most active communities.
2. ***Recruit.*** Find internet users who want to talk about the industry and recruit them for joining the new social media property.
3. ***Evaluate platforms.*** Decide whether the format should be a blog, pure online community, or social network.
4. ***Engage.*** Plan ways to get the community members to talk and upload content.
5. ***Measure.*** Identify metrics that will measure the success of the effort. For example, number of comments posted or number of members.
6. ***Promote:*** Plan ways to advertise or build a buzz in the social media and with search engines so the new community will attract users.
7. ***Improve.*** Use the metrics to continuously improve the community.

Note that many of these steps follow good CRM principles (see Chapter 15). For example, community members are more loyal because of the social bond they form with the company or the salesperson (such as Dell's IdeaStorm site). Also, organizations should be authentic, honest, and transparent in all their posts, otherwise they'll be found out, and it will create lots of negative conversation in the social media.

Podcasts

A **podcast** is a digital media file available for download online to computers, music players, tablets, or smartphones. Podcasts began with purely audio files for the iPod and other MP3 players, but now users can download video podcasts ("vidcasts" or "videocasts") for use on many types of receiving appliances. The line between video podcasts and other online video is quite fuzzy. Twenty-one percent of all internet users have downloaded a podcast (according to Pew Internet & American Life research—see Chapter 7), and nearly 18 percent of companies offer them (according to digital agency cScape's customer engagement research).

It seems that purely audio podcasts are in limited use as an IMC tool, especially in light of the popularity of online video; however, some companies are using them quite successfully. For example, the Eastman Kodak Company records interviews with professional photographers and offers them as podcasts on iTunes. Kodak notes that many other professionals like to listen to the podcasts during their long commute to work. Other companies offering podcasts to build their brands include media (e.g., Comedy Central, ESPN, and *The New York Times*), music (e.g., MTV and Quincy Jones), sports (e.g., HBO and the NBA), and technology firms (e.g., Diggnation and CNET).

E-Mail

Direct marketing includes such techniques as telemarketing, outgoing e-mail, and postal mail—of which catalog marketing is a big part. Due to the internet, paper-based direct marketing is declining so rapidly that the U.S. Postal Service (USPS) is close to declaring bankruptcy (this is also due to rising expenses, particularly employee pension costs). Targeted online ads and other forms of advertising and sales promotions that solicit a direct response are also considered direct marketing. For simplicity, and because e-mail is still so important, we focus our discussion of direct marketing communication on this application and its shorter offspring, **text messaging**—also called **short message services (SMS)**. In Chapter 15, we discuss the customer relationship–building implications of e-mail.

With over 3 billion e-mail accounts worldwide and trillions of e-mails flying over the internet worldwide annually, it is still one of the internet's killer applications (royal.pingdom .com). E-mail remains the most important communication technique for building customer relationships, as evidenced by the 75.4 percent of marketers investing in e-mail campaigns (according to the Direct Marketing Association). E-mail is the most often used marketing tactic in the B2B market, used by 84 percent of the business respondents according to a survey conducted by MarketingProfs and Forrester Research.

E-mail has not been replaced by RSS feeds, blogs, or social networking, in spite of the many people predicting its demise. Instead, marketers integrate e-mail with social media, as noted in Chapter 14. E-mail is still used to build a buzz about products. However, response rates for e-mail pale in comparison to many offline IMC tactics, as shown in Exhibit 12.11 (data gathered from over 29 billion e-mails). However, the study also notes that physical direct mail response rates have declined by 25 percent since 2003 and that even with the higher cost of direct postal mail, the metrics are about the same for physical and electronic mail: The average cost per order (or lead) for direct mail was $51.40 as compared to $55.24 for e-mail ("2012 Response Rate. . .," 2012).

E-mail has several advantages over postal direct mail. First, it requires no postage or printing charges. Second, e-mail offers an immediate and convenient avenue for direct response to Web and social media sites using hyperlinks. Third, and perhaps most important, e-mail can be automatically individualized to meet the needs of specific users—beyond just using a name in the e-mail. Similarly, marketers use e-mail for behavioral targeting. For example, an Expedia customer receives an e-mail about a particular travel destination after he or she searched flights on the Web site. Finally, e-mail is quicker than postal mail.

Conversely, e-mail must be delivered, opened, and acted upon in order to work. E-mail's disadvantages include the difficulty of making it though an ISP's **spam filters** (in 2004 AOL became famous for blocking nearly 80 percent of

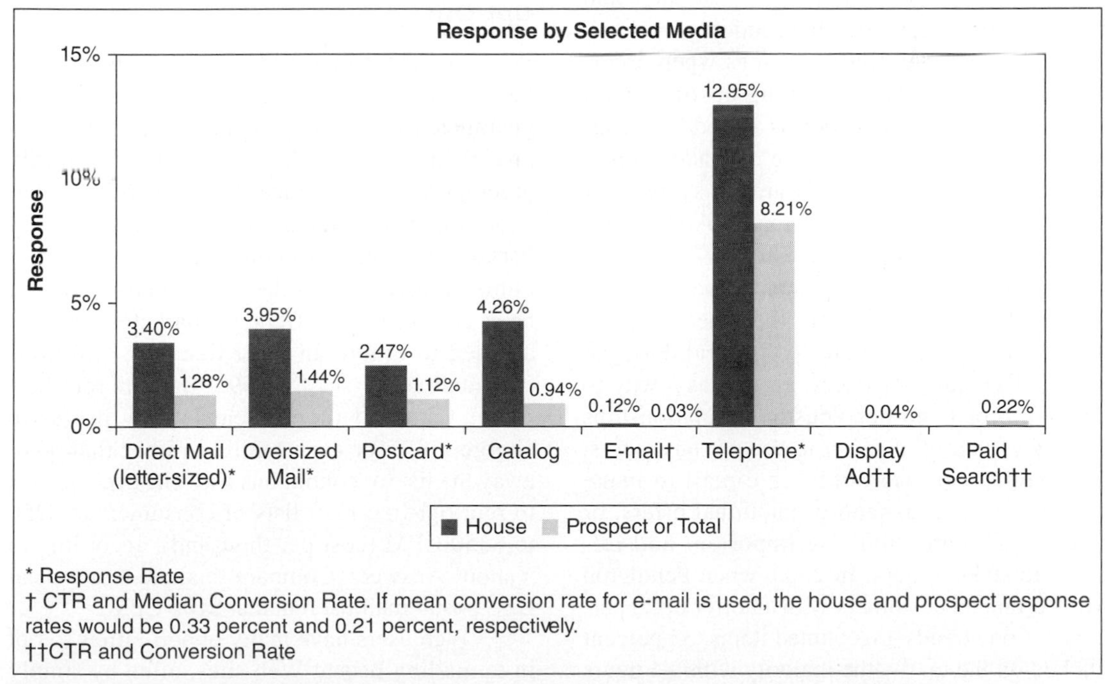

EXHIBIT 12.11 Response by Selected Media in 2012 *Source:* Data from the Direct Marketing Association (available at newdma.org)

incoming e-mail, and it still blocks 75 percent of the e-mails coming to members each day). E-mail software, such as Microsoft Outlook, also uses spam filtering at the user's computer. According to several sources, 71 to 95 percent of e-mail worldwide is spam. Various estimates suggest that anywhere from 17 to 60 percent of legitimate e-mail is caught in spam filters. Consumers are much more upset about spam than they are about unsolicited postal mail and might not open anything looking like spam.

Then there is the difficulty in finding and maintaining appropriate e-mail lists. Lists can be built in any of three ways: (1) generated through Web site registrations, subscription registrations, or purchase records (the most responsive list members); (2) rented from a list broker; or (3) harvested from some newsgroup postings or online e-mail directories—though this practice is questionable for reasons to be mentioned shortly. Even though nearly 91 percent of the U.S. population sends or reads e-mails (Chapter 7), at this time it is difficult to match a list of these e-mail addresses with individual customers and prospects in a firm's database unless the e-mail address owner supplies it, such as when ordering products online or signing up for e-mail announcements. And as soon as a good list exists, individuals often change their e-mail addresses—a problem because no forwarding system for abandoned e-mail addresses exists like the ones for telephone and postal addresses.

E-marketers must remember that e-mail is not simply postal mail minus the paper and postage. E-mail offers the chance for real dialogue with individual customers, as well as a way to develop broad and deep customer relationships instead of merely using it to acquire customers. Companies can use outgoing e-mail to make announcements, to send promotional offers, or to communicate anything important and relevant to stakeholders. In 2006, when Pendleton Mills e-mailed customers with an offer of 20 percent off on already-discounted items, 33 percent clicked on the mail—the majority within 3 hours of the mailing's start. When Amazon tested free shipping on orders over $49 in 2001 and over $25 in 2003, CEO Jeff Bezos sent a message to Amazon's customers informing them of the new offering. Microsoft e-mails registered users when new software patches are available for download. Many firms send out periodic e-mail newsletters, an excellent tool for communicating with clients; small wonder that most U.S. online customers enjoy receiving them. E-mail newsletters are a growth area because they provide many benefits:

- Regularly and legitimately promote the company name to clients.
- Personalize the communication with tailored content.
- Position the company as an expert on a subject.
- Point recipients back to the company Web site or social media properties.
- Make it easy for clients to pass along the information to others.
- Occasionally pay for themselves by carrying small advertisements.

Permission Marketing: Opt-In, Opt-Out

When renting e-mail address lists from list brokers, marketers should search for lists that are guaranteed to be 100 percent opt-in. The opt-in qualification means that users have voluntarily given permission to receive commercial e-mail about topics of interest to them. Other types of lists are compiled from outside sources, such as public information—these recipients will not be as responsive to offers, so marketers are best advised to ignore an offer like this: "millions of e-mail addresses for $99." Brokers rent lists rather than sell them because they prefer to charge a fee for each mailing rather than give away the list for continuous use. The average cost to rent opt-in e-mail lists of consumers is $250 to $350 CPM (cost per thousand), according to Yahoo! Answers. Compare this rate to a typical B2C postal mail list rental at $100 CPM.

Web users have many opportunities to opt in to mailing lists at Web sites, often by simply checking a box and entering an e-mail address. Research shows that lists with opt-in members get much higher response than do lists without. Marketing messages to opt-in lists can generate response rates of up to 90 percent, because these are interested users. For instance, Ticketmaster reported a 90 percent click-through on a mailing list offering additional merchandise to Bruce Springsteen fans who had already bought a ticket for an upcoming concert. Opt-in lists may be successful, in large part, because users often receive coupons, cash, or products for responding.

When opting out, users have to uncheck the box on a Web page to prevent being put on the e-mail list. Some marketers question this practice because users do not always read a Web page thoroughly enough to evaluate the meaning of checked boxes and, therefore, may be surprised and upset at receiving e-mail later. Some U.S. legislators have proposed laws banning opt-out e-mail.

Opt-in techniques are part of a marketing strategy called **permission marketing**: An opt-in form of marketing in which advertisers present marketing communication messages to consumers who agree to receive them. According to Seth Godin (1999), permission marketing is about turning strangers into customers. How to make this conversion? Ask people what they are interested in, ask permission to send them information, and then do it in an entertaining, educational, or interesting manner.

Rules for Successful E-Mail Marketing

Knowing how to use e-mail that gets through spam filters is opened by recipients, and is acted upon is as much science as art. The Direct Marketing Association, among others, constantly reports on the most effective techniques. Obviously, tactics vary by industry, but the following are some general guidelines:

- Use opt-in to build your lists because your reputation for being customer oriented is more important than having a large list.
- Check your e-mail reputation to see if it will make it through ISP filters. Check e-mail blacklists and use a service such as Return Path's Sender Score Reputation Manager, which screens for 60 reputation variables.
- Use an e-mail address that is professional. Senders from Yahoo!, Hotmail, and even Gmail are more likely to be blocked than company or education e-mail addresses. For example, the best e-mail address is Firstname.Lastname@companyname.com or Firstname.Lastname@university.edu.
- Make it easy for users to unsubscribe. This builds trust.
- Use microsegmentation, sending offers to smaller lists of relevant customers and personalize them.
- A small improvement in creative layout and multimedia use in e-mail can raise response rates up to 75 percent, according to MailerMailer.com. Test HTML e-mail approaches to see which pulls best for various offers.
- Give recipients plenty of opportunities to engage with the e-mail and act on the offer. High-performing e-mails offer an average of 27 links per message, according to the Peppers and Rogers Group (1to1.com).
- Use metrics to track the open rates, response rates, and return of investment (ROI). For instance, one author recently sent an e-mail to 178 recipients on an opt-in list using the Constant Contact e-mail service. There were seven bounces for bad e-mail addresses (3.9%), one opt-out, 92 opens (53.8%), and 19 clicks on various links in the mail (20.7%). We can look to see exactly which recipients were in each category and who clicked on each link. Also, consider the cost of nonresponses that may contribute to lower brand equity if your mail is perceived as spam (and narrow the list afterward).

As previously mentioned, many organizations study effective e-mail marketing. They provide lots of advice about what works, considering everything from how to build the best opt-in list, to the creative look and subject lines, and to the unsubscribe Web page and how it might be used to build relationships. The previous list was just a sampling—much more information is available online for e-mail marketers.

Spam

Now for the dirty side of e-mail marketing. Internet users do not like unsolicited e-mail because it shifts the burden of selectivity from the sender to the recipient. Users developed the term *spam* as a pejorative reference to this type of e-mail. It was made illegal in the United States with the CAN-SPAM Act; however, thus far the act appears to have little ability to stop spam (see Chapter 5). Marketers must be careful because viral marketing can work in reverse as well. Recipients of e-mail perceived as spam can vent their opposition to thousands of users in blogs and social networks, and to friends on e-mail lists, thereby quickly generating negative publicity for the organization. To avoid this outcome, many companies post anti-spam policies on their Web sites (see Nike.com for a good example).

Spammers routinely harvest e-mail addresses from newsgroup/community postings and then spam all the newsgroup members. Spam lists can also be generated from public directories such as those provided by many universities to look up student e-mail addresses. Spammers often hide their return e-mail addresses so that the recipients cannot reply. Other unscrupulous tactics include spamming through a legitimate organization's e-mail server so that the message appears to come from an employee of that organization.

Incidentally, spam is a problem in the B2B market as well as in the B2C market. Editorial staffs from the media complain about getting spam from public relations personnel at firms. Some measures have been put in place to limit spam. Many moderated groups filter spam and hide members' e-mail addresses in posts, and most e-mail programs offer users the option to filter spam as well. Also, a number of suits filed by ISPs seek to recover costs from spammers for the strain on their systems from the tremendous number of spam messages. Remember that all unsolicited e-mail is considered spam; still, as with direct mail, when the e-mail is appropriate and useful to the recipient, it is often welcomed, unsolicited or not.

It is increasingly common for opt-in lists to remind users that they are not being spammed. Usually a disclaimer appears right at the beginning of the message, "You are receiving this message because you requested to be notified about. . ." The message also advises users how they can easily unsubscribe from the list. This notification is important because many users do not realize that they opted-in—especially if they did so far in the past or in an unrelated context.

Privacy

Databases drive e-mail marketing. Such a database requires collecting personal information, both online and offline, and using it to send commercial e-mail, customized Web pages, display ads, and more. Astute marketers have found that consumers will readily give personal information to firms that use it to provide value and that do not share it with others unless given permission. For example, Amazon.com has implicit permission to collect customers' purchase information in the database and serve it collectively to others looking for book recommendations. Users don't mind this service because they receive valuable information and their privacy is guarded on an individual level. Amazon also has permission to send customers e-mail notification about books that might interest each individual. When Amazon announced that it would share customer databases with partners, it faced a huge media backlash. This reaction proves, once again, that firms desiring to build customer relationships must guard the privacy of customer data. Note that internet privacy protection is much stricter in Europe. Most European countries have much stricter regulations that protect any use of personal data by internet companies, including e-mail addresses. For example, it is against the law in Germany to post a picture of someone else in Facebook without their permission.

The use of spyware for gathering information from personal computers is also a huge privacy issue (see the "Let's Get Technical" box on spyware). User privacy was discussed more thoroughly in Chapter 5.

LET'S GET TECHNICAL

Spyware

A goofy-looking purple gorilla keeps popping up on your screen, and you do not know where it came from. Its prevalence and persistence is getting on your nerves. However, it is potentially performing much more damage behind the scenes. The purple gorilla is part of a spyware program, known as Bonzi Buddy, which can broadcast your personal information onto the internet. But just how do you get rid of the pesky guy?

As far too many internet users have experienced, spyware is everywhere on the net. Any type of program that is downloaded to your computer that collects information about you can be considered spyware. Spyware can be downloaded and installed on your computer without you ever knowing, and it can also transmit the information it collects about you to a third party without being detected. For example, common spyware programs send a list of the MP3s on your computer or a list of the Web sites you recently visited. They can also send the contents of your address book or password and banking information.

Spyware programs that collect information about your surfing habits to feed you with focused advertisements are often considered adware. Spyware programs that perform malicious activity, such as retrieving your bank account number, are called malware. The information that is collected is stored in large databases. Adware is extremely common online (such as Google's Double-Click network), and a Web site owner can distribute it to visitors in order to track their viewing habits and preferences. Although Web site owners and developers can use this information to make sites more in-tune with customer preferences, they are more interested in this information because of its ability to sell advertising space.

Web site owners can obtain the adware software from media networks. The purpose of media network companies is to track and record the behavior of online consumers. The information is stored in large databases and is used to target consumers. When you visit a site that is associated with the media network, the adware is downloaded and starts monitoring your internet usage. As it records your usage, it can determine certain demographic information about you. For example, if you visit babystyle.com, it might infer that you are a new parent or grandparent. Media networks lease the advertising space on Web sites and, in turn, sell it to advertisers. The media network then uses your profile to provide targeted advertisements the next time you visit a site in its association, such as a banner ad sold to a diaper company. When advertisers purchase ads from the media network, they are guaranteed a certain number of impressions, or the number of times their ad is displayed on a user's page.

In order for spyware to infect a computer, the computer user must visit a Web site that has the spyware program embedded in the programming code for the Web site. Spyware can also be triggered accidentally by the user when installing a regular program that is infested with spyware.

The origin of spyware is actually cookies, which are small files downloaded to and stored on the user's computer. Cookies were used by Web developers to collect usability information and were generally harmless. For example, sites that recognize who you are when you visit them most likely stored a cookie on your computer and read it upon your return to the site. The user could use his or her browser's settings to accept or reject cookies.

Today's spyware can be extremely dangerous because the information collected can end up anywhere. Spyware can also do any of the following:

- Flood your computer with pop-up advertisements.
- Send spam to your e-mail inbox.
- Slow down your internet connection speed.
- Slow down your computer's performance.
- Crash your computer.

Thousands of different spyware programs exist online. Names of software to watch out for include: CoolWebSearch, Internet Optimizer aka DyFuCa, Zango, HuntBar aka WinTools or Adware, Websearch, Movieland aka Moviepass.tv or Popcorn .net, and Zlob Trojan.

(continued)

Software that specifically finds and removes spyware should be installed on all computers that are connected to the internet. Some antivirus software companies have developed product line extensions to handle spyware. Popular and reliable anti-spyware programs include AdAware, Spybot, and Pest Patrol. Microsoft even offers a free anti-spyware program, Windows Security Essentials, with its Windows 7 operating system. In addition to being free, the Microsoft product does not slow down the computer as much as some other products on the market. Nonetheless, the easiest way to reduce spyware instances on your computer is to not download something unless you know it is from a reliable source.

Text Messaging

Short message services (SMS) are up to 160 characters of text sent by one user to another over the internet, usually with a cell phone or smartphone. Twitter messages are similar; however, they are only 140 characters in length and sent via mobile phone to the Twitter.com site instead of exchanged between phones. In the United States, SMS is usually commonly known as **text messaging** and is used by a majority of mobile phone users. It is different from **instant messaging (IM)**—short messages sent among users who are online at the same time (used by 38 percent of internet users). IM is used both by consumers and by employees (who have a quick question needing attention). Most commercial use of IM today involves the ads delivered to IM screens as users send messages to one another (such as movie ads presented to AOL's subscribers using its AIM product). Multimedia message service (MMS) involves multimedia content, but is not commonly in use yet because handheld receiving appliances often have difficulties receiving large image or video files in the text message function.

SMS differs from e-mail because users can receive the messages instantly and inexpensively on mobile phones. SMS uses a store-and-send technology that holds messages for only a few days. When users send short text messages, they are charged either by cell phone minutes or by the message, but the cost is minimal compared to using the cell phone for a conversation. In addition, accessing SMS is easy because users do not have to open e-mail or other software to send or receive. Instead, they simply type the message on the phone keyboard. In Japan, consumers are reportedly so adept at this that they have created what is called the "thumb culture" (because they rapidly type out messages using their thumbs), and now this culture has spread worldwide.

According to Nielsen Mobile, the biggest users are teenagers, with 3,146 messages a month—10 messages for every hour they are not sleeping or in school (although some of these may indeed be while they are in school because some use a high-frequency ring tone that older teachers cannot hear). SMS use continues to grow in all industrialized nations.

How can marketers capitalize on SMS use? Most experts agree that marketers can build relationships by sending permission-based information to customers when and where they want to receive it. To be successful, the messages should be short, personalized, interactive, and relevant. Some customers might want to receive an SMS warning about pending natural disasters from their insurance firm, an SMS notification of an upcoming flight delay, or notification of an overnight shipment. Travelers receive a text message warning when their cell phone is connecting to an expensive network abroad. In Germany, opt-in customers of local clubs receive text messages each week that announce the band playing during the upcoming weekend.

In one interesting example, Heineken, the global beer brand, used an SMS sales promotion to capitalize on the British pub tradition of quiz nights. Typically, a quiz night consists of a loyal pub customer shouting out a series of questions to which other customers answer on paper score sheets. Winners receive free pints or meals. Using a combination of online and offline promotion, Heineken placed point-of-purchase signs in pubs inviting customers to call a phone number from cell phones or other mobile devices, and type in the word *play* as a text message (SMS). In response, the customer received a series of three multiple-choice questions to answer. Correctly answering all the questions scored a food or beverage prize to be redeemed by giving a special verifiable number to the bartender—and 20 percent of all players won. "Feedback was that it was a great promotion . . . consumers found it fun and sellers found it to be a hook," said Iain Newell, marketing controller at Interbrew, which owns the Heineken brand.

Online Events

Online events are designed to generate user brand interest, draw traffic to a site, or generate revenue with paid admission. Perhaps the most memorable early commercial online event occurred in 1999 when Victoria's Secret held a Web-based live fashion show. The company announced it in advertisements in *The New York Times*, Super Bowl football game, and other traditional media. The event drew 1.2 million visitors, an 82 percent increase in Web traffic and the firm's Web servers could not handle all the traffic.

Companies and organizations can hold seminars (usually called "Webinars"), workshops, and discussions online. Holding online events in which clients get to "talk to" senior or prestigious people may be seen as one more valuable reason for being a client of a particular organization. It also saves considerable time and cost compared to holding or attending a physical seminar. Also, when business people attend online webinars, they register, creating leads for personal selling

CVENT is an online firm that provides clients with a Web interface for inviting and registering potential attendees to either online or offline special events (cvent.com). It is particularly strong because it also allows for registrant online payment and travel arrangements, and gives client firms business intelligence to improve event participation in the future (such as conversion rates and post-event surveys). Using CVENT, the marketing director for Nasdaq (stock exchange) doubled the response rate and reduced marketing costs by 92 percent. Likewise, WebEx provides a space for online meetings and Webinars.

Meetup.com users form special interest groups by location and then arrange offline meetings. Local residents can post to a calendar in Meetup.com that is searchable by local area. Facebook and Evite.com allow individuals to create events, such as a party, and invite a list of people via e-mail. The invitees can respond with a "yes," "no," or "maybe," and post a comment.

SALES PROMOTION OFFERS

Online sales promotion tactics can build brands, build databases, and support increased online or offline sales, but like offline promotions, most do not help to build customer relationships in the long term. Online sales promotion works, especially to entice consumers to change their behavior in the short term (e.g., visit a Web site, register online, purchase in the next week). Marketers report three to five times higher response rates with online promotions than with direct postal mail. Whereas most offline sales promotion tactics are directed to businesses in the distribution channel, online tactics are directed primarily at consumers—with the exception of Webinars, as previously mentioned. As with offline consumer sales promotions, many are used in combination with advertising. Sales promotions are popular display ad content. Sales promotion activities include coupons, discounts, rebates, product sampling, contests, sweepstakes, and premiums (free or low-cost gifts). Of these promotion types, only coupons, sampling, discounts, and contests/sweepstakes are widely used on the internet.

Coupons

Online coupons had great promise in the internet's early days but did not gain widespread acceptance until the economy declined in the United States. According to one estimate, 92.5 million people will use online coupons by the end of 2012

("Digital Coupons Rival. . .," 2012). In this study, 27 percent of respondents said they preferred online coupons because of their convenience, as compared with 33 percent, who still preferred print coupons. Incidentally, those who like digital coupons prefer getting them via e-mail.

Sampling

Some sites allow users to sample digital products prior to purchase. Many software companies provide free download of fully functional demo versions of their software. The demo normally expires in 30 to 60 days, after which time users can choose to purchase the software or remove it from their system. Online music stores allow customers to sample short clips of music before downloading the song or ordering the CD. Market research firms often offer survey results as a sampling to entice businesses to purchase reports. For example, comScore Media Metrix posts the results of its monthly survey of top Web sites for prospects to see, use, and, thus, perhaps discover a need to purchase more in-depth data.

Contests, Sweepstakes

Many sites hold contests and sweepstakes to draw traffic and keep users returning. Contests require skill (e.g., trivia answer or photo upload) whereas sweepstakes involve only a pure chance drawing for the winners. Just as in the brick-and-mortar world, these sales promotion activities create excitement about brands and entice customers to visit a retailer. They persuade users to move from page to page on a Web site, thus increasing the length of time on a site (called site "stickiness"). If sweepstake offers are changed regularly, users will return to the site to check out the latest chance to win.

ContestHound.com, a sweepstakes and contest directory originating in 1999, does an excellent job of consolidating promotions from many Web sites. This site gets nearly 200,000 visitors a year, and 10 percent are double opt-in newsletter subscribers. Its three key sites also offer other entertainment and personalization tactics such as games, a newsletter, and an affiliate program to engage customers. ContestHound uses both e-commerce and media models—the revenue comes from paid ads and affiliate programs to which they belong. It posts about 20 new contests a day. One of their craziest and most popular long-running promotions involved winning 24 rolls of toilet paper (one winner a month).

In one popular promotion, Wendy's restaurants and the Canadian TSN sports TV network offered the 2012 Wendy's "Kick for a Million" sweepstakes and contest. Contestants entered online and TSN drew one sweepstakes winner from the 14 million entries. The finalist had a chance at $1 million Canadian by kicking a field goal during the halftime of a Wendy's Canadian Football League game. The 2012 winner did not win the million (kicking a field goal from the 50-yard line), but he did win a $25,000 gift card, a Nissan Titan PRO-4X, and $42,000 in cash—$1,000 per yard the ball traveled (see wendys.tsn.ca).

Virtual Worlds

These are sites where users take the form of avatars and socialize in an online space of their own making. Companies create a presence in metaverses such as Second Life, or create their own virtual world to support commerce, such as Webkinz—where children enter a key code from a stuffed Webkinz animal they purchased at a brick-and-mortar retailer, then create a life online for their animal, while connecting with others doing the same (see webkinz.com). In Second Life, companies can create a virtual storefront, multimedia event or talk/lecture, contest, and can also create blogs. They can publish a URL containing streaming audio or video content, so that other Second Life residents will view their content and subscribe. Companies can also participate in Second Life media, such as providing content for the in-world radio and television stations. Naturally, all of this content must be enticing enough for in-world residents or it will not be consumed. Other interesting tactics include offering visitors branded items, such as clothing containing logos (every avatar wants that Calvin Klein Beanie hat!). Finally, some companies use their avatars as promotional vehicles, engaging other avatars in conversation about the brand and offering sales promotions, such as coupons. For example, the Nesquik Bunny avatar hops around Second Life, attending various events (see secondlife.com).

Online Games

Games can be played on three types of hardware: consoles, PCs, and portable devices. Zynga, Inc. produces online games and sells virtual products to players who use real currency to buy them. In "FishVille," for example, the company successfully sells a virtual, translucent, anglerfish and other fish for $3 to $4 each. Some players spend thousands of dollars a month on virtual skyscrapers in "CityVille" or imaginary chickens in "FarmVille" (TraderMark, 2011).

Advergames combine online advertising and gaming, featuring a company's product. They are used to draw site traffic and build brands in both business-to-business (B2B) and business-to-customer (B2C) markets and are growing in popularity online. For instance, consumers can test drive a Toyota online or play any number of exciting games at the Nickelodeon Web site, such as SpongeBob's Pizza Toss (nick.com). During the fall back-to-school season in 2008, JCPenney created a Facebook game called Dork-Dodge for girls on Facebook. Players had to navigate their way past undesirable boyfriends to get to their dream date. The retailer also had an interactive video (a modern-day take on the movie *The Breakfast Club*) where users could choose clothes from JCPenney for the actors. Advergames are unabashedly commercial by nature, but if they are fun and exciting, players will enjoy them and tell their friends. The advergame is an important tactic that acknowledges the consumer's increasing power by engaging users with entertaining product-related content.

Online Gifting

GroupCard's application allows retailers to sell group gift cards on their own Web sites and social networking pages. What is unique about this app is that the customer who creates the card can circulate it to many others, who then can add additional personalized messages and contribute a dollar amount via PayPal. GroupCard also offers collaborative gifting so that a group of people can combine funds for a gift certificate redeemable at the merchant's own Web properties (see groupcard.com)

JibJab allows users to create videos and eCards using images of friends or family. Consumers upload a headshot from their computers and drag it into the hilarious and charming videos, then send the link to the person in the headshot, or post it on a social network. These can quickly become viral, and more people visit the site to pay $1.99 to download the video or $12 a year to make more eCards and videos (see sendables.jibjab.com).

Branded Mobile Apps

Many companies create branded mobile applications and widgets that support social interactions and user contributions. In fact 45 percent of companies already have branded apps and another 31 percent planned to create them by the end of 2012 ("Marketers Challenged to Keep. . ., " 2012). "**Widgets** are mini Web applications that are used to distribute or share content throughout the social Web, downloaded to a mobile device or desktop, or accessed on a Website or blog," according to the IAB ("IAB Social Media. . ., " 2010). The content in widgets can be branded information, games, or other types of interactive content. For example, Nike + iPod Sports Kit is an application that measures the distance and pace of a user's walk or run in the physical world. It uses a unit embedded in the shoes that communicates with any iPod. Nike+ has many such apps. We could write an entire book about branded apps! Suffice to say that with the increase in mobile device adoption and internet access; all but the smallest companies will have a mobile presence because that is where the customers are.

QR Codes and Mobile Tags

QR codes are barcodes that appear as many black modules in a small square white background (see Exhibit 12.12). These barcodes were first

EXHIBIT 12.12 QR Code to Author's Web Site

developed for the automobile industry in 1994 to track inventory; however, they are now an extension of offline paid media that engages internet users. Consumers who have the mobile tag reader application can scan a QR code appearing in a print or outdoor advertisement by taking a picture or scanning with their phones. This immediately transports the user to a Web or social media site for more information on the brand, contest, or other information provided by the brand online. QR code scanning can present a user with an online movie trailer, wallpaper for download, text-based information on an event location and time, in a form of dynamic promotions. As of June 2011, 14 million users had scanned a QR code from their mobile phones (Pozin, 2012).

At the time of this writing, marketers are placing QR codes on physical objects, such as ads, and by scanning them, consumers will be transported to Facebook and record an immediate "like"—just as would happen when they click the "like" button on a Web site with a computer mouse. Google has also incorporated QR codes into Google Places, so this is a tactic that might become quite important for social media promotions in the future. Companies can generate QR codes for free at many Web sites and incorporate them in printed materials, such as ads and business cards (e.g., ZXing Project, BeQRious, Delivr, or Kaywa).

Many believe that QR codes are dying a quick death. This is likely because many marketers are not using them appropriately. Not too many users would scan a QR code they see on a billboard or at the bottom of an ad unless there was some incentive. We saw a real estate magazine with expensive homes for sale, and each had a QR code taking the reader to a video showing the inside of the home. On the magazine cover, a sales promotion offered a hefty coupon to a local restaurant that was received via one of the QR codes as a surprise. This kind of approach encourages users to scan codes. QR codes must offer incentives, such as entertainment, information or discounts. What do you think—are QR codes worthless or not?

Mobile tagging, however, is growing. A mobile tag is a two-dimensional image usually in a retail store. Shoppers can scan the tag with their smartphone and receive coupons or information.

Location-Based Marketing

A few marketers have experimented with location-based marketing, including promotional offers that are pushed to mobile devices and customized based on the user's physical location. Google is on the leading edge with its local search (Exhibit 12.13). On the iPhone, users simply type a business type into the map function, such as "pizza restaurant," and Google immediately returns a map with pizza restaurant locations near their current location. Other phone platforms also offer maps, navigation, and store locators, and more than 25 percent of U.S. phone users have used their mobile phones to access location-based services, according to eMarketer. Imagine receiving a short text message on your cell phone offering a 20 percent off your favorite boutique while driving in the neighborhood! For example, 27 shopping malls across the United States now can send deals to opt-in consumers in the mall via text messages (Murphy, 2011). Other uses include connecting with their friends and family by exchanging location information (discussed in Chapter 14).

Social Networks

Social networks are nodes of individuals or organizations that are connected based on common values, ideas, friendships, and so forth. They are based on the idea of six degrees of separation—that each

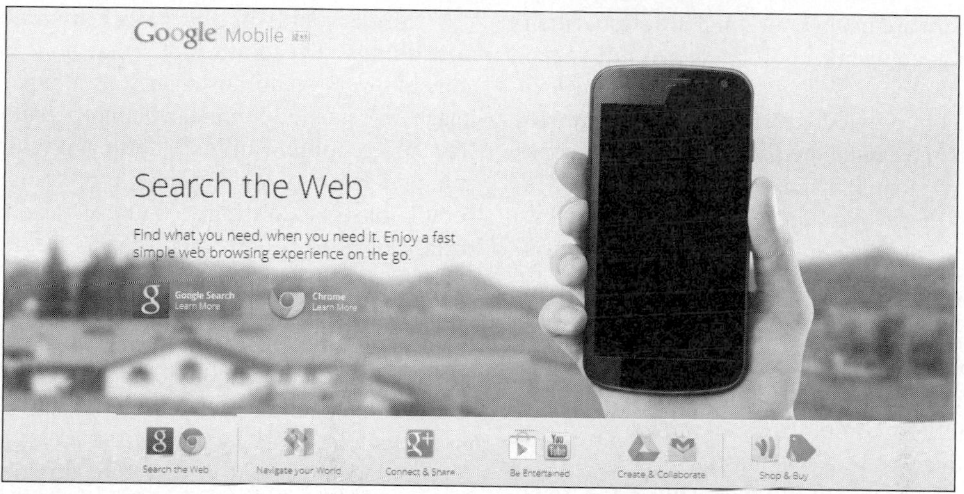

EXHIBIT 12.13 Google Leads the Field with Local Search *Source:* Google.com

individual is connected to every other individual in the network by up to six other people. If you join LinkedIn, a business network, you might be only six contacts away from the CEO of a Fortune 100 company. All it takes is introductions from the individuals between you and him. Social networks come in both business and personal varieties, but the lines are blurring as businesses build a presence where customers and prospects hang out.

Because today's customer researches brands online and learns about products from other customers in social media, businesses want to join in and influence the conversations—or start them when launching a new product. Social networks are one good place to do that, as long as marketers realize that they are not purely for selling but, instead, for communicating with, and learning from, users. And many don't: One study in December 2011 found that nearly all branded Facebook pages directed users to the Web site, and only 50 percent of them engaged Facebook users in conversation on the pages ("Listen, Engage, Build," 2012). Ninety percent of companies with over 100 employees participate in social media, according to an eMarketer.com estimate. Facebook is the giant, hitting 1 billion users in October 2012 and experiencing 2.02 billion visits during that month (according to facebook .com and experian.com). YouTube is next with 800 million unique visits and over 4 billion hours of videos watched in October 2012 (see youtube .com press room). The next eight networks, in terms of share of visits, experienced 236.8 million visitors total in October (Exhibit 12.14).

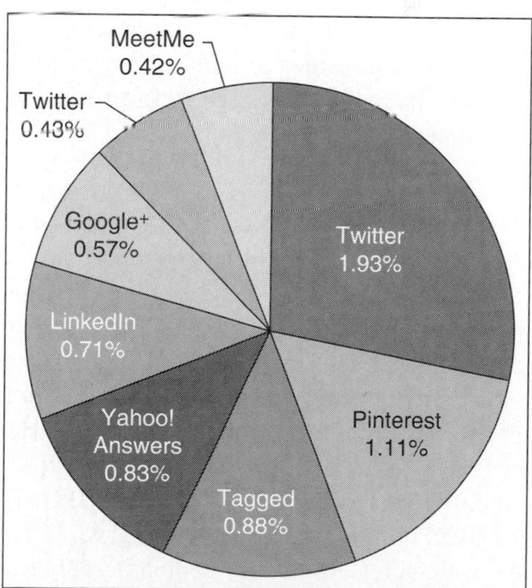

EXHIBIT 12.14 Social Network Share of Visits in October 2012 (Facebook and YouTube had 58.8% and 24.6%, respectively, and are included in this calculation but not on the chart) *Source:* Data from experian.com

There are many books and articles written about how companies build a successful social network presence. We've already discussed several ideas in previous chapters, and Chapter 14 discusses the earned media aspect: "likes," comments, and sharing by fans and followers. Suffice it to say here that top-performing company Facebook pages are those that build fan numbers by engaging users in compelling ways:

- Update the page often so there is a reason for fans to return frequently, but keep it consistent to the brand image.
- Include compelling activities (such as games, polls, and contests).
- Add attention-getting content to the timeline (e.g., videos, commercials, event announcements, status updates, and consumer uploaded content.
- Use clear calls-to-action (such as "like" us or "visit our Web site").
- Post frequently to maintain the conversation with fans. It is about being social and fun to make the brand likable.
- Listen carefully to the comments that can help the brand improve.
- Use Facebook "insights," a free service that allows companies to monitor page and app activity. Use this to keep improving the content so it is more engaging.

It is not only about inbound marketing. Ads and other paid promotions can also drive people to the social network pages (discussed in Chapter 13).

It is informative to learn from the companies that are the most successful at gathering Facebook fans and "likes." The Facebook page with the most fans in January 2012 was the Facebook Official Page (58.5 million fans), second was Texas Hold 'em Poker (55.5 million fans), and third was Eminem (50.9 million fans) (Obinna, 2012). The most liked company in August 2012 was Coca-Cola, which created its page content largely from fans and artists in music, film, and television—thus, gathering 47.8 million likes (Felix, 2012). Disney was second with 37.8 million likes because it has a casual, happy tone, and 268 sub-fan pages for discussion.

Some social networks are also called **microblogs**. These are blogs that hold micro content—very small posts, such as a hyperlink, image, or sentence comment. Tumblr.com offers free micro content blogs: "To make a simple analogy: If blogs are journals, tumblelogs are scrapbooks," according to Tumblr. Users can form groups or follow each other's frequently updated posts. Twitter is an even smaller mini blog, formed around the question: "What are you doing right now?" Members send text messages of up to 140 characters that post to their Twitter space. Friends follow each other's "tweets" either on computers or via incoming text messages to smartphones. Currently, Lady Gaga is the top "twitterholic" with over 31 million followers.

How do businesses use Twitter? CNN posts breaking news tweets and has over 3 million followers. Many executives use Twitter to talk about what is happening in the company and gain feedback and ideas from followers. Companies can tweet about their business and product offerings, announce sales promotions, and entice Twitter followers (as well as their own followers) to visit the virtual or brick-and-mortar store. For example, Virgin American gave away free flights to Tweeters with large numbers of followers to entice talk about the company's new Toronto, Canada, route.

Finally consultants, such as Andy Beal, often post links and images from conferences so that he is breaking news on the latest technologies in his field. His followers then click on links to his Web site or contact him for consulting. Collin Loretz promoted a WordPress blog workshop, WordCamp, on a dedicated Facebook page and answered questions via Twitter. This microblog, also a social network, is not just for social activity: 62 percent send their "tweets" from work.

It is extremely important to send interesting and informational posts on a microblog and not use a "hard sell" as the major topic of the tweet. People on Twitter want to know "what are you doing?" and "what can you tell me" not "what are you selling?" A smart marketer will conceal the promotional message in the post or comment, such as when someone with a lot of followers gets paid to tweet where she is going to eat. A smart marketer will present himself as a subject area expert who happens to work at a particular company in the field. Twitter is cost effective for replacing other customer touch points, such as direct mail, trade shows, and paper newsletters.

COORDINATING INTERNET AND TRADITIONAL MEDIA IMC PLANS

In a survey of 3,300 marketers, roughly 25 percent extensively integrated social media with both offline and online tactics, according to a Marketing Sherpa survey (see marketingsherpa.com).

The primary goal of marketers has always been to become monomaniacally customer driven and build long-term relationships that bring revenue to the company. Some owned and paid media don't allow for social interactions, such as some traditional Web sites or online ads. Traditional marketing communication media only allow one-way communication, yet these are still important for building brand awareness (e.g., an ad in the Super Bowl that reaches 60 percent of the population), creating desire and interest, and moving prospects and customers to purchase (e.g., a coupon or calendar event listing in the Sunday print newspaper). Yet, marketing is moving more to the concept of inbound marketing, as mentioned in Chapter 1, because it entices customers and earns their attention.

Today, marketers face a mashup of owned, paid, and earned media that can carry the promotional tools of advertising, sales promotion, direct marketing, public relations, and personal selling. The guiding force for selecting appropriate tools and media is the communication objectives in desired target markets. For example, if a company's goal is to sell its new software package to accountants, it could do any of the following: (1) use PR by describing the software on its own Web site and with a social media press release, (2) use Twitter to talk about software needs in the industry and offer codes for free sample downloads (sales promotion), (3) include recommendations from current customers on a LinkedIn page, (4) upload a video demonstration with software tutorials, or (5) advertise in a traditional print accounting industry magazine and on the industry's Web site (including testimonials from the LinkedIn pages). All this could direct prospects to a Web site where they can download a free sample and purchase it after a 30-day trial. This would be much more effective than giving away free iPads on Facebook, because that tactic does not align with the campaign goals or target market.

There are many other tactical ways to integrate marketing communications media, and they primarily involve providing links to all the Web and social media sites in all promotional media and integrating positive conversation into various appropriate media.

The main thing to remember is that the traditional and some internet media carry corporate monologues, while social media contain dialogs with target markets: Both play a role, but the dialog is becoming much more important and is more true to the well-accepted company goal of customer-driven marketing.

Search Engine Optimization

Search engine optimization (SEO) is the process of maximizing the number of visitors to a Web or social media site by ensuring that either (1) the site name and links appear high on a search engine results page for appropriate key words or (2) ads on search engine sites get a high click-through. This reflects two types of SEO: natural search (also called organic search) and paid search. The latter is a form of paid media, discussed in Chapter 13. Here we focus on natural search as relates to owned media. **Search marketing** is an umbrella term that refers to the act of marketing via search engines, whether through improving rank in listings, purchasing paid listings, or a combination of these and other search engine–related activities.

Search marketing is a complex art and science that combines the intricacies of human behavior, linguistic preferences, marketing techniques, analytics, Web site usability, and technology to drive qualified visitors to a Web site and convert them into customers.

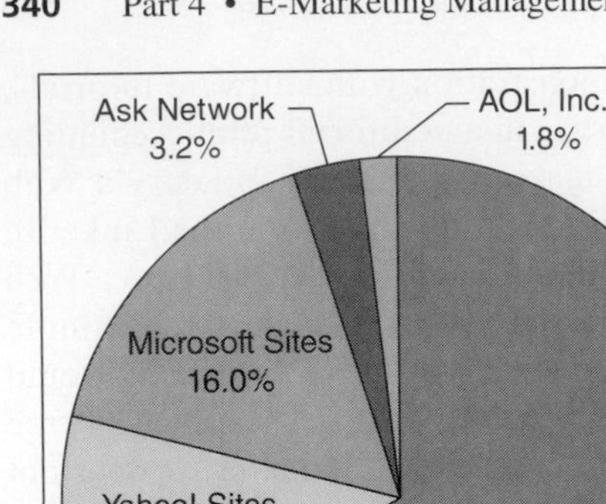

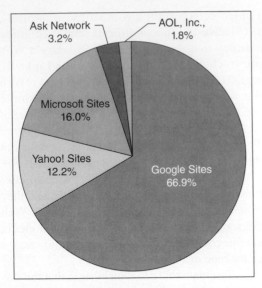

EXHIBIT 12.15 Search Engine Market Share in October 2012 *Source:* Data from comscore.com

Search engines are **reputation aggregators**—Web sites that rank other Web sites, products, retailers, or other content according to some rating system. An aggregator gathers sites by category, value, and popularity and displays them in some organized fashion. These sites rely heavily on user input for their rankings.

The giant is Google, with 66.9 percent market share (Exhibit 12.15). Google ranks search engine results page (SERP) links partially based on popularity—the number of quality sites linking to each site. Many authors call Google a "reputation engine" instead of a search engine because of the way it determines these rankings. Users visit Google because the search engine results pages are so relevant and not just an unordered list of pages with just the keyword in them, with little regard to popularity. Heavy focus on meeting the needs of site visitors is what propelled Google to number one search engine.

Other reputation aggregators include social media niche sites with search capability, such as YouTube for video and TripAdvisor for hotel ratings. We discuss these in the vertical search section that follows.

NATURAL SEARCH **Natural search** is a search marketing strategy involving optimizing a Web site so it will appear as close to the first search engine results page as possible (sometimes called "organic search"). Natural search is critical because with 4.7 billion search queries on Google each day (in 2011), most searchers will click on a link in the first page of search engine results pages (SERP), and few scroll onto subsequent pages.

There are many ways for a site to inch its way to page one, but first it is important to understand that every reputation aggregator uses somewhat different criteria for ranking content. Google uses an ever-changing algorithm with over 200 variables, one of the most important of which is popularity as measured partially by relevant incoming links to a site (thus, its nickname as reputation engine). Companies wanting to optimize their site for Google will seek as many relevant and high-quality incoming links as possible.

Another important tactic involves **keywords**—the words users type into the search query box to find what they seek. When Web sites are optimized in both their (1) content and (2) HTML meta tags that hold keywords, it will make it easy for search engines to know how to categorize the site and to provide a relevant match when users actually type in those keywords. Meta tags are not seen by visitors unless they choose to view the page source code. For example, these are the actual keywords used by eBay.com: "ebay, electronics, cars, clothing, apparel, collectibles, sporti ng goods, ebay, digital cameras, antiques, tickets, jewelry, online shopping, auction, online auction." When someone types one or more of those words in Google, the search engine will consider the match as one of the 200 variables. Google finds the keywords both in the Web site text and headlines and in the HTML tags.

To discover the best keywords, companies (1) use Web logs to see what words their visitors type into search engines before arriving at their sites; (2) use Web tools, such as Google's AdSense keyword auctions, to discover the keywords used in their industry so they can find unique words for their site (e.g., *vintage jewelry* instead of *jewelry*); and (3) by polling customers and prospects to see

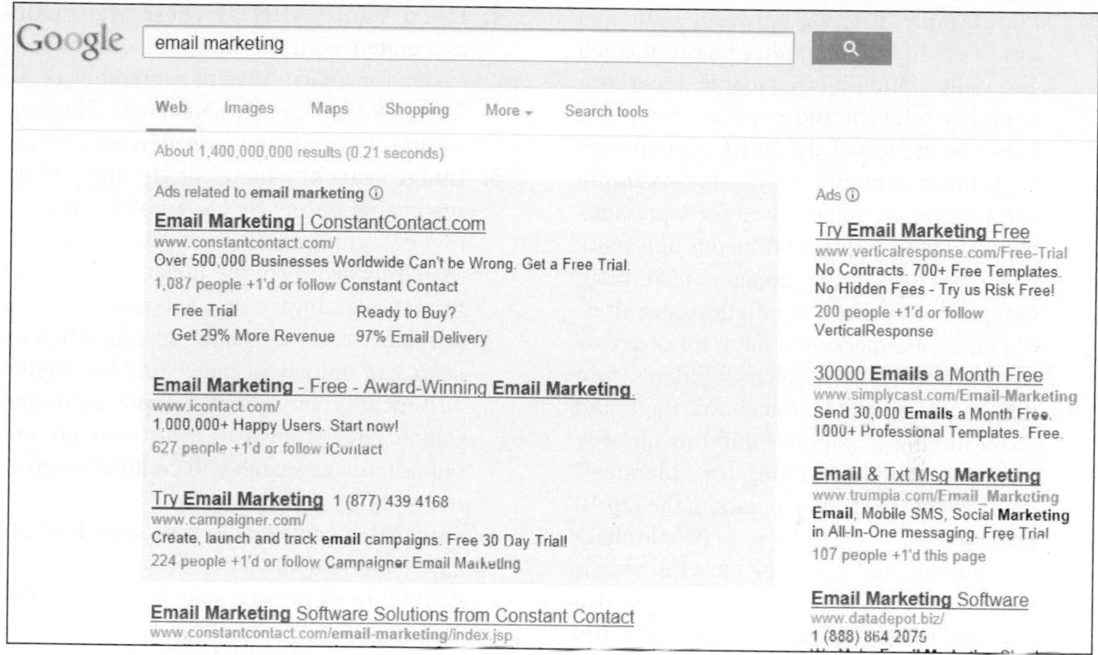

EXHIBIT 12.16 Search for E-mail Marketing *Source:* google.com

what words they actually use when looking for firms in the industry. Organizations also carefully craft the text on their pages to reflect this content, including even purposefully using different spellings of keywords that searchers might use (e.g., *email* and *e mail*). Oftentimes, experimentation is the best way to see which words actually produce the highest click-throughs to a Web site.

Exhibit 12.16 shows a search for "e-mail marketing" in Google. On the left side, at the bottom, Constant Contact grabbed the number one natural result spot for these keywords—quite a feat in a crowded field of vendors. Note that all the other sites are paid search results.

SEO is a topic that fills many books, so we will discuss only a few principles here, which relate to social media and positive earned media. Visit the Google Webmaster pages for more information.

1. **Spread fresh content all over the Web.** The more sites and social media pages a company or brand maintains, the more links will appear on search engine results pages. This is important because when others post negative content in social media, this content will briefly appear on page one in the search results. However, these will be quickly replaced by current, positive Web content from brand owners, such as images, podcasts, videos, press releases and articles. For example, when searching for "Will it Blend," the branded microsite appears first on the results page. This is followed by three YouTube videos, the Blendtec company YouTube channel, a Wikipedia entry, the company's Facebook page, and then two social media columns about the company's blenders and fascinating campaign—one a humorous and positive parody of the viral videos ("Will the blender blend itself?").
2. **Relevance and popularity.** Google judges relevance by incoming links to a Web page and the popularity of the site based on clicks from a SERP or number of "likes" or comments on a Facebook page.

For example, if it is a musician's site and lots of credible similar sites link to it (such as a radio station blog), Google assumes it is highly relevant and popular, moving it closer to the top of the SERP. Companies seek these inbound links—for example one blogger we interviewed for a previous book asked to be linked from our university pages because ".edu" domains have more Google credibility than do dot-com sites. Social media marketers put a lot of cross-links to various sites, such as linking from the microsite to the Facebook page and cross-linking to pages within the site. For example, when searching for "blender," the Blendtec Web site appears in the top 10 links because of the millions of people clicking, linking, and watching the viral videos on YouTube and its microsite. Google also defines "relevance" as individual-specific using social graphs (friend connections), so if you search for "the best restaurant" in your town the top result might well be one that your Facebook friends rated highly on Yelp.com, whereas someone else's SERP will reflect what their friends commented upon in other social media sites.

3. **Optimize content.** A search engine's automated robots search Web sites to see which words are the most important, partially by looking at topic headings, page titles (words that appear on the browser tabs), URL names, meta tags, and other things in large font. This means that marketers must understand their audiences' desired benefits and search habits so they can select key words to populate the sites used by target markets for searching. For example, the Student Loan Down blog about student loans and Wells Fargo bank financing uses 29 key words in its meta tag but only three of them rank in Google's first SERP—these are the one used in the name of the blog as well (see blog.wellsfargo.com). This site needs to revise its key words to focus on a smaller number to be used throughout the content.
4. **Use a Vanity URL.** These are usually associated with a brand name to make it easier for a customer to remember (e.g., facebook.com/YourBrandName). The vanity url is typically mentioned in advertising.
5. **Image search.** Increasingly, images are searchable online by the graphics, not the text descriptions. Google allows users to search for words in the image and by size, format (e.g., jpg), color, and more. TinEye provides "reverse image" search, whereby users can upload an image and the engine will locate it anywhere it is posted online (catch your friends posting your picture online). Image search will continue to grow in capability and use.
6. **Integrate social media and search strategy.** Google now considers social media activity in its organic search rankings. For example, a tweet that gets 1,000 retweets will boost a page higher in the rankings than one that gets 10 retweets. Bing considers the number of "likes" in its rankings.
7. **SEO tactics constantly change.** Google is famous for adjusting its search algorithm (several hundred times a year) both to improve results and so that sleazy site owners cannot spam the system (such as putting key words in white text all over a white background so search engines are able to read it but users do not). For example, Google introduced "Panda" and "Penguin" in 2011 and 2012 to refine the search algorithm so that site quality and social media conversation ranked higher and pages with much advertising, especially above the fold, ranked lower. Google also announced a penalty for over-optimizing pages for search, trying to level the playing field. This means that marketers must constantly watch developments and change tactics accordingly. We recommend visiting searchengineland.com, searchenginewatch.com, and seomoz.org for the latest developments and capabilities. Especially worth watching because *Forbes Magazine* predicted the death of SEO by 2014. We'll see.

In one example of what not to do, Nevada's former governor, Jim Gibbons, posted images from appearances, a blog, and his authored white papers all on the official Nevada government Web site (nv.gov). When the citizens became critical of his decisions and social behavior, a search for "Jim Gibbons" brought the nv.gov page first and then nine links to criticism on other sites. Some of these lasted for several years on the first page of SERP and could have been bounced to later pages, if the governor had spread fresh content, such as, putting images on Flickr, making a unique URL for his blog, creating Facebook and Twitter accounts, and inserting content in Wikipedia and elsewhere that would appear in the first 10 links on the SERP for his name.

Note that, although password-protected sites such as Facebook and Twitter are crawled by search engines for public display in the SERP, users have to log onto these sites in order to follow the link. If a company wants its content to appear on Google and be easily viewed, it will create a public page that is available to people who are not required to be logged onto the site. Moreover, Facebook provides its own powerful search engine for users who are logged in, and there are many specialized search engines for social media sites, such as Cue and Boolshaka. Companies work to be sure their content is listed by these specialty companies, who usually allow submissions if the search robots have not yet found the sites.

As with any social strategy, companies working on an SEO program first work to understand the Web behaviors and sites used by their target market and influentials in terms of publishing and sharing content. They then set SEO goals and monitor the results.

VERTICAL SEARCH **Vertical search** is site-specific search on very specialized topics, such as travel, online retailers, or books. As compared with general search engines, such as Google and Bing, vertical sites are destinations for fewer users seeking very specific content. For example, in 2012 Tripadvisor.com had 75 million reviews and opinions about various hotels worldwide. Someone seeking a hotel in New York City or Bangkok can search the TripAdvisor site and get a listing of hotels ranked by popularity, with hundreds of reviews and several traveler photos per hotel. Thus, hotels want to be listed on this vertical search site. This social media site capitalizes on the fact that people trust others like themselves more than they trust the company Web sites.

Other vertical search site examples include ZoomInfo and LinkedIn (people search), Guru.com (vendor search in B2B market), Autobytel (automobile search), CareerBuilder (jobs), Retrevo (consumer electronics), YouTube (video), and iTunes (music). The B2B Infomat fashion engine provides access to over 350,000 fashion designers, showrooms, retailers, manufacturers, and more, and DPRWorld helps dentists find everything from whitening agents to anesthesia.

Companies need to learn whether or not there are vertical sites for their industries and then to see if they are also indexed by the general search engines. Marmite, the English food spread, has a Facebook page with over 360,000 people liking the site—its Facebook link appears fourth in a Google search. Conversely, the Marmite Hate Party site has over 156,000 people liking it—this is what we love about the social media, both as consumers and companies. We get to learn what consumers don't like about our products and save tons of market research money.

Vertical search is a growing area because it helps users find what they are looking for quickly—20 percent of online users search at vertical sites, according to iProspect. A consumer seeking a local pizza restaurant might do better at a Yelp vertical search or mobile application than at a general search engine, where the local entries will be buried among thousands of similar businesses nationwide (although Google now lists local results on some SERPs).

The pricing models on some vertical search sites include directory submission fee, cost per click, and cost per action, as well as the traditional cost per thousand (CPM) impressions. When the directory content is user generated, such as with Tripadvisor.com, advertisers can pay for display ads on the site or can enter comments in response to reviews for free.

In the next section, you will learn about how companies measure owned media.

OWNED MEDIA PERFORMANCE METRICS

With so many owned media choices that take a lot of participation effort, how can a marketer know which are worth the investment? The most important answer is it depends on the market and communication objectives. Referring back to Exhibit 12.1, if sales is the goal, then the number and dollars of sales are the key metrics, along with the costs, such as cost per click and ROI. If brand awareness is the goal, marketers will need a survey to determine if awareness improved (although site visits is one indicator).

For company-owned Web sites and blogs, marketers use Web analytics, such as number of unique visitors, time on each page, conversion to sales, and so forth (discussed in Chapter 2). Google Analytics is a free service that provides many metrics to determine the efficacy of these types of pages. For example, companies can learn the number of daily visitors to each page, where users visited immediately prior to landing on their site, and the country from which they are accessing the site (based on IP addresses). Other metrics for owned media follow:

- Podcasts: number of downloads and length of time listening.
- Online events: number in attendance, number of questions asked (if it is a Webinar).
- Virtual world: number visiting the company property, how long they stay, and whether or not they interact with the various features.
- Online games: number playing, length of time in the game, purchase of virtual properties, and clicks on game links.
- Branded mobile apps: number of downloads, updates, and number of actions that are built into the app (such as "checking in" with a location-based app or earned media "shares").
- QR codes: number of scans and actions taken at the site destination.
- Web landing pages: exit rate (view and leave the page), click-through rate, and conversion rate.

Social media metrics are different from standard Web site metrics because users interact with branded media in many different ways. Initially, companies want to know how many fans and followers they have, number of visits and return visits, and cost per fan (especially the staff time cost). As well there are engagement metrics, such as, when an internet user views an online video, he or she might spend 4 minutes viewing it, but another might stop it immediately. And if the user uploads, comments on, and likes or shares a branded video, this brand interaction is counted (see Chapters 2 and 14 for more detail on engagement metrics).

Next, we move to metrics for measuring sales promotion and direct marketing effectiveness.

Sales Promotion Metrics

Marketers want to know how their sales promotions contribute to the overall communication goals. For example, if the firm desires increased Web site traffic, how much came from the online contest? What was the conversion rate to sales at the site? As with all metrics, the selected measures depend on campaign goals. Software and music suppliers will want to measure the number of users who sampled their free online samples (e.g., 30-day trial for software or listen to a music sample), and how many subsequently purchased the product.

As an example, Russell Athletics teamed with ESPN in 2003 to draw traffic to ESPN.com and build a database of prospects for Russell Athletics (Linkner, 2004). The athletic apparel company created an online contest based on its sponsorship of college football's Bowl Championship Series (BCS). Russell ran television spots on the ESPN Motion video channel that encouraged viewers to visit ESPN.com to pick 10 winners in the BCS. The highest-scoring winners each week received Russell Athletic jerseys and the top entry over a longer time period received a trip to the BCS Championship game. To measure the campaign's success, Russell Athletics and ESPN gathered the following metrics:

- 500,000 viewed the Russell Athletics television spot (traffic to ESPN.com objective).
- 21 million visited ESPN.com (number of impressions on the site).
- 85,000 men in the target age group visited the game site.
- 20,000 of the target group entered the game.
- 34 percent of contest participants asked for ongoing communication from Russell Athletics (database objective).

Obviously marketers must plan to collect this information prior to beginning the sales promotion campaign and continuously monitor the results. Online technologies make it easy.

Direct Marketing Metrics

Response rate and ROI are the most appropriate metrics for any direct marketing campaign. Additionally, many firms use direct tactics to build databases and measure success in terms of customer information growth. E-mail marketers collect metrics on every mouse click, desiring to know which offers pull best (A/B testing), which message content brings the greatest response, when is the best time to send e-mail for maximum response (by the way, it is Monday between 6 A.M. and 10 A.M. Eastern time), and so forth.

E-mail receives a widely varied and generally low click-through to the sponsor's Web site; however, as we've already said, the right list and offer can yield very high click-throughs. Interestingly, e-mail provides the highest ROI of any direct media, at $42.08 on average ("Print's Place in . . . ," 2010).

SMS marketers also study responses other than simple click-through. In a study of more than 200 SMS campaigns, the response performance was outstanding (enpocket.com):

- 94 percent of messages were read by recipients.
- 23 percent showed or forwarded messages to a friend.
- 15 percent to 27 percent of recipients responded to SMS campaigns.
- Cost per response was $1.92, returning a better ROI than direct postal mail.

Chapter Summary

Integrated marketing communication (IMC) is a cross-functional process for planning, executing, and monitoring brand communications with the goal of profitably acquiring, retaining, and growing customers. When making decisions about marketing communication tools, companies consider the results they would like to achieve in moving consumers through the steps of awareness, interest, desire, and action (AIDA model) or the steps of "think, feel, do" in the hierarchy of effects model. Companies develop social media strategies and plan specific tactics to increase consumer awareness, influence attitude, and encourage behavior.

The five traditional marketing communication tools are advertising, public relations, sales promotion, direct marketing, and personal selling. In planning IMC campaigns, companies can now move beyond traditional tools and "1 to 1" (one marketer, one recipient) and "1 to many" (one marketer, multiple recipients) into "many to many" (many consumers using social media to communicate with each other). Owned media carry marketing communication messages on channels that are owned and therefore partially or entirely controlled by the marketer. Paid media are properties owned by others paid to carry marketer-controlled promotional messages (such as advertising). Organizations have the most reach and the least control over earned media, with "many to many" conversations generated by others (such as internet users' opinions).

Communication media are communication channels used to disseminate news, information, entertainment, and promotional messages. In contrast, social media blend technology and social interactions for co-creation of content and value. Content marketing involves creating and publishing content offline and online on Web sites and in social media. As a result, digital content functions as inbound marketing to attract customers and prospects, with appropriate content available when and where users seek information.

Among the most commonly used owned media are: company Web sites (to provide information, entertain, build communities, and serve as a communication channel with customers); blogs (to disseminate views, attract site visitors, engage in conversations, and support expert standing); support forums and communities (for customers and prospects to discuss topics of interest, provide product ideas, or seek assistance); podcasts (to support brand-building); e-mail (for building relationships and encouraging direct response); text messaging (for instant communication and relationship-building); online events (to generate interest, build traffic, or generate revenue); sales promotion (such as coupons); virtual worlds (to encourage engagement); online games (to engage users with product-related content); online gifting (for revenue); branded mobile apps (to support social interactions); QR codes (to provide more information); location-based marketing (to reach users who are at or near a marketing location); social networks (connecting individuals for business or personal reasons). Given the many choices of owned, paid, and earned media, organizations have to make decisions based on their communication objectives in desired target markets.

Search engine optimization (SEO) is the process of maximizing the number of visitors to a Web site or social media site by landing the site name and link high on search engine results (natural or organic search) or attracting clicks on ads that appear on search engine sites (paid search). Natural search strategies depend on tactics such as site quality, achieving many relevant and high-quality incoming links or on selecting appropriate keywords. Vertical search refers to site-specific search on specialized topics like travel or books. Marketers can use a variety of metrics to measure owned media performance, depending on the market and the objectives. For podcasts, the firm can measure number of downloads and length of time listening; for online events, the number of visitors in attendance; for QR codes, the number of scans and actions taken. Some metrics used to evaluate sales promotion performance include the conversion rate to sales at the Web site and the number of online samples distributed. Some metrics for evaluating direct marketing include response rate, ROI, best time for response, and cost per response.

Exercises

REVIEW QUESTIONS

1. What is integrated marketing communication (IMC), and why is it important?
2. Why do marketers keep the AIDA or hierarchy of effects model in mind when planning social media strategy?
3. What are the five traditional marketing communication tools, and what are some social media platform examples of each?
4. How do the reach and control of marketing communications in owned, paid, and earned media differ?
5. What is marketing public relations (MPR), and how can an organization use its Web site as owned media for this purpose?
6. Why would a company use e-mail or text messaging instead of postal direct mail for marketing?
7. How are advergames used in marketing?

8. What are the marketing benefits of initiating, participating in, and influencing conversations on social networks?
9. How does natural search differ from paid search and vertical search?
10. Why is search engine optimization an important consideration for the company's owned media strategy?

DISCUSSION QUESTIONS

11. **Will It Blend? Story.** What other owned media do you think this company could use to build its brand online? Explain your rationale.
12. **Will It Blend? Story.** How do the videos create earned media? Are there any other things the company could do to engage users to create more earned media?
13. "Great products + Weak branding = Weak sales." The CEO of Blendtec said this before his *Will It Blend?* videos became an internet sensation. How does the hierarchy of effects model explain the CEO's comment and the sales results that followed this marketing success?
14. Why would a company prefer the control of owned media over the extended reach of the "many to many" model?
15. What are the possible marketing consequences of not having an effective search engine optimization strategy?
16. As a consumer, how are you likely to react when you see that a company representative tweets a comment about a specific topic after other consumers have opened the conversation? What guidelines would you recommend that marketers follow for joining such conversations?
17. Have you scanned any QR codes? Do you think marketers should include QR codes in their IMC plans? Why or why not?
18. Which could be more important to an airline selling seats on its flights: a general search engine or a vertical search site? Explain your answer.

WEB ACTIVITIES

19. Locate the microsite for a specific brand, marketing campaign, or new product. Based on your experience finding this site and looking at its landing page, what changes would you like to see included in A/B testing, and why? List at least three specific items to be tested and explain your rationale for each test.
20. Visit the Ikea Web site (ikea.com) and click on the "Ask Anna" chat bot link at the top of the page. Try asking Anna two or three questions about Ikea's merchandise or policies. Is this chat bot helpful? What two or three suggestions can you offer for making Ask Anna even more effective for customer support?
21. Use your favorite search engine to locate a blog written by a company CEO. How often does the CEO blog, and what topics are represented in recent posts? What marketing objectives do you think this blog is intended to achieve? List two other Web pages that are linked to this blog (or that should be linked to this blog), and explain why these links make sense. If you could ask this CEO a question to be answered on the blog, what would it be?
22. Conduct a search for a nationally advertised consumer product using only its brand name, and analyze the first page of search results. Who sponsors the Web site at the very top of the results page? How many owned paid search links do you see? How relevant are the top six search results? Which keywords do you think this brand should use to optimize its site for natural search?
23. Visit the home page of a major retailer such as Macy's (macys.com) or Target (target.com). Does this retailer offer consumers the opportunity to sign up for promotional messages delivered via e-mail or text messages (or both)? What does the retailer do to entice visitors to sign up? How is it using permission marketing? Also follow any links to see this retailer's presence in social media and participation in online conversation. What else do you think this retailer should do to accomplish its marketing communication objectives through social media?

CHAPTER 13

E-Marketing Communication: Paid Media

This chapter explores paid media, the second of the three elements of content marketing used to communicate with customers and prospects. In addition to learning about the latest trends and specific uses of paid media, you will examine some of the pricing models that apply when marketers select these tools. Finally, you will see how advertisers use metrics to evaluate the effectiveness and efficiency of paid media.

After reading this chapter, you will be able to:

- Outline the characteristics, benefits, and limitations of paid media.
- List the most important paid media techniques and discuss how and when advertisers use each.
- Explain the three unique aspects of social networks that attract advertisers to paid social media.
- Describe some of the advertising tactics offered by the most popular social media sites, virtual worlds, and online video sites.
- Discuss the various ways in which marketers can reach target audiences through mobile advertising and paid search.
- Highlight how paid media can move B2B prospects through the marketing purchase funnel.
- Identify some key metrics used by advertisers to determine the effectiveness and efficiency of paid media.

• 92 percent of global consumers say they trust earned media (word-of-mouth and recommendations from friends and family) above all other forms of advertising. 68 percent of consumers trust reviews more when they see both good and bad scores, while 30 percent suspect censorship or faked reviews if there aren't any negative comments or reviews (Source: Reevoo.com, January 2012).

• In Poland, one of the country's main banks, ***BZ WBK***, hosts the ***Bank Pomysłów*** ("Bank of Ideas"), where customers can publicly suggest how the bank could improve its service or introduce new facilities. Ideas can be voted up or down by other customers, and the bank has implemented over 300 customer suggestions.

Lenovo Wins Big with Paid Media

Lenovo is a Chinese company selling computers and other electronic items. It is headquartered in Hong Kong but maintains operational headquarters in the United States. In 1995, it acquired IBM's personal computer business and became the second-largest PC seller in 2011. Lenovo sells to both businesses and individual consumers.

This multinational company advertises both in traditional media and online. In 2008, Lenovo began using Google display advertising for remarketing (a tactic that involves communicating with users who previously visited a Web site). The Google display network contains a variety of Web sites, from news to blogs, and advertisers can place video, text, image, or interactive ads on specific sites anywhere in the network. Remarketing allowed Lenovo to tag visitors at its own Web site and show them specific ads while on another site in the Google display network.

Lenovo tagged site visitors displaying three different behaviors; general visitors, those who abandoned shopping carts, and those who purchased on the site. It could then present tailored ads elsewhere, based on this user behavior on Lenovo. For example, general visitors got ads featuring discounts on laptops, those who abandoned shopping carts saw ads with 5 to 10 percent discounts on the exact laptop or product they viewed, and online purchasers received ads offering laptop accessories, such as laptop bags.

Did it work? Yes! In late 2010, those coming from Lenovo's Google Display ads resulted in 20 percent of total site orders and advertising expenses dropped due to this specific targeting. Lenovo continues to use this remarketing strategy and many metrics to tweak tags and ads for maximum effectiveness and efficiency (see Google Display Network Success Stories and lenovo.com for more).

PAID MEDIA

Lenovo used paid media to entice its target market to visit the Lenovo-owned media Web site. As you learned in Chapter 12, paid media are properties that are paid by an organization to carry its promotional messages, as when Lenovo paid Google to present narrowly targeted ads on its Display Network. The terms *paid media* and *advertising* are often used interchangeably, as you'll note in this chapter. However, there are a few paid media tactics that don't quite fit the definition of advertising, such as paid product placement in virtual worlds or online games and sponsored tweets.

The line between physical (also called traditional or offline) and digital platforms (often called nontraditional or online) for paid marketing communication messages is blurring more every day. For example, Current.com allows users to submit video "pods" on its Web site, with the highest voted videos being played on Current's cable television programming. Now that U.S. television programming is completely digital and as more sites like iTunes, Hulu.com, and Akimbo.com offer online television and movie viewing on computers and MP3 players, the meaning of the terms *offline* and *online* will continue to lose their distinction—the same fate awaits the terms *traditional media* (newspapers, magazines, TV, radio, and outdoors) and *nontraditional media* (everything else, including digital media). Already, newspaper ads and articles are often accessible in either location.

Note also that the medium is not the appliance: TV programming can carry content and ads that are seen on television, mobile phone, and the computer; radio audio transmission can come into many devices, and so forth. Many of the media shown in Exhibit 12.3 can be delivered on a TV set, tablet computer, or elsewhere. In this environment, the most effective tactics will be those that integrate IMC tools to reach their target markets effectively and efficiently (at the lowest cost)—regardless of the communication channel. This is especially important and different because of the high level of multitasking among consumers, as mentioned in previous chapters. To do this, marketers must know the capabilities, strengths, and weaknesses of each medium.

Paid media can engage target markets, moving them to owned media and resulting in social media conversation (earned media). Great content will not stay trapped in owned media but will spread (such as the *Will It Blend?* videos or excellent white papers). Paid media often also carries sales promotions, such as the discounts offered by Lenovo in its display ads. This cycle of owned, paid, and earned media can also result in increased e-commerce sales.

Internet paid media parallels traditional media advertising, in which companies create content, draw an audience to their Web sites or mobile apps, and then sell space to outside advertisers (such as with television advertising). Sometimes it is confusing online, such as when a company includes something that looks like a banner ad promoting its own products on its Web site. The key is exchange—if a firm pays money or barters with goods for space in which to put the marketing message it creates, the content is considered paid media. In Chapter 11, we discussed how firms create revenue streams from selling advertising space, but this chapter discusses the flipside: buying advertising space from someone else to reach a firm's markets. These specific definitions are meaningless to consumers (who view all branded messages as advertising), but they are important to marketers because various MarCom tools help to accomplish various specific goals.

In this chapter, we begin with the trends in paid media and then move on to various types. We conclude with pricing models and metrics for monitoring paid media effectiveness.

TRUST IN PAID MEDIA

Do you trust ads? Globally, consumers trust earned media the most, followed by owned media, and then paid media. The most trusted digital media include branded Web sites, opt-in e-mails, coupons (owned media), and recommendations from like-minded people and social network contacts (earned media). Exhibit 13.1

Global Trust in Media

PAID	OWNED	EARNED
42% search ads[1] 36% video ads[1] 36% social network ads[1] 33% banner ads[1] 33% mobile ads[1] 29% text ads[1] 25% paid ads[3]	58% branded Web sites[1] 50% e-mails (opt-in)[1] 43% coupons/offers[3] 31% brand photos & videos[3] 30% social network pages[3]	65% persons like yourself[2] 62% contacts recommending product[3]

EXHIBIT 13.1 Proportion of Consumers Expressing Trust in Media *Sources:* 1. Nielsen Trust in Advertising Survey 2011 (blog.nielsen.com), 2. Edelman Global Trust Barometer, (trust.edelman.com), 3. Vision Critical Study (U.S. only) (womma.org)

displays the results of several studies that put most paid media at the bottom of the trust scale. Incidentally, Nielsen found that consumers don't trust traditional paid media much either: TV ads (47 percent), magazine ads (47 percent), and newspaper ads (46 percent) ("Earned, Owned Media. . .," 2012). And it goes downhill from there for ads before movies and radio ads.

According to Nielsen, mobile ads are the least trusted (only 33 percent trust mobile display ads and 29 percent trust text ads). Conversely, several studies have noted that ad recall is greater in social media and the movement of consumers to social media means that ad dollars are flowing to social media properties. Thus, marketers want to create authentic ads that drive traffic to their great owned content.

Even though a majority of consumers love to hate advertising, they usually recognize that someone has to pay for free content in the media. Nonetheless, in addition to the much disliked Web page pop-up ads, there are some online formats that frustrate users, according to usability testing by the Catalyst Group (see catalystnyc.com). Here are the "dirty ten" that online marketers would be wise to avoid: Banner ads below headers, ads that look like content (e.g., some sponsorships), dancing ads (across the Web page), auto-expanding half-page ads, banners next to logos, billboards in the top right corner, Google text links interrupting content, ads with hidden close buttons, interstitials (taking over the entire screen), and other page takeovers. In short—most interrupt advertising. Nonetheless, paid media are still very effective for building awareness and moving users to owned media: Online advertising is growing, as discussed next.

INTERNET ADVERTISING TRENDS

Internet advertising in the United States began with the first series of banner ads on Hotwired .com on October 27, 1994. One of these ads, sponsored by AT&T, simply invited users to "click here" with no graphics or animation. The ad ran for 12 weeks, cost $30,000, and received an amazing 30 percent click-through. Compare this ratio to the less than 1 percent click-through rates on banner ads in 2012. That means fewer than 10 people in 1,000 click on an ad. Interestingly, only 16 percent of internet users click on ads at all (down from 32 percent in 2007), and 8 percent of users account for 85 percent of all clicks, according to comScore research. In its report, comScore suggests that online display ads improved online and offline sales and Web site visits even if people didn't click on the ads. This means that the online brand

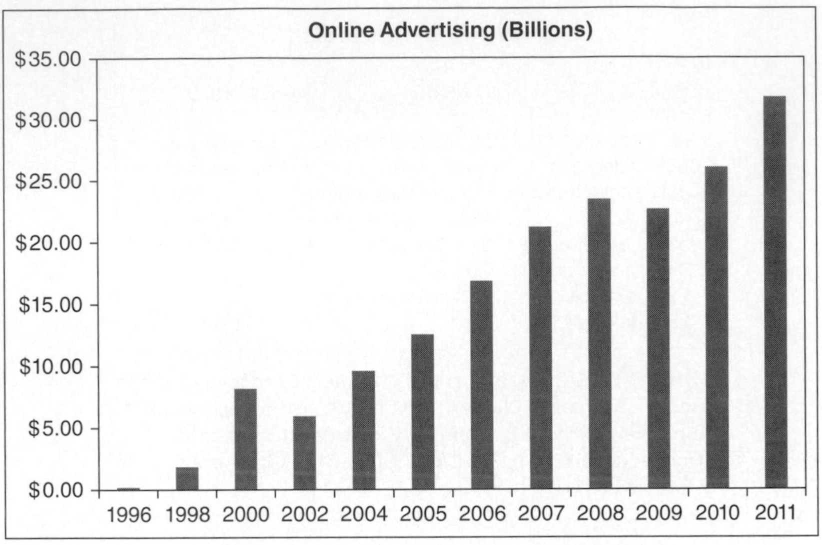

EXHIBIT 13.2 U.S. Internet Advertising Expenditure, 1996–2011
Source: PricewaterhouseCoopers LLP/IAB Internet Advertising Revenue Reports

communication effects increased sales in the absence of positive direct response metrics.

U.S. online advertising reached $1 billion in 1998, grew quickly to $8.2 billion in 2000, dropped a bit in 2001–2002 due to the economic recession, and continued to grow to $31 billion in 2011 with a small drop-off due to the economic crisis in 2009 (Exhibit 13.2). Predictions of 2012 online spending showed an average of a 23 percent increase (the first half of 2012 exhibited a 14 percent increase over 2011). Global online ad spending reached $84.8 billion in 2011 (O'Leary, 2012). Most advertisers realize that the internet is an important medium for reaching their target markets. This is especially true for retailers, who spend the most of any industry for paid media online ($7.1 billion in 2011), according to the Interactive Advertising Bureau (IAB) (Exhibit 13.3).

To understand the context of advertiser spending on the internet, consider that total advertising expenditures in the United States alone during 2012 were expected to reach $169.5 billion (Indvik, 2012). In other words, in 2012, internet firms with space to sell might capture 23.3 percent of advertiser dollars and, for the first time ever, this surpasses the amount spent on traditional print advertising.

PAID MEDIA FORMATS

Anything goes with paid media online: text—from a sentence to pages of story—graphics, sound, video, hyperlinks, or an animated car driving through a page. A paid search ad, prompted by keywords, is the most important technique (see Exhibit 13.4). Keyword search is the paid part of a larger strategy called search marketing, as discussed in Chapter 12. Mobile advertising is the fastest-growing category, nearly doubling from the first half of 2011 to 2012 (from $636 million to $1.2 billion).

Many of these ads also have interactive capability, allowing action between consumers and producers. This occurs when the advertiser provides a link, game, or direct purchase shopping cart within the ad, and the consumer can click on the ad to activate a drop-down menu or other interactive feature. For example, Virgin America created an interactive ad that allows users to vote for their favorite in-flight feature: (1) plugs at every seat; (2) MP3s, movies, and TV; or (c) fresh food and mixed drinks. The bottom of the ad indicates the number of people voting and if the ad was placed in a social network, how many of the voters are the user's friends.

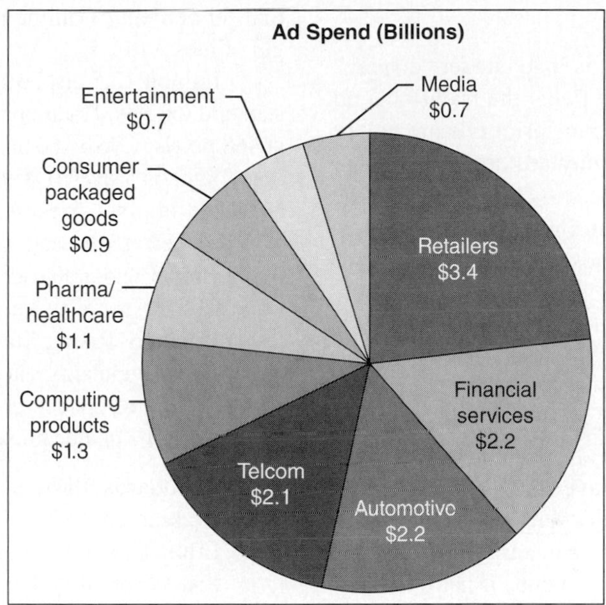

EXHIBIT 13.3 U.S. Internet Advertising Expenditure by Industry in First Half of 2012 *Source:* Pricewaterhouse-Coopers LLP/IAB Internet Advertising Revenue Reports

Display ads are the second-largest spending category, with a little over 20 percent of online marketers' advertising dollars followed by classified ads and the fast-growing mobile ad category. It is interesting to note how ad formats have changed over the years, reflecting the intense competition for audience attention in an environment where consumers are in charge. Next, we discuss several interesting or commonly used advertising formats. Then, due to their importance, we present mobile, social media, and search engine paid media in separate sections.

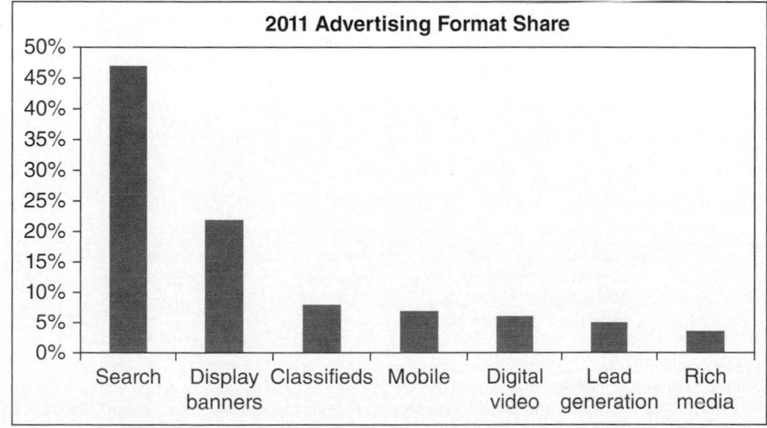

EXHIBIT 13.4 Proportion of Advertising Dollars by Format in 2011
Source: PricewaterhouseCoopers LLP/IAB Internet Advertising Revenue Reports.

Display Ads

Note that the banner ad is listed under "display" in Exhibit 13.4. This reflects the traditional ad nomenclature—traditional print ads are called display ads. Online **display ads** are embedded in Web pages, allowing users to click through to the advertiser's site and can include text, graphics, and animation. These ads usually contain more graphics and white space than text, and include traditional banners and many additional sizes. Display ad revenues in 2011 totaled $11.1 billion (22 percent of all online ad revenue).

The Interactive Advertising Bureau (IAB) has proposed standard dimensions for display ads. It is important to have standardized formats so that Web site owners renting ad space and advertisers purchasing it can easily agree on the space and creative requirements. It helps companies to create a standard ad for use on many sites, versus having to make many different versions, and it helps the media design pages that allow for insertion of standard ad sizes. The IAB claims that 80 percent of online marketers follow these guidelines.

Exhibit 13.5 displays many of the display ad standard formats. Traditional banners are rectangular at 468 pixels wide by 60 pixels tall (one **pixel** is one dot of light on a screen). The ad sizes in Exhibit 13.5 are listed in pixel sizes. Although many sizes are standard, newer sizes and formats break through the online clutter and grab user attention better than do standard sizes, so things keep changing.

"Display Rising Stars" in Exhibit 13.5 are increasing in popularity and use, including billboard, filmstrip, portrait, sidekick, and slider. Following are some of the unique properties of each:

- Billboards allow users to close the ad by clicking an "x."
- Filmstrips are divided into five segments that scroll through a window when the user interacts with the ad.
- Portraits allow for up to three interactive segments cycling through the space, driven by user interactivity.

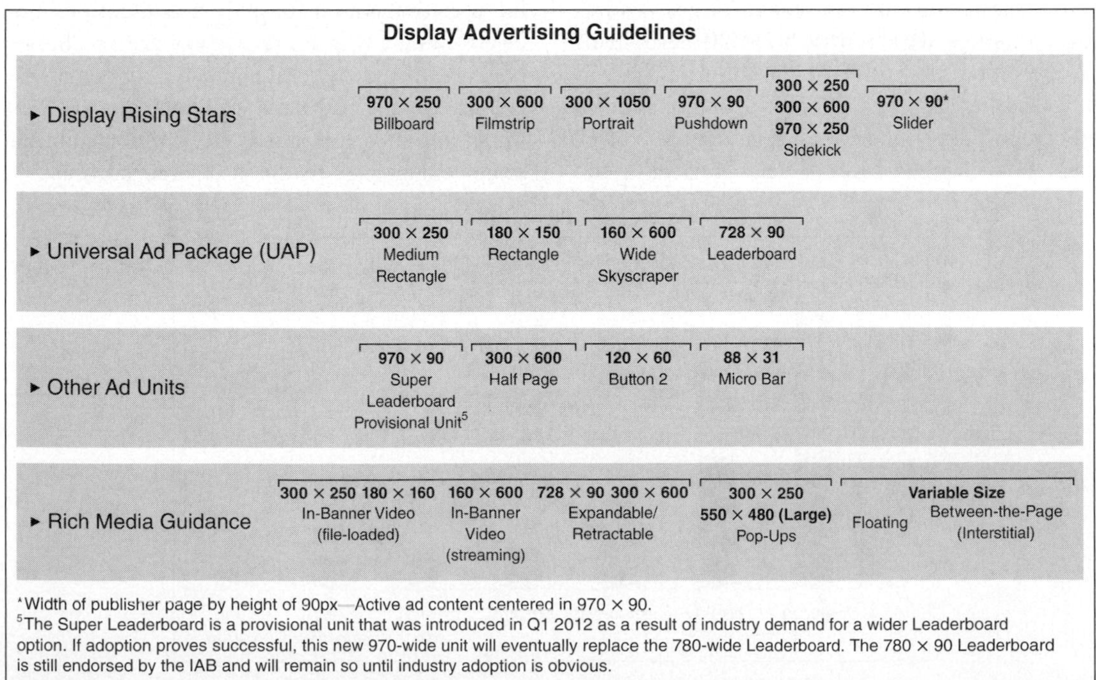

EXHIBIT 13.5 IAB Display Advertising Guidelines in 2012 *Source:* Internet Advertising Bureau (iab.net)

- Sidekick starts as the sizes listed, but the user can click to open it to 970 × 550 pixels of interactivity. A slider does something similar, but starts at screen bottom prior to a user clicking to open it to a larger size.

The Universal Ad Package (UAP) includes four sizes that can be displayed all over a publisher's Web site for gaining more impressions and possible click-throughs. "Other ad units" are simply additional sizes available to advertisers. Display ads also appear as overlays on videos; however, these account only for 6.9 percent of all online advertising (Reese, 2011).

One wonders why so many advertisers still use display ads for direct response when the click-through rates are so low. The answer is that (1) display ads help build brand awareness when viewed by site visitors and (2) carefully targeted display ads can generate high click-through rates, such as experienced by Lenovo.

Two additional types of display ads are a bit different from the previously discussed types: Rich media ads and contextual ads.

Rich Media Ads

All ads in this category are highly interactive, at least offering click-through to the advertiser's Web site, where the transaction or any other objective is achieved. Some rich media display ads enhance the interactivity by sensing the position of the mouse on the Web page and animating faster as the user approaches. Other ads have built-in games or videos. Still others have drop-down menus, check boxes, and search boxes to engage and empower the user. All of the following formats can be rich media (see Exhibit 13.5 and the IAB.net site for more on some of these):

- **In-banner video ad:** Similar to a banner ad, except that instead of a static or animated image, actual moving video clips are displayed without the viewer having to open a video window. These can be delivered as automatic streaming or be user-activated.
- **Expandable/retractable ad:** These become larger, sometimes filling an entire Web page. They can be automated or user-activated.
- **Pop-up:** A new window that opens in front of the current one, displaying an advertisement, or entire Web page.
- **Pop-under:** Similar to a pop-up except that the window is loaded or sent behind the current window so that the user does not see it until they close one or more active windows.
- **Floating ad:** An ad that moves across the user's screen or floats above the content. These can be animations, such as, the Energizer bunny hopping across the page.
- **Interstitial ad: Interstitial ad** is also called "between-the-page," this represents a full page ad that appears before the requested page content or as the user clicks between pages. Occasionally this type of ad can appear over a Web page as well.
- **Wallpaper ad:** An ad that changes the background of the page being viewed.
- **Trick banner:** A banner ad that looks like a dialog box with buttons. It simulates an error message or an alert.
- **Map ad:** Text or graphics linked from, and appearing in or over, a location on an electronic map such as on Google Maps.

One downside of video, animated, and highly **interactive display ads** is that they require more bandwidth. Keeping banner file sizes small reduces the time that they take to load. Another downside is that the aggressive types can irritate users, similar to all interrupt advertising (such as pop-ups). Alternatively, they can definitely engage users if appropriate to the market.

Contextual Advertising

Ad servers maintain an inventory of display ads from clients and serve them into Web sites as appropriate users are viewing particular pages. **Contextual advertising** occurs when an ad system scans a Web page for content and serves an appropriate ad, such as an ad for tickets to a concert on a music site. Google's AdSense gives sites special JavaScript code to put into their HTML site code so that relevant ads can be sent into the page. Microsoft adCenter and many others offer this service and pay site owners when the ad appears on their sites.

Behavioral advertising is another form of contextual advertising, but follows user behavior instead of Web page text. Used by Lenovo in the Google Display Network, one behavioral advertising approach is called **remarketing**—a tactic that involves communicating with users who previously visited a Web site. This occurs when advertising networks track user click behavior, usually through cookie files placed on their hard drive, then present ads to the user based on their previous behavior. For example, when you search for a particular CD, an ad for that CD might appear on Amazon.com on a subsequent visit. This is accomplished via ad networks that maintain a large number of Web site clients. The largest ad networks are search engines—for example, the Google AdWords program has a network that reaches 80 percent of U.S. internet users (i.e., over 245 million people). The Web site owner gets paid when users click on the targeted ads.

Facebook also offers very specific ad targeting based on profile information (more on this later). Contextual advertising is good microsegmentation for marketers and good for users who receive relevant ads at the precise moment they want information. Contextual advertising tends to yield higher click-through rates because the ads are relevant to the user's needs.

E-Mail Advertising

Sometimes, the least expensive type of online advertising is **e-mail advertising**—paid content embedded in another firm's e-mail. Advertisers purchase space in the e-mail sponsored by others, often an e-mail newsletter. For example, the Law Marketing Association sells a 50-word text ad with a 75 by 75 pixel graphic logo for inclusion in its e-mail newsletter to legal firm marketers and consultants for $500 a month (see lawmarketing.com). In another example, eMarketer.com sends "eMarketer FYI" e-mails to its regular newsletter subscribers that include graphical ads and links to white paper downloads from other companies (and are paid for this). Note that HTML and multimedia e-mail messages sent from a firm directly to internet users are owned content, not paid media.

Text Link Ads

These are ads that are simply a hyperlink placed in specific text in a blog post or other owned media content—including content downloaded by mobile phone users. In a hypothetical example, a flower shop might buy a specified number of links for the word *rose* on many blogger sites, and these would have a hyperlink to the flower shop's Web site. The goal of these ads is to raise a site's rankings in the search engines. For example, a furniture store bought three keywords in a large number of related Web sites, and in over a 1-year period, the store moved from a rank of 97 to 4 in a Google Search Engine results page (SERP) for those three keywords (see textlinkbrokers.com for other success stories).

Sponsored Content

Sponsorships integrate editorial content and paid media based on either underwritten (someone else's content) or advertiser-created content. Most traditional media clearly separate content from advertising; women's magazines are an exception. Food advertisers usually barter for recipes that include their products in these magazines, and fashion advertisers get mentions of their clothing in articles. This practice pleases advertisers because it gives them additional exposure and creates the impression that the publication endorses their products. The IAB has observed the following types of online sponsorships: content creation, mobile/Web applications, branded interaction, contests/sweepstakes, games, podcasts, polls/surveys, and trivia.

For example, a food company might pay for space on a cooking blog or wiki to insert recipes using its products as ingredients (e.g., Hershey's Brownie Recipe). Astrology.com sponsors an astrology quiz on iVillage.com, a site for women. This adds value for site users and revenue for iVillage. This looks like content from the site, but is actually paid for space. Companies also can pay bloggers directly to endorse products by writing positive reviews. A problem with sponsored content, however, is that bloggers often do not disclose that they are being paid (or receiving gifts) for their endorsements, even though the recent U.S. Federal Trade Commission guidelines require this disclosure. If they do not tell and are found out, they can be exposed with a huge and negative amount of discussion online (and possible federal action). Nonetheless, 54 percent of marketers have paid for sponsored blog posts ("Marketers Rely Most...," 2012).

PayPerPost runs a marketplace where advertisers can find bloggers, online photographers, and podcasters who are willing to endorse advertisers' products (payperpost.com). It claims to create 220 million impressions of sponsored content a month in social media. A company begins by registering with PayPerPost and describing the type of endorsement it wants and how much it is willing to pay. A hotel, for example, might post a request for people willing to write a 50-word blog entry about their property or upload a video of themselves enjoying the hotel facilities. Bloggers create the blog post and then inform PayPerPost, which checks to see that the content matches what the advertiser asked for, and PayPerPost arranges payment. Note that the PayPerPost bloggers *are* required to disclose that they are being paid for their posting.

Some people worry about the ethics of sponsorships when consumers cannot easily identify the content author(s). Perhaps this problem is not significant because many users view the entire Web as one giant advertisement. However, when advertising is passed off as locally generated content, it can potentially lower user trust in the Web site and hurt brand image. To address this important issue, the IAB established a panel to set standards for sponsor disclosure in this type of advertising.

Note that Facebook and Twitter also have sponsored content. You'll read about this in the social media section, later in this chapter.

Classified Ads

Classified ads are placed both by individual consumers and by companies. These usually use text, but may also include photos. The ads are grouped according to classification (e.g., cars and rentals) and tend to be an inexpensive format. Classified ads can be found on dedicated sites (e.g., craigslist.org and superpages.com), as well as online newspapers, exchanges, and Web portals. In many cases, posting regular-size classified ads is free, but placing them in a larger size, in color, or with some other noticeable features is done for a fee. Craigslist postings are free for most citizens, but it covers operating costs by charging a fee for job listings and apartments for rent in large cities. Many daily newspapers have suffered big financial losses due to the classified ad business moving to the free Craigslist.

Product Placement

Online gaming creates huge special-interest communities. There are many types of online games with social interaction, from two-player chess to Massively Multiplayer Online Role Playing Games (MMORPG)—sporting thousands of players moving about as avatars at the same time. Some games have storylines or plots, with players accomplishing goals and developing in skill and power, and others are completely nonstructured, with players designing the action. World of Warcraft may be the most popular MMORPG, with 10 million monthly subscribers worldwide. Advertisers are keenly interested in online games because they reach a broad spectrum of demographics and the players actually like to see product placement in the games. This is because it makes the games seem more real. This is similar to movie product placement offline. For example, the online music video game Guitar Hero often has advertisements on the stage behind the musicians. Some games include billboards or signs on walls behind the players.

Television programming also includes product placement. For example, a show like *The Handyman* might have branded tools used for fixing up houses. *American Idol* is famous for including a Coca-Cola in each of the judge's hands. Now that these programs are seen online via Hulu, Netflix, and more, this can also be considered paid online media product placement. In the social media world, product mentions in tweets, blogs, and elsewhere are the new age of product placement, as discussed later in this chapter.

Emerging Formats

On the internet, anything goes and novelty gains attention. This is fertile ground for the creative advertiser, who constantly devises new ways to reach target markets with online advertising. Downloadable widget ads are one of the latest trends. Kraft Foods offers a widget that once installed on a consumer's desktop will automatically send a different recipe every day. Yahoo! has nearly 5,000 widgets, some of which offer shopping assistance—such as one that searches for Amazon.com deals or finds products at Sears .com. Internet users are attracted to novel things online, so new formats are usually attention getting and help to build brand awareness and motivate purchase.

SOCIAL MEDIA ADVERTISING

Social media sites sell space to advertisers who wish to reach the site's audience. In this section, we will discuss paid media on the most important of these sites. In 2011, two-thirds of marketers conducted social media advertising campaigns and 18 percent said they planned to do so within the next year, according to research from The Pivot Conference ("Advertisers Begin to Look . . .," 2011). Furthermore, 54 percent of those marketers running social media ads were very satisfied with the results for achieving campaign objectives. This research discovered the four main objectives for this branded content paid by advertisers in social media (as cited in Solis, 2011): build brand awareness (17 percent), engage existing customers (13 percent), increase the size of community (friends, followers, and fans: 12 percent), and drive traffic to an online destination (12 percent). Advertisers also used social media to introduce new products, build databases, and gain feedback from users.

Thus, paid social media are for building awareness, creating positive brand attitudes, collecting valuable information about customers, and motivating actions such as joining a community, clicking through to a site, and purchase. To drive sales, they require a compelling reason to click. For example, the fast-food chain Chick-fil-A ran a successful Facebook free-sample sales promotion engagement ad campaign; clicking on the ad revealed a form to receive a mail-in coupon.

Advertising spending on social media is predicted to grow 15 to 34 percent faster than search advertising over the next 5 years, according to Forrester Research. Part of this growth is for display ad space on blogs and other social media. However, display ads do not take advantage of the unique properties of social networks, such as Facebook—namely, high user interactivity and free sharing of individual profiles and photos. Social networks have three unique aspects:

- ***Personal profile.*** Social networks contain personal profiles' data, including the member's name, image and other pictures, demographic information (e.g., age, gender, and location of residence), interests, career/student status, and membership groups. These data are freely shared and usable by marketers for customizing advertising.
- ***Social data graph.*** Companies can make a map or list of all the connections between individuals to discover the network size for like-minded people.
- ***Interpersonal interaction data.*** Marketers can capture information about the amount and timing of interactions among network friends.

In contrast, behavioral targeting, discussed previously, sends appropriate display ads, Web pages, or e-mail based on the user's click behavior when viewing Web sites. Many companies have created advertising platforms that capitalize on social media's unique features. Social media ads use these data for specific targeting and user engagement.

Advertising is the major current revenue source for social media companies. Advertisers are willing to pay a great deal for placing ads and running promotions in social networks because of the large number of visitors in the networks and the amount of time they spend there. They find it effective. In one Marketing Sherpa study, 56 percent of marketers found paid media on blogs and other social media sites to be somewhat very effective (available at bakasmedia.com).

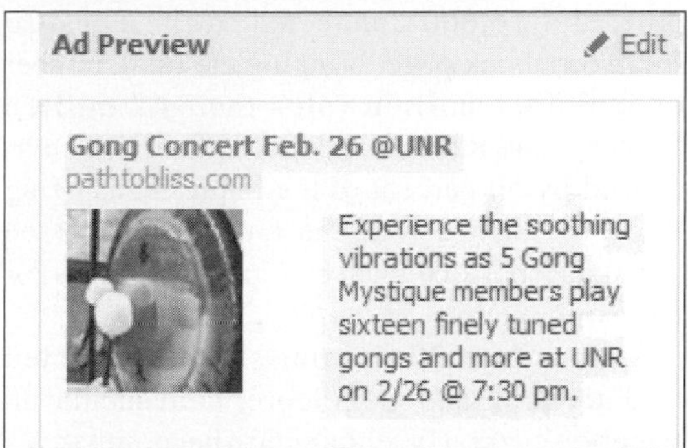

EXHIBIT 13.6 Facebook Ad Placed by the Author

Paid Media on Facebook

Advertisers can reach over 1 billion active members by advertising on the Facebook social network, with over 50 percent of users logging in on any given day, according to Facebook.com. However, most advertisers prefer more narrow targeting to reach their well-defined markets, and this can easily be done via member profile information. Exhibit 13.6 is a Facebook ad placed by one author to promote a gong concert. When placing the ad, the marketer selects the desired target profile. For this ad, the criteria were Facebook users with the following in their profiles:

- live in the United States
- live within 50 miles of Reno, NV
- are aged 18 and older
- who like meditation, tai chi, reiki, power now, sound healing, metaphysics, meditating, Buddhism, Deepak Chopra, and spirituality or yoga

This narrow targeting resulted in 4,980 Facebook users, all of whom were presented the ad on their walls and would likely be interested and able to attend the Reno concert. The cost of the ad was based on the number clicking on it, at a rate of $0.88 per click.

This narrow targeting is important for global advertisers because Facebook is available in more than 70 different languages on the site, and over 75 percent of active users live outside of the United States. Facebook ads can include interactive features, link to other brand content, and are very easy to create. Advertisers simply upload an image and type the text right into the Facebook template. Facebook offers excellent metrics to see how many people were presented the ad, and whether or not they took an action, like clicking on a link. Furthermore, advertisers can set a maximum daily budget.

In another example, PepsiCo India ran a "Reach Block" on Facebook in February 2011. Reach Block allows advertisers to specify a particular demographic they want to reach, such as all users 18–20 years old. This market will see the ad a maximum of five times a day. In this example, PepsiCo used a geographic target: The Reach Block ad appeared on Facebook pages of all Indian Facebook users. The campaign enticed users to watch video content from a television ad called "Change the Game," and to vote on the cricket umpire's style via a video plus poll. PepsiCo also used a Premium Video Like Ad, encouraging users to watch the ad, "Like" it, and connect to the Pepsi India page. Finally, a third ad drove users to the PepsiCo India micro site, where they could upload a headshot of themselves to create an avatar that would wear clothing with a Pepsi logo on it and dance and cheer around on their desktop for India's cricket team. Users could share the avatar with friends.

The Reach Block video ads were viewed over 19 million times, 53,000 people took the poll, and 16,000 connected to the PepsiCo India Facebook page, bringing the total number of fans to 1 million (plus their 42 million friends). The Reach Block became viral, as evidenced by 50 percent of the impressions being those of "friends" of the target market (see ads.ak.facebook.com advertising case studies for more information).

In a late 2012 joint study conducted by Facebook and ComScore, paid media on Facebook greatly enhanced the company's reach. For example, the top 100 Facebook pages reached 5.4 times as many users by adding paid media (Cohen, 2012). Focusing on three brands, including Samsung Mobile USA, the study also found that users exposed to paid media were more likely than average Facebook users to shop and purchase from these companies.

Facebook Sponsored Stories

In January 2011, Facebook added an interesting feature called *sponsored story*, which integrates social endorsement into ads. This is a great tactic because a Facebook member's friends are likely in the same target market for any particular product. When members chat with friends and notify them that they "checked into" a place or "like it," for instance at Starbucks, a boxed "sponsored story" will appear on the Facebook page with the logo of Starbucks (fee paid to Facebook). Furthermore, the name Starbucks will also appear in the user's news feed (another fee paid to Facebook). This feature has a few variations (e.g., uploaded photos). Users have the option to delete the boxed advertisement. This kind of advertising can increase word-of-mouth conversation as well. There are several types of sponsored stories (all paid for by advertisers):

- **Domain stories** happen when a user "likes" a Web site while on the site. Immediately a post goes into the user's Facebook news feed, saying something to the effect: "Travis likes X site."
- **Page like stories** are similar; however, the news feed post occurs when a user "likes" a product's Facebook page.
- **Check in stories** occur when a user checks in via Facebook at a retail location. When the advertiser pays for this type of sponsored story, the user's friends will see the check in.
- **Page post stories** allow marketers to turn favorable posts on their own Facebook pages into ads.
- **App Used/Shared Game Played stories** are shown to the friends who also use apps or games.

Social Ads

A social ad has three criteria: profile data, interaction data, and social graph (friend connections). Thus, data to create these ads come automatically from the user's profile data, social data (friends/connections), and interaction data (data about the user's interaction with friends). For example, if a Facebook user went to a particular movie and liked it, a social ad would be populated with this information. The ad is then presented to the Facebook friends that she selected to view it and, thus, share her excitement about this new movie (or product). A social ad also can include interactive features such as polling, votes, sharing, and other types of engagement with the ad.

In general, when companies incorporate social networks into ads, Facebook advertising is quite effective. One study of 800,000 Facebook users showed a big increase in ad recall, awareness, and purchase intent for the Facebook ads of 14 different brands—this occurred when the homepage ads mentioned the friends of users who were already fans of the advertised brand (Neff, 2010).

Twitter's "Promoted Tweets," "Trends," and "Accounts"

Barking at Facebook's heels, Twitter is a strong competitor for advertisers' dollars. According to Learmonth (2011), Twitter launched its first ad product—*promoted tweets*—in 2010 and netted $45 million in ad dollars. That was due in part to the enthusiasm among brands like Virgin America, Coke, Ford, and Verizon to give the untried format a whirl. Learmonth estimates the ad revenue to be $150 million in 2011 and $250 million in 2012. **Promoted tweets** are ads that appear as content at the top of a Twitter search page or a user's timeline. They can be targeted to Twitter users by geographic location and by whose Twitter streams they follow. Users can interact with promoted Tweets just as they can with organic Tweets. **Promoted trends** are ads placed on hot topics in Twitter that are presented near a user's timeline. **Promoted account ads** are featured in search results and in the "Who to Follow section." These ads help users find others with similar interests.

Using these paid media vehicles, advertisers can target Twitter users by 350 very narrow interests, such as movies that are musicals. Companies can also target @username to reach users with similar interests as the original account holder, not simply their followers.

Another interesting trend is that famous Twitter account holders often get paid to send tweets. For example, Kim Kardashian gets paid $10,000, Snoop Dogg $8,000, and Charlie Sheen $50,000 per tweet ("Kim Kardashian, Snoop . . .," 2012). These celebrities tweet when they visit a retailer, like Best Buy or a restaurant, and the innocuous tweets do not seem like the paid media that they are. One study found that 47.3 percent of marketers had paid for sponsored Tweets in 2012 ("Marketers Rely Most. . .," 2012).

LinkedIn Advertising

The LinkedIn social network is great for advertising to narrowly targeted business professionals. Advertisers can use the LinkedIn DirectAds product to target by (1) job title and function, (2) industry or company size, (3) seniority or age, or (4) LinkedIn Group membership. Advertisers have the choice of paying for the number of impressions or clicks (see more in the pricing model discussion later in this chapter). According to Matt Johnson of uTest, LinkedIn is their most effective online media, generating 50 percent of inbound links (see linkedin.com for more information).

Advertising in Second Life

Interestingly, it is possible to advertise in virtual worlds. For instance, in Second Life, companies can pay virtual clubs, stores, or malls to put up posters or kiosks featuring brand information and links and can even provide "teleports" to the company's virtual property. There are ad networks available in-world so that advertisers can spread their messages throughout various properties and pay for either number of ads displayed or per click on the ads.

Paid Media in Online Videos

Organizations can place ads before, during, or after videos on a number of different sites, including YouTube and Vimeo. The types of ads include the following:

- In-stream videos are ad units that show before or during the video playback, such as pre-roll, mid-roll, and video takeovers (ad takes over the entire video screen for a short time). These are usually 15 to 30 seconds in length.
- Interactive banners and buttons run over or within the video content during play.
- Branded player skins allow companies to surround the video with their branded images. Note that text, banners, and rich media ads can also surround the video.
- In-text video ads are displayed when the viewer rolls the mouse over relevant words shown during the video play.
- Various sizes include banners, marquees, expandable ads, and full screen takeovers.

Nearly all of these allow for interactivity. Viewers can click through to an advertiser's Web site, Facebook, or Twitter page. Also, special buttons allow click-through to get store or dealer locations, see related videos, and receive special promotions or simply to share the video (automatically offered on YouTube but not at all video sites). As well, video ads must be prepared to play automatically for the three screens: television, computer, and smartphone.

Just as with the Google Display Network, several companies offer video network ad serving. According to comScore, in October 2012 there were 10.9 billion streaming video ads (68.2 per viewer) for 3.8 billion ad minutes of viewing pleasure ("Top 5 Video . . . ," 2012). The leading network servers and their share of market were BrightRoll (16.8 percent), Google Sites (16.1 percent), Hulu (14.2 percent), and LiveRail (11.4 percent). This was the first time that Google's network fell from first place—amazing because Google owns YouTube.

Note that advertisers pay only if viewers watch at least 30 seconds or to the end of the ad. That is, when viewers click to skip the ad after a few seconds, advertisers do not have to pay for the placement. Recall from Chapter 7 that 71 percent of internet users watch videos on social media sites; this type of paid media space is very important for marketers.

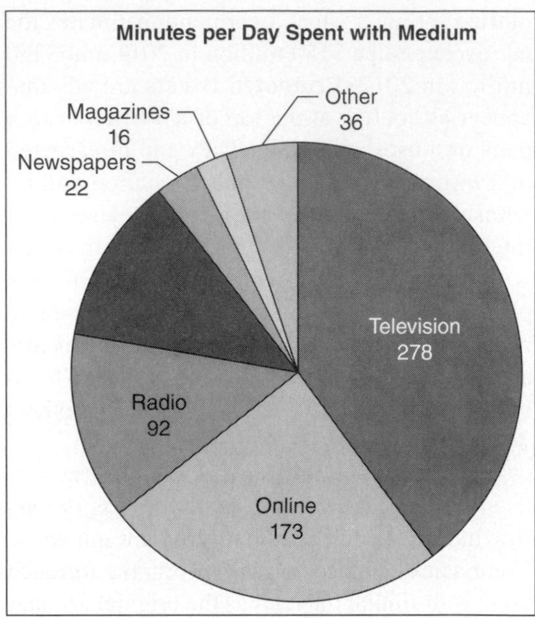

EXHIBIT 13.7 Consumer Time Spent with Each Medium in 2012 *Source:* eMarketer.com ("Trends for 2013. . .,'" 2012).

MOBILE ADVERTISING

Forward-thinking marketers are closely watching developments in the mobile device market. Smartphones and tablets have high penetration, and several companies predict that mobile internet usage will surpass computer internet usage by 2014. While mobile advertising is still only 6 percent of the online advertising pie (Exhibit 13.4), according to the *Economist*, "Marketers hail the mobile phone as advertising's promised land." This is partly because consumers spend 82 minutes a day in nonvoice activities on the phone (Exhibit 13.7).

E-marketer predicts that mobile advertising will reach $2.61 billion in 2012 ("Advertisers Will Spend. . .," 2012). The reason for its fast growth also has to do with Google's mobile search advertising options, the increase of display advertising space available, and the number of mobile networks for placing ads (such as Google's AdMob and Apple's iAd). Note that the lion's share of mobile ad spend goes to mobile search (45 percent), followed by banners and rich media (30.7 percent), and text/video messaging (19.6 percent) ("Advertisers Will Spend. . .," 2012). This ratio is not likely to change much, partially because it parallels computer ad spending proportions. Following are the mobile advertising formats available to marketers:

- ***Paid search.*** Advertisers can buy keywords that appear as sponsored links on mobile search engine results pages. Because of limited screen sizes, these ads must be short and relevant in order to attract click-throughs.
- ***Display ads.*** Users pull content from mobile Web sites and banners, flash, or other types of ad formats come along for the ride. In Virgin Mobile's "Sugar Mama" campaign, it offered cell phone owners free minutes in exchange for viewing mobile ads. For example, viewing a 45-second ad while on the Web got them one free minute of cell talk time, and receiving text message ads or completing online questionnaires got them more free minutes. According to Ultramercial, the company running the campaign, Virgin Mobile gave away over 10 million free minutes by mid-campaign.

- ***Full screen takeovers.*** Say Publishing offers a mobile display ad platform involving an ad image taking over the entire mobile screen (saymedia.com). They can also provide this as an interstitial.
- ***Messaging.*** Short message services (SMS) have broader reach than many other formats because even the lowest-end phone can receive text messages, but not all can receive larger display ads or videos. Text ads are also included with other types of content.
- ***Location-based ads.*** These are often text based, relying on GPS (discussed more thoroughly in Chapters 12 and 14).
- ***Video.*** These ads are a slowly growing area because they take up a lot of bandwidth and thus are lengthy to download.
- ***Voice.*** While still quite rare, voice ads can play before or after a voicemail or conversation.
- ***Apps.*** The iPhone and iPad put mobile apps on the map. Advertisers can use apps as a sampling for products (freemium model), or they can send ads with an application to offset the user's free purchase price. Tapjoy offers an ad marketplace, offering consumers virtual rewards or extra content within an app in exchange for completing some action (registering, subscribing, taking a survey, and so forth). Advertisers pay Tapjoy for this service.

Following rapid mobile use growth, the Interactive Advertising Bureau and Mobile Marketing Association (MMA) are quickly trying to define advertising formats and pricing models. It is difficult for advertisers because mobile phones have many different screen sizes and resolutions. For example, the MMA has specified four different banner sizes based on several different "aspect ratios" of a screen—aspect ratio refers to the screen width by height (e.g., the iPhone has a 2 by 3 aspect ratio and a television screen has a 4 by 3 ratio). For a 6 by 1 aspect ratio phone screen, an extra large banner ad would be 300 by 50 pixels, but for a 4 by 1 aspect ratio screen it would be 300 by 75 pixels. Is your head spinning yet? This is what mobile advertisers have to go through when trying to send banner ads to cell phones.

Which platform to choose? It all depends on the marketing goals of the campaign, the target market demographics and behavior, and other things marketers consider for any advertising format choice. See Exhibit 13.8 for a matrix showing which IMC goals are best for selected mobile advertising goals, according to the Interactive Advertising Bureau.

Mobile ads are a new area with great promise and many unanswered questions. An important current debate involves whether mobile users would rather pay for content or receive advertising-sponsored content. This is analogous to television—the audience can pay for cable TV programming with no commercials or receive advertising-sponsored programming from stations. In one survey, only 9 percent of phone users would be very likely, and 25 percent somewhat

	Display Ad	SMS	Location Based	Paid Search	Video	Voice	Apps
Branding	3		3		3	3	3
Drive-to-mobile site	3	3	3	3	3		3
Click to call		3	3	3		3	3
Dialog with customer		3				3	3
Lead generation	3	3		3			3
Direct sales	3		3	3			3

EXHIBIT 13.8 Mobile Advertising Venues by Campaign Goal *Source:* Adapted from "IAB Mobile Buyer's Guide." Available at iab.net

likely, to be receptive to receiving ads—even if they were opt-in ads ("Mobile Metrics to Know," 2010). However, because 43 percent of mobile phone users access the internet daily from their phones, this low consumer interest doesn't seem to be discouraging marketers—after all, consumers hate advertising but they still view it if relevant to them, and if these are creatively conceived and executed.

Several major issues may affect the future of mobile advertising. First, wireless bandwidth is currently small, so additional advertising content interferes with quick download of the requested information. Second, the smaller screen size of cell phones and smartphones greatly limits ad size. Third, it requires different techniques to track advertising effectiveness, and this is an emerging field. Finally, many mobile users must pay their service provider by the minute or amount of data downloaded while accessing the internet—and many do not want to pay for the time it takes to receive ads. In spite of these issues, content-sponsored advertising on mobile devices is likely to increase in the future.

Do mobile ads work? A Nielsen study of iPhone users compared Apple's iAds involving Campbell Soup Company as an advertiser against similar TV ads (Patel, 2011). Those who were exposed to one of Campbell's iAd campaigns had higher brand recall than those who had seen similar TV ads. The 5-week study showed that those seeing an iAd remembered the brand "Campbell's" five times more often than TV ad respondents, and the ad messaging three times more often.

PAID SEARCH

Paid search occurs when an advertiser pays a search engine a fee for directory submission, for inclusion in a search engine index, or to display its ad when users type in particular keywords. Paid search has been the paid media giant since 2006, capturing nearly half of all online advertising dollars in 2011 (Exhibit 13.4). Marketers spent $14.8 billion on paid search (advertising) in 2011, an increase of 27 percent from 2010. Internet users click on paid search ads (also called "sponsored links") 25 percent of the time, according to HubSpot. Three tactics currently prevail when it comes to paid search marketing: keyword advertising, paid inclusion, and directory listings.

Keyword advertising at search engine sites prompts sponsored text or display ads to appear on the SERPs (Search Engine Results Pages). For example, advertisers can buy the word *automobile*, and when users search using that word, the advertiser's banner or text message will appear on the resulting page. A review of Exhibit 12.16 shows the advertisers who bought the term *e-mail marketing* as sponsored links on the top and right of the natural SERP links. Google.com orders the ads by price paid in a keyword bidding process, the landing page URL, and the click-through rate. Thus, the most relevant ad tops the list of sponsored links on the page. Most advertisers use word groupings that describe the business rather than relying on a single word. They also use "negative" keywords to remove words that don't apply, such as a dinner-only restaurant using "restaurant" and then "lunch" and "breakfast" as negative words because it is open only for dinner. There are many other criteria, such as industry categories, and as with natural search, paid search is always changing.

Google also sends contextual ads for display on other Web sites in its AdSense program, as previously mentioned (site owners get paid whenever a user clicks on the ad at their site or in a video and so forth). See the Let's Get Technical box to understand how search engines work.

Paid inclusion occurs when sites receive guaranteed indexing in a search engine. This service is offered by many search engines, except for Google—which does not offer paid inclusion, preferring to keep the natural search results purely based on its algorithm. Sites can submit URLs both to Google and to Yahoo! for free. Doing this accelerates the time to get into the index, although the search crawlers will eventually find the site. Paid inclusion doesn't guarantee position in the SERP—other factors used for ranking determine the position there. Sometimes search engines indicate paid inclusion with the term *sponsored link*.

LET'S GET TECHNICAL

Search Engines

You've just been hired as a junior executive in the marketing department. You'd like to make a good impression. Your manager hands you a study showing that most visitors to your company's Web site find the site using a search engine. She asks you to improve your site's ranking on the search engines. You have no idea where to begin and you are worried about looking bad. Fortunately, you've heard about services that help improve search engine rankings. If only you could remember what they are called and how they work.

The Web contains billions of pages. Realistically it would be impossible for the search engines to search the entire Web every time someone types in a search term. The task would take days to complete. Therefore, search engines actually do the searching up to a month in advance and store the results in a huge database. They send automatic programs called **spiders** out on the Web to go from site to site, page by page, and word by word, as shown in Exhibit 13.9. These spiders build up a massive index or database of all the words found, where they are found, how many times they appear on each page, and so on.

When users type in a search term, they are actually querying this database. Because it is an indexed database, the query returns the results almost instantly. The results are generally returned in order of relevance, with the most relevant site appearing first. But how does the search engine define relevance?

It is the search engine's job to figure out which sites are most likely to be relevant to the search term. Here the spider aids it. The spider does more than just count words. It also looks for the location of those words on the page and the **frequency** with which they appear. For example, if the word is in the title of a page, it is given a higher relevance value than a word appearing in the body text. A word appearing multiple times also earns a higher ranking.

So why not combine these ideas and repeat the keyword multiple times at the top of the page to fool the spider? The spiders are also trained to avoid sites that attempt to trick them by repeating words many

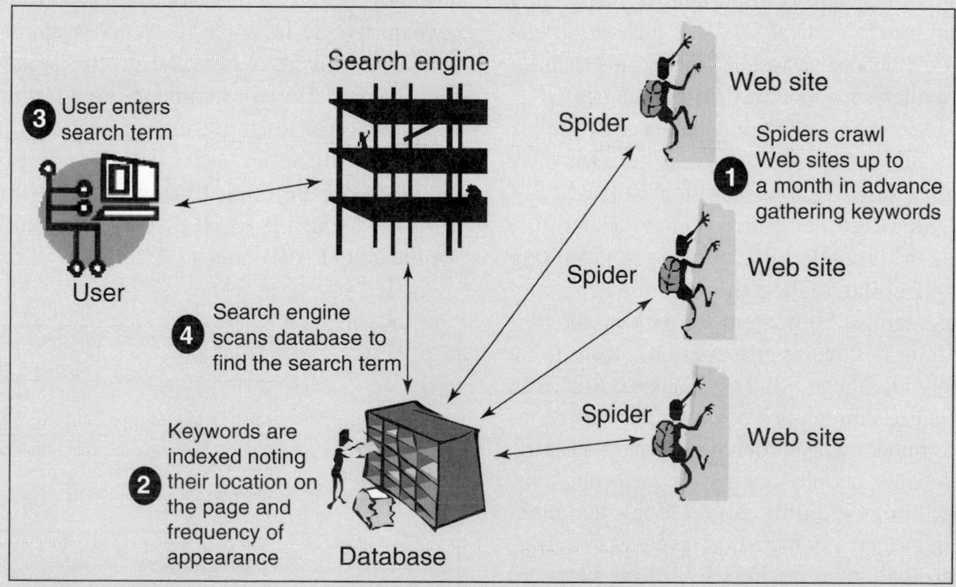

EXHIBIT 13.9 How Search Engines Work

(continued)

times in a row. One technique is to ignore repeats that are not separated by at least, say, seven other words. This guards against someone loading a page with, for example, "Mazda, Mazda, and Mazda." Google will even punish sites that attempt to work the system by plummeting their search engine ranking.

Search engines also take two other off-page considerations into account—how many sites link to a particular site and how many times users have clicked through to a site. Both links and click-throughs are indicators of a site's popularity.

So again why not just make a bunch of dummy sites that link to your site? Why not sign onto the search engine thousands of times and click through to your site to improve your ranking? The search engines are trained to spot both behaviors and compensate accordingly. The actual techniques used are becoming trade secrets because producing a search engine that returns truly useful results is actually a point of product differentiation and, therefore, provides a competitive advantage. Nonetheless, one Web site, Search Engine Watch (searchenginewatch.com), reveals many of the secrets of each search engine.

E-marketers would like their sites to appear high in the search engine rankings—preferably on the first page—above the fold—meaning that they show without scrolling. One way to gain this placement is to purchase paid listings usually triggered by keywords in the search term. Another way is to hire a company that studies the search engines to determine their algorithms for ranking pages. The analysis provides information that can be used to redesign pages so they will rise in the rankings. Some of these companies have rather catchy names, such as MoreVisibility and SpiderBait.

Directory submission is when an organization pays to be included in a searchable directory. For example, Yahoo! includes products in its shopping pages at a cost-per-click (CPC) fee and includes local business listings in its local directory ($299 for most businesses and $600 for adult content sites). Directory submission is important for many other search engines in vertical markets, such as job listing fees in Craigslist or business listings in Business.com. Note that some directory listings are free.

Paid search is commonly called pay per click (PPC) because advertisers pay whenever users click on the ads. Google charges between $0.15 and $15 per click; however, depending on the popularity of keywords the monthly bill can range from $100 to millions of dollars. Click-through rates can vary from 0 percent to 50 percent, so picking the best keywords is key if advertisers don't want to be surprised with a huge bill. For example, American Meadows used the names of particular flowers as keywords rather than "gardening" because it got too many clicks for people looking for gardening tools and other things it didn't carry. Google and other search engines greatly increased revenues for advertisers and their own pockets by selling keyword ads because the user is more open to messages that relate to the context of their online activity.

As an example, Carolina Rustica, a furniture store in North Carolina, used the Google AdWords program, and by selecting appropriate search key words increased sales by 50 percent each year from 2002 to 2011 (see Google.com AdWords in its Advertising section for more success stories). Google AdWords is a very complex service to use because it involves appropriate selections for keywords, ad group (several ads in one subject area), language, geographic area, run dates, and formulating an ad headline and text that will capture user clicks. Plus, of course, deciding on the click-through rate for bidding purposes. Exhibit 13.10 displays the guidelines for the actual AdWords ad design.

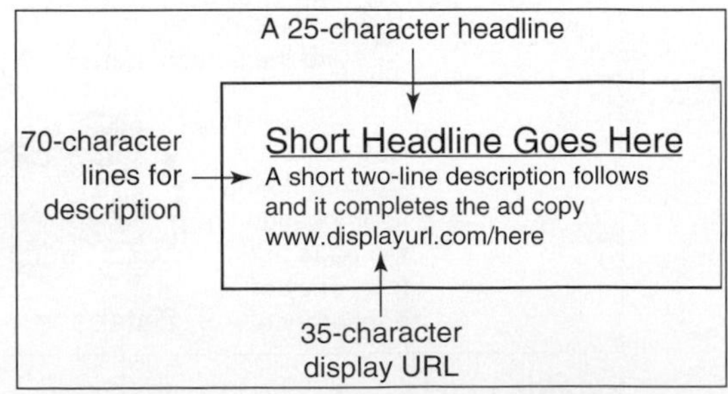

EXHIBIT 13.10 Google AdWords Copy Design

WHICH MEDIA TO BUY?

Advertisers pay for space on Web and social media sites, mobile phones, and in e-mail, as previously mentioned. But how do they decide which media vehicles to purchase? Beyond the target, product, and campaign goals, marketers consider media characteristics, effectiveness, and efficiency. Each medium has unique characteristics for achieving goals—much of which has already been discussed. For example, television is good for building awareness and branding because it reaches the masses for some programs, and the internet can be used well for branding but is especially well suited for direct response, such as registering, purchasing, and so forth. And of course, the level of trust consumers have in each medium is important.

Media planners want both effective and efficient media buys. **Effectiveness** means reaching and gaining the attention of the target market, and **efficiency** means doing so at the lowest cost.

Effective Internet Buys

Once a company decides to use paid media, it faces the question of which vehicle (individual paid medium) to use. As noted earlier, media planners look for the media with audiences that closely match the brand's target markets. Marketers use many innovative digital strategies to reach narrowly targeted markets, including social media and e-mail ads sent using proprietary databases.

Advertisers trying to reach the largest number of users through keyword targeting will buy space with search engines. Regardless of these large sites, the Web is less effective at reaching the masses than some network television, but is better at reaching niche markets. This reason explains the huge growth in vertical search marketing and keyword advertising.

It is difficult to generalize about the most effective media because it varies widely based on many factors. In a study of 297 marketing and public relations "social media power users," online video and blogs topped the list of effective media; however, all were very effective at reaching campaign goals.

Weather.com used search marketing effectively in 2006 to drive traffic to its lifestyle content pages (weather considerations for golf, skiing, weddings, allergies, and so forth). Its goals were to increase page views by 45 percent a year, maintain leadership in the weather category (with 30 percent of all weather category search clicks coming to Weather.com), and drive lifestyle page visits because they have the highest revenue value. To do this, they planned a keyword advertising campaign. Weather.com marketers tested two key phrases for its wedding pages—for people planning outdoor weddings away from home. The phrase "wedding planner" brought 1.5 visits to Weather.com per unique visitor, 3.6 Web pages per visit, and 5.2 pages per unique visitor. The term *outdoor wedding* did better, with 1.8 visits per unique visitor, 6.6 pages per visit, and 12.0 pages per unique visitor. Thus they settled on "outdoor wedding" for their keyword ad buy. "Our analytics data drives 95 percent of our decisions. We want to make sure what we changed worked and have data to back up our decisions," according to Marketing Director Derek Van Nostran.

Paid media can be quite effective at moving B2B prospects through the marketing purchase funnel. Bizo conceived a purchase funnel for the business market, as shown in Exhibit 13.11.

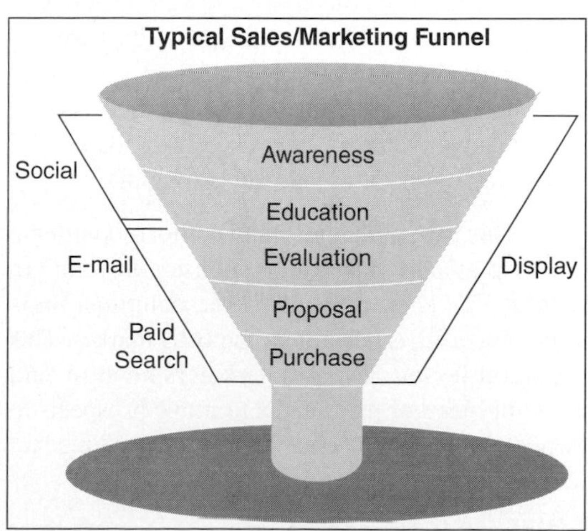

EXHIBIT 13.11 How Paid Media Move Prospects through the Purchase Funnel *Source:* Bizo (Business Audience Marketing). bizo.com

First, prospects become aware of the product and then they need to learn what its benefits are as compared to competition (education). Next prospects evaluate options and then often ask for a proposal from the seller. Hopefully this results in a purchase and the prospect emerges from the funnel as a customer. It should be noted that not every prospect goes through all these steps in order. Also, other than the proposal stage, this is very similar to the consumer market funnel.

According to Bizo, "display advertising gives marketers the opportunity to touch prospects at every stage of the funnel." As seen in Exhibit 13.11, Bizo recommends using social display ads for awareness and education and e-mail ads and paid search for the evaluation, proposal, and purchase stages. Their reasoning follows from B2B market studies:

- ***Top of the funnel.*** Bizo cites studies showing increases in awareness, aided brand recall, and Web site visits after users were exposed to display advertising.
- ***Mid-funnel.*** Bizo cites a ZDNet study showing a large increase in engagement and download of Web content after seeing display ads.
- ***Bottom of the funnel.*** When combined with paid search tactics, display ads prompted increases in conversions to sales, increases in event registrations, and click-through rates. Further, comScore found a 119 percent sales lift when paid search and display ads were paired (see "Bizo Data Sheet Display by the Numbers" at bizo.com).

This is remarkable, when compared with the low display and search ad response rates cited in Exhibit 12.11. It appears that the combination is more powerful, especially in the B2B market. This is a good lesson because marketers need to find the right blend of paid media to move prospects to owned media and generate positive earned media.

Efficient Internet Buys

If the audience for certain media vehicles matches the firm's target (*effective* buy), advertisers examine particular metrics to determine the most efficient buy. To measure efficiency *before* buying advertising space, media buyers use three important metrics: CPM (cost per thousand impressions) and two performance-based models: CPA (cost per action) and CPC (cost per click). Exhibit 13.12 displays performance-based models as preferred in early 2012 (this has not changed for years).

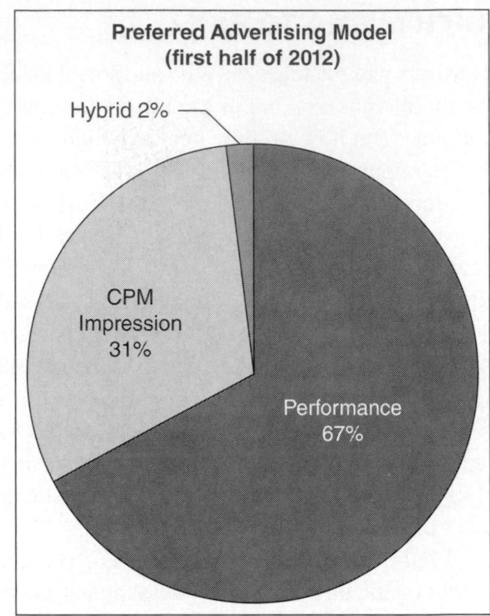

EXHIBIT 13.12 Proportion of Advertising Dollars by Preferred Advertising Pricing Model: PricewaterhouseCoopers LLP/IAB Internet Advertising Revenue Reports.

CPM is calculated by taking the ad's cost, dividing it by the audience size, and then multiplying by 1,000 [(cost ÷ audience) × 1,000]. Internet audience size is counted using **impressions**: the number of times an ad was served to unique site visitors, regardless of whether or not they looked at it. For example, a full banner ad at MediaPost.com, an advertising and media internet portal, received 2.4 million impressions and cost $168,000 a month for a CPM of $70. This pricing model is often used for sponsorships, gaming, and video ads. CPM is used because it allows for efficiency comparisons among various media and *vehicles* within the media (e.g., a particular video or Web site). Magazines are usually the most expensive medium to reach 1,000 readers; radio is often the least expensive.

Cost per action (CPA) includes social actions, such as the number of chocolate gifts sent to friends, number of posts to a profile, number of comments to a blog, number of users who play a game or view a video trailer, number of site registrations, or number of fans as a result of an advertisement. It is also commonly used in affiliate programs. For example, when a blogger recommends a book and a user clicks on the image to land on Amazon.com, the blogger will be paid if the user buys the book (not simply for clicking).

Cost per click (CPC) is a performance-based payment, often called **pay per click** (PPC). This includes schemes such as payment for each click on the ad, payment for each conversion (sale), or payment for each sales lead or new registered user.

Google AdWords, Facebook, and many other sites use a bidding process for paid ads. Sometimes called **real-time bidding (RTB)**, the advertiser only buys the number of impressions they want at a predefined price. For example, the Facebook ad in Exhibit 13.6 was bid at a maximum of $1.20 per click with a $50 total budget for the 2-week campaign, and based on other competing bids the final CPC price was $0.88. An ad using the RTB pricing model appears higher or lower in a list of ads depending on the price level of other bids (and other factors). This type of pricing is beneficial to advertisers but risky for Web sites, which must depend partially on the power of the client's ad and product to yield click-throughs for revenues. Nonetheless, RTB represents an increasing number of ad buys in addition to search advertising, and several companies predict this model will grow to as much as 25 percent of all ad purchases by 2016.

There are many other pricing models online. Some of these include the following:

- Cost per install (CPI) is the cost charged for a unique installation of a widget or other application included in a social media page.
- Cost per engagement (CPE) is the cost of each user-defined engagement, such as submission of branded content generated by the user (CGM), entries to a contest, votes/polls, reviews or comments, ratings, engagement with interactive ads, replies to, clicks or favorites, a Promoted Tweet, or other social actions (clicking on "Like" button or a "thumb up/down" icon).
- Cost per visitor (CPV) is the price paid for each visitor coming from an ad to the advertiser's site.

In one interesting example, JC Penney hired Gigya to create a widget that allowed its teen market to add hats, mustaches, and other fun things to photos of their friends using a social network application. Called "Stuck on You," the campaign paid the social media property using a CPI model and realized 2.9 million installations by users in 2008–2009. Furthermore, there were over 43 clicks for every widget install (engagement), and an average of 22 friends was reached each time a user engaged with the widget ("Social Media Buyer's Guide," 2010).

The paid media pricing models are also used during and after an IMC campaign to measure its effectiveness. At this point, we turn to paid media metrics.

PAID MEDIA PERFORMANCE METRICS

There are hundreds of performance metrics to choose among, but the best ones will be those that closely match the campaign's objectives. If it is purchasing, measure the number of sales, dollar amounts, and ROI that came from the ad. If it is branding, measures could include the percentage increase in positive conversations or blog comments about the brand, number of video views, increase in number of fans or friends, number of widget shares, and so forth. As mentioned in Chapter 12, marketers often use A/B testing to see which landing page pulled best. They also use this type of testing to test various display ads or other paid media tactics. Regardless, most marketers still rely heavily on click-through metrics as a starting

Metric	Definition/Formula	Proportion Using (Percentage)
Web site page views and registrations	Number viewing the pages and number registering at the site	64[1]
Click-Through Rate (CTR)	Number of clicks as percent of total impressions	60.0[2]
Volume and origin of site traffic	Number of visitors coming from different sources, such as Google or referring sites	60.0[1]
Lead generation	Number of people who are potential buyers	48.7[2]
New account acquisition or opportunities	Number of new accounts or likely accounts	48.0[1]
Search prominence and site preference	Ranking on search engine results pages based on keyword searches	46.0[1]
Incremental sales	Number of additional sales	40.0[2]
Return on investment (ROI)	Tactic profit/investment	38.4[2]
Incidence of content downloads	Number of users downloading white papers, and other content	37.0[1]
Transactions and/or subscriptions	Number of users purchasing or subscribing	37.0[1]
Brand awareness or reputation	As measured by survey or blog sentiment analysis	31.5[2]
Requests for information	Number requesting	27.3[2]
Engagement with Web content	Various measures, such as incoming e-mail or content download/upload	22.2[2]
Increased knowledge of customers	Database information increase	19.8[2]
Media impressions	Number of users exposed to a medium where ad or other communication is presented	16.6[2]
Redemption rates	Number redeeming coupons or other offers	14.7[2]
Do not measure effectiveness		4.0[2]

EXHIBIT 13.13 IMC Metrics and Proportion of Marketers Using Them *Sources:* 1. "Is the Click Still King?" 2010 (CMO Council study, as found on eMarketer.com). 2. "Is the Click Still King?" 2010 (Chief Marketer survey, as found on eMarketer.com)

point because it is an easy measure to get and helps to compare various tactics—for example, did the e-mail or display ad generate a higher click-through? Exhibit 13.13 displays many popular paid media metrics and the proportion of advertisers using them.

Effectiveness Evidence

When viewed as a direct-response medium, display ads are generally ineffective: Only 0.2 percent of all users click on them. However, many individual firms have received stunning click-through results with carefully targeted offers to prospects. Other tactics motivating action in one study include sponsored search engine links (40 percent), banner ads (28 percent), and pop-up ads (19 percent). This means that the 0.2 percent click-through for banners may not fully appreciate the effectiveness of this format, in terms of brand awareness and subsequent search activity.

According to research, when display ads are considered as branding media, they increase brand awareness and message association, and they build brand favorability and purchase intent (see iab.net). In many studies, online ads that were bigger or contained rich multimedia delivered an even greater impact. For example, skyscrapers and large rectangles are more effective than standard-size banners in increasing brand awareness and purchase intent, and video is the best. One thing hasn't changed in years—bigger and more novel ads are noticed more frequently.

Increasing evidence indicates that online and offline advertising work well together, such as with the Wendy's "Kick for a Million" sweepstakes and contest (described in Chapter 12), the large number of people who research online and shop offline, and the sometimes huge Web site visitations experienced by internet companies after advertising in the Super Bowl television event.

The best online paid media tactic depends on the target, competition, company, offer, and how novel, engaging, relevant, and creative the tactic is. Paid search and e-mail are validated in many other studies as being effective tactics, but don't forget that it all depends—a creative and scientific e-marketer can make the lowly banner ad a stellar tactic if used adroitly.

Metrics Example

To see how a firm evaluates the effectiveness of its internet advertising buy, consider the actual internet buy made by iGo, an online retailer selling batteries and small electronic devices by catalog and online (Exhibit 13.14). Many different forms of online advertising are represented in this buy, from a simple text link to buttons,

Type	Yearly Impressions	Est. Click %	Cost @ Est. Conv. %	# Visitors	# Orders	$4.24 CPM
E-commerce text link	400,000,000	0.20	0.60	800,000	4,800	1,856,000
Shopping Channel						
Computing—anchor	8,500,000	3.00	2.00	255,000	5,100	39,440
Computing—sponsor	1,700,000	3.00	2.00	51,000	1,020	7,888
Homepage	10,000,000	1.10	1.50	110,000	1,650	46,400
Computing Channel						
ROS	40,000,000	1.10	1.50	440,000	6,600	185,600
Section front pages	3,500,000	1.10	1.50	38,500	578	16,240
Homepage	2,100,000	0.75	1.00	15,750	158	9,744
Homepage text link	7,200,000	0.75	1.00	54,000	540	33,408

(continued)

Type	Yearly Impressions	Est. Click %	Cost @ Est. Conv. %	# Visitors	# Orders	$4.24 CPM
News Portal						
Selected sections	10,000,000	1.10	1.50	110,000	1,650	46,400
Technology	5,000,000	1.10	1.50	55,000	825	23,200
Shopping section	200,000	1.10	1.50	2,200	33	928
ROS sticky ads	5,000,000	0.75	1.00	37,500	375	23,200
ROS banners	11,000,000	0.75	1.00	82,500	825	51,040
Portal (6.5 months)						
Homepage—button	6,000,000	0.75	1.00	45,000	450	27,840
Homepage—text link	6,000,000	0.75	1.00	45,000	450	27,840
Office computing	50,000	0.75	1.00	375	4	232
Office computing	300,000	0.75	1.00	2,250	23	1,392
BCentral ROS	6,000,000	0.75	1.00	45,000	450	27,840
Link exchange	20,000,000	0.75	1.00	150,000	1,500	92,800
Portal Co-Promotion						
Promo main page	75,000,000	1.10	1.50	825,000	12,375	348,000
Sweepstakes						
Banners linked sweeps	4,000,000	1.10	1.50	44,000	660	18,560
Promo button	6,000,000	1.10	1.50	66,000	990	27,840
Button on sweeps site	1,000,000	1.10	1.50	11,000	165	4,640
Portal Package						
Transition Ads-1	2,000,000	1.10	1.50	22,000	330	9,280
Mid page Ads-2	1,000,000	1.10	1.50	11,000	165	4,640
Mid page Ads-3	5,000,000	1.10	1.50	55,000	825	23,200
Mid page Ads-4	5,000,000	1.10	1.50	55,000	825	23,200
A-column Ads-5	5,400,000	1.10	1.50	59,400	891	25,056
	646,950,000	**0.54**	**1.27**	**3,487,475**	**44,255**	**3,001,848**

EXHIBIT 13.14 iGo.com $3 Million Dollar Advertising Buy *Source*: Adapted from information provided by Brian Casey, iGo

banners, and content sponsorships at major portals (names removed to protect confidentiality). This spreadsheet shows estimated click-through percentage, conversion to people who might order, number of visitors that might visit the iGo site from the ad, number of orders expected, and cost of the ad. Exhibit 13.15 displays several effectiveness measures: average order value and more. Based on the annual profit and loss estimate from this campaign, it appears to generate more than half a million dollars in profits as well as drawing nearly 3.5 million visitors to iGo.com—folks who may develop into long-term customers.

Variables	
AOV	$140
Incremental order (annual)	0.60
Gross margin	0.36
Click rate	0.54%
Conversion	1.27%
Annual P&L	
Revenue	$6,195,735
Incremental revenue	3,717,441
Total revenue	**$9,913,176**
COGS	(6,344,433)
Advertising cost	(3,001,848)
Total	**$566,895**
CPM	**$4.24**
Cost per order (CPO)	**67.83**
Cost per click (CPC)	**0.86**
Total visitors	**3,487,475**

EXHIBIT 13.15 iGo Effectiveness Measures *Source:* Adapted from information provided by Brian Casey, iGo

Chapter Summary

Many media are paid to carry an organization's promotional messages such as online advertising, product placement, and sponsored tweets. Paid media are generally used to build awareness, move users to owned media, and, ultimately engage them in earned media. The most important paid media technique is paid search advertising, followed by display banner ads, classified ads, mobile ads, and social media. Paid display ads include rich media ads such as in-banner video ads, expandable/retractable ads, pop-up and pop-under windows, floating ads, interstitial ads, wallpaper ads, trick banner ads, and map ads, as well as contextual advertising and behavioral advertising. In addition, e-marketers may use e-mail ads, sponsored content, product placement, or text link ads as part of their paid media.

Advertisers use paid social media to build brand awareness, create positive brand attitudes, gather information about customers, and motivate user actions such as joining a community, clicking through to a site, or making a purchase. They can take advantage of three unique aspects of social networks: profile data (knowing the personal profile of members), social graph (mapping connections between members), and interaction data (capturing data about members' personal interactions). In particular, the narrow targeting available through paid Facebook, Twitter, and LinkedIn ads enables organizations to reach well-defined markets. Advertising is also available in virtual worlds such as Second Life and before, during, or after online videos on YouTube and other sites.

Because of the high penetration and heavy consumer usage of mobile devices, marketers see great promise in mobile advertising. Paid search occurs when an advertiser pays a search engine for directory submission, for inclusion in a search engine index, or to display its ad when users type in specific keywords. When selecting media vehicles, companies look not just at the target, product, and campaign goals, but also at media characteristics, effectiveness (reaching the target audience), and efficiency (reaching the right audience at the lowest cost). Paid media can move prospects through the marketing purchase tunnel from awareness and education to evaluation, proposal, and purchase. Three important efficiency metrics for paid media are cost per thousand impressions (CPM), cost per action (CPA), and cost per click (CPC). To evaluate paid media performance, advertisers use metrics that relate to the campaign's objectives, recognizing that techniques such as display ads can also have a powerful impact on brand awareness, association, favorability, and purchase intent.

Exercises

REVIEW QUESTIONS

1. How has usage of internet advertising changed over the years? In light of this trend, how is spending on internet advertising expected to change in the future?
2. What is an online display ad and what are some of its standard formats?
3. What are some types of rich media ads, and what are their general advantages and disadvantages?
4. Why does contextual advertising tend to produce higher click-through rates?
5. How does sponsored content help advertisers reach their audiences?
6. What three unique aspects of social network accounts, in large part, account for the expected rise in spending in social media advertising?
7. What are some of the options advertisers have when they use Facebook, Twitter, LinkedIn, or Second Life as paid media?
8. What issues are likely to affect the future of mobile advertising?
9. How does keyword advertising differ from paid inclusion and directory submission?
10. Why must advertisers be concerned about both the effectiveness and efficiency of media buys?
11. Which types of paid media tend to be most effective at each stage of the B2B purchase funnel?
12. How and why would an advertiser measure efficiency according to CPM, CPA, and CPC?

DISCUSSION QUESTIONS

13. **The Lenovo Story.** Do you think customers might be upset if they found out Lenovo was using remarketing and keeping track of their behavior online? Why or why not?
14. **The Lenovo Story.** Identify at least five other types of paid media that might work for Lenovo, including Facebook. Explain why each might be a good idea for this company.
15. Why do you think consumers have less trust in paid media than they do in earned media or owned media?
16. Knowing that companies are always experimenting with new sizes and formats of online display ads to attract user attention and break through clutter, why would the Interactive Advertising Bureau continue to propose standard dimensions for display ads?
17. From the marketer's perspective, what are the advantages and disadvantages of the types of display ads listed in Exhibit 13.5? From the consumer's perspective?
18. What ethical issues seem to be raised by the use of online-sponsored content and product placement? How would you recommend that a marketer improve transparency when it uses such paid media?

WEB ACTIVITIES

19. Conduct a Google search to locate three recent news articles about "Lenovo internet advertising." Which, if any, of the paid media described in this chapter has Lenovo used during the past year, and which does it appear to be planning to use in the future? Is the company continuing its remarketing strategy, as described in the chapter-opening example? Prepare a brief written or oral report summarizing what you've learned and include your recommendations for metrics Lenovo should use to evaluate paid media performance.

20. Select a large retailer or a particular product and conduct an internet search for one example each of its paid media, owned media, and earned media. What do you think are the marketer's objectives for each? What differences and similarities do you notice among these media? Which do you personally find the most engaging, and why?

21. Visit the Google page that describes its Google Ads Display Network. What types of formats can advertisers display through this network? What kinds of targeting tools can advertisers use to get their messages to the right audience? How does Google explain the pricing model for ads on this network?

22. Go to the Interactive Advertising Bureau's homepage (iab.net). Browse some of its links to guidelines and best practices. Choose two of the ideas mentioned in these guidelines and best practices, and explain why they're important for advertisers, based on the concepts and principles discussed in this chapter.

23. On Facebook's homepage (facebook.com), click on the "create an ad" link at the bottom, read about how Facebook advertising works, and then look at the questions. If you were considering whether to participate as an advertiser, what additional questions would you ask of a Facebook representative?

24. Visit the homepage of the Mobile Marketing Association (mmaglobal.com), look for the link to case studies, and read one. What was the advertiser trying to achieve? What type of mobile advertising did it use, and why? How did it measure performance? What other metrics, if any, can you suggest to evaluate both effectiveness and efficiency?

CHAPTER 14

E-Marketing Communication: Earned Media

This chapter examines why and how companies plan, implement, and evaluate e-marketing communication initiatives for earned media, the third element of the online content strategy. You will learn about the techniques that marketers use to engage users, encourage collaborative content creation, manage the firm's reputation online, and monitor earned media activities.

After reading this chapter, you will be able to:

- Describe the five levels of user engagement and explain what each means for earned media.
- Explain the role of trust in earned media and its implications for consumer behavior.
- List some key techniques for engaging users and discuss the importance of each.
- Outline the marketing benefits of engaging consumers in collaborative content creation.
- Highlight seven ways in which companies can attract users and move them up the engagement ladder.
- Discuss how a company can build, maintain, monitor, and repair its reputation online.
- Identify specific metrics used to monitor, measure, and refine earned media activities.

- Consumers' desire to broadcast their lives on social media is truly unabated and "liking" things is an integral part of that. 2011 began the first initiatives to bridge the offline physical world with online liking.

- ***C&A*** introduced special Facebook-integrated clothing hangers across stores in Brazil. The hangers display the number of times items have been "Liked" on the brand's Facebook store, updated in real time, so that shoppers can see the popularity of specific products.

Dell Starts Listening

Dell Computer has always been America's darling with its high-quality equipment, direct distribution model, and great customer service. Yet, in June 2005, Dell was brought to its knees by a single blogger—Jeff Jarvis of BuzzMachine.com:

"I just got a new Dell laptop and paid a fortune for the four-year, in-home service. . . . The machine is a lemon and the service is a lie. . . . DELL SUCKS. DELL LIES. Put that in your Google and smoke it, Dell."

This post brought a hailstorm of similar customer service complaints that lasted for nearly 2 years, and this issue has come to be known as "Dell's Hell." What happened?

Wanting to pare costs, Dell followed a current trend and outsourced its technical customer service to a firm in India in the early 2000s. Things looked great as costs dropped and market share increased to 28.8 percent the following year (2004), according to the global market intelligence firm IDC. However, complaints about the customer service also increased: Better Business Bureau complaints rose by 23 percent and Dell's customer satisfaction declined by 6.3 percent, according to a University of Michigan survey. A 2005 Google search for "Dell customer service problems" returned nearly 3 million links. Clearly the outsourcing strategy was not having the desired effect.

Like many companies, Dell decided to sit tight for a year and wait for the online complaint storm to pass. When it didn't stop, Dell appointed a digital media manager to "deal" with the internet chatter. Lionel Menchaca initiated several Dell blogs in multiple languages as mechanisms for handling customer complaints and ideas, and to have conversations with stakeholders about the problems and Dell's actions to fix them. IdeaStorm.com is a notable blog and social medium where users post ideas and vote on them, with the best percolating to the top. Dell responds to the ideas, makes changes in the company, and reports on the progress. In the first 3 months, IdeaStorm gathered 5,000 ideas, over 20,000 comments, and more than 350,000 idea endorsements. These resulted in over 20 changes in the company (see Beal and Strauss, 2008, for more on "Dell's Hell").

EARNED MEDIA

Dell learned the hard way that companies must listen to individual customers online or pay a dear price. Listening was only a start—Dell found that a company can benefit by truly engaging stakeholders in conversation and using what it learned to improve the company. Dell's experience was a wake-up call to marketers in the early days of the social media. Finally, marketers were being forced to act on the concept that they must deliver on their brand promises or be exposed in a big way online.

Well-executed owned and paid media can drive prospects and customers through the steps from awareness to product purchase, repurchase, and into long-term customer loyalty. However, earned media have a multiplier effect, intensifying and spreading the communication messages far and wide online (e.g., 1 + 1 = 5). Marketing communication is shifting from purely impression based (e.g., ads) to recommendation based (social media posting). When marketers offer compelling reasons for people to share online content, "like" on Facebook, write comments, pin on Pinterest, or retweet, it has the effect of increasing marketing spend effectiveness.

Earned media is like physical word-of-mouth on steroids: a social megaphone. When someone posts a positive comment about a product on her Facebook wall, it serves as a recommendation to friends. Recall from Chapter 12 that earned media occur when "individual conversations become the channel" on blogs, product review sites, news sites, many other places, and in comments on owned media pages and everywhere else they are allowed.

Earned media can be initiated by the company through branded content distribution, such as entertaining YouTube videos about the product, press releases (public relations), or other activities intended to engage users, such as placing social hooks on company brand and microsites (e.g., Facebook register, subscribe or "like," Digg, Delicious, RSS, and other buttons). Companies also put "follow us" links to these social sites in e-mail messages sent to customer or prospect databases. Earned media can have a direct cost associated with it, such as when the company sponsors a contest or creates content that spreads, but it has no financial cost when it is user conversation. By definition, earned media are created by others, and companies have little to no control over this user-generated content (UGC). This communication can get ugly very quickly—and often does. Professional and citizen journalists share their own opinions and experiences all over the social media via computers and mobile phones, sometimes while company marketing personnel are sleeping. This is a fast-paced social media world and marketers are having a hard time keeping up.

Before discussing the types of earned media, it is important to understand the possible levels of internet user engagement.

USER ENGAGEMENT LEVELS

Engagement occurs among and between the company and internet users, who are actively discussing the brand. This is compared to traditional media, which allows only passive exposure, such as when a consumer is watching television. Occasionally, however, traditional media will prompt engagement when the consumer writes an e-mail to the magazine editor or sends a text to a friend about a television program. Traditional media can also prompt communication to companies about their brands when designed for this purpose, such as awarding a prize to the first 100 people who comment on a company Facebook page or the *American Idol* voting by text message. However, it is not as easy for consumers to engage when they receive the information in traditional media and must move to the computer or smartphone to respond. Company-owned Web sites can also engage customers by offering content downloading and uploading, Web page personalization, and one-to-one contact opportunities.

There are many levels of user engagement online. It is important for a company to review its marketing communication objectives and understand what proportion of its customers and prospects operate at each hierarchy of effects level (from awareness through behavior), so that it can use social media for positive discussion online and collaboration with customers. Forrester's Social Technographics™ framework includes seven levels of engagement (recall Exhibit 8.11), and this company has data about the entire internet population for comparison to an individual company's consumers. Evans and McKee (2011) also suggest a four-level engagement ladder that moves engagement beyond simple owned and paid media consumption to earned media discussion. Exhibit 14.1 displays an iteration of these two models, displaying the five levels of engagement from least to most engaged: consume, connect, collect, create, and collaborate.

1. The least engaged internet users **consume** only online content. They read blogs, view videos and photos, listen to podcasts, and read the reviews and opinions expressed by others occupying higher levels of engagement on Web sites and forums.

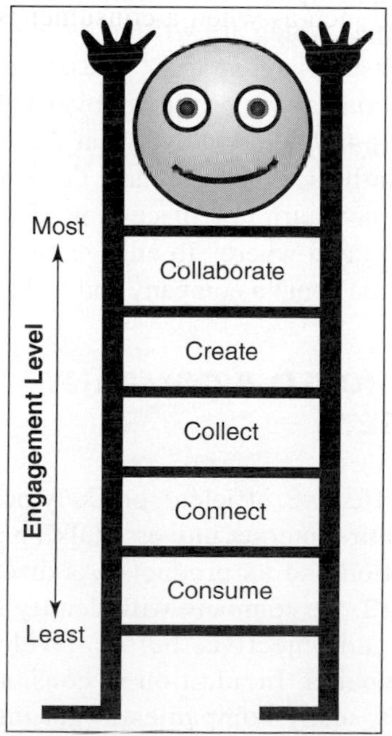

EXHIBIT 14.1 Five Levels of Internet User Engagement

2. At the next level, users **connect** with others by creating a profile on a social network, such as by "friending" on Facebook, or joining Tripadvisor or other sites that require registration to read the social media content. These consumers do not actively post anything, however. Connecting is a low-risk level of engagement that allows people to participate in small steps. Another way to connect is through a social gathering, happening either online or offline and that is facilitated by a site allowing groups to coordinate these meetings. For example, St. Supéry winery used meetup.com to create a global celebration of a wine—they called it #Cabernet Day (the "#" is a Twitter hash tag). In a 24-hour time period, over 1,000 people online and 75 in real life met to celebrate, purchase, and drink the wine. Many messages were also posted on social network sites and YouTube, and there were even check-ins via Foursquare (Bakas, 2010).
3. Consumers who **collect** information go through a process of filtering content and tagging what they find valuable in social media sites. This could include Delicious for bookmark sharing and Flickr or Facebook for photo tagging, or "liking" someone else's content. Collectors might also subscribe to RSS feeds on blog sites so that they can actively read content of interest. Finally, collectors show their preferences by voting in polls online. For example, collector shoppers at Sears.com have the option of sharing prom dresses they like with their Facebook friends using a feature called Prom Premier 2011. Sears supplemented the option with an ad campaign placed on Facebook.
4. Moving up the engagement ladder, **creators** actually write or upload original multimedia content to Web sites, such as videos to YouTube, photos to Facebook, or music and podcasts to iTunes. This involves creating content—which is at a higher level than simply voting on someone else's

content. These consumers write product reviews/ratings, create their own blogs/Web pages, and comment on other people's blogs, contribute to wiki sites (e.g., eHow and Wikipedia), and generally add much more to the social media content.

5. Finally, the most engaged customers **collaborate** with the company when they work with others in discussion to find ways to improve products. For example, CNN offers iReporter, where users send in videos of breaking news, which can result in CNN sending a company reporter to the event for a story. Another example is Dell's IdeaStorm site, where users post questions and product problems and others view and vote the posts as important concerns or not (as mentioned in the opening story). Dell then responds on the status of each idea. As we are writing this, the top idea is to standardize power cables for laptops (as voted on by 41,600 "collectors"). Finally, Twitter's hash tag (#), marking keywords and topics in Tweets, was actually created by Twitter users. This type of collaboration helps companies and bloggers improve products.

Forrester's Technographics' research indicates that 68 percent of internet users join social networks; however, the numbers lessen at the deeper levels of engagement—for example, 24 percent created content in 2011 (see Exhibit 8.11). In the next sections, you will see how companies engage customers to create earned media product discussion and multimedia content uploading.

ENGAGING INDIVIDUALS TO PRODUCE EARNED MEDIA

When a couple becomes engaged to be married, they are expressing their trust, commitment, and caring for each other—this is also true when a brand seeks this kind of love from its markets and wants them to talk about the products. **Engagement** occurs when internet users consume, connect, or collaborate with brands, companies, or each other.

Trust is a key component of word-of-mouth communication resulting from customer engagement. According to a 2012 A.C. Nielsen study, consumers trust other consumers' opinions online 70 percent of the time and recommendations from people they know 92 percent of the time. This is in contrast to the 58 percent who trust branded Web sites and fewer that trust advertising, either offline or online (see marketingcharts.com). Edelman, a leading U.S. public relations firm, found in 2012 that 65 percent of its over 5,000 respondents in 23 countries trust "persons like themselves" for credible information about a company. This is in contrast to the only 38 percent who trust the company CEO (see trust/edelman.com for more information). "A person like yourself" is someone who shares similar interests or friends—either in person or in a social network. For example, when planning trips or on the road, travelers visit the largest travel site, Tripadvisor.com, to check out the 50 million reviews and opinions of hotels and sites in 30 countries, which are written by other travelers as they are planning trips. Thus, when people post opinions about products, over half of the readers are likely to believe what they say, and this will influence their purchase decisions.

We now turn to a discussion of the "who, what, how, and where" to engage customers in conversation about a company and its brands.

WHO SHOULD A COMPANY ENGAGE?

It is not effective, efficient, or likely possible to get the entire internet universe talking about an organization and its products. As discussed in Chapter 12, the company will identify its target markets and objectives before developing an IMC campaign. In addition to consumers and prospects, many companies target influential bloggers and social network members, such as Arianna Huffington's *Huffington Post* internet newspaper/blog, with its 9,000 contributing bloggers and over 29 million page views per weekday (according to quantcast.com).

Social Media Influencers

Companies identify social media influencers, such as Arianna Huffington, in two ways. First, they can observe and participate in conversations in social media locations where people discuss their industries. This will help them see who is active and has the most Facebook fans or friends, Flickr comments, Tumblr or Twitter subscribers, or simply the most comments on posts. For example, the eMarketing Association group in LinkedIn had over 478,000 members in 2012, and by clicking on the "members" tab, companies can see the list of "This Week's Top Influencers." These influencers, along with the group creator (Robert Fleming), are the members who have the most followers in LinkedIn and contribute the most to the conversation. For a B2B company selling products to e-marketers, this is an ideal source for building a buzz with influential social media participants.

The second way to find influentials is to use a service such as Klout, Inc. (klout.com). Klout measures 35 variables for each of over 80 million social network participants and ranks them based on (1) the number of people they reach, (2) how much influence participants have on their followers (e.g., number of "likes" or "retweets"), and (3) how influential the person's network members are. The result is a Klout Score from 1 to 100, with the top-scored people having the most social media influence. Klout also lists the topics these influencers write about and their social media style (e.g., broadcaster or specialist). Klout also has a perks program that puts together high-Klout score users with brands they are likely to care and write about, such as Starbucks, Audi, Virgin America, and Dove—who all offer free products to high Klout score individuals (Griffith, 2011). As of this writing, Canadian pop/R&B singer, songwriter, and actor Justin Bieber was the only person with a perfect 100 Klout score.

Traditional Journalists

The term *earned media* was coined prior to the advent of the internet. It referred to journalists writing or reporting on stories about companies and brands in traditional media, such as newspapers, television, and magazines. These same journalists now generate earned media in their online versions of these media.

The top 25 print newspapers in the United States have a combined daily circulation of 13.7 million readers (and 5.3 million online readers), according to the Audit Bureau of Circulation's 2012 figures. However, the top five general news Web sites in 2010 attracted 140 million monthly visitors (Yahoo! News, MSNBC Digital Network, AOL News, CNN Digital Network, and NYTimes.com), according to Nielsen//NetRatings. For this reason, and because users find news themselves via online searches, companies usually include a press room with releases about brands on their Web sites, and also send them electronically via e-mail or the Web to media firms for publishing. The resulting brand publicity is the result of most company MPR strategies.

The traditional press release is a typed document that includes the "what, when, where, who, and why" of something newsworthy the company sends to journalists for possible inclusion in print or online media (e.g., a new product announcement). Many companies include these text-heavy press releases as links on their Web sites, or worse, as PDF files for download (worse because journalists can't pick up smaller pieces of the text very easily). This is changing. Now bloggers and other social media journalists want to gain quick bits of information and expert quotes on topics they are writing about. Because they want to include images, video, and text information for articles, news releases are beginning to become social media friendly. Exhibit 14.2 is a model social media press release created by Shift Communications, to be used on company Web sites. It includes the important facts and is largely interactive, providing links to company-created multimedia and white papers (note that

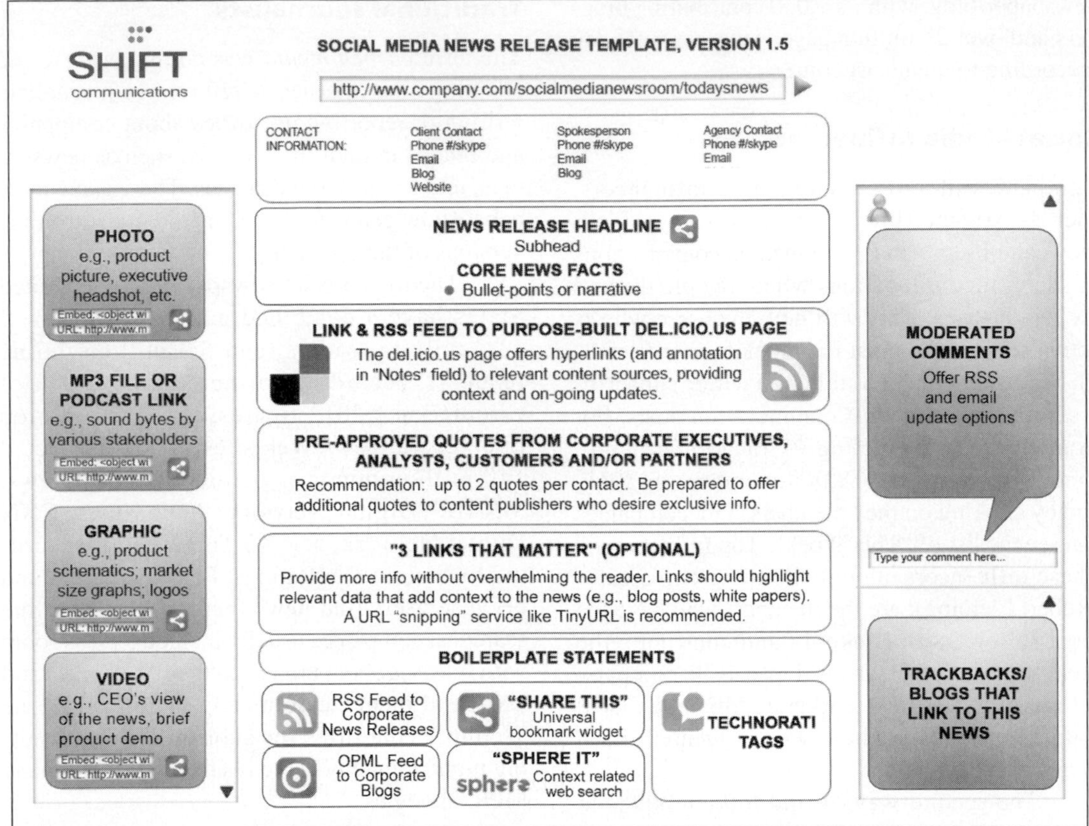

EXHIBIT 14.2 Social Media Friendly Press Release *Source:* Shift Communications (shiftcomm.com)

the social media logos are on the press release as links but deleted in the exhibit due to intellectual property concerns). It is especially social media friendly because it allows journalists to pick up short bits of information and easily pass these along using an RSS button, Delicious bookmark link, or paste it into a Wikipedia article, and more. For example, a blogger or *New York Times* reporter can easily find a quote from the company to include in an article without sifting through long documents. This means that company news can move around the internet quickly as these small information bits are shared: more earned media. The large PR firm, Edelman, uses this type of press release. The social media press release is the brainchild of Todd Defren, who also created a social media newsroom template for company Web sites, similar to what is being used by Google and others (see shiftcomm.com).

TECHNIQUES FOR ENGAGING USERS

Most social media, and many Web sites and mobile apps, provide space and tools for earned media content. You have read about many of them in this book, such as there are many sites that allow multimedia content upload (YouTube and Flickr), comments, bookmarking (Delicious), tagging (Flickr and Facebook), reviews, recommendations, and more. In the following sections, we focus on just a few important or new techniques not yet fully described in other chapters.

Viral Marketing

Viral marketing is a bad name for a great technique. When individuals forward e-mail to friends or share Facebook newsfeed posts or YouTube videos, they are using what we like to call *word-of-mouse*. **Viral marketing** is the online equivalent of word-of-mouth and sometimes referred to as word-of-mouse, which occurs when individuals forward content to each other through e-mail or social media sharing.

This is analogous to the spread of physical or computer viruses. It is the opposite of the sales funnel, which narrows as prospects drop off to fewer customers, as shown in Exhibit 14.3. The viral funnel increases brand exposure as content circulates.

Viral marketing can be delivered by offline word-of-mouth or online when users forward e-mail or multimedia content to others. A viral video is any video that is passed electronically, from person to person, regardless of its content. This is done via the "share" link on YouTube or simply by sending an e-mail link to the video. Viral marketing was used by the founder of Hotmail, a free e-mail service that grew from zero to 12 million subscribers in its 18 initial months, and to more than 50 million subscribers in about 4 years. Each e-mail sent via Hotmail carried an invitation for free Hotmail service. (See the Let's Get Technical Box for information about instant messaging.)

As with all engagement strategies, successful viral marketing programs involve appealing content that has a high chance of spreading. For example in 2011, 72 million links were shared a day on Facebook ("E-Mail + Twitter + Facebook," 2011).

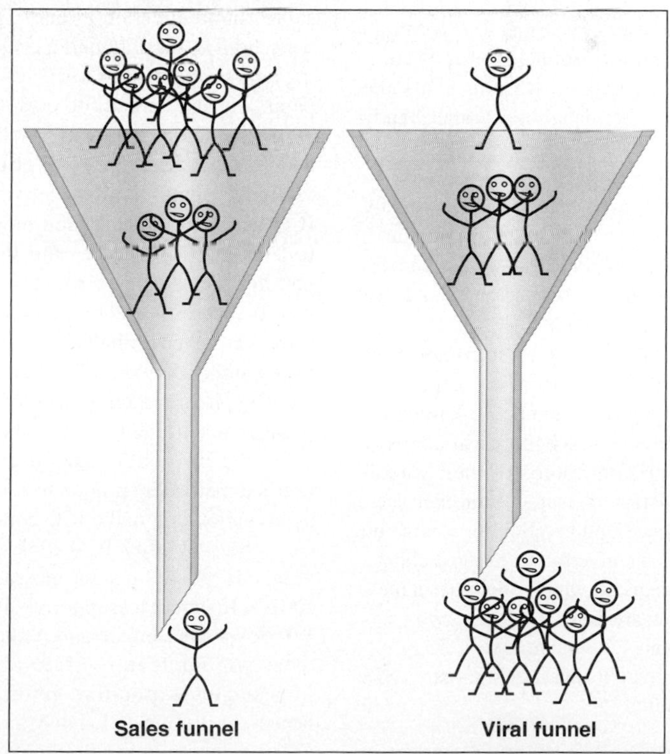

EXHIBIT 14.3 Viral Marketing Turns the Sales Funnel Upside Down

LET'S GET TECHNICAL

Instant Messaging

Your company has two offices: one in the United States and one in India. As the director of marketing and public relations, it is your responsibility to facilitate communication between the product development team in India and the marketing and sales teams in the United States. Due to budget limitations, you need a low-cost, reliable solution, and the phone company has been unwilling to negotiate beyond its corporate packages. The teams are currently communicating via e-mail, but they are disappointed with the lag time—it often takes 45 minutes to get a simple question answered. An old technology—instant messaging (IM)—is now being reapplied in the business world, and it is changing the way businesspeople communicate worldwide.

IM has taken internet users by storm. Even though e-mail was the most rapidly adopted form of communication to date, instant messaging beats the speed of e-mail and maintains all of its other handy features.

Once the user is logged on, he or she views a list of contacts, which is often referred to as a buddy list or contact list. The list indicates each contact's status: online, offline, away, or idle. The list updates dynamically as friends and associates enter and exit the online world.

Sometimes instant messaging usernames are exchanged instead of e-mail addresses, especially among students of all ages. Students are known for displaying their entire days' schedules in an away message, thereby apprising friends of their whereabouts. To send an instant message to another user, the user has to be online. Double-clicking a name on the buddy list initiates a conversation in most clients. A separate window opens, in which one types a message, such as: "hi, how are you?" Only the two users can see the message and subsequent text.

In addition to instant messages, most clients offer a variety of features:

- *Chat rooms.* Multiple users can all engage in one conversation.
- *Hyperlinks.* Users can send each other active links to Web sites.
- *Files.* Users instant messaging each other can send files (e.g., Microsoft Word documents) to one another.
- *Talk.* With a microphone and speakers attached to the PC, users can talk to each other over the internet.
- *Videoconference.* With a Web camera connected to the PC, users can engage in videoconferencing.
- *Streaming information.* Up-to-date news, stock quotes, and other information can be displayed in the client application.

ICQ ("I Seek You") is considered to be the first instant messaging client. In November 1996, four Israeli entrepreneurs founded Mirabilis, Ltd., the company that developed ICQ. The thought behind the instant messaging concept was to create interpersonal communication online. The four noticed that the world was quickly adopting surfing and browsing online, and wanted to create a simple solution for people to find and talk to each other. Just 6 months after its release, ICQ had 850,000 registered users and was considered the "World's Largest Internet Online Communication Network." By May 2002, ICQ had been downloaded more than 200 million times from CNET.com, and ICQ claimed to have 150 million registered users in 2004. ICQ believes that its success is due to viral marketing, for the software was never formally marketed. Emanuel Rosen, expert author on word-of-mouth marketing, discusses the ICQ phenomenon in his book titled *The Anatomy of Buzz.* According to Rosen, the "marketing" occurs when the ICQ client asks users if it can scan the user's e-mail address book to send friends and family an invitation to join the ICQ community.

Shortly after ICQ took off, other Web providers developed instant messaging clients. Today, AOL's Instant Messenger rivals ICQ. Microsoft's Windows Messenger and Yahoo! Messenger also offer similar features free of charge. Windows Messenger is popular among businesspersons because it is preinstalled in Microsoft Windows.

As the number of clients available increased, avid users faced a dilemma—friends they wanted to talk to were all using different clients. Rival firms attempted to retain market share by refusing to allow their clients to interoperate. The Internet Engineering Task Force (IETF) has not been able to gain agreement on a standard protocol for instant messaging. As a result, utilities were developed to allow users to communicate with users of different clients all at once. Examples include Pidgin, Trillian, Adium, and Miranda.

After the success of instant messaging using stand-alone clients, large software developers took note and began adding the feature to corporate communication packages. Microsoft's Office Communication Server allows companies to run their own instant messaging network. This approach addresses security and privacy issues that companies often face. Office Communication Server interfaces with Microsoft Office and SharePoint, which is a file-sharing and team-collaboration package. Microsoft developers claim that instant messaging fits better with these programs so that the conversation is discussed in context.

Very similar to instant messaging is text messaging on cell phones. Texting allows sending text messages and pictures between cell phones over the cell phone network as opposed to the internet. Texting is a huge revenue source for cell phone providers. They charge a premium for a service that costs them very little to provide.

Although corporate instant messaging solutions have been on the market for a few years, they have not been widely adopted. Most companies use one of two tactics: Use free clients to communicate within the company or block instant messaging completely.

Viral marketing has long been a favorite strategy of online marketers pushing youth-oriented products. For example, marketers might distribute a small game program or a video embedded within a sponsor's e-mail that is easy to forward. By releasing a few thousand copies of the game to some consumers, vendors hope to reach hundreds of thousands of others. Also known as *advocacy marketing*, viral marketing, if properly used, can be effective, efficient, and relatively inexpensive.

Viral marketing can be very successful with entertaining videos (especially on YouTube) that are spread via e-mail and by microbloggers (e.g., Twitter). Following are some successful viral campaigns:

- Burger King's The Subservient Chicken campaign, running from 2004, is an extremely successful example of viral marketing from a microsite with an interactive video (subservientchicken.com). Users type commands and the chicken performs them, sometimes quite humorously. The chicken had received over 450 million views as of 2011. It is particularly relevant and appropriate for the brand because users can type a command, such as "dance," and the chicken will dance in the video—supporting Burger King's "Have it your way" advertising slogan.
- Old Spice is credited with the fastest-growing online viral video campaign. In mid 2010, the ad agency put TV star, Isaiah Mustafa, in a bathroom set and had him answer 186 posts to Twitter, Facebook, and other social media sites. The video had 6.7 million views in just 1 day and 23 million within 3 days.

Every company wants to create content that goes viral, but few accomplish this feat. The content has to be entertaining or mysterious, match popular culture, and gain user attention. In a sea of online content and information overload, sometimes even the best content does not go viral.

One downside of a viral strategy is that several e-mail hoaxes have been spread this way. Viral marketing has also been criticized by consumers because of a concern over unsolicited e-mails, which many see as an invasion of privacy.

Viral Blogging

Viral blogging is when bloggers conduct viral marketing activities. Viral blogging can be very effective with the use of tools such as Twitter. Many retailers entice WOM marketing by bloggers. For example, Paramount wanted to build awareness and box office sales for a sneak preview of the modestly budgeted *Super 8* science fiction film, which opened on June 10, 2011. Paramount sent a single Tweet and purchased advertising on Twitter via two Promoted Trends—one fairly early and the other a day before the premier. The sneak preview generated $1 million in box office sales, and the opening weekend for the film surpassed Paramount's goals by 52 percent (see the case studies at business.twitter.com).

Stormhoek Vineyards initiated successful viral marketing on social networks (stormhoek.com). The company first offered a free bottle of wine to bloggers. Within 6 months, about 100 of these bloggers posted voluntary comments about the winery on their own blogs. Most had positive comments that were read by their readers and by other bloggers. The Stormhoek example raises an interesting question: Can bloggers be bought? The criticism is that bloggers are not required to disclose that they are being paid (or receiving gifts) for their endorsements. Companies can pay bloggers directly to endorse products, or do so via an intermediary, such as PayPerPost.

Multimedia Sharing

Users upload many types of media for others to view, rate, and comment on, or build channels of other people's media. Following are the main types of sites used for this purpose, along with examples:

- ***Photos and art.*** Flickr (with 4 billion photos), Photobucket, and deviantArt.
- ***Video.*** YouTube (with nearly 75% market share and serving 1 billion videos a day), Vimeo, and traditional news sites.
- ***Live casting.*** **Live casting** enables live audio or video streaming directly from a mobile phone, tablet internet device, PC, or Mac to a Web site for viewing by others. Examples: Skype, Justin.tv, and LiveCast.
- ***Music.*** Here we are referring to sites that allow users to share and comment on music playlists or original music, not copyright-protected music files. Examples: MySpace Music, Pandora, and ShareTheMusic.
- ***Presentations.*** These are uploaded, usually from PowerPoint, MS Word, or PDF documents, and then freely shared and commented upon. Examples: SlideShare and Scribd.

Amazon, Barnes and Noble, and other online booksellers allow anyone to self-publish content by uploading a digital eBook and selling it for download by iPad, PC, Kindle, and other digital book readers. For example, 26-year-old Amanda Hocking could not find a publisher for her young-adult paranormal novels, so she began selling them at online bookstores for $0.99 to $2.99 per digital download. In January 2011, she sold 450,000 copies of the nine titles (Memmott, 2011)! Hocking earned between 30 and 70 percent of the sales price. This self-publishing capitalizes on consumer behavior trends—one survey indicated that 20 million people read eBooks. It also cuts out the book publishing middlemen and allows the online booksellers to offer many products created by consumer authors. Incidentally, Amazon also allows users to upload DVD, CD, MP3, and video content created by users for sales on the site.

Many other social media sites benefit by allowing users to upload digital multimedia content. CNN's iReport accepts video, photos, and audio from citizen journalists who are on the scene of breaking news. The best content is shown on the site, and some receive iReport awards. iTunes and Amazon allow musicians to upload digital music files for sale on their sites. Musicians cannot upload music directly, but must go through a distributor, such as CD Baby (the largest Indie online music store), who helps them obtain a bar code and ascertains that the intellectual property belongs to the said musician.

Obviously, YouTube, Flickr, and many other multimedia sites contain only user-created content. Their business models entice users to upload content, draw many eyeballs, and sell advertising.

Wikis

Wikis are Web sites that allow users to post, edit, and organize multimedia content. This is closely related to crowdsourcing and user-generated content. Examples include Wikipedia (encyclopedia), Wikihow (how-to-do site), and Wikispaces (education). For example, Demand Media Inc.'s eHow has over 2 million articles and videos created by consumers and professionals covering 30 categories and every topic from house and garden tips to business ideas. All content is created by site users and screened by site editors for quality and value (see ehow.com)

Wikis are important because a consultant can edit definitions and add material to a site like Wikipedia or Wikihow and become known as an expert. When added to other tactics like reviewing products and books or answering Yahoo! questions in his field of expertise, the consultant is building a thought leadership niche: type in his or her name and it comes up in lots of different places showing his or her expert area. Some companies, people, and brands are important enough to be allowed their own Wikipedia entries and marketers take advantage of this.

Ratings and Reviews

Prior to a purchase, consumers like to collect information, such as what brand to buy, from which vendor, and at what price. Online customers do this via shopping aids (e.g., comparison shopping agents), looking at product review sites such as Epinions, and conducting research at company sites and other sources. Ratings and reviews in social networks facilitate commerce, both online and offline. According to Gartner Inc., the majority of online customers already rely on social networks to guide them in purchase decisions (according to *Techshout.com*). Shoppers resort to friends, fans, followers, and other experienced customers. With peer-to-peer engagement through social media and high consumer trust in acquaintances, retailers recognize that their customers' voices can be an extremely strong marketing tool for building sales and improving products. Therefore, retailers want to hear what the customers say. A variety of tools is available to engage shoppers online:

- **Customer ratings and reviews.** This is feedback from real customers, integrated into an e-commerce product page, a social network page, a customer's review site, or in customer news feeds (e.g., Amazon.com, iTunes, Buzzillions, and Epinions). Yelp and Google local pages are two other important review sites. Customer ratings can be summarized by votes or polls.
- **Expert ratings and reviews.** The view from the independent voice of authority, whether professional or prosumer—professional consumer, can be integrated into an e-commerce product page, a social network page, a product review site, an online magazine, and/or in news feeds (e.g., Metacritic and CNET Reviews).
- **Business reviews.** These sites hold reviews for everything from local restaurants and retailers to national brands and professionals. Examples: Yelp, RateMDs, and Rate My Professors.
- **Community questions and answers.** These sites are especially valuable to professionals who want to build a thought leadership niche, demonstrating their knowledge when answering questions in their specialty area. Examples: Yahoo! Answers and WikiAnswers (a Wiki and a community Q&A site).
- **Sponsored reviews.** These are paid-for reviews written by either customer bloggers or experts on social media platforms (e.g., SponsoredReviews and PayPerPost). Expert and sponsored reviews are often generated in video format.
- **Consumer conversations.** People communicate via e-mail, blog, live chat, discussion groups, and tweets, in both original posts

and subsequent comments. Monitoring conversations yields rich data for market research, product improvements (collaboration), and customer service.

- **Customer testimonials.** Customer stories and case studies are often published on a social media site that allows comments and discussion (e.g., Bazaarvoice site reviews).

Ratings and reviews have been a cornerstone of e-commerce since 1995 (e.g., at Amazon.com) and are a proven solution for boosting traffic volume, conversions (from surfing a site to buying), and increasing average order value. Reviews may result in word-of-mouse marketing through social influence and in promoting purchase decisions with credible information. Bazaarvoice measured the impact of ratings and reviews as boosting Web site conversion rates by up to 25 percent. Interestingly, negative reviews appear not to have a detrimental effect on sales; we do not live in a five-star world, and apparently shoppers find positive ratings more believable when they also see negative ratings.

Social Recommendations and Referrals

Whereas ratings and reviews usually are visible to all, social recommendations and referrals are personal endorsements designed to realize value for customers and advocates. The in-store analogy for this strategy is when consumers ask a fellow shopper for advice. Often, social recommendations take the form of online versions of traditional customer-get-customer and referral-rewards programs (e.g., Sky TV's "Introduce a Friend"), but can also use syndication tools via Twitter and Facebook to share recommendations with friends, fans, and followers. These are closely related to ratings and reviews, and are sometimes integrated with them.

Traditional online product review companies such as Amazon.com, Bazaarvoice, and Power Reviews have advised many consumers. Up-and-coming social shopping start-ups such as ShopSocially, Swipely, and Bee Bargains now encourage *conversations* about purchases. The product recommendations come from people consumers know and are thus more trustworthy than reviews by strangers (recall the trust statistics previously mentioned). It will be interesting to see if this kind of model for product recommendations will eventually replace traditional general Web site recommendations, and what products, services, and price ranges customers will use with traditional methods.

Many vendors provide infrastructure and services for soliciting recommendations. For example, ThisNext (thisnext.com) is a social commerce site where people *recommend* their favorite products so others can discover what is best to buy online. It blends two powerful elements of real-world shopping otherwise lost for online consumers: word-of-mouth recommendations from trusted sources and the ability to browse products in the way that naturally leads to discovery. ThisNext has also developed a suite of distribution tools for bloggers, online communities, and e-commerce sites. Another special site, productwiki.com, collects product reviews from people all over the world. Users can edit and change the product information.

Sometimes social shopping portals that bundle ratings and reviews with recommendations also provide shopping tools: A prime example is provided in the Kaboodle shopping community. Common recommendation methods follow:

- **Social bookmarking. Social bookmarking** sites allow users to share their favorite Web sites and comments on them online, such as StumbleUpon.com. Delicious.com provides a free Web browser plug-in so that users can simply click on a button to bookmark a Web site. Once done, a Delicious window opens and asks for text tags, which are used to categorize the bookmark. Social bookmarking is powerful because users can click through to other users who have bookmarked the same articles to see what else they are reading on the same topic. It is a great resource for individual or collaborative research, and a tool we've used to indicate assigned class reading lists. It is even better for marketers wanting to create a buzz about a white paper, blog post, or other online article, and that is why a Delicious bookmark icon appears near such articles.

- **Referral programs.** These involve financial rewards for customers and partners who refer new customers (e.g., Groupon and Gilt). These programs give social media sites the opportunity to make money when a user clicks from the site to the retailer and purchases a product. For example, the Amazon.com Associate Program provides bloggers and others with banner ads, book or CD images for their sites; the site owner gains revenue by sending its audience to purchase at Amazon.com. You can find examples of this on blogs where the authors have a sidebar of "books I like" or simply recommend books on a topic of discussion, complete with a link to Amazon.com.
- **Social recommendations.** Personal shopping recommendations are based on profile similarities with other customers (e.g., Apple Genius Recommendations, Amazon Recommendations, and Netflix Cinematch).
- **Social news.** Users submit links to online news stories on **social news** sites and then readers vote or comment on which are the best ones. Examples: Digg and Reddit.
- **Other innovative methods.** Companies such as Honk and StyleFeeder automate personal recommendations based on algorithms, comparing similarities between customer purchasing histories and profiles. Amazon's collaborative filtering software presents product recommendations by displaying additional titles purchased by consumers who also purchased the same book or CD.

E-Mail

E-mail is not dead. Facebook and other social sites require valid e-mail addresses when users sign up. The task for marketers is to integrate e-mail and social media, and many studies show that the majority of marketers plan to do this. For example, Yahoo!, Gmail, and Outlook .com (formerly Hotmail) allow integration with Facebook contacts. When users open their e-mail inbox, they might only see e-mail from Facebook friends. Facebook will integrate friends with e-mail contacts and much more. This means that companies need to be on user contact lists or their e-mail messages might not be viewed.

In one study, nearly 60 percent of marketers said they planned to use "follow us" links in e-mail messages, so recipients could click and be transported to the Facebook, Twitter, or other social media page (GetResponse survey, as cited in eMarketer.com). Other e-mail tactics: 64 percent said they planned to include "sign-up" forms for Facebook-type pages, 53 percent said they would place links to e-mail messages on social media pages, and 47 percent said they'd include options to share the e-mail with others.

KFC, the fast-food chicken restaurant, wanted to build awareness and create a buzz for its new Double Down sandwich (two fried chicken patties surrounding bacon and cheese). KFC sent an e-mail announcement to 3 million registered males between the ages of 18 and 30 at the KFC.com Web site, according to Rich Maynard, PR Manager (as cited in Marketing News). Immediately the social media started carrying commentary about the plusses and minuses of this product. KFC started getting calls from journalists about the buzz before the product was even on the shelf. Much of the talk centered on the unhealthy aspects of the sandwich. Social media monitoring revealed an increase in both brand awareness and negative news about the sandwich. Had KFC also engaged in the social media talk and announced the sandwich on its Facebook page, this would have been an integrated effort. Sometimes companies do the reverse: Undertake social media campaigns instead of e-mail campaigns because they find their e-mail blasts caught in spam filters, unseen by customers and prospects. In fact, social media has overtaken e-mail as the most popular consumer activity, especially for the younger markets.

Groupon used a fascinating and humorous engagement technique to entice customers to

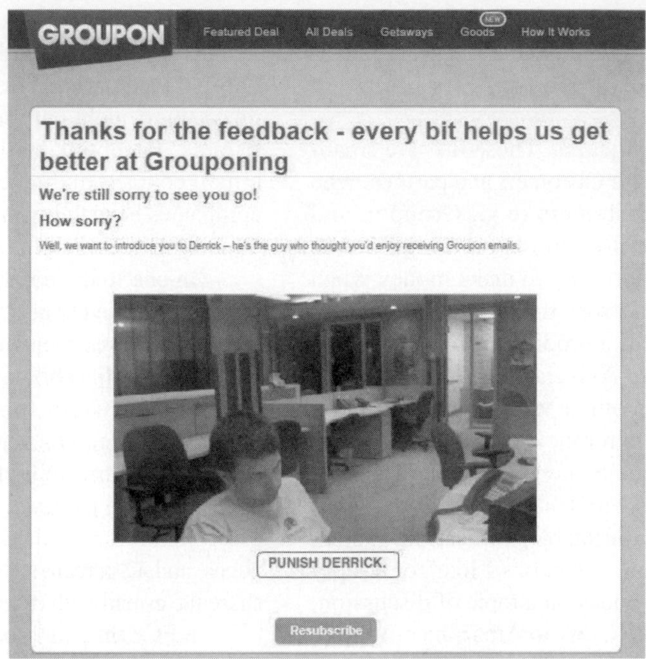

EXHIBIT 14.4 Groupon Encourages Customers to Remain on the E-Mail List *Source:* Reprinted with permission from Groupon (groupon.com)

continue receiving their e-mail messages about special offers. When customers click the link in an e-mail to unsubscribe, they are transported to a Web page that said "We're still sorry to see you go! How sorry? Well, we want to introduce you to Derrick—he's the guy who thought you'd enjoy receiving Groupon mails" (Exhibit 14.4). Then, the user can press a button to "Punish Derrick." The video shows a coworker walking in, speaking to Derrick, and then throwing a glass of water on his face! After that, the user can choose to resubscribe. This likely keeps some people on the mailing list or at least gives them a very positive feeling about the brand.

Social Media Site Discussions

The social media are full of comments from users, and many relate to products, companies, and brands. As well, users share images and videos, pin images on Pinterest, and upload product images from Instagram and to Flickr. Another form of earned media occurs when users submit a link to an online news story and it appears on digg.com. On this site, additional readers can "Digg" the story, and the more who do so, the higher on the page the story appears (this is similar to a Facebook "like"). At this writing the number-one story was "Cold Comfort," about the above-average temperatures globally in 2012, with over 10,000 Diggs.

Blog conversations occur with lengthy lists of comments, especially in the B2B market, where professionals share information on various topics. For example, Brian Solis writes about social media, technology, and business and has a huge following, often gathering many comments to his posts. He creates informative infographics and writes on cutting-edge, provocative, and interesting topics. Who has the most comments? Timico's Trefor Davies wrote a blog to support the UK's Royal National Lifeboat Institution and gathered 100,000 blog comments in a 24-hour period. This was recognized as the most comments on a blog by the *Guinness Book of World Records* ("World Record Attempt . . . ," 2012).

The way to engage users on business blogs is to write timely, interesting, and current content. And to include buttons so users can easily "like" on Facebook, Tweet, recommend on Google+, and share on LinkedIn.

Speaking of "like," Facebook made this term famous, but does it matter how many likes a company page receives? In a study about the "Meaning of Like," a research company found reasons for not hitting the "like" button on a Facebook brand page ("What Do Facebook . . . ," 2011):

- 54 percent do not want to be bombarded with ads or messages,
- 45 percent do not want companies to have access to profile information,
- 31 percent do not want to push things into friends' networks,
- 29 percent do not want companies to contact them through Facebook, and
- 23 percent did not see the benefit of doing so.

In contrast, Facebook members who do "Like" a company or brand have certain expectations: Gain access to exclusive content, events, or sales (58 percent); receive discounts or promotions through Facebook (58 percent); receive updates about the company in newsfeed (47 percent); the company can post updates, photos, or videos on newsfeed (39 percent); the name of the company, brand, or organization to show up on my profile (37 percent); the company will contact me through other channels (24 percent); and do not expect anything to happen (37 percent).

In one interesting blog post, Paul Dunay wrote an analysis about why brands fail to convert Facebook fans into paying customers (Exhibit 14.5). His motivation was Hubspot's finding that although 93 percent of internet adult users are on Facebook, only 1 percent of a brand's Facebook fans ever visit the company Web site. His advice covers many of the things discussed in this chapter, beginning with the importance of engaging customers immediately. On Dunay's blog, he entices engagement by offering subscription options (e-mail, RSS, and podcast updates) and connection options (e-mail, Google+, Friend on Facebook, Follow on Twitter,

Social Media Darwinism
Those That Don't Adapt Become Irrelevant
by Paul Dunay

10 Reasons Brands Fail to Convert Facebook Fans into Paying Customers

1. Failure to Get Past the First Step (try to engage visitors immediately)
2. Poor Text and Visuals (must be relevant to brand and visitors)
3. Stagnant Page Content (use consistent fresh content)
4. Inconsistent or Sloppy Branding (Facebook page and Web site with consistent brand elements)
5. Confused Calls-to-Action (make clear offers on Facebook)
6. Too Many Clicks (create only a few clicks to target content)
7. Mystery Visitors (compile Facebook user profiles)
8. Preconceived Notions (use Facebook-specific campaigns)
9. Ineffective Plugin Use (integrate "like" buttons, recommendations, and comment boxes well)
10. Sticking to Stand-alone Metrics (integrate Facebook with other shopping stats)

EXHIBIT 14.5 How to Convert Facebook Fans into Paying Customers *Source*: pauldunay.com

and Network on LinkedIn). Readers can also listen to his blog in iTunes podcasts (see pauldunay.com). This is a good example of many ways to engage blog readers.

Community Discussion/Forums

Online forums, also called bulletin boards, are areas where users can post e-mail messages on selected topics for other users to read (as discussed in Chapter 12). A large public newsgroup forum is the Usenet, which has 35,000 groups (accessed at groups.google.com) and contains community discussion about product experiences, among other topics. The Usenet has over 1 billion messages, beginning in 1981 (far predating the Web in 1993). Although the Usenet is no longer the most-used forum, it holds a special place in the hearts of all geeks who have been online since the beginning. For us, it seems that the internet has come back to its Usenet roots with the advent of the social media—an internet for, by, and about users. Google and Yahoo! Groups carry on the Usenet tradition with private and public text-based groups for collaboration and sharing common interests (Exhibit 14.6). Businesses use Google Groups for international business meetings, product question and answer forums, and more (in 47 languages).

Widgets and Social Apps

Marketers use widgets and social applications to engage social media users. Widget content can include brand information in contests or games, be sponsorships or calls for action, or be user generated. If a company knows, for instance, that a Facebook member lives in Los Angeles, is 28 years old, and surfs, a surf shop can send a surf-related widget that allows for sharing with friends—who likely also surf. For example, see the movie widget created by the author to simulate a social network widget (Exhibit 14.7). Note that the Facebook member's name and profile photo are automatically put into the widget, which can then be passed to friends in the network. Godiva Chocolate wanted to engage with younger prospects and build the brand image of quality and excellence. It created an "I love chocolate" widget and Facebook friends sent over 1 million virtual chocolate gifts to each other within 2 weeks—some were Godiva branded and some were generic. Godiva's Facebook fan page grew to 15,000 members as

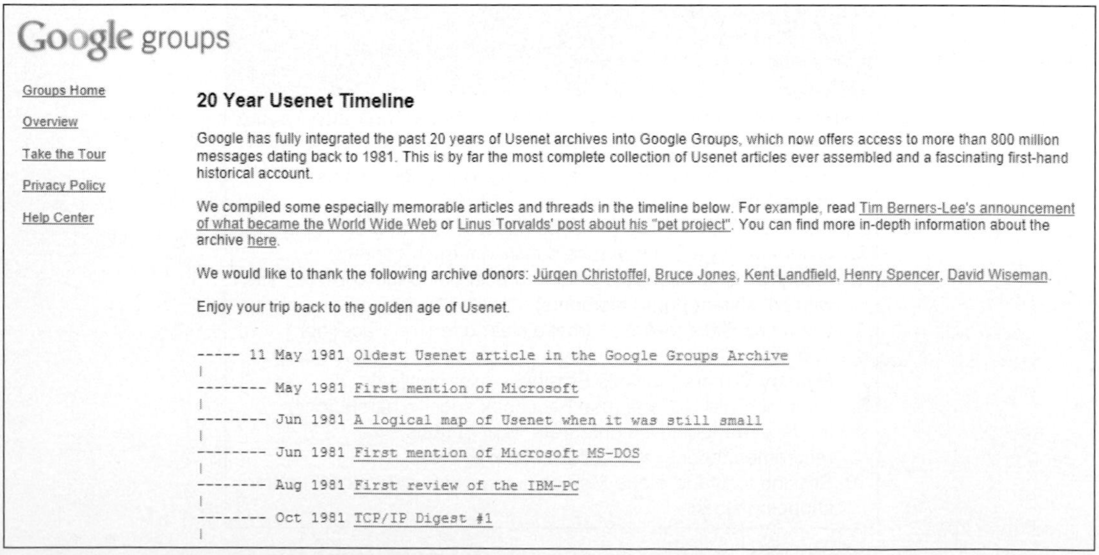

Google groups

Groups Home
Overview
Take the Tour
Privacy Policy
Help Center

20 Year Usenet Timeline

Google has fully integrated the past 20 years of Usenet archives into Google Groups, which now offers access to more than 800 million messages dating back to 1981. This is by far the most complete collection of Usenet articles ever assembled and a fascinating first-hand historical account.

We compiled some especially memorable articles and threads in the timeline below. For example, read Tim Berners-Lee's announcement of what became the World Wide Web or Linus Torvalds' post about his "pet project". You can find more in-depth information about the archive here.

We would like to thank the following archive donors: Jürgen Christoffel, Bruce Jones, Kent Landfield, Henry Spencer, David Wiseman.

Enjoy your trip back to the golden age of Usenet.

```
----- 11 May 1981 Oldest Usenet article in the Google Groups Archive
|
-------- May 1981 First mention of Microsoft
|
-------- Jun 1981 A logical map of Usenet when it was still small
|
-------- Jun 1981 First mention of Microsoft MS-DOS
|
-------- Aug 1981 First review of the IBM-PC
|
-------- Oct 1981 TCP/IP Digest #1
|
```

EXHIBIT 14.6 Google Groups Houses the Usenet *Source*: Courtesy of google.com

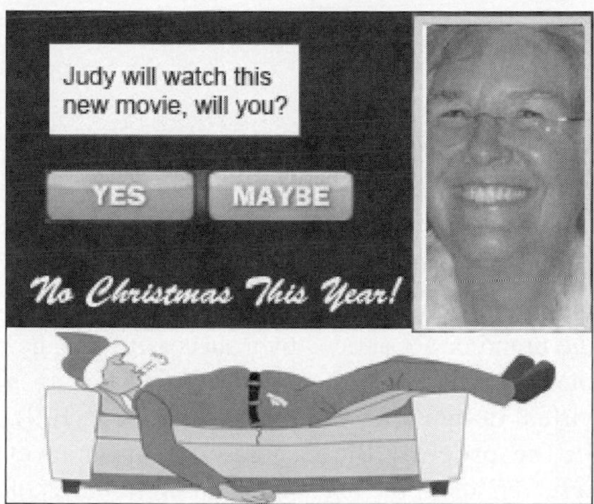

EXHIBIT 14.7 Social Network Movie Widget

a result. Companies such as Friend2Friend and Product Pulse create widgets for advertisers that allow for voting, gaming, gifting, user-created content, and more.

Apps are not only for smartphones and tablets—they appear on Web sites and social media as well. Facebook features hundreds of thousands of third-party software applications on its site. One popular application area is travel. For example, one specific application is "Where I've Been," which is a map that highlights places where users have visited or hope to visit. Visitors can plan trips, organize group travel, and find and rate free in-home accommodations (e.g., at Couchsurfing.org). This information can be sold to travel-oriented vendors, who in turn advertise their products to Facebook members. Other important apps include the following:

- Facebook messenger allows users to send messages to friends' mobile phones anytime, from a phone, tablet, or computer. This app made history at the SXSW conference (South by Southwest) as attendees messaged friends about all the new technology and gadgets they encountered.
- Pinterest has grown astronomically since its inception. We've mentioned this several times already as a site where users can "pin" images and make collections for others to see (and click on for purchase).
- Instagram allows users to take photos, add filters, and upload to the Instagram site. People then can share the photo on Facebook, Twitter, and Tumblr. This aids commerce because people often take images while in restaurants, bars, and retailers.
- Mashups. These include many types of Web site combinations to engage consumers. One notable example is Google Places, which allows business owners to list their business name and location so that mobile and computer users can find the business location on a Google Map. Lil' Piddlers Pet Grooming & Boutique in Oakland Park, Florida, realized a 30 percent increase in sales within 5 years of using Google Places (see google.com/"places for business" for other success stories).

We could fill a book with lists of apps that create earned media about companies, products, and brands. We'll stop with one more important one: location-based services (LBS).

Location-Based Services (LBS)

LBS is a business model for m-commerce (mobile-commerce). It is based on knowing where customers are located via a global positioning system (GPS) chip in their smartphones. A basic idea is that users who have a GPS-enabled smartphone can let their friends know their location. Users can also find restaurants and other places recommended by people they know, or "check in" while at stores, clubs, bars, and restaurants.

Checking in has its privileges: Once it is known that a person is in or near a certain business, the company can send an automated text, e-mail, or even a phone call offering discounted products, coupons, or services. For example, one restaurant near the author's campus offers patrons a free drink for checking in with Foursquare via their smartphones. In another example, the Milwaukee restaurant, AJ Bombers, had 1,400 people check in on Foursquare 6,000 times total in a 3-month period, thus increasing sales by 110 percent (Chaffey, 2010). Visitors also received a free cookie for writing a tip on Foursquare.

This business model was not too successful prior to the use of social media. Many customers were not interested, and those with GPS shut it off for privacy concerns. The situation changed with the introduction of social networks. The nature of location-based marketing changed to being social, entertaining, and rewarding; vendor promotion came as an add-on enticement.

The major players in this area are Foursquare, Yelp, and Facebook Places.

- **Foursquare.** With over 10 million users, Foursquare works via a smartphone app or its mobile Web site. Using GPS, Foursquare identifies the user's location. Friends, also on Foursquare, can see the users' locations once they have "checked in." Businesses offer award points for checking in and the person who checks in the most often during a 60-day time period will be designated "Mayor" of the business. Universities are also in Foursquare. Do you think it would increase class attendance to offer an incentive to the College Mayor? It works for many businesses, who offer free gifts or food to those who check in.
- **Yelp.** Just 8 years old, Yelp had 84 million visitors in 19 countries in the third quarter of 2012 (see yelp.com). At that time there were 33 million reviews of local businesses. Business owners (from retailers to dentists) set up Yelp accounts that allow site visitors to review the company and to respond to user posts. Yelp's mobile app also allows users to check into local businesses via their smartphones.
- **Facebook places.** Users can easily add a location to their Facebook text-based or photo posts. This can either be a specific business or event or just be a general city location. They can decide which friends will see the location and also receive notification when tagged by a friend.

There are many other techniques and examples that allow for successful customer engagement in a brand or organization's messages to generate earned media. Finally, we move to the gold at the top of the engagement ladder: user collaboration.

COLLABORATIVE CONTENT CREATION BY CONSUMERS

As previously mentioned, the most engaged customers help the company improve products and promotions because they either care deeply about the brand or are enticed by a successful engagement technique (recall The LEGO Group's virtual design uploads, discussed in Chapter 9). In the process, the company gains market research about the behaviors and preferences of its markets. At the simplest level, when you visit an automobile company's Web site and click around to change the color of the car and give it leather seats and other options, you are helping the company learn about consumer preferences as it captures your online click stream—and this will guide its future product design. Collaborative content creation is crowdsourcing at its best.

You've read about several companies using crowdsourcing to solicit product ideas, such as Dell and Starbucks. Another important crowdsourcing trend involves user-generated advertising. Frito Lay offers internet users \$1 million, a free trip to the Super Bowl, and the chance to work with an ad agency to create winning 30-second television commercials about the Doritos brand chips. The winning spot each year is aired at the game. Since its inception in 2007, consumers have submitted over 19,000 ads, according to sponsor, PepsiCo. This promotion was so successful that winners typically end up in of the top three spots in *USA Today*'s Super Bowl Ad Meter. General Motors (GM) tried the same strategy, providing consumers' video, audio, and images to use in constructing commercials. It worked well for GM, too; however, there was a negative backlash—approximately 20 percent of the entries had superimposed text mentioning the Chevy Tahoe's part in using up the world's oil and causing global warming. These videos were posted as ad parodies on YouTube and received lots of press. The moral: In an online environment where everyone is a journalist, expect your

EXHIBIT 14.8 The San Francisco County Transportation Authority Uses Crowdsourcing
Source: Courtesy of the San Francisco County Transportation Authority

underbelly to be exposed. Regardless, GM felt the campaign was a huge success.

Advertisers continue to experiment with user-created ads for good reason—one study found that consumers believe companies with customer-created ads are more friendly (68 percent), creative (56 percent), and innovative (55 percent) than those that use only professional advertising (according to AMA and Opinion Research Corporation research). Also, recall that consumers trust each other more than they trust companies, so consumer-created advertising is an appropriate tactic.

The San Francisco County Transportation Authority (SFCTA) used a crowdsourcing campaign that combined offline and online IMC. It posted ads in the city busses (in both English and Chinese), inviting citizens to propose ways to spend the $64 billion transportation budget from 2012 through 2040. Titled "How would you invest San Francisco's transportation dollars: be the City's budget czar for a day!," it consists of a Web page (sfbudgetczar.com) that guides users through a series of transportation spending options under three expenditure categories: maintenance and operations, programs, and capital projects (Exhibit 14.8). The site operates like an online game, and participants are put into a drawing for $50 transit passes. The campaign ran from October through November 2012, and approximately 600 people participated. You'll also note a QR code in the ad for easy access to the Web site.

Crowdfunding involves raising money online for new product ideas, or for political campaigns, and nonprofit causes. As you read previously, trendwatching.com noted that in 2011 crowdfunded platforms raised $1.4 billion. Sites such as Kickstarter.com assist ordinary citizens in raising money for their creative projects.

HOW DO COMPANIES ENTICE ENGAGEMENT?

As Oscar Wilde famously noted, "The only thing worse than being talked about is not being talked about." How do companies engage their markets, gaining trust and guiding people from passive content consumption, up the ladder to sparking positive brand conversations and viral activity? This involves creating content and promotions that encourage people to interact with the brand and then tag, bookmark, or rate the content and share opinions with others via comments and recommendations in the social media. Because they can reach millions of people when they share, it is like the old-fashioned word-of-mouth on steroids.

As with all effective promotions, three basic criteria must be met—delivering the right message to the right messengers in the right media. Accomplishing this requires a deep understanding of the audience's needs, behaviors, and motivations, and constant earned media monitoring.

Social media participants want to be informed, entertained, appreciated, and not bombarded with interruptive brand messages, seen in the following engagement principles and examples.

Provide High-Quality, Timely, Unique, and Relevant Information

When companies like eMarketer, A.C. Nielsen, ComScore, or Forrester release statistics from their primary research, bloggers will write about it, giving their interpretations for readers to comment upon and share. For example, internet marketing consultant Andy Beal started the Marketing Pilgrim blog in 2005. He begins his day in the wee hours by reading his RSS streams from over 100 sites he follows. He then writes a blog post about the latest news announced by Google or another company and gives his expert analysis on what it means to internet marketers. Beal built his consulting business from the blog followers, sells advertising space on his blog, participates in many interviews with mainstream media, has added a team of experts to write articles, and is consistently in the top 10 media and marketing blogs, as rated by *Advertising Age* (see marketingpilgrim.com). In the eMarketing LinkedIn group mentioned previously, Fleming posted a very provocative short article: "Social Media Has Ruined Marketing," and this quickly received nearly 600 comments, creating a very lively discussion that continues a year later.

Create Entertaining Content

Consumers will watch and share video commercials and other company-created content that is entertaining, irreverent, interesting, or unusual. For example, Blendtec created a series of infomercials showing the power of its new consumer market blenders (recall the opening story from Chapter 12). The videos showed the company CEO blending everything from a garden rake to golf balls, glow sticks, and an iPad. The iPhone 4 blending video alone received 3.5 million views within 13 months, and the blended iPhone remnants received over $900 on eBay in 2007. As of October 2012, all the Blendtec videos had received a total of 204,352,346 views on YouTube, an undetermined amount on the Willitblend.com microsite, and have had an "amazing impact" on company sales, according to the company CEO, Tom Dickson (see YouTube and willitblend.com for more details).

Offer Competitions

Many people love to compete and win prizes. For example, the Microsoft Windows 7 launch included a "School Pride" sales promotion campaign, asking site visitors to vote on videos created by middle or high school students who hoped to win a computer lab makeover. Microsoft used a social graph that allowed voters to invite friends and followers to vote as well. Microsoft experienced a 75 percent increase in traffic during the competition (Dhalokia, 2011). A **social graph** is a drawing showing the interconnection of social network members. Incidentally, Washington's Whatcom Middle School won the competition, and this provided another opportunity for social media activity and publicity from Microsoft and its partner, NBC.

Appeal to Altruism

People like to share stories, videos, and other content about social causes. For example, the

American Red Cross ran a blood donation drive to assist residents after the storms that battered the East Coast of the United States in 2011. Instead of providing the paper sticker for the donor's clothing ("I gave blood"), the Red Cross made a virtual status badge that people could share on their social networks, encouraging friends and followers to make blood donation appointments. If blood donors checked in via Foursquare, they could "shout" a 140-character post to friends that they were currently giving blood, and this would unlock a special donor badge that appeared on the user's Foursquare profile and would be automatically sent to a Twitter feed (Behlmann, 2010).

Make an Exclusive Offer

The social psychology principle of "scarcity" often motivates people to take action immediately. For example, sales promotion discounts and free sample product offers with expiration dates often engage recipients. Artists and movie producers often release songs or trailers for viewing by their fan bases, prior to release to the general public. American rapper, Pitbull, went further when promoting his CD, *Planet Pit*, by telling fans that if they sent an early release online track link to friends, and three visited the Web site to listen, the original fan would get to unlock three additional bonus tracks from the CD (Dhalokia, 2011).

Reward Influentials and Fans

Following the famous Pareto rule, that 80 percent of the business comes from 20 percent of the customers, most of the buzz about a brand comes from a small number of fans. If Andy Beal or the Huffington Post continuously writes about a company, they should be rewarded. Rewards of appreciation can take the form of exclusive information, first chance at breaking news, or a free gift—such as the chance to review a new product that they get to keep, an exclusive offer, or a special discount. Following the principles of customer relationship management (Chapter 15), a brand will do well to occasionally appreciate its important fans. Foursquare allows this by awarding "mayor" status to the people who check in the most number of days during a 60-day time period at a particular location. Frito Lay made the Guinness World Records title in April 2011 for the most new "likes" on its Facebook page (1,571,161) and rewarded fans by giving away 24,000 bags of chips, via coupons, to the first fans who registered (see press releases at fritolay.com). Finally, Intel displays pictures on its Intel Web site and gives welcome gifts, a laptop computer, and more to its "Network Hall of Fame—Intel Black Belt Software Developers." Award winners are community members who contribute their expertise and experience in posts to the Intel Software Network (see software.intel.com). Incidentally, this is a good way for consultants to build awareness of their services online.

Incentivize Group Behavior

Following the social psychology principle of reciprocity, customers can be motivated to participate in social media if offered an incentive up front (versus the "thank-you" type reward just mentioned). For example, Oscar Mayer gave consumers an offline discount coupon to an initial product trial of its Oscar Mayer Selects hot dogs. They added a deal sweetener: Share a "Taste-a-Monial" review of the product and receive a second coupon. The twist was that for every 5,000 people who shared Taste-a-Monials, the coupon value increased by $0.50 until the consumer could receive a full free pack of the hot dogs. Using the scarcity principle, the offer was limited to a short time period (Dhalokia, 2011).

A key principle of enticing engagement is to make it easy for users. For instance, most social media and many Web sites provide one-click buttons for "liking," tagging, bookmarking (e.g., offering a Delicious button), subscribing via an RSS feed button (which can rapidly spread the content), and sharing content on social networks. Many sites also allow users to register with one click, using their Facebook, or other social network profile. For example, BostInnovation provides information on happenings in the Boston area. The site implemented Gigya's social login application so that users could register, login, share, and comment directly on the site. This resulted in a 58 percent increase in commenting activity, according to the site cofounder, Kevin McCarthy (see case studies at gigya.com).

Thus far, we have been painting a rosy picture of customer engagement and all the good it can do for a brand or organization. As hard as marketers try to deliver a good product and respect consumer communication preferences, things can quickly go downhill with earned media, such as what happened with the General Motors UGC advertising. The moral is, in an online environment where everyone is a critic, expect the brand's underbelly to be exposed. This brings us to an important topic: How can a company manage its brand messages and reputation in the Wild West environment of earned media?

REPUTATION MANAGEMENT ONLINE

In February 2011, Egyptian citizens used social media to organize protests against President Hosni Mubarak, high unemployment, and rising prices. They used Facebook, Twitter, and YouTube until the government blocked all WiFi and cell networks. This didn't stop the people, who then used dial-up phone modems to connect and organize protests. Ultimately, Mubarak fell from power. If social media conversation can bring down the government of Egypt, what can it do to a company, brand, or CEO?

Kitchen Aid, the appliance producer, found out very quickly in 2012 when the social media manager sent a tweet from the company @KitchenAidUSA twitter account that spoke badly of the then-candidate Barack Obama, saying something to the effect that his grandmother died 3 days before he became president the first time because she knew it wasn't going to go well with him as president. That 140-character message created a fast and huge backlash against well-regarded Kitchen Aid, until the company sent an apology Tweet to the Twitter community and directly to Obama, taking full responsibility for its social media and employee mismanagement ("Kitchen Aid—Bad Tweets. . .," 2012).

Reputation is a belief in the mind of the beholder. Abraham Lincoln is attributed to saying that "character is like a tree and reputation like a shadow. The shadow is what we think of it and the tree is the real thing." Thus, an entity's reputation is based on what other people think of it, not what it thinks of itself. With earned media, there is plenty of opportunity for other people to shape the reputations of a company, its brands, and its employees. Brands and companies have lost a great deal of control over their images and reputations, and must now monitor, engage, and participate in social media conversations or pay the consequences. In a survey of 28 public boards of directors, Edelman found consensus that reputational risk was among corporate America's greatest challenges in 2011 (for more information, see edelman.com).

Marketers must remember that although viral videos and other branded content is a plus, it is quite often changed as it gets passed along the internet. The message will be distorted (such as a mashup of a company video posted on YouTube) and oftentimes the message will turn negative. An example is the numerous YouTube videos showing the Mentos brand mints exploding out of soda bottles.

In another example, Greenpeace UK, the activist not-for-profit organization working for a green and peaceful world, posted a video on YouTube to build awareness of a perceived problem. Nestlé, the maker of Kit Kat candy bar, was purchasing palm oil extracted from forests in Indonesia, thus ruining the Indonesian rainforests, which pushed the orangutans toward extinction. The video entitled "Have a Break?" showed an office worker taking a break by eating a Kit Kat bar. When he bit into it, blood gushed from the chocolate bar.

The video received 476,328 views by 2011; however, the damage really escalated on Nestlé's Facebook page. Immediately after the March 17, 2010, video post, viewers began complaining about the palm oil harvesting with comments on the company's Facebook page. Some of the protesters created a graphic imitation of the Kit Kat candy bar package, replacing the brand name with the word *Killer* in the same font, or stamping the package with bloody orangutan footprints. They made this image their profile picture on Facebook so every post on the Nestlé page included this image.

Nestlé responded by saying that it would delete any comments that contained the altered image. This inappropriate response created a blogstorm and many more posts, and shifted the conversation away from the core issue of deforestation and animal slaughter to Nestlé's ineptitude in social media. Nestlé debated with commenters, defending its decision to censor profile pictures, and then started deleting comments as well. It got very nasty. Eventually, the Nestlé executive running the Facebook page posted an apology and said they would stop deleting comments.

What really is amazing is the speed at which this happened:

- March 17, 2010: Greenpeace video posted on YouTube.
- March 18: 190 Facebook complaints and thousands of Tweets in response.
- March 19 at 2:26 AM: Nestlé responds on Facebook with the plan to delete the "Killer" bar logo profile pictures and comments.
- March 19 at 1:29 PM: Nestlé apologizes on Facebook and stops deleting the posts.

Several companies analyzed the social media conversations after this incident. One found that social media conversations including both terms *Nestlé* and *Facebook* jumped by 40 percent on March 19, 2010, and that 16 percent of this conversation was negative, 66 percent neutral, and 16 percent positive (according to the former blog.biz360.com).

Quality, transparency, and trust principally influence company and brand reputations, according to the Edelman 2012 Trust survey. In order to be trusted, an entity must be reliable, of high quality, authentic, transparent, and follow through on its promises. Marketers often describe a brand as a promise to deliver promoted benefits, and if they do not follow through on that promise, they are open to attack in the social media. For example, if an automobile does not get the advertised gas mileage, a customer will lose some degree of trust in the company/brand and likely talk about this gas mileage disparity online on product review sites, or in social networks or blogs. Transparency occurs when companies honestly and quickly reveal the truth before or during a reputation crisis. If they hide the truth and later are discovered, the negative social media conversation will escalate. Transparency includes honest conversation in social media and revealing product improvement processes, such as Dell does in its IdeaStorm microsite previously discussed.

Consider the following statistics:

- In 2011, only 53 percent of the world trusted companies do "what is right" (according to the 2012 Edelman Trust Survey).
- Twenty-five percent of searches for the world's 20 largest brands return links to user-generated content (Falls and Deckers, 2012). Search engines rank as the first place people go for information about a company, according to the Edelman Global Trust Survey.
- Thirty-four percent of bloggers post opinions about product and brands, and these are read by those people who follow and trust the blogs (Falls and Deckers, 2012).
- Only 14 percent of people trust advertisements (Falls and Deckers, 2012). This is likely because the intent of advertising is to persuade consumers by presenting only the positive about a product (in contrast, recall the high number of people who trust people like themselves).
- When a company is distrusted, 57 percent of the people will believe negative information after hearing it one to two times, whereas only 15 percent will believe positive information after hearing it once or twice (according to the 2011 Edelman Trust Survey).

- Trust has value: When a company is trusted, 51 percent will believe the positive information after hearing it one to two times, and only 25 percent will believe negative information after hearing it once or twice (according to the 2011 Edelman Trust Survey).

Beyond social media participant responses to company actions, people often make attacks in the middle of the night, surprising the companies who are the objects of these attacks, such as the one that happened to Nestlé.

Which Reputations Matter?

Brand and company reputations are very important. Sixty-three percent of a company's market value is attributable to reputation, according to a global survey conducted by PR firm Weber Shandwick ("Safeguarding Reputation," 2006). This PR company also noted that (1) 66 percent of executives think it is harder to recover from reputation failure than to build and maintain a reputation and (2) it takes U.S. companies 3.2 years to fully recover from a damaged reputation. Just think about how British Petroleum is still suffering from its oil spill incident in 2010.

In an interesting example, Brazilian creative agency, Moma Propaganda, was stripped of two awards and prohibited from entering the Cannes Lions International Festival of Creativity for a year. The agency entered two fake ads for Kia Motors Brazil—"fake" meaning that it created the ads for the competition—but the ads were neither approved by Kia nor run in any traditional or online media. Cannes discovered this when it came across the firestorm of social media conversation, which criticized the campaign for overtones of lust and pedophilia. This incident created reputation-damaging publicity for both the agency and Kia Motors Brazil, until the latter said it had neither seen nor approved the ads (Wentz and Penteado, 2011).

A company's CEO's reputation is linked closely to the company reputation. PR firm Burson-Marsteller's survey of company decision-makers found that favorable CEO reputations resulted in over 90 percent of respondents (1) purchasing stock in the company, (2) believing in the company when the news is negative, and (3) recommending the company as a good business partner (Gaines-Ross, 2003). Often, the reputations of other company executives also affect the company. For example, the reputations of job recruiters in a company can make a big difference when trying to attract good employees (Shih, 2011). Successful recruiters build their reputations on LinkedIn, and this helps them build good relationships with previous job candidates and new hires.

Recently, there has been a great deal of talk and information about using the social media for personal branding. This especially applies to consultants, sales people, and other professionals, as well as to college students who are about to enter the job market.

Build, Maintain, Monitor, Repair, Learn

The reputation management process includes four steps: build, maintain, monitor, and repair. Many of the techniques for implementing these steps are elsewhere in the book so we just touch upon it here. There are many promotional techniques for *building* a strong reputation, but it all starts with the company's actions. As previously mentioned, most social media reputation crises happen because of something the company does or does not do. Given positive actions, the company can use owned or paid media and join the conversation in earned social media to communicate its benefits to consumers and other stakeholders. This book gives many examples of how companies do this, such as engaging social media participant customers and prospects where they hang out online, and building good customer relationships (Chapter 15).

Maintaining positive reputations requires constant internet and offline media monitoring, and then sometimes participating when things go awry. We say "sometimes" because companies decide whether or not to respond based on three factors: (1) how valuable is the poster to the company? (2) how much potential does the comment contain for creating reputation damage? and (3) how widely can the discussion travel in social media (Flynn, 2012)? For example, if the comment came from a high-value customer or influential journalist, the company will respond immediately, sometimes by direct e-mail to the author. Conversely, if the poster is a low-value customer or a competitor and does not seem like a big enough conversation to spread far, the company might ignore the comment (mostly due to time constraints). Interestingly, one survey of marketers found that in response to customer complaints or questions, 29 percent seldom or never respond to them on Twitter and 17 percent said the same for Facebook posts ("How Well Do Companies. . .," 2011). These may be low-value complaints, but this same study found that 22 percent of companies do not even know if their customers use social media to comment on company products, so we suspect that many reputations are declining unnoticed by marketers.

The Nestlé example shows the need to *monitor* social media conversation 24/7 and assign appropriate personnel to Facebook and other social media for beneficial user interactions. Xbox was found to be the fastest brand to respond to customer queries on Twitter, with an average response time of 2 minutes and 42 seconds, whereas one study found the fastest U.S. retailer responses took over 4 hours ("Who's Ignoring Their Customers?" 2011). It is also critically important to understand and fix the underlying problem, if possible, prior to responding to bloggers and other social media detractors. Without substance, responses to a crisis can be seen as empty promises to social media participants.

When a company creates a Facebook business page, by default, it allows other Facebook members—potentially including disgruntled customers or sleazy competitors—to post on the Facebook Wall, or comment on what the company has posted. However, if the page owner turns off the feature that allows others to write on the Wall, people may wonder what the company fears or is hiding. Turning off the feature also precludes great customer fan conversations that could promote the products and services better than the company could do (because people trust others like them online). Companies can delete posts, but that may only encourage the post author to scream louder about being censored, as it did with Nestlé. Most social media marketing experts advise deleting only the most offensive or vulgar posts, while trying to address the rest as constructively as possible. In fact, this is how a company can learn things that will improve its products and processes.

For example, Coca-Cola has 33 million fans on its Facebook page worldwide, with 80 percent living outside the United States. The company uses geotags so that fans see relevant posts in their own language, based on the poster's IP (internet protocol) address (e.g., someone posting from .de would see only German language posts). Coke posted something it thought would appeal to fans about the Day of the Student. Unfortunately, there was a glitch in the geotagging on Facebook and, for 10 minutes, U.S. fans saw this text in Portuguese instead of English. This created a firestorm of comments from U.S. fans, the likes of "Speak English or @#* die (bad word deleted)!" Apparently, U.S. fans think that Coke is an American brand and should stay that way. Coca-Cola removed the Portuguese post and all the offensive comments from its wall. Sometimes it is surprising to see what will upset customers.

Repairing reputations can take an average of 3.2 years, as previously mentioned. This involves fixing the fundamental problems causing the crisis, communicating the solutions to important stakeholders, and enticing social media participants to spread the conversation.

Most good companies *learn* from criticism in social media and act upon what they hear. Negative comments add authenticity in balancing a company's one-sided owned and paid media but, when handled well, can boost reputations and sales. Product reviews, complaints, and positive suggestions help them improve products, processes, and Web content. The best way to encourage this type of posting is by hosting a conversation on the company's own social media and Web properties so it becomes easier to identify, learn, and then respond that changes have been made (if warranted).This kind of dialog often prevents complaints from becoming viral as well. For example, My Starbucks Idea site has several hundred thousand users and accepts ideas in product, experience, and involvement categories. The microsite lists recent ideas as they are sent via Twitter and Facebook, or posted on the microsite, and then reports on "ideas in action." Users can click on each idea to see its status and add comments. This is a brilliant way to learn from customers without doing expensive market research, and it yields a lot more actionable data as well.

One important way to avoid unwarranted reputation crises involves building a reputation management system in company-owned social media.

Reputation Management Systems

Reputation management systems use various criteria and technologies for monitoring and protecting reputations. This is a solution that helps companies initiate and monitor reputations. For example, most social media platforms have a member profile feature, which allows others to see more about who is posting on the medium, and also to view statistics about the member's activity. Furthermore, many social networks require a reply to an automated outgoing e-mail so they know the user actually resides at that e-mail address. eBay and other social commerce sites have feedback systems so that buyers can rate sellers for all future buyers to see. Similarly, Slashdot uses a "karma" rating system, and others also have systems where users can rate the reviews and even the ratings of other users. These reputation management systems help build authenticity and trust in contributors to the conversation.

Facebook grew and beat MySpace partially because of its reputation management system. It engaged users and built trust through e-mail authentication, privacy settings, and building the site around relationships in the offline world (Shih, 2011). Facebook started as a site for Harvard and other Ivy League schools, adding to its credibility.

In another reputation management system example, Rosetta Stone is a maker of software for language translation. It is mostly a B2B organization. To get the most out of social media, Rosetta Stone uses a strategy and software to control its customer interaction on Facebook. The strategy involves both human intervention and an investment in software to help monitor its social networking presence. Specifically, the company software helps to monitor Wall posts and respond to them appropriately. Rosetta Stone uses Parature, Inc. software to scan fan Wall posts, add them to a database, and flag those that need a response from the company. This solution is handy because it all occurs on a special Facebook support tab and separates fans chatting among themselves from discussions involving company customer service representatives (Carr, 2010).

EARNED MEDIA PERFORMANCE METRICS

As you've read elsewhere, a company specifies which metrics will be used to measure marketing communication success, and then uses these measures as feedback to (1) see if the campaign objectives were met and (2) continually refine the strategies and tactics to enhance performance. Chapter 2 discussed many social media metrics that apply to earned media in the areas of awareness/exposure, brand health, engagement, action, and innovation. These include elements such as number of likes and shares, number of ideas uploaded, share of voice, and sentiment analysis. For company-owned channels (owned media), some of these earned media metrics apply if the action was on the company's own sites or pages, such as number of comments posted to a company's blog, or sentiment in a forum on a company's Web site. Following is a summary of additional metrics that apply to earned media:

- **General earned media metrics.** Number of users who interact with an application or ad, and time spent viewing a video, playing a game, or listening to music. Also the growth of social media fans and communities.

- Individual engagement, determined as interaction with a brand in a way that the brand defines as meaningful. It may be dependent on creative, for example, number of video views, bookmarks, photo uploads, or creation of user-generated content from content supplied by the company relating to the brand.
- Social engagement, defined as interaction with brand assets, which has peer-to-peer(s) impact:
  - Conversation contributions, size, density
  - Comments, ratings, and reviews, discussion boards, forum activity
  - Content shared, status updates made
- Growth of followers (Twitter), fans, friends
- RSS subscribers
- Media attention/press coverage/buzz
- Traffic (link-backs from newsfeed items or status updates to brand pages)
- Search equity from links to a brand site sent by users into a social environment (status update, blog post, comment)

EXHIBIT 14.9 Earned Media Metric Examples *Source*: "IAB Social Media Booklet," (2010). Available at iab.net

- **Actions taken by users.** Number of downloads for a white paper, MP3 music file, ring tone, or other content; number of bookmarks for a Web site at a social bookmarking site such as Delicious.com; number of uploads for user-created video, photo, or other multimedia content to a Web site; number of ratings at a book or online retailer; and number of games played, coupons downloaded, polls voted, and invitations accepted to an online event.
- **Conversations on blogs and elsewhere.** Number of comments, tweets/retweets; conversation sentiment as positive/negative; conversation reach—number of visitors viewing a conversation; number of relevant conversation comments; and dates of first and last comment post.

See Exhibit 14.9 for the Interactive Advertising Bureau's earned media sample metrics for social media.

Social Media Dashboard

With so many social and earned media to monitor and reputations that can be damaged in a matter of hours, how can a company keep track? We discussed Google Alerts in Chapter 6, and here we present the much more sophisticated social media dashboard. It is software that pulls in company, brand, or any keyword mentions from any social media and displays them all in one place. This makes it easy for companies to monitor conversations and also displays selected metrics. Many companies are rushing to compete in this space—see Exhibit 14.10 for the Radian6 dashboard. It gives a 360° view of social media channels and allows daily, weekly, or monthly comparisons for up to a year. It shows whether the trend is positive or negative and builds a word cloud of keyword mentions in conversations, and metrics allow marketers to keep track of the effects.

Are you dizzy yet? There are many complexities to social engagement measurement, and marketers are just beginning to find robust ways for collecting these important Web 2.0 metrics as relates to their IMC goals. We'll leave you with one final example to enliven this long list of metrics. In 2007, Jeep automobiles decided to engage more deeply with its already tight brand community. The "Jeep Experience" featured a showcase on Jeep.com, which aggregated social media branded profiles and conversations from its own Jeep Facebook, MySpace, YouTube, and Flickr pages (using RSS feeds). The showcase page was also infused with Jeep company content in several areas: Community (branded

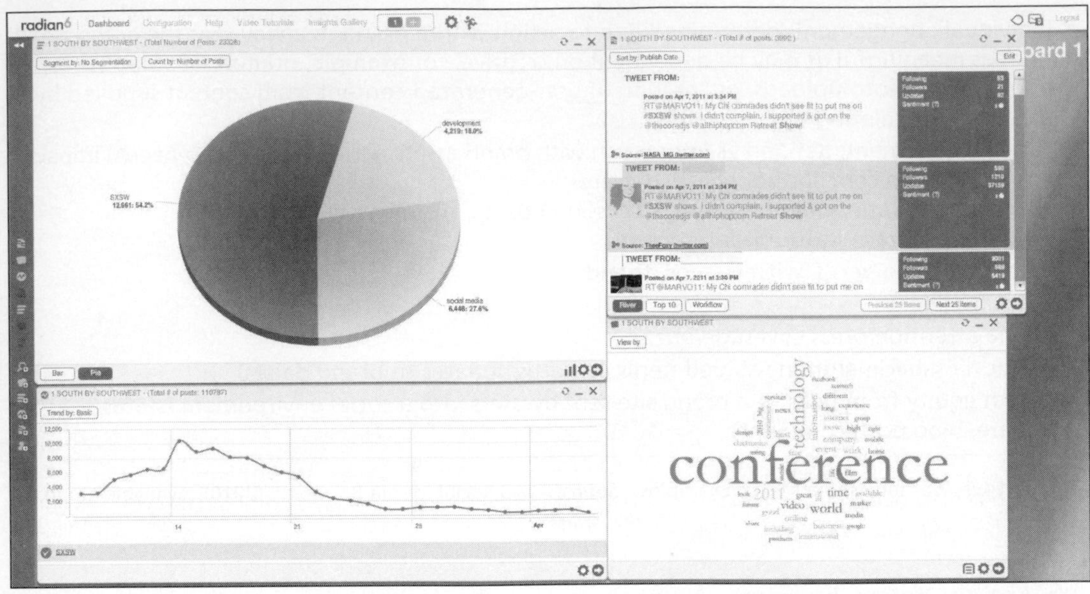

EXHIBIT 14.10 Radian6 Social Media Dashboard *Source*: © radian6, reproduced with permission

social media profiles and content), news, Jeep events, action sports (for Jeep-sponsored events), and more ("IAB Social Media Buyer's Guide," 2010). Now for the performance metrics actually used by Jeep:

- Average time on the Jeep experience site was 14.53 minutes.
- The Jeep Facebook page had 350,000 fans.
- Seventeen percent of the visitors to the Jeep Experience pages compared Jeep vehicles, versus only 7 percent of visitors to the Web site alone (Jeep.com).
- Twelve percent of Jeep Experience visitors searched vehicle inventory, versus only 9 percent on Jeep.com.
- Fifteen percent of Jeep Experience visitors searched to locate a dealer, versus 11 percent on Jeep.com.

These are very impressive results for a campaign that had no advertising and involved engaging visitors at purely company-owned social media sites. Without these metrics, Jeep would not have known whether or not the time investment paid off.

Chapter Summary

Earned media is the third element of content strategy, resulting from owned media and paid media efforts. Unlike traditional media, which involves passive exposure, earned media is the result of user engagement. Engagement can occur at five levels: (1) when internet users consume online content (the lowest level of engagement); (2) when users connect with others online, such as by registering for a social network; (3) when users collect information, such as by filtering and tagging content on social media sites; (4) when users create original social media content, such as posting YouTube videos; and (5) when users collaborate with a company (the highest level of engagement), such as by suggesting ideas for product improvement. Compared with company-generated communications, consumers tend to put more trust in recommendations from people they know and in user-generated online reviews, and opinions. Because of this trust, earned media can have a significant influence on buying decisions.

Among the key techniques for engaging users to produce earned media are viral marketing, in which individuals forward content to each other; viral blogging, with bloggers participating in viral marketing activities; multimedia sharing, in which users upload photos, video, music playlists, live audio/video, or presentations to share with others; wikis, where users can post, edit, and organize multimedia content; product ratings and reviews, which can influence purchasing online and offline; social recommendations and referrals, such as referral programs; e-mail; social media site conversations; community forums and discussions; widgets and social apps; and location-based services.

Collaborative content creation, a form of crowdsourcing, is at the high end of the engagement ladder. The marketing benefits include learning more about the behaviors and preferences of target markets, receiving new product ideas from users, and receiving user-generated advertising ideas and materials via crowdsourcing. Crowdfunding involves raising money online for new product ideas, political campaigns, or nonprofit causes.

Techniques companies can use to attract users and move them up the engagement ladder include: (1) providing information that is of high quality, timely, unique, and relevant; (2) creating content that is entertaining, irreverent, interesting, or unusual; (3) devising competitions where users can win prizes; (4) appealing to users' altruism and interest in social causes; (5) making an exclusive offer that motivates immediate action; (6) rewarding influentials and fans; and (7) offering upfront incentives.

Building a strong, positive reputation for the company, its brands, and its executives starts with what the company does (or does not do), not just what and how it promotes itself. Maintaining positive reputations requires constant monitoring of internet and offline media, and then determining whether or not to respond to comments. Repairing a reputation takes years, but this is a worthwhile process because the company can open a dialog and learn from any criticism. Finally, a number of metrics apply to earned media, including: (1) general metrics such as number of users who interact with a communication or other element, and growth in community, or number of fans; (2) actions taken by users, such as number of downloads or uploads; and (3) number and sentiment of conversations on blogs, microblogs, and elsewhere. Some companies use a social media dashboard to monitor selected metrics.

Exercises

REVIEW QUESTIONS

1. What are the five levels of user engagement? Provide an example of each.
2. In addition to consumers and prospects, which two groups should companies seek to engage for earned media?
3. How are viral marketing and viral blogging used to generate word-of-mouse?
4. Explain how shoppers use or contribute content to the seven forms of online reviews and ratings.
5. Why should marketers be aware of the role of trust when planning for earned media?
6. How do social recommendations and referrals differ from ratings and reviews?
7. Why are many companies integrating e-mail and social media for marketing communication?
8. What are location-based services, and how do users and marketers benefit from them?
9. In what ways does collaborative content creation help companies?

10. Which reputations should a company monitor and seek to manage? Be specific.
11. As part of the decision about responding to a comment or complaint in online or offline media, what three questions should a company ask?
12. What is a social media dashboard, and why would a company use it?

DISCUSSION QUESTIONS

13. **The Dell Story.** Identify several ways that Dell could engage customers in a positive way, using techniques in this chapter.
14. **The Dell Story.** What might Dell have done to manage its online reputation better? Acting as Dell's consultant, give the company advice that would keep it out of this kind of trouble in the future.
15. What techniques from this chapter can you adapt to manage your personal brand and reputation? List at least six tactics you might use, and why.
16. Based on the idea that "reputation is a belief in the mind of the beholder," can a firm realistically take the initiative to manage its reputation online?
17. Do you think that marketers are losing control of brand images due to the social media? Why or why not?
18. Which level of engagement best describes your online behavior? How could your favorite brand move you to a higher level using the principles in this chapter?
19. Once consumers engage in collaborative content creation on behalf of a brand, what are the implications for recommendations and referrals, reputation, and purchasing?
20. If "viral marketing turns the sales funnel upside down," as shown in Exhibit 14.3, what are the potential consequences when viral marketing spreads a negative message about a company, product, or brand?
21. Should companies put more emphasis on earned media instead of investing in paid media and owned media? Explain your answer.

WEB ACTIVITIES

22. Search Google images for "social media dashboards." Look at several dashboards and follow their links to the companies that created them. Which one would you recommend that a large consumer goods company, such as Coca-Cola, use to monitor and manage mentions online? Explain the reasoning behind your recommendation.
23. Visit a business news site such as **businessweek.com** or **forbes.com** and search for an article about the reputation of a company, product, brand, or executive. What happened, and what was the effect on the company? What role did social media play in this situation? What could the company have done differently to monitor, protect, and repair its reputation online?
24. Check out your personal reputation online by searching for your name on Google. If you were a job recruiter, would you hire yourself based on what you find? Why or why not? What can you do online to improve your reputation and your chances in the job market?
25. Visit the Web site of the Interactive Advertising Bureau at **iab.net**. What information does its wiki feature? Select one entry in the wiki and look at its source and its history. Why would a marketing manager or the employee of an advertising agency contribute to this wiki?
26. Visit **yelp.com** and read the reviews for a restaurant, a store, or another business in your area. How many and what kinds of reviews and ratings do you see? How might the ratings and sentiment of these reviews affect the behavior of someone making a decision about buying from that business? What is Yelp doing to get users engaged and move them up the engagement ladder?

CHAPTER 15

Customer Relationship Management

The main objective of this chapter is to provide you with an overview of the purpose and process of building a company's relationship capital through customer relationship management (CRM). You will learn about relationship marketing's three pillars, CRM's benefits, social CRM, and the nine building blocks needed for effective and efficient e-marketing CRM.

After reading this chapter, you will be able to:

- Define customer relationship management and identify the major benefits to e-marketers.
- Outline the three pillars of relationship marketing for e-marketing.
- Describe social CRM and how it relates to traditional CRM.
- Discuss the nine major components needed for effective and efficient CRM in e-marketing.
- Highlight some of the company-side and client-side tools that e-marketers use to enhance their CRM processes.
- Differentiate CRM metrics by customer life cycle stage.

- Everyday great "customer service" will of course forever be crucial: a 2011 American Express survey found that 70 percent of American consumers were willing to spend more with brands that provided a great service, and a whopping 60 percent thought brands weren't thinking enough about the service experience.

- When ***Virgin America*** upgraded its reservation system in November 2011, a number of passengers experienced difficulties and complained via Twitter and Facebook. Rather than delete the negative comments, or reply with a generic apology, Virgin America replied to each and every customer about the particular problem that they had encountered, sending over 12,000 direct messages in the weeks after the upgrade.

The Best Buy Story

Best Buy Co., Inc. is the eleventh-largest U.S. e-commerce retailer, with $50 billion in revenue and over 160,000 employees. It is famous for its "Blue Shirt" store sales force and "Geek Squad" employees who deliver technology solutions to homes and offices. The company has 1.6 billion customers per year who visit its physical and online stores. With 1 billion online visitors and a multichannel strategy, how can the company maintain the type of communication and customer satisfaction to maintain that huge number of customer relationships? Best Buy initiated several social media tactics just for this purpose, as described next.

In 2008 Best Buy initiated the Best Buy Community online. Six hundred thousand customers a quarter post 20,000 messages and view over 22 million pages of content. They chat with the Blue Shirts, Geek Squad Agents, and each other. Users can ask and answer questions, rate answers, and give "kudos" for the best replies. There are also several blogs on the community site. According to the Best Buy Community Manager, this tactic has yielded $5 million in benefits to the company (see forums.bestbuy.com).

Best Buy uses Twitter to engage customers (@twelpforce). It is particularly important for a consumer electronics retailer to be available for answering technology questions quickly. This can retain customers and bring more business to Best Buy. For example, one person tweeted a question about using Nintendo 3DS and within 6 minutes a Blue Shirt responded with details about which systems the Nintendo games can be played on.

BBYFeed is an extension of @twelpforce and provides access to the company's knowledge database. A recent check of the tweets to BBYFeed showed a very active discussion about things such as how to get gift cards, the cost of a camcorder, and problems with delivery schedules.

It is interesting that Best Buy employees are available to immediately answer user questions in social media platforms (including its Facebook page). Mobile computing aids employees as well as customers. And everyone benefits in the end.

Sources: bestbuy.com, bbyfeed.com, and lithium.com case studies.

BUILDING CUSTOMER RELATIONSHIPS, 1:1

Best Buy develops long-term customer relationships one at a time (1:1), not unlike those developed by neighborhood retailers in the early 1900s—except that information technology allows the company to handle millions of these close relationships. A Best Buy customer enjoying this type of employee access and high satisfaction is brand loyal, and will not easily be enticed away by competition. This customer will slowly spend an increasing amount of money on additional products and services, and also refer others. According to *Harvard Business Review* authors Thomas Jones and Earl Sasser, "Increased customer loyalty is the *single most* important driver of long-term performance." *Business 2.0* calls **relationship capital** the most important asset a firm can have ("Relationships Rule," 2000). In an environment of customer control, where attention is a scarce commodity, an organization's ability to build and maintain relationships with customers, suppliers, and partners may be more important than a firm's land, property, and financial assets. It is this relationship capital that provides the foundation of future business.

This approach represents a major shift in marketing practice: from mass marketing to individualized marketing, and from focusing on acquiring lots of new customers to retaining and building more business from a smaller base of loyal high-value customers. Although many B2B companies have practiced customer relationship management for a long time, now organizations in the consumer services market (e.g., Amazon.com) and even marketers of consumer packaged goods, such as Best Buy, work to build long-term customer relationships, 1:1. How can a maker of canned dog food profitably build relationships with each consumer? Internet technologies can facilitate relationship marketing in many new ways, yet many companies that purchase and install relationship management technologies are losing money on them. This chapter explains the process, identifies key internet tools, and presents the case for a consumer-centric customer relationship management focus throughout the entire supply chain.

RELATIONSHIP MARKETING DEFINED

Marketers named this customer focus *relationship marketing* (also *1:1 marketing*). As originally defined, **relationship marketing** is about establishing, maintaining, enhancing, and commercializing customer relationships through promise fulfillment (Grönroos, 1990). Usually companies try to build profitable, mutually beneficial relationships in the long term (versus the short term). Promise fulfillment means that when companies make offers in their marketing communications programs, customer expectations will be met through actual brand experiences. For example, an offer on the Stash Tea Web site homepage promises a free box with the purchase of three but the order page does not confirm this offer, and the total quantity shown on the final order is only three. If four do not arrive, the customer will likely consider buying tea from competitor Twinings next time. Even when the four boxes arrive, the suspense may erode some of the customer's trust in the firm. Similarly, good relationships are built when company personnel meet the promises made by salespeople and promotional messages.

An organization using relationship marketing focuses on wallet share more than market share. **Wallet share** is the amount of sales a firm can generate from one customer over time and, thus, reflects a focus on retention and growth rather than an acquisition focus (market share). For instance, Amazon wants to sell hardware, music, household appliances, and more to each customer who buys a book. Relationship marketing differentiates individual customers based on need rather than differentiating products for target groups—such as buyers of novels by a particular author. It will be more profitable for Best Buy to identify its best customers, get

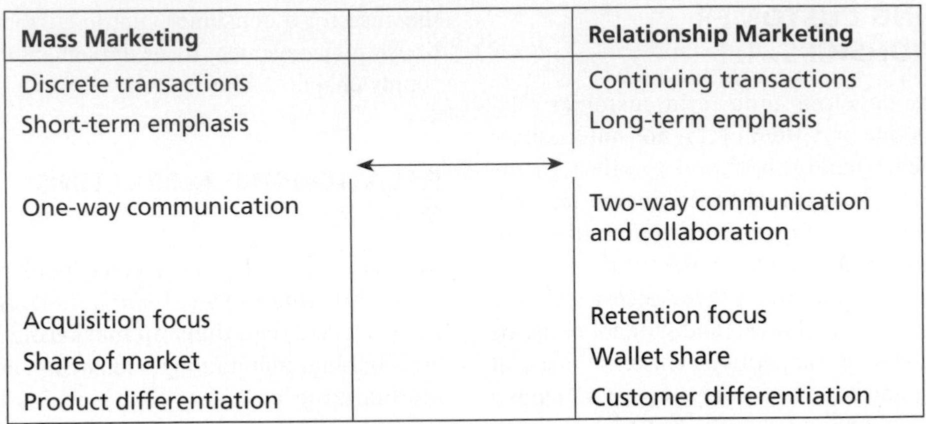

Mass Marketing		Relationship Marketing
Discrete transactions		Continuing transactions
Short-term emphasis	⟷	Long-term emphasis
One-way communication		Two-way communication and collaboration
Acquisition focus		Retention focus
Share of market		Wallet share
Product differentiation		Customer differentiation

EXHIBIT 15.1 Continuum from Mass Marketing to Relationship Marketing

to know them individually, and suggest additional products based on their needs than to spend all its efforts on acquiring new customers. If Best Buy is successful, clients will eventually buy all their consumer electronic products and services from the company (greater wallet share). Best Buy saves on promotion and price discounting expenditures by spending time on customer retention versus customer acquisition. Exhibit 15.1 displays a summary of these ideas, comparing mass marketing to relationship marketing.

Few companies fall on either end of the continuum but instead use varying strategies for different products and markets. For example, Procter & Gamble must differentiate its brands of laundry detergent for sale to the masses; however, it tries to build relationships with mothers who will buy increasing numbers of P&G products over the years, from Ivory powder for washing baby clothes and Pampers diapers to Crest toothpaste for the family and Olay cosmetics for themselves.

STAKEHOLDERS

Most companies also use relationship marketing techniques to build mutually supportive bonds with stakeholders other than consumers, such as employees and supply chain companies. Organizations can establish and maintain relationships with many different stakeholder groups. The four most affected by internet technologies are the following:

1. ***Employees.*** It is difficult for a firm to persuade buyers when employees are not happy (recall the Zappos story in Chapter 11). When Yahoo! introduced its new position, "The Life Engine," it gave away a Harley-Davidson motorcycle to one of 800 employees who wrote the best reason that Yahoo! was their life engine. This prize generated excitement among employees for the new positioning strategy. Because many employees are instrumental in building relationships with customers, it is critical for them to have training and access to data and systems used for relationship management. In fact, some observers say that many relationship management programs fail due to lack of employee training and commitment.
2. ***Business customers in the supply chain.*** With partner relationship management (PRM), companies build and maintain relationships with other businesses for the purpose of buying and selling both upstream and downstream. First are business customers: the B2B market. Procter & Gamble works with numerous wholesale and retail intermediaries, using internet technologies and databases to facilitate these relationships. Second are a company's suppliers. General Electric uses the internet to receive bids from its suppliers,

a system that not only lowers transaction costs but also enhances competition and speeds order fulfillment.

3. ***Lateral partners.*** Other businesses, not-for-profit organizations, or governments join with the firm for some common goal but not for transactions with each other. CargoNet Transportation Community Network, a consortium of 200,000 shippers, handled 250 million trade-related documents a year at its peak, for Hong Kong shippers at the world's busiest port. The internet facilitates its partner relationship management (PRM) through document tracking and customer service for manufacturers; ocean, rail, truck, and air carriers; banks; insurance companies; and governments associated with CargoNet (eds.com).
4. ***Consumers.*** These individuals are the end users of products and services. Marketers must differentiate between business customers and final consumers because different tactics are usually employed in the B2C and B2B markets.

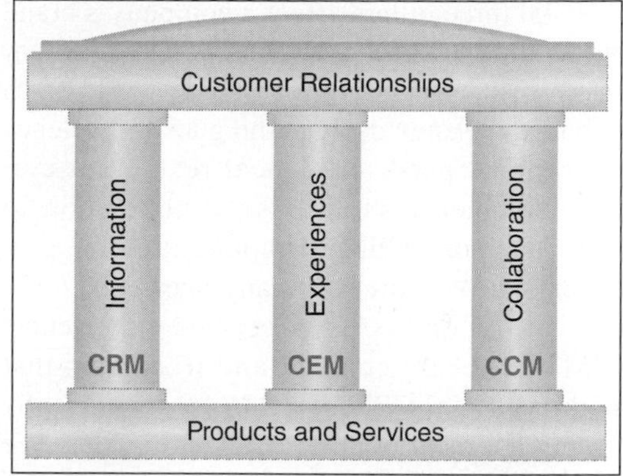

EXHIBIT 15.2 Three Pillars of Relationship Management *Source*: Thompson, Bob (2009). "How to Use Social Media to Improve Customer Service and Cut Costs." Courtesy of Customer Think Corp.

THREE PILLARS OF RELATIONSHIP MARKETING

Today, relationship marketing involves much more than promise fulfillment. It means two-way communication with individual stakeholders, one at a time (1:1). How can a company understand individual customer or partner needs without asking what they are and listening to the answers? Fortunately, the internet's social media allow companies to listen much better than ever before (recall the Dell story in Chapter 14).

One forward-thinking CEO, Bob Thompson, believes that relationship marketing has three pillars that support customer relationships with the company's products and services (Exhibit 15.2). The first is **customer relationship management (CRM)**—the process of targeting, acquiring, transacting, servicing, retaining, and building long-term relationships with customers that add value both to the organization and to the customer. CRM is based on data, information, customer insight, and knowledge, as will be discussed in this chapter. A company needs lots of data to know how its tactics work at acquiring, retaining, and building customer relationships. The second pillar is **customer experience management (CEM)**. As coined by Bernd Schmitt in 2003, CEM "represents the discipline, methodology and/or process used to comprehensively manage a customer's cross-channel exposure, interaction and transaction with a company, product, brand or service." The difference between CRM and CEM is very slight because they both have the end goal of building loyal customers. CRM focuses more on the internal processes to maximize customer value in the long term and CEM more on the customer expectations and touch point satisfaction/dissatisfaction (customer value). CEM can refer to one transaction experience or the sum of all transactions over the duration of the relationship. Both CRM and CEM are controlled by the marketer, who designs marketing mix strategies to build and maintain customer relationship value.

In contrast, the final pillar is controlled by customers but monitored and directed by companies whenever possible, and grew from the social media explosion: **customer collaboration management (CCM)**, a strategy to engage customers in relationship-building conversation, often through social media. CCM is also called CRM 2.0 and social CRM.

All three pillars affect a company's brand image and revenue growth. CEM is used for nearly every product in the offline world, such as the way Disney designs the guest experience at its theme parks or a local restaurant creates an ambience and trains servers on how to treat customers. CEM is important online as it relates to a Web site, company marketing communication, or customer service experience. CCM is a recent concept and it appears that the terms social *CRM* or *CRM 2.0* are currently gaining the most popular use for this idea. We want to make you aware of these pillars and the growing CCM area, but integrate their discussion under the umbrella of the more often-used CRM terminology (social CRM). This thinking follows Forrester Research's social media experts: "Social CRM augments social networking to serve as a new channel within existing end-to-end CRM processes and investments" (in a paper by R "Ray" Wang and Jeremiah Owyang with Christine Tran, edited by Charlene Li).

CUSTOMER RELATIONSHIP MANAGEMENT (CRM 1.0)

CRM is an oft misused term that many companies use to refer to the software and other technology used to implement CRM solutions. As you'll see, CRM is much more—it is a philosophy, strategy, and process. It includes all three pillars and other tenets of relationship marketing and is grounded in customer data and conversations, and facilitated by technology. Increasingly, organizations recognize that if they don't keep their customers happy, someone else will. Many have experienced one sweet tweet to increase sales and one sour tweet to hurt the business.

SOCIAL CUSTOMER RELATIONSHIP MANAGEMENT (CRM 2.0)

Social CRM (CRM 2.0) retains all the tenets of CRM 1.0; however, it adds social media technology and customer collaborative conversations to the process (Exhibit 15.3). Social

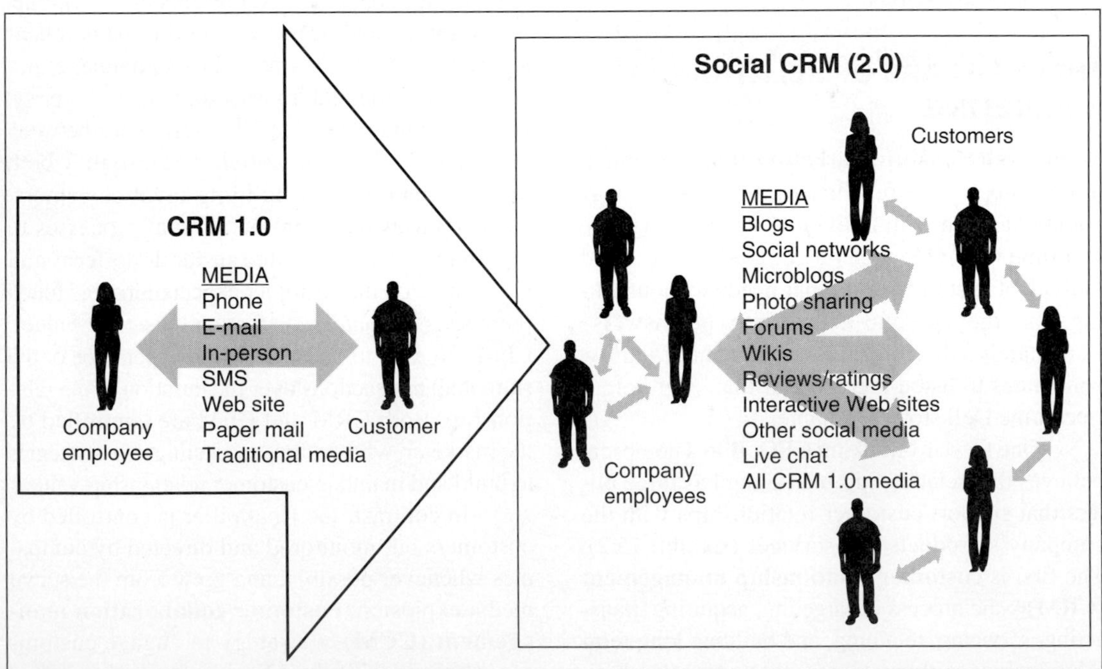

EXHIBIT 15.3 CRM Evolves Using Social Media

CRM means that companies must interact with customers on their terms, and not based solely on the company's data, strategy and desires. Social CRM extends CRM 1.0, but does not replace it. In CRM 1.0, customers would forward e-mails to friends or talk in business meetings about products. Social CRM added more conversation among customers due to social media and gave companies many additional media for building long-term customer relationships (and sales).

Social CRM adds many benefits to companies, such as monitoring and improving reputations; learning more about customer needs, wants, and problems; improving target market selection and revenue potential; gathering data for market research on products and customer service; decreasing customer service costs; and identifying new revenue opportunities. Similarly, social CRM helps customers by getting quick problem resolution, finding unbiased product information more easily from other customers, interacting with companies easily, and improving customer satisfaction.

Qantas Airlines learned social CRM the hard way. A saxophone player protested on Facebook when he learned of a policy change: After 20 years of carrying his sax on the plane, now musical instruments had to be checked and carried in the plane's cargo area. He checked his sax and incurred $1,200 worth of damage on one flight. The sax player started a Qantas boycott on Facebook, and more than 8,700 musicians and others joined the group. Qantas discovered the group protest and subsequently changed the policy to allow smaller instruments on the plane ("Facebook Chorus Ends . . .," 2011).

Social CRM adds new technologies to CRM 1.0. Marketers need to rethink many of their current CRM strategies and tactics, as did Best Buy with its Twitter accounts and forums. Marketers are also wondering how to find the staff time to monitor conversations and manage all these 1:1 interactions with customers and prospects. Fortunately, many suppliers have stepped up to assist, as you saw in previous chapters, with the social media metrics dashboards.

The explosion of social media has marketers putting "social" in front of many strategies, such as social CRM. This reminds us of the early days of the Web when marketers put "e" in front of everything (e.g., e-mail and e-marketing). Such is the way with new technology. Because social CRM simply adds new media, strategies, and tactics to traditional CRM, we organize the rest of this chapter using the basic tenets of CRM and simply add social CRM methods to current strategy and tactics.

CRM Benefits

The benefits of CRM include those previously mentioned and increased revenue from better prospect targeting, increased wallet share with current customers, and retaining customers for longer periods of time. These benefits are quantified through databases that help companies understand their customers better and use this knowledge to build loyalty and optimize lifetime value (LTV). CRM tactics can also decrease costs, resulting in greater profitability. Finally, social CRM tactics help companies work with individual customers and manage their all-important reputations in the social media.

Most companies use prospect and customer data to build mathematical models that help them perform more effective customer segmentation. Effective segmentation allows them to define prospect and customer profiles that are most likely to respond favorably to particular promotional offers, or simply to identify the best segment of prospects for current or new products.

Most businesses spend more money acquiring new customers than they spend keeping current customers—but this approach is usually a mistake. The cost of acquiring a new customer is typically five to seven times higher than the cost of retaining a current one, as shown in Exhibit 15.4. For example, assume that a company budgets $3,000 to acquire six customers, and the cost of acquiring each is $500. Because retaining customers costs one-fifth less (on average), that same $500 could be spent enticing five customers to stay at a cost of $100 each. If instead

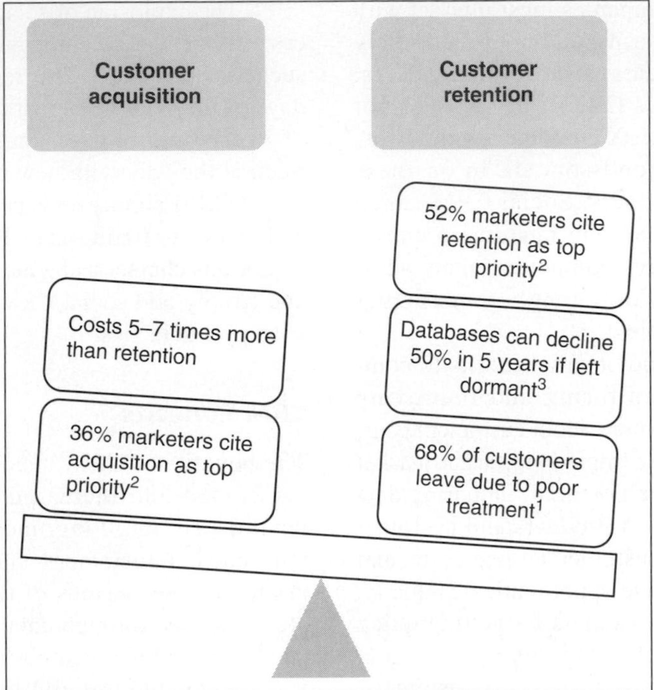

EXHIBIT 15.4 Maximizing Number of Customers through Customer Retention *Sources:* [1] "Biz Dev: Customer Acquisition vs Retention" 2012. Available at www.r-2w.com; [2] "52% of Marketers Say Customer Retention is Top Priority" 2012. Available at www.mediabuyerplanner.com; [3] "Small Business Marketing Strategies – Customer Retention Vs Customer Acquisition" 2009. Available at www.businessfast4ward.com

of spending $3,000 on gaining six customers, a firm spent $1,500 on three new customers, and $1,500 on customer retention, it would be 12 customers ahead. Fortunately, most marketers now understand this and that is why a majority see customer retention as a top priority.

One reason that retention is less costly than acquisition is reduced promotion costs, both for advertising and for discounts. Additionally, higher response rates to promotional efforts yield more profits. Sales teams can be more effective when they get to know individual customers well. Another reason CRM makes sense is that loyal customers are experienced customers. They know the products well, and they know who to call in the firm when they have questions. Loyal customers cost less to service. Plus they post positive reviews online and tell their social network friends about it.

Having more customers leads to more sales. However, acquiring and retaining customers is only part of the equation. A firm must also attempt to increase the amount purchased by each customer. For example, Southwest Airlines and most online travel agents send e-mails to customers when the airfare to a destination of interest to them drops and to offer special hotel and car rental deals.

In addition to buying more, satisfied customers recommend Web sites, stores, and products to their friends in e-mail, social networks, and other social media. Word-of-mouth communication among customers has been called the heart of CRM. Positive word-of-mouth can attract many new customers, but negative word-of-mouth can drive them away. One classic study reported that each dissatisfied customer tells 10 people about the unhappy experience; of 13 percent of dissatisfied customers each tells 20 people how bad the company and its products were (Sonnenberg, 1993). The internet outdates this offline statistic because now each dissatisfied customer can tell thousands with one keystroke in Facebook. For example, one consumer created a Twitter account, @BPGlobalPR "because the oil spill had been going on for almost a month and all British Petroleum had to offer were [bad swear word deleted] PR statements. No solutions, no urgency, no sincerity, no nothing" (see streetgiant.com). The consumer took it upon himself to pose as a PR person and write humorous Tweets that "trashed" BP, gathering 100,000 followers in the process. This kind of extensive word-of-mouth is accomplished through e-mail, special-interest groups, blogs, microblogs, social networks, personal Web pages, and many other online media. Obviously, it was negative, but British Petroleum could learn from this social media event.

One key CRM benefit is its cost-saving advantage. Consider the following:

- One study estimated that U.S. businesses saved $155 billion between 1998 and 2000 by using internet technology for both CRM and supply chain management (SCM) (interactive.wsj.com). In more current 2010 example, one CEO posted on the CRMAdvocate blog that his company saved 10 percent of staff costs through CRM software streamlining of information flow and work process automation.
- A 5 percent increase in customer retention translates to 25 percent to 125 percent profitability in the B2B market.

CRM BUILDING BLOCKS

Although companies understand CRM's benefits and are investing heavily in CRM software, as many as 70 percent lose money on this investment. Thus, businesses are trying to determine what works and what doesn't, knowing that they have to get it right to win—especially as the social media create a loss of marketing control. This section focuses on the nine important CRM components used for e-marketing, based on a Gartner Group CRM model (see Exhibit 15.5). According to Gartner, "CRM initiatives need a framework to ensure that programs are approached on a strategic, balanced and integrated basis. Such a framework will maximize benefits to the enterprise and its customers."

1. **CRM Vision**: Leadership, value proposition
2. **CRM Strategy**: Objectives, target markets

3. **Customer Experience Management (CEM):** Requirements, expectations, satisfaction, feedback, interaction
4. **Customer Collaboration Marketing (CCM):** Creating and monitoring content, listening, measuring, integrating into CRM technology

5. **Organizational Collaboration** Culture and structure Customer understanding People, skills, competencies Incentives and compensation Employee communication Partners and suppliers

6. **CRM Processes**: Customer life cycle, knowledge management
7. **CRM Information**: Data, analysis, one view across channels
8. **CRM Technology**: Applications, architecture, infrastructure
9. **CRM Metrics**: Value, retention, satisfaction, loyalty, cost to serve

EXHIBIT 15.5 Nine Building Blocks for Successful CRM *Source*: Adapted from Gartner Group. Available at gartner.com. (Note that this model was adapted in 2003 and more current information may be available at gartner.com.)

1. CRM Vision

Many organizations purchase expensive CRM software just because it is becoming a necessary component of successful competition. It is no wonder that so many projects fail. Some estimates note that more than twice as many companies with successful CRM strategies spent time working with employees before and while implementing CRM systems. It is the employees, and not the software, that make successful CRM.

Management must start with a vision that fits the company culture and makes sense for the firm's brands and value propositions. This involves both technology and employee collaboration with customers. Some say that the main reason CRM projects fail is because companies do not realize how pervasive they are and underestimate the costs. For example, when a company installs CRM software to integrate data from the Web site, social media, and brick-and-mortar retail operations, customer service reps need training and must be committed to the initiative. Some customer service reps bypass CRM software because it is easier to do it the old way. As well, management needs to embrace social media and put structures in place for employee interactions, as did Best Buy. To be successful, the CRM vision must start at the top and filter throughout the company to keep the firm completely customer focused.

The privacy policy also needs a vision supported by key executives. Marketers have access to lots of information about every customer and prospect, and that information is stored in databases and used for marketing communications. One key aspect of this vision is how to guard customer privacy.

GUARDING CUSTOMER PRIVACY Use of customer data is very important to marketers, yet the temptation to overuse it must be balanced by the need to satisfy customers and not anger them. The burden is on marketers to use customer and prospect information responsibly, both for their own business health and for the image of the profession. In one 2009 study, 30 percent of internet users said they were concerned about the amount of information available about them on the Web (Pew Internet & American Life Project). This is down from 92 percent 10 years ago, but is still a substantial number. Actions taken by social network users to limit personal information access include changing privacy settings to limit access (65 percent); deleting people from social network friend's lists (56 percent); blocking certain updates from some people (52 percent); filtering updates posted by friends (41 percent); deleting comments posted by others on a profile page (36 percent); removing names from photo tags (30 percent); and regretting previous postings, photos, or videos (12 percent). Nonetheless, consumers are unaware of the extent to which real-time profiling and other techniques monitor their online behavior—and marketers must address this issue before regulators make them do it. For instance, Facebook made a huge mistake in late 2007 when it published customer purchasing behavior on profile pages. One Facebook user purchased an item at Overstock.com using her personal e-mail address, and then saw a description of what she bought on her Facebook Profile news feed. The Facebook-sponsored stories discussed in Chapter 13 reveal a lot about individual behavior and whereabouts.

CRM is based on trust. Customers must believe that the information they give companies when they purchase online, in e-mail, or in other ways will be used responsibly. It means using the information to improve the relationship by tailoring goods, services, and marketing communications to meet individual needs. It means allowing consumers to request removal of their information from databases, to opt out of e-mail lists, and not to share information with other companies unless permission is granted.

Another important privacy issue concerns intrusions into people's lives. Junk mail, spam, and repeated telephone calls requesting account upgrades by a cable or internet service provider are all examples of interrupt-type marketing messages that can upset consumers.

What's a marketer to do? The answer is twofold: Build relationships through dialog and better target profiling. Companies must listen to customers and prospects and give them what they want. If a consumer wants to receive e-mail from American Airlines, great. If not, the firm should remove that customer from the list, perhaps checking once a year to see whether the status has changed. Why? Organizations know that retention and development of customer relationships are more profitable than one-time customer transactions, and that relationship capital is one of the firm's strongest assets. Second, marketers can use consumer information to build more precise target profiles. Instead of sending a mass e-mail to everyone who visits the site, how about sending individual or small group e-mails to people who might actually need a car for the flight they just booked at the site? Individuals do not get upset with companies who send valuable and timely information to them.

TRUSTe To help Web sites earn the trust of their users, an independent, nonprofit privacy initiative named TRUSTe was created. TRUSTe provides its seal and logo to any Web site meeting its philosophies, as stated on the site (Exhibit 15.6). Note how well these and the following information requirements fit with good CRM practices:

- Adopting and implementing a privacy policy that factors in the goals of your individual Web site as well as consumer anxiety over sharing personal information online.
- Posting notice and disclosure of collection and use practices regarding personally identifiable information (data used to identify, contact, or locate a person) via a posted privacy statement.
- Giving users choice and consent over how their personal information is used and shared.
- Putting data security and quality and access measures in place to safeguard, update, and correct personally identifiable information.

In addition, site owners must publish the following information on their sites to gain the TRUSTe seal (truste.org):

1. What personal information is being gathered by your site?
2. Who is collecting the information?

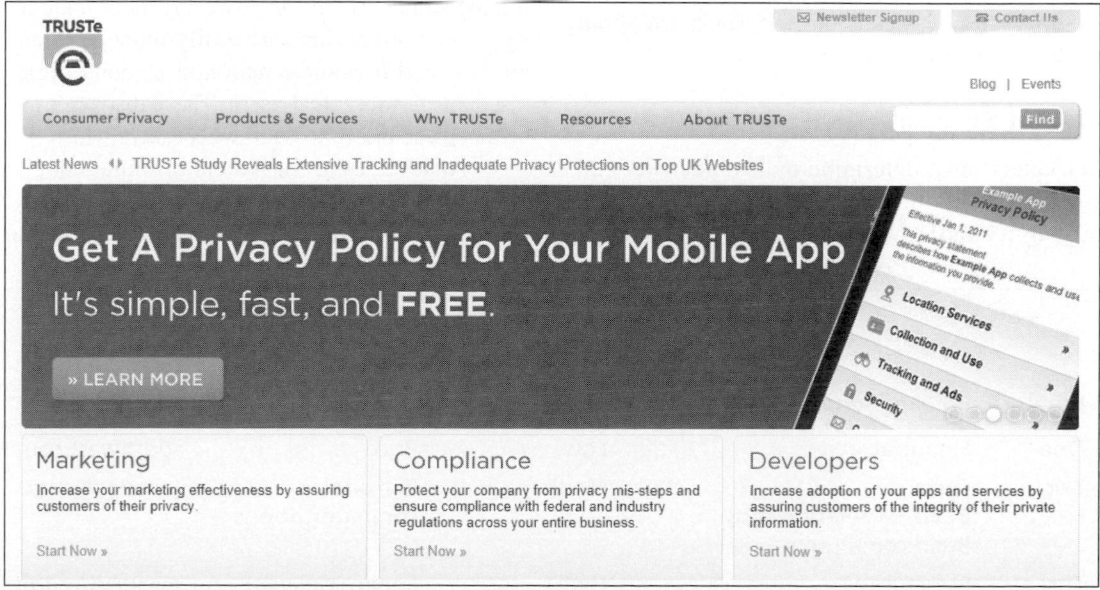

EXHIBIT 15.6 TRUSTe Builds User Trust *Source*: truste.org

3. How will the information be used?
4. With whom will the information be shared?
5. What are the choices available to users regarding collection, use, and distribution of their information? (You must offer users an opportunity to opt out of internal secondary uses as well as third-party distribution for secondary uses.)
6. What are the security procedures in place to protect users' collected information from loss, misuse, or alteration? (If your site collects, uses, or distributes personally identifiable information such as credit card or social security numbers, accepted transmission protocols, including encryption, must be in place.)
7. How can users update or correct inaccuracies in their pertinent information? (Appropriate measures must be taken to ensure that personal information collected online is accurate, complete, and timely, and that easy-to-use mechanisms are in place for users to verify that inaccuracies have been corrected.)

Other organizations also provide guidelines for internet privacy. The American Marketing Association has a code of ethics for internet marketing, dealing primarily with privacy and intellectual property. See Chapter 5 for more about the legal aspects of privacy.

2. CRM Strategy

Marketers must determine their objectives and strategies for initiating CRM programs and buying technology or setting up social media accounts. These objectives may involve any stakeholders (employees, business customers, partners, or consumers) and will likely entail targeting, acquiring, retaining, and growing specified relationships. The B2B market is different from the B2C market due to its CRM focus on lead generation and follow-up for salespeople (often using the subsequently discussed Sales Force Automation [SFA] software).

Many of these CRM goals refer to customer loyalty. Most companies would be delighted if they had customers who proudly wore their brand name on clothing and tried to talk others into buying the brand on Facebook—like customers of Harley-Davidson and Apple Computer. Chapter 9 discussed five levels of relationship intensity (awareness, identity, connection, community, and advocacy). Thus, an important CRM strategy is trying to move customers upward to advocacy.

Another CRM goal involves building bonds with customers that transcend the product experience itself. Some experts suggest that relationship marketing is practiced on three levels (see Exhibit 15.7). The strongest relationships are formed if all three levels are used and if the product itself actually satisfies buyers. At level one, marketers build a financial bond with customers by using pricing strategies. At this lowest level of relationship, price promotions are easily imitated. Many airlines send periodic e-mail notification of price discounts to individual users. These discounts can be timed and priced to build wallet share.

At level two, marketers stimulate social interaction between customers and the company, and among customers themselves. According to

Level	Primary Bond	Potential for Sustained Competitive Advantage	Main Element of Marketing Mix	Web Example
One	Financial	Low	Price	southwest.com
Two	Social Build 1:1 relationships Build community	Medium	Personal communications	facebook.com
Three	Structural	High	Service delivery	my.yahoo.com

EXHIBIT 15.7 Three Levels of Relationship Marketing *Source*: Based on Berry and Parasuraman (1991)

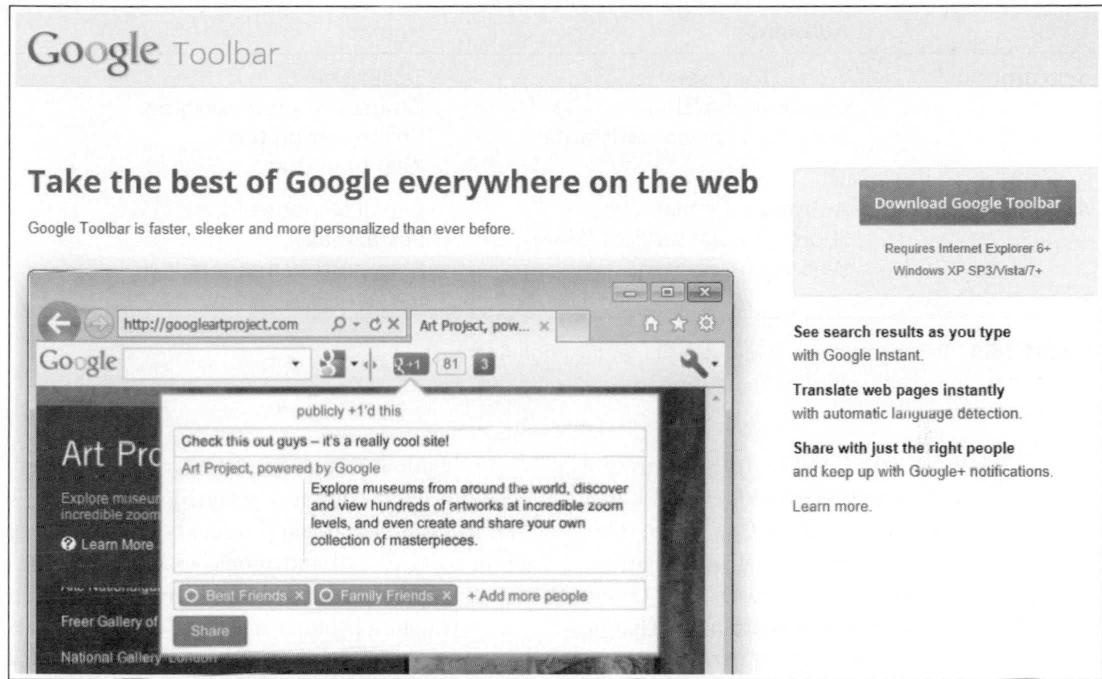

EXHIBIT 15.8 Google Downloadable Toolbar *Source*: google.com

eMarketer, 9 out of 10 interactions with customers are nontransactional communication, thus demonstrating this strategy. Social media participation is an important way to forge level-two relationships and strengthen loyalty (as discussed in Chapters 12–14). Social CRM fits well at this level.

At level three, relationship marketing relies on creating structural solutions to customer problems. **Structural bonds** form when companies add value by making structural changes that facilitate the relationship. For example, the Google toolbar for Internet Explorer assures Google search use by customers installing it (Exhibit 15.8). All of the major Web portals and social networks create structural bonds with their users. Services such as My Yahoo! allow consumers to customize their interface to Yahoo! so it lists local weather and movies, personal stock portfolios, and news of interest to them. Once consumers invest the time and effort to customize this interface, they will be reluctant to switch to another portal.

Social networks combine levels two and three: They create community and structural bonds. When customers create profiles on Facebook or LinkedIn, they spend time learning how to use the sites and they invest by uploading content. Thus, customers are likely to stick with the few social networking sites they use. Even TripAdvisor has this structural bond because customers have to register in order to log on and rate hotels.

3. Customer Experience Management

Amazon.com continually demonstrates its commitment to the customer experience. The great majority of its stated goals involve customer service and fewer involve sales and profits, but of course this customer mentality results in higher sales.

Most customers want a good experience resulting in brand loyalty as much as the companies they patronize want it. Being a consumer can be difficult because of constant bombardment by marketing communications and unlimited product

	Automated	Human
Synchronous	Web 1:1 self-service Online transactions Shop bots (virtual assistants)	Telephone Online instant messaging Collaboration tools Real-time chat
Asynchronous	Automated e-mail Short message services (SMS) Web forms	E-mail response Postal mail Blog posts/comments Social media comments

EXHIBIT 15.9 Relationships over Multiple Communication Channels

choices. Jagdish Sheth (1995) wrote that from a consumer's perspective, the basic tenet of CRM is choice reduction. That holds true today. This notion suggests that consumers want to patronize the same Web site, social network, and online booksellers because doing so is efficient. That is, consumers do not want to spend their days contemplating which brand of toothpaste to buy or how to find a good search engine. Many consumers are "loyalty prone," searching for the right product or service and then sticking with it as long as the promises are more or less fulfilled. Many customers buy from Amazon.com because of good previous experiences, the convenience of having personal preferences on file, one-click ordering, and the familiar interface, regardless of price.

Customers generally like to patronize stores, services, and Web sites where they are treated like individuals with important needs and where they know those needs will be met, "satisfaction guaranteed." Users believe the company cares when they get an e-mail about operating system upgrades to their smartphone, addressed to them by name that refers to the exact product purchased. They care less when they get frequent communication pushing for general service upgrades. They feel more brand loyalty when Amazon sends an e-mail announcing a new book by an author they enjoy. Of course, companies must learn to answer e-mails sent from customers as well. Listening to hundreds of thousands of customers one at a time in e-mail or social media can be difficult and expensive, but it satisfies customers.

Customers' preferences for communicating with each company vary by individual as well as by situation and product type. Customers might want to call and speak with a live representative about an account problem, go to a Web site to research product information, use e-mail to complain about a service problem, send a tweet to Best Buy's @twelpforce, and so forth. Exhibit 15.9 displays these options covering many technologies, using both automated and human intervention for both synchronous (simultaneous) and asynchronous communication. This exhibit reinforces the importance of the internet in creating valued customer experiences and the idea that companies must be adept at many different technologies and processes, putting the focus on customers and their preferences, not the company's capabilities.

CUSTOMER SERVICE Customer service permeates every stage of customer acquisition, retention, and development practices, although most service occurs postpurchase when customers have questions or complaints. Customer service is an important part of the customer experience and a critical strategic component for 91 percent of companies, according to Forrester Research. However, in Forrester's survey, over half (57 percent) said that their customer service function is at or below average and only 4 percent closely monitor the quality of customer interactions. No wonder customers are bad-mouthing companies in the social media.

Key customer experience technology tools include e-mail, online live chat either through customer service representatives or through animated shop bots, social media comments, and Web self-service through frequently asked questions, and more. Mercedes-Benz uses its "teleweb" technology. The consumer types a question into a form on the Web site and receives an immediate phone call from a Mercedes representative. The consumer and representative can then discuss the question while viewing the same Web pages. In fact, software now allows customer service reps on the telephone with a customer to take control of the user's mouse and guide the customer around the company Web site. E-mail, customized Web landing pages, live Web chat, and package tracking using smartphones are just a few of the customer service techniques described throughout this chapter. Regardless of technique, online or offline, customer service is critical to building long-term customer relationships.

4. Customer Collaboration Management

As previously mentioned, this pillar of relationship management has been variously called social CRM, CRM 2.0, and customer collaboration management (or customer collaboration marketing). CCM recognizes the change from a transaction focus online to an interaction focus. "We've moved from the transaction to the interaction with customers, though we haven't eliminated the transaction—or the data associated with it . . . Social CRM focuses on engaging the customer in a collaborative conversation in order to provide mutually beneficial value in a trusted and transparent business environment," according to CRM expert, Paul Greenberg.

Interaction with customers allows companies to collect data necessary for CCM and to evaluate strategy effectiveness on a continuous basis. Peppers and Rogers (1997, p. 15) call this interaction a "learning relationship."

A **learning relationship** between a customer and an enterprise gets smarter and smarter with each individual interaction, defining in ever more detail the customer's own individual needs and tastes.

The idea here is that both the company and the customer learn from each experience and interaction. In any perfect relationship, this ongoing experience equates to increased trust, loyalty, and an increasing share of business for the company, with peace of mind for the customer. The internet is uniquely positioned to deliver on this promise. When a company adopts this philosophy, it is a learning organization.

Customer collaboration management is content, people, and interaction driven, while traditional CRM is data driven. People create and upload content about brands, and companies attempt to engage internet users in their brand-related content. For example, throughout this book you've seen examples of YouTube videos about brands, uploaded both by consumers (Greenpeace about Nestlé) and by companies (Will it Blend?), all toward the end goal of company/customer collaboration. Even the detractors, such as the British Petroleum post @BPGlobalPR, are motivated by helping the company do right.

Thus, CCM is about managing customer relationships and experiences by creating and monitoring online content. This means listening to the online chatter using technology such as Google Alerts and social media dashboards to assist in this difficult endeavor. It means responding to legitimate content posters, with the goal of enhancing their brand experience. It involves posting content that consumers and business buyers find valuable, interesting, or entertaining—as evidenced by the success of the top blogs. This brings to mind an old saying: "We have two ears and one mouth for a reason." Listening is more important than talking when a company is selling. The Altimeter Group summarizes CCM requirements well with its 5 Ms (Wang and Owyang, 2010):

1. ***Monitoring.*** Provides listening capabilities to filter out noise from the social sphere, encapsulates both metrics and measurement, and extracts insights that make measurement more effective.

2. ***Mapping.*** Identifies social media relationships, linking social profiles to customer records for providing a holistic experience.
3. ***Management.*** Systems bring CRM processes to life. Without a purpose, social data is not actionable, thus, business rules and processes are needed to triage the right information to the right teams in real time.
4. ***Middleware.*** These are technologies that glue the social world to the enterprise. Social CRM connects to nearly every customer facing system. Data will have to seamlessly flow between systems and advanced dashboards that provide intelligence.
5. ***Measurement.*** What you can't measure you can't improve; therefore organizations must be able to benchmark what's been done.

5. Organizational Collaboration

Within the company, cross-functional teams join forces to focus on customer satisfaction to create a CRM culture (such as the numerous Blue Shirts and Geek Squad members posting in the social networks). Outside the organization, when two or more companies join forces, the results often exceed what each firm might have accomplished alone—whether it is in the distribution channel or a nontransactional-type collaboration. In fact, some marketers believe that today's marketplace consists of supply chain competition, not individual firm competition. For instance, Amazon and Toys"R"Us teamed up to form the online baby retail site Babies"R"Us (at toysrus.com). Amazon's online retail expertise combined with the toy merchandising expertise of Toys"R"Us benefits both partners and the site's customers.

In the following sections, we discuss two important collaboration techniques that capitalize on internet properties: CRM–SCM integration and extranets.

CRM–SCM INTEGRATION CRM usually refers to front-end operations, meaning that companies work to create satisfying experiences at all customer touch points: telephone calls to customer service reps, e-commerce purchases at online stores, e-mail and Facebook contact, and so forth. This challenge is substantial because different employees and computer systems collect various types of information, which somehow must be integrated into appropriate customer records. In one study sponsored by Jupiter Communications, three phone calls were made to *Forbes* magazine asking why two renewal offers were different. The interviewer got three different explanations. Fortunately several companies now provide software to address this issue. For example, the Aspect Relationship Portal assists CRM staff by integrating all customer contact media—phone, fax, e-mail, and Web—with front- and back-office operations (aspect.com).

In the online environment of customer control, however, even consistently good customer service is not enough. With technological advances and interoperability, online retailers can seamlessly link the back-end (e.g., inventory and payment) with the front-end CRM system and the entire supply chain management system (SCM). The entire supply chain can work together to single-mindedly focus on meeting consumer needs and make higher profits in the process. It all centers, of course, on information (Exhibit 15.10).

Imagine that a customer orders a particular shirt from a clothing retailer's Web site. In the past, if the shirt was out of stock, the customer might see a Web screen with that message or an e-mail notification. With an integrated CRM–SCM system, however, the system can instantly check inventory levels at the retailer and notify the customer that it is not available—usually this information appears right on the product page. The next generation of CRM–SCM integration would allow immediate inventory checking at the wholesaler or manufacturer to determine availability. Then the system could notify the customer during the ordering process and offer options: Wait 2 weeks for delivery from the manufacturer or consider a similar shirt currently in

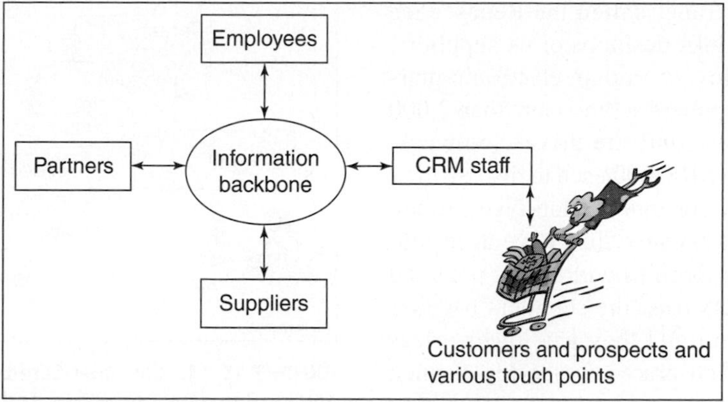

EXHIBIT 15.10 CRM–SCM Integration

stock, for example. This option message would improve customer service and experience if done with a pop-up window featuring a live customer service rep helping the customer. Lands' End, Toyota, and Intuit are three of many sites using LivePerson software, which offers Web site integration with live customer service reps in real time (liveperson.com).

Connecting customers with supply chain businesses provides several advantages. First, all companies will share transaction data so that inventories can be kept low (thus, lowering costs). If producers and wholesalers constantly receive data about consumer orders, they can produce goods in a timely manner. Second, upstream companies can use the data to design products that better meet consumer needs (see the co-designing discussion in Chapter 9). Third, if customer service reps have up-to-the-minute information about product inventories, they will be able to better help consumers immediately. Catalog companies are already fairly accomplished at this task, but the process breaks down when supplier companies are several levels upstream from the retailer.

As more companies integrate CRM and SCM activities, they will become more responsive to individual customer needs. For example, Levi's Personal Pair program used electronic scanners to send precise measurements directly to the factory for individualized jeans, and Dell and BlueNile (jewelry) produce and ship customized products within days. Conversely, this type of integration is quite difficult when a firm has many different channels for its brands and when each firm uses different software and hardware to manage its internal systems. Nevertheless, the systems for integration are currently available and are helping companies become market winners.

EXTRANET Extranets are two or more intranet networks that are joined for the purpose of sharing information. If two companies link their proprietary intranets, they would have an extranet. By definition, extranets are proprietary to the organizations involved. Companies participating in an extranet have formed a structural bond, the third and strongest level of relationship marketing. It is the use of extranets that allows CRM–SCM integration.

Electronic Data Systems (EDS) is a Dallas-based firm that provides enterprise-wide computer desktop services from procurement to network management for large clients. The word *enterprise* means that EDS focuses on all the computer desktops in an entire company, bringing them together in a network. In 1998, the firm managed more than 736,000 desktops, both internally and externally, in 19 countries. EDS created an innovative extranet called the Renascence Channel, which links desktops of its suppliers, clients, and employees into an electronic marketplace. Forty suppliers selling more than 2,000 software products fund the private network, paying $25,000 to $100,000 each to display their products and services in a catalog-type format. Suppliers benefit because they have access to and can build relationships with lots of potential buyers. The buyers trust the suppliers because EDS selected them and they pay lower prices because suppliers' costs are lower in this channel: One vendor reported a drop in order-processing expenses from $150 to $25 per item. Buyers benefit by having desktop access to convenient product information, click-of-a-mouse purchasing, product delivery tracking, online training, and expedited delivery. The Renascence Channel both creates a barrier to entry for suppliers not part of the network and presents switching costs for companies using the channel's services. The Renascence Channel is a good example of relationship building in the B2B market using internet technology.

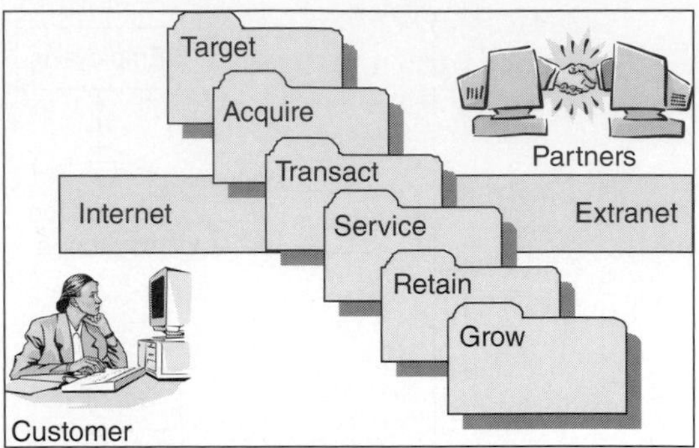

EXHIBIT 15.11 Customer Care Life Cycle
Source: Based on a speech by Tod Famous, Cisco Systems

6. CRM Processes

Customer relationship management involves an understanding of the customer care life cycle, as presented in Exhibit 15.11. Companies monitor and attract customers, both online and offline, as they progress through the stages: target, acquire, transact, service, retain, and grow. This process begins with the e-marketing plan when companies select target markets. However, opportunities often arise when a new target group appears at the Web site—such as when Brooks Brothers noted a large number of Japanese users at the site. Thus, the cycle is circular in nature: For example, while servicing customers a new target may emerge. This important cycle is based on one central tenet of CRM that bears repeating—it is better to retain and grow customers than to focus only on customer acquisition. Of course, not all customers go through this process—some do less business with the firm or leave to transact with a competitor. Sometimes companies try to reacquire these customers, as when Netflix sends e-mails to customers who have cancelled their accounts, with the line "We want you back" and an offer of free movies for a certain period.

There are many CRM processes. In this section we present a customer churn cycle that works both for retention and for increasing customer value. Then we discuss two important CRM processes using internet technologies: sales force automation and marketing automation.

HEAR NOW OR GONE TOMORROW This is the name of a report, created by Nice and Peppers & Rogers Group, to describe the importance of listening to customers and gathering interaction data across all marketing channels. These data help organizations predict who is likely to leave, how to keep them, and how to make changes to the marketing program to keep others from leaving. Companies use this six-step process to focus on reducing customer defection through the customer care life cycle.

1. Companies obtain transactional, behavioral, and interaction data about prospects, business customers, and end consumers through personal disclosure, automated tracking through the sales force, customer service encounters, bar code scanners at retailers, and Web site/social media activity.
2. Every piece of user information goes into a database that helps companies identify who

is at risk of defecting. This step entails statistical modeling.

3. Segment customers using value analysis based on behavior, demographics, and so forth, to determine which individuals might leave.
4. Identify the root cause for possible defection by evaluating product/service flaws, competitive offers, or promotions that are not working.
5. Fix this with a retention program that might involve promotional offers and real-time recommendations while customers are online.
6. Measure the program effectiveness in terms of customer retention.

We present this model because it also works in the CRM process for identifying the company's best customers. *Best* is described in many different ways, such as highest value, longest loyalty, highest frequency of purchase, and so on. CRM allows marketers to leverage their resources by investing more in the most lucrative customers. The idea is not new but what is new is that technology allows companies to identify high-value customers and respond with offers in real time over the internet. Value differentiation pays off: When a plastics firm focused on its most profitable customers, it cut its customer base from 800 to 90 and increased its revenues by 400 percent (Renner, 2000). However, not all companies have high- and low-value customers. According to the Peppers & Rogers Group, differentiation by valuation is not profitable unless a firm can say that at least half of its profits come from 20 percent or fewer of its customers (the four- and five-star customers in Chapter 10).

Some customers are clearly not profitable and, thus, should be "fired" so that the company can allocate resources profitably. For example, Continental Airlines identified 35,000 customers in the five-star tier and 400,000 four-star level customers. These customers get extra services, such as being put on a competitor's flight immediately when the customer's Continental flight is cancelled (Kupper, 2004). This attention has resulted in an extra $200 in annual revenue from each four-star customer and $800 each for five-star customers. Continental doesn't exactly fire low-value customers, but simply does not give them the same high level of service as it does to high-value customers. Casinos operate the same way—high rollers get anything they want and low spenders might get only a buffet discount. Casino management knows the difference because customers use player cards in slot machines that are networked and always collect data on spending patterns.

Tripadvisor.com has 5 million registered users at its travel Web site. It continually sends special reward offers to those who had posted hotel reviews, thus differentiating and rewarding the customers who engage by uploading content. A recent e-mail to one author offered a special digital badge for posting just one more hotel review.

Once a company identifies prospects and differentiates customers according to characteristics, behavior, needs, or value, it can consider customizing offerings to various segments or individuals—either as a retention campaign or to increase current customer value. **Customization** occurs when companies tailor their marketing mixes to meet the needs of small target segments, even to the individual level, using electronic marketing tools. Products, marketing communication messages, and dynamic pricing can all be tailored to individuals and delivered over the internet in a timely manner. These approaches were not possible before the internet except with very high-priced products such as manufacturing equipment. Through customization, companies can zero in on the precise needs of each prospect and customer and build long-term, profitable relationships.

Some writers use the term *personalize* when referring to customization. **Personalization** involves ways that marketers individualize in an impersonal computer networked environment. For example, Web sites may greet users by name or automatically send an e-mail to individuals with personal account information. We use the term *customization* because it refers to much more than automated personalization.

Now, how to put this model into operation for retaining and building customer value?

BUILD A DYNAMIC CUSTOMER PROFILE With billions of daily e-mails and millions of tweets and Facebook posts and updates, how can a marketer keep up? Lyris, Inc. summarizes this current problem by suggesting that marketers gather data to profile each customer as reflected by his interactions with a brand at many touch points. "From a customer's perspective, his or her dynamic profile would look something like this:

- What I've bought.
- What I've browsed.
- What devices I use.
- When I'm online.
- Where I've visited online.
- My current status.
- What I like and dislike.
- Who my friends are ("Field Guide to . . .," 2012).

From a marketer's perspective, the dynamic customer profile includes the data in Exhibit 15.12. Armed with this demographic, attitudinal, and behavioral information, marketers can make precise decisions to move the consumer through the CRM process from targeting and acquisition to repeat purchase. Marketers can also (1) group customers into profitable segments, (2) use the data to engage customers and deliver value, (3) integrate the data into current CRM databases, and (4) integrate data from offline sources, such as call centers and physical retail stores. All this can be accomplished in an automated fashion using databases and other technologies.

British interiors and gift store, Graham & Green, tested this system. The company has a large e-mail database and had been sending two product-related e-mails a week to the entire database with a 20 percent open rate. The company then sent an e-mail offering a home accessory discount to those who had visited the home accessories pages on its Web site and realized a 49 percent open rate and 1.1 percent conversion to purchase. Several additional tests produced similar results. This type of behavioral targeting is data driven and helps to build customer relationships and sales. Many companies, including Lyris, offer the technology solutions to make this work well.

SALES FORCE AUTOMATION (SFA) "Increase your sales, not your sales force," proclaims SFA software. Used primarily in the B2B market, SFA allows salespeople to build, maintain, and access customer records; manage leads and accounts; manage their schedules; and more. In relation to

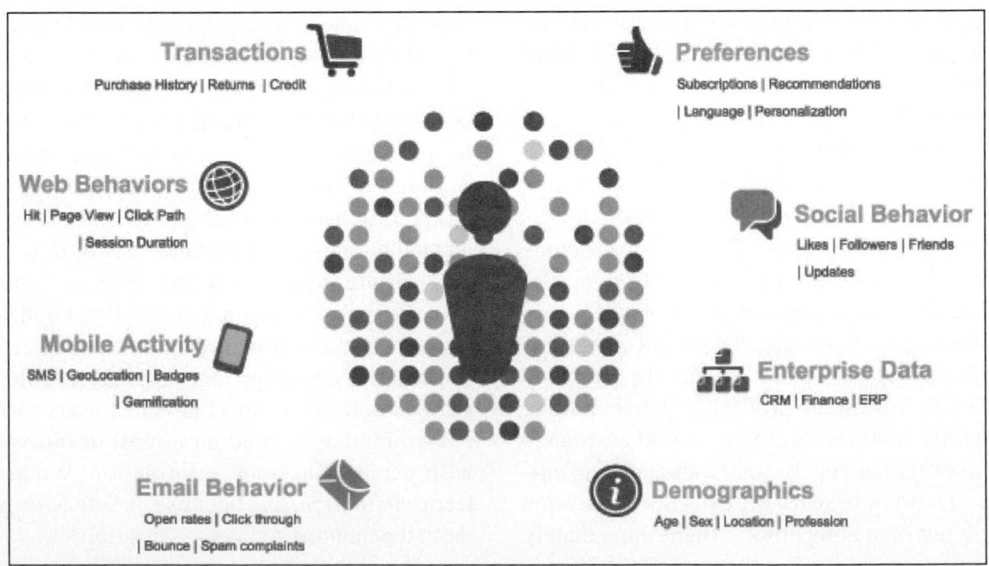

EXHIBIT 15.12 Building a Dynamic Customer Profile *Source*: Image courtesy of Lyris, Inc. lyris.com

e-marketing, SFA helps the sales force acquire, retain, and grow customers by accessing customer and product data from the company's data warehouses, both while in the office and on the road. Salespeople can also send the results of sales calls and activity reports to the data warehouse for access by others. Up-to-date customer and prospect records help customer service reps and others build customer relationships. As an example, SFA leader Salesforce.com's software claims to drive sales productivity and revenues, improve customer service, facilitate partner relationship management by integrating data, improve marketing of multichannel campaigns, improve Web 2.0 content distribution, and evaluate sales operations through performance metrics.

Notably, Salesforce.com also has tools to monitor brand conversation in the social media, helping companies respond quickly: customer collaboration management in a CRM tool.

MARKETING AUTOMATION **Marketing automation** activities aid marketers with effective targeting, efficient marketing communication, and real-time monitoring of customer and market trends. Marketing automation software usually takes data from Web sites and databases, and turns it into reports for fine-tuning CRM efforts, such as shown in Exhibit 15.12. Software solutions include e-mail campaign management, database marketing, market segmentation, Web site log analysis, and more.

Marketing automation is a powerful marketing solution for CRM. SAS, business intelligence and predictive analytics software provider, offers the following marketing automation benefits with its software (sas.com): an integrated customer view, customer life cycle management, customer targeting, analytics, and integrated support for all business units. Companies using this software can develop multichannel communication campaigns, understand their results, and store all data in one technology solution.

7. CRM Information

As you have read up to this point, information is the lubricant of CRM. The more information a firm has, the better value it can provide to each customer and prospect in terms of more accurate, timely, and relevant offerings. Many companies entice customers to provide additional information over time by engaging them in blogs, product reviews, or through e-commerce transactions. For example, Orbitz.com first requests a simple e-mail address from those who want information about discount offers and subsequently asks about vacation preferences so as to provide more relevant e-mailings. A customer who provides increasingly more personal information shows enough trust in the firm to invest in the relationship.

Sometimes companies gather this type of information under the guise of entertainment. For example, the Mini Cooper automobile gains valuable information about the preferences of site visitors by allowing them to configure the perfect car online, using 10 million possible option combinations (miniusa.com).

Companies gain much information from customers less intrusively by tracking their behavior electronically. Information technology allows companies to move beyond the traditional segment profiling (e.g., Generation X) to detailed profiles of individuals. For example, when product bar code scanner data collected at the checkout is combined with a store shopping card, the company can identify individual customer purchases over time. On the internet, software tracks a user's movement from page to page, indicating how much time was spent on each page, whether the user made a purchase, the type of computer and operating system, and more. Companies can track which sites users visited before and after theirs, and use this information to guess which competitive products are under consideration and to learn about users' interests. Tracking user behavior is valuable to both users and companies, but it has its critics because of privacy considerations, as previously mentioned.

Now a customer can telephone the customer service representative to discuss a product purchased in the brick-and-mortar store last week, refer to an e-mail sent yesterday, and post about it on his or her Facebook account—with the data all stored in the database under one customer record. This approach is known as having a 360° customer view, or one view across channels. In her book, Customers.com, Patricia Seybold (1998) identified eight critical success factors for building successful e-business relationships with customers. Even over a decade later, these factors remain a good springboard to understanding how internet technologies facilitate customer relationship management using e-marketing.

1. ***Target the right customers.*** Identify the best prospects and customers and learn as much about them as possible.
2. ***Own the customer's total experience.*** This factor refers to the customer **share of mind** or share of wallet previously discussed.
3. ***Streamline business processes that impact the customer.*** This task can be accomplished through CRM–SCM integration and monomaniacal customer focus.
4. ***Provide a 360° view of the customer relationship.*** Everyone in the firm who touches the customer should understand all aspects of that customer's relationship with the company. For example, customer service reps should know all customer activity over time and understand which products and services might benefit that particular customer.
5. ***Let customers help themselves.*** Provide Web sites and other electronic means for customers to find things they need quickly and conveniently, 24/7.
6. ***Help customers do their jobs.*** Especially in the B2B market, if a firm provides products and services to help customers perform well in their businesses, they will be loyal and pay a premium for the help. Many supply chain management electronic processes facilitate this factor.
7. ***Deliver personalized service.*** Customer profiling, privacy safekeeping, and marketing mix customization all aid in delivering personalized services electronically.
8. ***Foster community.*** Enticing customers to join in communities and social networks of interest that relate to a firm's products is one important way to build loyalty.

8. CRM Technology

Technology greatly enhances CRM processes. Incoming toll-free numbers, electronic kiosks, fax-on-demand, voice mail, and automated telephone routing are examples of technology that assist in moving customers through the life cycle. The internet, however, is the first fully interactive and individually addressable low-cost multimedia channel—it forms the centerpiece of a firm's CRM abilities. Cookies, Web site logs, bar code scanners, automated Web monitoring (such as Google Alerts), social media, and other tools help to collect information about consumer behavior, conversations, and characteristics. Databases and data warehouses store and distribute these data from online and offline touch points, thus allowing employees to develop marketing mixes that better meet individual needs.

Here we discuss do-it-yourself tools that aid organizations in customizing products to groups of customers or individuals, versus all-in-one software packages. These include "push" strategies that reside on the company's Web and e-mail servers and "pull" strategies that are initiated by internet users. The difference is important, because companies have more control over push techniques.

COMPANY-SIDE TOOLS Exhibit 15.13 displays important tools used to push customized information to users. Visitors are generally unaware that marketers are collecting data and using these technologies to customize offerings.

Cookies Cookie files are the reason that customers returning to Amazon.com get a greeting by name, and that users don't have to remember passwords to every site for which they are registered. Cookie files allow ad-server companies to see the path users take from site to site and thus serve display advertising relevant to user interests. Finally, cookies keep track of shopping baskets and other tasks so that users can quit in the middle and return to the task later.

Web analytics By performing **Web analytics**, companies can do many things, not the least of which is to customize Web pages based on visitor behavior. Web analytics are tools that

Company-Side Tools (push)	Description
Cookies	Cookies are small files written to the user's hard drive after visiting a Web site. When the user returns to the site, the company's server looks for the cookie file and uses it to personalize the site.
Web log analysis	Every time a user accesses a Web site, the visit is recorded in the Web server's log file. This file keeps track of which pages the user visits, how long the user stays, and whether the user purchases.
Data mining	Data mining involves the extraction of hidden predictive information in large databases through statistical analysis.
Behavioral targeting	Behavioral targeting occurs when software tracks a user's movements through a Web site and then sends appropriate Web content at a moment's notice.
Collaborative filtering	Collaborative filtering software gathers opinions of like-minded users and returns those opinions to the individual in real time.
Outgoing e-mail/ Distributed e-mail	Marketers use e-mail databases to build relationships by keeping in touch with useful and timely information. E-mail can be sent to individuals or sent *en masse* using a distributed e-mail list.
Social media	A firm may listen to users on blogs or social networks, and build community by providing a space for user conversation on the Web site.
iPOS terminals	Interactive point-of-sale terminals are located on a retailer's counter and used to capture data and present targeted communication.

EXHIBIT 15.13 Selected E-Marketing "Push" Customization Tools

collect and display information about user behavior on a Web site (see Chapter 2). Software, such as WebTrends, also tells which sites the users visited immediately before arriving, what keywords they typed in at search engines to find the site, user domains, and much more.

AutoTrader.com uses Web analytics to transform 25 million rows of daily Web log data into marketing knowledge. This firm is an automotive marketplace offering more than 2 million new and used vehicles with price comparisons, performance reviews, and financing and insurance resources. More than 6 million monthly visitors view more than 200 million pages, including pages where advertisers sell cars. To make sense of it all, AutoTrader created the *Management Dashboard,* a marketing tool powered by SAS statistical data analysis software. The dashboard reports on the following:

- Visitor demographics and customer behavior online—analyzed by U.S. region.
- Analytics about the advertisements served on the site Web pages.
- Key site metrics such as number of visitors, and the makes and models of cars viewed.

As an example, SAS software evaluates 30 million monthly vehicle searches, categorizing them by city, state, and zip code, as well as make, model, year, and price. The regional sales force can then quickly answer inquiries about Web traffic in different localities. The firm also uses an Oracle database, extracting e-mails, leads, and other information to generate more than 100 month-to-date reports for marketing managers. AutoTrader learns many things from these analyses. First, it knows which vehicles are in demand in various regions, which helps participating car dealers and individual sellers. Second, it can fine-tune the Web site based on traffic patterns. Third, and most important, AutoTrader can demonstrate the value of advertising on its site. Advertisers receive automatically generated reports about how many times their cars were viewed, how many visitors asked for a map to the brick-and-mortar location, and how many e-mail inquiries were received about the cars. Finally, these reports help AutoTrader bill its e-commerce partners.

Data Mining Marketers don't need *a priori* hypotheses to find value in databases but use software to find patterns of interest. For example, Nissan used E.piphany software to increase its sophistication with up-selling and cross-selling. Prior to using the software, Nissan would simply attempt to sell the same model of automobile as previously owned to a repeat customer. Using E.piphany data mining software, Nissan identified a group of affluent, loyal customers with children aged 19 to 24 years living at home, who purchased the Sentra model. Nissan used this information to cross-sell Sentras to other customers fitting the same profile. Even though Nissan did not use the Web, it is a great e-marketing application.

Behavioral Targeting This occurs when software tracks a user's movements through a Web site and then sends appropriate Web content at a moment's notice. Amazon uses it when it presents recently viewed products on its home page when a return customer visits. Google's DoubleClick uses it when sending ads as users click through several different Web sites. This targeting uses data warehouse information to help marketers understand the characteristics and behavior of specific target groups.

American Express has used behavioral targeting for years: It sends bill inserts to groups of customers based on their previous purchasing behavior. What's new is that this type of targeting can be done online inexpensively via e-mail and customized Web pages. For example, the software could be set to use the following rule: If a customer orders a Dave Matthews Band CD, display a Web page offering a concert T-shirt. TokyoPop.com, a site targeted at Generation Y, carries behavioral targeting over to all its affiliate sites. Every time a TokyoPop registered member visits an affiliate site, it serves rule-based content, advertising, or offers. This targeting builds relationships because members are presented with relevant and timely offers, which increases their business with TokyoPop.

Consumers visiting Greatcoffee.com are greeted with personalized Web content on their *first visit*! The site doesn't know who the users are because they have never entered information at the site nor have been given a cookie file from GreatCoffee (Peppers, 2000). So how is it done? The site uses behavioral profiling to match a database of anonymous cookie files from Angara. This company's e-commerce targeting service purchased more than 20 million anonymous cookie files with demographic and geographic data from companies such as Dell (all personal information is removed first). When users surf the Web sites at Angara's clients, such as Greatcoffee.com, this database is accessed and relevant Web page content served. For example, if Angara matches a new user's IP address and other easily obtained information and the database shows that the user lives in California, the site might display the greeting, "Drink our coffee, win free San Francisco Giants tickets." This directed ad happens in less than half a second and has increased surfer-to-buyer conversion to twice the normal amount in some segments. In addition, the reorder rate at Greatcoffee.com is 60 percent versus 5 percent before using Angara's service.

Collaborative Filtering Individuals often seek the advice of others before making decisions. Similarly, collaborative filtering software gathers the recommendations of an entire group of people and presents the results to a like-minded individual.

BOL.com, an international media and entertainment store (owned by Germany's DirectGroup Bertelsmann), uses Net Perceptions collaborative filtering software to observe how users browse and buy music, software, games, and more at its site. The more time a user spends at the site, the more BOL.com will learn about user behavior and preferences, and the better able it will be to present relevant products ("learning relationship"). BOL .com notes that it realized increased revenues from using this software and achieved a positive ROI within months.

Outgoing E-Mail As discussed in earlier chapters, outgoing e-mail from firm to customer is still the internet's "killer app." E-mail is used to communicate with individuals or lists of individuals in an effort to increase their purchases, satisfaction, and loyalty. E-mail sent to distribution lists is redistributed to the entire subscription list. Many companies maintain e-mail distribution lists for customers and other stakeholders. Automated e-mail confirming purchase or shipping activities assured customers that the company is taking care of them.

Permission marketing dictates that customers will be pleased to receive e-mail for which they have opted in. MyPoints rewards consumers with points and gift certificates, all for reading targeted e-mail ads and shopping at selected sites. MyPoints client companies pay a fee for these e-mails, part of which goes directly to customers as points. MyPoints advertises "responsible" e-mail messaging, meaning that consumers agree to receive commercial messages within their e-mails. Conversely, spam does not build relationships but instead focuses solely on customer acquisition. The internet provides the technology for marketers to send 500,000 or more e-mails at the click of a mouse, and all for less than the cost of one postage stamp. Relationship-building e-mail requires sending e-mails that are valuable to users, sending them as often as users require, and offering users the chance to be taken off the list at any time. It means talking and listening to consumers as if they were friends.

Exhibit 15.14 displays an outgoing e-mail from HubSpot, a company that provides software

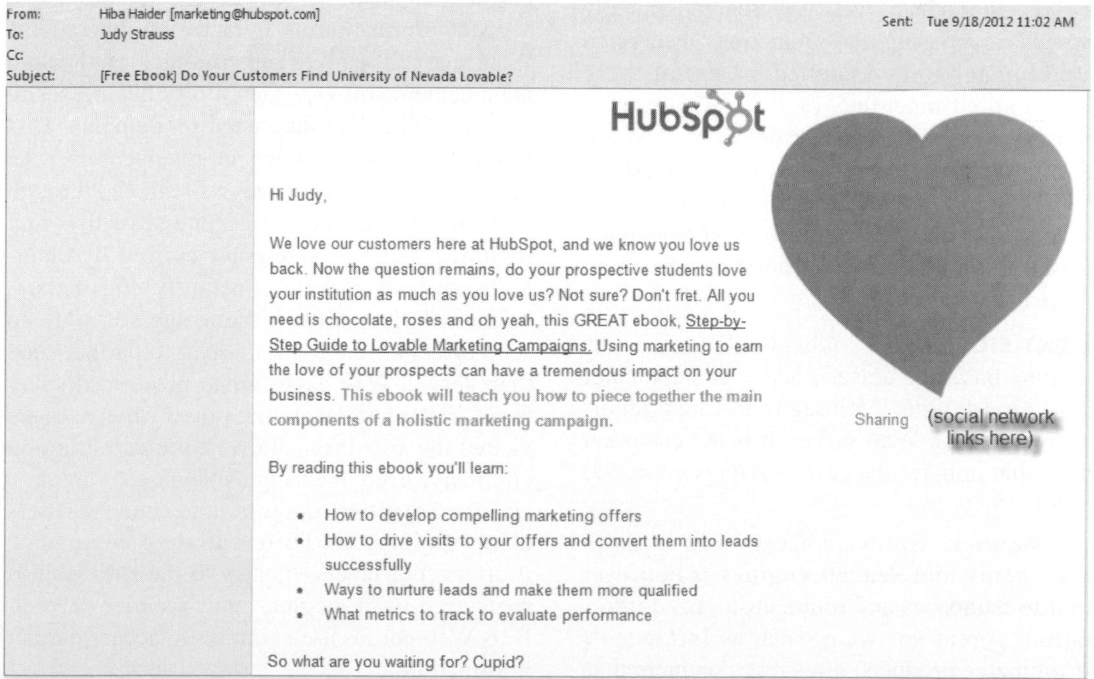
From: Hiba Haider [marketing@hubspot.com]
To: Judy Strauss
Cc:
Subject: [Free Ebook] Do Your Customers Find University of Nevada Lovable?
Sent: Tue 9/18/2012 11:02 AM

HubSpot

Hi Judy,

We love our customers here at HubSpot, and we know you love us back. Now the question remains, do your prospective students love your institution as much as you love us? Not sure? Don't fret. All you need is chocolate, roses and oh yeah, this GREAT ebook, Step-by-Step Guide to Lovable Marketing Campaigns. Using marketing to earn the love of your prospects can have a tremendous impact on your business. This ebook will teach you how to piece together the main components of a holistic marketing campaign.

By reading this ebook you'll learn:

- How to develop compelling marketing offers
- How to drive visits to your offers and convert them into leads successfully
- Ways to nurture leads and make them more qualified
- What metrics to track to evaluate performance

So what are you waiting for? Cupid?

Sharing (social network links here)

EXHIBIT 15.14 Showing Customers That You Care *Source:* © 2012 By Hubspot, Inc. Used By Permission

and guidance for inbound marketing. It offers a free eBook about "Lovable Marketing Campaigns." The e-mail expresses caring for HubSpot's customers and shows by example how its client companies might want to treat their customers in order to build good long-term relationships.

Social Media Companies build community and learn about customers and products through blogs, social networks, and bulletin board/newsgroup e-mail postings all over the Web, and at its Web site (for government examples, see Exhibit 15.15). Analysis of these exchanges is used in the aggregate to design marketing mixes that meet user needs. For example, if many consumers log onto a Caribbean Chat at Expedia, it might feature special tours of Caribbean islands during the next week (expedia.com). Expedia sends e-mail offers to users who participate in the conversation.

iPOS Terminals **iPOS terminals** are small customer-facing machines near the brick-and-mortar cash register, used to record a buyer's signature for a credit card transaction. They are important because they can gather survey and other data as well as present individually targeted advertising and promotions. Federated Department Stores installed 34,000 of these Web-enabled machines in 2001. The retailer used signature data to see whether women are buying their own clothing, as well as clothing for male family members, and it planned to use the terminals to send images and personalized messages—all generated from a database and sent over the internet.

CLIENT-SIDE TOOLS Client-side tools come into play based on a user's action at a computer or mobile device. Although the tools generally reside on a Web server, it is the customer "pull" that initiates the customized response. See Exhibit 15.16.

Agents Software agents such as shopping agents and **search engines** match user input to databases and return customized information. Agent software, such as Inference's k-Commerce products, often relies on more than one interaction. For example, a user might type "computer" on the Dell site and then be presented with either laptop or desktop options. This process continues until the search is narrowed. Similarly, when visitors to Google use a keyword search, they receive a text-based ad based on the word they entered along with a customized Web page of Web site links. For example, if a user types "automobile" into the search box, an ad for Toyota might be returned along with the list of relevant sites. Agents are the basis of all shopping comparison sites, such as BizRate.com.

Individualized Web Portals The *Wall Street Journal*'s online edition allows individual customers to create a personalized Web page based on keywords of interest. This capability is particularly helpful for business readers who want to monitor stories about their competitors. The *Wall Street Journal* creates a structural bond with individual customers, thereby boosting loyalty—something that was unheard of prior to the internet.

Individualized Web portals are more often used to build relationships in the B2B market rather than in the B2C market. It is through these portals that supply chains access inventory and account information and track various operations. Webridge sells partner and customer relationship management software that allows businesses to access all the data they need on demand. This resource represents a huge improvement over the previous method, where buyers searched through piles of brochures, catalogs, and price lists that included many products not carried by channel partners and were constantly out-of-date. InFocus Systems used Webridge software to send offers of interest via e-mail to partners and then served Web pages customized to display those featured products and prices when partners visited the site. Primedia, a health care training company, used Webridge software to create a site for hospitals, doctors, and other partners using its services. Differentiating customers, it offers four layers of entry to the site: visitor, registered user, member, and premier partner. B2B Web portals use extranets to access partner information.

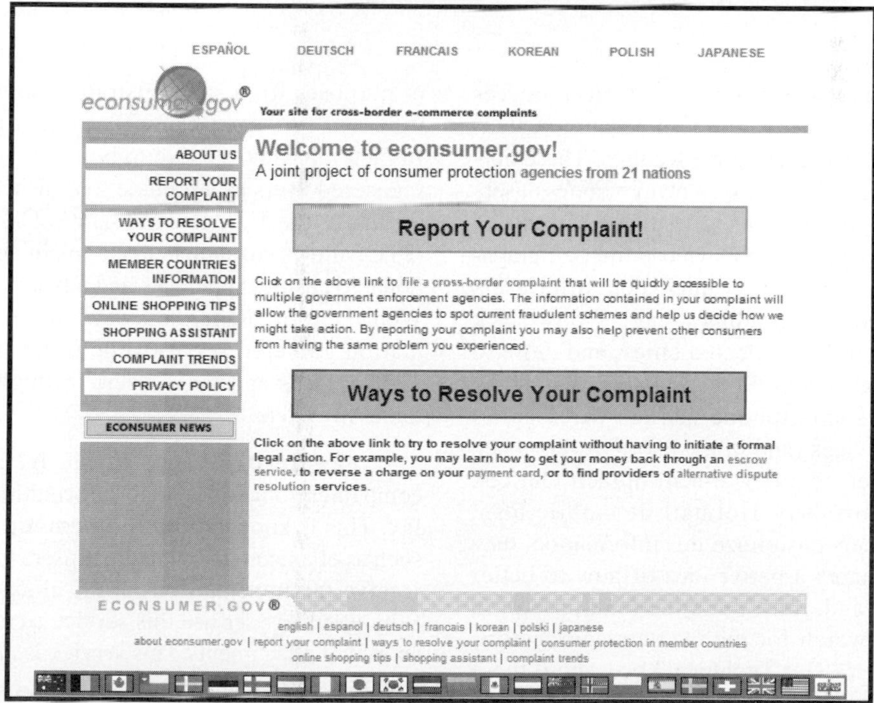

EXHIBIT 15.15 Chat Opportunities between the U.S. Government and Its Citizens *Sources:* state.gov and econsumer.gov

Client-Side Tools (Pull)	Description
Agents	Agents are programs that perform functions on behalf of the user, such as search engines and shopping agents.
Individualized Web portals	Personalized Web pages that users can easily configure at Web sites such as MyYahoo! and many others.
Wireless data services	Wireless Web portals send data to customer cell phones, pagers, and PDAs, such as the Palm Treo.
Web forms	Web form (or HTML form) is the technical term for a form on a Web page that has designated places for the user to type information for submission.
Fax-on-demand	With fax-on-demand, customers telephone a firm, listen to an automated voice menu, and select options to request a fax be sent on a particular topic.
Incoming e-mail	E-mail queries, complaints, or compliments initiated by customers or prospects comprise incoming e-mail and is the fodder for customer service.
RSS feeds	Really simple syndication feeds are an XML format designed for sharing headlines and other Web content.

EXHIBIT 15.16 Selected E-Marketing "Pull" Customization Tools

Wireless Data Services Wireless data services are included as a separate tool because of their rapid growth and distinctive features. These portals are remarkable because many wireless users want only optimized pages due to the screen size of wireless devices and download time for graphics. Services such as AvantGo.com offer users ad-sponsored news headlines, sports scores, stock quotes, weather in selected cities, and more to users on pagers; and iPhone's applications serve the wireless smartphone market. Microsoft's wireless services (and others) notify users when they've received a new e-mail in their Outlook account (formerly Hotmail at mobile.msn.com). As users customize this information, they give companies a better idea of how to better serve them and, thus, build the relationship. In the future, watch for mobile data aggregators. See the "Let's Get Technical" box about these "third screens."

Web Forms Many corporate Web sites sport Web forms, using them for a multitude of purposes from site registration, communication, and survey research to product purchase. In fact, many sites strive to build the number of registered users as a prelude to transactions. For example, the U.S. Federal Trade Commission (FTC) allows consumers to complain about questionable business practices and advertising via its Web site form. Regardless of purpose, the information gathered serves to help the firm build relationships and move users through the customer life cycle.

Fax-on-Demand In the B2B market, companies sometimes want information sent via fax. This is known as **fax-on-demand**. Services such as eFax.com allow internet users to send and receive fax transmissions at the eFax Web site. Why would a user use this service as opposed to an e-mail attachment? This service is appropriate when the document is not in digital form, a signature is needed, or internet access is not available so the document cannot be sent as an e-mail attachment. Also, eFax is handy for users who do

LET'S GET TECHNICAL

Mobile Trends

As you stroll through the supermarket on Sunday afternoon, you suddenly realize that you have forgotten to buy peanut butter. In what aisle do they stock the 20 different varieties of peanut butter? And how are you going to know which size is the best price? Then you remember, the supermarket is now offering a wireless access in the store to a searchable floor plan, weekly specials, and unit price calculator for every item. You are once again relaxed as you pull out your iPhone.

Are Your Web Sites Ready?

Many classic marketing strategies hinged on the concept of giving potential customers information about a product or service right when they are likely to need it, such as an advertising billboard stating "McDonald's, Exit 11, Turn Left" or automatic coupon dispensers attached to the shelves at the grocery store. The interesting part of these strategies is that the information was in a form that the potential customers could use: a large billboard readable from the highway and a pocket-sized coupon for use at checkout.

These days, potential customers are hungry for information on their smart devices, which include iPhones, PDAs, Pocket PCs, Tablet PCs, iPads, and any combination of these products. Today's customers want their smart device to be just that—smart. Just as the classic marketing strategists did, today's e-marketer must also provide information for potential customers in a form that is easy to use for the customer. In other words, Web sites and online services should be developed specially for smart devices, using industry standards. Specially designed Web sites and online services should also be tested before distribution to the public. For example, frozen Web pages (fixed height and width) are difficult for Pocket PC users to view. To view the information, they must scroll both down and to the right. A better solution is liquid Web pages that allow the information to be resized to the width of the device's screen.

The Third Screen

Information technology visionaries are nicknaming the screen of mobile devices the "third screen." The first was television, the second was the personal computer, and the third includes a variety of mobile devices. The unique aspect of these screens is that users take them just about everywhere, especially the iPhone. The iPhone works off of both regular phone networks and the faster 3G and 4G networks. The iPhone is a fully functioning internet device with a very intuitive and easy-to-use interface. Interestingly, the iPhone also cannibalizes Apple's iPod market since the iPhone duplicates iPod functionality and then some.

Although mobile devices are convenient for users because of their size, portability, and organizer functions, they are even more convenient when they are able to access wireless networks. Popular mobile devices can access one or more of the available wireless networks: wireless phone signals, WiFi internet hotspots, and Bluetooth wireless networks. The type of network that the mobile device can access depends on the hardware it possesses.

As the ability to access wireless networks and the speed of data transfer on the networks increase, services for mobile devices are becoming more prevalent. MobiTV converts the content of such stations as MSNBC, Fox, ABC, and the Discovery Channel. The speed needed for streaming content should be at least 10 frames per second and ideally 24 or 30. MobiTV will even let you pause a show on one device and then pick up where you left off on another!

Advertisers have long used the "first screen" to reach their target market, and the question of whether advertising dollars will support the "third screen" is being asked. Most current content converters have not included advertisements, except for MobiTV. The company feels that it should provide genuine television programming to their customers, and that includes the commercials. MobiTV sells advertisements in the same spaces where cable operators insert their ads. And due to the nature of the mobile phone, viewers have bonus interactive features, such as clicking a button to get more information on a product.

not want to leave their fax machines online constantly. eFax will notify users by e-mail if a fax is waiting and they can download it when convenient. Adobe's Acrobat has become very sophisticated with digital signature capabilities, perhaps signaling the eventual demise of the fax machine.

Incoming E-mail Post transaction customer service is an important part of the customer care life cycle. Normally the Web sites include a feedback button or form that delivers an e-mail message to the corporation. Often an automated customer service program acknowledges the message via e-mail and indicates that a representative will be responding shortly. Research shows that most companies are getting much better at responding to incoming e-mail in a timely manner. Companies should include feedback options online only if they have staff in place to respond: E-mail addresses on a Web site imply a promise to reply. Some companies, such as Apple Computer, do not provide e-mail feedback from their Web sites, opting instead for automated telephone routing.

RSS Feeds Really simple syndication (RSS) allows users to subscribe to blogs and Web sites. Subscribers will receive notification as soon as there is new information posted, either in e-mail or through an RSS feed reader—for example, RssReader or the many social media dashboards now available. This technology creates a structural bond, tying user to content originator, in a way that enhances the relationship. For instance, subscribers to CNN feeds in e-mail and at Twitter will receive breaking news headlines, which increase their loyalty to CNN.

CRM Software As previously mentioned, CRM, CEM, and CCM success depend on all nine building blocks, not simply technology. Nonetheless, technology and software are what grease the CRM wheel, allowing companies to gather, interpret, and use masses of customer and prospect data. There are software companies in every aspect of CRM. For example, BusinessSoftware.com presents a list of the top 10 in each area relating to CRM. Well-recognized CRM software market share leaders include SAP, Oracle, Salesforce.com, Amdocs, and Microsoft. It is a complex group of products, which is another reason that marketers must heed the nine building blocks, setting objectives and strategies first, and being sure that CRM is a top-down management philosophy. Remember that most CRM software installations fail because the firm did not take steps to fix their objectives and gain buy-in and feedback from employees at every step. The opportunities for wasting money on the wrong application are endless.

9. CRM Metrics

E-marketers use numerous metrics to assess the internet's value in delivering CRM performance—among them are ROI, cost savings, revenues, customer satisfaction, and especially the contribution of each CRM tactic to these measures. Recall that all e-marketing performance measures assess specific tactics from different perspectives, and that the metrics of choice depend on the company's goals and strategies. Refer to the Balanced Scorecard in Chapter 2 and note the metric dashboard generated for customers of Salesforce.com (Exhibit 15.17). Here we present a few of the common metrics used to track customers' progress through the customer life cycle in Exhibit 15.18. One study named the three most important to be customer retention rates (89 percent using the metric), ROI (89 percent using), and **customer lift**—increased response or transaction rates (93 percent).

Armed with this and other information about what makes customers value the company's products, organizations attempt to increase conversion and retention rates, reduce defection rates, and build average order value (AOV) and profits per customer over time (acquire, retain, grow). For example, cars.com lists more than 1.8 million new and used cars for sale by 12,000 dealers, classified advertisers, and individuals. In 2005, it used salesforce.com to facilitate the hundreds of thousands of annual transactions and 25,000 daily inquiries handled by 180 agents in many locations. As a result, agent productivity increased from six

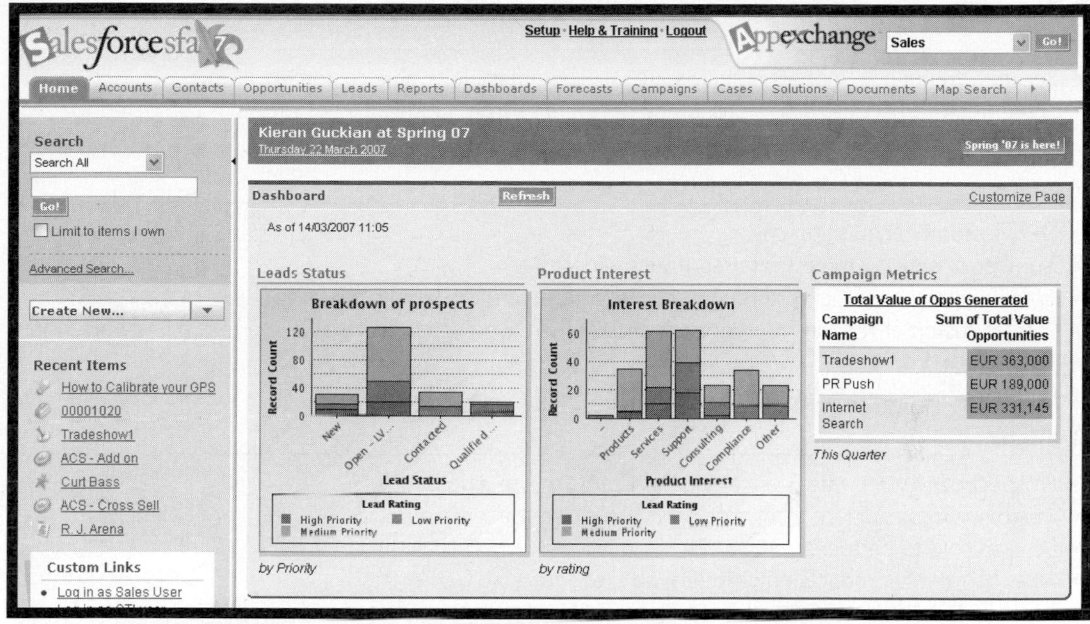

EXHIBIT 15.17 Metrics Scoreboard Generated by Salesforce.com Software *Source*: ©salesforce.com, inc. All rights reserved. Copyrights in image owned by salesforce.com and featured here with permission

to nine cases an hour, from 600 to 800 dealers per agent, and from 8,500 to 14,000 for-sale-by-owner customers per agent (see modelmetrics.com).

In addition to performance improvements, many companies use some of these methods to identify the least profitable customers and minimize interactions with them. The point is not to treat some customers poorly but to try to minimize the time invested in servicing low-profit customers.

One important CRM metric deserves discussion—**customer lifetime value (LTV)**. "Customer Lifetime Value is the expected profit that you will realize from sales to a particular customer in the future," according to Arthur Hughes, founder of the Database Marketing Institute. Exhibit 15.19 displays an LTV calculation over a 3-year period. In the first year, the company gained 100,000 customers; however, only 60 percent were retained into year two. The table is fairly self-explanatory except the "discount rate" refers to the interest rates into the future. Future revenue is worth less in the present year because of future interest rates. This is the net present value of future revenue. There are a few notable conclusions from this table:

- The retention rate in years two and three is higher than in year one: Retained customers are more loyal than new customers.
- In this example, newly acquired customers do not become profitable until the second and third years. This is quite common because of high customer acquisition costs.
- Marketing costs decline over time, reflecting the concept that it costs more to acquire than to retain customers. In fact, it is not often profitable to acquire new customers in the first year.

Marketers use market segmentation to identify which customers have the highest lifetime value, and court them accordingly. They can also calculate possible retention rates and LTV prior to undertaking marketing campaigns, to analyze possible profits. This example shows why most marketers spend more effort retaining than acquiring customers.

Target
• Recency, frequency, monetary analysis (RFM)—identifies high-value customers • Share of customer spending—proportion of revenues from high-value customers as compared to low-value customers
Acquire
• New customer acquisition cost • Number of new customers referred from partner sites • Campaign response—click-throughs, conversions, and more from Chapters 12 and 14 • Rate of customer recovery—proportion of customers who drop away that the firm can lure back using various offers • Number of product recommendations in social media
Transact
• Prospect conversion rate—percentage of visitors to site who buy • Customer cross-sell rate from online to offline, and the reverse • Services sold to partners • Sales of a firm's products on partner Web sites • Average order value (AOV)—dollar sales divided by the number of orders for any given period • Referral revenue—dollars in sales from customers referred to the firm by current customers • Sales leads from internet to closure ratio
Service
• Customer satisfaction ratings over time (see Cisco opening story) • Time to answer incoming e-mail from customers • Number of complaints
Retain
• Customer attrition rate—proportion who don't repurchase in a set time period • Percentage of customer retention—proportion of customers who repeat purchase • Sentiment of blog and other social media conversations (positive/negative discussion)
Grow
• Lifetime value (LTV)—net present value of the revenue stream for any particular customer over a number of years • AOV over time—increase or decrease • Average annual sales growth for repeat customers over time • Loyalty program effectiveness—sales increase over time • Number of low-value customers moved to high value

EXHIBIT 15.18 CRM Metrics by Customer Life Cycle Stage

TEN RULES FOR CRM SUCCESS

Many organizations lose money with their CRM efforts. This prompted Chris Selland, managing director of Reservoir Partners, to write a white paper about how to succeed with CRM applications for e-marketing. Following are his 10 rules, along with explanations from material in this chapter (see frontrange.com for more).

1. ***Recognize the customer's role.*** It is all about the customer, as evidenced by the

	Acquisition Year	Second Year	Third Year
Customers	100,000	60,000	42,000
Retention Rate	60%	70%	80%
Orders per Year	1.8	2.5	3
Avg Order Size	$90	$95	$100
Total Revenue	$16,200,000	$14,250,000	$12,600,000
Costs	70%	65%	65%
Cost of Sales	$11,340,000	$9,262,500	$8,190,000
Acquisition/Mkt. Cost	$55	$20	$20
Marketing Costs	$5,500,000	$ 1,200,000	$840,000
Total Costs	$16,840,000	$10,462,500	$9,030,000
Gross Profit	($640,000)	$3,787,500	$3,570,000
Discount Rate	1	1.16	1.35
Net Present Value (NPV)	($640,000)	$3,265,086	$2,644,444
Cumulative NPV Profit	($640,000)	$2,625,086	$5,269,531
Customer LTV	($6)	$26	$53

EXHIBIT 15.19 Customer LTV Calculation *Source:* Copyright 2012 by The Database Marketing Institute, Ltd. used with permission. Arthur Hughes may be reached at dbmarketing.com

rise in social media and the balance of control shifting from companies to customers. Customer relationship management may be a misnomer because successful companies don't "manage customers" but provide technology so that customers can manage their relationships with the company.

2. ***Build a business case.*** Before investing in CRM technology or processes, it is important to examine the cost versus predicted benefits. Don't forget the impact of costs such as employee training and staff. Put the metrics in place, as discussed in building block 9.
3. ***Gain buy-in from end users to executives.*** Many CRM installations fail because no one uses them. SFA from companies such as Salesforce.com provides tremendous benefits but only if the sales force is trained and ready.
4. ***Make every contact count.*** CRM means integrating data from all customer touch points, and it is likely that much of these data already exist in databases. Before starting, a company should determine how it can integrate all customer or partner data into the system.
5. ***Drive sales effectiveness.*** If the CRM application involves a sales force, companies should ensure that the system helps salespeople close more deals, and is not simply used to manage the metrics such as sales costs and close ratios.
6. ***Measure and manage the marketing return.*** Marketing is bigger than sales and often responsible for generating sales leads. Good CRM solutions will monitor the marketing expenditures and their role in revenues—things such as mailing list management and how leads flow through an organization.
7. ***Leverage the loyalty effect.*** Customer service is one of the three CRM facets, and although most companies consider it a cost, it plays a huge part in retaining customers and building wallet share. CRM initiatives

can monitor customer service efforts to see how they help increase customer loyalty, and, thus, add to profitability.

8. ***Choose the right tools and approach.*** This chapter covered many types of technology solutions for CRM from enterprise-wide tools to smaller tactics focusing on individual aspects of CRM. It is important that marketers evaluate these tools and not leave it to information technology personnel alone. As well, CRM applications can be purchased and installed on the company servers or "leased" on a contract basis, such as with the Salesforce.com solution. Which fits the problem most adequately?
9. ***Build the team.*** Although an effective CRM solution begins with vision from the top, it is critical to build the right team before purchasing the software and beginning the training. The team might include members from marketing, IT, sales, and finance.
10. ***Seek outside help.*** It is often worthwhile to hire a consultant to assist, especially if the company has little experience with CRM.

Chapter Summary

Marketers have practiced relationship marketing for some time; however, internet technologies made it possible to manage many relationships one at a time. In the move from mass marketing to relationship marketing, the emphasis has become long-term customer retention rather than many discrete transactions with new customers. The three pillars of relationship management are customer relationship management (CRM), customer experience management (CEM), and customer collaboration management (CCM)—also called CRM 2.0 and social CRM. Social CRM is an extension of CRM 1.0, involving social media to build profitable customer relationships. Social CRM adds many benefits to both companies and consumers.

Customer relationship management is used to create and maintain relationships with employees, business customers in the supply chain, lateral partners, and final consumers. CRM's benefits include cost-effective acquisition, retention, and growth of current customers as well as word-of-mouth referrals. The Gartner Group amended model of CRM covers nine building blocks: CRM vision, CRM strategy, customer experience management, customer collaboration management, organizational collaboration, CRM processes, CRM information, CRM technology, and CRM metrics.

The CRM vision must include guarding of customer privacy and building user trust. CRM strategy starts by defining what the company wants to accomplish with CRM technology. Relationship intensity ranges from awareness (the lowest intensity) to advocacy (the highest intensity). Three relationship levels mark the bonds that e-marketers build with customers. The highest level of CRM involves creating structural bonds that raise switching costs and build loyalty. E-marketers need to think about the experience of their valued customers, how customers prefer to interact with companies, and how they can forge ties through community building.

An important trend in CRM is the integration with supply chain management (SCM). When the firm's front end, back end, and supply chain all focus on the consumer, value is delivered, satisfaction is increased, and the firm has a competitive edge. The customer care life cycle covers the stages of targeting, acquiring, transaction, servicing, retaining, and growing customers by identifying customers, differentiating customers, and customizing the marketing mix for targeted segments or individuals—customization. CRM depends on information and on technology using company-side tools (including cookies, Web site logs, data mining, behavioral targeting, collaborative filtering, outgoing e-mail, social media, and iPOS terminals) and client-side tools (including agents, experiential marketing, individuals' Web portals, wireless data services, Web forms, fax-on-demand, incoming e-mail, and RSS feeds). Then e-marketers use a variety of software for implementation and metrics to assess the performance and value of using the internet for CRM. The chapter concludes with 10 rules for successful CRM.

Exercises

REVIEW QUESTIONS

1. Explain why relationship capital is the foundation of future business.
2. Define relationship marketing and contrast it with mass marketing.
3. Compare and contrast CRM, CEM, and CCM.
4. Define social CRM and tell how it relates to traditional CRM.
5. What are the main benefits of CRM?
6. Why do companies use sales force automation and marketing automation?
7. What are the nine building blocks of CRM?
8. What are the five levels of relationship intensity, and why do e-marketers strive to move customers to the top level?
9. Why do e-marketers see social media as an important aspect of CRM?
10. What are the advantages of CRM–SCM integration? Give an example.
11. What are the six stages in the customer care life cycle?
12. Explain how data mining, real-time profiling, collaborative filtering, and outgoing e-mail help companies customize offerings.
13. How are company-side and client-side customization tools different? Explain your answer.
14. What are the 10 rules of CRM success, according to Reservoir Partners?

DISCUSSION QUESTIONS

15. The Best Buy Story. Explain how Best Buy practiced the three relationship management pillars.
16. The Best Buy Story. What additional CRM techniques do you think Best Buy could use to step it up even more and increase sales in the process?
17. Explain the difference between wallet share and share of market.
18. Describe differences among the three pillars of relationship marketing.
19. Do you agree with the idea that social CRM is simply an extension of CRM 1.0, or do you think it is different enough to spawn an entire new field? Explain.
20. If good relationship marketing means firing a company's least profitable or most costly customers, suggest how it might be accomplished without causing them to criticize the company to their friends.
21. Explain how the customer benefits from CRM–SCM integration.
22. Do you agree with the statement that the customer's goal in relationship marketing is choice reduction? Are consumers really such creatures of habit? Why or why not?
23. Which tools do you think are more powerful for building relationships—company-side tools or client-side tools? Why?
24. Compare and contrast the concept of differentiating customers with that of differentiating products.
25. As a consumer, would you be more likely to buy from a Web site displaying the TRUSTe logo than from a competing Web site without the TRUSTe affiliation? Explain your answer.

WEB ACTIVITIES

26. Register at two Web sites and see if you get e-mail from these. Identify the ways in which those sites attempt to build relationship with you: Evaluate the sites as well as the incoming e-mail.
27. Find a company online that you think does a poor job with relationship marketing. Suggest a strategy by which it could build in phases toward a structural relationship with its customers.
28. Visit Amazon.com and list all of the ways it personalizes and customizes the site to retain and increase your business.

APPENDIX A

Internet Penetration Worldwide as of December 31, 2011

Facebook Users as of March 31, 2012

Nation	Population	Internet Users	Internet Penetration (%)	Facebook Users
Iceland	311,058	304,129	97.80	210,220
Norway	4,691,849	4,560,572	97.20	2,561,820
Sweden	9,088,728	8,441,718	92.90	4,519,780
Luxembourg	503,302	459,833	91.40	190,020
Greenland	57,670	52,000	90.20	25,720
Australia	21,766,711	19,554,832	89.80	n/a
Netherlands	16,847,007	15,071,191	89.50	5,759,840
Denmark	5,529,888	4,923,824	89.00	2,835,120
Finland	5,259,250	4,661,265	88.60	2,078,880
New Zealand	4,290,347	3,625,553	84.50	n/a
Switzerland	7,639,961	6,430,363	84.20	2,727,600
United Kingdom	62,698,362	52,731,209	84.10	30,470,400
Niue	1,311	1,100	83.90	n/a
Korea, South	48,754,657	40,329,660	82.70	6,376,160
Germany	81,471,834	67,364,898	82.70	22,123,660
Liechtenstein	35,236	28,826	81.80	11,880
Canada	34,030,589	27,757,540	81.60	17,113,220
Belgium	10,431,477	8,489,901	81.40	4,634,220
Andorra	84,825	68,740	81.00	36,760
Japan	126,475,664	101,228,736	80.00	7,684,120
Bermuda	68,679	54,687	79.60	28,820
Brunei Darussalam	401,890	318,900	79.40	234,060
Slovakia	5,477,038	4,337,868	79.20	1,889,160
United States	313,232,044	245,203,319	78.30	157,418,920
Estonia	1,282,963	993,785	77.50	447,620
Singapore	4,740,737	3,658,400	77.20	2,602,880
France	65,102,719	50,290,226	77.20	23,544,460
Faroe Islands	49,267	37,500	76.10	29,880
Monaco	30,539	23,000	75.30	36,800
Austria	8,217,280	6,143,600	74.80	2,766,540

Nation	Population	Internet Users	Internet Penetration (%)	Facebook Users
Guernsey & Alderney	65,068	48,300	74.20	440
Slovenia	2,000,092	1,420,776	71.00	670,660
Czech Republic	10,190,213	7,220,732	70.90	3,502,420
Israel	7,473,052	5,263,146	70.40	3,469,020
Taiwan	23,071,779	16,147,000	70.00	11,877,620
Latvia	2,204,708	1,540,859	69.90	319,300
Gibraltar	28,956	20,200	69.80	18,800
United Arab Emirates	5,148,664	3,555,100	69.00	2,909,860
Hong Kong	7,122,508	4,894,913	68.70	3,752,160
Argentina	41,769,726	28,000,000	67.00	17,581,160
Ireland	4,670,976	3,122,358	66.80	2,093,960
Qatar	848,016	563,800	66.50	481,400
Spain	46,754,784	30,654,678	65.60	15,682,800
Hungary	9,976,062	6,516,627	65.30	3,751,300
Malta	408,333	262,404	64.30	191,940
Poland	38,441,588	23,852,486	62.00	7,524,220
Malaysia	28,728,607	17,723,000	61.70	12,365,780
Lithuania	3,535,547	2,103,471	59.50	983,440
Croatia	4,483,804	2,656,089	59.20	1,452,300
Chile	16,888,760	10,000,000	59.20	9,020,800
Palestine (West Bk.)	2,568,555	1,512,273	58.90	914,660
Italy	61,016,804	35,800,000	58.70	20,889,260
Tokelau	1,384	800	57.80	n/a
Vatican City State	832	480	57.70	20
Oman	3,027,959	1,741,804	57.50	422,180
Bahrain	1,214,705	694,009	57.10	346,220
Serbia	7,310,555	4,107,000	56.20	3,173,440
Uruguay	3,308,535	1,855,000	56.10	1,479,580
Colombia	44,725,543	25,000,000	55.90	15,799,320
Macao	573,003	308,797	53.90	204,920
Cook Islands	11,124	6,000	53.90	n/a
San Marino	31,817	17,000	53.40	8,240
Cyprus	1,120,489	584,863	52.20	553,860
Macedonia	2,077,328	1,069,432	51.50	879,540
Portugal	10,760,305	5,455,217	50.70	4,174,000
Montenegro	661,807	328,375	49.60	292,700

Nation	Population	Internet Users	Internet Penetration (%)	Facebook Users
Guam	183,286	90,000	49.10	n/a
Morocco	31,968,361	15,656,192	49.00	4,408,340
Bulgaria	7,093,635	3,464,287	48.80	2,386,800
Jersey	94,161	45,800	48.60	820
Albania	2,994,667	1,441,928	48.10	1,060,760
Armenia	2,967,975	1,396,550	47.10	282,700
Greece	10,760,136	5,043,550	46.90	3,562,120
Iran	77,891,220	36,500,000	46.90	n/a
Belarus	9,577,552	4,436,800	46.30	409,120
French Polynesia	294,935	132,674	45.00	n/a
Turkey	78,785,548	35,000,000	44.40	30,963,100
Russia	138,739,892	61,472,011	44.30	5,237,420
Azerbaijan	8,372,373	3,689,000	44.10	782,000
Costa Rica	4,576,562	2,000,000	43.70	1,638,420
Saudi Arabia	26,131,703	11,400,000	43.60	5,148,240
Panama	3,460,462	1,503,441	43.40	895,700
Puerto Rico	3,989,133	1,698,301	42.60	1,361,020
Kuwait	2,595,628	1,100,000	42.40	898,560
Bosnia-Herzegovina	4,622,163	1,955,277	42.30	1,268,560
Man, Isle of	84,655	35,600	42.10	30,660
Dominican Republic	9,956,648	4,120,801	41.40	2,514,120
Tuvalu	10,544	4,300	40.80	n/a
Venezuela	27,635,743	10,976,342	39.70	9,579,200
Kyrgyzstan	5,587,443	2,194,400	39.30	75,380
Romania	21,904,551	8,578,484	39.20	4,161,340
Brazil	203,429,773	79,245,740	39.00	35,158,740
China	1,336,718,015	513,100,000	38.40	447,460
Seychelles	89,188	33,900	38.00	19,880
Mexico	113,724,226	42,000,000	36.90	30,990,480
Tunisia	10,629,186	3,856,984	36.30	2,955,260
Reunion (FR)	834,261	300,000	36.00	236,880
Kazakhstan	15,522,373	5,448,965	35.10	452,200
Northern Marianas	46,050	15,980	34.70	n/a
Peru	29,248,943	9,973,244	34.10	7,886,820
New Caledonia	256,275	87,420	34.10	n/a
Ukraine	45,134,707	15,300,000	33.90	1,686,500

Nation	Population	Internet Users	Internet Penetration (%)	Facebook Users
Vietnam	90,549,390	30,516,587	33.70	3,173,480
Moldova	4,314,377	1,429,154	33.10	221,220
Christmas Island	1,402	464	33.10	n/a
Lebanon	4,143,101	1,367,220	33.00	1,444,200
Norfolk Island	2,169	700	32.30	n/a
Jordan	6,508,271	1,987,400	30.50	2,226,220
Philippines	101,833,938	29,700,000	29.20	27,724,040
Nigeria	155,215,573	45,039,711	29.00	4,312,060
Maldives	394,999	114,100	28.90	120,020
Cape Verde	516,100	148,800	28.80	83,940
Palau	20,956	5,980	28.50	n/a
Georgia	4,585,874	1,300,000	28.30	907,620
Thailand	66,720,153	18,310,000	27.40	14,235,700
Ecuador	15,007,343	4,075,500	27.20	4,075,500
Uzbekistan	28,128,600	7,550,000	26.80	128,780
Egypt	82,079,636	21,691,776	26.40	10,475,940
Kenya	41,070,934	10,492,785	25.50	1,325,020
Mauritius	1,303,717	323,494	24.80	312,640
Paraguay	6,459,058	1,523,273	23.60	954,980
Indonesia	245,613,043	55,000,000	22.40	43,523,740
Micronesia	106,836	22,213	20.80	n/a
Kosovo	1,825,632	377,000	20.70	n/a
El Salvador	6,071,774	1,257,380	20.70	1,257,380
Syria	22,517,750	4,469,000	19.80	n/a
Bolivia	10,118,683	1,985,970	19.60	1,482,800
Fiji	883,125	162,880	18.40	n/a
Sao Tome & Principe	179,506	31,012	17.30	4,640
Guatemala	13,824,463	2,280,000	16.50	1,740,660
Senegal	12,643,799	1,989,396	15.70	694,220
Pakistan	187,342,721	29,128,970	15.50	6,412,960
Cuba	11,087,330	1,702,206	15.40	n/a
South Africa	49,004,031	6,800,000	13.90	4,954,280
Bhutan	708,427	98,728	13.90	65,660
Algeria	34,994,937	4,700,000	13.40	3,328,800
Honduras	8,143,564	1,067,560	13.10	1,067,560

Nation	Population	Internet Users	Internet Penetration (%)	Facebook Users
Uganda	34,612,250	4,178,085	12.10	387,080
Zimbabwe	12,084,304	1,445,717	12.00	n/a
Sri Lanka	21,283,913	2,503,194	11.80	1,235,080
Tonga	105,916	12,487	11.80	n/a
Saint Helena (UK)	7,700	900	11.70	n/a
Nicaragua	5,666,301	663,500	11.70	663,500
Tanzania	42,746,620	4,932,535	11.50	437,040
Mongolia	3,133,318	355,524	11.30	458,700
Yemen	24,133,492	2,609,698	10.80	436,500
Tajikistan	7,627,200	794,483	10.40	34,640
India	1,189,172,906	121,000,000	10.20	45,048,100
Marshall Islands	67,182	6,540	9.70	n/a
Sudan	45,047,502	4,200,000	9.30	n/a
Kiribati	100,743	8,959	8.90	n/a
Gambia	1,797,860	159,012	8.80	82,860
Vanuatu	224,564	19,172	8.50	n/a
Ghana	24,791,073	2,085,501	8.40	1,205,420
Wallis & Futuna	15,398	1,300	8.40	n/a
Botswana	2,065,398	167,180	8.10	199,180
Djibouti	757,074	61,320	8.10	42,260
Laos	6,477,211	527,400	8.10	156,160
Rwanda	11,370,425	818,048	7.20	127,680
Congo	4,243,929	295,132	7.00	81,640
Gabon	1,576,665	108,845	6.90	94,940
Namibia	2,147,585	148,414	6.90	148,420
Swaziland	1,370,424	95,122	6.90	62,540
Nepal	29,391,883	2,031,245	6.90	1,396,800
Samoa	193,161	12,816	6.60	n/a
Zambia	13,881,336	882,170	6.40	206,700
Equatorial Guinea	668,225	42,024	6.30	21,200
Libya	6,597,960	391,880	5.90	464,700
Angola	13,338,541	744,195	5.60	361,420
Togo	6,771,993	356,300	5.30	84,480
Mayotte (FR)	209,530	10,620	5.10	11,460
Eritrea	5,939,484	283,699	4.80	20,120

Nation	Population	Internet Users	Internet Penetration (%)	Facebook Users
Comoros	794,683	37,472	4.70	13,340
Solomon Islands	571,890	26,907	4.70	n/a
Cote d'Ivoire	21,504,162	968,000	4.50	n/a
Malawi	15,879,252	716,400	4.50	127,780
American Samoa	67,242	3,040	4.50	n/a
Lesotho	1,924,886	83,813	4.40	31,480
Mozambique	22,948,858	975,395	4.30	191,080
Iraq	30,399,572	1,303,760	4.30	1,550,840
Afghanistan	29,835,392	1,256,470	4.20	257,440
Cameroon	19,711,291	783,956	4.00	481,280
Nauru	9,322	340	3.60	n/a
Bangladesh	158,570,535	5,501,609	3.50	2,520,680
Mauritania	3,281,634	100,333	3.10	87,160
Cambodia	14,701,717	491,480	3.10	449,160
Benin	9,325,032	744,195	3.00	134,920
Mali	14,159,904	414,985	2.90	132,520
Central African Rep.	4,950,027	123,800	2.50	105,580
Guinea-Bissau	1,596,677	37,123	2.30	n/a
Turkmenistan	4,997,503	110,924	2.20	5,860
Papua New Guinea	6,187,591	125,000	2.00	n/a
Chad	10,758,945	190,863	1.80	26,760
Burundi	10,216,190	176,040	1.70	31,460
Madagascar	21,926,221	352,135	1.60	219,620
Burkina Faso	16,751,455	230,562	1.40	103,680
Congo, Dem. Rep.	71,712,867	915,400	1.30	643,220
Somalia	9,925,640	106,000	1.10	75,500
Guinea	10,601,009	95,823	0.90	43,720
Sierra Leone	5,363,669	48,520	0.90	50,320
Niger	16,468,886	128,749	0.80	43,880
Ethiopia	90,873,739	622,122	0.70	511,240
Liberia	3,786,764	20,000	0.50	n/a
Myanmar	53,999,804	110,000	0.20	n/a
Timor-Leste	1,177,834	2,361	0.20	n/a

Sources: Based on *Internet World Stats: Usage and Population Statistics*. Available at internetworldstats.com/stats.htm.

APPENDIX B

Glossary

A/B testing When there are two versions of a Web page with similar content and images for testing which performs better.

access control Laws and standards that enable persons to reasonably regulate the information that they are giving up.

advergame A combination of online advertising and gaming, where the user sees products and services in the game itself.

advertising Any paid form of nonpersonal presentation and promotion of ideas, goods, or services by an identified sponsor (Kotler and Armstrong, 2011).

affiliate program A link to an e-tailer's Web site, put in by firms to make a commission on all purchases by referred customers.

agent An intermediary who represents either the buyer or the seller, does not take title to the goods, and makes a commission for work completed.

aggregation The gathering of products from multiple suppliers so that the consumer can have more choices in one location.

AIDA model Stands for awareness, interest, desire, and action and is one of the **hierarchy of effects** models.

AIO Activities, interests, and opinions of consumers.

atmospherics The in-store ambiance created by retailers.

attention economy The idea that infinite information is available but the demand for it is limited by human capacity.

Balanced Scorecard An enterprise performance management system that links strategy to measurement by asking firms to set goals and subsequent performance metrics in four areas: customer, internal, innovation and learning, and financial.

banner ad A rectangular space appearing on a Web site, paid for by an advertiser, which allows the user to click through to the advertiser's Web site.

bar code scanner A real-space primary data collection technique by which information is gathered offline at brick-and-mortar retail stores and is subsequently stored and used in marketing databases.

barter A negotiation where seller costs for producing the good or service represent the pricing floor, under which no profit is made. Above that floor, marketers have the freedom to set a price that will draw buyers from competing offers. Between cost and price is profit.

behavioral advertising Another form of contextual advertising, but follows user behavior instead of Web page text.

behavioral targeting Occurs when software tracks a user's movements through a Web site and then sends appropriate Web content at a moment's notice.

benefit segmentation A variable in behavioral segmentation where marketers form groups of consumers based on the benefits they desire from the product.

big data Data sets that are so big that they are difficult to manage with currently available software.

blogs Also known as *Web logs*. Web sites where entries are listed in reverse chronological order and readers can comment on any entry.

boot viruses These viruses reside on removable disks and destroy operating systems when users mistakenly boot the computer with a disk inserted.

born global firms These understand that the Web, along with e-mail and VoIP communications, such as Skype, enable them to tap global markets immediately.

brand communication Advertising and other marketing communication tactics that create a distinctly favorable image that customers associate with a product when considering buying decisions.

brand equity The intangible value of a brand, measured in dollars.

broker An intermediary that brings buyers and sellers together but doesn't represent either side. Like agents, brokers are paid by either the buyer or the seller.

build to order A complex product that is created as it is ordered, which helps to eliminate inventory and reduce cost.

business intelligence The gathering of secondary and primary information about competitors, markets, customers, and more.

business model A method by which the organization sustains itself in the long term, which includes its value proposition for partners and customers as well as its revenue streams.

business-to-business (B2B) The marketing of products to businesses, governments, and institutions for use in the business operation, as components in the business products, or for resale.

business-to-consumer (B2C) The marketing of products to the end consumer.

business-to-government (B2G) The marketing of products to government institutions.

buyer cooperative (buyer aggregator) A type of online purchasing agent that brings buyers together for the purpose of buying in larger quantities and, thus, reducing prices.

cable modem Allowing transmission of internet traffic over the cable TV wire connected to the home, with a speed of transmission over a cable modem ranging between 500 Kbps and 2.5 Mbps.

CDA (Computer Decency Act) Legislation added, in 1996, to the federal Telecommunications Act of 1934 making it a criminal act to send an obscene or indecent communication to a recipient who was known to the sender to be under 18 years of age.

chat bots Automated 1:1 discussion on a site: also called virtual agents, virtual assistants, and avatars.

citizen journalists Internet users who contribute their perspectives by posting content to online blogs, forums, and Web sites, usually without editorial review.

CIVETS Emerging market economies: Colombia, Indonesia, Vietnam, Egypt, Turkey, and South Africa.

click-through Determined when a Web surfer clicks on a banner or another ad that is hyperlinked to the advertiser's site.

client-side Refers to activities that occur on the user's computer, such as writing and sending e-mail.

client-side data collection Information about consumer surfing is gathered right at the user's PC (e.g., the cookie file).

cloud computing A network of online Web servers in remote locations from the company, used to store and manage data.

collaborative filtering This software gathers opinions of like-minded users online and returns those opinions to the individual in real time.

common law Decisions, presumptions, and practices traditionally embraced by Anglo-American courts.

communications media These are communication channels used to disseminate news, information, entertainment, and promotional messages.

community building Firms build Web sites to draw groups of special interest users.

competitive intelligence (CI) The analysis of the industries in which a firm operates as input to the firm's strategic positioning and to understand competitor vulnerabilities.

consumer-to-consumer (C2C) Business transaction from one consumer to another. Once limited to classified advertising and garage sales, C2C has now grown due to the popularity of online auctions.

content analysis This is the examination of text or images in order to evaluate the communication content.

content filtering A process by which Web users may block unwanted material.

content marketing This is a strategy involving creating and publishing content on Web sites and in social media.

content publishing (brochureware) Used by every firm that has a Web site. Content refers to any text, graphics, audio, or video online that informs or persuades.

content sponsorship An e-commerce business model that involves companies selling online Web site space or e-mail space to advertisers.

contextual advertising Occurs when an ad system scans a Web page for content and serves an appropriate ad.

continuous replenishment The concept of "scan one, make one—and deliver it fast"; helps to eliminate inventory and reduce cost.

conversion The proportion of all Web site visitors who actually purchase on that visit.

Cookie files are small data files written to a user's hard drive when visiting a site.

COPPA (Children's Online Privacy Protection Act) Requires that Web sites and other online media that knowingly collect information from children 12 years of age or under (1) provide notice to parents; (2) obtain verifiable parental consent prior to the collection, use, or disclosure of most information; (3) allow parents to view and correct this information; (4) enable parents to prevent further use or collection of data; (5) limit personal information collection for a child's participation in games, prize offers, or related activities; and (6) establish procedures that protect the confidentiality, security, and integrity of the personal information collected.

copyright A protection of the right to publish or duplicate the expressions of ideas.

cost per click Total advertisement cost divided by number of clicks on an ad or hyperlink.

cost per order Total ad cost divided by the number of orders.

cost per thousand (CPM) The cost to deliver 1,000 impressions in a physical or digital medium. (CPM is calculated by taking the ad's cost, dividing it by the audience size, and then multiplying by 1,000 [(cost ÷ audience) × 1,000].)

crowdfunding This involves raising money online for new product ideas or for political campaigns and non-profit causes.

crowdsourcing This is the practice of outsourcing ads, product development, and other tasks to people outside the organization.

customer collaboration management (CCM) (also called *CRM 2.0* and *social CRM*) CCM is a strategy to engage customers in relationship-building conversation, often through social media.

customer experience management (CEM) CEM "represents the discipline, methodology and/or process used to comprehensively manage a customer's cross-channel exposure, interaction and transaction with a company, product, brand or service" (as coined by Bernd Schmitt in 2003).

customer lifetime value "LTV" is the expected profit that a company will realize from sales to a particular customer in the future (Hughes, 2012).

customer lift Increasing the response rates from promotions; increasing transaction rates.

customer profiling Use of data warehouse information to help marketers understand the characteristics and behavior of specific target groups.

customer relationship management (CRM) CRM is the process of targeting, acquiring, transacting, servicing, retaining, and building long-term relationships with customers that add value both to the organization and to the customer.

customization The third step in the CRM process (identify, differentiate, and customize) in which firms tailor their marketing mixes to meet the needs of small target segments, even to the individual level, using electronic marketing tools; sometimes refers to technology that allows consumers to cater the Web site to suit their own needs.

cybersquatting A type of trademark violation that involves the registration of domains that resemble or duplicate the names of existing corporations or other entities.

database marketing Collecting, analyzing, and disseminating electronic information about customers, prospects, and products in order to increase profits.

data mining Extraction of hidden predictive information from the warehouse via statistical analysis in order to find patterns and other information in databases.

data warehouse Repository for an entire organization's historical data (not just marketing data), designed specifically to support analyses necessary for decision making.

demographics The characteristics of populations.

diaspora communities When a large number of people leave their home country and live together in a common neighborhood or city abroad, they become part of a diaspora community, often wanting to maintain a relationship with their homeland.

differential advantage 1. A property of any product that is able to claim a uniqueness over other products in its category. To be a differential advantage, the uniqueness must be communicable to customers and have value for them. The differential advantage of a firm is often called its distinctive competences. 2. An advantage unique to an organization; an advantage extremely difficult to match by a competitor (Reprinted with permission from American Marketing Association's Online Marketing Dictionary).

digital divide The distinction between countries and between different groups of people within countries; between those who have real access to information and communications technology and are using it effectively, and those who don't.

digital video recorder (DVR) Hard drives that can let viewers pause live shows or record up to 160 hours of television programming. Also knows as *personal video recorder (PVR)*.

dilution The diminishment of the ability to identify or distinguish a good or a service.

direct distribution Refers to a type of e-commerce in which manufacturers sell directly to consumers, eliminating intermediaries such as retailers (the Dell model). Also called *direct selling*.

direct marketing Direct marketing is an interactive process of addressable communication that uses one or more . . . media to effect, at any location, a measurable sale, lead, retail purchase, or charitable donation, with this activity analyzed on a database for the development of ongoing mutually beneficial relationships between marketers and customers, prospects, or donors (*The Power of Direct Marketing*, 2011–2012).

Directory submission When an organization pays to be included in a searchable directory.

direct-response advertising Seeking to create action such as inquiry or purchase from consumers as a result of seeing the ad.

discontinuous innovations New-to-the-world products never seen before, such as music CDs and the television at their introductions.

disintermediation The process of eliminating traditional intermediaries. Eliminating intermediaries has the potential to reduce costs because each intermediary must add to the price of the product in order to make a living.

display ads These are embedded in Web pages, allowing users to click through to the advertiser's site and can include text, graphics, and animation.

disruptive innovation A special category of discontinuous innovation that changes the existing market in a drastic way (sometimes called disruptive technology).

distribution channel A group of interdependent firms that works together to transfer product from the supplier to the consumer. The transfer may either be direct or employ a number of intermediaries.

Digital Millennium Copyright (DMCA) Act A complex piece of legislation that contains several provisions, among granting internet service providers (ISPs) protection from acts of user infringement as long as certain procedures are followed, including the prompt reporting and disabling of infringing material, and criminalizing the circumvention of software protections and the development or distribution of circumvention products.

domain name The unique name that identifies a Web site, such as company.com. It is also called an **IP address (internet protocol).**

DSL (digital subscriber line) Technology that refers to a family of methods (nine variations) for transmitting at speeds up to 8 Mbps (8 million bits per second) over a standard phone line.

dynamic pricing The strategy of offering different prices to different customers.

early adopters The next 13.5 percent to purchase the product, after the innovators, who comprise the first 2.5 percent. Early adopters are eager to buy new products, but they are more community minded than innovators and tend to communicate with others about new products.

earned media When individual conversations become the channel: messages about a company that are generated by social media authors (such as bloggers); traditional journalists on media Web sites; and by internet users who share opinions, experiences, insights, and perceptions on Web sites and mobile applications.

e-business See *electronic business.*

e-business model A method by which the organization sustains itself in the long term using information technology, which includes its value proposition for partners and customers as well as its revenue streams.

e-business strategy The deployment of enterprise resources for capitalizing on technologies to reach specified objectives and ultimately improve performance and create sustainable competitive advantage.

e-commerce Use of digital technologies such as the internet and bar code scanners to enable the buying and selling process. E-commerce is about transactions through distribution channels and e-tailing.

ECPA (Electronic Communication Privacy Act) Legislation, similar to the Fair Credit Reporting Act, which provides sanctions for misuse of consumer data.

electronic data interchange (EDI) The computerized exchange of information between organizations in order to avoid paper forms. The classic use of EDI is to eliminate purchase requisitions between firms.

effectiveness The extent to which choices made maximize a company's competitive advantage.

efficiency Generally referring to the relative costs of delivering media audiences.* See *cost per rating point* and *cost per thousand.*

efficient market A market in which customers have equal access to information about products, prices, and distribution.

electronic business (e-business) The continuous optimization of a firm's business activities through digital technology. This term and *e-commerce* are often used interchangeably.

electronic check A consumer's authorization for a third-party Web site to pay a specific amount in a transaction and withdraw funds from the user's checking account.

electronic commerce (e-commerce) The subset of e-business focused on transactions that includes buying/selling online, digital value creation, virtual marketplaces and storefronts, and new distribution channel intermediaries. This term and *e-business* are often used interchangeably.

electronic marketing (e-marketing) The use of information technology in the processes of creating, communicating, and delivering value to customers, and for managing customer relationships in ways that benefit the organization and its stakeholders.

electronic money Also called *e-money* or *digital cash*, a system that uses the internet and computers to exchange payments electronically.

e-mail advertising The least expensive type of online advertising, generally consisting of a few sentences of text embedded in another firm's e-mail content.

e-marketing strategy A marketing strategy using information technology.

emerging economies Those with low levels of gross domestic product (GDP) per capita that are experiencing rapid growth.

enforcement The process through which users have effective means to hold data collectors accountable to their policies.

engagement This occurs when internet users connect or collaborate with brands, companies, or each other.

enterprise resource planning (ERP) Back-office operations such as order entry, purchasing, invoicing, and inventory control that allow organizations to optimize business processes while lowering costs.

environmental factors The online legal, political, and technological environments that can greatly influence marketing strategies, alter the composition of the internet audience, and affect the quality of material that can be delivered to them. These factors also affect laws regarding taxation, access, copyright, and encryption on the internet.

environmental scan Continual task of observing factors that affect a firm's operations; includes economic analysis as well as social and demographic trends.

ethical code A statement outlining proper behaviors of participants as developed by trade associations, commercial standards groups, and the professions.

ethics A general endeavor that takes into account the concerns and values of society as a whole.

evaluation plan System of tracking effectiveness, put in place before the site is launched, whereby the site is continually assessed after it is created and published.

exchange A basic concept in marketing that refers to the act of obtaining a desired object from someone else by offering something in return.

extensible markup language (XML) The next generation of HTML that allows Web browsers to pull information from databases on the fly and display in Web pages.

extranet is an intranet to which proprietary networks are joined for the purpose of sharing information. If two companies link their intranets, they would have an extranet. Extranets are proprietary to the organizations involved.

fax-on-demand Customers telephone a firm, listen to an automated voice menu, and through selecting options request that a fax be sent on a topic of interest.

fixed pricing A price set by sellers, which buyers must take or leave. Also called *menu pricing*.

flash sales These are limited-time offers for site members to purchase a product at a deep discount.

focus group A qualitative methodology that attempts to collect in-depth information from a small number of participants.

folksonomy The technology behind classification techniques for online media, such as collaborative tagging or social bookmarking.

fraud The use of deception and false claims to obtain profit.

freemium This is a combination of "free" and "premium," where companies offer a basic product for free and then provide upgraded versions for a fee. This pricing model is commonly used for technology products, such as mobile apps.

frequency The number of times consumers are exposed to an advertising message.

FTC (Federal Trade Commission) Administrative agency concerned with making laws responsive to particular situations by promulgating rules and opinions within the sectors of its expertise.

FTP (file transfer protocol) The procedure whereby files are transferred from the designer's computer to the Web server; used in the publication of Web pages.

geographics Separation of large markets into smaller groupings according to country, region, state, city, community, or block divisions.

geographic segment pricing A company sets different prices when selling a product in different geographic areas.

geolocation This includes many different technologies to locate an internet-enabled device (and its owner) at its physical world address: For example WiFi, GPS (global positioning satellite coordinates), or simply IP addresses (internet protocol).

GPRS (general packet radio service) Also known as *3G* (third-generation) mobile phone technology, supporting a wide range of bandwidths for receiving and sending e-mail and large amounts of data and for Web browsing in many different countries.

group member event sites Allow an individual to form a public group that can be joined by anyone who shares the interest—and then use the group to post meetings.

hierarchy of effects model Device that attempts to explain the impact of marketing communication. It assumes that consumers go through a series of stages when making product decisions and that communication messages are designed to assist that movement.

hostile applets Programs that can be used to surreptitiously access and transmit data on hard drives, including e-mail addresses, credit card records, and other account information.

HTML (hypertext markup language) A coding system that allows content to be viewed in Web browsers. This system is standard for all Web pages.

IMC (integrated marketing communication) See *integrated marketing communication.*

image recognition Technology that sees the content within an image.

impressions The number of times an ad was served to unique site visitors, regardless of whether they looked at it.

inbound marketing Web companies getting found online, as opposed to interrupting customers to get them to pay attention to the Web site, products, and so forth.

in-depth interviews (IDI) A semistructured conversation with a small number of subjects.

indirect distribution channel A typical indirect channel that includes suppliers, a manufacturer, wholesalers, retailers, and end consumers.

individualized targeting See *micromarketing.*

infomediary An online organization that aggregates and distributes information, acting as a personal agent for Web users.

instant messaging Short messages sent among users who are online at the same time.

Internet Corporation for Assigned Names and Numbers (ICANN) The organization responsible for the administration of the internet name and address system and for resolving conflicts that surround the assignment and possession of domains.

integrated marketing communication (IMC) A cross-functional process for planning, executing, and monitoring brand communications designed to profitably acquire, retain, and grow customers.

interactive display ads The most advanced stage of the banner; an ad that may sense the position of the mouse on the Web page and begin to animate faster as the user approaches; have built-in games, or have drop-down menus, check boxes, and search boxes to engage and empower the user.

intermediary A firm that appears in the channel between the supplier and the consumer and specializes in performing functions more efficiently than the supplier could.

internet As relates to marketing strategy, the internet is a global network of interconnected networks (technology), a medium for communication with stakeholders, and a distribution channel for digital products.

internet telephony Use of the internet to carry simultaneous digitized voice transmission. Also called *Voice over Internet Protocol (VoIP).*

interstitial ad Java-based ads that appear while the publisher's content is loading.

intranet A network that runs internally in a corporation but that uses internet standards such as HTML and browsers; can be thought of as a mini-internet but only for internal corporate consumption.

IP address (internet protocol) See *URL* and *domain name*. All three terms are used interchangeably.

iPOS terminals Small customer-facing machines near the brick-and-mortar cash register, used to record a buyer's signature for a credit card transaction.

jurisdiction The legal term that describes the ability of a court or other authority to gain control over a party; traditionally based on physical presence, but now less certain within the online world commonality of physical location.

keyword advertising Banner ads or links on a search query return page based on the keywords entered by the user at a search engine.

keywords The words users type into the search query box to find what they seek.

knowledge management (KM) The process of managing the creation, use, and dissemination of knowledge.

laggards The last 16 percent of buyers of new products, who are traditional, generally of lower socioeconomic status, and who often adopt a product when newer products have already been introduced.

landing page This is a unique page that appears after a user clicks on a link associated with that Web site.

Lanham Act Legislation that protects trademarks registered with the government and some not registered with the government.

law An expression of values, normally created for broader purposes, with the goal of addressing national or sometimes international populations, and made by legislatures such as Congress or Parliament, enforced by executives or agencies, and interpreted by the courts.

learning relationship A learning relationship between a customer and an enterprise that gets smarter and smarter with each individual interaction, defining in ever more detail the customer's own individual needs and tastes.

least developed countries (LDCs) These are those countries with the world's poorest economies.

license Contractual agreement made between consumers and software vendors that allows the buyer to use the product but restricts duplication or distribution.

lifetime value (LTV) See *customer lifetime value.*

live casting Enables live audio or video streaming directly from a cell phone, mobile internet device, PC, or Mac to a Web site for viewing by others.

local event sites Allow residents to post to a calendar that is searchable by local area.

location-based marketing delivers local and relevant content to a user's mobile device using GPS technology.

logistics This includes physical distribution activities such as transportation and inventory storage, as well as the function of aggregating products.

lower-cost products Products introduced to compete with existing brands by offering a price advantage. The internet spawned a series of free products with the idea of building market share so the firm would have a customer base for marketing other products owned by the firm. For example, Eudora Light, the e-mail reader software, was an early entry with this strategy.

macroenvironment All stakeholders, organizations, and forces external to the organization.

macro viruses These are viruses that attach to data files and infect common desktop applications when users open the infected data file.

manufacturer's agents (seller aggregators) An entity that represents more than one seller, and, in the virtual world, generally creates Web sites to help an entire industry sell products.

market differences Ways in which two country markets exhibit dissimilar characteristics, such as different languages, cultural behaviors, buying behaviors, and so on.

market intelligence The procedure in which marketers continually scan the firm's macroenvironment for threats and opportunities.

market opportunity analysis (MOA) Analysis conducted by a firm upon reviewing the marketing environment, focusing on finding and selecting among market opportunities. A traditional market opportunity analysis includes both demand and supply analyses. The demand portion reviews various market segments in terms of their potential profitability. Conversely, the supply analysis reviews competition in selected segments that are under consideration.

market similarity Ways in which two country markets exhibit similar characteristics, such as similar languages, cultural behaviors, buying behaviors, and so forth.

market targeting The process of selecting the market segments that are most attractive to the firm.

marketing automation These are activities aiding marketers with effective targeting, efficient marketing communication, and real-time monitoring of customer and market trends.

marketing concept The idea that an organization exists to satisfy customer wants and needs while meeting organizational objectives.

marketing information system (MIS) The system of assessing information needs, gathering information, analyzing it, and disseminating it to marketing decision makers. In a separate context, MIS also refers to management information systems—a field of study in many business schools.

marketing public relations (MPR) Brand-related activities and nonpaid, third-party media coverage to positively influence target markets.

marketing segmentation The process of aggregating individuals or businesses along similar characteristics that pertain to the use, consumption, or benefits derived from a product or service.

mass customization The internet's unique ability to individualize marketing mixes electronically and automatically to the individual level.

mass marketing See *undifferentiated targeting.*

metatags HTML statements, which describe a Web site's contents, which allow search engines to identify sites relevant to topics of their inquiries.

microblogs A type of blog, but with very short sentence fragments, or just an image or hyperlink.

microenvironment Stakeholders and forces internal to the organization.

micromarketing Individualized targeting.

microsite A Web site designed for a narrow purpose, with only three to five pages.

millennials A consumer segment born between 1974 and 1994 (also called *Generation Y*).

mobile commerce (m-commerce) This occurs when consumers make a transaction with a smartphone or other mobile device.

multichannel marketing The use of more than one sales channel, such as online, brick and mortar, and catalog.

multimedia The audio and video experience that is not prevalent yet on the internet due primarily to lack of sufficient bandwidth for its transmittal.

natural search An SEO strategy involving optimizing a Web site so it will appear as close to the first search engine results page as possible.

near-field communication (NFC) This involves two smartphones or a smartphone and another device that communicate by touching each other or being in very close proximity.

new-product lines Lines introduced when firms take an existing brand name and create new products in a completely different category. For example, General Foods applied the Jell-O brand name to pudding pops and other frozen delights.

newsgroup Communities of interest that post e-mails on electronic bulletin boards (e.g., Usenet, which is organized around topics or products).

niche marketing A firm's selection of one segment and development of one or more marketing mixes to meet the needs of that segment.

No Electronic Theft (NET) Act Legislation that confers copyright protection for computer content and imposes sanctions when infringement is committed for commercial or private financial gain, or by the reproduction or distribution of one or more copies of copyrighted works having $1,000 or more in retail value.

notice A statement to users to make them aware of a site's information policy before data are collected.

omni-channel shopping This is the shopper's perspective of multichannel marketing, describing the way consumers move seamlessly through many shopping channels: Web, brick and mortar store, computer, mobile device, catalog, and so forth.

online agents Represent either the buyer or the seller and earn a commission for their work.

online auctions The auction-style sale of merchandise via the internet.

online brokers Intermediaries who assist in purchase negotiations without actually representing either buyers or sellers.

online exchange Electronic forum in which buyers and sellers meet to make transactions.

online extensions A lower-risk strategy for marketers introducing a new-product line.

online observation The monitoring of people's behavior in relevant situations, such as consumer chatting and e-mail posting through chat rooms, bulletin boards, or mailing lists.

online panel A panel of people who are paid to be the subject of marketing research. Also called *single-source data systems* or *opt-in communities.*

open buying on the internet (OBI) An electronic data interchange (EDI) that supports the sharing of internal information with value chain partners.

opt-in Occurs when users voluntarily agree to receive commercial e-mail about topics that might be of interest to them by simply checking a box and entering an e-mail address. Also called *permission marketing*.

opt-out Similar to opt-in; however, users have to uncheck the box on a Web page to prevent being put on the e-mail list.

outsource To contract services from external firms in order to accomplish internal tasks.

owned media Media that carry communication messages from the organization to internet users on channels that are owned and, thus, at least partially controlled by, the company.

page tags One pixel on a page that is invisible to users. (A pixel is one dot of light on a computer screen.)

paid inclusion Occurring when sites receive guaranteed indexing in a search engine.

paid media These are properties owned by others who are paid by the organization to carry its promotional messages (e.g., advertising).

paid search Occurring when an advertiser pays a reputation aggregator a fee for listing, directory submission, inclusion in a search engine index, or to display their ad when users type in particular keywords.

Pareto principle The generalization that 80 percent of a firm's business usually comes from the top 20 percent of customers.

patent The registered protection of inventions and the ability to reproduce or manufacture an inventor's product.

pay per click advertising Sometimes called cost per action (CPA), this is an advertising model whereby the advertiser pays a predetermined amount to the Web site for each visitor who clicks on the ad. Advertisers may also pay for each conversion (sale), each sales lead, or each newly registered user.

paywall Some Web content is hidden and available only to users who pay a fee for access.

performance metrics Specific measures designed to evaluate the effectiveness and efficiency of an organization's operations.

permission marketing An opt-in form of marketing in which advertisers present marketing communication messages to consumers who agree to receive them.

personal event sites Allow individuals to create events, such as a party, and invite a list of people via e-mail.

personal selling Personal interactions between a customer's and the firm's sales force for the purpose of making sales and building customer relationships (Kotler and Armstrong, 2011).

personalization Methods of individualizing an impersonal computer networked environment (e.g., Web sites that greet users by name, providing personalized information).

PICS (platform for internet content selection rules) An application that allows for the filtering of sites deemed inappropriate for minors.

piracy Installing computer software or other copyrighted intellectual property (such as music or movies) that the individual did not purchase.

pixel One dot of light on a computer or television screen.

podcast A digital media file available for download online to computers, music players, tablets, or smartphones.

portal A point of entry to the internet that combines diverse content from many sources.

positioning A strategy to create a desired image of a company and its products in the minds of a chosen user segment.

price The amount of money charged for a product or service. More broadly, price is the sum of all the values (such as money, time, energy, and psychic cost) that buyers exchange for the benefits of having or using a good or service.

price dispersion The observed spread between the highest and lowest price for a given product.

price elasticity The variability of purchase behavior with changes in price.

price leadership The lowest-priced product entry in a particular category.

price negotiation A company negotiates prices with individual customers, who can comprise segments of those online.

price transparency The idea that both buyers and sellers can view all competitive prices for items sold online.

primary data Information gathered for the first time to solve a particular problem. It is usually more expensive and time-consuming to gather than secondary data, but conversely, the data are current and generally more relevant to the marketer's specific problem. In addition, primary data have the benefit of being proprietary and, thus, unavailable to competitors.

privacy Topic of much debate, including issues of the Warren and Brandeis concept of a right to be left alone, often referred to as the seclusion theory; access control, which places its emphasis on laws and standards that enable persons to reasonably regulate the information that they are giving up; and autonomy that identifies private matters such as those necessary for a person to make life decisions.

probability sample A sample selected in such a way that each item or person in the population being studied has an equal likelihood of being included in the sample.

promoted account ads These are featured in Twitter search results and in the "Who to Follow section."

promoted trends Ads placed on hot topics in Twitter that are presented near a user's timeline.

promoted tweets Ads that appear as content at the top of a Twitter search page or a user's timeline.

promotional pricing Special deals in price that retailers use to encourage a first purchase, to encourage repeat business, or to close a sale.

proxy server A system that stores frequently used information closer to the end user to provide faster access or to reduce the load on another server; also serves as the gateway to the internet.

psychographics These are a consumer's personality, values, lifestyle, activities, interests, and opinions (**AIO**).

public relations Building good relations with the company's various publics by obtaining favorable publicity; building up a good corporate image; and handling or heading off unfavorable rumors, stories, and events (Kotler and Armstrong 2011).

purchasing agents Represent buyers. In traditional marketing, they often forge long-term relationships with one or more firms; on the internet, however, they represent any number of buyers, often anonymously.

pure play A business that began only on the internet, even if it subsequently added a brick-and-mortar presence.

QR codes Bar codes that appear as many black modules in a small square white background.

radio frequency identification (RFID) Tags used to transmit a signal to scanners, which detect the presence of the RFID tag in products, credit cards, or even under a person or animal's skin.

real-space data collection This primary data collection refers to technology-enabled approaches to gather information offline that is subsequently stored and used in marketing databases, such as bar code scanners at retail stores.

real-time bidding (RTB) The advertiser only buys the number of impressions they want at a predefined price.

real-time profiling The use of special software to track a user's movements through a Web site, and then compile and report on the data at a moment's notice.

referral revenue Dollars in sales from customers referred to the firm by current customers.

relationship capital A firm's ability to build and maintain relationships with customers, suppliers, and partners: The total value of these relationships to a firm in the long term is its relationship capital.

relationship marketing The process of establishing, maintaining, enhancing, and commercializing customer relationships; its long-term customer orientation involves ongoing interactive communication between a firm and selected stakeholders and focuses on individual customers 1:1.

remarketing A tactic that involves communicating with users who previously visited a Web site.

repositioned products Current products that are either targeted to different markets or promoted for new uses.

repositioning The process of creating a new or modified brand, company, or product position.

reputation aggregator A Web site that ranks other Web sites, products, retailers, or other content according to some rating system.

reputation management systems These use various criteria and technologies for monitoring and protecting reputations.

respondent authenticity A disadvantage of online research in which it is difficult to determine whether respondents are who they say they are.

retailers Buy products from manufacturers or wholesalers and sell them to consumers. Retailers can operate either offline or online.

return on investment (ROI) A measure of investment success. It is calculated by dividing net profit by total assets (fixed plus current).

revenue streams Cash flows that may come from Web site product sales, advertising sales, and agent commissions.

reverse auction An exchange arrangement in which individual buyers enter the price they will pay for particular items at the purchasing agent's Web site, and sellers can agree to pay that price or not.

revisions of existing products Products that are introduced as "new and improved" and, thus, replace the old product. On the internet, firms are continually improving their brands to add value and remain competitive.

RFM analysis A scan of the database for three criteria: recency, frequency, and monetary value. This process allows firms to target offers to the customers who are most responsive, thus saving promotional costs and increasing sales.

RSS (really simple syndication) An easy XML format designed for sharing headlines and other Web content.

safe harbor Provisions for the protection of EU citizen data.

sales promotion Short-term incentives to encourage the purchase or sale of a product or service (Kotler and Armstrong, 2011).

sampling An arrangement in which users are allowed to sample a digital product prior to purchase. For example, software companies provide a free 30- to 60-day trial and online music stores give 30-second sound clips to customers.

search engine A Web site that scans the Web, searching for matches for the user's keywords, and returns a list of Web sites that might have the desired information.

search engine optimization (SEO) The process of maximizing the number of visitors to a Web or social media site by ensuring that either (1) the site name and links appear high on a search engine results page for appropriate key words or (2) ads on search engine sites get a high click-through.

search marketing The act of marketing a Web site via search engines, whether through improving rank in listings, purchasing paid listings, or a combination of these and other search engine-related activities.

seclusion Warren and Brandeis theory outlining the concept of the right to be left alone.

secondary data Information that has been gathered for some other purpose but is useful for the current problem; can be collected more quickly and less expensively than primary data.

second-generation shopping agents Shopping agents that measure value and not just price.

segmentation basis Dividing the market by the general categories of demographics, geographic location, psychographics, and behavior, each of which has a number of variables.

segmentation variables Variables used by marketers to identify and profile groups of customers.

segmented pricing Setting the price of a good or service at two or more levels, based on segment differentiation rather than cost alone.

self-regulation The private sector's ability to rapidly identify and resolve problems specific to its areas of competence.

selling agent An entity that represents a single firm to help it move products and normally works for a commission.

semantic Web An extension of the current Web in which information is given a well-defined meaning.

server-side data collection Information about consumer surfing that is gathered and recorded on the Web server.

secure electronic transaction (SET) A vehicle for legitimizing both the merchant and the consumer as well as protecting the consumer's credit card number. Under SET, the card number is never directly sent to the merchant. Rather a third party is introduced to the transaction with whom both the merchant and consumer communicate to validate one another as well as the transaction.

sentiment This is the proportion of online conversation about a brand that is positive, negative, or neutral.

share of mind Refers to relationship marketing focusing on customer development in the long term: maintaining and enhancing. A firm using this kind of relationship marketing differentiates individual customers based on need rather than differentiating products for target groups.

Share of voice (SOV) The proportion of online conversations about one brand versus its competitors.

shopping agents Programs that allow the consumer to rapidly compare prices and features within product categories. Shopping agents implicitly negotiate prices downward on behalf of the consumer by listing companies in order of best price first.

short message services (SMS) 160 characters of text, using a store-and-delivery technology, sent by one user to another over the internet, usually with a cell phone or PDA. Also called *text messaging.*

situation analysis Review of the existing marketing plan and any other information that can be obtained about the company and its brands, examination of environmental factors related to online marketing, and development of a market opportunity analysis.

social bonding Stimulated social interaction between companies and customers resulting in a more personalized communication and brand loyalty.

social bookmarking These sites allow users to share their favorite Web sites and comments on them online, such as StumbleUpon.com.

social CRM (CRM 2.0) This strategy retains all the tenets of CRM 1.0, however, adds social media technology and customer collaborative conversations to the process.

social commerce is a piece of e-commerce that uses social media and consumer interactions to facilitate online sales.

social graph This is a drawing showing the interconnection of social network members.

social media One media type with one differentiating characteristic: They blend technology and social interactions for the co-creation of content and value. That is, people use them for social interactions and conversations.

social media optimization A component of search engine optimization that uses an optimal variety of social media sites for building awareness of a product, brand, event, or Web site.

social network aggregation The process of collecting content from several social networks or providing user consolidation of all his or her network profiles, all on one site.

social networking The practice of expanding the number of one's business and social contacts by making connections through individuals online.

social networks Nodes of individuals or organizations that are connected based on common values, ideas, friendships, and so forth.

social news Sites where users submit links to online news stories and readers vote or comment on which are the best ones.

social sign-in Also called social log in, this occurs when members use social media sites to register or sign into another Web site.

spam Unsolicited e-mail, either sent to users or posted on an electronic bulletin board.

spam filter A program that has the capability of blocking unsolicited e-mails.

spider Automatic programs in search engines that search the Web from site to site, page by page, and word by word in order to build up a massive index or database of all the words found, where they were found, how many times they appear on each page, and so on. It is this database that is actually queried when you type in a search term.

sponsorship Integration of editorial content and advertising on a Web site. The sponsor pays for space and creates content that appeals to the publisher's audience.

spoofing A manipulation of the average person's lack of knowledge—and understanding of exactly how information is displayed, transferred, or stored—which provides opportunities for novel deceptions and is often used to extract sensitive information by leading a user to believe that a request is coming from a reputable source, such as an ISP or credit card company.

strategic e-marketing The design of marketing strategy that capitalizes on the organization's electronic or information technology capabilities to reach specified objectives.

strategic planning The "process of developing and maintaining a strategic fit between the organization's goals and capabilities and its changing market opportunities" (Kotler and Armstrong, 2010).

strategy The means to achieve a goal.

streaming video Content sent to the user's computer as it is viewed versus sending an entire file before the user can view it. Audio is also streamed to a user's computer.

structural bonds Relationships created when firms add value by making structural changes that facilitate the relationship with customers and suppliers.

supply chain management (SCM) The behind-the-scenes coordination of the distribution channel to deliver products effectively and efficiently to customers. Also called *integrated logistics*.

switchers Consumers who do not show any specific brand loyalty but generally go for the best price.

SWOT Strengths, weaknesses, opportunities, and threats analysis. SWOT analysis objectively evaluates the company's strengths and weaknesses with respect to the environment and the competition.

syndicated research Data collected regularly using a systematic process, such as the Nielsen television ratings. This is secondary data for the companies who purchase it.

synergy Result that occurs when two or more firms join in a business relationship in which the results often exceed what each firm might have accomplished alone.

tagging involves attaching keywords to video, photos, or text to help users find the desired content.

technographics Segments of online shoppers as identified by Forrester Research. Consumers fall into one of 10 groups based upon their attitude toward technology, income as an indicator of shopping behavior, and primary motivation to go online.

telecenters Small shops with three to ten computers that offer internet connections to the general public in simply furnished settings.

telematics A communication system in an automobile that uses a global positioning system (GPS) for interactive communication between firms and drivers.

text messaging See *short message services (SMS).*

third-party logistics The outsourcing of logistics such that a third party manages the company's supply chain and provides value-added services such as product configuration and subassembly.

tipping point That moment when an emerging trend or phenomenon becomes so big that it becomes irreversible.

trademark A brand name. A trademark or service mark includes any word, name, symbol, device, or any combination, used or intended to be used to identify and distinguish the goods/services of one seller or provider from those of others, and to indicate the source of the goods/services (definition from uspto.gov).

transactional functions The process of matching product to buyer needs, negotiating price, and carrying out the transaction.

TRIPs (Trade Related Intellectual Property Rights) A 1995 agreement that is part of the World Trade Organization's (WTO) program of international treaties.

Trojan horses These programs do not replicate and often appear as legitimate software. This virus-like program can do damage to the computer and open doors to let hackers enter the computer to do damage.

twinsumers These taste "twin consumers" share similar opinions, buying patterns, entertainment, and other behaviors.

ubiquitous application An application that is able to function in the course of nearly any online session without a user's knowledge or control.

UNCITRAL (United Nations Commission of International Trade Law) The governing body that established the Model Law on Electronic Commerce to provide for global uniformity in digital commerce.

Uniform Computer Information Transactions Act (UCITA) A model that, if adopted by the states, would govern all legal agreements pertaining to software transactions, including sales.

universal product code (UPC) Also called the *bar code*, a symbol scanned by retailers, wholesalers, and manufacturers for the purpose of inventory management.

URL (uniform [or universal] resource locator) This is a Web site address. It is also called an **IP address (internet protocol)** and a **domain name.**

Usenet Worldwide network of thousands of computer systems with a decentralized administration. The Usenet systems exist to transmit postings to special-interest newsgroups.

value Benefits minus costs.

value chain (integrated logistics) The supply chain, the manufacturer, and the distribution channel viewed as an integrated system.

value segment pricing The seller recognizes that not all customers provide equal value to the firm, and segments by high, medium, and low value—and pricing accordingly.

vertical search A site-specific search on very specialized topics, such as travel, online retailers, or books.

viral marketing The online equivalent of word-of-mouth and referred to as word-of-mouse, which occurs when individuals forward content to each other through e-mail or social media sharing.

virtual magistrate A mediation-oriented program developed to resolve online disputes.

virtual mall A model similar to a shopping mall in which multiple online merchants are hosted at a Web site.

virtual worlds Sites where users can take the form of avatars and socialize in an online space of their own making.

visitor A user who visits a site, but does not distinguish between one-time and repeat visitors.

voice of the customer A systematic approach for incorporating the needs of customers into the design of customer experiences (Forrester Research).

voice-over-internet protocol (VoIP) The term used to refer to internet telephony that relies on the Web to transmit phone calls, thus eliminating long-distance charges.

wallet share The amount of sales a firm can generate from one customer over time, which reflects the focus on customer retention versus acquisition (market share).

Web 2.0 This refers to second-generation internet technologies behind blogs, wikis, social networks, product review sites, image and video upload sites, and even Google Maps.

Web analytics Tools that collect and display information about user behavior on a Web site.

Web form Technical term for a Web page that has designated places for the user to type information. Many corporate Web sites sport Web forms, using them for a multitude of purposes from site registration and survey research to product purchase.

Web site content The text, graphics, video, and audio that are displayed on a Web page, which can also include interactive features such as search tools, forms, purchase options, and e-mail.

Web site log Data about how long users spend on each page, how long they are at the site, and what path they take through the site, among other things.

wholesalers These intermediaries buy products from the manufacturer and resell them to retailers.

widgets Mini Web applications that are used to distribute or share content throughout the social Web, downloaded to a mobile device or desktop, or accessed on a Website or blog ("Social Media Guide," 2010).

wiki Web sites that allow users to post, edit, and organize multimedia content.

wireless The transmission of communication signals that relies on towers to relay the signals in a mode similar to that of cell phones.

worms These viruses reproduce rapidly throughout a computer's memory, destroying the stored information and eating up resources.

yield management A strategy used most often by the travel industry to optimize inventory management through frequent price changes.

APPENDIX C

References

Note: References for Chapter 5 are displayed at the end of this list.

"1-800-Flowers.com, Inc. Reports Continued Positive Trends in Revenues, EBITDA and EPS From Continuing Operations for its Fiscal 2012 Fourth Quarter and Full Year." (2012). Available at investor.1800flowers.com.

"2011 Annual Survey of Market Research Professionals." (2011). Available at MarketResearchCareers.com.

"2012 Shopping Outlook." (2012). Available at pricegrabber.com.

"2012 Response RateTrends Report." (2012). Available at newdma.org.

"21% of US Pay TV Subscribers Report Cutting or Shaving the Cord." (2012). Available at marketingcharts.com.

Abraham, Jack. (2011). "Commerce 3.0: Online Research, Offline Buying." Available at ecommercetimes.com.

AdMob by Google. (2011). "Tablet Survey." Available at services.google.com.

"Advertisers Begin to Look Beyond Facebook and Twitter." (2011). *eMarketer*. Available at emarketer.com.

"Advertisers Will Spend $2.61 Billion on Mobile This Year." (2012). Available at emarketer.com.

Afuah, Allan, and Christopher Tucci. (2001). *Internet Business Models and Strategies*. New York: McGraw-Hill/Irwin.

Aho, Karen. (2011). "The 2011 Customer Service Hall of Fame." Available at money.msn.com.

Arno, C. (2012). "CIVETS: New Global Marketing Opportunities in Emerging Economies." Available at searchenginewatch.com.

"Are Marketers Missing Multichannel Opportunities?" (2012). Available at emarketer.com.

Arnold, Catherine. (2004). "Marketers Discover Weblogs' Power to Sell—Minus the Pitch." *Marketing News* (March 15).

Bakas, R. (2010). "How to Engage a Global Audience." Available at rickbakas.com.

Barker, Dennis. (2012). "Outsourcing Enables 21st Century Focus Groups." Available at bpooutcomes.com.

Beal, Andy, and Judy Strauss. (2008). *Radically Transparent: Monitoring and Managing Reputations Online*. Indianapolis, Indiana: Wiley and Sons, Inc.

Behlmann, E. (2010). "Red Cross Unlocks a Blood Donor Badge on Foursquare." Available at bizjournals.com.

Berners-Lee, Tim, James Hendler, and Ora Lassila. (2001). "The Semantic Web." *Scientific American* (May). Available at scientificamerican.com.

Bold, W., and Davidson, W. (2012). "Mobile Broadband: Redefining Internet Access and Empowering Individuals." In Dutta, S., and Bilbao-Osorio, B. (Eds.), *The Global Information Technology Report 2012: Living in a Hyperconnected World*. Available at weforum.org.

Brown, Eryn. (2002). "Slow Road to Fast Data." *Fortune* (March 18), pp. 170–172.

Bruner, Rick, and Kathryn Koegel. (2005). "Target Demographics, Before and After." *DoubleClick Report*. Available at doubleclick.com.

Budis, Christian. (2004). "Recreational Equipment Inc. (REI)." Working paper.

Case, Karl, and Ray Fair. (2001). *Principles of Economics*. Upper Saddle River, NJ: Prentice Hall.

Chaffey, D. (2010). "Social Location-Based Marketing." Available at smartinsights.com.

Chao, E. (2012). "A Soap Set in the Favelas." Available at online.wsj.com.

Chowney, Vikki. (2012). "11 Examples of f-Commerce for 2012." Available at econsultancy.com.

CIW Team Staff. (2012). "China Search Engine Market Share by Revenue Q1 2012." Available at chinainternetwatch.com.

CNNIC. (2010). "Statistical Survey Report on Internet Development in China." Available at cnnic.net.cn.

Cohen, David. (2012). "Facebook, ComScore Study Touts Benefits of Paid Media, Even for Larger Brands." Available at allfacebook.com.

comScore. (2012). "2012 Mobile Future in Focus." Available at comscore.com.

Curioso, Walter, et al. (2007). "Opportunities for Providing Web-Based Interventions to Prevent Sexually Transmitted Infections in Peru." *PloS Medicine Online Journal*. Available at medicine.plosjournals.org.

Dhalokia, S. (2011). "5 Ways to Encourage Customers to Share Your Content." Crowdfactory Whitepaper. Available at crowdfactory.com.

"Digital Coupons Rival Print Counterparts in Effectiveness." (2012). Available at emarketer.com.

"Does Online Marketing Really Lead to Offline Buying?" (2002). Presentation at the Advertising Research Foundation Annual Convention. Available at powersearch2.thearf.org.

Duncan, Tom. (2002). *Using Advertising and Promotion to Build Brands*. New York: McGraw Hill-Irwin.

Duncan, Tom, and Frank Mulhern. (Eds.). (2004). "A White Paper on the Status, Scope, and Future of IMC." The IMC Symposium (March).

"Earned, Owned Media More Trusted Than Paid." (2012). Available at marketingprofs.com.

"E-Biz Strikes Again!" (2004). *BusinessWeek Online* (May 10). Available at businessweek.com.

Economist. (2009). "The Power of Mobile Money." Available at people.ucsc.edu.

Egyptians Flock to New Net Plan. (2002). *Wired* (June 25). Available at wired.com.

Elliott, Stuart. (2009). "Letting Consumers Control Marketing: Priceless." *The New York Times* (October 9). Available at nytimes.com.

"E-Mail + Twitter + Facebook" (2011). Lyris. Available at lyris.com.

"eMarketer Mobile Roundup." (2012). Available at emarketer.com.

"Emerging Countries Lead Broadband." (2009). Available at point-topic.com.

Evans, D., and J. McKee. (2010). "Social Media Marketing." Indianapolis, IN: Wiley Publishing, Inc.

"Facebook Chorus Ends Instrument Luggage Ban." (2011). *Taipei Times*. Available at taipeitimes.com.

Facebook Solidifies Hold on Social Sign-Ins. (2012). Available at emarketer.com.

Falls, Jason and Erik Deckers (2012). "No Bullshit Social Media." Indianapolis, IN: Que Publishing.

False Hopes on Fantasy Island." (2003) *Business 2.0* (December), p. 38.

Farivar, Cyrus. (2004). "New Ways to Pay." *Business 2.0* (August), p. 26.

Felix, Samantha. (2012). "The 20 Most-Liked Facebook Companies Ever." Available at businessinsider.com.

"Field Guide to Customer Digital Engagement." (2012). Available at lyrislabs.com.

Flynn, N. (2012). *The Social Media Handbook*. Indianapolis, IN: Wiley Publishing, Inc.

Gallagher, James. (2010). "Duke Study: TiVo Doesn't Hurt TV Advertising." *Triangle Business Journal* (January 3). Available at bizjournals.com.

Griffith, E. (2011). "Getting Your Klout Out." *AdWeek*. Available at adweek.com.

Gaines-Ross, Leslie. (2003). *CEO Capital*. Hoboken, NJ: John Wiley & Sons Inc.

Gartner, Inc. (2010). "Hype Cycle for E-Commerce, 2010, Gene Alvarez." (August 3).

Gemius, Vladimir. (2009). "E-Commerce 2009: Trends and Attitudes Research into Czech Internet Users." Available at gemius.pl.

Ghemawat, P. *(*2007). "Redefining Global Strategy: Crossing Borders in a World Where Differences Still Matter." Cambridge, MA: Harvard University Press.

Ghosh, Shikhar. *(*1998). "Making Business Sense of the Internet." *Harvard Business Review* (March–April), pp. 126–135.

Gladwell, M. *(*2000). *Tipping Point*. New York: Little Brown.

"Global Marketers Say Management Keen on Customer Data Insights." *(*2012). Available at marketingcharts.com.

Godin, Seth. *(*1999). *Permission Marketing*. New York: Simon and Schuster.

Goldwyn, Craig. *(*2012). *"The Art of the Cart: Why People Abandon Shopping Carts."* Available at visibility.tv.

Grönroos, Christian. *(*1990). "Relationship Approach to Marketing in Service Contexts: The Marketing and Organizational Behavior Interface." *Journal of Business Research*, 20 (January), pp. 3–11.

Gruener, Jamie. *(*2001). "How to Measure Storage ROI." *Network Connections*, pp. 8–10.

Harrison, Matt. *(*2010). "Dunkin' Donuts Uses Social Media to Drive Positive Brand Engagement." Available at wave.wavemetrix.com.

Hinshaw, D. *(*2012). "In Nigeria, Rising Dreams of Web Commerce." Available at online.wsj.com.

"How Well do Companies Respond to Customer Complaints?" *(*2011). *eMarketer*. Available at emarketer.com.

Huynh, S. *(*2012). "Mobile Internet Users Will Soon Surpass PC Internet Users Globally." Available at blogs.forrester.com.

"IAB Social Media Buyer's Guide." *(*2010). Available at iab.net.

Indvik, Lauren. *(*2012). "Online Ad Spending to Surpass Print for First Time in 2012 [STUDY]." Available at mashable.com.

"iOS and Android Adoption Explodes Internationally." *(*2012). Available at blog.flurry.com.

"iPhone App Business Models: Paid Versus Free." *(*2010). Available at smartpassiveincome.com.

ITU. *(*2006a). "The World Telecommunication/ICT Development Report 2006." Available at foss.org.my.

ITU. *(*2006b). "ITU Internet Report 2006: Digital Life." Available at itu.int.

ITU. *(*2012). "The State of Broadband 2012: Achieving Digital Inclusion for All." Available at broadbandcommission.org.

Jeanette, Jean-Pierre, and H. David Hennessy. *(*2002). *Global Marketing Strategies*. Boston: Houghton Mifflin Company.

Jones, R. *(*2011). "5 Ways to Measure Social Media." *ClickZ* (August 22). Available at clickz.com.

Kim, G. *(*2010). "Social Media Buyer's Guide." Available at.iab.net.

"Kim Kardashian, Snoop Dogg Get Paid HOW Much to Tweet?" *(*2012). Available at huffingtonpost.com.

King, Julia, and Thomas Hoffman. *(*1999). "Pace of Change Fuels Web Plans; Sites Must Shift Offering Every 60 Days to Thrive." *Computer World* (July 5), p. 1.

"Kitchen Aid—Bad Tweet Happen to Good Brands Who Don't Manage Social Media Risk Properly." *(*2012). Available at pammarketingnut.com.

Kotler, Philip, and Gary Armstrong. *(*2010). *Principles of Marketing*. 13th ed. Upper Saddle River, NJ: Prentice Hall.

Kupper, Phillip. *(*2004). "How Continental Airlines Interprets and Uses CRM." Working paper.

Laseter, Tim, David Torres, and Anne Chung. *(*2001). "Oasis in the Dot-Com Delivery Desert." *Strategy + Business*, 24, pp. 28–33.

"Leaders in Mobile Phone Adoption." *(*2012). Available at googlemobileads.blogspot.com.

Learmonth, M. *(*2011). "Study: Twitter Ad Revenue Grows to $150M in 2011." Available at adage.com.

Linkner, Josh. *(*2004). "Interactive Promos Engage Buyers." *Marketing News* (June 15), p. 13.

"Listen, Engage, Build." *(*2012). HFNYK. Available at img-cdn.centro.net.

"Live Chat Performance Benchmarks." *(*2012). Available at boldchat.com.

Lunden, Ingrid. (2012). "Nielsen: U.S. Consumers the Most Likely to Pay for Content on a Tablet. . . Except When It's News." Available at techcrunch.com.

Lutz, Ashley. (2012). "Gamestop to J.C. Penney Shut Facebook Stores." Available at bloomberg.com.

Maniewicz, Mario. (2009). "Information Society Statistical Profiles 2009: Africa." Available at itu.int.

"Marketers Buzz About ROI." (2010). Available at emarketer.com.

"Marketers Challenged to Keep Pace with Mobile, Social." (2012). Available at emarketer.com.

"Marketers Find Less Than Half of Analytics Useful for Decision-Making." (2012). Available at emarketer.com.

"Marketers Rely Most on Blog Posts and Twitter to Reach Their Audience." (2012). Available at emarketer.com.

"Marketers Struggle to Link Digital Data to 'Big Data' Picture." (2012). Available at emarketer.com.

"Media CEOs Look to Smartphones, Tablets for Digital Growth." (2012). Available at emarketer.com.

Meeker, Mary. (2012). "Internet Trends—D10 Conference." Available at kpcb.com.

Mei, Yin. (2012). "5 Chinese Social Networks You Need to Watch." Available at mashable.com.

Memmott, C. (2011). "Authors Catch Fire with Self-Published e-Books." *USA TODAY*. Available at usatoday.com.

"Mobile Wallets Have Uphill Climb to Consumer Acceptance." (2012). Available at emarketer.com.

Modahl, Mary. (2000). *Now or Never*. New York: HarperBusiness.

"More Than One in Six Visitors to Travel Sites Are Also Pinterest Users." (2012). Available at emarketer.com.

"Multichannel Is a Must for Beauty and Personal Care." (2012). Available at emarketer.com.

Murphy, Samantha. (2011). "Malls Send Geo-fencing Texts to Lure Shoppers to Stores." Available at mashable.com.

"Nielsen: Facebook's Ads Work Pretty Well." Ad Age Digital. Available at adage.com

"New eGlobal Report." (2000). *Business Wire*. Available at lexis-nexus.com (accessed on March 28, 2000).

Nutley, M. (2010). "Forget E-Commerce; Social Commerce Is Where It's at." Available at marketingweek.co.uk.

Obinna, Egbule. (2012). "Facebook Pages with Most Fans." Available at onwaweb.com.

O'Leary, Noreen. (2012). "GroupM: Global Web Ad Spend Up 16 Percent in 2011." Available at adweek.com.

"Online Vehicle Shopping Influences Dealership Choice According to Study from Polk, Autotrader.com***."*** (2011). Available at polk.com.

Palacios, Ivan. (2002). "Transforming the Digital Divide into a Digital Opportunity." Workshop presentation at APEC Workshop on e-Business and Supply Chain Management, Bangkok, Thailand. Available at ecommerce.or.th.

Palis, Coureney. (2012). "The Worst Kinds of Tweets: Study." Available at huffingtonpost.com.

Patel, K. (2011). "Apple, Campbell's Say IADs Twice as Effective as TV." Available at adage.com.

Pellegrino, Robert, Doug Amyx, and Kimberly Pellegrino. (2002). "A Methodology for Assessing Buyer Behavior: Price Sensitivity and Value Awareness in Internet Auctions." Working paper.

Peppers, Don. (2000). "Getting to Know You Without Knowing You." *Peppers and Rodgers Newsletter* (Spring). Available at 1to1.com.

Perez, Sarah (2011). "Mobile Game Prices Decline, but Revenue Up." Available at readwriteweb.com.

Polasik, M., and Fiszeder, P. (2010). "Factors determining the acceptance of payment methods by online shops in Poland." Available at networkworld.com.

Ponnaiya, Elzaurdia, and Sanjay Ponnaiya. (1999). "The Distribution of Survey Contact and Participation in the United States: Construction a Survey Based Estimate." *Journal of Marketing Research*, 36, pp. 286–294.

"Portals Vital for Users and Marketers." (2010). Available at emarketer.com.

Pozin, Ilya. *(*2012). "Are QR Codes Dead?" Available at forbes.com.

"Print's Place in Multichannel Retailing." *(*2010). Available at emarketer.com.

Radding, Alan. *(*2001). "A Tale of Two Users." *Network Connections*, p. 20.

Ray, Michael L. *(*1973). "Communication and the Hierarchy of Effects." In P. Clarke (Ed.), *New Models for Mass Communication Research*. Beverly Hills, CA: Sage Publications, pp. 147–175.

Reed, B. *(*2012). "Global broadband Snapshot: Hong Kong Trounces Rest of World." Available at networkworld.com.

Reese, S. *(* 2011). "Quick Stat: Online Video Will Account for 6.9% of Online Ads This Year." Available at emarketer.com.

"Relationships Rule." *(*2000). *Business 2.0* (May), pp. 303–319.

Renner, Dale. *(*2000). "Closer to the Customer: Customer Relationship Management and the Supply Chain." *Andersen Consulting*. Available at renner.ascet.com.

"Retailers Experiment with Varied, Personalized Pricing." *(*2012). Available at emarketer.com.

Rhoads, Christopher. *(*2007). "What's the Hindi Word for dot.com?" *Wall Street Journal* (October 11).

Ridley, Kirstin. *(*2007). "Global Mobile Phone Use to Pass Record 3 Billion." *Reuters News* (June 27). Available at reuters.com.

"Running Smoothly: Online Shoe Sales in the US Industry Market Research Report Now Available from IBISWorld." *(*2012). Available at prweb.com.

"Safeguarding Reputation." *(*2006). Weber Shandwick Research Report. Available at reputationrx.com.

Sarno, David. *(*2009). "Twitter Creator Jack Dorsey Illuminates the Site's Founding Document." *Los Angeles Times*. Available at latimesblogs.latimes.com.

Seybold, Patricia. *(*1998). Customers.com. New York: Random House.

Shannon, S. *(*2012). "Britain's Surprise Shopaholics: Nigerians." Available at businessweek.com.

Shih, Clara. *(*2011). "The Facebook Era." Upper Saddle River, NJ: Pearson Education, Inc.

"Shopper Sentiment: How Consumers Feel About Shopping In-Store, Online, and via Mobile." *(*2012). Available at blog.nielsen.com.

Sloan, Paul. *(*2011). "Jack Dorsey: Twitter's Business Model Based on 'Serendipity.'" *CNET News*. Available at news.cnet.com.

"Smartphones Turn Millions More Americans into Mobile Shoppers." *(*2012). Available at emarketer.com.

"Social Media Report: Facebook Pages in Armenia." *(*2012). Available at socialbakers.com.

"Social Media Share of Voice-Converse, Adidas, New Balance, Nike and Under Armour." *(*2009). Available at istrategylabs.com.

Solis, Brian. *(*2011). "Report: The Rise of the Social Advertising." Available at briansolis.com.

Sonnenberg, Frank. *(*1993). "If I Had Only One Client." *Sales and Marketing Management*, 56 (November), p. 4.

Spector, Robert. *(*2000). Amazon.com*: Get Big Fast*. New York: HarperBusiness.

Stanhope, Joe. *(*2011). "The State of Online Testing 2011." Available at forrester.com.

State of the Global Mobile Industry Annual Assessment. *(*2012). Available at navdeep-manaktala.com.

"State of Media Consumer Usage Report." *(*2011). The Nielsen Company. Available at slideshare.net.

Stokes, Tracy. *(*2012). "How Social Media is Changing Brand Building." Available at forrester.com.

"Super Buzz or Super Blues?" *(*2008). *Nielsen Media Company Webcast* (January 3). Available at netratings.com.

Tang, Fang-Fang, and Xiaolin Xing. *(*2003). "Pricing Differences Between Dotcoms and Multi-Channel Retailers in the Online Video Market." *Journal of the Academy of Business and Economics* (March). Available at findarticles.com.

Taylor, Colleen. *(*2012). "VC Funding to Web Startups Hits Decade-Long High in 2011." Available at gigaom.com.

Terdiman, Daniel. (2005). "Study: Wikipedia as Accurate as Britannica." *CNET News*. Available at news.com.

"The Elegance of Simplicity: Creating Experiences That Drive Purchase." (2012). Available at socialmediatoday.com.

"The Mobile Difference—Tech User Types." (2009). Pew Internet & American Life Project. Available at pewinternet.org/Infographics/The-Mobile-Difference—Tech-User-Types.aspx Accessed September 17, 2012.

"The Power of Direct Marketing." (2011–2012 Edition). Direct Marketing Association. Available at the dma.org.

"The State of Inbound Marketing 2010." (2012). Available at hubspot.com.

Togan-Egrican, A., English, C., and Klapper, L. (2012). "Credit Cards and Formal Loans Rare in Developing Countries." Available at gallup.com.

TraderMark. (2011). "WSJZ: Zynga—Virtual Products, Real Profits." *iStock Analyst*. Available at istockanalyst.com.

U.S. State Department. (1998). "The Global Landmine Crisis." *Hidden Killers*. Available at state.gov.

Voskresensky, Mitya (2011). Google Research about Smartphone Usage in 2011. Available at slideshare.net and google.com.

Wang, R. Ray, and Jeremiah Owyang. (2010). "Social CRM: The New Rules of Relationship Management." (March 5).

Wentz, L., and C. Penteado. (2011). "Banned from Cannes." Available at creativity-online.com.

"What Do Facebook Users Expect from Brands?" (2011). *eMarketer*. Available at emarketer.com.

"What is Big Data?" (2012). Available at ibm.com.

"Who's Ignoring Their Customers?" (2011). Conversocial. Available at conversocial.com.

"Why do People Overpay on eBay." (2011). Available as a consumer post in a forum on deals.woot.com.

Wolfinbarger, Mary, and Mary Gilly. (2001). "Shopping Online for Freedom, Control and Fun." *California Management Review*, 43, p. 39.

"Women and Mobile: A Global Opportunity." (2009). Available at gsmworld.com.

World Internet Project. (2010). "World Internet Project Press Release Report." Available at worldinternetproject.net.

"World Record Attempt for Most Blog Post Comments Underway for Charity." (2012). Available at electricpig.co.uk.

Notes for Chapter 5

[1] ***American Marketing Association,*** *Statement of Ethics* (Chicago, IL, American Marketing Association, 2008).

[2] www.dhs.gov/files/events/stop-think-connect.shtm.

[3] www.getsafeonline.org.

[4] ***S. Warren and L. Brandeis, The Right to Privacy, 4 Harvard Law Review 193*** (1890).

[5] 381 U.S. 479 (1965).

[6] 410 U.S. 113 (1973).

[7] ***Restatement (Second) of Torts § 652*** (1977).

[8] ***Lane v. Facebook, Inc., No. 08-03845*** (N.D. Cal., filed Aug. 12, 2008).

[9] ***In re Google Buzz User Privacy Litigation, No. 10-00672*** (N.D. Cal., filed February 17, 2010)

[10] ***Elec. Privacy Info. Ctr. v. F.T.C., 844 F. Supp. 2d 98, 100-101*** (D.D.C. 2012).

[11] ***For more information on recent privacy cases please go to: business.ftc.gov/legal-resources/8/35.***

[12] ***W. Adkinson, J. Eisenach, and T. Lenard,*** *Privacy Online: A Report on the Information Practices and Policies of Commercial Web Sites* (The Progress & Freedom Foundation, 2002). Available at www.pff.org.

[13] ***Timothy R. McVeigh v. William Cohen, et al., 983 F. Supp. 215*** (D.D.C. 1998).

[14] ***Children's Online Privacy Protection Act of 1998, 15 U.S.C. 6501 et seq.***

[15] ***Federal Trade Commission, Children's Online Privacy Protection Rule, Final Rule, 16 CFR 312*** (1999). Available at http://www.ftc.gov/privacy/privacyinitiatives/COPPARule_2005SlidingScale.pdf.

[16] ***Fair Credit Reporting Act, 15 USC 1681*** (1992).

[17] ***Electronic Communications Protection Act*** (ECPA) 18 USC §2510–21, 2701–11 (1994).

[18] www.the-dma.org/library/guidelines/onlineguidelines.shtml.

[19] ***In re Northwest Airlines Privacy Litigation, No. 04–126*** (D. Minn., June 6, 2004).

[20] ***Consumer Data Privacy in a Networked World: A Framework for Protecting Privacy and Promoting Innovation in the Global Digital Economy*** (February 23, 2012). Available at www.whitehouse.gov/sites/default/files/privacy-final.pdf.

[21] ***OECD, Recommendations of the Council Concerning Guidelines Governing the Protection of Privacy and Transborder Flows of Personal Data*** (September 23, 1980). For more information please see: OECD, *The Evolving Privacy Landscape: 30 Years after the OECD Privacy Guidelines* (2011), available at www.oecd.org/dataoecd/22/25/47683378.pdf.

[22] *Directive 95/46/EC of the European Parliament and of the Council of 24 October 1995 in the protection of individuals with regard to the processing of personal data and on the free movement of such data*, Article 1.

[23] ***Updated Safe Harbor Principles are available at*** http://export.gov/safeharbor/.

[24] ***Commission of the European Communities, Commission Staff Working Document: The implementation of Commission Decision 520/2000/EC on the adequate protection of personal data provided by the Safe Harbour privacy Principles and related Frequently Asked Questions issued by the US Department of Commerce*** (October 20, 2004). Available at ec.europa.eu/justice/policies/privacy/docs/adequacy/sec-2004-1323_en.pdf.

[25] *Directive 2002/58/EC of the European Parliament and of the Council of 12 July 2002 concerning the processing of personal data and the protection of privacy in the electronic communications sector.*

[26] ***Regulation of the European Parliament and of the Council of 25 January 2012 on the protection of individuals with regard to the processing of personal data and on the free movement of such data*** (General Data Protection Regulation). Available at ec.europa.eu/justice/data-protection/document/review2012/com_2012_11_en.pdf.

[27] ec.europa.eu/justice/data-protection/document/review2012/factsheets/6_en.pdf.

[28] ***Personal Data (Privacy) Ordinance*** (Hong Kong, 1995).

[29] ***Code on Access to Information*** (Hong Kong, 1995).

[30] ***Personal Information Protection Act*** (Japan, 2003).

[31] ***Personal Information Protection Act*** (South Korea, 2011).

[32] ***Personal Data Protection Bill*** (Singapore, 2012). As per September 30, 2012 (the date when this chapter was revised) the bill has passed its initial hearing in the Parliament.

[33] ***Federal Trade Commission,*** *Privacy Online: A Report to Congress,* (June 1998). Available at www.ftc.gov/reports/privacy3/toc.htm.

[34] ***ftc.gov/os/2012/03/120326privacyreport.pdf.***

[35] 35 U.S.C. §101 et seq.

[36] ***Amazon.com v. Barnesandnoble.com*** (W.D. Wash., filed October 21, 1999).

[37] ***Bilski v. Kappos, 130 S. Ct. 3218***(2010).

[38] ***Bilski v. Kappos, 130 S. Ct. 3227-3229***(2010).

[39] 17 U.S.C. §§107 and 109 (1998).

[40] 17 U.S.C. §506(a) (as amended 1997).

[41] 17 U.S.C. §512 et seq. (1998).

[42] 17 U.S.C. §1201 et seq. (1998).

[43] ***Electronic Frontier Foundation,*** *Unintended Consequences: Three Years Under the DMCA*, May 3, 2002.

[44] ***WIPO Copyright Treaty, adopted by the Diplomatic Conference on December 20, 1996, WIPO Doc. CRNR/DC/94*** (1996), and *WIPO Performances and Phonograms Treaty*, adopted by the Diplomatic Conference on December 20, 1996, WIPO Doc. CRNR/DC/95 (1996).

[45] ***Stop Online Piracy Act, H.R.3261, 112th Cong.*** (2011).

[46] ***Preventing Real Online Threats to Economic Creativity and Theft of Intellectual Property Act, 112th Cong., S. 968*** (2011).

[47] ***Ian Paul, Were SOPA/PIPA Protests a Success? The Results Are In*** (PCWorld, 2012). Available at www.pcworld.com/article/248401/were_sopapipa_protests_a_success_the_results_are_in.html.

[48] www.sopastrike.com/.

[49] ***Macon Phillips, Obama Administration Responds to We the People Petitions on SOPA and Online Piracy*** (The White House Blog, 2012). Available at www.whitehouse.gov/blog/2012/01/14/obama-administration-responds-we-people-petitions-sopa-and-online-piracy.

[50] 15 U.S.C. §1051 et seq.

[51] 15 U.S.C. §1125 et seq.

[52] 15 U.S.C. §1125(c).

[53] 15 U.S.C. §1125.

[54] ***Playboy Enterprises, Inc. v. Calvin Designer Label, 985 F. Supp. 1220*** (N.D. Cal. 1997).

[55] ***Playboy Enterprises, Inc. v. Welles, 279 F.3d 796*** (9th Cir. 2002).

[56] ***Estée Lauder Inc. v. The Fragrance Counter and Excite, Inc.*** (S.D.N.Y. complaint filed March 5, 1999).

[57] ***Ticketmaster Corp. v. Microsoft Corp., No. 97–3055 DDP*** (D. Cal. filed April 28, 1997).

[58] ***Washington Post v. TotalNEWS, Inc., 97 Civ. 1190*** (PKL) (S.D.N.Y., filed February 28, 1997).

[59] ***Kelly v. Arriba Soft Corp., 336 F.3d 818*** (9th Cir. 2003).

[60] ***Perfect 10, Inc. v. Amazon.com, Inc., 508 F.3d 1059-1062*** (9th Cir. 2007).

[61] ***M. A. Mortenson Co. v. Timberline Software, 998 P.2d 305*** (Wash. 2000).

[62] ***Groff v. America Online, 1998 WL 307001*** (R.I. Super. Ct., May 27, 1998).

[63] 18 USC §1831 et seq.

[64] ***New England Circuit Sales v. Randall, No. 96–10840-EFH*** (D.Mass., June4, 1996).

[65] www.ndasforfree.com/UTSA.html.

[66] ***eBay, Inc. v. Bidder's Edge, Inc., 100 F.Supp. 2d 1058*** (N.D. Cal. 2000).

[67] *Directive 96/9/EC of the European Parliament and of the Council of March 11, 1996 on the legal protection of databases.*

[68] ***Cyber Promotions, Inc. v. America Online, Inc., 948 F.Supp. 436*** (E.D. Pa. 1996).

[69] ***America Online v. Christian Brothers, No. 98 Civ. 8959*** (DAB) (HBP) (S.D. N.Y., December 14, 1999).

[70] 15 U.S.C. §7701 et seq.

[71] ***Intel Corp. v. Hamidi, 1 Cal Rptr. 3d 32*** (Cal. 2003).

[72] ***267623 Ontario Inc. v. Nexx Online, No. C20546/99*** (Ontario Super. Ct., June 14, 1999).

[73] 47 U.S.C. §230(c)(1) [Communications Decency Act of 1996].

[74] ***Zeran v. America Online, 129 F.3d 327*** (4th Cir. Va. 1997), cert. denied, 524 U.S. 937 (1998).

[75] 117 S.Ct. 2329 (1997).

[76] ***United States et al. v. American Library Association, Inc., et al., 539 US 194*** (2003).

[77] ***Zippo Manufacturing Company v. Zippo Dot Com, Inc., 952 F. Supp. 1119*** (W.D.Pa., January 16, 1997).

[78] ***Digital Control Inc. v. Boretrontics, Inc., 161 F. Supp. 2d 1183*** (W.D. Wash. 2001).

[79] ***ALS Scan, Inc. v. Robert Wilkins, 142 F. Supp. 2d 793*** (D.Md. 2001).

[80] ***Net2Phone, Inc. v. Superior Court, 109 Cal. App. 4th 583*** (Cal. Ct. App. 2003).

[81] vmag.vcilp.org/.

[82] www.arbiter.wipo.int/center/index.html.

[83] http://www.uncitral.org/pdf/english/texts/electcom/05-89450_Ebook.pdf.

[84] www.etrust.org.

INDEX

D

M

N

O

Q

R

S

T

U